Race, Class, and Gender: *An Anthology*

OTHER WADSWORTH TITLES OF RELATED INTEREST IN SOCIOLOGY

Susan A. Basow, *Gender Stereotypes: Traditions and Alternatives,* 2nd ed.

Dennis Gilbert and Joseph A. Kahl, *The American Class Structure,* 4th ed.

Gary Kessler, *Voices of Wisdom: A Multicultural Reader*

Bernice Lott, *Women's Lives: Themes and Variations in Gender Learning*

Martin N. Marger, *Race and Ethnic Relations: American & Global Perspectives,* 2nd ed.

Martin N. Marger, *Elites and Masses: An Introduction to Political Sociology,* 2nd ed.

Charlotte O'Kelly and Larry S. Carney, *Women and Men in Society: Cross-Cultural Perspectives on Gender Stratification,* 2nd ed.

Barbara J. Risman and Pepper Schwartz, *Gender in Intimate Relationships: A Microstructural Approach*

Robert Staples, *The Black Family: Essays and Studies,* 4th ed.

RACE, CLASS, and GENDER

An Anthology

Margaret L. Andersen
University of Delaware

Patricia Hill Collins
University of Cincinnati

Wadsworth Publishing Company
Belmont, California
A Division of Wadsworth, Inc.

Editor: *Serina Beauparlant*
Editorial Assistant: *Marla Nowick*
Production Editor: *Karen Garrison*
Designer: *Cynthia Schultz*
Print Buyer: *Karen Hunt*
Permissions Editor: *Jeanne Bosschart*
Cover: *Cynthia Schultz*
Signing Representative: *Ron Shelly*
Compositor: *Omegatype Typography*
Printer: *Arcata Graphics, Fairfield*
Cover Art: *Hans Hofmann,* Summer Night's Dream, *1958, oil on canvas, 52 × 60¹/₄.*
Albright-Knox Art Gallery, Buffalo, New York. Gift of Seymour H. Knox, 1958.

This book is printed on acid-free paper that meets
Environmental Protection Agency standards for
recycled paper.

2 3 4 5 6 7 8 9 10—96 95 94 93 92

Library of Congress Cataloging in Publication Data

Race, class, and gender : an anthology / [compiled by] Margaret L.
  Andersen, Patricia Hill Collins.
      p.   cm.
    Included bibliographical references.
    ISBN 0-534-13566-8 (acid-free paper)
    1. United States—Social conditions—1980– 2. United States—Race
relations. 3. Social classes—United States. 4. Sex role—United
States. 5. Homosexuality—United States. 6. Discrimination—United
States. I. Andersen, Margaret L. II. Collins, Patricia Hill.
HN59.2.R32 1992
305–dc20   91-20038

Contents

ENVISIONING CHANGE

Preface

This book analyzes the interrelationship of race, class, and gender and explores how they have shaped the experiences of all people in the United States. Race, class, and gender are interlocking categories of experience that affect all aspects of human life. We want readers to conceptualize them as interactive systems, not just as separate features of experience or variables in sociological equations. While race, class, and gender can be seen as different axes of social structure, individual persons experience them simultaneously. The term *double jeopardy* has, for example, been used to describe the oppression of women of color by race as well as gender. However, we do not think of race and gender oppression in additive terms, an implication of phrases such as *double* and *triple jeopardy*. Rather, race, class, and gender are part of the whole fabric of experience for all groups, not just women and people of color.

We have avoided a "social problems approach" to the study of race, class, and gender because we want readers to move away from thinking only in a problem-centered framework. Race, class, and gender are indeed the basis for many social problems, but a problems-based approach tends to portray people primarily as victims while ignoring their independent views of the society in which they live and other groups within it. A problems-based approach also tends to see oppressed groups only through the perspective of the more privileged, relegating those who most suffer under race, class, and gender oppression to the status of "others." This reproduces the hierarchical viewpoints that have permeated traditional thinking. Instead, we think it is more revealing to study groups in their own right and to see the relationship of all groups to the structure of race, class, and gender relations throughout society.

As a result, we do not think we should talk only about women when talking about gender or people of color when talking about race. Race, class, and gender affect the experience of all, so it is important to study men when analyzing gender, to study whites when analyzing race, and to study the experience of all classes when analyzing class. And, if we are thinking in an inclusive way, we will think about women, not just men, when studying race; Latinos and people of color when thinking about class; and women and men of color when studying gender.

In addition, we should not relegate the study of racial-ethnic groups, the working class, and women only to subjects marked explicitly as race, class, or gender studies. As categories of social experience, race, class, and gender shape all social institutions and systems of meaning; thus, it is important to think about people of color, different class experiences, and women in analyses of all social institutions and belief systems.

Once we understand that race, class, and gender are simultaneous and intersecting systems of relationship and meaning, we also see the different ways that other categories of experience intersect in society. Age, religion, sexual orientation, physical ability, region, and ethnicity also shape systems of privilege and inequality. Rather than segregate these subjects into separate sections, we have integrated them throughout the book, although, for reasons of space, we could not include as much as we would have liked. We do not have a separate section on sexuality, for example, because we do not want readers to conclude that heterosexual privilege is only significant when thinking about sexual identity. Just as white privilege and male privilege shape institutional structures, so heterosexual privilege structures all dominant institutions. We have included homosexual experience in the discussion of different social institutions and the discussion of identity and consciousness, rather than segregating these experiences into a separate discussion of sexuality. We also recognize age as a structural category of experience by including material on different age groups throughout the book. And we have integrated the experiences of different racial-ethnic groups throughout the book. Although links among the structures of race, class, and gender exist in the United States and the experiences of groups worldwide, here we focus only on race, class, and gender in the United States.

The reconstruction of existing ways of thinking to become more inclusive requires many transformations. One necessary transformation is the language we use to describe and define different groups. As Robert Moore describes in his essay in Part Three, language reflects many assumptions about race, class, and gender. The term *minority*, for example, marginalizes groups, making them seem outside the mainstream or majority culture. Even worse, the phrase *nonwhite*, which social scientists routinely use, defines groups in terms of what they are not and assumes whites to have the universal experiences against which all other groups are measured. We have consciously avoided use of both terms throughout this book. We have capitalized *Black* in our writing because of the specific historical experience, varied as it is, of African-Americans in the United States. We have not capitalized *white* because white has not represented a marked historical experience in the same sense that Black experience has. We realize this is an arguable point, but we wanted to make our decision explicit.[1]

Language becomes especially problematic when we want to talk about features of experience that different groups share. Using shortcut terms, like *Hispanic* or *Latino* and even *women of color*, homogenizes distinct experiences. Even the term *white* falsely unifies experiences across such factors as ethnicity, region, and gender, to name a few. But, at times, we want to talk of common experiences across different groups and so we have used the labels *Latino* and *women of color* to do so. Unfortunately, describing groups in this way reinforces basic categories of oppression. We do not know how to resolve this problem, but want readers to be aware of the limitations and significance of language as they try to think more inclusively about diverse group experiences.

The focus of this book is on the institutional, or structural, basis for race, class, and gender relations. The book is organized in four parts. Part One contains personal reflections on the ways race, class, and gender shape individual and collective experiences. These articles provide a fresh beginning point for social thought because they put those who have traditionally been excluded at the center of our thoughts. Part Two focuses on race, class, and gender as distinct, but interlocking, systems of experience to provide conceptual grounding for the rest of the book. Though we do not see them as separate systems, we treat them separately here to see their intersections more clearly. In Part Three, we examine how race, class, and gender shape the organization of social institutions, and as a result, how diverse groups experience race, class, and gender differently. Finally, we conclude by looking at the process of social change in Part Four. Oppression generates resistance, so we look at the meaning of activism and its connection to the conditions in which people live. The final section of *Race, Class, and Gender: An Anthology* also includes articles by writers whose ideas are both inclusive and visionary. We see these articles as providing the ideals for change that inform the spirit of this book.

Throughout the book, we include analytical works that explore the different dimensions of race, class, and gender as they exist in social institutions and the experiences of different groups. We searched for articles that were not only conceptually and theoretically informed but also accessible to under-

---

[1]We have followed this practice in our own writing, but have used the originally published form in articles reprinted here.

graduate readers and centered in personal experiences. Although it is important to think of race, class, and gender as analytical categories, we do not want
to lose sight of how they affect human experiences and feelings. Thus, we
include personal narratives that are reflective and analytical. The subjects of
race, class, and gender generate strong feelings, and we wanted to include
articles that would encourage empathy between and among different groups.
We think that more personal accounts generate empathy and also help us
connect personal experiences to social structural conditions.

We have tried to be as inclusive of all groups as possible, representing the
richness of difference and diversity within the United States. It is impossible
to include all historically and presently marginalized groups in one book, so
we encourage readers to explore the many other works available. We have
selected materials that explain the relationships among race, class, and gender
in ways that illuminate the experiences of many groups, not just those about
whom an article is specifically written. As we begin to untangle the structure
of race, class, and gender relations, we can better see both the commonalities
and differences that different historical experiences have generated.

In compiling this volume, we regretted having to delete many fine writings
by different groups of people. Other times, our ability to be inclusive was
hampered by an absence of articles. For example, we found it especially
difficult to find articles about men, and Black men in particular, with an
inclusive perspective on race, class, and gender. We understand that developing truly inclusive thinking and teaching is a long-term process, one involving
both personal, intellectual, and political change. We do not claim to be perfect
in this regard; reconstructing knowledge to be inclusive is a long-term historical process. Measuring one's place in this process against some assumed end
point is a judgment that is as hierarchical as the systems of knowledge we are
trying to change. Our own teaching and thinking have been transformed by
developing this book; we imagine many changes still to come.

ACKNOWLEDGMENTS

An anthology rests on the efforts of more people than the editors alone. This
book has been inspired by our work with scholars and teachers around the
country who are working to make their teaching and writing more inclusive
and sensitive to the experiences of all groups. Over the years of our own
collaboration, we have each been enriched by the work of people trying to
make higher education a fairer and more equitable institution. This book
grows from several of those projects, most particularly the Memphis State
Center for Research on Women Curriculum Workshops and the American
Sociological Association Minority Opportunity Summer Training Program.

These two programs provided the context for many of our discussions, as well as places to work together. We thank Chuck Bonjean, Marion Coleman, Bonnie Thornton Dill, Elizabeth Higginbotham, Clarence Lo, Lionel Maldonado, Carole Marks, Cora Marrett, Howard Taylor, and Lynn Weber for providing the space and time in which to work. More importantly, we thank them for the companionship, encouragement, and vision that inspires our work.

Many other people contributed to the development of this book. We thank Tina Dunhour and Rachel Levy, now graduates of the University of Delaware, for advising us from students' perspectives about the articles we selected; we also thank Rachel for the work she did in helping us proceed on schedule. We thank Maxine Baca Zinn, David Ermann, Alison Graham, Ken Haas, and Tina Hancock for suggestions about potential articles to be included. We appreciate the support provided by our two institutions, with special thanks to Helen Gouldner, Dean of the College of Arts and Science and Richard B. Murray, Provost, University of Delaware, and Joseph Caruso, Dean of the College of Arts and Sciences and Tony Perzigian, Acting Head of the Department of African-American Studies, University of Cincinnati, for providing funds that supported the completion of this book. Linda Prusak deserves a special thanks for her work, especially in organizing and tracking down permissions. We also thank Anna Marie Brown, Nancy Benderoth, Sadie Wright Oliver, and Roderick W. Williams for their invaluable secretarial support. We hope they know how much we value their work.

Several reviewers gave extensive and valuable comments that assisted us in developing the manuscript. We thank Judith Barker, Ithaca College; Marsha Douglass, Holy Names College; Karen Dugger, Bucknell University; Mary E. Galvin, SUNY-Albany; Tom Gerschick, University of Michigan; Linda Grant, University of Georgia; Roxanne Lin, University of Vermont; Tom Lough, Kent State University; Margo MacLeod, Yale University; Margaret Nash, SUNY-Cortland; Daisy Quarm, University of Cincinnati; Ronnie Steinberg, Temple University; Mary F. Stuck, SUNY-Oswego; Verta Taylor, Ohio State University; and Kathryn Ward, Southern Illinois University. Also, thanks to Marla Nowick, in particular for her work compiling the contributors' biographical sketches. We are most appreciative of Serina Beauparlant, our editor. She was unwavering in her enthusiasm for this project and provided expert guidance, assistance, and support throughout the project.

Developing this book has been an experience based on friendship, hard work, travel, and fun. We want especially to thank Valerie, Patrice, Roger, and Richard for giving us the support, love and time we needed to do this work well. This book has deepened our friendship, as we have grown more committed to transformed ways of thinking and being. We are lucky to have had such rich times together while working on this project.

About the Editors

Margaret L. Andersen is Professor of Sociology and Women's Studies at the University of Delaware where she also serves as Associate Provost for Instruction. She is the author of *Thinking About Women: Sociological Perspectives on Sex and Gender* and *Social Problems* (with Frank R. Scarpitti). She is currently the editor of *Gender & Society*.

Patricia Hill Collins is Associate Professor of African-American Studies and Sociology at the University of Cincinnati. She is the author of *Black Feminist Thought: Knowledge, Consciousness, and the Politics of Empowerment*, which won the C. Wright Mills Award in 1991.

About the Contributors

Paula Gunn Allen is Professor of English at UCLA. She was awarded the Native American Prize for Literature in 1990. That same year her anthology of short stories, *Spider Woman's Granddaughters*, was awarded the American Book Award, sponsored by the Before Columbus Foundation, and the Susan Koppleman Award. A major Native American poet, writer, and scholar, she's published seven volumes of poetry, a novel, a collection of essays, and two anthologies. Her prose and poetry appear widely in anthologies, journals, and scholarly publications.

Evelyn Torton Beck is Professor and Director of the Women's Studies Program at the University of Maryland–College Park and a member of the Jewish Studies Program. She is the author of *Kafka and the Yiddish Theater* (1971), *The Prism of Sex: Essays in the Sociology of Knowledge* (with Julia Sherman, 1979), and *Nice Jewish Girls: A Lesbian Anthology* (1982, rev. ed. 1989). She has lectured and written widely on Jewish women's studies, lesbian studies, anti-Semitism in the women's movement, feminist transformations of knowledge, and feminist pedagogy.

Mary Frances Berry is Professor of History at the University of Pennsylvania and past president of the Organization of American Historians. She is the author of *Why ERA Failed: Politics, Women's Rights, and the Amending Process of the Constitution*, among other books, and is a former member of the U.S. Civil Rights Commission.

Note: Not all contributors provided biographical information.

Samuel Betances is an educator, sociologist, commentator, comedian, author, and media personality. As Professor of Sociology at Northeastern Illinois University in Chicago for the past eighteen years, he has taught in almost every area of the discipline. In addition, he has led the battle for bilingual education and better racial relations. But more than any other achievement, Samuel Betances' name has become synonymous with building positive synergy through ethnic diversity.

John Blassingame is Professor of History at Yale University. He is the author of *Slave Community: Plantation of Life in the Antebellum South* and editor of *Slave Testimony: Two Centuries of Letters, Speeches, Interviews, and Autobiographies*, among numerous other books and articles.

Robert Blauner is Professor of Sociology at University of California, Berkeley. He teaches courses on race and ethnicity, the sociology of men's experiences, and interviewing/oral history. In addition to *Black Lives/ White Lives* (1989), he has written *Alienation and Freedom* (1964) and *Racial Oppression in America* (1972).

Peter Blood is a marriage and family therapist for the Institute for Christian Counseling and Therapy. He writes about and leads retreats focusing on men's issues. He is the editor of *Rise Up Singing* and is editorial director for the *Sing Out* publication.

Edna Bonacich is Professor of Sociology and Ethnic Studies at the University of California, Riverside. She is currently conducting research on issues of race, class, and gender oppression in the Los Angeles garment industry. She is working with the ILFWU in hopes that the research may benefit the workers.

Olivia Castellano is Professor of English at California State University, Sacramento, where she teaches composition, Chicano literature, and creative writing. She holds an M.A. in Social Anthropology and was a Stanford Fellow in Modern Thought and Literature in 1976. She has published three collections of poetry: *Blue Mandolin–Yellow Field* (1980), *Blue Horse of Madness* (1983), and *Spaces That Time Missed* (1986).

Sucheng Chan is Professor of History and Chair of the Asian American Studies Program at the University of California, Santa Barbara. She is the author of *This Bittersweet Soil: The Chinese in California Agriculture, 1860–1910* (which won three awards), *Asian Californians*, and *Asian Americans: An Interpretive History*. She has also edited four books and written dozens of articles.

Johnnetta B. Cole was named the first African-American woman president of Spelman College in 1987, the largest women's college in Georgia. Dr. Cole's scholarship centers on cultural anthropology, Afro-American studies, and women's studies.

Nancy Diao currently works in banking. She spent ten years as a community organizer in the San Francisco Bay Area Asian Community. She was born in Beijing, China.

Bonnie Thornton Dill earned her Ph.D. at New York University after working for a number of years in antipoverty and open admissions programs in New York. She is currently Professor of Women's Studies at the University of Maryland, College Park. She was the founding director of the Center for Research on Women at Memphis State University. She has contributed articles to such journals as *Signs, Journal of Family History*, and *Feminist Studies* and is currently editing the book *Women of Color in American Society* for Temple University Press. She is also conducting research on single mothers, race, and poverty in the rural South with a grant from the Aspen Institute and the Ford Foundation.

Diana Dujon teaches welfare organizing and is an administrator at the College of Public and Community Service of the University of Massachusetts, Boston. She is a co-founder of Advocacy for Resources for Modern Survival, a Boston welfare-rights group.

D. Stanley Eitzen earned his Ph.D. from the University of Kansas and is Professor of Sociology at Colorado State University. With Maxine Baca Zinn, he has written *Diversity in Families, In Conflict and Order*, and *Social Problems*. He has also written *Elite Deviance* (with David R. Simon), *Criminology* (with Doug A. Timmer), and *Sociology of North American Sport* (with Geroge H. Sage).

Marilyn Frye is Professor of Women's Studies and Philosophy at Michigan State University. She writes about feminism and lesbianism primarily for the lesbian community and the society for Women in Philosophy (Midwestern). She has a Ph.D. in Philosophy from Cornell University, and has written *The Politics of Reality: Essays in Feminist Theory*.

Henry Louis Gates, Jr., is currently Professor of English at Duke University. He is the author of *The Signifying Monkey: A Theory of African-American Literature* and *Reading Black/Reading Feminist: A Critical Anthology*. He is the

General Editor of the Schomburg Library of Nineteenth-Century Black Women Writers, a major collection of rare works of fiction, poetry, autobiography, biography, essays, and journalism written by nineteenth-century black women.

Jewelle Taylor Gibbs is Professor of Social Welfare at the University of California, Berkeley.

Judy Gradford works with Transition House, a Cambridge, Massachusetts, battered-women's shelter. She is a co-founder of Advocacy for Resources for Modern Survival and a board member of DBHN.

Rayna Green is currently Director of the American Indian Program at the National Museum of American History, Smithsonian Institution. She has served on several faculties, public institutions, and nonprofit boards. She has written several books, including *That's What She Said: Contemporary Fiction and Poetry by Native American Women*, and *Native American Women: A Contextual Bibliography*, and many essays on American Indians and American culture. She is also known for her work in museum exhibitions, performance production, television, and radio.

Jacquelyn Dowd Hall earned her Ph.D. at Columbia University. She is Director of the Southern Oral History Program and Julia Cherry Spruill Professor of History at the Unversity of North Carolina, Chapel Hill. She is currently at work on a study of class, race, and sexuality in the twentieth-century South.

Evelynn Hammonds is a doctoral candidate in History of Science at Harvard University, where she is completing her dissertation. She is also currently a visiting scholar in the School of Natural Science at Hampshire College. Her most recent publication, "Conflicts and Tensions in the Feminist Study of Gender and Science" (with Helen Longino), appears in *Conflicts in Feminism*, edited by Evelyn Fox Keller and Marianne Hirsch.

Elizabeth Higginbotham is Associate Professor in the Department of Sociology and Social Work at Memphis State University and a member of the research faculty at their Center for Research on Women. She received her Ph.D. from Brandeis University. She has written widely on race, class, and gender, including articles on incorporating women of color into the college curriculum. She is currently completing a book on educated Black women entitled *Too Much to Ask: The Cost of Black Female Success*.

Robert A. Hummer is a doctoral candidate in Sociology at Florida State University. His areas of interest include social stratification and demography. Current projects include the specification of processes that lead to infant mortality differentials across race/ethnic groups and the understanding of health and mortality differentials between women and men.

June Jordan, a poet and scholar, has published twenty books to date. Currently, she is Professor of African-American Studies and Women's Studies at the University of California, Berkeley.

Kathleen Kautzer wrote her Ph.D. dissertation on the Older Women's League for Brandeis University. She has been a union organizer of clerical workers and is the daughter of a displaced homemaker.

Martha Kirkpatrick is a Clinical Professor of Psychiatry at UCLA where she participated in Robert Stoller's Gender Identity Research Group. She is the editor of *Women's Sexual Development* and *Women's Sexual Experience*, and also has a private practice in Los Angeles.

Tracy A. M. Lai is Professor of History/Coordinated Studies, with an emphasis on multicultural education, at Seattle Central Community College. Her writing is inspired by her experiences organizing in the Asian community and her work with student and international support movements. She is a founding member of Unity Organizing Committee, a new national organization promoting social change.

George Lakey is an activist, teacher, and author of five books. He has conducted over 1,000 workshops on four continents and was already leading men's conferences in the mid-1970s. He has initiated social change projects in civil right, neighborhood development, economic conversion, and peace, and was a founder of the Movement for a New Society. An openly gay grandfather of four, he frequently lectures at major colleges and universities.

Donna Langston has worked a variety of jobs: as secretary, waitress, factory worker, and on an oil refinery crew. She is a Jewish lesbian who was raised and spent the majority of her adult life in an urban, working class/poor background. She is co-editor of *Changing Our Power* and Associate Professor of Women's Studies at Mankato State University.

Audre Lorde grew up in the West Indian community of Harlem in the 1930s, the daughter of immigrants from Grenada. She attended Hunter College (later becoming Professor of English there), ventured to the American expatriate community in Mexico, and participated in the Greenwich Village scene of the early 1950s. She has visited Cuba and Grenada. She is a major figure in the lesbian and feminist movements. Among her works are *Sister Outsider*, *Zami: A New Spelling of My Name*, *Uses of the Erotic*, *Chosen Poems Old and New*, *The Black Unicorn*, and *From a Land Where Other People Live*.

Arturo Madrid is a native of New Mexico but has lived elsewhere over the past thirty years, including California, New Hampshire, Minnesota, and Washington, D.C. Trained as an analyst of literary texts, he has spent most of his life reading and reacting to social texts. He has also worked as an administrator, government official, and institution builder. Currently, he serves as President of the Tomas Rivera Center, a national institute for policy studies on Hispanic issues.

Patricia Yancey Martin is Daisy Parker Flory Alumni Professor of Sociology at Florida State University. She specializes in formal organizations, social stratification (primarily gender), and the social organization of work. She has recently published a theoretical paper on feminist organizations and is completing a book-length study of 130 organizations in Florida that deal with rape victims.

Leanita McClain was the first black member of the editorial board of the *Chicago Tribune*. She died at age 32 by taking her own life. According to her obituary in *Time* magazine (June 11, 1984), her death followed bouts of depression brought on by the strain of being a role model and by the furor resulting from an article she wrote about racial politics in Chicago. Her essays and articles are collected in *A Foot in Each World*.

Peggy McIntosh is Associate Director of the Wellesley College Center for Research on Women. She is founder and codirector of the National SEED Project on Inclusive Curriculum. She consults widely throughout the country and the world with college and school faculty who are creating gender-fair and multicultural curricula. She has written many articles on women's studies, curriculum change, and systems of unearned privilege. She has also taught at the Bearley School, Harvard University, Trinity College (Washington, D.C.), the University of Denver, the University of Durham (England), and Wellesley College. She is contributing editor to *Women's Studies Quarterly* and a consulting editor to *SAGE: A Scholarly Journal on Black Women*.

Michael Messner is Professor of Sociology at the University of Southern California and is the author of *Sport, Men, and Gender Order: Critical Feminist Perspectives*, as well as *Men's Lives* (with Michael Kimmel).

Roslyn Arlin Mickelson is Associate Professor of Sociology and Adjunct Associate Professor of Women's Studies at the University of North Carolina, Charlotte. She received her Ph.D. from UCLA in 1984. Her work examines race, class, and gender inequality in educational processes and outcomes. Currently, she is investigating business-led school reforms and their implications for educational equity.

Cherríe Moraga is a poet, essayist, editor, and playwright. She is author of *Loving in the War Years—Lo que nunca paso por sus labios*, a collection of essays and poetry. She co-edited the ground-breaking anthology *This Bridge Called My Back: Writing by Radical Women of Color* and *Cuentos*, the first collection of stories by Latina feminists published in the United States. She has completed three full-length plays: *Giving Up the Ghost*, which premiered at Theatre Rhinoceros in 1989; *Shadow of a Man*, presented by Brava! for Women in the Arts and the Eureka Theatre in 1990; and *Heroes and Saints*, which was commissioned by the Los Angeles Theatre Center and is scheduled for production by Brava! in 1992.

David Mura is the author of *Turning Japanese: Memoirs of a Sansei*, *After We Lost Our Way* (poetry), and *A Male Grief: Notes on Pornography and Addiction*. His creative nonfiction and poems have appeared in *Mother Jones*, *The New Republic*, *The National*, *Partisan Review*, and *The Graywolf Annual V: Multi-Cultural Literacy*. He has recently created a performance piece on his identity as a Japanese-American male and is now adapting it for video.

Felix M. Padilla is Associate Professor of Sociology at DePaul University. He is the author of *Latino Ethnic Consciousness: The Case of Mexican Americans and Puerto Ricans in Chicago*, *Puerto Rican Chicago*, and *The Gang as an American Enterprise*. His research focuses on the social psychology of Latino consciousness, and he edits a journal on Latino social science.

Roberta Praeger is a long-time Cambridge, Massachusetts, activist who has worked on housing, welfare, and women's issues.

Bernice Johnson Reagon is currently employed by the Smithsonian Institution, American History Department, in Washington, D.C.

Adrienne Rich is a feminist poet and essayist. Her numerous collections of poetry include *Diving into the Wreck, A Wild Patience Has Taken Me This Far, Dream of a Common Language, Your Native Land, Your Life*, and *Time's Power*. Other works include *On Lies, Secrets and Silence: Selected Prose: 1966–1978, Blood, Bread, and Poetry: Selected Prose, 1979–1985*, and *Of Woman Born: Motherhood as Experience and Institution*.

Karen K. Russell holds a degree from Harvard Law School and is the daughter of basketball great Bill Russell.

Jake Ryan is Professor of Political Science at Ithaca College and the author (with Charles Sackray) of *Strangers in Paradise: Academics from the Working Class* (1984).

Charles Sackray is Associate Professor of Economics at Bucknell University. He teaches economic principles and courses on Marx and on the relationship between contemporary theater and the modern economy. He has written *The Political Economy of Urban Poverty* (1973) and (with Jake Ryan) *Strangers in Paradise: Academics from the Working Class* (1984).

Stephen Samuel Smith recently received his Ph.D. from Stanford Unviersity. His dissertation investigated the effects of governmental violence on political participation in the United States. He is currently Assistant Professor of Political Science at Winthrop College in South Carolina where he teaches the politics of education, public policy, and urban politics.

Gloria Steinem is among the country's most widely read and critically acclaimed feminist writers. Her contributions to the women's movement have made her one of the most influential women in America. She co-founded *Ms.* magazine, the national feminist monthly, in 1972. She is a best-selling author whose works include *Outrageous Acts and Everyday Rebellions* and *Marilyn: Norma Jeane*. She is currently writing *The Bedside Book of Self-Esteem*, to be published in 1991.

Dottie Stevens is a Boston-area welfare-rights and poor people's activist, a co-founder of Advocacy for Resources for Modern Survival, and a board member of DBHN.

Robyn I. Stone earned her Ph.D. in Public Health at the University of California, Berkeley. She currently is Senior Policy Analyst at Project HOPE's Center for Health Affairs outside Washington, D.C. She has spoken and published widely in the areas of long-term care reform, informal caregiving, and the feminization of poverty among the elderly.

Emily Warn earned her M.A. in creative writing at the University of Washington. She is the author of three collections of poetry: *The Leaf Path*, *The Book of Esther*, and *Highway Suite*. Her essays and reviews have appeared in *The Bloomsbury Review*, *ERGO*, *The Literary Center Quarterly*, and *Backbone Magazine*. Her writing awards include Pushcart Outstanding Writer, Washington and Idaho State Arts Commissions writer-in-residence, Seattle Arts Commission Independent Artist Grant, and King County Arts Commission Publication Prize. She currently works as a technical writer and editor in Seattle and is also working on her next collection of poems.

Gaye Williams graduated in 1983 from Radcliffe–Harvard College. She has served as Acting Archivist at the Bethune Museum Archives National Historic Site. She is also an activist who tries to combine scholarship, politics, and art to affect change.

Deborah Woo is a sociologist in Community Studies at the University of California, Santa Cruz. She earned her Ph.D. from the University of California, Berkeley, in 1983. Her research focuses on issues of cultural diversity, ethnic stratification, and the ideological or theoretical framework that shapes social relations within a particular context. Her writings relate these issues to mental health, literature, law, and education.

Gloria Yamato is currently the Community Relations Associate for the Pacific Northwest Regional Office of the American Friends Service Committee. She is also the acting Executive Director for ACT/fra, an organization for community-based social/economic change. She has contributed essays to *Changing Our Power* and *Making Face, Making Soul/Haciendo Caras*.

Maxine Baca Zinn is Professor of Sociology and Senior Research Associate in the Julian Samora Research Institute at Michigan State University. Her areas of study include family, race, and gender, with a focus on making the discipline of sociology more race and gender inclusive. She is currently writing a book with Bonnie Thornton Dill on women of color.

I

Reconstructing Knowledge: Toward Inclusive Thinking

We begin this book by asking, Who has been excluded from what is known and how might we see the world differently if we acknowledged and valued the experiences and thoughts of those who have been excluded? Over the centuries Western thought has been centered in the experiences of a privileged few whose particular views of the world and experience within it have shaped what is known. How else can we explain the idea that democracy and egalitarianism were defined as central cultural beliefs in the nineteenth century while millions of African-Americans were enslaved? Why have social science studies been generalized to the whole population while being based only on samples of men? The exclusion of women, African-Americans, Latinos, Native Americans, gays and lesbians, and other groups from formal scholarship has resulted in distortions and incomplete information not only about the experiences of excluded groups but also about the experience of more privileged groups. Thus, the development of women's studies has also changed the way we see men; the study of racial-ethnic groups has transformed our understanding of white experiences, as well.

This exclusionary thinking has been increasingly challenged by scholars and teachers who want to include the diversity of human experience in the construction and transmission of knowledge. Those who ask us to think more inclusively want to open up the way the world is viewed, making the experience of previously excluded groups more visible and central in the construction of knowledge. Inclusive thinking shifts our perspective from the white, male-centered forms of thinking that have characterized much of Western thought. Thinking inclusively means putting the experiences of those who have been excluded at the center of thought so that we can better understand the intersections of race, class, and gender in the experiences of all groups, including those with privilege and power.

The selections in this book ask the reader to consider the experience of those who have been silenced before. Ask yourself, "How does the world look different if we put the experiences of those who have been excluded at the center of our thinking?" The six articles in Part One show the limits of existing knowledge by providing personal accounts of what exclusion means and how it feels. We have selected personal accounts that reflect the diverse experiences people have because of race, class, gender, and/or sexual orientation. These accounts document the diversity of experience within the United States by describing how exclusion shapes individual and collective consciousness. As a result, we begin to see how diverse experiences can shape the concepts and theories we develop in the academy. Together, they suggest new possibilities for thinking inclusively and imagining a society that would be more enabling for everyone.

In "Missing People and Others," Arturo Madrid tells how exclusion and marginalization in the educational curriculum has affected us all. Madrid describes his schooling as a denial of the specific experience of Latinos, Asian Americans, Native Americans, and all groups together considered to be "other." He asks us to consider what it feels like to be the missing person. As we read his account, we see how education has contributed to exclusion, by marginalizing the history of Chicanos and groups considered to be "other."

Likewise, David Mura, a third-generation, middle-class Japanese American, speaks in "Strangers in the Village" of the gap that racism creates between him and his white friends. He, like Madrid, sees the all-white images that pervade education and the dominant culture. These images deny, for all people, the complexity of human life. In the end, as Mura poignantly relates, knowing others is also a way of knowing ourselves.

In "La Güera" Cherríe Moraga writes about her developing awareness of her class, race, and sexual identity. Like the other authors here, Moraga tells us what exclusion has meant in her experience and how it feels. Her essay also reveals the intersections of race, class, and gender with the system of compulsory heterosexuality—that is, the institutionalized structures and beliefs that define and enforce heterosexual behavior as the only natural and permissible form of sexual expression. For Moraga, acknowledging her lesbian identity deepened her understanding of her mother's oppression as a poor Chicana. Moraga also reminds us of the importance of breaking the silences that protect oppression.

Readers should keep the accounts of Madrid, Mura, and Moraga in mind as they read the remainder of this book. What new experiences, understandings, theories, histories, and analyses do these readings inspire? What does it take for a member of one group (say a white male) to be willing to learn from and value the experiences of another (for example, a Chicana lesbian)? For example, in her essay "Report from the Bahamas," June Jordan, herself a Black woman, shows her student, a white Catholic Irish woman, finding common ground with her South African classmate. There are no simple or singular answers to these questions, but recentering our frame of reference can reshape what we know, both formally and in everyday life. But this is not just an intellectual exercise; as Paula Gunn Allen shows in her article on Native American women, it is a matter of survival. Resisting systems of oppression means revising the ideas about ourselves and others that have been created as a part of a system of social control.

Reading these articles shows us the radical shift that thinking inclusively requires. Such a shift begins with valuing the experiences of those who have been excluded and questioning the assumptions made about all groups. When we begin to take a more inclusive perspective, divisions between privileged and underprivileged, oppressor and oppressed are challenged because we start to see race, class, and gender as intersecting systems of experience. For example, white women and women of color share some common experiences based on their gender, but their racial experiences are distinct. Moreover, experiences within the race/gender system are further conditioned by one's class. For example, as Johnnetta Cole points out in an article in Part Two, gender is manifested differently, depending on one's race and class.

June Jordan's essay "Report from the Bahamas" is a model of this inclusive thinking. In it she begins from her own experience as a black, middle-class, well-educated woman and reflects on her connections with other women in different locations in the race, class, gender system. In doing so, she finds connections in surprising places, while also understanding the differences that distinguish our experiences.

Engaging oneself at the personal level is critical to thinking inclusively. Changing one's mind is not just a matter of assessing facts and data, though that is important, but it also requires examining one's feelings. That is why we begin with personal narratives. Unlike more conventional forms of sociological data (such as surveys, interviews, and even direct observations), personal accounts are more likely to elicit emotional responses. Traditionally, social science has defined emotional engagement as an impediment to objectivity. Sociology, for example, has emphasized rational thought as the basis for social action and has often discouraged more personalized reflection. But the capacity to reflect on one's experience is what makes us distinctly human. Personal documents tap the private, reflective dimension of life, enabling us to see the inner life of others and revealing our own lives more completely. The idea that objectivity is best reached only through rational thought is a specifically Western and masculine way of thinking—one that we challenge throughout this book.

However, including personal narratives is not meant to limit our level of understanding to individuals. As sociologists, we study individuals in groups as a way of revealing the social structures shaping collective experiences. Through doing so, we discover our common experiences and see the impact of the social structures of race, class, and gender on our experiences. Marilyn Frye's article, "Oppression," introduces the structural perspective that lies at the heart of this book. She distinguishes oppression from suffering, pointing out that many individuals suffer in society, but that oppression is structured into the fabric of social institutions. Using the metaphor of a bird cage, Frye artfully explains the concept of social structure. Looking only at an individual wire in a cage does not reveal the network of wires forming a cage. Likewise, social structure refers to the patterns of behavior, belief, resource distribution, and social control that constitute society. Although experienced at the individual level, race, class, and gender are embedded in social structures. Individual experience reveals these structures to us, but change cannot be limited to individuals alone.

As the authors in this section show, the strength and richness of our society are in its diversity, but the potential of this diversity will only be realized through social structures that value and protect all human experiences. To reconstruct what we know, we begin with the experiences of those who have been excluded. In so doing, we build a system of knowledge that ensures the survival of us all.

Shifting the Center

MISSING PEOPLE AND OTHERS:
Joining Together to Expand the Circle

Arturo Madrid

1

I am a citizen of the United States, as are my parents and as were their parents, grandparents, and great-grandparents. My ancestors' presence in what is now the United States antedates Plymouth Rock, even without taking into account any American Indian heritage I might have.

I do not, however, fit those mental sets that define America and Americans. My physical appearance, my speech patterns, my name, my profession (a professor of Spanish) create a text that confuses the reader. My normal experience is to be asked, "And where are *you* from?"

My response depends on my mood. Passive-aggressive, I answer, "From here." Aggressive-passive, I ask, "Do you mean where am I originally from?" But ultimately my answer to those follow-up questions that ask about origins will be that we have always been from here.

Overcoming my resentment I will try to educate, knowing that nine times out of ten my words fall on inattentive ears. I have spent most of my adult life explaining who I am not. I am exotic, but—as Richard Rodriguez of *Hunger of Memory* fame so painfully found out—not exotic enough . . . not Peruvian, or Pakistani, or Persian, or whatever.

I am, however, very clearly *the other*, if only your everyday, garden-variety, domestic *other*. I've always known that I was *the other*, even before I knew the vocabulary or understood the significance of being *the other*.

From: *Change* 20 (May/June 1988): 55–59. Reprinted by permission.

I grew up in an isolated and historically marginal part of the United States, a small mountain village in the state of New Mexico, the eldest child of parents native to that region and whose ancestors had always lived there. In those vast and empty spaces, people who look like me, speak as I do, and have names like mine predominate. But the *americanos* lived among us: the descendants of those nineteenth-century immigrants who dispossessed us of our lands; missionaries who came to convert us and stayed to live among us; artists who became enchanted with our land and humanscape and went native; refugees from unhealthy climes, crowded spaces, unpleasant circumstances; and, of course, the inhabitants of Los Alamos, whose socio-cultural distance from us was moreover accentuated by the fact that they occupied a space removed from and proscribed to us. More importantly, however, they—*los americanos*—were omnipresent (and almost exclusively so) in newspapers, newsmagazines, books, on radio, in movies and, ultimately, on television.

Despite the operating myth of the day, school did not erase my otherness. It did try to deny it, and in doing so only accentuated it. To this day, schooling is more socialization than education, but when I was in elementary school— and given where I was—socialization was everything. School was where one became an American. Because there was a pervasive and systematic denial by the society that surrounded us that we were Americans. That denial was both explicit and implicit. My earliest memory of the former was that there were two kinds of churches: theirs and ours. The more usual was the implicit denial, our absence from the larger cultural, economic, political and social spaces— the one that reminded us constantly that we were *the other*. And school was where we felt it most acutely.

Quite beyond saluting the flag and pledging allegiance to it (a very intense and meaningful action, given that the U.S. was involved in a war and our brothers, cousins, uncles, and fathers were on the front lines) becoming American was learning English and its corollary—not speaking Spanish. Until very recently ours was a proscribed language—either *de jure* (by rule, by policy, by law) or *de facto* (by practice, implicitly if not explicitly; through social and political and economic pressure). I do not argue that learning English was not appropriate. On the contrary. Like it or not, and we had no basis to make any judgments on that matter, we were Americans by virtue of having been born Americans, and English was the common language of Americans. And there was a myth, a pervasive myth, that said that if we only learned to speak English well—and particularly without an accent—we would be welcomed into the American fellowship.

Senator Sam Hayakawa notwithstanding, the true text was not our speech, but rather our names and our appearance, for we would always have an accent, however perfect our pronunciation, however excellent our enunciation, however divine our diction. That accent would be heard in our pigmentation, our physiognomy, our names. We were, in short, *the other*.

Being *the other* means feeling different; is awareness of being distinct; is consciousness of being dissimilar. It means being outside the game, outside the circle, outside the set. It means being on the edges, on the margins, on the periphery. Otherness means feeling excluded, closed out, precluded, even disdained and scorned. It produces a sense of isolation, of apartness, of disconnectedness, of alienation.

Being *the other* involves a contradictory phenomenon. On the one hand being *the other* frequently means being invisible. Ralph Ellison wrote eloquently about that experience in his magisterial novel *The Invisible Man*. On the other hand, being *the other* sometimes involves sticking out like a sore thumb. What is she/he doing here?

If one is *the other*, one will inevitably be perceived unidimensionally; will be seen stereotypically; will be defined and delimited by mental sets that may not bear much relation to existing realities. There is a darker side to otherness as well. *The other* disturbs, disquiets, discomforts. It provokes distrust and suspicion. *The other* makes people feel anxious, nervous, apprehensive, even fearful. *The other* frightens, scares.

For some of us being *the other* is only annoying; for others it is debilitating; for still others it is damning. Many try to flee otherness by taking on protective colorations that provide invisibility, whether of dress or speech or manner or name. Only a fortunate few succeed. For the majority, otherness is permanently sealed by physical appearance. For the rest, otherness is betrayed by ways of being, speaking or of doing.

I spent the first half of my life downplaying the significance and consequences of otherness. The second half has seen me wrestling to understand its complex and deeply ingrained realities; striving to fathom why otherness denies us a voice or visibility or validity in American society and its institutions; struggling to make otherness familiar, reasonable, even normal to my fellow Americans.

I am also a missing person. Growing up in northern New Mexico I had only a slight sense of our being missing persons. *Hispanos*, as we called (and call) ourselves in New Mexico, were very much a part of the fabric of the society and there were Hispano professionals everywhere about me: doctors, lawyers, school teachers, and administrators. My people owned businesses, ran organizations and were both appointed and elected public officials.

To be sure, we did not own the larger businesses, nor at the time were we permitted to be part of the banking world. Other than that, however, people who looked like me, spoke like me, and had names like mine, predominated. There was, to be sure, Los Alamos, but as I have said, it was removed from our realities.

My awareness of our absence from the larger institutional life of society became sharper when I went off to college, but even then it was attenuated by the circumstances of history and geography. The demography of Albuquerque still strongly reflected its historical and cultural origins, despite the influx of Midwesterners and Easterners. Moreover, many of my classmates at the University of New Mexico in Albuquerque were Hispanos, and even some of my professors were.

I thought that would obtain at UCLA, where I began graduate studies in 1960. Los Angeles already had a very large Mexican population, and that population was visible even in and around Westwood and on the campus. Many of the groundskeepers and food-service personnel at UCLA were Mexican. But Mexican-American students were few and mostly invisible, and I do not recall seeing or knowing a single Mexican-American (or, for that matter, black, Asian, or American Indian) professional on the staff or faculty of that institution during the five years I was there.

Needless to say, persons like me were not present in any capacity at Dartmouth College—the site of my first teaching appointment—and, of course, were not even part of the institutional or individual mind-set. I knew then that we—a "we" that had come to encompass American Indians, Asian-Americans, black Americans, Puerto Ricans, and women—were truly missing persons in American institutional life.

Over the past three decades, the *de jure* and *de facto* segregations that have historically characterized American institutions have been under assault. As a consequence, minorities and women have become part of American institutional life, and although there are still many areas where we are not to be found, the missing persons phenomenon is not as pervasive as it once was.

However, the presence of *the other*, particularly minorities, in institutions and in institutional life, is, as we say in Spanish, *a flor de tierra*; spare plants whose roots do not go deep, a surface phenomenon, vulnerable to inclemencies of an economic, political, or social nature.

Our entrance into and our status in institutional life is not unlike a scenario set forth by my grandmother's pastor when she informed him that she and her family were leaving their mountain village to relocate in the Rio Grande Valley. When he asked her to promise that she would remain true to the faith and continue to involve herself in the life of the church, she assured him that she would and asked him why he thought she would do otherwise.

"Doña Trinidad," he told her, "in the Valley there is no Spanish church. There is only an American church." "But," she protested, "I read and speak English and would be able to worship there." Her pastor's response was: "It is possible that they will not admit you, and even if they do, they might not accept you. And that is why I want you to promise me that you are going to go to church. Because if they don't let you in through the front door, I want you to go in through the back door. And if you can't get in through the back door, go in the side door. And if you are unable to enter through the side door I want you to go in through the window. What is important is that you enter and that you stay."

Some of us entered institutional life through the front door; others through the back door; and still others through side doors. Many, if not most of us, came in through windows and continue to come in through windows. Of those who entered through the front door, some never made it past the lobby; others were ushered into corners and niches. Those who entered through back and side doors inevitably have remained in back and side rooms. And those who entered through windows found enclosures built around them. For despite the lip service given to the goal of the integration of minorities into institutional life, what has occurred instead is ghettoization, marginalization, isolation.

Not only have the entry points been limited: in addition, the dynamics have been singularly conflictive. Gaining entry and its corollary—gaining space—have frequently come as a consequence of demands made on institutions and institutional officers. Rather than entering institutions more or less passively, minorities have, of necessity, entered them actively, even aggressively. Rather than taking, they have demanded. Institutional relations have thus been adversarial, infused with specific and generalized tensions.

The nature of the entrance and the nature of the space occupied have greatly influenced the view and attitudes of the majority population within those institutions. All of us are put into the same box; that is, no matter what the individual reality, the assessment of the individual is inevitably conditioned by a perception that is held of the class. Whatever our history, whatever our record, whatever our validations, whatever our accomplishments, by and large we are perceived unidimensionally and are dealt with accordingly.

My most recent experience in this regard is atypical only in its explicitness. A few years ago I allowed myself to be persuaded to seek the presidency of a large and prestigious state university. I was invited for an interview and presented myself before the selection committee, which included members of the board of trustees. The opening question of the brief but memorable interview was directed at me by a member of that august body. "Dr. Madrid," he asked, "why does a one-dimensional person like you think he can be the president of a multi-dimensional institution like ours?"

If, as I happen to believe, the well-being of a society is directly related to the degree and extent to which all of its citizens participate in its institutions, we have a challenge before us. One of the strengths of our society—perhaps its main strength—has been a tradition of struggle against clubbishness, exclusivity, and restriction.

Today, more than ever, given the extraordinary changes that are taking place in our society, we need to take up that struggle again—irritating, grating, troublesome, unfashionable, unpleasant as it is. As educated and educator members of this society, we have a special responsibility for leading the struggle against marginalization, exclusion, and alienation.

Let us work together to assure that all American institutions, not just its precollegiate educational and penal institutions, reflect the diversity of our society. Not to do so is to risk greater alienation on the part of a growing segment of our society. It is to risk increased social tension in an already conflictive world. And ultimately it is to risk the survival of a range of institutions that, for all their defects and deficiencies, permit us the space, the opportunity, and the freedom to improve our individual and collective lot; to guide the course of our government, and to redress whatever grievances we have. Let us join together to expand, not to close the circle.

STRANGERS IN THE VILLAGE   2

David Mura

Recently, in *The Village Voice*, a number of articles were devoted to the issue of race in America. Perhaps the most striking article, "Black Women, White Kids: A Tale of Two Worlds," was about Black women in New York City who take care of upper-middle-class and upper-class white children. Merely by describing the situation of these Black women and recording their words, the article pointed out how race and class affects these women's lives: "As the nanny sits in the park watching a tow-haired child play, her own kids are coming home from school; they will do their homework alone and make dinner."

From: Rick Simonson and Scott Walker (eds.), *Multicultural Literacy: Opening the American Mind* (St. Paul, Minn.: Graywolf Press, 1988), pp. 135–153. Reprinted by permission.

None of the white people who employed these nannies seemed at all cognizant of the contradictions of this description. Instead the whites seemed to view the Black nannies as a natural facet of their lives, an expected privilege. Yet, on another less-conscious level, the whites appeared to have misgivings that they could not express. One of the nannies, named Bertha, talked about how she objected to the tone of voice her employer, Barbra, used: "You wait a minute here, Barbra. I'm not a child," Bertha would tell Barbra, "I can talk to you any way I want. This is a free country, it's not a commie country." Every time Bertha and Barbra have an argument, Barbra buys Bertha presents: "She bought me shoes, a beautiful blouse, a Mother's Day present . . . she's a very generous person. She's got a good heart." But Bertha doesn't really like the presents. "It always made me feel guilty. To tell you the truth about it, I never had too many people give me presents, so it just made me feel bad.

"Another reason we don't get along," Bertha continues, "is she always trying to figure me out. See, I'm a very complicated person. I'm a very moody person . . . I'm independent. I figure I can deal with it myself. And we would sit there, I could just feel her eyes on me, and I'd have to get up and leave the room . . . She just wants you to be satisfied with her all the time . . . She wants me to tell her I love you. I just can't."

The author of the article says that sometimes Barbra seems to want love and sometimes she seems to want forgiveness. "But perhaps for most white people, a black person's affection can never mean more than an act of absolution for historical and collective guilt, an affection desired not because of how one feels about that particular person but because that person is black."

As a middle-class third-generation Japanese-American, I read this article with mixed feelings. On one level, I have much more in common with Bertha's employer, Barbra, than I do with Bertha. Although at one time Japanese-Americans worked in jobs similar to Bertha's and were part of the lower class, by my generation this was not the case. I grew up in the suburbs of Chicago, went to college and graduate school, married a pediatrician who is three-quarters WASP and one-quarter Jewish. Although I will most likely assume a large portion of our child care when we have children, my wife and I will probably use some form of outside child care. Most likely, we would not employ a Black nanny, even if we lived in New York City, but I could not help feeling a sense of guilt and shame when I read the article. I could understand Barbra's wish to use acts of kindness to overlook inequalities of class and race; her desire to equate winning the affections of a Black servant with the absolution of historical and collective guilt. I would not, in the end, act like Barbra, but I do recognize her feelings.

At the same time, I also recognize and identify with the anger Bertha feels toward her white employer. In part, Bertha's anger is a recognition of how profoundly race has affected her and Barbra's lives, and also that Barbra does not truly understand this fact. Although generalizations like this can sometimes be misused—more about this later—American culture defines white middle-class culture as the norm. As a result, Blacks and other colored minorities, must generally know two cultures to survive—the culture of middle-class whites and their own minority culture. Middle-class whites need only to know one culture. For them, knowledge of a minority culture is a seeming—and I use the word "seeming" here purposely—luxury; they can survive without it.

On a smaller scale than Bertha I have experienced the inability of members of the white majority to understand how race has affected my life, to come to terms with the differences between us. Sometimes I can bridge this gap, but never completely; more often, a gulf appears between me and white friends that has previously been unacknowledged. I point out to them that the images I grew up with in the media were all white, that the books I read in school—from Dick and Jane onwards—were about whites and later, about European civilization. I point out to them the way beauty is defined in our culture and how, under such definitions, slanted eyes, flat noses, and round faces just don't make it. And as I talk, I often sense their confusion, the limits of their understanding of the world. They become angry, defensive. "We all have experiences others can't relate to," they reply and equate the issue of race with prejudice against women or Italians or rich people. Such generalizations can sometimes be used to express sympathy with victims of prejudice, but as used by many whites, it generally attempts to shut down racial anger by denying the distinct causes of that anger, thereby rendering it meaningless. Another form of this tactic is the reply, "I think of you just as a white person," or, a bit less chauvinistically, "I think of you as an individual." While, at one time in my life, I would have taken this for a compliment, my reply now is, "I don't want to be a white person. Why can't I be who I am? Why can't you think of me as a Japanese-American *and* as an individual?"

I'd like to leave these questions a moment and, because I'm a writer, take up these themes in terms of literature. In my talks with whites about race, I very quickly find myself referring to history. As many have pointed out, America has never come to terms with two fundamental historical events: the enslavement of Blacks by whites and the taking of this continent by Europeans from the Native Americans and the accompanying policies of genocide. A third historical event that America hasn't come to terms with—and yet is closer to doing so than with the other two—is the internment of Japanese-Americans during World War II. Although some maintain that the camps were caused simply by wartime hysteria, the determining factors were racism and a desire for the property owned by the Japanese-Americans. . . .

Knowing the history behind the camps, knowing that during the internment the lives of many Japanese-Americans, particularly the Issei (first generation), were permanently disrupted; knowing the internment caused the loss of millions of dollars of property, I, as a Japanese-American, feel a kinship to both Blacks and Native Americans that I do not feel with white Americans. It is a kinship that comes from our histories as victims of injustice. Of course, our histories are more than simply being victims, and we must recognize that these histories are also separate and distinct, but there is a certain power and solace in this kinship.

This kinship is reinforced by our current position as minorities in a white-dominated culture. For instance, when Blacks or Native Americans or Chicanos complain about their image in the media, it is a complaint I easily understand. I myself have written a number of pieces about this subject, analyses of the stereotypes in such films as *Rambo* or *Year of the Dragon*. Recently, I read a play by a Sansei playwright, Philip Kan Gotanda, *Yankee Dawg You Die*, and I was struck by the similarities between this play about two Japanese-American actors and Robert Townsend's *Hollywood Shuffle*, a film about a Black actor trying to make it in Hollywood.

In both works, the actors must struggle with the battle between economics and integrity, between finding no parts or playing in roles that stereotype their minority. In *Hollywood Shuffle*, we see the hero, clearly a middle-class Black, trying and failing to portray a pimp in his bathroom mirror. Later in the film, there is a mock Black acting school where Black actors learn to talk in jive, to move like a pimp, to play runaway slaves, to shuffle their feet. In *Yankee Dawg You Die*, a young third-generation Japanese-American actor, Bradley, is fired at one point because he will not mix up his r's and l's when playing a waiter. Throughout the play, he keeps chastizing an older Japanese-American actor for selling out, for playing stereotyped "coolie" and "dirty Jap" parts. Essentially, what Bradley is accusing Vincent of being is a Tom:

> The Business. You keep talking about the business. The industry. Hollywood. What's Hollywood? Cutting up your face to look more white? So my nose is a little flat. Fine! Flat is beautiful. So I don't have a double fold in my eye-lid. Great! No one in my entire racial family has had it in the last 10,000 years.
>
> My old girlfriend used to put scotch tape on her eyelids to get the double folds so she could look more "cau-ca-sian." My new girlfriend—she doesn't mess around, she got surgery. Where does it stop? "I never turned down a role." Where does it begin? Vincent? Where does it begin? All that self hate. You and your Charlie Chop Suey roles.

Vincent tells Bradley that he knows nothing about the difficulties he, Vincent, went through: "You want to know the truth? I'm glad I did it . . . in some small way it is a victory. Yes, a victory. At least an oriental was on the screen acting, being seen. We existed!" At this point, the scene slides into a father and son mode, where the father-figure, Vincent, tells Bradley that he should appreciate what those who went before him have done; it's easy now for Bradley to spout the rhetoric of Asian-American consciousness, but in the past, such rhetoric was unthinkable. (Earlier in the play, when Vincent says, "I do not really notice, or quite frankly care, if someone is oriental or caucasian . . ." Bradley makes a certain connection between Asian-American rights and other liberation movements. "It's Asian, not oriental," he says. "Asian, oriental. Black, negro. Woman, girl. Gay, homosexual.")

But Bradley then gets on a soapbox and makes a cogent point, though a bit baldly, and I can easily imagine a young Black actor making a similar argument to an old Black actor who has done Stepin Fetchit roles:

> You seem to think that every time you do one of those demeaning roles, all that is lost is your dignity . . . Don't you realize that every time you do a por- trayal like that millions of people in their homes, in movie theatres across the country will see it. Be influenced by it. Believe it. Every time you do any old stereotypic role just to pay the bills, you kill the right of some Asian-American child to be treated as a human being. To walk through the school yard and not be called a "chinaman gook" by some taunting kids who just saw the last Rambo film.

By the end of the play, though, it's clear Bradley's been beaten down. After scrambling through failed audition after audition, wanting to make it in the business, he cries when he fails to get a role as a butler because he doesn't know kung fu. He also reveals he has recently had his nose fixed, à la Michael Jackson.

What do the similarities I've been pointing out mean for an Asian-American writer? Recently, there have been a spate of books, such as Allan Bloom's *The Closing of the American Mind*, which call for a return to the classics and a notion of a core-cultural tradition; these critiques bemoan the relativism and "nihilism" of the sixties and the multicultural movements which, in the name of "tolerance," have supposedly left our culture in a shambles. Unfortunately, such critics never really question the political and historical bases of cultural response. If they did, they would understand why, contrary to Allan Bloom, other minority writers represent a valuable resource for Asian-American writers and vice versa: our themes and difficulties are similar; we learn from each other things we cannot receive from a Saul Bellow or John Updike or even Rousseau or Plato.

It is not just the work of Asian-American writers like Gotanda that sustain me. I know a key point in my life was when I discovered the work of Frantz Fanon, particularly his book, *Black Skin, White Masks*. My experience with that work and others like it shows why multiculturalism, for a member of a racial minority, is not simply tolerance, but an essential key to survival.

In his work, Fanon, a Black psychologist, provides a cogent analysis of how a majority can oppress a minority through culture: it makes the victim or servant identify with the ruler and, in so doing, causes the victim to direct whatever anger he/she feels at the situation towards himself/herself in the form of self-hatred.

> In the Antilles . . . in the magazines, the Wolf, the Devil, the Evil Spirit, the Bad Man, the Savage are always symbolized by Negroes or Indians; since there is always identification with the victor, the little Negro, quite as easily as the little white boy, becomes an explorer, an adventurer, a missionary "who faces the danger of being eaten by the wicked Negroes" . . . The black school boy . . . who in his lessons is forever talking about "our ancestors, the Gauls," identifies himself with the explorer, the bringer of civilization, the white man who carries truth to the savages—an all-white truth . . . the young Negro . . . invests the hero, who is white, with all his own aggression—at that age closely linked to sacrificial dedication, a sacrificial dedication permeated with sadism.

This passage can be taken as another version of Bradley's speech to Vincent on the effects of stereotypes on an Asian-American child.

Fanon was incredibly aware of how the economic, social, and political relations of power create and warp an individual's psychic identity. He was quick to point out that psychic sickness does not always find its source in the neuroses of an individual or that individual's family, but in the greater sickness of a society. In such cases, for the individual to become healthy, he or she must recognize that society is sick, and that the ideas he or she has received from that society are part of that sickness.

In short, what Fanon recognized and taught me was the liberating power of anger.

After reading Fanon and the Black French poet from Martinique, Aime Cesaire, I wrote a number of poems in which I chose to ally myself with people of color, anti-colonialist movements, and a non-Eurocentric consciousness. When writing these poems, I was aware of how such poems can often become vehicles for slogans and cheap rhetoric; still I tried to discover a language with a denseness which would prevent such reduction, increase thought, and turn words like "gook" and "nigger" against their original meaning, bending and realigning the slang of racism. Here is the ending of one of those poems:

> . . . and we were all good niggers, good gooks and japs, good spics and
> rice eaters saying mem sab, sahib, bwana, boss-san, señor, father, heart-
> throb oh honored and most unceasing, oh devisor and provider of our own ob-
> sequious, ubiquitous ugliness, which stares at you baboon-like, banana-like,
> dwarf-like, tortoise-like, dirt-like, slant-eyed, kink-haired, ashen and pansied
> and brutally unredeemable, we are whirling about you, tartars of the air all the
> urinating, tarantula grasping, ant multiplying, succubused, hothouse hoards
> yes, it us, it us, we, we knockee, yes, sir, massa, boss-san, we tearee down
> your door!

I was scared at first by the anger of this poem, but I also saw it as an answer, an antidote to the depression I had been feeling, a depression brought on by a lack of self-worth and by my dropping out of English graduate school. As my therapist had told me, depression is the repression of anger and grief. In my diary I wrote about the unlocking of this repression:

> In the first stages of such a process, one can enter a position where the
> destruction of one stereotype creates merely a new stereotype, and where the
> need to point out injustice overwhelms and leaves the writing with a baldness
> that seems both naive and sentimental. Still, the task must be faced, and what
> I am now trying to do in both my writing and my life is to replace self-hatred
> and self-negation with anger and grief over my lost selves, over the ways my
> cultural heritage has been denied to me, over the ways that people in Amer-
> ica would assume either that I am not American or, conversely, that I am just
> like them; over the ways my education and the values of European culture
> have denied that other cultures exist. I know more about Europe at the time
> when my grandfather came to America than I know about Meiji Japan. I know
> Shakespeare and Donne, Sophocles and Homer better than I know Zeami,
> Bashō or Lady Murasaki. This is not to say I regret what I know, but I do regret
> what I don't know. And the argument that the culture of America is derived
> from Europe will not wipe away this regret.

I am convinced if I had not read Fanon, if I had not reached these insights, and gone on to explore beyond white European culture, I would have died as a writer and died spiritually and psychically as a person. I would have ended up denying who I am and my place in history. Thus, I think that to deny a people a right to determine their own cultural tradition is a type of genocide.

Of course, arguing for multiculturalism is not the same thing as saying that, as a minority writer, I don't need to read the works of European culture. It's not a case of either/or. As Carlos Fuentes remarked, "We [Latin Ameri-cans] have to know the cultures of the West even better than a Frenchman or an Englishman, and at the same time we have to know our own cultures. This sometimes means going back to the Indian cultures, whereas the Europeans feel they don't have to know our cultures at all. We have to know Quetzalcoatl and Descartes. They think Descartes is enough." I think Fuentes would agree with Jesse Jackson that there was something wrong with those students who greeted his appearance at Stanford with the chant, "Hey hey, ho ho/Western culture's got to go." As Jackson pointed out, Western culture was their culture. It is difficult to strike an appropriate balance.

. . . If we ignore the specifics of the situation of our own minority group, in essence we both deny who we are and our own complexity. We also run the risk of using our victimhood as a mask for sainthood, of letting whatever sins the white race has committed against us become a permanent absolution for us, an excuse to forgo moral and psychological introspection.

. . . It is intoxicating after years of feeling inferior, after years of hating oneself, it is so comforting to use this rage not just to feel equal to the oppressor, but superior, and not just superior, but simply blameless and blessed, one of the prophetic and holy ones. It is what one imagines a god feels like, and in this state one does feel like a god of history, a fate; one knows that history is on one's side, because one is helping to break open, to recreate history. And how much better it is to feel like a god after years of worshipping the oppressor as one.

But once one can clearly describe all this, one realizes that such a stance represents a new form of hubris, an intoxicating blindness: human beings are not gods, are not superior to other human beings. Human beings are fallible, cannot foresee the future, cannot demand or receive freely the worship of others. In aligning one's rage with a sense of superiority, one fails to recognize how this rage is actually fueled by a sense of inferiority: one's own version of history and views on equality need, on some level, the approval, the assent, the defeat of the oppressor. The wish for superiority is simply the reverse side of feeling inferior, not its cure. It focuses all the victim's problems on the other, the oppressor. Yet until it is recognized how one has contributed to this victimhood, the chains are still there, inside, are part of the psyche. Conversely, liberation occurs only when one is sure enough of oneself, feels good enough, to admit fault, admit their portion of blame.

Given the difficulty of this process, it's no wonder so many stumble in the process or stop midway through. And it is made much more difficult if the oppressor is especially recalcitrant, is implacable towards change. When this happens, fresh wound after fresh wound is inflicted, causing bundle after bundle of rage: bitterness then becomes too tempting; too much energy is required to heal. . . .

Here I return to the fundamental historical events I mentioned earlier in this essay: the enslavement of Blacks, the taking of Native American land and the genocidal policies that accomplished it. One can think of other related historical events: the internment camps, the Asian-Exclusion act, the conditions of the Asian workers building the American railroads, the conditions of migrant farm workers and illegal aliens. The list could go on and on. But that is to point out the obvious. What is not so obvious is how the laws of property in our society have served to make permanent what was stolen in the past. Those who bought my grandparents' property for a song still benefit from that property today; there has been no compensation, just as there has been no compensation to Blacks for the institution of slavery or to Native Americans for the taking of a continent and the destruction of their peoples and culture. And as long as there is no movement toward a just compensation, the collective guilt will remain.

And yet I also recognize that a just compensation is not possible. The wrongs are too great, run too far back in history, and human beings are fallible and forgetful. Justice demands too high a price.

Therefore we must settle for less, for a compromise. The concept of white collective guilt reminds us of this compromise, that there has been and probably will always be a less than even settling of the debt. However whites protest that they want equality and justice, they are, in the end, not willing to pay the price. And when those they have wronged call for the price, the reaction of whites is almost always one of anger and resentment.

Now, in this situation, the whites have two choices. When they accept the concept of collective guilt, they admit that they feel unjustifiable anger and resentment at any measure that threatens any part of their privileged position, much less any of the measures that approach just compensation. When whites don't admit collective guilt, they try to blame racial troubles on those who ask for a just settlement and remain baffled at the anger and resentment of the colored minorities.

Whether in the area of culture or in economic relations, these choices remain. In the realm of culture in America, white European culture has held the floor for centuries; just as with any one-sided conversation, a balance can only be achieved if the speaker who has dominated speaks less and listens more. That is what conservative cultural critics are unwilling to do; for them there is no such thing as collective guilt, much less the obligation such guilt bestows. It is not just that the colored minorities in America need to create and receive their own cultural images, nor that, for these minorities, the culture of the Third World and its struggles against white-dominated cultures provides insights into race in America that cannot be found in European literature. This much ought to seem obvious. But there is more: only when whites in America begin to listen to the voices of the colored minorities and the Third World will they come to understand not just those voices but also themselves and their world. Reality is not simply knowing who we think we are, but also what others think of us. And only with this knowledge will whites ever understand what needs to be done to make things equal.

The situation in the *Voice* article on nannies is no different: without admitting the concept of collective guilt, the white middle-class Barbra remains unable to comprehend her nanny Bertha, unable to understand what this Black woman feels. Ultimately, Barbra does not want to admit that the only way she is going to feel comfortable with Bertha is if they meet as equals; that society must be changed so that Barbra and her children will not enjoy certain privileges they have taken as rights. In short, Barbra and other whites will have to give up power; that is what it means to make things equal. At the same time she must admit that no matter how much she works for change, how much society changes, there will never, on this earth, be a just settling of accounts. That is the burden she has to take up; she may think it will destroy her, but it will not. And, ultimately, this process would not only help Bertha to meet and know Barbra as an equal, but for Barbra to understand and accept who she is, to know herself.

LA GÜERA

3

Cherríe Moraga

It requires something more than personal experience to gain a philosophy or point of view from any specific event. It is the quality of our response to the event and our capacity to enter into the lives of others that help us to make their lives and experiences our own.

Emma Goldman[1]

I am the very well-educated daughter of a woman who, by the standards in this country, would be considered largely illiterate. My mother was born in Santa Paula, Southern California, at a time when much of the central valley

From: Cherríe Moraga and Gloria Anzaldúa (eds.), *This Bridge Called My Back: Radical Writings by Women of Color* (New York: Kitchen Table Press, 1983), pp. 27–34. Copyright © 1983 by Cherríe Moraga. Reprinted by permission of the author and the publisher.

1. Alix Kates Shulman, "Was My Life Worth Living?" *Red Emma Speaks.* (New York: Random House, 1972), p. 388.

there was still farm land. Nearly thirty-five years later, in 1948, she was the only daughter of six to marry an anglo, my father.

I remember all of my mother's stories, probably much better than she realizes. She is a fine story-teller, recalling every event of her life with the vividness of the present, noting each detail right down to the cut and color of her dress. I remember stories of her being pulled out of school at the ages of five, seven, nine, and eleven to work in the fields, along with her brothers and sisters; stories of her father drinking away whatever small profit she was able to make for the family; of her going the long way home to avoid meeting him on the street, staggering toward the same destination. I remember stories of my mother lying about her age in order to get a job as a hat-check girl at Agua Caliente Racetrack in Tijuana. At fourteen, she was the main support of the family. I can still see her walking home alone at 3 a.m., only to turn all of her salary and tips over to her mother, who was pregnant again.

The stories continue through the war years and on: walnut-cracking factories, the Voit Rubber factory, and then the computer boom. I remember my mother doing piecework for the electronics plant in our neighborhood. In the late evening, she would sit in front of the T.V. set, wrapping copper wires into the backs of circuit boards, talking about "keeping up with the younger girls." By that time, she was already in her mid-fifties.

Meanwhile, I was college-prep in school. After classes, I would go with my mother to fill out job applications for her, or write checks for her at the supermarket. We would have the scenario all worked out ahead of time. My mother would sign the check before we'd get to the store. Then, as we'd approach the checkstand, she would say—within earshot of the cashier—"oh honey, you go 'head and make out the check," as if she couldn't be bothered with such an insignificant detail. No one asked any questions.

I was educated, and wore it with a keen sense of pride and satisfaction, my head propped up with the knowledge, from my mother, that my life would be easier than hers. I was educated; but more than this, I was "la güera": fair-skinned. Born with the features of my Chicana mother, but the skin of my Anglo father, I had it made.

No one ever quite told me this (that light was right), but I knew that being light was something valued in my family (who were all Chicano, with the exception of my father). In fact, everything about my upbringing (at least what occurred on a conscious level) attempted to bleach me of what color I did have. Although my mother was fluent in it, I was never taught much Spanish at home. I picked up what I did learn from school and from over-heard snatches of conversation among my relatives and mother. She often called other lower-income Mexicans "braceros," or "wet-backs," referring to herself and her family as "a different class of people." And yet, the real story was that my family, too, had been poor (some still are) and farmworkers. My mother can remember this in her blood as if it were yesterday. But this is something she would like to forget (and rightfully), for to her, on a basic economic level, being Chicana meant being "less." It was through my mother's desire to protect her children from poverty and illiteracy that we became "anglocized"; the more effectively we could pass in the white world, the better guaranteed our future.

From all of this, I experience, daily, a huge disparity between what I was born into and what I was to grow up to become. Because, (as Goldman suggests) these stories my mother told me crept under my "güera" skin. I had no choice but to enter into the life of my mother. *I had no choice.* I took her life into my heart, but managed to keep a lid on it as long as I feigned being the happy, upwardly mobile heterosexual.

When I finally lifted the lid to my lesbianism, a profound connection with my mother reawakened in me. It wasn't until I acknowledged and confronted my own lesbianism in the flesh, that my heartfelt identification with and empathy for my mother's oppression—due to being poor, uneducated, and Chicana—was realized. My lesbianism is the avenue through which I have learned the most about silence and oppression, and it continues to be the most tactile reminder to me that we are not free human beings.

You see, one follows the other. I had known for years that I was a lesbian, had felt it in my bones, had ached with the knowledge, gone crazed with the knowledge, wallowed in the silence of it. Silence *is* like starvation. Don't be fooled. It's nothing short of that, and felt most sharply when one has had a full belly most of her life. When we are not physically starving, we have the luxury to realize psychic and emotional starvation. It is from this starvation that other starvations can be recognized—if one is willing to take the risk of making the connection—if one is willing to be responsible to the result of the connection. For me, the connection is an inevitable one.

What I am saying is that the joys of looking like a white girl ain't so great since I realized I could be beaten on the street for being a dyke. If my sister's being beaten because she's Black, it's pretty much the same principle. We're both getting beaten any way you look at it. The connection is blatant; and in the case of my own family, the difference in the privileges attached to looking white instead of brown are merely a generation apart.

In this country, lesbianism is a poverty—as is being brown, as is being a woman, as is being just plain poor. The danger lies in ranking the oppressions. *The danger lies in failing to acknowledge the specificity of the oppression.* The danger lies in attempting to deal with oppression purely from a theoretical base. Without an emotional, heartfelt grappling with the source of our own oppression, without naming the enemy within ourselves and outside of us, no authentic, non-hierarchical connection among oppressed groups can take place.

When the going gets rough, will we abandon our so-called comrades in a flurry of racist/heterosexist/what-have-you panic? To whose camp, then, should the lesbian of color retreat? Her very presence violates the ranking and abstraction of oppression. Do we merely live hand to mouth? Do we merely struggle with the "ism" that's sitting on top of our own heads?

The answer is: yes, I think first we do; and we must do so thoroughly and deeply. But to fail to move out from there will only isolate us in our own oppression—will only insulate, rather than radicalize us.

To illustrate: a gay male friend of mine once confided to me that he continued to feel that, on some level, I didn't trust him because he was male; that he felt, really, if it ever came down to a "battle of the sexes," I might kill him. I admitted that I might very well. He wanted to understand the source of my distrust. I responded, "You're not a woman. Be a woman for a day. Imagine being a woman." He confessed that the thought terrified him because, to him, being a woman meant being raped by men. He *had* felt raped by men; he wanted to forget what that meant. What grew from that discussion was the realization that in order for him to create an authentic alliance with me, he must deal with the primary source of his own sense of oppression. He must, first, emotionally come to terms with what it feels like to be a victim. If he—or anyone—were to truly do this, it would be impossible to discount the oppression of others, except by again forgetting how we have been hurt.

And yet, oppressed groups are forgetting all the time. There are instances of this in the rising Black middle class, and certainly an obvious trend of such "unconsciousness" among white gay men. Because to remember may mean giving up whatever privileges we have managed to squeeze out of this society by virtue of our gender, race, class, or sexuality.

Within the women's movement, the connections among women of different backgrounds and sexual orientations have been fragile, at best. I think this phenomenon is indicative of our failure to seriously address ourselves to some very frightening questions: How have I internalized my own oppression? How have I oppressed? Instead, we have let rhetoric do the job of poetry. Even the word "oppression" has lost its power. We need a new language, better words that can more closely describe women's fear of and resistance to one another; words that will not always come out sounding like dogma.

What prompted me in the first place to work on an anthology by radical women of color was a deep sense that I had a valuable insight to contribute, by virtue of my birthright and background. And yet, I don't really understand first-hand what it feels like being shitted on for being brown. I understand much more about the joys of it—being Chicana and having family are synonymous for me. What I know about loving, singing, crying, telling stories, speaking with my heart and hands, even having a sense of my own soul comes from the love of my mother, aunts, cousins . . .

But at the age of twenty-seven, it is frightening to acknowledge that I have internalized a racism and classism, where the object of oppression is not only someone outside of my skin, but the someone inside my skin. In fact, to a large degree, the real battle with such oppression, for all of us, begins under the skin. I have had to confront the fact that much of what I value about being Chicana, about my family, has been subverted by anglo culture and my own cooperation with it. This realization did not occur to me overnight. For example, it wasn't until long after my graduation from the private college I'd attended in Los Angeles, that I realized the major reason for my total alienation from and fear of my classmates was rooted in class and culture. CLICK.

Three years after graduation, in an apple-orchard in Sonoma, a friend of mine (who comes from an Italian Irish working-class family) says to me, "Cherríe, no wonder you felt like such a nut in school. Most of the people there were white and rich." It was true. All along I had felt the difference, but not until I had put the words "class" and "color" to the experience, did my feelings make any sense. For years, I had berated myself for not being as "free" as my classmates. I completely bought that they simply had more guts than I did—to rebel against their parents and run around the country hitch-hiking, reading books and studying "art." They had enough privilege to be atheists, for chrissake. There was no one around filling in the disparity for me between their parents, who were Hollywood filmmakers, and my parents, who wouldn't know the name of a filmmaker if their lives depended on it (and precisely because their lives didn't depend on it, they couldn't be bothered). But I knew nothing about "privilege" then. White was right. Period. I could pass. If I got educated enough, there would never be any telling.

Three years after that, another CLICK. In a letter to Barbara Smith, I wrote:

> I went to a concert where Ntosake Shange was reading. There, every-thing exploded for me. She was speaking a language that I knew—in the deepest parts of me—existed, and that I had ignored in my own feminist stud-ies and even in my own writing. What Ntosake caught in me is the realization that in my development as a poet, I have, in many ways, denied the voice of my brown mother—the brown in me. I have acclimated to the sound of a white language which, as my father represents it, does not speak to the emotions in my poems—emotions which stem from the love of my mother.
> The reading was agitating. Made me uncomfortable. Threw me into a week-long terror of how deeply I was affected. I felt that I had to start all over

again. That I turned only to the perceptions of white middle-class women to speak for me and all women. I am shocked by my own ignorance.

Sitting in that auditorium chair was the first time I had realized to the core of me that for years I had disowned the language I knew best—ignored the words and rhythms that were the closest to me. The sounds of my mother and aunts gossiping—half in English, half in Spanish—while drinking cerveza in the kitchen. And the hands—I had cut off the hands in my poems. But not in conversation; still the hands could not be kept down. Still they insisted on moving.

The reading had forced me to remember that I knew things from my roots. But to remember puts me up against what I don't know. Shange's reading agitated me because she spoke with power about a world that is both alien and common to me: "the capacity to enter into the lives of others." But you can't just take the goods and run. I knew that then, sitting in the Oakland auditorium (as I know in my poetry), that the only thing worth writing about is what seems to be unknown and, therefore, fearful.

The "unknown" is often depicted in racist literature as the "darkness" within a person. Similarly, sexist writers will refer to fear in the form of the vagina, calling it "the orifice of death." In contrast, it is a pleasure to read works such as Maxine Hong Kingston's *Woman Warrior*, where fear and alienation are described as "the white ghosts." And yet, the bulk of literature in this country reinforces the myth that what is dark and female is evil. Consequently, each of us—whether dark, female, or both—has in some way *internalized* this oppressive imagery. What the oppressor often succeeds in doing is simply *externalizing* his fears, projecting them into the bodies of women, Asians, gays, disabled folks, whoever seems most "other."

> call me
> roach and presumptuous
> nightmare on your white pillow
> your itch to destroy
> the indestructible
> part of yourself
>
> Audre Lorde[2]

But it is not really difference the oppressor fears so much as similarity. He fears he will discover in himself the same aches, the same longings as those of

---

2. From "The Brown Menace or Poem to the Survival of Roaches," *The New York Head Shop and Museum* (Detroit: Broadside, 1974), p. 48.

the people he has shitted on. He fears the immobilization threatened by his own incipient guilt. He fears he will have to change his life once he has seen himself in the bodies of the people he has called different. He fears the hatred, anger, and vengeance of those he has hurt.

This is the oppressor's nightmare, but it is not exclusive to him. We women have a similar nightmare, for each of us in some way has been both oppressed and the oppressor. We are afraid to look at how we have failed each other. We are afraid to see how we have taken the values of our oppressor into our hearts and turned them against ourselves and one another. We are afraid to admit how deeply "the man's" words have been ingrained in us.

To assess the damage is a dangerous act. I think of how, even as a feminist lesbian, I have so wanted to ignore my own homophobia, my own hatred of myself for being queer. I have not wanted to admit that my deepest personal sense of myself has not quite "caught up" with my "woman-identified" politics. I have been afraid to criticize lesbian writers who choose to "skip over" these issues in the name of feminism. In 1979, we talk of "old gay" and "butch and femme" roles as if they were ancient history. We toss them aside as merely patriarchal notions. And yet, the truth of the matter is that I have sometimes taken society's fear and hatred of lesbians to bed with me. I have sometimes hated my lover for loving me. I have sometimes felt "not woman enough" for her. I have sometimes felt "not man enough." For a lesbian trying to survive in a heterosexist society, there is no easy way around these emotions. Similarly, in a white-dominated world, there is little getting around racism and our own internalization of it. It's always there, embodied in some one we least expect to rub up against.

When we do rub up against this person, *there* then is the challenge. *There* then is the opportunity to look at the nightmare within us. But we usually shrink from such a challenge.

Time and time again, I have observed that the usual response among white women's groups when the "racism issue" comes up is to deny the difference. I have heard comments like, "Well, we're open to *all* women; why don't they (women of color) come? You can only do so much . . ." But there is seldom any analysis of how the very nature and structure of the group itself may be founded on racist or classist assumptions. More importantly, so often the women seem to feel no loss, no lack, no absence when women of color are not involved; therefore, there is little desire to change the situation. This has hurt me deeply. I have come to believe that the only reason women of a privileged class will dare to look at *how* it is that *they* oppress, is when they've come to know the meaning of their own oppression. And understand that the oppression of others hurts them personally.

The other side of the story is that women of color and working-class women often shrink from challenging white middle-class women. It is much easier to rank oppressions and set up a hierarchy, rather than take responsibility for changing our own lives. We have failed to demand that white women, particularly those who claim to be speaking for all women, be accountable for their racism.

The dialogue has simply not gone deep enough.

I have many times questioned my right to even work on an anthology which is to be written "exclusively by Third World women." I have had to look critically at my claim to color, at a time when, among white feminist ranks, it is a "politically correct" (and sometimes peripherally advantageous) assertion to make. I must acknowledge the fact that, physically, I have had a *choice* about making that claim, in contrast to women who have not had such a choice, and have been abused for their color. I must reckon with the fact that for most of my life, by virtue of the very fact that I am white-looking, I identified with and aspired toward white values, and that I rode the wave of that Southern California privilege as far as conscience would let me.

Well, now I feel both bleached and beached. I feel angry about this—the years when I refused to recognize privilege, both when it worked against me, and when I worked it, ignorantly, at the expense of others. These are not settled issues. That is why this work feels so risky to me. It continues to be discovery. It has brought me into contact with women who invariably know a hell of a lot more than I do about racism, as experienced in the flesh, as revealed in the flesh of their writing.

I think: what is my responsibility to my roots—both white and brown, Spanish-speaking and English? I am a woman with a foot in both worlds; and I refuse the split. I feel the necessity for dialogue. Sometimes I feel it urgently.

But one voice is not enough, nor two, although this is where dialogue begins. It is essential that radical feminists confront their fear of and resistance to each other, because without this, there *will* be no bread on the table. Simply, we will not survive. If we could make this connection in our heart of hearts, that if we are serious about a revolution—better—if we seriously believe there should be joy in our lives (real joy, not just "good times"), then we need one another. We women need each other. Because my/your solitary, self-asserting "go-for-the-throat-of-fear" power is not enough. The real power, as you and I well know, is collective. I can't afford to be afraid of you, nor you of me. If it takes head-on collisions, let's do it: this polite timidity is killing us.

As Lorde suggests in the passage I cited earlier, it is in looking to the nightmare that the dream is found. There, the survivor emerges to insist on a future, a vision, yes, born out of what is dark and female. The feminist movement must be a movement of such survivors, a movement with a future.

REPORT FROM THE BAHAMAS

4

June Jordan

I am staying in a hotel that calls itself The Sheraton British Colonial. One of the photographs advertising the place displays a middle-aged Black man in a waiter's tuxedo, smiling. What intrigues me most about the picture is just this: while the Black man bears a tray full of "colorful" drinks above his left shoulder, both of his feet, shoes and trouserlegs, up to ten inches above his ankles, stand in the also "colorful" Caribbean salt water. He is so delighted to serve you he will wade into the water to bring you Banana Daquiris while you float! More precisely, he will wade into the water, fully clothed, oblivious to the ruin of his shoes, his trousers, his health, and he will do it with a smile.

I am in the Bahamas. On the phone in my room, a spinning complement of plastic pages offers handy index clues such as CAR RENTAL and CASINOS. A message from the Ministry of Tourism appears among these travellers tips. Opening with a paragraph of "WELCOME," the message then proceeds to "A PAGE OF HISTORY," which reads as follows:

> New World History begins on the same day that modern Bahamian history begins—October 12, 1492. That's when Columbus stepped ashore—British influence came first with the Eleutherian Adventurers of 1647—After the Revolutions, American Loyalists fled from the newly independent states and settled in the Bahamas. Confederate blockade-runners used the island as a haven during the War between the States, and after the War, a number of Southerners moved to the Bahamas . . .

There it is again. Something proclaims itself a legitimate history and all it does is track white Mr. Columbus to the British Eleutherians through the Confederate Southerners as they barge into New World surf, land on New World turf, and nobody saying one word about the Bahamian people, the Black peoples, to whom the only thing new in their island world was this weird succession of crude intruders and its colonial consequences.

This is my consciousness of race as I unpack my bathing suit in the Sheraton British Colonial. Neither this hotel nor the British nor the long ago Italians nor the white Delta airline pilots belong here, of course. And every

---

From: June Jordan, *On Call: Political Essays* (Boston: South End Press, 1985), pp. 39–49. Reprinted by permission.

time I look at the photograph of that fool standing in the water with his shoes on I'm about to have a West Indian fit, even though I know he's no fool; he's a middle-aged Black man who needs a job and this is his job—pretending himself a servile ancillary to the pleasures of the rich. (Compared to his options in life, I am a rich woman. Compared to most of the Black Americans arriving for this Easter weekend on a three nights four days' deal of bargain rates, the middle-aged waiter is a poor Black man.)

We will jostle along with the other (white) visitors and join them in the tee shirt shops or, laughing together, learn ruthless rules of negotiation as we, Black Americans as well as white, argue down the price of handwoven goods at the nearby straw market while the merchants, frequently toothless Black women seated on the concrete in their only presentable dress, humble themselves to our careless games:

"Yes? You like it? Eight dollar."

"Five."

"I give it to you. Seven."

And so it continues, this weird succession of crude intruders that, now, includes me and my brothers and my sisters from the North.

This is my consciousness of class as I try to decide how much money I can spend on Bahamian gifts for my family back in Brooklyn. No matter that these other Black women incessantly weave words and flowers into the straw hats and bags piled beside them on the burning dusty street. No matter that these other Black women must work their sense of beauty into these things that we will take away as cheaply as we dare, or they will do without food.

We are not white, after all. The budget is limited. And we are harmlessly killing time between the poolside rum punch and "The Native Show on the Patio" that will play tonight outside the hotel restaurant.

This is my consciousness of race and class and gender identity as I notice the fixed relations between these other Black women and myself. They sell and I buy or I don't. They risk not eating. I risk going broke on my first vacation afternoon.

We are not particularly women anymore; we are parties to a transaction designed to set us against each other.

"Olive" is the name of the Black woman who cleans my hotel room. On my way to the beach I am wondering what "Olive" would say if I told her why I chose The Sheraton British Colonial; if I told her I wanted to swim. I wanted to sleep. I did not want to be harassed by the middle-aged waiter, or his nephew. I did not want to be raped by anybody (white or Black) at all and I calculated that my safety as a Black woman alone would best be assured by a multinational hotel corporation. In my experience, the big guys take customer complaints more seriously than the little ones. I would suppose that's one reason why they're big; they don't like to lose money anymore than I like to be bothered when I'm trying to read a goddamned book underneath a palm tree I paid $264 to get next to. A Black woman seeking refuge in a multinational corporation may seem like a contradiction to some, but there you are. In this case it's a coincidence of entirely different self-interests: Sheraton/cash = June Jordan's short run safety.

Anyway, I'm pretty sure "Olive" would look at me as though I came from someplace as far away as Brooklyn. Then she'd probably allow herself one indignant query before righteously removing her vacuum cleaner from my room; "and why in the first place you come down you without your husband?"

I cannot imagine how I would begin to answer her.

My "rights" and my "freedom" and my "desire" and a slew of other New World values; what would they sound like to this Black woman described on the card atop my hotel bureau as "Olive the Maid"? "Olive" is older than I am and I may smoke a cigarette while she changes the sheets on my bed. Whose rights? Whose freedom? Whose desire?

And why should she give a shit about mine unless I do something, for real, about hers?

It happens that the book that I finished reading under a palm tree earlier today was the novel, *The Bread Givers,* by Anzia Yezierska. Definitely autobiographical, Yezierska lays out the difficulties of being both female and "a person" inside a traditional Jewish family at the start of the 20th century. That any Jewish woman became anything more than the abused servant of her father or her husband is really an improbable piece of news. Yet Yezierska managed such an unlikely outcome for her own life. In *The Bread Givers,* the heroine also manages an important, although partial, escape from traditional Jewish female destiny. And in the unpardonable, despotic father, the Talmudic scholar of that Jewish family, did I not see my own and hate him twice, again? When the heroine, the young Jewish child, wanders the streets with a filthy pail she borrows to sell herring in order to raise the ghetto rent and when she cries, "Nothing was before me but the hunger in our house, and no bread for the next meal if I didn't sell the herring. No longer like a fire engine, but like a houseful of hungry mouths my heart cried, 'herring—herring! Two cents apiece!' " who would doubt the ease, the sisterhood of conversation possible between that white girl and the Black women selling straw bags on the streets of paradise because they do not want to die? And is it not obvious that the wife of that Talmudic scholar and "Olive," who cleans my room here at the hotel, have more in common than I can claim with either one of them?

This is my consciousness of race and class and gender identity as I collect wet towels, sunglasses, wristwatch, and head towards a shower.

I am thinking about the boy who loaned this novel to me. He's white and he's Jewish and he's pursuing an independent study project with me, at the State University where I teach whether or not I feel like it, where I teach without stint because, like the waiter, I am no fool. It's my job and either I work or I do without everything you need money to buy. The boy loaned me the novel because he thought I'd be interested to know how a Jewish-American writer used English so that the syntax, and therefore the cultural habits of mind expressed by the Yiddish language, could survive translation. He did this because he wanted to create another connection between us on the basis of language, between his knowledge/his love of Yiddish and my knowledge/my love of Black English.

He has been right about the forceful survival of the Yiddish. And I had become excited by this further evidence of the written voice of spoken language protected from the monodrone of "standard" English, and so we had grown closer on this account. But then our talk shifted to student affairs more generally, and I had learned that this student does not care one way or the other about currently jeopardized Federal Student Loan Programs because, as he explained it to me, they do not affect him. He does not need financial help outside his family. My own son, however, is Black. And I am the only family help available to him and that means, if Reagan succeeds in eliminating Federal programs to aid minority students, he will have to forget about furthering his studies, or he or I or both of us will have to hit the numbers pretty big. For these reasons of difference, the student and I had moved away from each other, even while we continued to talk.

My consciousness turned to race, again, and class.

Sitting in the same chair as the boy, several weeks ago, a graduate student came to discuss her grade. I praised the excellence of her final paper; indeed it had seemed to me an extraordinary pulling together of recent left brain/right brain research with the themes of transcendental poetry.

She told me that, for her part, she'd completed her reading of my political essays. "You are so lucky!" she exclaimed.

"What do you mean by that?"

"You have a cause. You have a purpose to your life."

I looked carefully at this white woman; what was she really saying to me?

"What do you mean?" I repeated.

"Poverty. Police violence. Discrimination in general."

(Jesus Christ, I thought: Is that her idea of lucky?)

"And how about you?" I asked.

"Me?"

"Yeah, you. Don't you have a cause?"

"Me? I'm just a middle-aged woman: a housewife and a mother. I'm a nobody."

For a while, I made no response.

First of all, speaking of race and class and gender in one breath, what she said meant that those lucky preoccupations of mine, from police violence to nuclear wipe-out, were not shared. They were mine and not hers. But here she sat, friendly as an old stuffed animal, beaming good will or more "luck" in my direction.

In the second place, what this white woman said to me meant that she did not believe she was "a person" precisely because she had fulfilled the traditional female functions revered by the father of that Jewish immigrant, Anzia Yezierska. And the woman in front of me was not a Jew. That was not the connection. The link was strictly female. Nevertheless, how should that woman and I, another female connect, beyond this bizarre exchange?

If she believed me lucky to have regular hurdles of discrimination then why shouldn't I insist that she's lucky to be a middle class white Wasp female who lives in such well-sanctioned and normative comfort that she even has the luxury to deny the power of the privileges that paralyze her life?

If she deserts me and "my cause" where we differ, if, for example, she abandons me to "my" problems of race, then why should I support her in "her" problems of housewifely oblivion?

Recollection of this peculiar moment brings me to the shower in the bathroom cleaned by "Olive." She reminds me of the usual Women's Studies curriculum because it has nothing to do with her or her job: you won't find "Olive" listed anywhere on the reading list. You will likewise seldom hear of Anzia Yezierska. But yes, you will find, from Florence Nightingale to Adrienne Rich, a white procession of independently well-to-do women writers. (Gertrude Stein/Virginia Woolf/Hilda Doolittle are standard names among the "essential" women writers.)

In other words, most of the women of the world—Black and First World and white who work because we must—most of the women of the world persist far from the heart of the usual Women's Studies syllabus.

Similarly, the typical Black History course will slide by the majority experience it pretends to represent. For example, Mary McLeod Bethune will scarcely receive as much attention as Nat Turner, even though Black women who bravely and efficiently provided for the education of Black people hugely outnumber those few Black men who led successful or doomed rebellions against slavery. In fact, Mary McLeod Bethune may not receive even honorable mention because Black History too often apes those ridiculous white history courses which produce such dangerous gibberish as The Sheraton British Colonial "history" of the Bahamas. Both Black and white history courses exclude from their central consideration those people who neither killed nor conquered anyone as the means to new identity, those people who took care of every one of the people who wanted to become "a person," those people who still take care of the life at issue: the ones who wash and who feed and who teach and who diligently decorate straw hats and bags with all of their historically unrequired gentle love: the women.

> *Oh the old rugged cross*
> *on a hill far away*
> *Well I cherish the old rugged cross*

It's Good Friday in the Bahamas. Seventy-eight degrees in the shade. Except for Sheraton territory, everything's closed.

It so happens that for truly secular reasons I've been fasting for three days. My hunger has now reached nearly violent proportions. In the hotel sandwich shop, the Black woman handling the counter complains about the tourists; why isn't the shop closed and why don't the tourists stop eating for once in their lives. I'm famished and I order chicken salad and cottage cheese and lettuce and tomato and a hard boiled egg and a hot cross bun and apple juice.

She eyes me with disgust.

To be sure, the timing of my stomach offends her serious religious practices. Neither one of us apologizes to the other. She seasons the chicken salad to the peppery max while I listen to the loud radio gospel she plays to console herself. It's a country Black version of "The Old Rugged Cross."

As I heave much chicken into my mouth tears start. It's not the pepper. I am, after all, a West Indian daughter. It's the Good Friday music that dominates the humid atmosphere.

> *Well I cherish the old rugged cross*

And I am back, faster than a 747, in Brooklyn, in the home of my parents where we are wondering, as we do every year, if the sky will darken until Christ has been buried in the tomb. The sky should darken if God is in His heavens. And then, around 3 p.m., at the conclusion of our mournful church service at the neighborhood St. Phillips, and even while we dumbly stare at the black cloth covering the gold altar and the slender unlit candles, the sun should return through the high gothic windows and vindicate our waiting faith that the Lord will rise again, on Easter.

How I used to bow my head at the very name of Jesus: ecstatic to abase myself in deference to His majesty.

My mouth is full of salad. I can't seem to eat quickly enough. I can't think how I should lessen the offense of my appetite. The other Black woman on the premises, the one who disapprovingly prepared this very tasty break from my fast, makes no remark. She is no fool. This is a job that she needs. I suppose she notices that at least I included a hot cross bun among my edibles. That's something in my favor. I decide that's enough.

I am suddenly eager to walk off the food. Up a fairly steep hill I walk without hurrying. Through the pastel desolation of the little town, the road brings me to a confectionary pink and white plantation house. At the gates, an unnecessarily large statue of Christopher Columbus faces me down, or tries to. His hand is fisted to one hip. I look back at him, laugh without deference, and turn left.

It's time to pack it up. Catch my plane. I scan the hotel room for things not to forget. There's that white report card on the bureau.

"Dear Guests:" it says, under the name "Olive." "I am your maid for the day. Please rate me: Excellent. Good. Average. Poor. Thank you."

I tuck this momento from the Sheraton British Colonial into my notebook. How would "Olive" rate *me*? What would it mean for us to seem "good" to each other? What would that rating require?

But I am hastening to leave. Neither turtle soup nor kidney pie nor any conch shell delight shall delay my departure. I have rested, here, in the Bahamas, and I'm ready to return to my usual job, my usual work. But the skin on my body has changed and so has my mind. On the Delta flight home I realize I am burning up, indeed.

So far as I can see, the usual race and class concepts of connection, or gender assumptions of unity, do not apply very well. I doubt that they ever did. Otherwise why would Black folks forever bemoan our lack of solidarity when the deal turns real. And if unity on the basis of sexual oppression is something natural, then why do we women, the majority people on the planet, still have a problem?

The plane's ready for takeoff. I fasten my seatbelt and let the tumult inside my head run free. Yes: race and class and gender remain as real as the weather. But what they must mean about the contact between two individuals is less obvious and, like the weather, not predictable.

And when these factors of race and class and gender absolutely collapse is whenever you try to use them as automatic concepts of connection. They may serve well as indicators of commonly felt conflict, but as elements of connection they seem about as reliable as precipitation probability for the day after the night before the day.

It occurs to me that much organizational grief could be avoided if people understood that partnership in misery does not necessarily provide for partnership for change: *When we get the monsters off our backs all of us may want to run in very different directions.*

And not only that: even though both "Olive" and "I" live inside a conflict neither one of us created, and even though both of us therefore hurt inside that conflict, I may be one of the monsters she needs to eliminate from her universe and, in a sense, she may be one of the monsters in mine.

I am reaching for the words to describe the difference between a common identity that has been imposed and the individual identity any one of us will choose, once she gains that chance.

That difference is the one that keeps us stupid in the face of new, specific information about somebody else with whom we are supposed to have a connection because a third party, hostile to both of us, has worked it so that the two of us, like it or not, share a common enemy. *What happens beyond the idea of that enemy and beyond the consequences of that enemy?*

I am saying that the ultimate connection cannot be the enemy. The ultimate connection must be the need that we find between us. It is not only who you are, in other words, but what we can do for each other that will determine the connection.

I am flying back to my job. I have been teaching contemporary women's poetry this semester. One quandary I have set myself to explore with my students is the one of taking responsibility without power. We had been wrestling ideas to the floor for several sessions when a young Black woman, a South African, asked me for help, after class.

Sokutu told me she was "in a trance" and that she'd been unable to eat for two weeks.

"What's going on?" I asked her, even as my eyes startled at her trembling and emaciated appearance.

"My husband. He drinks all the time. He beats me up. I go to the hospital. I can't eat. I don't know what/anything."

In my office, she described her situation. I did not dare to let her sense my fear and horror. She was dragging about, hour by hour, in dread. Her husband, a young Black South African, was drinking himself into more and more deadly violence against her.

Sokutu told me how she could keep nothing down. She weighed 90 lbs. at the outside, as she spoke to me. She'd already been hospitalized as a result of her husband's battering rage.

I knew both of them because I had organized a campus group to aid the liberation struggles of Southern Africa.

Nausea rose in my throat. What about this presumable connection: this husband and this wife fled from that homeland of hatred against them, and now what? He was destroying himself. If not stopped, he would certainly murder his wife.

She needed a doctor, right away. It was a medical emergency. She needed protection. It was a security crisis. She needed refuge for battered wives and personal therapy and legal counsel. She needed a friend.

I got on the phone and called every number in the campus directory that I could imagine might prove helpful. Nothing worked. There were no institutional resources designed to meet her enormous, multifaceted, and ordinary woman's need.

I called various students. I asked the Chairperson of the English Department for advice. I asked everyone for help.

Finally, another one of my students, Cathy, a young Irish woman active in campus IRA activities, responded. She asked for further details. I gave them to her.

"Her husband," Cathy told me, "is an alcoholic. You have to understand about alcoholics. It's not the same as anything else. And it's a disease you can't treat any old way."

I listened, fearfully. Did this mean there was nothing we could do?

"That's not what I'm saying," she said. "But you have to keep the alcoholic part of the thing central in everybody's mind, otherwise her husband will kill her. Or he'll kill himself."

She spoke calmly. I felt there was nothing to do but to assume she knew what she was talking about.

"Will you come with me?" I asked her, after a silence. "Will you come with me and help us figure out what to do next?"

Cathy said she would but that she felt shy: Sokutu comes from South Africa. What would she think about Cathy?

"I don't know," I said. "But let's go."

We left to find a dormitory room for the young battered wife.

It was late, now, and dark outside.

On Cathy's VW that I followed behind with my own car, was the sticker that reads BOBBY SANDS FREE AT LAST. My eyes blurred as I read and reread the words. This was another connection: Bobby Sands and Martin Luther King Jr. and who would believe it? I would not have believed it; I grew up terrorized by Irish kids who introduced me to the word "nigga."

And here I was following an Irish woman to the room of a Black South African. We were going to that room to try to save a life together.

When we reached the little room, we found ourselves awkward and large. Sokutu attempted to treat us with utmost courtesy, as though we were honored guests. She seemed surprised by Cathy, but mostly Sokutu was flushed with relief and joy because we were there, with her.

I did not know how we should ever terminate her heartfelt courtesies and address, directly, the reason for our visit: her starvation and her extreme physical danger.

Finally, Cathy sat on the floor and reached out her hands to Sokutu.

"I'm here," she said quietly, "Because June has told me what has happened to you. And I know what it is. Your husband is an alcoholic. He has a disease. I know what it is. My father was an alcoholic. He killed himself. He almost killed my mother. I want to be your friend."

"Oh," was the only small sound that escaped from Sokutu's mouth. And then she embraced the other student. And then everything changed and I watched all of this happen so I know that this happened: this connection.

And after we called the police and exchanged phone numbers and plans were made for the night and for the next morning, the young South African woman walked down the dormitory hallway, saying goodbye and saying thank you to us.

I walked behind them, the young Irish woman and the young South African, and I saw them walking as sisters walk, hugging each other, and whispering and sure of each other and I felt how it was not who they were but what they both know and what they were both preparing to do about what they know that was going to make them both free at last.

And I look out the windows of the plane and I see clouds that will not kill me and I know that someday soon other clouds may erupt to kill us all.

And I tell the stewardess No thanks to the cocktails she offers me. But I look about the cabin at the hundred strangers drinking as they fly and I think even here and even now I must make the connection real between me and these strangers everywhere before those other clouds unify this ragged bunch of us, too late.

OPPRESSION

5

Marilyn Frye

It is a fundamental claim of feminism that women are oppressed. The word "oppression" is a strong word. It repels and attracts. It is dangerous and dangerously fashionable and endangered. It is much misused, and sometimes not innocently.

From: Marilyn Frye, *The Politics of Reality* (Trumansburg, N.Y.: The Crossing Press, 1983), pp. 1–16. Reprinted by permission.

The statement that women are oppressed is frequently met with the claim that men are oppressed too. We hear that oppressing is oppressive to those who oppress as well as to those they oppress. Some men cite as evidence of their oppression their much-advertised inability to cry. It is tough, we are told, to be masculine. When the stresses and frustrations of being a man are cited as evidence that oppressors are oppressed by their oppressing, the word "oppression" is being stretched to meaninglessness; it is treated as though its scope includes any and all human experience of limitation or suffering, no matter the cause, degree or consequence. Once such usage has been put over on us, then if ever we deny that any person or group is oppressed, we seem to imply that we think they never suffer and have no feelings. We are accused of insensitivity; even of bigotry. For women, such accusation is particularly intimidating, since sensitivity is one of the few virtues that has been assigned to us. If we are found insensitive, we may fear we have no redeeming traits at all and perhaps are not real women. Thus are we silenced before we begin: the name of our situation drained of meaning and our guilt mechanisms tripped.

But this is nonsense. Human beings can be miserable without being oppressed, and it is perfectly consistent to deny that a person or group is oppressed without denying that they have feelings or that they suffer. . . .

The root of the word "oppression" is the element "press." *The press of the crowd; pressed into military service; to press a pair of pants; printing press; press the button.* Presses are used to mold things or flatten them or reduce them in bulk, sometimes to reduce them by squeezing out the gases or liquids in them. Something pressed is something caught between or among forces and barriers which are so related to each other that jointly they restrain, restrict or prevent the thing's motion or mobility. Mold. Immobilize. Reduce.

The mundane experience of the oppressed provides another clue. One of the most characteristic and ubiquitous features of the world as experienced by oppressed people is the double bind—situations in which options are reduced to a very few and all of them expose one to penalty, censure or deprivation. For example, it is often a requirement upon oppressed people that we smile and be cheerful. If we comply, we signal our docility and our acquiescence in our situation. We need not, then, be taken note of. We acquiesce in being made invisible, in our occupying no space. We participate in our own erasure. On the other hand, anything but the sunniest countenance exposes us to being perceived as mean, bitter, angry or dangerous. This means, at the least, that we may be found "difficult" or unpleasant to work with, which is enough to cost one one's livelihood; at worst, being seen as mean, bitter, angry or dangerous has been known to result in rape, arrest, beating and murder. One can only choose to risk one's preferred form and rate of annihilation.

Another example: It is common in the United States that women, especially younger women, are in a bind where neither sexual activity nor sexual inactivity is all right. If she is heterosexually active, a woman is open to censure and punishment for being loose, unprincipled or a whore. The "punishment" comes in the form of criticism, snide and embarrassing remarks, being treated as an easy lay by men, scorn from her more restrained female friends. She may have to lie and hide her behavior from her parents. She must juggle the risks of unwanted pregnancy and dangerous contraceptives. On the other hand, if she refrains from heterosexual activity, she is fairly constantly harassed by men who try to persuade her into it and pressure her to "relax" and "let her hair down"; she is threatened with labels like "frigid," "uptight," "man-hater," "bitch" and "cocktease." The same parents who would be disapproving of her sexual activity may be worried by her inactivity because it suggests she is not or will not be popular, or is not sexually normal. She may be charged with lesbianism. If a woman is raped, then if she has been heterosexually active she is subject to the presumption that she liked it (since her activity is presumed to show that she likes sex), and if she has not been heterosexually active, she is subject to the presumption that she liked it (since she is supposedly "repressed and frustrated"). Both heterosexual activity and heterosexual nonactivity are likely to be taken as proof that you wanted to be raped, and hence, of course, weren't *really* raped at all. You can't win. You are caught in a bind, caught between systematically related pressures.

Women are caught like this, too, by networks of forces and barriers that expose one to penalty, loss or contempt whether one works outside the home or not, is on welfare or not, bears children or not, raises children or not, marries or not, stays married or not, is heterosexual, lesbian, both or neither. Economic necessity; confinement to racial and/or sexual job ghettos; sexual harassment; sex discrimination; pressures of competing expectations and judgments about *women*, *wives* and *mothers* (in the society at large, in racial and ethnic subcultures and in one's own mind); dependence (full or partial) on husbands, parents or the state; commitment to political ideas; loyalties to racial or ethnic or other "minority" groups; the demands of self-respect and responsibilities to others. Each of these factors exists in complex tension with every other, penalizing or prohibiting all of the apparently available options. And nipping at one's heels, always, is the endless pack of little things. If one dresses one way, one is subject to the assumption that one is advertising one's sexual availability; if one dresses another way, one appears to "not care about oneself" or to be "unfeminine." If one uses "strong language," one invites categorization as a whore or slut; if one does not, one invites categorization as a "lady"—one too delicately constituted to cope with robust speech or the realities to which it presumably refers.

The experience of oppressed people is that the living of one's life is confined and shaped by forces and barriers which are not accidental or occasional and hence avoidable, but are systematically related to each other in such a way as to catch one between and among them and restrict or penalize motion in any direction. It is the experience of being caged in: all avenues, in every direction, are blocked or booby trapped.

Cages. Consider a birdcage. If you look very closely at just one wire in the cage, you cannot see the other wires. If your conception of what is before you is determined by this myopic focus, you could look at that one wire, up and down the length of it, and be unable to see why a bird would not just fly around the wire any time it wanted to go somewhere. Furthermore, even if, one day at a time, you myopically inspected each wire, you still could not see why a bird would have trouble going past the wires to get anywhere. There is no physical property of any one wire, *nothing* that the closest scrutiny could discover, that will reveal how a bird could be inhibited or harmed by it except in the most accidental way. It is only when you step back, stop looking at the wires one by one, microscopically, and take a macroscopic view of the whole cage, that you can see why the bird does not go anywhere; and then you will see it in a moment. It will require no great subtlety of mental powers. It is perfectly *obvious* that the bird is surrounded by a network of systematically related barriers, no one of which would be the least hindrance to its flight, but which, by their relations to each other, are as confining as the solid walls of a dungeon.

It is now possible to grasp one of the reasons why oppression can be hard to see and recognize: one can study the elements of an oppressive structure with great care and some good will without seeing the structure as a whole, and hence without seeing or being able to understand that one is looking at a cage and that there are people there who are caged, whose motion and mobility are restricted, whose lives are shaped and reduced.

The arresting of vision at a microscopic level yields such common confusion as that about the male door-opening ritual. This ritual, which is remarkably widespread across classes and races, puzzles many people, some of whom do and some of whom do not find it offensive. Look at the scene of the two people approaching a door. The male steps slightly ahead and opens the door. The male holds the door open while the female glides through. Then the male goes through. The door closes after them. "Now how," one innocently asks, "can those crazy womenslibbers say that is oppressive? The guy *removed* a barrier to the lady's smooth and unruffled progress." But each repetition of this ritual has a place in a pattern, in fact in several patterns. One has to shift the level of one's perception in order to see the whole picture.

The door-opening pretends to be a helpful service, but the helpfulness is false. This can be seen by noting that it will be done whether or not it makes any practical sense. Infirm men and men burdened with packages will open doors for able-bodied women who are free of physical burdens. Men will impose themselves awkwardly and jostle everyone in order to get to the door first. The act is not determined by convenience or grace. Furthermore, these very numerous acts of unneeded or even noisome "help" occur in counterpoint to a pattern of men not being helpful in many practical ways in which women might welcome help. What *women* experience is a world in which gallant princes charming commonly make a fuss about being helpful and providing small services when help and services are of little or no use, but in which there are rarely ingenious and adroit princes at hand when substantial assistance is really wanted either in mundane affairs or in situations of threat, assault or terror. There is no help with the (his) laundry; no help typing a report at 4:00 a.m.; no help in mediating disputes among relatives or children. There is nothing but advice that women should stay indoors after dark, be chaperoned by a man, or when it comes down to it, "lie back and enjoy it."

The gallant gestures have no practical meaning. Their meaning is symbolic. The door-opening and similar services provided are services which really are needed by people who are for one reason or another incapacitated— unwell, burdened with parcels, etc. So the message is that women are incapable. The detachment of the acts from the concrete realities of what women need and do not need is a vehicle for the message that women's actual needs and interests are unimportant or irrelevant. Finally, these gestures imitate the behavior of servants toward masters and thus mock women, who are in most respects the servants and caretakers of men. The message of the false helpfulness of male gallantry is female dependence, the invisibility or insignificance of women, and contempt for women.

One cannot see the meanings of these rituals if one's focus is riveted upon the individual event in all its particularity, including the particularity of the individual man's present conscious intentions and motives and the individual woman's conscious perception of the event in the moment. It seems sometimes that people take a deliberately myopic view and fill their eyes with things seen microscopically in order not to see macroscopically. At any rate, whether it is deliberate or not, people can and do fail to see the oppression of women because they fail to see macroscopically and hence fail to see the various elements of the situation as systematically related in larger schemes.

As the cageness of the birdcage is a macroscopic phenomenon, the oppressiveness of the situations in which women live our various and different lives is a macroscopic phenomenon. Neither can be *seen* from a microscopic perspective. But when you look macroscopically you can see it—a network of forces and barriers which are systematically related and which conspire to the immobilization, reduction and molding of women and the lives we live. . . .

ANGRY WOMEN ARE BUILDING:

Issues and Struggles Facing American Indian Women Today

6

Paula Gunn Allen

The central issue that confronts American Indian women throughout the hemisphere is survival, *literal survival*, both on a cultural and biological level. According to the 1980 census, population of American Indians is just over one million. This figure, which is disputed by some American Indians, is probably a fair estimate, and it carries certain implications.

Some researchers put our pre-contact population at more than 45 million, while others put it at around 20 million. The U.S. government long put it at 450,000—a comforting if imaginary figure, though at one point it was put at around 270,000. If our current population is around one million; if, as some researchers estimate, around 25 percent of Indian women and 10 percent of Indian men in the United States have been sterilized without informed consent; if our average life expectancy is, as the best-informed research presently says, 55 years; if our infant mortality rate continues at well above national standards; if our average unemployment for all segments of our population—male, female, young, adult, and middle-aged—is between 60 and 90 percent; if the U.S. government continues its policy of termination, relocation, removal, and assimilation along with the destruction of wilderness, reservation land, and its resources, and severe curtailment of hunting, fishing, timber harvesting and water-use rights—then existing tribes are facing the threat of extinction which for several hundred tribal groups has already become fact in the past five hundred years.

In this nation of more than 200 million, the Indian people constitute less than one-half of one percent of the population. In a nation that offers refuge, sympathy, and billions of dollars in aid from federal and private sources in the form of food to the hungry, medicine to the sick, and comfort to the dying, the indigenous subject population goes hungry, homeless, impoverished, cut out of the American deal, new, old, and in between. Americans are daily made aware of the worldwide slaughter of native peoples such as the Cambodians, the Palestinians, the Armenians, the Jews—who constitute only a few groups faced with genocide in this century. We are horrified by South African apartheid and the removal of millions of indigenous African black natives to what is there called "homelands"—but this is simply a replay of nineteenth-century U.S. government removal of American Indians to reservations. Nor do many even notice the parallel or fight South African apartheid by demanding an end to its counterpart within the borders of the United States. The American Indian people are in a situation comparable to the imminent genocide in many parts of the world today. The plight of our people north and south of us is no better; to the south it is considerably worse. Consciously or unconsciously, deliberately, as a matter of national policy, or accidentally as a matter of "fate," *every single government*, right, left, or centrist in the western hemisphere is consciously or subconsciously dedicated to the extinction of those tribal people who live within its borders.

Within this geopolitical charnel house, American Indian women struggle on every front for the survival of our children, our people, our self-respect, our value systems, and our way of life. The past five hundred years testify to our skill at waging this struggle: for all the varied weapons of extinction pointed at our heads, we endure.

We survive war and conquest; we survive colonization, acculturation, assimilation; we survive beating, rape, starvation, mutilation, sterilization, abandonment, neglect, death of our children, our loved ones, destruction of our land, our homes, our past, and our future. We survive, and we do more than just survive. We bond, we care, we fight, we teach, we nurse, we bear, we feed, we earn, we laugh, we love, we hang in there, no matter what.

Of course, some, many of us, just give up. Many are alcoholics, many are addicts. Many abandon the children, the old ones. Many commit suicide. Many become violent, go insane. Many go "white" and are never seen or heard from again. But enough hold on to their traditions and their ways so that even after almost five hundred brutal years, we endure. And we even write songs and poems, make paintings and drawings that say "We walk in beauty. Let us continue."

Currently our struggles are on two fronts: physical survival and cultural survival. For women this means fighting alcoholism and drug abuse (our own and that of our husbands, lovers, parents, children);[1] poverty; affluence—a destroyer of people who are not traditionally socialized to deal with large sums of money; rape, incest, battering by Indian men; assaults on fertility and other health matters by the Indian Health Service and the Public Health Service; high infant mortality due to substandard medical care, nutrition, and health information; poor educational opportunities or education that takes us away from our traditions, language, and communities; suicide, homicide, or similar expressions of self-hatred; lack of economic opportunities; substandard housing; sometimes violent and always virulent racist attitudes and behaviors directed against us by an entertainment and educational system that wants only one thing from Indians: our silence, our invisibility, and our collective death.

A headline in the *Navajo Times* in the fall of 1979 reported that rape was the number one crime on the Navajo reservation. In a professional mental health journal of the Indian Health Services, Phyllis Old Dog Cross reported that incest and rape are common among Indian women seeking services and that their incidence is increasing. "It is believed that at least 80 percent of the Native Women seen at the regional psychiatric service center (5 state area) have experienced some sort of sexual assault."[2] Among the forms of abuse being suffered by Native American women, Old Dog Cross cites a recent phenomenon, something called "training." This form of gang rape is "a punitive act of a group of males who band together and get even or take revenge on a selected woman."[3]

These and other cases of violence against women are powerful evidence that the status of women within the tribes has suffered grievous decline since contact, and the decline has increased in intensity in recent years. The amount of violence against women, alcoholism, and violence, abuse, and neglect by women against their children and their aged relatives have all increased. These social ills were virtually unheard of among most tribes fifty years ago, popular American opinion to the contrary. As Old Dog Cross remarks:

> Rapid, unstable and irrational change was required of the Indian people if they were to survive. Incredible loss of all that had meaning was the norm. Inhuman treatment, murder, death, and punishment was a typical experience for all the tribal groups and some didn't survive.
>
> The dominant society devoted its efforts to the attempt to change the Indian into a white-Indian. No inhuman pressure to effect this change was overlooked. These pressures included starvation, incarceration and enforced education. Religious and healing customs were banished.

> In spite of the years of oppression, the Indian and the Indian spirit sur-
> vived. Not, however, without adverse effect. One of the major effects was the
> loss of cultured values and the concomitant loss of personal identity . . . The
> Indian was taught to be ashamed of being Indian and to emulate the non-
> Indian. In short, "white was right." For the Indian male, the only route to be
> successful, to be good, to be right, and to have an identity was to be as much
> like the white man as he could.[4]

Often it is said that the increase of violence against women is a result of various sociological factors such as oppression, racism, poverty, hopelessness, emasculation of men, and loss of male self-esteem as their own place within traditional society has been systematically destroyed by increasing urbaniza-tion, industrialization, and institutionalization, but seldom do we notice that for the past forty to fifty years, American popular media have depicted American Indian men as bloodthirsty savages devoted to treating women cruelly. While traditional Indian men seldom did any such thing—and in fact among most tribes abuse of women was simply unthinkable, as was abuse of children or the aged—the lie about "usual" male Indian behavior seems to have taken root and now bears its brutal and bitter fruit.

Image casting and image control constitute the central process that American Indian women must come to terms with, for on that control rests our sense of self, our claim to a past and to a future that we define and that we build. Images of Indians in media and educational materials profoundly influence how we act, how we relate to the world and to each other, and how we value ourselves. They also determine to a large extent how our men act toward us, toward our children, and toward each other. The popular American media image of Indian people as savages with no conscience, no compassion, and no sense of the value of human life and human dignity was hardly true of the tribes—however true it was of the invaders. But as Adolf Hitler noted a little over fifty years ago, if you tell a lie big enough and often enough, it will be believed. Evidently, while Americans and people all over the world have been led into a deep and unquestioned belief that American Indians are cruel savages, a number of American Indian men have been equally deluded into internalizing that image and acting on it. Media images, literary images, and artistic images, particularly those embedded in popular culture, must be changed before Indian women will see much relief from the violence that destroys so many lives.

To survive culturally, American Indian women must often fight the United States government, the tribal governments, women and men of their tribe or their urban community who are virulently misogynist or who are threatened by attempts to change the images foisted on us over the centuries by whites. The colonizers' revisions of our lives, values, and histories have devastated us at the most critical level of all—that of our own minds, our own sense of who we are.

Many women express strong opposition to those who would alter our life supports, steal our tribal lands, colonize our cultures and cultural expressions, and revise our very identities. We must strive to maintain tribal status; we must make certain that the tribes continue to be legally recognized entities, sovereign nations within the larger United States, and we must wage this struggle in many ways—political, educational, literary, artistic, individual, and communal. We are doing all we can: as mothers and grandmothers; as family members and tribal members; as professionals, workers, artists, shamans, leaders, chiefs, speakers, writers, and organizers, we daily demonstrate that we have no intention of disappearing, of being silent, or of quietly acquiescing in our extinction.

NOTES

1. It is likely, say some researchers, that fetal alcohol syndrome, which is serious among many Indian groups, will be so serious among the White Mountain Apache and the Pine Ridge Sioux that if present trends continue, by the year 2000 some people estimate that almost one half of all children born on those reservations will in some way be affected by FAS. (Michael Dorris, Native American Studies, Dartmouth College, private conversation. Dorris has done extensive research into the syndrome as it affects native populations in the United States as well as in New Zealand.)

2. Phyllis Old Dog Cross, "Sexual Abuse, a New Threat to the Native American Woman: An Overview," *Listening Post: A Periodical of the Mental Health Programs of Indian Health Services*, vol. 6, no. 2 (April 1982), p. 18.

3. Old Dog Cross, p. 18.

4. Old Dog Cross, p. 20.

II

Conceptualizing Race, Class, and Gender

In 1988, white women working year-round, full time earned $18,823 (median income); white men, $28,262. Black women earned $16,867, Black men, $20,716; Latino women earned $15,201, Latino men, $18,190.[1] Such data indicate that racism and sexism continue to affect the distribution of economic resources. But we need not look at economic figures to see the persistence of race, sex, and class inequality. The reappearance of racial hostilities on college campuses is further evidence of the continuation of racist practices and beliefs. Yet, despite this and other evidence, as Robert Blauner shows in his article "The Ambiguities of Racial Change," whites continue to be optimistic in their assessment of racial progress. They say they are tired of hearing about racism and that whites have done all they can to eliminate racial discrimination. Blacks are less sanguine about racial progress, and they are more aware of the nuances of racism. Although overt discrimination has been lessened, marked differences by race are still evident in such comparisons as employment, political representation, schooling, and other basic measures of group well-being.

At the same time, class divisions in the United States are becoming more marked. In the nation's cities and towns, homelessness has become increasingly apparent even to casual observers. Middle-class people feel that their way of life is slipping away—a feeling supported by data showing increasing economic polarization. Moreover, Black family income as a proportion of white family income remains virtually the same as in 1970 (approximately 60 percent); for Latinos, the gap has grown. At the same time, wealth is increasingly concentrated in the hands of a few.

Many people believe that sexism is disappearing. More women are entering the labor force; many have moved into jobs traditionally reserved for men, sometimes leaving the impression that women are doing well. But how real have their gains been? The gap between women's and men's income did close slightly through the 1980s; however, most analysts agree that the decreased gap reflects a drop in male wages. The most dramatic gains in economic status have been for younger women in professional jobs. The majority of women remain concentrated in gender-segregated occupations with low wages, little opportunity for mobility, and stressful conditions. This is particularly true for women of color who are more likely to be in occupations that are race and gender segregated. And, for women heading their own households, poverty persists at alarmingly high rates. By 1988, more than half of Black and Latino families and 30 percent of white families headed by women were officially categorized as poor. Income and occupational data do not tell the full story for women. High rates of violence against women, whether in the home, on campus, in the workplace, or on the streets, indicate the continuing devaluation and danger for women in this society.

Such facts show that race, class, and gender are inextricably intertwined, and they compel us to think about the structure of race, class, and gender relations in society. Although some people believe that race, gender, and class divisions are relics of the past, they are deeply embedded in the structure of social institutions. In Part Two, we focus on race, class, and gender as separate systems of oppression but with the purpose of conceptualizing how each structures and intersects with the others. For example, we want readers to understand how race and class structure gender relations and how gender and race structure class relations. We look at each factor distinctly only to provide a foundation for understanding their interlocking nature.

We also examine race, class, and gender relations from an institutional, or structural, perspective. Institutions are "fairly stable social arrangements and practices" that persist over time.[2] Locating race, class, and gender oppression in the structure of social institutions provides a different frame for analysis than does analysis of individuals only. For example, individual racism is one person's belief in the superiority of one race over another. Individual racism is related to prejudice, a hostile attitude toward a person who is presumed to have the negative characteristics associated with a group to which he or she belongs. Institutional racism is more systematic than this. Institutional racism is a system of beliefs and behaviors by which a group defined as a race is oppressed, controlled, and exploited because of presumed cultural or biological characteristics.[3] Racism is not the same thing as prejudice, although prejudice is one manifestation of racism. The concept of institutional racism reminds us that racism is not just a matter of belief but is also embedded in a system of power relations. Institutional racism evolves over time.

In this definition of institutional racism, note first that racism is systematic—it is part of society's structure, not just present in individual bigots. As Jenny Yamato discusses in her article, racism can be intentional or unintentional. In a racist system, well-meaning white people benefit from racism even if they have no intention of behaving like a racist. Second, racism creates a built-in system of privilege. As Yamato suggests, different groups internalize it in different forms of consciousness. Peggy McIntosh's essay, "White Privilege and Male Privilege," describes how racial privilege becomes most invisible to those who benefit most from it, even though it structures the everyday life of both white people and people of color. Third, the institutional basis of racism means that eliminating racism requires fundamental change in social institutions.

A final point embedded in this definition is that the meaning of *race* itself reflects institutionalized racist practices and beliefs. "Race" is a social-historical-political concept.[4] Who defines one's race? Should it matter? Many people believe that to not be a racist means one must be color blind—that is, not recognize or place significance on a person's racial background and identity. But to ignore the significance of race in a society where racial groups have distinct historical and contemporary experiences is to deny the reality of their group experience. As Karen Russell points out in "Growing Up with Privilege and Prejudice," being color blind in a society structured on racial privilege means everybody is assumed to be "white." She is offended by the comments of her friends who say, "But, I never think of you as Black."

Racism does not exist in a vacuum. As we have said, race, gender, and class are intersecting systems—experienced simultaneously, not separately. Do not think of any one category in the absence of the others. Race, for example, is also structured differently, depending on class and gender. For example, Karen Russell, the daughter of a basketball star, grew up with relative class privilege. Although this provided her a good education and other opportunities, it did not eliminate racism from her experience. And, as Leanita McClain tells us in "The Middle-Class Black's Burden," being Black and middle class creates tensions and incongruities of its own.

We can consider class in a parallel way to this discussion of racism. Class, like gender and race, involves both objective and subjective dimensions. Objectively, the class system differentially structures group access to material resources, including economic, political, and social resources. But, in addition to giving some groups more privileges than others, class shapes social relationships. The personal narratives of Bob Cole and Leanita McClain included here describe how different groups and people experience class. Bob Cole, for example, was raised working class and discusses the shame he experienced when he entered academia—an institution with its own set of class expectations. His narrative shows how he learned the rules of the class system and then used his growing class consciousness to resist class oppression.

The subjective dimensions of class are also evident in the ideology of class. *Ideology* refers to a system of beliefs that distort reality at the same time that they justify the status quo. As we learn from the articles by Edna Bonacich and Donna Langston, the class system in the United States has been supported by the myth that we live in a classless society. This myth serves the dominant class, making class privilege seem like something one earns, not something that is deeply embedded in the institutions of society. Langston and Bonacich also suggest that systems of privilege and inequality (by race, class, and gender) are least visible to those who are most privileged by them and who, in turn, control the resources to define the dominant cultural belief systems. This is perhaps why men more than women deny that patriarchy exists, why whites more than Blacks believe racism is disappearing, and why the privileged, not the poor, are more likely to believe that one gets ahead through hard work.

Finally, the articles on gender in this section illustrate how gender, like race, is a socially constructed experience, not a biological imperative. Sociologists distinguish between the terms *sex* and *gender* to emphasize this point. Sex refers to one's biological identity as male or female; gender refers to the systematic structuring of relationships between women and men in social institutions. Gender is a learned identity, but, as with race, it cannot be understood at the individual level alone. Gender is structured in social institutions, including work, families, mass media, and education. And again, changing gender relations is not just a matter of changing individual attitudes. Transformation of institutional structures requires change in consciousness and collective activism.

The ideology of sexism supports the system of gender relations, just as the ideology of racism supports the system of race relations. Like racism, sexism is a system of beliefs and behaviors by which a group is oppressed, controlled, and exploited because of presumed gender differences. Sexism is manifested in individually held beliefs and social behaviors and is embedded in cultural symbols. It supports the gender inequalities that are structured into social institutions. Homophobia—the fear of homosexuality—is part of the system of social control that legitimates and enforces gender oppression. It supports the system of compulsory heterosexuality, the institutionalized power and privilege given to heterosexual behavior and identification. If only heterosexual forms of gender identity are "normal," then gays and lesbians become ostracized, oppressed, and defined as "socially deviant."

The articles here show, however, that women are not oppressed in the same ways by gender. Race and class create significant differences among women. As Johnetta Cole notes in "Commonalities and Differences," women share many features of gender oppression, but the specific form of their experience depends on race and class, as well. Oliva Espín, for example, describes how the particular histories of Latinas shape their gender and sexual identities. Tracy Lai writes of the specific forms of gender oppression that Asian-American women experience. Peggy McIntosh's essay reminds us that although white women are oppressed by gender, they enjoy the privileges of race and, in some cases, class and heterosexual identification. Evelyn Torton Beck's discussion also shows the ways in which anti-Semitism, hatred of Jewish people, mingles with sexism, racism, and homophobia.

Institutionalized gender relations shape men's, as well as women's experiences. But as Peter Blood, Alan Tuttle, and George Lakey show in "Understanding and Fighting Sexism: A Call to Men," not all men benefit equally from patriarchy. Depending on their race and class, men experience gender differently. Michael Messner shows how men's experiences and choices in sports are conditioned by race, class, and gender.

Throughout Part Two, keep the concept of social structure in mind. Race, class, and gender are often discussed in terms of cultural difference, but they are also part of the institutional framework of society. A structural analysis studies the intersections of race, class, and gender within institutions and within individuals' experiences in those institutions. The articles in this section demonstrate how race, class, and gender influence individual and group experience.

1. U.S. Department of Commerce, Bureau of the Census, *Money Income and Poverty Status in the United States: 1988 (Advance Data from the March 1989 Current Population Survey)*. Series P-60, no. 166 (Washington, D.C.: U.S. Government Printing Office, October 1989).

2. Louis L. Knowles and Kenneth Prewitt, *Institutional Racism in America* (Englewood Cliffs, N.J.: Prentice-Hall, 1970), p. 5.

3. Robert Blauner, *Racial Oppression in America* (New York: Harper & Row, 1972).

4. Michael Omi and Howard Winant, *Racial Formation in the United States: From the 1960s to the 1980s* (New York: Routledge & Kegan Paul, 1986).

Race and Racism

THE AMBIGUITIES OF RACIAL CHANGE 7

Robert Blauner

Sitting in the park one hot summer afternoon in 1981, Florence Grier pointed to a group of black men, mostly in their early twenties, just standing around. There was no work for them, and the likelihood was small that there ever would be. Until that situation changes, Mrs. Grier told me, she would continue to question how much had been accomplished during the activist sixties, and she would continue to be pessimistic about the future, especially because the schools were not preparing black youngsters to do much more than stand around.

Like many of the people I reinterviewed (black as well as white), Florence Grier experienced measurable improvement in her own circumstances during the 1970s. But she saw herself as the highly unusual exception—as did many of the Afro-Americans I talked to. They reported extremely positive changes in their own lives coupled with a skeptical, even negative, assessment of the progress of black people as a group.[1]

With some exceptions, whites were much more positive about racial change. After the turbulence of the sixties, they were tired of the racial issue and wanted to put it behind them. They were also impressed by the success of integration. They have seen blacks and other minorities come into the places where they work or study, become visible in politics, the media, and the arts.

From: Robert Blauner, *Black Lives, White Lives: Three Decades of Race Relations in America* (Berkeley: University of California, 1989). Copyright © 1989 The Regents of the University of California. Reprinted by permission.

But the relatively few middle-class success stories and "superstars" the whites see don't seem that significant to the blacks, who focus instead on those who are poor, jobless, in jail, or on drugs—struggling folks rarely seen by whites in the course of their daily lives, but whom successful blacks know as friends, neighbors, or even relatives.

Blacks are inevitably more sensitive than whites to the nuances of racism. They are alert to its various and varying forms and make more distinctions as to what has changed and what has not. In their view, today's racism is more subtle, and therefore harder to fight, than the overt discrimination of earlier times. When they were excluded from a school or a job or from political participation, they could fight to open the doors, to become part of "the system." Today, people are in those doors, or halfway in, or at least a few have entered. But once inside, they still encounter barriers. They feel that the deck is stacked, and not in their favor.

There is truth to both the black and the white perspectives on contemporary racism: they focus on different aspects of a complex picture of two decades of uneven racial change. The black perspective, I believe, reflects more of a long-term historical outlook and a deeper and more comprehensive understanding of the ambiguities of progress and stagnation. In the last two decades we have seen both a greater acceptance of people of color and a disquieting return of bigotry and racial hatred. The situation is further complicated because the degree of change varies markedly from city to city and by social institution, and because black America itself is so split between those who are "making it" and those who have been left behind. One of the few sure generalizations is that the South has changed more profoundly than the North or the West.

NORTH AND SOUTH

During the 1970s and 1980s race relations in the South have varied by county and city, as the vastly different experiences of Florence Grier and Howard Spence on returning to their hometowns suggest. . . . Nonetheless, and despite an increase in Klan activity in the 1980s, there will be no return to the traditional forms of racial segregation in the southern states. While neither the "slavemaster" nor the "slave" mentality is dead, black southerners will no longer be intimidated from voting, exerting political influence, or defending themselves against racial attacks.

Southern blacks still lag behind whites economically, educationally, and politically. But school desegregation is more advanced in the South than in the North (despite the private academies whites use to circumvent it), and southern cities have made more progress than northern ones in reducing the still prevalent residential segregation.[2] Most scholars agree that the South's superior performance reflects a stronger commitment to change, though in part the region simply had further to go because of its segregationist and discriminatory patterns. In southern cities especially, the northern pattern of black bifurcation—a growing middle class *and* a growing underclass—is replacing the more cohesive community of the past. Too, an old-fashioned racism remains entrenched in many places. At the University of Mississippi and other southern colleges, white students flaunt the Confederate flag as the number of blacks on campus increases.[3]

Despite the virtual elimination of Jim Crow practices, segregation and even resegregation continue on a de facto basis, both in the South and in the North. More blacks now live in suburban and better urban neighborhoods, but metropolitan areas are increasingly divided into predominantly white suburbs and central cities that are becoming more black, more brown, and more Asian (with the arrival of new immigrants). Despite some improvements during the 1970s, Reynolds Farley's observation holds for southern cities as well: "Chicago, St. Louis, and Cleveland were almost as segregated as they would have been if a law mandated that all blacks must live in exclusively black blocks and whites in exclusively white ones"; and in many cities "black and white students go to separate schools, just as they did when 'separate but equal' was the guiding principle."[4]

Another measure of change during the 1970s and 1980s is the success of blacks in electoral politics. In June 1988 black mayors were leading most of our largest cities and were presiding over many medium-sized cities as well. Although in some cases this has meant administering the almost unsolvable urban problems of economically depressed, largely minority central cities for a larger white power structure, this new political influence has democratized access to municipal and public service jobs and has helped consolidate the economic position of the black middle class.

At the local level, the rise in black elected officials has been spectacular, particularly in the South, where their number quadrupled between 1969 and 1979.[5] The tenure of blacks on school boards, city councils, and in state legislatures and the election of black sheriffs and police chiefs have made a real difference in many communities.

Yet the degree of underrepresentation remains as impressive as the gains. Although 12 percent of the voting-age population is black, fewer than 1.5 percent of political officeholders are black.[6] Parity would call for twelve blacks in the U.S. Senate—there are none. Even in Mississippi, where blacks constitute 37 percent of the population, only 10 percent of the state representatives are black.[7] Gerrymandering and devices such as runoff elections continue to limit black political power, especially in the South.

Moreover, this new political influence often benefits middle-class blacks more than the poor and the working class. In Oakland, California, where blacks dominate city politics, police officers typically treat middle-class blacks courteously, while in poor neighborhoods reports of continuing harassment have prompted lawsuits against the city.[8] And the ability of mayors to respond to the urban poor has diminished as the federal government has reduced its financial support and revenue-sharing programs.

Finally, the continuing importance of race in the political arena is suggested by the growing polarization in the 1984 and 1986 elections. Middle-class and working-class blacks vote overwhelmingly Democratic, whereas white have been moving toward Republican candidates.[9]

THE BLACK MIDDLE CLASS

Discrimination in hiring and in training programs has lessened significantly over the past two decades, and affirmative action has had an effect in public-sector jobs and in the larger private companies. But small businesses (the fastest-growing segment of the economy) are not governed by the same equal opportunity standards, and expanding companies of all sizes can ensure a predominantly white work force by locating new plants and offices in areas where few blacks live.[10]

On-the-job discrimination persists. It is usually subtle, but not always so. A sociological study of members of the black elite has found that "racism remains a major obstacle in their mobility and in interaction with whites" because whites, in particular white males, feel threatened by upwardly mobile blacks, particularly black men.[11]

But the striking growth of the black middle class is one of the most significant legacies of the civil rights movement. Almost one-quarter of all black families had incomes of more than $25,000 (in constant dollars) in 1982, compared to only 8.7 percent in 1960. Among employed blacks the proportion who hold middle-class jobs increased from 13.4 percent in 1960 to 37.8 percent in 1981.[12] The proportion is even higher for women, whose rapid movement into the white-collar ranks accounted for much of the growth in the black middle class during the 1970s: by 1980 almost half of all employed black women (49.3 percent) were working in clerical, sales, professional, or managerial positions.[13]

This occupational mobility is a product of affirmative action, the expansion of public-sector employment, and, especially, higher levels of education.

The number of black college students increased from 340,000 to more than a million between 1966 and 1982. In 1980 some 80 percent of black college students were attending predominantly white institutions, rather than the traditional Negro colleges.[14] However, black dropout rates have been extremely high at the mainstream schools, and since the economic downturn in the early 1980s fewer black high school graduates have been going on to college. From 1980 to 1984 black college enrollment dropped 3 percent nationwide,[15] a decline that has deepened even during the improved economic conditions of the middle and late eighties.

Overall, a much smaller proportion of blacks than of whites has arrived in the middle class, and blacks are more concentrated in the lower middle class.[16] Compared to whites, employment in the public sector accounts for a much higher (and increasing) proportion of the black middle class. Even in professional occupations, blacks tend to be in the lower-paying, lower-prestige fields, though there have been impressive increases in law and medicine since 1978. Among black middle-class families, even more so than among whites, two paychecks are the norm; indeed, a middle-class income is often the result of two working-class wages. A higher proportion of married black women work than married white women, and their average earnings more nearly equal their husbands', since black women have reached parity with white women in occupations and earnings, whereas the gap between black men and white men remains extremely wide.[17]

With a more precarious economic status, the black middle class is highly vulnerable to economic recession, government budget cuts, and even changes in affirmative action policy.[18] Thus the black middle class still lags behind its white counterpart in its ability to transmit its favored class position to its children. Part of this situation is financial: in Bart Landry's 1976 survey, the wealth of middle-class whites was almost two and a half times that of middle-class blacks.[19] But part of it is situational: despite the exodus from the ghetto, many middle-class blacks remain there, and even in partly integrated neighborhoods they cannot always protect their children from the atmosphere of the streets, the pressure of peers, and the inadequacies of the schools.

Even with its newfound purchasing power, the black middle class has no significant influence on the nation's economy or on corporate decision making. In the nation's one thousand largest companies there were only three black senior executives in 1979, four in 1985. There are no black-owned firms in *Fortune*'s list of the five hundred largest corporations, and none of these corporations has a black chief executive officer.[20]

Yet the new black middle class is not a transitory phenomenon; it is not a minuscule stratum; and it is not composed only of marginally middle-class aspirants. In cities such as Atlanta, Philadelphia, New York, Los Angeles,

Chicago, Oakland, and Washington, significant numbers of blacks are entering the upper-middle-class ranks. Despite the problems, the upward mobility of many Afro-Americans during the past three decades has been unprecedented in American history.

THE BLACK UNDERCLASS

But these gains have had little meaning for poor blacks still trapped in deteriorating ghettos. Members of this underclass have less hope for the future today than they did in the sixties. Traditionally, the ghettos were the meeting ground for both poor and more successful blacks, the site of a shared identity and sense of community, because racism and discrimination limited the possibilities of life for all black people. But the very successes of the middle class have created a class polarization that has weakened this sense of unity. When middle-class blacks find better housing and schools in integrated or previously white neighborhoods, the ghetto is deprived of their economic contributions and their influence as models of success.

Between 1959 and 1970 the percentage of blacks classed as poor fell sharply, from 55 percent to 34 percent. But since then there has been little progress: in 1979 the black poverty rate was 33 percent; in 1986 it was 31 percent. Worse yet, the number of poor blacks increased from 7.1 million in 1970 to 9.7 million in 1982. Although the majority of poor people are white, the proportion who are black rose during the sixties and seventies, from 25 percent to 31 percent.[21] The situation has worsened in the eighties: the lowest-earning quintile of black families had 22 percent less purchasing power in 1984 than they did in 1980.[22] Half of all black children are growing up in poverty today.

The seventies and eighties have been particularly difficult for urban black teenagers and young adults as jobs have continued to move to suburbs, rural areas, and the predominantly white areas of the sunbelt. Blue-collar manufacturing work is disappearing, and young blacks who do not finish high school and college cannot compete for the new jobs in the white-collar, service, and high-tech industries. Between 1949 and 1979 the proportion of black eighteen- and nineteen-year-olds not in school and neither employed nor looking for work increased from 22 percent to 42 percent.[23] And from 1971 to 1980 unemployment among those teenagers *in* the labor force (working or actively looking for work) increased from 26 percent to 40 percent in New York, from 36 percent to 55 percent in Chicago, to name two cities.[24]

Unsuccessful in school and unable to find legitimate work, many young black males turn to hustling and crime. National statistics for 1980 attribute

51 percent of all violent juvenile crime to black youths. More than 90 percent of the victims of these crimes were other blacks; homicide has become the leading cause of death for young black males *and* females. In 1979 alone, 15 percent of blacks aged sixteen to nineteen were arrested. Today, black men constitute 46 percent of the prison population, and blacks are jailed at a rate eight times higher than that of whites.[25]

Traditionally, black men were more likely than white men to be either working or looking for work. But today fewer than two-thirds of black men participate in the labor force, and about half of them are either unemployed or employed only part time.[26] During the early seventies the official black unemployment rate was twice the white rate; today it is almost three times as high.

Although black women in the labor force made impressive gains in the 1970s, they have been hard hit by the "feminization of poverty." More unmarried black women are having children, and fewer black men have the steady incomes needed to marry and support a family. Separation and divorce rates are rising. In the mid-eighties 43 percent of all black families were headed by a single parent, and one-parent families accounted for 73 percent of black families below the poverty line. Single-parent families are increasing in the middle class as well. More than half of all black children live with one parent—almost always the mother.[27]

All these developments have seriously undermined the integrity and the unity of the black community. Joblessness and single-parent households have weakened the inner-city nuclear family, and extended families are not as strong as they once were. Even in street life there is less solidarity than in the sixties, as drugs and crime divide the community and create a climate of fear. The increasing distance between the classes makes it harder for Afro-Americans to speak with a unified voice. And an unwelcome by-product of integration has been the weakening of the traditional institutions of the black community. Black businesses, black colleges, and even the black church now compete with white and integrated institutions.

THE RACIAL CLIMATE

In the 1960s, despite the backlash, many white people tended to be sympathetic to black demands for equal opportunity and integration and to feel that black poverty and suffering were the result of objective structures of racial discrimination. But beginning in the seventies and intensifying in the eighties, a conservative zeitgeist has brought forth a very different attitude. No longer are centuries of slavery and racism, or even present-day lack of opportunities, used to explain black disadvantage. Pointing to state and federal civil rights laws, whites presuppose that blacks now have a fair chance to succeed and that affirmative action even gives them an unfair advantage. So, these whites argue, if blacks remain poor and unemployed, it's nobody's fault but their own—especially considering how well Asian-Americans are progressing.* As sociologist Troy Duster puts it: "Blacks have lost the moral advantage."

At the same time, individual blacks are more likely to be welcomed into formerly white worlds—if they meet white middle-class standards of acceptability. Integration and incorporation have taken place even in strategic aspects of culture and national symbolism: black history has become part of the curriculum in many high schools and colleges, and Martin Luther King's birthday is a national holiday in all but eleven states. On television, the Ed Bradleys report the news to nationwide audiences, the Dennis Richmonds (of Oakland's Channel 2) anchor local broadcasts, and in white households Bill Cosby's show is the most popular program, with white teenagers voting him their number one hero.[28]

Yet whites also made Bernhard Goetz a folk hero, identifying with his 1984 shooting of four black youths on a New York subway.[29] Black teenagers are viewed with fear and suspicion; welfare mothers, with anger and moral contempt. Thus public race relations, especially between strangers, remain tense. Racial friction is endemic in integrated schools, and incidents of racial conflict have been increasing throughout the eighties. But in situations where people know one another personally—at work, in neighborhood life—interracial contacts have improved markedly.

Whites are less likely today to see people of color in the global, undifferentiated mode of the classical racist tradition. Instead they view blacks more often in terms of class, reserving most of their animus for the poor and protesting too much that blacks similar to themselves would be welcome in their neighborhoods. Because class prejudice is the more acceptable attitude, it is sometimes used to conceal racial feelings.

William J. Wilson, in his very important sociological study *The Declining Significance of Race*, argued that since the late 1960s the "life chances" of black youths have been determined by their class position, not by the color of their skin.[30] Wilson is correct to emphasize the growing importance of class divisions in the black community. But class and race are not antithetical, nor

---

*Viewing Asian-Americans as a "model minority" and using their successes to denigrate Afro-Americans has become a commonplace argument of the neoconservatives, a group of scholars and social commentators who have achieved considerable influence in political and intellectual circles in the seventies and eighties.

are they reciprocals in a zero-sum relationship where "more class" must mean "less race." Race and class have always been closely connected in American life, and their separate influences cannot be easily unraveled. The black underclass is not simply a product of shifts in the economy and changes in the type and location of available jobs, as Wilson has argued. That blacks without marketable skills live in inner-city ghettos is also the result of centuries of overt discrimination and today's more subtle institutional racism.* Social class does loom more fateful in racial stratification, but the significance of race has not declined correspondingly. Despite the dismantling of discriminatory barriers and some improvement in white attitudes and in day-to-day relations between the races, the separation between blacks and whites, and the racism that feeds on this division, remains a powerful force in American life.

What has declined dramatically since the 1960s is *racial consciousness* and awareness. As Alice Kahn, a Bay Area columnist, capsulizes it: "The problems between black people and white people never got solved. We just stopped talking about them."[31]

I began this chapter by noting the differences between black and white respondents during the second round of interviews in 1978–79. By the third round of interviews in 1986, the two perspectives were somewhat closer. The whites were not quite as positive as they had been in the late seventies, largely, I think, because during the eighties the mass media have focused more on black *problems*, especially the plight of the underclass, than they did in the seventies. Here I discount the whites' personal experiences with blacks as a key factor, for most whites were still leading predominantly white lives. And the blacks I interviewed were less likely to focus only on negative trends. The passage of time has convinced them that at least some of the changes produced by the sixties are real and permanent, whereas eight years earlier they were much more skeptical. Too, over time, their intense initial disappointment in the failure of the sixties' promise of a fundamental, radical social transformation has softened such that they view more objectively the changes that have taken place.

Yet the differences in outlook persist. Whites remain more optimistic overall, more likely to believe that race relations and attitudes have continued to improve through the eighties. Blacks tend to be more fearful that opportunities are tightening up, that during the Reagan years progress has halted and gains have been lost. They are also much more likely to be seriously worried about their children's and grandchildren's futures.

---

*Wilson has moved closer to this position in his more recent works; see especially his *The Truly Disadvantaged: The Inner City, the Underclass, and Public Policy* (Chicago: University of Chicago Press, 1987).

NOTES

1. A similar paradox was reported in a 1986 *Washington Post*–ABC News poll of 1,022 blacks: 48 percent thought income and living conditions were worsening for most blacks, and only 14 percent thought these conditions were improving. But 28 percent said that conditions were improving for them personally, while only 23 percent said they were getting worse; *San Francisco Chronicle*, January 20, 1986.

2. Reynolds Farley, *Blacks and Whites: Narrowing the Gap?* (Cambridge: Harvard University Press, 1984), p. 35.

3. See Steve Milner, "The New South: The New Racism," *Western Journal of Black Studies* 12, no. 1 (Spring 1987): 39–46.

4. Farley, *Blacks and Whites*, pp. 34 and 199. Farley's overall assessment of racial change, however, is less negative than these two citations suggest.

5. In 1969 there were 1,185 black elected officials; in 1979 there were 4,607; Joint Center for Political Studies, *National Roster of Black Elected Officials* (Washington, D.C., 1980).

6. Ibid.

7. Theodore Cross, *The Black Power Imperative: Racial Inequality and the Politics of Nonviolence* (New York: Faulkner, 1984), pp. 321–22. On the role of gerrymandering and other political strategies that work against black candidates, see Cross's discussion on pp. 142–48.

8. *San Francisco Chronicle*, August 10, 1987.

9. *New York Times*/CBS News Poll, reported in *New York Times*, November 8 and November 19, 1984. A California poll one week before the 1984 presidential elections found whites preferring Reagan to Mondale 62 percent to 33 percent; for blacks the ratio was 8 to 77 percent.

10. On February 7, 1983, the *New York Times* reported that strategic relocation has become a widespread practice, because, as one company official put it: "Black workers were less reliable, less skilled, and easier to unionize" and the firms "wanted to avoid affirmative action."

11. Personal communication from Dr. Lois Benjamin, Central State University, Wilberforce, Ohio, on her preliminary research findings.

12. As Bart Landry explains, analysts disagree about whether to define *middle class* as a function of income, occupation, or life-style; see his *The New Black Middle Class* (Berkeley and Los Angeles: University of California Press, 1987). Data on income from William I. Taylor, "Access to Economic Opportunity," in *Minority Report: What Has Happened to Blacks, Hispanics, American Indians and Other Minorities in the Eighties*, edited

by Leslie W. Dunbar (New York: Pantheon, 1984); data on middle-class jobs from Landry, *New Black Middle Class*.

13. In contrast, only 38 percent of black women were white-collar workers in 1972; see Diane Westcott, "Blacks in the 1970s," *Monthly Labor Review*, June 1982, p. 20. It is also true that black women are still overrepresented in such traditional occupations as private household workers, cooks, and housekeepers; see National Committee on Pay Equity, *Pay Equity: An Issue of Race, Ethnicity, and Sex* (Washington, D.C., 1987), p. 31.

14. Taylor, "Access to Economic Opportunity," p. 31.

15. *Time* Magazine, November 11, 1985, p. 84; *New York Times* (national edition), December 3, 1986.

16. Landry, *New Black Middle Class*, pp. 108–10, 196–98.

17. Farley, *Blacks and Whites*, chaps. 2 and 3.

18. For example, the proportion of college faculty who were black doubled (from 3 to 7 percent) between 1970 and 1977, but blacks suffered disproportionate losses (36 percent) when 17,000 teaching positions were eliminated between 1977 and 1979; Cross, *Black Power Imperative*, p. 440.

19. Landry, *New Black Middle Class*, p. 148. See also *New York Times* (national edition), July 19, 1986.

20. Data on black senior executives in the nation's one thousand largest companies from John Naisbit, "Not Much Progress for Black Executives," *San Francisco Chronicle*, December 31, 1986. Data on Fortune 500 from Cross, *Black Power Imperative*, pp. 274–75.

21. Data from Farley, *Blacks and Whites*, p. 200; Cross, *Black Power Imperative*, chap. 12; U.S. Department of Commerce, *U.S. Statistical Abstracts*, 108th ed. (Washington, D.C.: Government Printing Office, 1988), p. 435.

22. Charles Hardy, "Black America, New Opportunities and New Problems," *San Francisco Examiner*, July 21, 1986. By 1986 there was some improvement: from 1982 to 1986 median family income for blacks increased 14 percent, according to the *New York Times* (national edition), July 31, 1987.

23. Cross, *Black Power Imperative*, pp. 245–46. Almost half of these black teenagers live in the fifteen largest metropolitan areas, where jobs are few; only 23 percent of white teenagers live in these largest cities.

24. Troy Duster, "Social Implications of the 'New' Black Urban Underclass," in *Poverty with a Human Face* (San Francisco: Public Media Center, 1985).

25. Data from Uniform Crime Reports; Duster, "Social Implications of the Underclass"; *Christian Science Monitor*, November 13, 1986.

26. Census reports show that 66.7 percent of all black men of working age were in the labor force (either working or actively seeking work) in 1979. Since then, the percentage has continued to decline: "The proportion of black males over the age of 16 who were employed dropped from 74 percent in 1960 to 56 percent in 1982"; Taylor, "Access to Economic Opportunity," p. 41.

27. Hardy, "Black America."

28. *San Francisco Chronicle*, December 19, 1986.

29. Lillian Rubin, *Quiet Rage: Bernie Goetz in an Age of Madness* (New York: Farrar, Straus & Giroux, 1986).

30. William J. Wilson, *The Declining Significance of Race: Blacks and Changing American Institutions* (Chicago: University of Chicago Press, 1978). Michael Hout and other social demographers have supported Wilson's claims by documenting the increasing role of social class in the occupational placement of Afro-Americans. Until the 1960s, race was so all-determining that blacks born into middle-class professional families were just as likely to end up in low-status jobs as blacks who were born poor; Hout, "Occupational Mobility of Black Men," *American Sociological Review* 49 (June 1984): 308–22.

31. Alice Kahn, *San Francisco Chronicle*, November 23, 1986.

SOMETHING ABOUT THE SUBJECT MAKES IT HARD TO NAME

8

Gloria Yamato

Racism—simple enough in structure, yet difficult to eliminate. Racism—pervasive in the U.S. culture to the point that it deeply affects all the local town folk and spills over, negatively influencing the fortunes of folk around the world. Racism is pervasive to the point that we take many of its manifestations for granted, believing "that's life." Many believe that racism can be dealt with

From: Jo Whitehorse Cochran, Donna Langston, and Carolyn Woodward (eds.), *Changing Our Power: An Introduction to Women's Studies* (Dubuque, Iowa: Kendall-Hunt, 1988), pp. 3–6. Reprinted by permission.

effectively in one hellifying workshop, or one hour-long heated discussion. Many actually believe this monster, racism, that has had at least a few hundred years to take root, grow, invade our space and develop subtle variations . . . this mind-funk that distorts thought and action, can be merely wished away. I've run into folks who really think that we can beat this devil, kick this habit, be healed of this disease in a snap. In a sincere blink of a well-intentioned eye, presto—poof—racism disappears. "I've dealt with my racism . . . (envision a laying on of hands) . . . Hallelujah! Now I can go to the beach." Well, fine. Go to the beach. In fact, why don't we all go to the beach and continue to work on the sucker over there? Cuz you can't even shave a little piece off this thing called racism in a day, or a weekend, or a workshop.

When I speak of *oppression*, I'm talking about the systematic, institutionalized mistreatment of one group of people by another for whatever reason. The oppressors are purported to have an innate ability to access economic resources, information, respect, etc., while the oppressed are believed to have a corresponding negative innate ability. The flip side of oppression is *internalized oppression*. Members of the target group are emotionally, physically, and spiritually battered to the point that they begin to actually believe that their oppression is deserved, is their lot in life, is natural and right, and that it doesn't even exist. The oppression begins to feel comfortable, familiar enough that when mean ol' Massa lay down de whip, we got's to pick up and whack ourselves and each other. Like a virus, it's hard to beat racism, because by the time you come up with a cure, it's mutated to a "new cure-resistant" form. One shot just won't get it. Racism must be attacked from many angles.

The forms of racism that I pick up on these days are 1) aware/blatant racism, 2) aware/covert racism, 3) unaware/unintentional racism, and 4) unaware/self-righteous racism. I can't say that I prefer any one form of racism over the others, because they all look like an itch needing a scratch. I've heard it said (and understandably so) that the aware/blatant form of racism is preferable if one must suffer it. Outright racists will, without apology or confusion, tell us that because of our color we don't appeal to them. If we so choose, we can attempt to get the hell out of their way before we get the sweat knocked out of us. Growing up, aware/covert racism is what I heard many of my elders bemoaning "up north," after having escaped the overt racism "down south." Apartments were suddenly no longer vacant or rents were outrageously high, when black, brown, red, or yellow persons went to inquire about them. Job vacancies were suddenly filled, or we were fired for very vague reasons. It still happens, though the perpetrators really take care to cover their tracks these days. They don't want to get gummed to death or slobbered on by the toothless laws that supposedly protect us from such inequities.

Unaware/unintentional racism drives usually tranquil white liberals wild when they get called on it, and confirms the suspicions of many people of color who feel that white folks are just plain crazy. It has led white people to believe that it's just fine to ask if they can touch my hair (while reaching). They then exclaim over how soft it is, how it does not scratch their hand. It has led whites to assume that bending over backwards and speaking to me in high-pitched (terrified), condescending tones would make up for all the racist wrongs that distort our lives. This type of racism has led whites right to my doorstep, talking 'bout, "We're sorry/we love you and want to make things right," which is fine, and further, "We're gonna give you the opportunity to fix it while we sleep. Just tell us what you need. 'Bye!!"—which *ain't* fine. With the best of intentions, the best of educations, and the greatest generosity of heart, whites, operating on the misinformation fed to them from day one, will behave in ways that are racist, will perpetuate racism by being "nice" the way we're taught to be nice. You can just "nice" somebody to death with naïveté and lack of awareness of privilege. Then there's guilt and the desire to end racism and how the two get all tangled up to the point that people, morbidly fascinated with their guilt, are immobilized. Rather than deal with ending racism, they sit and ponder their guilt and hope nobody notices how awful they are. Meanwhile, racism picks up momentum and keeps on keepin' on.

Now, the newest form of racism that I'm hip to is unaware/self-righteous racism. The "good white" racist attempts to shame Blacks into being blacker, scorns Japanese-Americans who don't speak Japanese, and knows more about the Chicano/a community than the folks who make up the community. They assign themselves as the "good whites," as opposed to the "bad whites," and are often so busy telling people of color what the issues in the Black, Asian, Indian, Latino/a communities should be that they don't have time to deal with their errant sisters and brothers in the white community. Which means that people of color are still left to deal with what the "good whites" don't want to ... racism.

Internalized racism is what really gets in my way as a Black woman. It influences the way I see or don't see myself, limits what I expect of myself or others like me. It results in my acceptance of mistreatment, leads me to believe that being treated with less than absolute respect, at least this once, is to be expected because I am Black, because I am not white. "Because I am *(you fill in the color)*, you think, "Life is going to be hard." The fact is life may be hard, but the color of your skin is not the cause of the hardship. The color of your skin may be used as an excuse to mistreat you, but there is no reason or logic involved in the mistreatment. If it seems that your color is the reason; if it seems that your ethnic heritage is the cause of the woe, it's because you've been deliberately beaten down by agents of a greedy system until you swallowed the garbage. That is the internalization of racism.

Racism is the systematic, institutionalized mistreatment of one group of people by another based on racial heritage. Like every other oppression, racism can be internalized. People of color come to believe misinformation about their particular ethnic group and thus believe that their mistreatment is justified. With that basic vocabulary, let's take a look at how the whole thing works together. Meet "the Ism Family," racism, classism, ageism, adultism, elitism, sexism, heterosexism, physicalism, etc. All these ism's are systematic, that is, not only are these parasites feeding off our lives, they are also dependent on one another for foundation. Racism is supported and reinforced by classism, which is given a foothold and a boost by adultism, which also feeds sexism, which is validated by heterosexism, and so it goes on. You cannot have the "ism" functioning without first effectively installing its flip-side, the internalized version of the ism. Like twins, as one particular form of the ism grows in potency, there is a corresponding increase in its internalized form within the population. Before oppression becomes a specific ism like racism, usually all hell breaks loose. War. People fight attempts to enslave them, or to subvert their will, or to take what they consider theirs, whether that is territory or dignity. It's true that the various elements of racism, while repugnant, would not be able to do very much damage, but for one generally overlooked key piece: power/privilege.

While in one sense we all have power we have to look at the fact that, in our society, people are stratified into various classes and some of these classes have more privilege than others. The owning class has enough power and privilege to not have to give a good whinney what the rest of the folks have on their minds. The power and privilege of the owning class provides the ability to pay off enough of the working class and offer that paid-off group, the middle class, just enough privilege to make it agreeable to do various and sundry oppressive things to other working-class and outright disenfranchised folk, keeping the lid on explosive inequities, at least for a minute. If you're at the bottom of this heap, and you believe the line that says you're there because that's all you're worth, it is at least some small solace to believe that there are others more worthless than you, because of their gender, race, sexual preference . . . whatever. The specific form of power that runs the show here is the power to intimidate. The power to take away the most lives the quickest, and back it up with legal and "divine" sanction, is the very bottom line. It makes the difference between who's holding the racism end of the stick and who's getting beat with it (or beating others as vulnerable as they are) on the internalized racism end of the stick. What I am saying is, while people of color are welcome to tear up their own neighborhoods and each other, everybody knows that you cannot do that to white folks without hell to pay. People of color can be prejudiced against one another and whites, but do not have an ice-cube's chance in hell of passing laws that will get whites sent to relocation camps "for their own protection and the security of the nation." People who have not thought about or refuse to acknowledge this imbalance of power/privilege often want to talk about the racism of people of color. But then that is one of the ways racism is able to continue to function. You look for someone to blame and you blame the victim, who will nine times out of ten accept the blame out of habit.

So, what can we do? Acknowledge racism for a start, even though and especially when we've struggled to be kind and fair, or struggled to rise above it all. It is hard to acknowledge the fact that racism circumscribes and pervades our lives. Racism must be dealt with on two levels, personal and societal, emotional and institutional. It is possible—and most effective—to do both at the same time. We must reclaim whatever delight we have lost in our own ethnic heritage or heritages. This so-called melting pot has only succeeded in turning us into fast food-gobbling "generics" (as in generic "white folks" who were once Irish, Polish, Russian, English, etc. and "black folks," who were once Ashanti, Bambara, Baule, Yoruba, etc.). Find or create safe places to actually *feel* what we've been forced to repress each time we were a victim of, witness to or perpetrator of racism, so that we do not continue, like puppets, to act out the past in the present and future. Challenge oppression. Take a stand against it. When you are aware of something oppressive going down, stop the show. At least call it. We become so numbed to racism that we don't even think twice about it, unless it is immediately life-threatening.

Whites who want to be allies to people of color: You can educate yourselves via research and observation rather than rigidly, arrogantly relying solely on interrogating people of color. Do not expect that people of color should teach you how to behave non-oppressively. Do not give into the pull to be lazy. Think, hard. Do not blame people of color for your frustration about racism, but do appreciate the fact that people of color will often help you get in touch with that frustration. Assume that your effort to be a good friend is appreciated, but don't expect or accept gratitude from people of color. Work on racism for your sake, not "their" sake. Assume that you are needed and capable of being a good ally. Know that you'll make mistakes and commit yourself to correcting them and continuing on as an ally, no matter what. Don't give up.

People of color, working through internalized racism: Remember always that you and others like you are completely worthy of respect, completely capable of achieving whatever you take a notion to do. Remember that the term "people of color" refers to a variety of ethnic and cultural backgrounds. These various groups have been oppressed in a variety of ways. Educate yourself about the ways different peoples have been oppressed and how they've resisted that oppression. Expect and insist that whites are capable of being good allies against racism. Don't give up. Resist the pull to give out the "people of color seal of approval" to aspiring white allies. A moment of appreciation is fine, but more than that tends to be less than helpful. Celebrate yourself. Celebrate yourself. Celebrate the inevitable end of racism.

WHITE PRIVILEGE AND MALE PRIVILEGE: *A Personal Account of Coming to See Correspondences Through Work in Women's Studies*

9

Peggy McIntosh

Through work to bring materials and perspectives from Women's Studies into the rest of the curriculum, I have often noticed men's unwillingness to grant that they are overprivileged in the curriculum, even though they may grant that women are disadvantaged. Denials that amount to taboos surround the subject of advantages that men gain from women's disadvantages. These denials protect male privilege from being fully recognized, acknowledged, lessened, or ended.

Thinking through unacknowledged male privilege as a phenomenon with a life of its own, I realized that since hierarchies in our society are interlocking, there was most likely a phenomenon of white privilege that was similarly denied and protected, but alive and real in its effects. As a white person, I

I have appreciated commentary on this paper from the Working Papers Committee of the Wellesley College Center for Research on Women, from members of the Dodge seminar, and from many individuals, including Margaret Andersen, Sorel Berman, Joanne Braxton, Johnnella Butler, Sandra Dickerson, Marnie Evans, Beverly Guy-Sheftall, Sandra Harding, Eleanor Hinton Hoytt, Pauline Houston, Paul Lauter, Joyce Miller, Mary Norris, Gloria Oden, Beverly Smith, and John Walter.

realized I had been taught about racism as something that puts others at a disadvantage, but had been taught not to see one of its corollary aspects, white privilege, which puts me at an advantage.

I think whites are carefully taught not to recognize white privilege, as males are taught not to recognize male privilege. So I have begun in an untutored way to ask what it is like to have white privilege. This paper is a partial record of my personal observations and not a scholarly analysis. It is based on my daily experiences within my particular circumstances.

I have come to see white privilege as an invisible package of unearned assets that I can count on cashing in each day, but about which I was "meant" to remain oblivious. White privilege is like an invisible weightless knapsack of special provisions, assurances, tools, maps, guides, codebooks, passports, visas, clothes, compass, emergency gear, and blank checks.

Since I have had trouble facing white privilege, and describing its results in my life, I saw parallels here with men's reluctance to acknowledge male privilege. Only rarely will a man go beyond acknowledging that women are disadvantaged to acknowledging that men have unearned advantage, or that unearned privilege has not been good for men's development as human beings, or for society's development, or that privilege systems might ever be challenged and *changed*.

I will review here several types or layers of denial that I see at work protecting, and preventing awareness about, entrenched male privilege. Then I will draw parallels, from my own experience, with the denials that veil the facts of white privilege. Finally, I will list forty-six ordinary and daily ways in which I experience having white privilege, by contrast with my African American colleagues in the same building. This list is not intended to be generalizable. Others can make their own lists from within their own life circumstances.

Writing this paper has been difficult, despite warm receptions for the talks on which it is based.[1] For describing white privilege makes one newly accountable. As we in Women's Studies work reveal male privilege and ask men to give up some of their power, so one who writes about having white privilege must ask, "Having described it, what will I do to lessen or end it?"

The denial of men's overprivileged state takes many forms in discussions of curriculum change work. Some claim that men must be central in the curriculum because they have done most of what is important or distinctive in

---

1. This paper was presented at the Virginia Women's Studies Association conference in Richmond in April, 1986, and the American Educational Research Association conference in Boston in October, 1986, and discussed with two groups of participants in the Dodge seminars for Secondary School Teachers in New York and Boston in the spring of 1987.

life or in civilization. Some recognize sexism in the curriculum but deny that it makes male students seem unduly important in life. Others agree that certain *individual* thinkers are male oriented but deny that there is any *systemic* tendency in disciplinary frameworks or epistemology to overempower men as a group. Those men who do grant that male privilege takes institutionalized and embedded forms are still likely to deny that male hegemony has opened doors for them personally. Virtually all men deny that male overreward alone can explain men's centrality in all the inner sanctums of our most powerful institutions. Moreover, those few who will acknowledge that male privilege systems have overempowered them usually end up doubting that we could dismantle these privilege systems. They may say they will work to improve women's status, in the society or in the university, but they can't or won't support the idea of lessening men's. In curricular terms, this is the point at which they say that they regret they cannot use any of the interesting new scholarship on women because the syllabus is full. When the talk turns to giving men less cultural room, even the most thoughtful and fair-minded of the men I know will tend to reflect, or fall back on, conservative assumptions about the inevitability of present gender relations and distributions of power, calling on precedent or sociobiology and psychobiology to demonstrate that male domination is natural and follows inevitably from evolutionary pressures. Others resort to arguments from "experience" or religion or social responsibility or wishing and dreaming.

After I realized, through faculty development work in Women's Studies, the extent to which men work from a base of unacknowledged privilege, I understood that much of their oppressiveness was unconscious. Then I remembered the frequent charges from women of color that white women whom they encounter are oppressive. I began to understand why we are justly seen as oppressive, even when we don't see ourselves that way. At the very least, obliviousness of one's privileged state can make a person or group irritating to be with. I began to count the ways in which I enjoy unearned skin privilege and have been conditioned into oblivion about its existence, unable to see that it put me "ahead" in any way, or put my people ahead, overrewarding us and yet also paradoxically damaging us, or that it could or should be changed.

My schooling gave me no training in seeing myself as an oppressor, as an unfairly advantaged person, or as a participant in a damaged culture. I was taught to see myself as an individual whose moral state depended on her individual moral will. At school, we were not taught about slavery in any depth; we were not taught to see slaveholders as damaged people. Slaves were seen as the only group at risk of being dehumanized. My schooling followed the pattern which Elizabeth Minnich has pointed out: whites are taught to think of their lives as morally neutral, normative, and average, and also ideal, so that when we work to benefit others, this is seen as work that will allow "them" to be more like "us." I think many of us know how obnoxious this attitude can be in men.

After frustration with men who would not recognize male privilege, I decided to try to work on myself at least by identifying some of the daily effects of white privilege in my life. It is crude work, at this stage, but I will give here a list of special circumstances and conditions I experience that I did not earn but that I have been made to feel are mine by birth, by citizenship, and by virtue of being a conscientious law-abiding "normal" person of goodwill. I have chosen those conditions that I think in my case *attach somewhat more to skin-color privilege* than to class, religion, ethnic status, or geographical location, though these other privileging factors are intricately intertwined. As far as I can see, my Afro-American co-workers, friends, and acquaintances with whom I come into daily or frequent contact in this particular time, place, and line of work cannot count on most of these conditions.

1. I can, if I wish, arrange to be in the company of people of my race most of the time.
2. I can avoid spending time with people whom I was trained to mistrust and who have learned to mistrust my kind or me.
3. If I should need to move, I can be pretty sure of renting or purchasing housing in an area which I can afford and in which I would want to live.
4. I can be reasonably sure that my neighbors in such a location will be neutral or pleasant to me.
5. I can go shopping alone most of the time, fairly well assured that I will not be followed or harassed by store detectives.
6. I can turn on the television or open to the front page of the paper and see people of my race widely and positively represented.
7. When I am told about our national heritage or about "civilization," I am shown that people of my color made it what it is.
8. I can be sure that my children will be given curricular materials that testify to the existence of their race.
9. If I want to, I can be pretty sure of finding a publisher for this piece on white privilege.
10. I can be fairly sure of having my voice heard in a group in which I am the only member of my race.
11. I can be casual about whether or not to listen to another woman's voice in a group in which she is the only member of her race.

12. I can go into a book shop and count on finding the writing of my race represented, into a supermarket and find the staple foods that fit with my cultural traditions, into a hairdresser's shop and find someone who can deal with my hair.

13. Whether I use checks, credit cards, or cash, I can count on my skin color not to work against the appearance that I am financially reliable.

14. I could arrange to protect our young children most of the time from people who might not like them.

15. I did not have to educate our children to be aware of systemic racism for their own daily physical protection.

16. I can be pretty sure that my children's teachers and employers will tolerate them if they fit school and workplace norms; my chief worries about them do not concern others' attitudes toward their race.

17. I can talk with my mouth full and not have people put this down to my color.

18. I can swear, or dress in secondhand clothes, or not answer letters, without having people attribute these choices to the bad morals, the poverty, or the illiteracy of my race.

19. I can speak in public to a powerful male group without putting my race on trial.

20. I can do well in a challenging situation without being called a credit to my race.

21. I am never asked to speak for all the people of my racial group.

22. I can remain oblivious to the language and customs of persons of color who constitute the world's majority without feeling in my culture any penalty for such oblivion.

23. I can criticize our government and talk about how much I fear its policies and behavior without being seen as a cultural outsider.

24. I can be reasonably sure that if I ask to talk to "the person in charge," I will be facing a person of my race.

25. If a traffic cop pulls me over or if the IRS audits my tax return, I can be sure I haven't been singled out because of my race.

26. I can easily buy posters, postcards, picture books, greeting cards, dolls, toys, and children's magazines featuring people of my race.

27. I can go home from most meetings of organizations I belong to feeling somewhat tied in, rather than isolated, out of place, outnumbered, un-heard, held at a distance, or feared.

28. I can be pretty sure that an argument with a colleague of another race is more likely to jeopardize her chances for advancement than to jeopardize mine.

29. I can be fairly sure that if I argue for the promotion of a person of another race, or a program centering on race, this is not likely to cost me heavily within my present setting, even if my colleagues disagree with me.

30. If I declare there is a racial issue at hand, or there isn't a racial issue at hand, my race will lend me more credibility for either position than a person of color will have.

31. I can choose to ignore developments in minority writing and minority activist programs, or disparage them, or learn from them, but in any case, I can find ways to be more or less protected from negative consequences of any of these choices.

32. My culture gives me little fear about ignoring the perspectives and powers of people of other races.

33. I am not made acutely aware that my shape, bearing, or body odor will be taken as a reflection on my race.

34. I can worry about racism without being seen as self-interested or self-seeking.

35. I can take a job with an affirmative action employer without having my co-workers on the job suspect that I got it because of my race.

36. If my day, week, or year is going badly, I need not ask of each negative episode or situation whether it has racial overtones.

37. I can be pretty sure of finding people who would be willing to talk with me and advise me about my next steps, professionally.

38. I can think over many options, social, political, imaginative, or professional, without asking whether a person of my race would be accepted or allowed to do what I want to do.

39. I can be late to a meeting without having the lateness reflect on my race.

40. I can choose public accommodation without fearing that people of my race cannot get in or will be mistreated in the places I have chosen.

41. I can be sure that if I need legal or medical help, my race will not work against me.

42. I can arrange my activities so that I will never have to experience feelings of rejection owing to my race.

43. If I have low credibility as a leader, I can be sure that my race is not the problem.

44. I can easily find academic courses and institutions that give attention only to people of my race.

45. I can expect figurative language and imagery in all of the arts to testify to experiences of my race.

46. I can choose blemish cover or bandages in "flesh" color and have them more or less match my skin.

I repeatedly forgot each of the realizations on this list until I wrote it down. For me, white privilege has turned out to be an elusive and fugitive subject. The pressure to avoid it is great, for in facing it I must give up the myth of meritocracy. If these things are true, this is not such a free country; one's life is not what one makes it; many doors open for certain people through no virtues of their own. These perceptions mean also that my moral condition is not what I had been led to believe. The appearance of being a good citizen rather than a troublemaker comes in large part from having all sorts of doors open automatically because of my color.

A further paralysis of nerve comes from literary silence protecting privilege. My clearest memories of finding such analysis are in Lillian Smith's unparalleled *Killers of the Dream* and Margaret Andersen's review of Karen and Mamie Fields' *Lemon Swamp*. Smith, for example, wrote about walking toward black children on the street and knowing they would step into the gutter; Andersen contrasted the pleasure that she, as a white child, took on summer driving trips to the south with Karen Fields' memories of driving in a closed car stocked with all necessities lest, in stopping, her black family should suffer "insult, or worse." Adrienne Rich also recognizes and writes about daily experiences of privilege, but in my observation, white women's writing in this area is far more often on systemic racism than on our daily lives as light-skinned women.[2]

In unpacking this invisible knapsack of white privilege, I have listed conditions of daily experience that I once took for granted, as neutral, normal, and universally available to everybody, just as I once thought of a male-focused curriculum as the neutral or accurate account that can speak for all. Nor did I think of any of these perquisites as bad for the holder. I now think that we need a more finely differentiated taxonomy of privilege, for some of these varieties are only what one would want for everyone in a just society, and others give license to be ignorant, oblivious, arrogant, and destructive. Before proposing some more finely tuned categorization, I will make some observations about the general effects of these conditions on my life and expectations.

In this potpourri of examples, some privileges make me feel at home in the world. Others allow me to escape penalties or dangers that others suffer. Through some, I escape fear, anxiety, insult, injury, or a sense of not being welcome, not being real. Some keep me from having to hide, to be in disguise, to feel sick or crazy, to negotiate each transaction from the position of being an outsider or, within my group, a person who is suspected of having too close links with a dominant culture. Most keep me from having to be angry.

---

2. Andersen, Margaret, "Race and the Social Science Curriculum: A Teaching and Learning Discussion." *Radical Teacher*, November, 1984, pp. 17–20. Smith, Lillian, *Killers of the Dream*, New York: W. W. Norton, 1949.

I see a pattern running through the matrix of white privilege, a pattern of assumptions that were passed on to me as a white person. There was one main piece of cultural turf; it was my own turf, and I was among those who could control the turf. I could measure up to the cultural standards and take advantage of the many options I saw around me to make what the culture would call a success of my life. *My skin color was an asset for any move I was educated to want to make.* I could think of myself as "belonging" in major ways and of making social systems work for me. I could freely disparage, fear, neglect, or be oblivious to anything outside of the dominant cultural forms. Being of the main culture, I could also criticize it fairly freely. My life was reflected back to me frequently enough so that I felt, with regard to my race, if not to my sex, like one of the real people.

Whether through the curriculum or in the newspaper, the television, the economic system, or the general look of people in the streets, I received daily signals and indications that my people counted and that others *either didn't exist or must be trying, not very successfully, to be like people of my race.* I was given cultural permission not to hear voices of people of other races or a tepid cultural tolerance for hearing or acting on such voices. I was also raised not to suffer seriously from anything that darker-skinned people might say about my group, "protected," though perhaps I should more accurately say *prohibited*, through the habits of my economic class and social group, from living in racially mixed groups or being reflective about interactions between people of differing races.

In proportion as my racial group was being made confident, comfortable, and oblivious, other groups were likely being made unconfident, uncomfortable, and alienated. Whiteness protected me from many kinds of hostility, distress, and violence, which I was being subtly trained to visit in turn upon people of color.

For this reason, the word "privilege" now seems to me misleading. Its connotations are too positive to fit the conditions and behaviors which "privilege systems" produce. We usually think of privilege as being a favored state, whether earned, or conferred by birth or luck. School graduates are reminded they are privileged and urged to use their (enviable) assets well. The word "privilege" carries the connotation of being something everyone must want. Yet some of the conditions I have described here work to systemically overempower certain groups. Such privilege simply *confers dominance*, gives permission to control, because of one's race or sex. The kind of privilege that gives license to some people to be, at best, thoughtless and, at worst, murderous should not continue to be referred to as a desirable attribute. Such "privilege" may be widely desired without being in any way beneficial to the whole society.

Moreover, though "privilege" may confer power, it does not confer moral strength. Those who do not depend on conferred dominance have traits and qualities that may never develop in those who do. Just as Women's Studies courses indicate that women survive their political circumstances to lead lives that hold the human race together, so "underprivileged" people of color who are the world's majority have survived their oppression and lived survivors' lives from which the white global minority can and must learn. In some groups, those dominated have actually become strong through *not* having all of these unearned advantages, and this gives them a great deal to teach the others. Members of so-called privileged groups can seem foolish, ridiculous, infantile, or dangerous by contrast.

I want, then, to distinguish between earned strength and unearned power conferred systemically. Power from unearned privilege can look like strength when it is, in fact, permission to escape or to dominate. But not all of the privileges on my list are inevitably damaging. Some, like the expectation that neighbors will be decent to you, or that your race will not count against you in court, should be the norm in a just society and should be considered as the entitlement of everyone. Others, like the privilege not to listen to less powerful people, distort the humanity of the holders as well as the ignored groups. Still others, like finding one's staple foods everywhere, may be a function of being a member of a numerical majority in the population. Others have to do with not having to labor under pervasive negative stereotyping and mythology.

We might at least start by distinguishing between positive advantages that we can work to spread, to the point where they are not advantages at all but simply part of the normal civic and social fabric, and negative types of advantage that unless rejected will always reinforce our present hierarchies. For example, the positive "privilege" of belonging, the feeling that one belongs within the human circle, as Native Americans say, fosters development and should not be seen as privilege for a few. It is, let us say, an entitlement that none of us should have to earn; ideally it is an *unearned entitlement*. At present, since only a few have it, it is an *unearned advantage* for them. The negative "privilege" that gave me cultural permission not to take darker-skinned Others seriously can be seen as arbitrarily conferred dominance and should not be desirable for anyone. This paper results from a process of coming to see that some of the power that I originally saw as attendant on being a human being in the United States consisted in *unearned advantage* and *conferred dominance*, as well as other kinds of special circumstance not universally taken for granted.

In writing this paper I have also realized that white identity and status (as well as class identity and status) give me considerable power to choose whether to broach this subject and its trouble. I can pretty well decide whether to disappear and avoid and not listen and escape the dislike I may engender in other people through this essay, or interrupt, answer, interpret, preach, correct, criticize, and control to some extent what goes on in reaction to it. Being white, I am given considerable power to escape many kinds of danger or penalty as well as to choose which risks I want to take.

There is an analogy here, once again, with Women's Studies. Our male colleagues do not have a great deal to lose in supporting Women's Studies, but they do not have a great deal to lose if they oppose it either. They simply have the power to decide whether to commit themselves to more equitable distributions of power. They will probably feel few penalties whatever choice they make; they do not seem, in any obvious short-term sense, the ones at risk, though they and we are all at risk because of the behaviors that have been rewarded in them.

Through Women's Studies work I have met very few men who are truly distressed about systemic, unearned male advantage and conferred dominance. And so one question for me and others like me is whether we will be like them, or whether we will get truly distressed, even outraged, about unearned race advantage and conferred dominance and if so, what we will do to lessen them. In any case, we need to do more work in identifying how they actually affect our daily lives. We need more down-to-earth writing by people about these taboo subjects. We need more understanding of the ways in which white "privilege" damages white people, for these are not the same ways in which it damages the victimized. Skewed white psyches are an inseparable part of the picture, though I do not want to confuse the kinds of damage done to the holders of special assets and to those who suffer the deficits. Many, perhaps most, of our white students in the United States think that racism doesn't affect them because they are not people of color; they do not see "whiteness" as a racial identity. Many men likewise think that Women's Studies does not bear on their own existences because they are not female; they do not see themselves as having gendered identities. Insisting on the universal "effects" of "privilege" systems, then, becomes one of our chief tasks, and being more explicit about the *particular* effects in particular contexts is another. Men need to join us in this work.

In addition, since race and sex are not the only advantaging systems at work, we need to similarly examine the daily experience of having age advantage, or ethnic advantage, or physical ability, or advantage related to nationality, religion, or sexual orientation. Professor Marnie Evans suggested to me that in many ways the list I made also applies directly to heterosexual privilege. This is a still more taboo subject than race privilege: the daily ways in which heterosexual privilege makes some persons comfortable or powerful, providing supports, assets, approvals, and rewards to those who live or expect to live in heterosexual pairs. Unpacking that content is still more difficult, owing to the deeper imbeddedness of heterosexual advantage and dominance and stricter taboos surrounding these.

But to start such an analysis I would put this observation from my own experience: The fact that I live under the same roof with a man triggers all kinds of societal assumptions about my worth, politics, life, and values and triggers a host of unearned advantages and powers. After recasting many elements from the original list I would add further observations like these:

1. My children do not have to answer questions about why I live with my partner (my husband).
2. I have no difficulty finding neighborhoods where people approve of our household.
3. Our children are given texts and classes that implicitly support our kind of family unit and do not turn them against my choice of domestic partnership.
4. I can travel alone or with my husband without expecting embarrassment or hostility in those who deal with us.
5. Most people I meet will see my marital arrangements as an asset to my life or as a favorable comment on my likability, my competence, or my mental health.
6. I can talk about the social events of a weekend without fearing most listeners' reactions.
7. I will feel welcomed and "normal" in the usual walks of public life, institutional and social.
8. In many contexts, I am seen as "all right" in daily work on women because I do not live chiefly with women.

Difficulties and dangers surrounding the task of finding parallels are many. Since racism, sexism, and heterosexism are not the same, the advantages associated with them should not be seen as the same. In addition, it is hard to isolate aspects of unearned advantage that derive chiefly from social class, economic class, race, religion, region, sex, or ethnic identity. The oppressions

---

3. "A Black Feminist Statement," The Combahee River Collective, pp. 13–22 in G. Hull, P. Scott, B. Smith, Eds., *All the Women Are White, All the Blacks Are Men, But Some of Us Are Brave: Black Women's Studies*, Old Westbury, NY: The Feminist Press, 1982.

are both distinct and interlocking, as the Combahee River Collective statement of 1977 continues to remind us eloquently.[3]

One factor seems clear about all of the interlocking oppressions. They take both active forms that we can see and embedded forms that members of the dominant group are taught not to see. In my class and place, I did not see myself as racist because I was taught to recognize racism only in individual acts of meanness by members of my group, never in invisible systems conferring racial dominance on my group from birth. Likewise, we are taught to think that sexism or heterosexism is carried on only through intentional, individual acts of discrimination, meanness, or cruelty, rather than in invisible systems conferring unsought dominance on certain groups. Disapproving of the systems won't be enough to change them. I was taught to think that racism could end if white individuals changed their attitudes; many men think sexism can be ended by individual changes in daily behavior toward women. But a man's sex provides advantage for him whether or not he approves of the way in which dominance has been conferred on his group. A "white" skin in the United States opens many doors for whites whether or not we approve of the way dominance has been conferred on us. Individual acts can palliate, but cannot end, these problems. To redesign social systems, we need first to acknowledge their colossal unseen dimensions. The silences and denials surrounding privilege are the key political tool here. They keep the thinking about equality or equity incomplete, protecting unearned advantage and conferred dominance by making these taboo subjects. Most talk by whites about equal opportunity seems to me now to be about equal opportunity to try to get into a position of dominance while denying that *systems* of dominance exist.

Obliviousness about white advantage, like obliviousness about male advantage, is kept strongly inculturated in the United States so as to maintain the myth of meritocracy, the myth that democratic choice is equally available to all. Keeping most people unaware that freedom of confident action is there for just a small number of people props up those in power and serves to keep power in the hands of the same groups that have most of it already. Though systemic change takes many decades, there are pressing questions for me and I imagine for some others like me if we raise our daily consciousness on the perquisites of being light-skinned. What will we do with such knowledge? As we know from watching men, it is an open question whether we will choose to use unearned advantage to weaken invisible privilege systems and whether we will use any of our arbitrarily awarded power to try to reconstruct power systems on a broader base.

GROWING UP WITH PRIVILEGE
AND PREJUDICE

10

Karen K. Russell

To our children . . . in the hope that they will grow up as we could not . . . equal . . . and understanding.

—William Felton Russell,
  William Frances McSweeny

In 1966, my father and his co-author dedicated his first autobiography, "Go Up for Glory." Today, in 1987, having just received my Doctor of Laws degree, I wonder if I can fulfill the dreams of my parents' generation. They struggled for integration, they marched for peace, they "sat in" for equality. I doubt they were naïve enough to think they had changed the world, but I know they hoped my generation would be able to approach life differently. In fact, we have been able to do things my parents never thought possible. But that is not enough.

I am a child of privilege. In so many ways, I have been given every opportunity—good grade schools, college years at Georgetown, the encouragement to pursue my ambitions. I have just graduated from Harvard Law School. My future looks promising. Some people, no doubt, will attribute any successes I have to the fact that I am a black woman. I am a child of privilege, and I am angry.

In "The Book of Laughter and Forgetting," Milan Kundera writes: "The struggle of man against power is the struggle of memory against forgetting." It seems that we have not come very far in that struggle in this country. We have entered the post–civil rights, post-feminist era, both movements I owe so much to. Meanwhile, my parents' dreams are still around us, still unrealized.

It is perhaps somewhat ironic that I came back for my postgraduate work to Boston, a city my father once described as the most racist in America. My father is Bill Russell, center for the Boston Celtics dynasty that won 11 championships in 13 years. Recently, I asked him if it was difficult to send me

From: *New York Times Magazine* 136 (June 14, 1987): 69–74. Copyright © 1987 by The New York Times Company. Reprinted by permission.

to school here. When he first went to Boston in 1956, the Celtics' only black player, fans and sportswriters subjected him to the worst kind of unbridled bigotry. When he retired from the National Basketball Association in 1969, he moved to the West Coast where he has remained.

I found his response to my question surprising. "I played for the Celtics, period," he said. "I did not play for Boston. I was able to separate the Celtics institution from the city and the fans. When I sent you to Harvard, I expected you to be able to do the same. I wanted you to have the best possible education and to be able to make the best contacts. I knew you'd encounter racism and sexism, and maybe, in some ways that's a good thing. If you were too sheltered, I'm afraid you'd be too naïve. If you were too sheltered, you might not be motivated to help others who do not have your advantages."

Looking back on my tenure at Harvard, I guess he was right; the last three years have opened my eyes, but law school was only part of it. I became much more aware of disparities in wealth, gender, status. The race issue had always been with me, but it hadn't occurred to me that my generation would still be saddled with so many other limitations.

Actually, people of my generation have a new breed of racism (and sexism and classism) to contend with. The new racism is more subtle, and in some ways more difficult to confront. Open bigotry is out, but there have been a number of overtly racist incidents recently, at Howard Beach in New York, for example, and on college campuses throughout the country. What provokes these incidents? The new racism seems to be partially submerged, coming out into the open when sparked by a sudden confrontation. Then there is the sort of comment Al Campanis, then a Los Angeles Dodgers vice president, made recently on the ABC News program "Nightline," that blacks "may not have some of the necessities" required to achieve leadership positions in baseball. Campanis continued that lacking necessities could be demonstrated in other areas: blacks are not good swimmers, he said, "because they don't have the buoyancy." (I've already ordered my "I'm Black and I'm Buoyant" bumper sticker.)

The Campanis incident is more than just your garden-variety, knee-jerk racism. I sincerely doubt that Campanis meant any harm to come from his remarks; in fact, he probably doesn't think of himself as a racist. But does it matter? How am I supposed to react to well-meaning, good, liberal white people who say things like: "You know, Karen, I don't understand what all the fuss is about. You're one of my good friends, and I never think of you as black." Implicit in such a remark is, "I think of you as white," or perhaps just, "I don't think of your race at all." Racial neutrality is a wonderful concept, but we are a long way from achieving it. In the meantime, I would hope that people wouldn't have to negate my race in order to accept me.

Last year, I worked as a summer law associate, and one day a white lawyer called me into her office. She told me, laughing, that her secretary, a young black woman, had said that I spoke "more white than white people." It made me sad; that young woman had internalized all of society's negative images of black people to the point that she thought of a person with clear diction as one of "them."

I am reminded of the time during college that I was looking through the classifieds for an apartment. I called a woman to discuss the details of a rental. I needed directions to the apartment, and she asked me where I lived. I told her I lived in Georgetown, to which she replied, "Can you believe the way the blacks have overrun Georgetown?" I didn't really know how to respond. I said, "Well, actually, I can believe that Georgetown is filled with blacks because I happen to be black." There was a silence on the other end. Finally, the woman tried to explain that she hadn't meant any harm. She was incredibly embarrassed, and, yes, you guessed it, she said, "Some of my best friends are. . . ." I hung up before she could finish.

I was afraid to come back to Boston. My first memory of the place is of a day spent in Marblehead, walking along the ocean shore with a white friend of my parents. I must have been 3 or 4 years old. A white man walking past us looked at me and said, "You little nigger." I am told that I smiled up at him as he went on: "They should send all you black baboons back to Africa." It was only when I turned to look at Kay that I realized something was wrong.

We lived in a predominantly Irish Catholic neighborhood in Reading, Mass. For a long time, we were the only black family there. It was weird to be the only black kid at school, aside from my two older brothers. I knew we were different from the other children. Notwithstanding that, I loved school. In 1968, in the first grade, we held mock Presidential elections, and the teacher kept a tally on the blackboard as she counted ballots. There were 20 votes for Hubert H. Humphrey, four or five votes for Richard M. Nixon and one vote for Dick Gregory. No one else in the classroom had heard of Gregory. I was mortified. But I had just done what the other kids had done: I had voted like my parents.

I think my brothers and I may have been spared some of the effects of racism because my father was a celebrity. But I know that his position also made us a bit paranoid. Sometimes it was hard to tell why other kids liked us, or hated us, for that matter. Was it because we had a famous father? Was it because we were black? We had one of those "fun" houses—lots of food, lots of toys, and, the coup de grace, a swimming pool. I was proud to have friends over. They were awed by my father's trophy case. Actually, so were we.

One night we came home from a three-day weekend and found we had been robbed. Our house was in a shambles, and "NIGGA" was spray-painted on the walls. The burglars had poured beer on the pool table and ripped up the felt. They had broken into my father's trophy case and smashed most of the trophies. I was petrified and shocked at the mess; everyone was very upset. The police came, and after a while, they left. It was then that my parents pulled back their bedcovers to discover that the burglars had defecated in their bed.

Every time the Celtics went out on the road, vandals would come and tip over our garbage cans. My father went to the police station to complain. The police told him that raccoons were responsible, so he asked where he could apply for a gun permit. The raccoons never came back.

The only time we were *really* scared was after my father wrote an article about racism in professional basketball for The Saturday Evening Post. He earned the nickname Felton X. We received threatening letters, and my parents notified the Federal Bureau of Investigation. What I find most telling about this episode is that years later, after Congress had passed the Freedom of Information Act, my father requested his F.B.I. file and found that he was repeatedly referred to therein as "an arrogant Negro who won't sign autographs for white children."

My father has never given autographs, because he thinks they are impersonal. He would rather shake a person's hand or look that person in the eye and say, "Pleased to meet you." His attitude has provoked racist responses, and these have tended to obscure the very basic issue of the right to privacy. Any professional athlete, and certainly any black professional athlete, is supposed to feel grateful to others for the fame he or she has achieved. The thoughtless interruptions, the insistence by fans that they be recognized and personally thanked for their support, never let up. I'll never forget the day I left for college at Georgetown. I had never been away from either parent for more than two weeks, and now I was moving 3,000 miles away. I was at the airport, saying goodbye to my friends and my family. I was crying so hard that I actually cried my contact lens out. And I was hugging my dad—it was a real Hallmark moment. A man came up, oblivious to the gathering, and said to him, "You're Wilt Chamberlain, aren't you?" We all turned to look at him as though he were crazy. He asked for an autograph. My father declined.

I always admired the way my father dealt with these intrusions. He never compromised his values. It would have been easier to acquiesce to the fans—or to a sponsor who offered him a lower fee than they would a white person for endorsing a product. But he would not. I struggle to emulate him.

I went to college with Patrick Ewing, whose playing style has been compared to my father's. Patrick came to Georgetown from the public high school in Cambridge, just a few blocks from the Harvard campus. I have a lot of sympathy for him. When he played in college, people in the stands—presumably educated people—held up signs that said "Patrick Ewing Can't Read Dis."

When my father first played for the Celtics, the fans called him "chocolate boy," "coon," "nigger,"—you name it, he was called it. Almost three decades later, Patrick Ewing was facing the same sort of treatment, and I was, in a way, reliving my father's experience in watching it happen. I never talked to Patrick about it because I respected his privacy. From being in public with my father, I knew how difficult it was to be someone like Patrick. Aside from everything else, when you're over 6 feet, 9 inches tall—as both of them are—it's hard to be inconspicuous. Your presence seems to make other people uncomfortable, and everyone seems to feel further compelled to speak to you. Still, I hoped Patrick knew he wasn't alone.

Several weeks ago, I heard on the news about a racial incident in Taunton, a town not far from Cambridge. It concerned two girls, high-school students and best friends. One was black, the other white. When the school yearbook arrived, it was discovered that the caption under the photograph of the white girl included the words "Nigger Lover." On the news, the school principal said that the incident was just an isolated "prank," not a racist act.

I remember a day in my own high school when a guy who was really popular walked by me in the hall and hissed "nigger" under his breath. I told one of my close friends, and she insisted that I must have misunderstood him, that he must have said "bigger." I felt betrayed.

I feel awful for those girls in Taunton. Adolescents can be really cruel. Adults may have the same thoughts, but they are not as likely to say them to your face. Not that the latter is necessarily an improvement. I could always pinpoint the source of the bigotry in my high school, but the new bigot is much harder to detect. Our society has taken to the presumption that racism—and sexism—no longer exist, and that any confrontations are the work of a few "bad actors." Given this myth, the person who complains about genuine harassment can expect to be seen as the source of conflict.

In Taunton, they crossed out the epithet in every copy of the yearbook. It would apparently have been too expensive to recall the edition. Too expensive for whom? . . .

My friends, from Harvard and elsewhere, reflect my fragmented background. I could never invite them all to the same party and survive. Nor can I meet them all on the same ground. At the law school, I made friends with fellow anti-apartheid protesters and members of a loose-knit group of leftists known as the counterhegemonic front. I have other friends whose politics I strongly disagree with. I have sometimes been drawn to the children of famous or wealthy parents because of an immediate sense of commonality; we know how to protect one another. One of my best friends is Chris Kennedy, son of Ethel and the late Robert F. Kennedy. We never use last names when introducing each other, because we resent people who remember only our last names. . . .

How will I deal with racism in my life? I have no brilliant solution. On a personal level, I will ask people to explain a particular comment or joke. When I have trouble hailing a cab in New York, as frequently happens—cabbies "don't want to go to Harlem"—I will copy down the medallion numbers and file complaints if necessary. On the larger level, I will work with others to confront the dilemma of the widening gap between the black middle class and the black lower class, a gap that must be closed if my generation is to advance the cause of racial equality.

Like many middle-class children who grew up accustomed to a comfortable life style, I will also have to work to balance the desire for economic prosperity with the desire to realize more idealistic goals.

If I do ever find a man and get married (after all those magazine and newspaper articles, I realize that I have a better chance of becoming a member of the Politburo!), will we want to raise our kids in a black environment? Sometimes I really regret that I didn't go to an all-black college. When I was in high school on Mercer Island, I didn't go out on dates. A good friend was nice enough to escort me to my senior prom. I don't know if I want my kids excluded like that. If it hadn't been my race, it might have been something else; I guess a lot of people were miserable in high school. Yet, I have to wonder what it would be like to be the norm.

I am concerned about tokenism. If I am successful, I do not want to be used as a weapon to defeat the claims of blacks who did not have my opportunities. I do not want someone to say of me: "See, she made it. We live in a world of equal opportunity. If you don't make it, it's your own fault."

I also worry about fallout from this article. One day during college, I was walking down the street when a photographer asked if he could take my picture for the Style section of The Washington Post. The photograph appeared with a caption that said I worked at a modeling agency, which I did—as a booking agent. Two things happened. I got asked out on some dates, which I didn't mind. And I received a letter that, accompanied by detailed anatomical description, said I was "a nigger bitch who has no business displaying your ugly body." What kind of letters and comments can I expect to receive as a result of this article? Although I am speaking as an individual, I run the risk of being depersonalized, even dehumanized, by others.

Daddy told me that he never listened to the boos because he never listened to the cheers. He did it for himself. I guess I have to, too.

FROM "KIKE" TO "JAP": How Misogyny, Anti-Semitism, and Racism Construct the "Jewish American Princess"

11

Evelyn Torton Beck

The stereotyping of the Jewish American woman as the JAP, which stands for Jewish American Princess, is an insult, an injury, and violence that is done to Jewish women. The term is used widely by both men and women, by both Jews and non-Jews. When gentiles use it, it is a form of anti-Semitism. When Jews use it, it is a form of self-hating or internalized anti-Semitism. It is a way of thinking that allows some Jewish women to harm other Jewish women who are just like them except for the fact that one is okay—she's *not* a JAP. The other is not okay—she's too JAPie. The seriousness of this term becomes evident when we substitute the words "too Jewish" for "too JAPie," and feel ourselves becoming considerably less comfortable.

When I speak on college campuses, young women frequently tell me that when someone calls them a Jew they are insulted because they know it's being said with a kind of hostility, but if someone calls them a JAP they don't mind because they frequently use this term themselves. They think the "J" in JAP really doesn't mean anything—it's just there. While everyone seems to know what the characteristics of a "Jewish American Princess" are, no one ever seems to think about what they are saying when they use the term. How is it that you don't have to be Jewish to be a JAP? If this is so, why is the word "Jewish" in the acronym at all? Words are not meaningless unless we choose to close our ears and pretend not to hear.

This subject is frequently trivialized, but when it is not, when we take it seriously, it makes us extremely tense. Why is that? I think it's because it takes us into several "war zones." It brings us in touch with Jew-hating, or anti-Semitism. It brings us in touch with misogyny, or woman-hating. And it brings us in touch with class-hatred, old money vs. nouveau riche. (Jews have classically been seen as intruders in the United States and have been resented for "making it.") It also puts us strongly in touch with racism. It is no accident

From: Evelyn Torton Beck, "From 'Kike' to 'JAP,' " in *Sojourner: The Women's Forum*, September 1988, pp. 18–20. Reprinted by permission.

that the acronym JAP is also the word used for our worst enemies in World War II—who were known as "the Japs." During World War II, posters and slogans saying "Kill Japs" were everywhere. It was a period in which slang terms were readily used in a pejorative way to identify many different minorities: "Japs," "Kikes," "Spics," "Wops," "Chinks" were commonplace terms used unthinkingly. And women were—and, unfortunately, still are—easily named "bitches," "sluts," and "cunts."

In such a climate, negative stereotypes easily overlap and elide. For example, in the popular imagination, Jews, "Japs," women and homosexuals have all been viewed as devious, unreliable, and power hungry. What has happened in the decades following World War II is that the "Japs," whom we de-humanized when we dropped our atom bomb on them, have subliminally merged in the popular imagination with "kikes" and other foreign undesirables. (The fact that in the 1980s Japan poses a serious economic threat to the United States should not be overlooked either.) While efforts to eradicate slurs against ethnic minorities have made it not okay to use explicitly ethnic epithets, women still provide an acceptable target, especially when the misogyny is disguised as supposedly "good-natured" humor. In this insidious and circuitous way, the Jewish American woman carries the stigmas of the "kikes" and "Japs" of a previous era. And that is very serious.

The woman, the Jewish woman as JAP has replaced the male Jew as the scapegoat, and the Jewish male has not only participated, but has, in fact, been instrumental in creating and perpetuating that image. I want to show how some of the images of Jewish women created in American culture by Jewish men provided the roots of the "Jewish American Princess." But first I want to provide a context for understanding the development of this image. I want to look at anti-Semitism in the United States, and at misogyny, and show how the merging of anti-Semitism and misogyny creates the Jewish American Princess.

Between 1986 and 1987 there was a 17 percent rise in anti-Semitic incidents in this country. Of these incidents, 48 percent occurred in the Northeast, and the highest rates of increase were in New York State; California, particularly Los Angeles; and Florida. These are all areas where there are high concentrations of Jews. On November 9 and 10, 1987, the anniversary of *Kristalnacht*, the Night of Broken Crystal, when Goebbels staged a mass "spontaneous pogrom" in Austria and Germany in 1938, swastikas were painted on entrances to synagogues in a number of different cities in the United States: Chicago, Yonkers, and others dotted across the country. Windows were smashed—not simply of Jewish-owned stores, but of identifiably Jewish businesses such as kosher meat markets, a kosher fish store, a Jewish book store—in five different neighborhoods, particularly in a Chicago suburb largely populated by Holocaust survivors. Having grown up in Vienna and having lived under the Nazis, the horror of that night resonated for me in a way that it might not for those who are much younger. But that these pogrom-like episodes happened on the eve of *Kristalnacht* cannot have been an accident, and the timing of these incidents should not be lost upon us.

In response to these attacks many members of the Jewish community wanted to hide the facts, and one member of the Jewish community in Chicago actually said, "The swastikas could have meant general white supremacy; they were not necessarily aimed at Jews." They just "happened" to be placed on synagogues, right? In the same way, it just "happens" that the word "Jewish" is lodged in the very negative image of this hideous creature known as the Jewish American Princess. Anyone who is aware of Jewish history and knows about the ridicule, defamation, and violence to which Jews have been subject will not be able to write this off so easily.

The Jewish American Princess phenomenon is not new; I (as well as other Jewish feminists) have been talking about it for at least ten years now, but only recently has it been given wide public attention. One reason for this is that it is beginning to be seen in the light of increased anti-Semitism and racism, particularly on college campuses. Dr. Gary Spencer, who is a *male* professor of sociology at Syracuse University (and it is unfortunate that his being male gives him credibility over women saying the same things) closely examined the library and bathroom graffiti of his school and interviewed hundreds of students on his campus and has concluded that "JAP"-baiting is widespread, virulent, and threatening to all Jews, not "just" Jewish women (which we gather might have been okay or certainly considerably less serious).

Spencer discovered that nasty comments about "JAPS" led to more generally anti-Semitic graffiti that said among other slogans, "Hitler was right!" "Give Hitler a second chance!" and "I hate Jews." He also discovered that there were certain places in which Jewish women—JAPS—were not welcome: for example, certain cafes where Jewish women were hassled if they entered. He also found that certain areas of the University were considered "JAP-free zones" and other areas (particular dorms) that were called "Jew havens." At The American University in Washington, D.C., largely Jewish residence halls are called "Tokyo Towers," making the racial overtones of "JAP" explicit. But let the parallels to Nazi occupied Europe not be lost upon us. Under the Nazis, movements of Jews were sharply restricted: there were many areas which Jews could not enter, and others (like ghettos and concentration camps) that they could not leave.

What I want to do now is to show how characteristics that have historically been attributed to Jews, primarily Jewish men, have been reinterpreted in terms of women: how misogyny combined with Jew-hating creates the Jewish American Princess. And I want you to remember that Jewish men have not only participated in this trashing, but they have not protected Jewish women when other men and women have talked about "JAPs" in this way. And this fact, I think, has made this an arena into which anyone can step—an arena that becomes a minefield when Jews step into it.

Jews have been said to be materialistic, money-grabbing, greedy, and ostentatious. Women have been said to be vain, trivial and shallow; they're only interested in clothing, in show. When you put these together you get the Jewish-woman type who's only interested in designer clothes and sees her children only as extensions of herself. The Jew has been seen as manipulative, crafty, untrustworthy, unreliable, calculating, controlling, and malevolent. The Jewish Princess is seen as manipulative, particularly of the men in her life, her husband, her boyfriend, her father. And what does she want? Their *money*! In addition, she's lazy—she doesn't work inside or outside the home. She is the female version of the Jew who, according to anti-Semitic lore, is a parasite on society; contradictorily, the Jew has been viewed both as dangerous "communist" as well as non-productive "capitalist." The cartoon vision of the Jewish American Princess is someone who sucks men dry: she is an "unnatural mother" who refuses to nurture her children (the very opposite of the "Jewish mother" whose willingness to martyr herself makes *her* ludicrous). And she doesn't "put out" except in return for goods; she isn't really interested in either sexuality or lovingness. We live in a world climate and culture in which materialism is rampant, and Jewish women are taking the rap for it. The irony is they are taking the rap from non-Jews and Jewish men alike—even from some Jewish women.

Another way in which Jewish women are carrying the anti-Semitism that was directed in previous eras at Jewish men is in the arena of sexuality. Jews have been said to be sexually strange, exotic. There are many stereotypes of Jewish men as lechers. The Jewish American Princess is portrayed as both sexually frigid (withholding) and as a nymphomaniac. Here we again see the familiar anti-Semitic figure of the Jew as controlling and insatiably greedy, always wanting more, combining with the misogynist stereotype of the insatiable woman, the woman who is infinitely orgasmic, who will destroy men with her desire. Like the Jew of old, the Jewish woman will suck men dry. But she is worse than "the Jew"—she will also turn on her own kind.

There are physical stereotypes as well: the Jew with the big hook nose, thick lips, and frizzy hair. The Jewish American Princess has had a nose job and her hair has been straightened, but she too has large lips (an image we immediately also recognize as racist). Jews are supposed to be loud, pushy, and speak with unrefined accents. Jewish American Princesses are said to come from Long Island and speak with funny accents: "Oh my Gawd!" The accent has changed from the lampooned immigrant speech of previous generations, but assimilation into the middle class hasn't helped the Jewish American Princess get rid of her accent. It doesn't matter how she speaks, because if it's Eastern and recognizably Jewish, it's not okay.

I also want to give you some idea of how widespread and what a money-making industry the Jewish American Princess phenomenon has become. There are greeting cards about the "JAP Olympics," with the JAP doing things like "bank-vaulting" instead of pole-vaulting. Or cross-country *kvetching* instead of skiing. In this card the definition of the Yiddish term *kvetch* reads: "an irritable whine made by a three-year-old child or a JAP at any age." So in addition to the all-powerful monster you also have the infantilization of the Jewish woman. And there are the Bunny Bagelman greeting cards: Bunny has frizzy hair, big lips, is wearing ostentatious jewelry—and is always marked as a Jew in some way. One of her cards reads, "May God Bless you and keep you . . . rich!" Or Bunny Bagelman is a professional, dressed in a suit carrying a briefcase, but this image is undermined by the little crown she incongruously wears on her head bearing the initials "JAP." There is also a Halloween card with a grotesque female figure; the card reads, "Is it a vicious vampire? No, it's Bunny Bagelman with PM syndrome!" In analyzing these kinds of cartoons, you begin to see how sexism is absolutely intertwined with anti-Semitism.

Such attacks devalue Jewish women and keep them in line. An incident reported by Professor Spencer at Syracuse University makes this quite evident. At a basketball game, when women who were presumed to be "JAPs" stood up and walked across the floor at half-time (and it happened to Jewish and non-Jewish women), 2,000 students stood up, accusingly pointed their fingers at them, and repeatedly yelled, "JAP, JAP, JAP, JAP, JAP" in a loud chorus. This was so humiliating and frightening that women no longer got out of their seats to go to the bathroom or to get a soda. This is a form of public harassment that is guaranteed to control behavior and parallels a phenomenon called "punching" at the University of Dar El Salaam, Tanzania. Here, when women were "uppity" or otherwise stepped out of line, huge posters with their pictures on them were put all over campus, and no one was to speak to them. If you spoke to these women, you were considered to be like them. This is a very effective way of controlling people.

The threat of physical violence against Jewish women (in the form of "Slap-a-JAP" T-shirts and contests at bars) is evident on many Eastern college campuses. A disc jockey at The American University went so far as to sponsor a "fattest JAP-on-campus" contest. That this kind of unchecked verbal violence can lead to murder is demonstrated by lawyer Shirley Frondorf in a recent book entitled *Death of a "Jewish American Princess": The True Story of a Victim on Trial* (Villard Books, 1988). Frondorf shows how the murder of a Jewish woman by her husband was exonerated and the victim placed on trial because she was someone who was described by her husband as "materialistic, who shopped and spent, nagged shrilly and bothered her husband at work"— in other words, she was a "JAP" and therefore deserved what she got. This account demonstrates the dangers inherent in stereotyping and the inevitable dehumanization that follows.

One of the most aggressively sexual forms of harassment of Jewish women, which amounted to verbal rape, were signs posted at a college fair booth at Cornell University that read, "Make her prove she's not a JAP, make her swallow." Part of the mythology is that the Jewish woman will suck, but she won't swallow. So you see that as the degradation of woman *as woman* escalates, the anti-Semitism also gets increasingly louder. In a recent Cornell University student newspaper, a cartoon offered advice on how to "exterminate" JAPS by setting up a truck offering bargains, collecting the JAPS as they scurried in, and dropping them over a cliff. While the word "Jew" was not specifically mentioned, the parallels to the historical "rounding up" of Jews and herding them into trucks to be exterminated in the camps during World War II can hardly be ignored. This cartoon was created by a Jewish man.

This leads me directly to the third thing I want to discuss, namely, how and why Jewish men have participated in constructing and perpetuating the image of the Jewish American Princess as monster. How is it that the Jewish Mother (a mildly derogatory stereotype that nonetheless contained some warmth) has become the grotesque that is the Jewish American Princess, who, unlike the Jewish Mother, has absolutely no redeeming features? Exactly how the Jewish Mother (created entirely by second generation American men who had begun to mock the very nurturance they had relied upon for their success) gave birth to the Jewish American Princess is a long and complex story. This story is intertwined with the overall economic success of Jews as a class in the United States, the jealousy others have felt over this success, and the discomfort this success creates in Jews who are fearful of living out the stereotype of the "rich Jew." It is also a likely conjecture that middle-class American Jewish men view the large numbers of Jewish women who have successfully entered the work force as professionals as a serious economic and ego threat.

We find the origins of the Jewish American Princess in the fiction of American Jewish males of the last three decades. In the '50s, Herman Wouk's *Marjory Morningstar* (nee Morgenstern) leaves behind her immigrant background, takes a new name (one that is less recognizably Jewish), manipulates men, has no talent, and is only interested in expensive clothing. The postwar Jewish male, who is rapidly assimilating into American middle-class culture and leaving behind traditional Jewish values, is creating the Jewish woman—the materialistic, empty, manipulative Jewish woman, the Americanized daughter who fulfills the American Dream for her parents but is, at the same time, punished for it. It looks as if the Jewish woman was created in the image of the postwar Jewish male but viewed by her creator as grotesque. All the characteristics he cannot stand in himself are displaced onto the Jewish woman.

In the '60s, Philip Roth created the spoiled and whiny Brenda Potemkin in *Goodbye, Columbus* at the same time that Shel Silverstein created his image of the perfect Jewish mother as martyr. Some of you may remember this popular story from your childhood. A synopsis goes something like this: "Once there was a tree and she loved the little boy. And he slept in her branches, and loved the tree and the tree was happy. And as the boy grew older, he needed things from her. He needed apples, so she gave him apples, and she was happy. Then she cut off her branches because the boy needed them to build a house. And she was happy. Then finally he needed her trunk because he wanted to build a big boat for himself. And she was happy. The tree gave and gave of herself, and finally the tree was alone and old when the boy returned one more time. By now, the tree had nothing to give. But the boy/man is himself old now, and he doesn't need much except a place on which to sit. And the tree said, 'An old stump is good for sitting and resting on. Come boy and sit and rest on me.' And the boy did, and the tree was happy." This "positive" entirely self-*less* mother, created as a positive wish fantasy by a Jewish man, very easily tips over into its opposite, the monstrous woman, the self-absorbed "JAP" who is negatively self-less. She has no center. She *is* only clothes, money, and show.

In concluding, I want to bring these strands together and raise some questions. Obviously Jews need to be as thoughtful about consumerism as others, but we need to ask why the Jewish woman is taking the rap for the consumerism which is rampant in our highly materialistic culture in general. We need to think about the image of the Jewish American Princess and the father she tries to manipulate. What has happened to the Jewish Mother? Why has she dropped out of the picture? If (as is likely true of all groups) some middle-class Jewish women (and men) are overly focused on material things, what is the other side of that? What about the middle-class fathers who measure their own success by what material goods they are able to provide to their wives and children and who don't know how to show love in any other way? Someone who doesn't know how to give except through material goods could easily create a child who comes to expect material goods as a proof of love and self-worth, especially if sexist gender expectations limit the options for women. We need to look more closely at the relationship between the "monster" daughter and the father who helped create her.

This brings up another uncomfortable subject—incest in Jewish families. We have to look carefully at the image of the "little princess" who sits on Daddy's lap and later becomes this monstrous figure. (My father thought it appropriate for me to sit on his lap until the day he died, well into his '80s, and I do not believe he was unusual in his expectations.) There are enough stories of incest in which we know that the father who sexually abuses his daughter when she is a child becomes quite distant when she reaches adolescence and may continue to abuse her in psychological ways. And the JAP image is a real form of psychological abuse. We need to look at these things to understand that this phenomenon is not trivial, and to understand how it undermines *all* Jewish women and particularly harms young women coming of age. It cannot do Jewish men such good either to think of their sisters, daughters, mothers, and potential girlfriends with such contempt.

Last, I want to say that we have many false images of Jewish families. There *is* violence in Jewish families, just as there is violence in families of all groups. It is time to put the whole question of the Jewish American Princess into the context of doing away with myths of all kinds. The Jewish family is no more nor less cohesive than other families, although there is great pressure on Jewish families to pretend they are. Not all Jewish families are non-alcoholic; not all Jewish families are heterosexual; not all Jews are upper or middle class; and not all are urban or Eastern. It's important that the truth of Jewish women's (and also Jewish men's) lives be spoken. Beginning to take apart this image of the Jewish American Princess can make us look more closely at what it is that we, in all of our diversity as Jews, are; what we are striving towards; and what we hope to become.

Class and Inequality

INEQUALITY IN AMERICA: *The Failure of the American System for People of Color*

12

Edna Bonacich

INTRODUCTION

Right before Christmas 1987 a Chicana was fired from food services on our campus, where she had been working as an assistant cook. She is a single mother with three children.[1] Her own mother suffers from epilepsy. She was making $150 a week and when she was fired she was faced with the prospect of not being able to pay next month's rent, let alone celebrating Christmas.

    According to university rules, food services have to be self-supporting, but cannot be run profitably on a campus of our size. For years the university

From: *Sociological Spectrum* 9(1) 1989, Hemisphere Publishing Corp., New York. Reprinted by permission.

I would like to thank Emily Abel, Lucie Cheng and Mary Sawyer for their helpful feedback on earlier drafts.

1. The style of this paper is more informal than most academic papers. This is purposeful. I am eager to get away from the dry abstraction of academic discourse. As I see it, the style of western academic writing is very much a part of the "white man's civilization," with its dualistic idealism, or division between thought and life. I am seeking a more integrated world view and want my method of communication to match the content. I realize that the imperatives of careerism often force us to speak and write in ways that are not authentic to us, and I am resisting this form of coercion. I hope that my audience will not close their ears to what I say just because my manner of presentation does not meet their preconceptions. Instead, I hope you will listen to its substance and check it against your own experience, against what you know in your hearts to be true.

lost money on it—around $50,000 a year. So they decided to bail out and subcontract to a private firm, the Marriott Corporation.

The decision to subcontract happens to have coincided with a union election victory among service workers in the University of California system, the first such victory in the system. When the union would actually be able to negotiate a pay raise was immaterial. Indeed the union was exceedingly weak and did not represent the self-organization of the workers. Instead, it operated as a Washington-based bureaucracy that saw the thousands of UC workers as a plum in its own organizational growth. Still, the university administration was quick to preclude any pay raises among the food services staff.

Marriott is managing to turn a losing operation into a profitable one. This miracle is achieved by paying the workers well below the university wage scale. Most of their employees, at least on our campus, are women of color. There are not a lot of other people who are "willing" to work for minimum wage and no benefits. Marriott is, of course, non-union.

The case against the woman who was fired consisted of tardiness and absences on the job. Perhaps the accusations had some validity. When a person is earning close to minimum wage there is not a lot of incentive to be a perfectly disciplined, eagerly loyal employee. Besides, her family circumstances made it difficult always to be punctual. There was no give in the situation that could allow for the exigencies of this employee's life. The management of food services claimed that they had given her every break, but they were operating on a tight budget and could not afford to hold on to an inefficient worker. The results might be unfortunate for this individual, but they were not a charity. They had a business to run. They had to balance their books.

And so the woman was left without a job right before Christmas. A group of us took her case to the campus administrator in charge of sub-contracting. He heard it and rejected it, siding with management that they could not afford to keep a nonpunctual worker. After learning of his decision, I went back alone one more time to make a humanitarian plea. I tried to draw a parallel to homelessness. Did he sanction it? Did he believe that, if persons could not pay their rent, they should be thrown out on the streets? Was not his action similar in this case? But I was wasting my time. "You can't coddle employees," he said. "We're in business to make money." He would not consider taking her back and giving her another chance. She was "poison" in his eyes, I assume because she had dared to challenge her firing and had managed to get a group around her to support her case. A politically aroused employee was indeed poison to this man.

Marriott claims it is not making a profit off food services on our campus, yet they take out six percent of the gross in "management fees," and the woman who manages the cafeteria for them makes a good salary. Money is certainly being made in this enterprise; it just is not going to the workers.

I am telling this little story in such detail because it illustrates some of the dynamics of capitalism and its racist manifestations. And it shows that even such seemingly benign institutions as the university are accomplices in the perpetuation of racial oppression in their daily operations. By handing over food services to Marriott, the University has allowed a kind of sweatshop to develop in its midst, a sweatshop that depends on the exploitation of women of color.

The university could have decided to subsidize food services. If they feel this is an important service to provide to the campus, they should be willing to pay for it. Other non-academic services, such as health and counseling centers, are supported by the campus and their employees are paid the university salary rates. But since food service workers are generally paid low wages, the competitive rates permit the university to save money. They can and do justify the special treatment of these workers by citing market conditions. If food service workers everywhere are paid poorly, why should campus food service employees be an exception?

So the poorly paid labor of a group of women of color is used to "subsidize" the mighty University of California. Wealth, as usual, is taken from the poor and transferred to the wealthy and privileged. The pathways of this transfer may be complicated and indirect, but the transfer occurs nonetheless. The university, Marriott, students, and faculty all have a little more money in their pockets because these women live so close to the margin.

Jesse Jackson captured this reality eloquently when he said to a group of poor people: "You are not the bottom. You are the foundation." What a profound inversion of the way this society normally looks at itself! And yet, how true are his words. As in the example I have just presented, the whole magnificent edifice of wealth and privilege in this society has been built on the suffering of poor people, large numbers of whom are people of color. . . .

INEQUALITY IN AMERICA

The United States is an immensely unequal society in terms of the distribution of material wealth, and consequently, in the distribution of all the benefits and privileges that accrue to wealth—including political power and influence. This inequality is vast irrespective of race. However, people of color tend to cluster at the bottom so that inequality in this society also becomes racial inequality. I believe that racial inequality is inextricably tied to overall inequality, and to an ideology that endorses vast inequality as justified and desirable. The special problems of racial inequality require direct attention in the process of attacking inequality in general, but I do not believe that the problem of racial inequality can be eliminated within a context of the tremendous disparities that our society currently tolerates. And even if some kind of racial parity, at the level of averages, could be achieved, the amount of suffering at the bottom would remain undiminished, hence unconscionable.

How unequal is the distribution of rewards in the United States? Typically this question is addressed in terms of occupation and income distribution rather than the distribution and control of property. By the income criterion, the United States is one of the more unequal of the Western industrial societies, and it is far more unequal than the countries of the Eastern European socialist bloc. The Soviet Union, for instance, has striven to decrease the discrepancy in earnings between the highest paid professionals and managers and the lowest paid workers, and as a consequence, has a much flatter income distribution than the United States (Szymanski 1979, pp. 63–9).

To take an extreme example from within the United States, in 1987 the minimum wage was $3.35 an hour, and 6.7 million American workers were paid at that level. That comes to $6,968 a year. In contrast, the highest paid executive, Lee Iacocca, received more than $20 million in 1986, or $9,615 per hour. In other words, the highest paid executive received more in an hour than a vast number of workers received in a year (Sheinkman 1987).

The excessive differences in income are given strong ideological justification—they serve, supposedly, as a source of incentive. Who will work hard if there is no pot of gold at the end, a pot that can be bigger than anyone else's? The striving for achievement leads to excellence, and we all are the beneficiaries of the continual improvements and advances that result.

Or are we? I believe a strong case can be made for the opposite. First of all, the presumed benefits of inequality do not trickle down far enough. The great advances of medical science, for example, are of little use to those people who cannot afford even the most basic health care. Second, instead of providing incentive, our steep inequalities may engender hopelessness and despair for those who have no chance of winning the big prize. When you have no realistic chance of winning the competition, and when there are no prizes for those who take anything less than fourth place, why should you run all out? Third, one can question how much inequality is necessary to raise incentives. Surely fairly modest inducements can serve as motivators. Does the person who makes $100,000 a year in any sense work that much harder than the person who makes the annual $7,000 wage? Altogether, it would seem that the justifications for inequality are more rationalizations to preserve privilege than they are a well-reasoned basis of social organization. The obvious wholesale waste of human capability (let alone life in and for itself) that piles up at the bottom of our system of inequality is testimony to the failure.

Even more fundamental than income inequality is inequality in the ownership of property. Here not only are the extremes much more severe, but the justification of incentives for achievement grow exceedingly thin. First, large amounts of property are simply inherited and the owner never did a stitch of work in his or her life to merit any of it. Second, and more important, wealth in property expands at the expense of workers. Its growth depends not on the achievements of the owner so much as on his or her ability to exploit other human beings. The owner of rental property, for example, gets richer simply because other people who have to work for a living cannot afford to buy their own housing and must sink a substantial proportion of their hard-earned wages into providing shelter. The ownership of property provides interest, rent or profit simply from the fact of ownership. The owner need only put out the capital itself to have the profits keep rolling in for the rest of his or her life.

The concentration of property in the United States is rarely studied—I assume because its exposure is politically embarrassing and even dangerous to those in power (who overlap substantially with, or are closely allied to those who own property). Only two such studies have been undertaken in the last 25 years, one in 1963 and one in 1983. The 1983 study was commissioned by the Democratic staff of the Congressional Joint Economic Committee (U.S. Congress 1986). It seems it may have been a political hot potato since shortly after its appearance, a brief 19-line article appeared in the *Los Angeles Times* stating that the committee withdrew some of its conclusions because of "an error in the figures" (*Los Angeles Times* 1986).

The 1983 study found that the top 0.5 percent of families in the United States owned over 35 percent of the net wealth of this nation. If equity in personal residences is excluded from consideration, the same 0.5 percent of households owned more than 45 percent of the privately held wealth. In other words, if this country consisted of 200 people, one individual would own almost half of the property held among all 200. The other 199 would have to divide up the remainder.

The remainder was not equally divided either. The top 10 percent of the country's households owned 72 percent of its wealth, leaving only 28 percent for the remaining 90 percent of families. If home equity is excluded, the bottom 90 percent only owned 17 percent of the wealth.

The super-rich top half of one percent consisted of 420,000 families. These families owned most of the business enterprises in the nation. They owned 58 percent of unincorporated businesses and 46.5 percent of all personally owned corporate stock. They also owned 77 percent of the value of trusts and 62 percent of state and local bonds. They owned an average of

$8.9 million apiece, ranging from $2.5 million up to hundreds of times that amount.

Forbes publishes an annual list of the 400 richest Americans (*Los Angeles Times* 1986). In 1986, 25 individuals owned over a billion dollars in assets. The richest owned $4.5 billion. That is a 10-digit figure. The four-hundredth person on the list owned $180 million. So the concentration of wealth at the very top is even more extreme than the Congressional study reveals. In 1986, for the first time, a Black man made the *Forbes* list—he owned $185 million in assets. The super rich property owners of this country are generally an all-white club.

By 1987, the number of billionaires in the country (as counted by *Forbes*) had grown from 26 in 1986 to 49 (*Forbes* 1987). The average worth of the top 400 had grown to $220 million apiece, a jump of 41 percent in one year. The top individual now owned $8.5 billion. Together, these 400 individuals commanded a net worth of $220 billion, comparable to the entire U.S. military budget in 1986, and more than the U.S. budget deficit, or total U.S. investment abroad.

RACIAL INEQUALITY

The gross inequalities that characterize American society are multiplied when race and ethnicity are entered into the equation. Racial minorities, especially Blacks, Latinos and Native Americans, tend to be seriously overrepresented at the bottom of the scale in terms of any measure of material well-being.

In the distribution of occupations Whites are substantially overrepresented in the professional and managerial stratum. They are almost twice as likely as Blacks (1.71 times) and Latinos (1.97 times) to hold these kinds of jobs. On the other hand, Blacks and Latinos are much more concentrated in the lower paid service sector, and the unskilled and semiskilled of operators, fabricators and laborers. Whereas only 27 percent of White employees fall into these combined categories, 47 percent of Blacks and 43 percent of Latinos are so categorized. Finally, even though the numbers are relatively small, Blacks are more than three times and Latinos more than twice as likely as Whites to work as private household servants. This most demeaning of occupations remains mainly a minority preserve (U.S. Department of Labor 1987).

Occupational disadvantage translates into wage and salary disadvantage. The median weekly earning of White families in 1986 was $566, compared to $412 for Latino families and $391 for Black families. In other words, Black and Latino families made about 70 percent of what White families made. Female-headed households of all groups made substantially less money. Both

Black and Latino female-headed families made less than half of what the average White family (including married couples) made (U.S. Department of Labor 1987).

Weekly earnings only reflect the take-home pay of employed people. In addition, people of color bear the brunt of unemployment in this society. In 1986, 14.8 percent of Black males, 14.2 percent of Black females, 10.5 percent of Latino males, and 10.8 percent of Latino females were unemployed officially. This compares to 6 percent of White males and 6.1 percent of White females (U.S. Department of Labor 1987).

The absence of good jobs or any jobs at all, and the absence of decent pay for those jobs that are held translates into poverty. Although the poverty line is a somewhat arbitrary figure, it nevertheless provides some commonly accepted standard for decent living in our society.

As of 1984, over one-third of Black households lived in poverty. If we include those people who live very close to the poverty line, the near poor, then 41 percent, or two out of five Blacks, are poor or near poor. For Latinos the figures are only slightly less grim, with over 28 percent living in poverty and 36 percent, or well over one-third, living in or near poverty. This compares to an official poverty rate of 11 percent for Whites.

Female-headed households, as is commonly known, are more likely to live in or near poverty. Over half of Black and Latino female-headed families are forced to live under the poverty line, and over 60 percent of each group live in or near poverty. The figures for White female-headed families are also high with over one-third living in or near poverty. But the levels for people of color are almost twice as bad (U.S. Bureau of the Census 1986).

The degree of racial inequality in property ownership is stark—more stark than the income and employment figures. . . . The average White family has a net worth of about $39,000, more than ten times the average net worth of about $3,000 for Black families. Latino families are only slightly better off, with an average net worth of about $5,000. The differences are even more marked among female-headed households. The average Black and Latino female-headed households have a net worth of only $671 and $478 respectively, less than 2 percent of the net worth of the average White household.

. . . The richest man in this country owned $8.5 billion in wealth in 1987 and there are a handful of others close behind him. Meanwhile, the average—not the poorest but the average—Black and Latino female-headed household only commands a few hundred dollars. How can one even begin to talk about equality of opportunity under such circumstances? What power and control must inevitably accompany the vast holdings of the billionaires, and what scrambling for sheer survival must accompany the dearth of resources at the bottom end? . . .

CAPITALISM AND RACISM

I want to consider the ways in which the American political-economic system is bound to racism. It is my contention that the racism of this society is linked to capitalism and that, so long as we retain a capitalist system, we will not be able to eliminate racial oppression. This is not to say that racism will automatically disappear if we change the system. If we were to transform to a socialist society, the elimination of racism would have to be given direct attention as a high priority. I am not suggesting that its elimination would be easily achieved within socialism, but it is impossible under capitalism.[2]

Stripped of all its fancy rationalizations and complexities, the capitalist system depends upon the exploitation of the poor by the rich. Property owners need an impoverished class of people so that others will be forced to work for them. We can see this in food services on my campus. And we can see it on a world-wide scale, where, for example, poor Latin American countries sent to American investors and lenders (between 1982 and 1987) $145 billion more than they took in. And they still owe a principal of $410 billion in foreign debt, and all the billions of dollars of interest payments that will accrue to that (*Los Angeles Times* 1987).

Capitalism depends on inequality. The truth is, the idea of equality cannot even be whispered around here. It is too subversive, too completely undermining of the "American way." Liberals, conservatives, Democrats and Republicans are all committed to the idea of inequality and so, no matter how much they yell at each other in Congressional hearings, behind the scenes they shake hands and agree that things are basically fine and as they should be.

Perhaps not everyone agrees with my formulation, but I do not think anyone can disagree that there is a commitment to economic inequality in this system and that no attempt is made to hide it. It is part of the official ideology. However the same cannot be said for racial inequality today. At least at the official level it is stated that race should not be the basis of any social or economic distinction. Thus it should, in theory, be possible to eliminate racial inequality within the system, even if we do not touch overall inequality.

Even though an open commitment to racial inequality has been made illegitimate in recent years as a consequence of the Civil Rights and related

---

2. There is a major debate around the question of race versus class. See, for example, Alphonso Pinkney (1984) and Michael Omi and Harold Winant. The question is raised: Which is more important, race or class? Some argue that race cannot be "reduced" to class and that it has independent vitality. A similar argument is made by some feminists regarding gender. I do not contend that race can be reduced to class, but I do not think that race and class are independent systems that somehow intersect with one another. This imagery is too static.

social movements, I believe that it remains embedded in this system. Before getting into the present dynamics of the system, however, let me point out how deeply racism is embedded in the historical evolution of capitalism. First of all, one can make the case that, without racism, without the racial domination implicit in the early European "voyages of discovery," Europe would never have accumulated the initial wealth for its own capitalist "take off." In other words, capitalism itself is predicated on racism (Williams 1966).

But setting aside this somewhat controversial point, European capitalist development quickly acquired an expansionist mode and took over the world, spreading a suffocating blanket of White domination over almost all the other peoples of the globe. The motive was primarily economic, primarily the pursuit of markets, raw materials, cheap labor and investment opportunities. The business sector of Europe, linked to the state, wanted to increase its profits. They sought to enhance their wealth (see Cheng and Bonacich 1984).

The belief in the inferiority of peoples of color, the belief that Europeans were bringing a gift of civilization, salvation, and economic development, helped justify the conquest. They were not, they could think to themselves, hurting anyone. They were really benefactors, bringing light to the savages.

The world order that they created was tiered. On the one hand, they exploited the labor of their own peoples, creating from Europe's farmers and craftsmen an ownerless White working class. On the other hand, of the conquered nationalities they created a super-exploited work-force, producing the raw materials for the rising European industries, and doing the dirtiest and lowest paid support jobs in the world economy. Because they had been conquered and colonized, the peoples of color could be subjected to especially coercive labor systems, such as slavery, indentured servitude, forced migrant labor and the like.

Both groups of workers were exploited in the sense that surplus was taken from their labor by capitalist owners. But White "free labor" was in a relatively advantaged position, being employed in the technically more advanced and higher paid sectors. To a certain extent, White labor benefited from the super-exploitation of colonized workers. The capital that was drained from the colonies could be invested in industrial development in Europe or the centers of European settlement (such as the United States, Canada, Australia, New Zealand and South Africa). The White cotton mill workers in Manchester and New England depended on the super-exploitation of cotton workers in India and the slave South, producing the cheap raw material on which their industrial employment was built.

Although the basic structure of the world economy centered on European capital and the exploitation of colonized workers in their own homelands, the expansion of European capitalism led to movement of peoples all over the globe to suit the economic needs of the capitalist class. Internal colonies, the products of various forms of forced and semiforced migrations, replicated the world system within particular territories.

The basic stratification of world capitalism, with workers of color at the foundation, remains in effect today. Women of color, in particular, are the most exploited of workers around the globe (see Fuentes and Ehrenreich 1983; Fernandez-Kelly 1983). Although race may not be overtly invoked in the exploitation of Third World peoples, the fact is that they are peoples of color who suffer external domination and must labor for "White" capitalists. In the case of South Africa, specifically racial oppression is openly endorsed. And the U.S. government's extremely weak response to this reality suggests the degree of their commitment to ending racism. But even if the racist government of South Africa collapses, as it inevitably will, U.S. capital still exploits people of color from Asia to Africa to Latin America, supporting regimes that enforce their ability to suck these nations dry.

Still, we can ask: Is it not possible that within the United States, a redistribution could occur that would eliminate the racial character of inequality? Could we not, with the banning of racial discrimination and even positive policies like affirmative action, restructure our society such that color is no longer correlated with wealth and poverty? This is what is meant by racial equality within capitalism. The total amount of human misery would remain unaltered, but its complexion would change.

Assimilationism

It seems to me that, even if people of color are fully distributed along the capitalist hierarchy, resembling the distribution of White people, that does not necessarily spell the end of racism. The very idea of such absorption is assimilationist. It claims that people of color must abandon their own cultures and communities and become utilitarian individualists like the White men. They must compete on the white man's terms for the White man's values.

The notion that the American system can be "color blind," a common conservative position, is, of course, predicated on the idea that one is color blind within a system of rules, and those rules are the White man's. Even though he claims they are without cultural content, this is nonsense. They are his rules, deriving from his cultural heritage, and he can claim that they are universal and culturally neutral only because he has the power to make such a claim stick. There is an implicit arrogance that the White man's way is the most advanced, and that everyone else ought to learn how to get along in it as quickly as possible. All other cultures and value systems are impugned as backward, primitive or dictatorial. Only Western capitalism is seen as the pinnacle of human social organization, the height of perfection (see Bonacich 1987 and Bonacich in press for an elaboration of these points).

The absurdity of such a position need scarcely be mentioned. The White man's civilization has not only caused great suffering to oppressed nationalities around the globe, but also to many of its own peoples. It has not only murdered and pillaged other human beings but has also engaged in wanton destruction of our precious planet, so that we can now seriously question how long human life will be sustainable at all.

Let me give an example of the way in which the White man's seemingly universal rules have been imposed. In 1887 the U.S. government passed the Allotment Act, authored by Senator Henry Dawes. This law terminated communal land ownership among American Indians by allotting private parcels of land to individuals. Dawes articulated the philosophy behind this policy:

> The head chief [of the Cherokee] told us that there was not a family in that whole nation that had not a home of its own. There was not a pauper in that nation, and the nation did not owe a dollar. . . . Yet the defect in the system was apparent. They have got as far as they can go, because they own their land in common. . . . There is no enterprise to make your home any better than that of your neighbor's. There is no selfishness, which is at the bottom of civilization. Until this people consent to give up their lands and divide them among their citizens so that each can own the land he cultivates, they will not make much progress (Wexler 1982).

Needless to say, the plans to coerce American Indians into participation in the White man's system of private property did not work out according to official plan. Instead, White people came in and bought up Indian land and left the Indians destitute. People who had not been paupers were now pauperized. It is a remarkably familiar story. The workings of an apparently neutral marketplace have a way of leaving swaths of destruction in their wake.

The Role of the Middle Class

The growth of a Black, Latino and Native American middle class in the last few decades also does not negate the proposition that racial inequality persists in America. In order to understand this, we need to consider the role that the middle class, or professional-managerial stratum, plays in capitalist society, irrespective of race. In my view, middle class people (including myself) are essentially the sergeants of the system. We professionals and managers are paid by the wealthy and powerful, by the corporations and the state, to keep things in order. Our role is one of maintaining the system of inequality. Our role is essentially that of controlling the poor. We are a semi-elite. We are given higher salaries, social status, better jobs, and better life chances as payment for our service to the system. If we were not useful to the power elite, they would not reward us. Our rewards prove that we serve their interests. Look at who pays us. That will give you a sense of whom we are serving (see Ehrenreich and Ehrenreich 1979).

We middle class people would like to believe that our positions of privilege benefit the less advantaged. We would like to believe that our upward mobility helps others, that the benefits we receive somehow "trickle down." But this is sheer self-delusion. It is capitalist ideology, which claims that the people at the top of the social system are really the great benefactors of the people at the bottom. The poor should be grateful to the beneficent rich elites for all their generosity. The poor depend on the wealthy; without the rich elites, where would the poor be? But of course, this picture stands reality on its head. Dependency really works the other way. It is the rich that depend on the poor for their well-being. And benefit, wealth and privilege flow up, not down.

The same basic truths apply to the Black and Latino middle class with some added features. People of color are, too often, treated as tokens. Their presence in higher level positions is used to "prove" that the American system is open to anyone with talent and ambition. But the truth is, people of color are allowed to hold more privileged positions if and only if they conform to the "party line." They are not allowed real authority. They have to play the White man's game by the White man's rules or they lose their good jobs. They have to give up who they are, and disown their community and its pressing needs for change, in order to "make it" in this system. . . .

The rising Black and Latino middle class is, more often than not, used to control the poor and racially oppressed communities, to crush oppression and prevent needed social change. The same is the case, as I have said, with the White middle class. However, there was an implicit promise that the election of Black and Latino political officials, and the growth of a professional and business stratum, would trickle down to the benefit of their communities. This has worked as well as trickle down theory in general. Regardless of the intentions of the Black and Latino middle class, the institutional structures and practices of capitalism have prohibited the implementation of any of the needed reforms. Black mayors, for example, coming in with plans of social progress, find themselves trapped in the logic of the private profit system and cannot implement their programs (see Lembeke in press).

This state of affairs is manifest on my campus. There has been a little progress in terms of affirmative action among the staff. However, if you look more closely, you discover that almost all of the Black and Chicano staff work under White administrators. Furthermore, those people with professional positions are highly concentrated in minority-oriented programs, like Student Affirmative Action, Immediate Outreach, Black and Chicano Student Programs and the like. Even here they are under the direction of White supervisors who ultimately determine the nature and limits of these programs.

What happens, more often than not, is that professional staff who are people of color become shock-absorbers in the system. They take responsibility for programs without having the authority to shape them. If recruitment or retention of students from racially oppressed communities does not produce results, it is the Black, Chicano and Native American professional staff who are held accountable, even though they could not shape a program that had any chance of succeeding. The staff people of color must accept the individualistic, meritocratic ethic of the institution and cannot push for programs that would enhance community development or community participation in the shaping of the university. They simply have to implement the bankrupt idea of plucking out the "best and brightest" and urging them to forsake their families and communities in the quest to "make it" in America.

Still, even if the ruling class can make use of people of color in middle class positions, I believe there are real limits to their willingness to allow enough redistribution to occur so that the averages across groups would become the same. The powerful and wealthy White capitalist class may be able to tolerate and even endorse "open competition" in the working and middle classes. However, they show no signs whatsoever of being willing to relinquish their own stranglehold on the world economy. They can play the game of supporting a recarving up of the tiny part of the pie left over after they have taken their share. Indeed, it is probably good business to encourage various groups to scramble for the crumbs. They will be so busy attacking each other that they will not think to join together to challenge the entire edifice.

The White establishment manipulates racial ideology. Even when it uses the language of colorblindness and equal opportunity, the words need to be stripped of their underlying manipulation. Right now it pays that establishment to act as though they are appalled by the use of race as a criterion for social allocation. But not too long ago, certainly within my memory, they were happy to use it openly. Have they suffered a real change of heart? Is a system that was openly built on racial oppression and that still uses it on a world scale, suddenly free from this cancer?

The truth is, a system driven by private profit, by the search for individual gain, can never solve its social problems. The conservatives promise that market forces will wipe out the negative effects of a history of racial discrimination. But this is a mirage. Wealth accrues to the already wealthy. Power and wealth enhance privilege. Nothing in the market system will change the fact that women of color are exploited in food services on my campus. The market system will not iron out this oppression. On the contrary, its operation sustains it. Only political opposition, only a demand for social justice, will turn this situation around. . . .

REFERENCES

Bonacich, Edna. 1989. "Racism in the Deep Structure of U.S. Higher Education: When Affirmative Action Is Not Enough." In *Affirmative Action and Positive Policies in the Education of Ethnic Minorities,* edited by Sally Tomlinson and Abraham Yogev. Greenwich, CT: JAI Press.

———. 1987. "The Limited Social Philosophy of Affirmative Action." *Insurgent Sociologist* 14:99–116.

Cheng, Lucie and Edna Bonacich. 1984. *Labor Immigration Under Capitalism: Asian Workers in the United States Before World War II.* Berkeley: University of California Press.

Ehrenreich, Barbara and John. 1979. "The Professional-Managerial Class." Pp. 5–45 in *Between Labor and Capital,* edited by Pat Walker. Boston: South End Press.

Fernandez-Kelly, Maria Patricia. 1983. *For We Are Sold, I and My People: Women and Industry in Mexico's Frontier.* Albany: State University of New York.

Forbes. 1987. "The 400 Richest People in America." 140 (October):106–110.

Fuentes, Annette and Barbara Ehrenreich. 1983. *Women in the Global Factory.* Boston: South End Press.

Lembeke, Jerry. Forthcoming. *Race, Class, and Urban Change.* Greenwich, CT: JAI Press.

Los Angeles Times. "Hemisphere in Crisis." December 29, 1987.

———. " 'Super Rich' Control Misstated by Study." August 22, 1986.

———. "Walton Still Tops Forbes List of 400 Richest Americans." October 14, 1986.

Omi, Michael and Harold Winant. 1986. *Racial Formation in the United States: From the 1960s to the 1980s.* New York: Routledge and Kegan Paul.

Pinkney, Alphonso. 1984. *The Myth of Black Progress.* Cambridge: Cambridge University Press.

Sacks, Karen Brodkin and Dorothy Remy. 1984. *My Troubles are Going to Have Trouble With Me: Everyday Trials and Triumphs of Women Workers.* New Brunswick, New Jersey: Rutgers University Press.

Sheinkman, Jack. 1987. "Stop Exploiting Lowest-Paid Workers." *Los Angeles Times* September 9.

Szymanski, Albert. 1979. *Is the Red Flag Flying? The Political Economy of the Soviet Union.* London: Zed Press.

U.S. Bureau of Census. 1986. Current Population Reports, Series P-60, No. 152. *Characteristics of the Population Below the Poverty Level: 1984.* Washington, D.C.: U.S. Government Printing Office.

U.S. Congress Joint Economic Committee. 1986. *The Concentration of Wealth in the United States: Trends in the Distribution of Wealth Among American Families.* Washington, D.C.: U.S. Government Printing Office.

U.S. Department of Labor, Bureau of Labor Statistics. 1987. *Employment and Earnings* 34:212. Washington, D.C.: U.S. Government Printing Office.

Wexler, Rex. 1982. *Blood of the Land: The Government and Corporate War Against the American Indian Movement.* New York: Vintage.

Williams, Eric. 1966. *Capitalism and Slavery.* New York: Capricorn.

TIRED OF PLAYING MONOPOLY?   13

Donna Langston

I. Magnin, Nordstrom, The Bon, Sears, Penneys, K mart, Goodwill, Salvation Army. If the order of this list of stores makes any sense to you, then we've begun to deal with the first question which inevitably arises in any discussion of class here in the U.S.—huh? Unlike our European allies, we in the U.S. are reluctant to recognize class differences. This denial of class divisions functions to reinforce ruling class control and domination. America is, after all, the supposed land of equal opportunity where, if you just work hard enough, you can get ahead, pull yourself up by your bootstraps. What the old bootstraps

From: Jo Whitehorse Cochran, Donna Langston, and Carolyn Woodward (eds.), *Changing Our Power: An Introduction to Women's Studies* (Dubuque, IA: Kendall-Hunt, 1988). Reprinted by permission.

theory overlooks is that some were born with silver shoe horns. Female-headed households, communities of color, the elderly, disabled and children find themselves, disproportionately, living in poverty. If hard work were the sole determinant of your ability to support yourself and your family, surely we'd have a different outcome for many in our society. We also, however, believe in luck and, on closer examination, it certainly is quite a coincidence that the "unlucky" come from certain race, gender and class backgrounds. In order to perpetuate racist, sexist and classist outcomes, we also have to believe that the current economic distribution is unchangeable, has always existed, and probably exists in this form throughout the known universe, i.e., it's "natural." Some people explain or try to account for poverty or class position by focusing on the personal and moral merits of an individual. If people are poor, then it's something they did or didn't do; they were lazy, unlucky, didn't try hard enough, etc. This has the familiar ring of blaming the victims. Alternative explanations focus on the ways in which poverty and class position are due to structural, systematic, institutionalized economic and political power relations. These power relations are based firmly on dynamics such as race, gender, and class.

In the myth of the classless society, ambition and intelligence alone are responsible for success. The myth conceals the existence of a class society, which serves many functions. One of the main ways it keeps the working-class and poor locked into a class-based system in a position of servitude is by cruelly creating false hope. It perpetuates the false hope among the working-class and poor that they can have different opportunities in life. The hope that they can escape the fate that awaits them due to the class position they were born into. Another way the rags-to-riches myth is perpetuated is by creating enough visible tokens so that oppressed persons believe they, too, can get ahead. The creation of hope through tokenism keeps a hierarchical structure in place and lays the blame for not succeeding on those who don't. This keeps us from resisting and changing the class-based system. Instead, we accept it as inevitable, something we just have to live with. If oppressed people believe in equality of opportunity, then they won't develop class consciousness and will internalize the blame for their economic position. If the working-class and poor do not recognize the way false hope is used to control them, they won't get a chance to control their lives by acknowledging their class position, by claiming that identity and taking action as a group.

The myth also keeps the middle class and upper class entrenched in the privileges awarded in a class-based system. It reinforces middle- and upper-class beliefs in their own superiority. If we believe that anyone in society really can get ahead, then middle- and upper-class status and privileges must be deserved, due to personal merits, and enjoyed—and defended at all costs.

According to this viewpoint, poverty is regrettable but acceptable, just the outcome of a fair game: "There have always been poor people, and there always will be."

Class is more than just the amount of money you have; it's also the presence of economic security. For the working class and poor, working and eating are matters of survival, not taste. However, while one's class status can be defined in important ways in terms of monetary income, class is also a whole lot more—specifically, class is also culture. As a result of the class you are born into and raised in, class is your understanding of the world and where you fit in; it's composed of ideas, behavior, attitudes, values, and language; class is how you think, feel, act, look, dress, talk, move, walk; class is what stores you shop at, restaurants you eat in; class is the schools you attend, the education you attain; class is the very jobs you will work at throughout your adult life. Class even determines when we marry and become mothers. Working-class women become mothers long before middle-class women receive their bachelor's degrees. We experience class at every level of our lives; class is who our friends are, where we live and work even what kind of car we drive, if we own one, and what kind of health care we receive, if any. Have I left anything out? In other words, class is socially constructed and all-encompassing. When we experience classism, it will be because of our lack of money (i.e., choices and power in this society) and because of the way we talk, think, act, move—because of our culture.

Class affects what we perceive as and what we have available to us as choices. Upon graduation from high school, I was awarded a scholarship to attend any college, private or public, in the state of California. Yet it never occurred to me or my family that it made any difference which college you went to. I ended up just going to a small college in my town. It never would have occurred to me to move away from my family for school, because no one ever had and no one would. I was the first person in my family to go to college. I had to figure out from reading college catalogs how to apply—no one in my family could have sat down and said, "Well, you take this test and then you really should think about . . ." Although tests and high school performance had shown I had the ability to pick up white middle-class lingo, I still had quite an adjustment to make—it was lonely and isolating in college. I lost my friends from high school—they were at the community college, vo-tech school, working, or married. I lasted a year and a half in this foreign environment before I quit college, married a factory worker, had a baby and resumed living in a community I knew. One middle-class friend in college had asked if I'd like to travel to Europe with her. Her father was a college professor and people in her family had actually travelled there. My family had seldom been able to take a vacation at all. A couple of times my parents were able—by saving all year—to take the family over to the coast on their annual two-week vacation. I'd seen the time and energy my parents invested in trying to take a family vacation to some place a few hours away; the idea of how anybody ever got to Europe was beyond me.

If class is more than simple economic status but one's cultural background, as well, what happens if you're born and raised middle-class, but spend some of your adult life with earnings below a middle-class income bracket—are you then working-class? Probably not. If your economic position changes, you still have the language, behavior, educational background, etc., of the middle class, which you can bank on. You will always have choices. Men who consciously try to refuse male privilege are still male; whites who want to challenge white privilege are still white. I think those who come from middle-class backgrounds need to recognize that their class privilege does not float out with the rinse water. Middle-class people can exert incredible power just by being nice and polite. The middle-class way of doing things is the standard—they're always right, just by being themselves. Beware of middle-class people who deny their privilege. Many people have times when they struggle to get shoes for the kids, when budgets are tight, etc. This isn't the same as long-term economic conditions without choices. Being working-class is also generational. Examine your family's history of education, work, and standard of living. It may not be a coincidence that you share the same class status as your parents and grandparents. If your grandparents were professionals, or your parents were professionals, it's much more likely you'll be able to grow up to become a yuppie, if your heart so desires, or even if you don't think about it.

How about if you're born and raised poor or working-class, yet through struggle, usually through education, you manage to achieve a different economic level: do you become middle class? Can you pass? I think some working class people may successfully assimilate into the middle class by learning to dress, talk, and act middle-class—to accept and adopt the middle-class way of doing things. It all depends on how far they're able to go. To succeed in the middle-class world means facing great pressures to abandon working-class friends and ways.

Contrary to our stereotype of the working class—white guys in overalls— the working class is not homogeneous in terms of race or gender. If you are a person of color, if you live in a female-headed household, you are much more likely to be working-class or poor. The experience of Black, Latino, American Indian or Asian American working classes will differ significantly from the white working classes, which have traditionally been able to rely on white privilege to provide a more elite position within the working class. Working-class people are often grouped together and stereotyped, but distinctions can be made among the working-class, working-poor and poor. Many working-class families are supported by unionized workers who possess marketable skills. Most working-poor families are supported by non-unionized, unskilled men and women. Many poor families are dependent on welfare for their income.

Attacks on the welfare system and those who live on welfare are a good example of classism in action. We have a "dual welfare" system in this country whereby welfare for the rich in the form of tax-free capital gain, guaranteed loans, oil depletion allowances, etc., is not recognized as welfare. Almost everyone in America is on some type of welfare; but, if you're rich, it's in the form of tax deductions for "business" meals and entertainment, and if you're poor, it's in the form of food stamps. The difference is the stigma and humiliation connected to welfare for the poor, as compared to welfare for the rich, which is called "incentives." Ninety-three percent of AFDC (Aid to Families with Dependent Children, our traditional concept of welfare) recipients are women and children. Eighty percent of food stamp recipients are single mothers, children, the elderly and disabled. Average AFDC payments are $93 per person, per month. Payments are so low nationwide that in only three states do AFDC benefits plus foodstamps bring a household *up to* the poverty level. Food stamp benefits average $10 per person, per week (Sar Levitan, *Programs in Aid of the Poor for the 1980s*). A common focal point for complaints about "welfare" is the belief that most welfare recipients are cheaters—goodness knows there are no middle-class income tax cheaters out there. Imagine focusing the same anger and energy on the way corporations and big business cheat on their tax revenues. Now, there would be some dollars worth quibbling about. The "dual welfare" system also assigns a different degree of stigma to programs that benefit women and children, such as AFDC, and programs whose recipients are primarily male, such as veterans' benefits. The implicit assumption is that mothers who raise children do not work and therefore are not deserving of their daily bread crumbs.

Anti-union attitudes are another prime example of classism in action. At best, unions have been a very progressive force for workers, women and people of color. At worst, unions have reflected the same regressive attitudes which are out there in other social structures: classism, racism, and sexism. Classism exists within the working class. The aristocracy of the working class—unionized, skilled workers—have mainly been white and male and have viewed themselves as being better than unskilled workers, the unemployed and poor, who are mostly women and people of color. The white working class must commit itself to a cultural and ideological transformation of racist attitudes. The history of working people, and the ways we've resisted many types of oppressions, are not something we're taught in school. Missing from our education is information about workers and their resistance.

Working-class women's critiques have focused on the following issues:

Education: White middle-class professionals have used academic jargon to rationalize and justify classism. The whole structure of education is a classist system. Schools in every town reflect class divisions: like the store list at the beginning of this article, you can list schools in your town by what classes of kids attend, and in most cities you can also list by race. The classist system is perpetuated in schools with the tracking system, whereby the "dumbs" are tracked into homemaking, shop courses and vocational school futures, while the "smarts" end up in advanced math, science, literature, and college-prep courses. If we examine these groups carefully, the coincidence of poor and working-class backgrounds with "dumbs" is rather alarming. The standard measurement of supposed intelligence is white middle-class English. If you're other than white middle-class, you have to become bilingual to succeed in the educational system. If you're white middle-class, you only need the language and writing skills you were raised with, since they're the standard. To do well in society presupposes middle-class background, experiences and learning for everyone. The tracking system separates those from the working class who can potentially assimilate to the middle class from all our friends, and labels us "college bound."

After high school, you go on to vocational school, community college, or college—public or private—according to your class position. Apart from the few who break into middle-class schools, the classist stereotyping of the working class as being dumb and inarticulate tracks most into vocational and low-skilled jobs. A few of us are allowed to slip through to reinforce the idea that equal opportunity exists. But for most, class position is destiny—determining our educational attainment and employment. Since we must overall abide by middle-class rules to succeed, the assumption is that we go to college in order to "better ourselves"—i.e., become more like them. I suppose it's assumed we have "yuppie envy" and desire nothing more than to be upwardly mobile individuals. It's assumed that we want to fit into their world. But many of us remain connected to our communities and families. Becoming college-educated doesn't mean we have to, or want to, erase our first and natural language and value system. It's important for many of us to remain in and return to our communities to work, live, and stay sane.

Jobs: Middle-class people have the privilege of choosing careers. They can decide which jobs they want to work, according to their moral or political commitments, needs for challenge or creativity. This is a privilege denied the working-class and poor, whose work is a means of survival, not choice (see Hartsock). Working-class women have seldom had the luxury of choosing between work in the home or market. We've generally done both, with little ability to purchase services to help with this double burden. Middle- and upper-class women can often hire other women to clean their houses, take care of their children, and cook their meals. Guess what class and race those "other" women are? Working a double or triple day is common for working-class women. Only middle-class women have an array of choices such as: parents put you through school, then you choose a career, then you choose when and if to have babies, then you choose a support system of working-class women to take care of your kids and house if you choose to resume your career. After the birth of my second child, I was working two part-time jobs—one loading trucks at night—and going to school during the days. While I was quite privileged because I could take my colicky infant with me to classes and the day-time job, I was in a state of continuous semi-consciousness. I had to work to support my family; the only choice I had was between school or sleep: Sleep became a privilege. A white middle-class feminist instructor at the university suggested to me, all sympathetically, that I ought to hire someone to clean my house and watch the baby. Her suggestion was totally out of my reality, both economically and socially. I'd worked for years cleaning other peoples' houses. Hiring a working-class woman to do the shit work is a middle-class woman's solution to any dilemma which her privileges, such as a career, may present her.

Mothering: The feminist critique of families and the oppressive role of mothering has focused on white middle-class nuclear families. This may not be an appropriate model for communities of class and color. Mothering and families may hold a different importance for working class women. Within this context, the issue of coming out can be a very painful process for working-class lesbians. Due to the homophobia of working-class communities, to be a lesbian is most often to be excommunicated from your family, neighborhood, friends and the people you work with. If you're working-class, you don't have such clearly demarcated concepts of yourself as an individual, but instead see yourself as part of a family and community that forms your survival structure. It is not easy to be faced with the risk of giving up ties which are so central to your identity and survival.

Individualism: Preoccupation with one's self—one's body, looks, relationships—is a luxury working-class women can't afford. Making an occupation out of taking care of yourself through therapy, aerobics, jogging, dressing for success, gourmet meals and proper nutrition, etc., may be responses that are directly rooted in privilege. The middle-class have the leisure time to be preoccupied with their own problems, such as their waistlines, planning their vacations, coordinating their wardrobes, or dealing with what their mother said to them when they were five—my!

The white middle-class women's movement has been patronizing to working-class women. Its supporters think we don't understand sexism. What we don't understand is white middle-class feminism. They act as though they invented the truth, the light, and the way, which they merely need to pass along to us lower-class drudges. What they invented is a distorted form of what working-class women already know—if you're female, life sucks. Only at least we were smart enough to know that it's not just being female, but also being a person of color or class, which makes life a quicksand trap. The class system weakens all women. It censors and eliminates images of female strength. The idea of women as passive, weak creatures totally discounts the strength, self-dependence and inter-dependence necessary to survive as work-ing-class and poor women. My mother and her friends always had a less-than-passive, less-than-enamoured attitude toward their spouses, male bosses, and men in general. I know from listening to their conversations, jokes and what they passed on to us, their daughters, as folklore. When I was five years old, my mother told me about how Aunt Betty had hit Uncle Ernie over the head with a skillet and knocked him out because he was raising his hand to hit her, and how he's never even thought about doing it since. This story was told to me with a good amount of glee and laughter. All the men in the neighborhood were told of the event as an example of what was a very acceptable response in the women's community for that type of male behavior. We kids in the neighborhood grew up with these stories of women giving husbands, bosses, the welfare system, schools, unions and men in general—hell, whenever they deserved it. For me there were many role models of women taking action, control and resisting what was supposed to be their lot. Yet many white middle-class feminists continue to view feminism like math homework, where there's only supposed to be one answer. Never occurs to them that they might be talking algebra while working-class women might be talking metaphysics.

Women with backgrounds other than white middle-class experience compounded, simultaneous oppressions. We can't so easily separate our experiences by categories of gender, or race, or class, i.e., "I remember it well: on Saturday, June 3, I was experiencing class oppression, but by Tuesday, June 6, I was caught up in race oppression, then all day Friday, June 9, I was in the middle of gender oppression. What a week!" Sometimes, for example, gender and class reinforce each other. When I returned to college as a single parent after a few years of having kids and working crummy jobs—I went in for vocational testing. Even before I was tested, the white middle-class male vocational counselor looked at me, a welfare mother in my best selection from the Salvation Army racks, and suggested I quit college, go to vo-tech school and become a grocery clerk. This was probably the highest paying female working-class occupation he could think of. The vocational test results sug-gested I become an attorney. I did end up quitting college once again, not because of his suggestion, but because I was tired of supporting my children in ungenteel poverty. I entered vo-tech school for training as an electrician and, as one of the first women in a non-traditional field, was able to earn a living wage at a job which had traditionally been reserved for white working-class males. But this is a story for another day. Let's return to our little vocational counselor example. Was he suggesting the occupational choice of grocery clerk to me because of my gender or my class? Probably both. Let's imagine for a moment what this same vocational counselor might have advised, on sight only, to the following people:

1. A white middle-class male: doctor, lawyer, engineer, business executive.
2. A white middle-class female: close to the same suggestion as #1 if the counselor was not sexist, or, if sexist, then: librarian, teacher, nurse, social worker.
3. A middle-class man of color: close to the same suggestions as #1 if the counselor was not racist, or, if racist, then: school principal, sales, management, technician.
4. A middle-class woman of color: close to the same suggestions as #3 if counselor was not sexist; #2 if not racist; if not racist or sexist, then potentially #1.
5. A white working-class male: carpenter, electrician, plumber, welder.
6. A white working-class female—well, we already know what he told me, although he could have also suggested secretary, waitress and dental hygienist (except I'd already told him I hated these jobs).
7. A working-class man of color: garbage collector, janitor, fieldhand.
8. A working-class woman of color: maid, laundress, garment worker.

Notice anything about this list? As you move down it, a narrowing of choices, status, pay, working conditions, benefits and chances for promotions occurs. To be connected to any one factor, such as gender or class or race, can make life difficult. To be connected to multiple factors can guarantee limited economic status and poverty.

WAYS TO AVOID FACING CLASSISM

Deny Deny Deny: Deny your class position and the privileges connected to it. Deny the existence or experience of the working-class and poor. You can even set yourself up (in your own mind) as judge and jury in deciding who qualifies as working-class by your white middle-class standards. So if someone went to college, or seems intelligent to you, not at all like your stereotypes, they must be middle-class.

Guilt Guilt Guilt: "I feel so bad, I just didn't realize!" is not helpful, but is a way to avoid changing attitudes and behaviors. Passivity—"Well, what can I do about it, anyway?"—and anger—"Well, what do they want!"—aren't too helpful either. Again, with these responses, the focus is on you and absolving the white middle class from responsibility. A more helpful remedy is to take action. Donate your time and money to local foodbanks. Don't cross picket lines. Better yet, go join a picket line.

HOW TO CHALLENGE CLASSISM

If you're middle-class you can begin to challenge classism with the following:

1. Confront classist behavior in yourself, others and society. Use and share the privileges, like time or money, which you do have.
2. Make demands on working-class and poor communities' issues—anti-racism, poverty, unions, public housing, public transportation, literacy and day care.
3. Learn from the skills and strength of working people—study working and poor people's history; take some Labor Studies, Ethnic Studies, Women Studies classes. Challenge elitism. There are many different types of intelligence: white middle-class, academic, professional intellectualism being one of them (reportedly). Finally, educate yourself, take responsibility and take action.

If you're working-class, just some general suggestions (it's cheaper than therapy—free, less time-consuming and I won't ask you about what your mother said to you when you were five):

1. Face your racism! Educate yourself and others, your family, community, any organizations you belong to; take responsibility and take action. Face your classism, sexism, heterosexism, ageism, able-bodiness, adultism. . . .
2. Claim your identity. Learn all you can about your history and the history and experience of all working and poor peoples. Raise your children to be anti-racist, anti-sexist and anti-classist. Teach them the language and culture of working peoples. Learn to survive with a fair amount of anger and lots of humor, which can be tough when this stuff isn't even funny.
3. Work on issues which will benefit your community. Consider remaining in or returning to your communities. If you live and work in white middle-class environments, look for working-class allies to help you

survive with your humor and wits intact. How do working-class people spot each other? We have antenna.

We need not deny or erase the differences of working class cultures but can embrace their richness, their variety, their moral and intellectual heritage. We're not at the point yet where we can celebrate differences—not having money for a prescription for your child is nothing to celebrate. It's not time yet to party with the white middle class, because we'd be the entertainment ("Aren't they quaint? Just love their workboots and uniforms and the way they cuss!"). We need to overcome divisions among working people, not by ignoring the multiple oppressions many of us encounter, or by oppressing each other, but by becoming committed allies on all issues which affect working people: racism, sexism, classism, etc. An injury to one is an injury to all. Don't play by ruling class rules, hoping that maybe you can live on Connecticut Avenue instead of Baltic, or that you as an individual can make it to Park Place and Boardwalk. Tired of Monopoly? Always ending up on Mediterranean Avenue? How about changing the game?

THE MIDDLE-CLASS BLACK'S BURDEN   14

Leanita McClain

I am a member of the black middle class who has had it with being patted on the head by white hands and slapped in the face by black hands for my success.

Here's a discovery that too many people still find startling: when given equal opportunities at white-collar pencil pushing, blacks want the same things from life that everyone else wants. These include the proverbial dream house, two cars, an above-average school and a vacation for the kids at Disneyland. We may, in fact, want these things more than other Americans because most of us have been denied them so long.

From: Leanita McClain, *A Foot in Each World: Essays and Articles* (Evanston, Ill.: Northwestern University Press, 1986). Reprinted by permission.

Meanwhile, a considerable number of the folks we left behind in the "old country," commonly called the ghetto, and the militants we left behind in their antiquated ideology can't berate middle-class blacks enough for "forgetting where we came from." We have forsaken the revolution, we are told, we have sold out. We are Oreos, they say, black on the outside, white within.

The truth is, we have not forgotten; we would not dare. We are simply fighting on different fronts and are no less war weary, and possibly more heartbroken, for we know the black and white worlds can meld, that there can be a better world.

It is impossible for me to forget where I came from as long as I am prey to the jive hustler who does not hesitate to exploit my childhood friendship. I am reminded, too, when I go back to the old neighborhood in fear—and have my purse snatched—and when I sit down to a business lunch and have an old classmate wait on my table. I recall the girl I played dolls with who now rears five children on welfare, the boy from church who is in prison for murder, the pal found dead of a drug overdose in the alley where we once played tag.

My life abounds in incongruities. Fresh from a vacation in Paris, I may, a week later, be on the milk-run Trailways bus in Deep South backcountry attending the funeral of an ancient uncle whose world stretched only 50 miles and who never learned to read. Sometimes when I wait at the bus stop with my attaché case, I meet my aunt getting off the bus with other cleaning ladies on their way to do my neighbors' floors.

But I am not ashamed. Black progress has surpassed our greatest expectations; we never even saw much hope for it, and the achievement has taken us by surprise.

In my heart, however, there is no safe distance from the wretched past of my ancestors or the purposeless present of some of my contemporaries; I fear such a fate can reclaim me. I am not comfortably middle class; I am uncomfortably middle class.

I have made it, but where? Racism still dogs my people. There are still communities in which crosses are burned on the lawns of black families who have the money and grit to move in.

What a hollow victory we have won when my sister, dressed in her designer everything, is driven to the rear door of the luxury high rise in which she lives because the cab driver, noting only her skin color, assumes she is the maid, or the nanny, or the cook, but certainly not the lady of any house at this address.

I have heard the immigrants' bootstrap tales, the simplistic reproach of "why can't you people be like us." I have fulfilled the entry requirements of the American middle class, yet I am left, at times, feeling unwelcome and stereotyped. I have overcome the problems of food, clothing and shelter, but I have not overcome my old nemesis, prejudice. Life is easier, being black is not.

I am burdened daily with showing whites that blacks are people. I am, in the old vernacular, a credit to my race. I am my brothers' keeper, and my sisters', though many of them have abandoned me because they think that I have abandoned them.

I run a gauntlet between two worlds, and I am cursed and blessed by both. I travel, observe and take part in both; I can also be used by both. I am a rope in a tug of war. If I am a token in my downtown office, so am I at my cousin's church tea. I assuage white guilt. I disprove black inadequacy and prove to my parents' generation that their patience was indeed a virtue.

I have a foot in each world, but I cannot fool myself about either. I can see the transparent deceptions of some whites and the bitter hopelessness of some blacks. I know how tenuous my grip on one way of life is, and how strangling the grip of the other way of life can be.

Many whites have lulled themselves into thinking that race relations are just grand because they were the first on their block to discuss crab grass with the new black family. Yet too few blacks and whites in this country send their children to school together, entertain each other or call each other friend. Blacks and whites dining out together draw stares. Many of my coworkers see no black faces from the time the train pulls out Friday evening until they meet me at the coffee machine Monday morning. I remain a novelty.

Some of my "liberal" white acquaintances pat me on the head, hinting that I am a freak, that my success is less a matter of talent than of luck and affirmative action. I may live among them, but it is difficult to live with them. How can they be sincere about respecting me, yet hold my fellows in contempt? And if I am silent when they attempt to sever me from my own, how can I live with myself?

Whites won't believe I remain culturally different; blacks won't believe I remain culturally the same.

I need only look in a mirror to know my true allegiance, and I am painfully aware that, even with my off-white trappings, I am prejudged by my color.

As for the envy of my own people, am I to give up my career, my standard of living, to pacify them and set my conscience at ease? No. I have worked for these amenities and deserve them, though I can never enjoy them without feeling guilty.

These comforts do not make me less black, nor oblivious to the woe in which many of my people are drowning. As long as we are denigrated as a group, no one of us has made it. Inasmuch as we all suffer for every one left behind, we all gain for every one who conquers the hurdle.

BOB COLE

15

My father was a coal miner for 40 years. My mother worked in factories during WWII and during my childhood and adolescence. They both graduated from the eighth grade and were rather intelligent, though not well-read. Around 1955 my home town, a boom and bust mining town for decades, went bust again. My father was over 50 and unemployable. It was the beginning of a bitter, degenerative period for him which lasted until his death twenty years later. My mother ran a small laundry for a while, then went back to the factory, making about $25 a week. I was ten years old.

I loved school and can still remember the smells and feelings of being in the first grade—oiled wooden floors, chalk, crayons, books. I was shy and a model student, properly respectful (or fearful as the occasion demanded), in awe of learning.

At about the same time I started school I began to go to church, and, in fact, school and church experiences sort of blend together in my memory at times. My parents were non-practicing Primitive Baptists. I chose to be a Methodist because I was invited to the church by my first grade teacher. I went alone. This, coupled with my love of school and my propensity to sit alone a lot, not fight and not raise hell, kept my parents from knowing how to deal with me.

Class differences in my town were pronounced, but not spoken of. Those with money and power got it primarily through the mining operations. Those without money were generally careful not to look the part; there was a cross-class norm that one ought not "put on." Everyone had a stake in being "common folk," but there still were differences. Since I was a clean-cut, church-going, patriotic (I won a VFW Voice of Democracy award in high school), poor, good student, there were many well-intentioned acts of paternalism. I was given money to go to church camp. The banker lent me money to buy a car, even though I was a junior in college and had no collateral. I appreciated such acts, and, upon reflection, still do. They did, however, serve

From: Jake Ryan and Charles Sackrey, *Strangers in Paradise: Academics from the Working Class* (Boston: South End Press, 1984). Reprinted by permission.

to reinforce my feeling of difference, my apartness from what appeared to be an "in-group."

Money was a problem for me when I was young. I once thought, in the seventh grade, I'd play baseball, until I found that I'd need to buy shoes and equipment. My father said, "Why do you want to do that?" I didn't. I also wanted to be in the band. My father said, "Why do you want to do that?" I really wanted it. My mother, the only breadwinner at that time, thought I should. They fought a bit, and I felt guilty. We only had $20 to $30 per week income, for four people—my niece was also living in our house. My mother arranged $5 a month payment plan and I joined the band, playing a cornet.

I was big, 5'7" and 160, in the eighth grade. The band needed a sousa-phone player. I was appointed. I taught myself to play and, being the only bass horn player, began to develop some confidence. I still loved school and was still a loner, preferring to sit by myself and read or think, rather than socialize. I had no close friends. I never spent the night in a friend's house. No one visited me, perhaps because of my home—there was no place for anyone else to sleep.

I remember shame attached to living in a shack, though many people in my town lived in the same conditions. My mother was a lousy housekeeper, and the house was basically uncleanable anyway. There was a sense of futility and cynicism, fostered by my father. When my mother or I attempted to clean house, he would encourage us to stop: "Why do you want to do that now?" He would clean and cook, and was pretty good at it, but the house was filthy most of the time.

Life at home seemed futile in many ways. I could not study after dark when I was in high school. My father went to bed at 8:30 at the latest, and in a four room house, if there was a light on, or noise, even walking, he would raise hell. I learned quickly to acquiesce. There was nowhere else to go, so I did my reading and work at school or before dark. At bedtime I either went to bed, or went and stood at the four-way stop in town and watched the cars go by.

I had no bedroom; my bed was in the kitchen. I had no privacy. Even the outhouse was only semi-private since there were holes between the boards.

Although I was encouraged to do my "homework," it was more for propriety's sake than for learning. Learning was important to a point; one should do well in school (meaning not fail) and become able to handle the practical aspects of living. Other than newspapers, *Grit*, and Western novels, we had no literature in the house. It wasn't that my home life was unhappy—I was very happy—it just wasn't conducive to planning for the future or for transcending class. To some measure school and community filled the gap.

I was absolutely naive about higher education. I was the first in my family to graduate from high school. Only recently was I reminded that I took SAT exams; I had no idea about such things at the time. I did very well, as it turned out. I was also something of a music "star," singing solos at school and church, winning awards with my tuba, and being the highly visible only bass player in a 100 piece band which was winning many awards.

One day a representative from a nearby college came to school and offered me a grant-in-aid, if I would major in music. The mines were still not running, so, being flattered, I accepted the offer and found myself in college. My father said, "Are you sure you want to do that?"

My first semester was awful. I was lonely, insecure, threatened, and broke, competing with people not only from Louisville, but from New York and Pennsylvania! The grant, coupled with an NDEA loan, gave me enough money to live on at a subsistence level, but I was still so concerned with money that I gauged the papers I wrote on their length; they had to be short. I couldn't afford the paper. I learned in the first semester that I couldn't read music. I also learned I could survive. Second semester, I changed my major to English (I could read), got a job, and connected with the Methodist Student Center.

My parents seemed not to want me to be a miner (although I believe my father would not have minded too much—he loved the mines). They both absolutely did not want me to work in a factory. They, like most people in my home town, wanted their children to "have it better" than they did, which meant to them I should work in a clean job or be a school teacher, preferably the former, and preferably in my home town. They were vaguely proud that I went to college, but could not comprehend why. When I decided to go to graduate school, in another state, they were agreeable, but totally uncomprehending. Here I was again, doing something weird. Why didn't I just come back home and teach?

In graduate school I was struck again by how much I didn't know, how much I hadn't read, how truly ignorant I was. The realization was more profound this time, and I reacted by beginning an anti-social, cynical period, closed socially, uncommunicative about my background, constructing a new self as I went along. The "good old boy" act still worked, but I began to see places and times when it was artificial, contrived, deceitful, even counterproductive. It also didn't fit me anymore. I did not want to be either a good old boy, or an arrogant know-it-all intellectual.

I was a good student, though my papers were still gauged on how many sheets of paper I'd need to buy. My background began to haunt me. My major professor wrote a recommendation for me that said, "given his background, he has done amazingly well." Though meant as a compliment, it hurt.

It was 1968, and I was burnt with academia. I decided to drop out, in a socially acceptable way, of course. There was a teaching job open in a Black school in middle Georgia. I took it. By this time, I had consciously destroyed my native Kentucky dialect. The job I took called for me to help the students, faculty and staff in this rural town to get rid of theirs. The reasoning behind the Program went: a major reason Blacks are raising hell and not fitting in is because they're different—they think, talk, and act differently than whites. It was thought, then, that if they changed the way they talked they could change the way they thought and acted.

The county was ninety per cent black, but it was run by whites. Blacks had, until 1962, gone to school in churches taught by whomever was available, for about three months a year, all the time they could take away from farming. There was massive illiteracy and poverty. The students were just beginning to develop a sense of awareness of any pride in blackness. The last thing the students needed was a poor-white-trash man trying to get them to talk white. I didn't try.

What I tried to do was to teach them how to organize messages—written and oral—to channel their blossoming hostility into an effective method for dealing with the white world, using and appreciating their own dialect. It was basically a failure. There were good moments, but they didn't trust me and had no reason to. I was, incidentally, making twice as much money as black teachers who had been teaching there five years or more. I learned some lessons about class and racial differences and power. I'm not sure the students learned anything. I felt like a white do-gooder who had raped the community.

I couldn't stay in Georgia. The draft was breathing down my neck, and in 1969 I ran north, taking a college teaching job. I was an outspoken liberal, for the most part. I had enough money finally to relax a bit and try to plan. Did I want a Ph.D.? What did I want to do? What could I do? How big was my bootstrap? I was teaching, mildly protesting, and fitting in rather well with university life. My friends were unassuming academics, from working class families. I shied away from the "big time" crowd and felt vaguely uncomfortable around them. I got married, fat, and comfortable.

Then, in August, 1970, at age 26, I was drafted. In ten days I went from a comfortable existence as a liberal "intellectual" college professor back to my roots—a nobody who, under threat, would shuffle for his superiors, ROTC lieutenants and working class sergeants trying to overcome their fears. My confidence was shaken to the core, and my fears, rooted in class and father fear came into focus again. My cynicism was made more solid; my romantic optimism faltered.

I survived basic training by relearning what my experience in factory work had taught me: learn the rules, do the work, keep your mouth shut, put your body on automatic pilot, and let your mind roam. It was more difficult to do since I was supposed to be learning to kill and was treated as a part of a distinctive young subculture: working-class, killing machines.

After the army I decided to go back to school. I was cynical, arrogantly class conscious and somewhat more politically radical. I could not work in industry. I didn't feel smart enough, nor the right "sort" to become a lawyer. The profession for which I seemed best suited was the academy. For that I needed a Ph.D. I wanted no part of hurdle jumping, so I chose a college close to my home town, which had a reputation as a degree mill.

It was at that college that I first began to feel I could actually become a scholar. It turned out not to be a degree mill. I was challenged, personally and academically. Again, I went into a new discipline, for which I had no preparation, and found myself doing well, achieving respect from peers and professors alike. I opened up to others. My confidence soared. Then my major professor decided to say "fuck it" to academia, and, mid-way through my dissertation pulled up stakes and left. My cynicism about what "doing well" means in academic institutions and in the world generally, grew. My introspection into my background relative to my future as a "scholar" began.

In 1978, I moved to the East Coast and was confronted again, this time more strongly than ever with class differences.

Gender and Sexism

COMMONALITIES AND DIFFERENCES

16

Johnnetta B. Cole

If you see one woman, have you seen them all? Does the heavy weight of patriarchy level all differences among US women? Is it the case, as one woman put it, that "there isn't much difference between having to say 'Yes suh Mr. Charlie' and 'Yes dear'?" Does "grandmother" convey the same meaning as "abuela," as "buba," as "gran'ma"? Is difference a part of what we share, or is it, in fact, *all* that we share? As early as 1970, Toni Cade Bambara asked: "How relevant are the truths, the experiences, the findings of white women to black women? Are women after all simply women?" (Bambara 1970: 9).

Are US women bound by our similarities or divided by our differences? The only viable response is *both*. To address our commonalities without dealing with our differences is to misunderstand and distort that which separates as well as that which binds us as women. Patriarchal oppression is not limited to women of one race or of one particular ethnic group, women in one class, women of one age group or sexual preference, women who live in one part of the country, women of any one religion, or women with certain physical abilities or disabilities. Yet, while oppression of women knows no such limitations, we cannot, therefore, conclude that the oppression of all women is identical.

Among the things which bind women together are the assumptions about the way that women think and behave, the myths—indeed the stereotypes—

about what is common to all women. For example, women will be asked nicely in job interviews if they type, while men will not be asked such a question. In response to certain actions, the expression is used: "Ain't that just like a woman?" Or during a heated argument between a man and a woman, as the voice of each rises and emotions run high, the woman makes a particularly good point. In a voice at the pitch of the ongoing argument, the man screams at her: "You don't have to get hysterical!"

In an interesting form of "what goes around comes around," as Malcolm X put it, there is the possibility that US women are bound together by our assumptions, attitudes toward, even stereotypes of the other gender. Folklorist Rayna Green, referring to women of the Southern setting in which she grew up, says this:

> Southern or not, women everywhere talk about sex. . . . In general men are more often the victims of women's jokes than not. Tit for tat, we say. Usually the subject for laughter is men's boasts, failures, or inadequacies ("come-uppance for lack of upcommance," as one of my aunts would say). Poking fun at a man's sexual ego, for example, might never be possible in real social situations with the men who have power over their lives, but it is possible in a joke. (Green 1984: 23–24)

That which US women have in common must always be viewed in relation to the particularities of a group, for even when we narrow our focus to one particular group of women it is possible for differences within that group to challenge the primacy of what is shared in common. For example, what have we said and what have we failed to say when we speak of "Asian American women"? As Shirley Hune notes (1982), Asian American women as a group share a number of characteristics. Their participation in the work force is higher than that of women in any other ethnic group. Many Asian American women live life supporting others, often allowing their lives to be subsumed by the needs of the extended family. And they are subjected to stereotypes by the dominant society: the sexy but "evil dragon lady," the "neuter gender," the "passive/demure" type, and the "exotic/erotic" type.

However, there are many circumstances when these shared experiences are not sufficient to accurately describe the condition of particular Asian American women. Among Asian American women there are those who were born in the United States, fourth and fifth generation Asian American women with firsthand experience of no other land, and there are those who recently arrived in the United States. Asian American women are diverse in their heritage or country of origin: China, Japan, the Philippines, Korea, India, Vietnam, Cambodia, Thailand, or another country in Asia. If we restrict ourselves to Asian American women of Chinese descent, are we referring to those women who are from the People's Republic of China or those from Taiwan, those from Hong Kong or those from Vietnam, those from San Francisco's Chinatown or those from Mississippi? Are we subsuming under "Asian American" those Pacific Island women from Hawaii, Samoa, Guam, and other islands under U.S. control? Although the majority of Asian American women are working-class—contrary to the stereotype of the "ever successful" Asians—there are poor, "middle-class," and even affluent Asian American women (Hune 1982: 1–2, 13–14).

It has become very common in the United States today to speak of "Hispanics," putting Puerto Ricans, Chicanos, Dominicans, Cubans, and those from every Spanish-speaking country in the Americas into one category of people, with the women referred to as Latinas or Hispanic women. Certainly there is a language, or the heritage of a language, a general historical experience, and certain cultural traditions and practices which are shared by these women. But a great deal of harm can be done by sweeping away differences in the interest of an imposed homogeneity.

Within one group of Latinas there is, in fact, considerable variation in terms of self-defined ethnic identity, such that some women refer to themselves as Mexican Americans, others as *Chicanas*, others as Hispanics, and still others as Americans. Among this group of women are those who express a commitment to the traditional roles of women and others who identify with feminist ideals. Some Chicanas are monolingual—in Spanish or English—and others are bilingual. And there are a host of variations among Chicanas in terms of educational achievements, economic differences, rural or urban living conditions, and whether they trace their ancestry from women who lived in this land well before the United States forcibly took the northern half of Mexico, or more recently arrived across the border that now divides the nations called Mexico and the United States.

Women of the Midwest clearly share a number of experiences which flow from living in the U.S. heartland, but they have come from different places, and they were and are today part of various cultures.

> Midwestern women are the Native American women whose ancestors were brought to the plains in the mid-nineteenth century to be settled on reservations, the black women whose fore-bears emigrated by the thousands from the South after Reconstruction. They are the descendants of the waves of Spanish, French, Norwegian, Danish, Swedish, Bohemian, Scottish, Welsh, British, Irish, German, and Russian immigrants who settled the plains, the few Dutch, Italians, Poles, and Yugoslavs who came with them. (Boucher 1982:3)

There is another complexity: when we have identified a commonality among women, cutting across class, racial, ethnic, and other major lines of difference, the particular ways that commonality is acted out and its consequences in the larger society may be quite diverse. Ostrander makes this point in terms of class:

> When women stroke and soothe men, listen to them and accommodate their needs, men of every class return to the workplace with renewed energies. When women arrange men's social lives and relationships, men of every class are spared investing the time and energy required to meet their social needs. When women run the households and keep family concerns in check, men of every class are freer than women to pursue other activities, including work, outside the home. But upper-class women perform these tasks for men at the very top of the class structure. . . . Supporting their husbands as individuals, they support and uphold the very top of the class structure. In this way they distinguish themselves from women of other social classes. (Ostrander 1984: 146)

Suppose that we can accurately and exclusively identify the characteristics shared by one particular group of women. For each of the women within that group, into how many other groups does she want to, or is she forced to, fit? Or can we speak of similarities only with respect to a group such as Puerto Rican women who are forty-three years old, were born in San Juan, Puerto Rico, migrated to New York City when they were five years old, work as eighth-grade school teachers, attend a Catholic church, are heterosexual, married, with two male and two female children, and have no physical disabilities?

Then there is that unpredictable but often present quality of individuality, the idiosyncrasies of a particular person. Shirley Abbott, describing experiences of growing up in the South, contrasts her mother's attitude and behavior toward the black woman who was her maid with what was the usual stance of "Southern white ladies."

> I don't claim that my mother's way of managing her black maid was typical. Most white women did not help their laundresses hang the washing on the line. . . . Compulsive housewifery had some part in it. So did her upbringing. . . . There was another motive too. . . . Had she used Emma in just the right way, Mother could have become a lady. But Mother didn't want to be a lady. Something in her was against it, and she couldn't explain what frightened her, which was why she cried when my father ridiculed her. (Abbott 1983: 78–79)

Once we have narrowed our focus to one specific group of women (Armenian American women, or women over sixty-five, or Arab American women, or black women from the Caribbean, or Ashkenazi Jewish women), the oppression that group of women experiences may take different forms at different times. Today, there is no black woman in the United States who is the legal slave of a white master: "chosen" for that slave status because of her race, forced to give her labor power without compensation because of the class arrangements of the society, and subjected to the sexual whims of her male master because of her gender. But that does not mean that black women today are no longer oppressed on the basis of race, class, and gender.

There are also groups of women who experience intense gender discrimination today, but in the past had a radically different status in their society. Contrary to the popular image of female oppression as being both universal and as old as human societies, there is incontestable evidence of egalitarian societies in which men and women related in ways that did not involve male dominance and female subjugation. Eleanor Leacock is the best known of the anthropologists who have carried out the kind of detailed historical analysis which provides evidence on gender relations in precolonial North American societies. In discussing the debate on the origins and spread of women's oppression, Leacock points out that women's oppression is a reality today in virtually every society, and while socialist societies have reduced it, they have not eliminated gender inequality. However, it does not follow that women's oppression has always existed and will always exist. What such arguments about universal female subordination do is to project onto the totality of human history the conditions of today's world. Such an argument also "affords an important ideological buttress for those in power" (Leacock 1979: 10–11).

Studies of precolonial societies indicate considerable variety in terms of gender relations.

> Women retained great autonomy in much of the pre-colonial world, and related to each other and to men through public as well as private procedures as they carried out their economic and social responsibilities and protected their rights. Female and male modalities of various kinds operated reciprocally within larger kin and community contexts before the principle of male dominance within individual families was taught by missionaries, defined by legal status, and solidified by the economic relations of colonialism. (Leacock 1979: 10–11)

Even when there is evidence of female oppression among women of diverse backgrounds, it is important to listen to the individual assessment which each women makes of her own condition, rather than assume that a synonymous experience of female oppression exists among all women. As a case in point, Sharon Burmeister Lord, in describing what it was like to grow up "Appalachian style," speaks of the influence of female role models in shaping the conditions of her development. In Williamson, West Virginia, she grew up knowing women whose occupations were Methodist preacher, elementary school principal, county sheriff, and university professor. Within her own family, her mother works as a secretary, writes poetry and songs, and "swims faster than any boy"; her aunt started her own seed and hardware store; one grandmother is a farmer and the other runs her own boarding house. Summarizing the effect of growing up among such women, Lord says:

> When a little girl has had a chance to learn strength, survival tactics, a firm grasp of reality, and an understanding of class oppression from the women around her, it doesn't remove oppression from her life, but it does give her a fighting chance. And that's an advantage! (Lord 1979: 25)

Finally, if it is agreed that today, to some extent, all women are oppressed, to what extent can a woman, or a group of women, also act as oppressor? Small as the numbers may be, there are some affluent black women. (In 1979, less than 500 black women had an income of over $75,000 a year. Four thousand black men had such an income, as compared to 548,000 white men who were in that income bracket [Marable 1983: 101–102].) Is it not possible that among this very small group of black women there are those who, while they experience oppression because of their race, act in oppressive ways toward other women because of their class? Does the experience of this society's heterosexism make a Euro-American lesbian incapable of engaging in racist acts toward women of color? The point is very simply that privilege can and does coexist with oppression (Bulkin et al. 1984: 99) and being a victim of one form of discrimination does not make one immune to victimizing someone else on a different basis. . . .

REFERENCES CITED

Abbott, S. 1983. *Womenfolks: Growing Up Down South*. New York: Ticknor and Fields.

Bambara, T. C., ed. 1970. *The Black Woman: An Anthology*. New York: Signet.

Boucher, S. 1982. *Heartwomen: An Urban Feminist Odyssey Home*. New York: Harper & Row.

Bulkin, E., M. E. Pratt, and B. Smith, eds. 1984. *Yours in Struggle*. Brooklyn, N.Y.: Long Haul Press.

Green, R. 1984. "Magnolias Grow in Dirt: The Bawdy Lore of Southern Women." In *Speaking for Ourselves*, M. Alexander, ed., pp. 20–28. New York: Pantheon.

Hune, S. 1982. Asian American Women: Past and Present, Myth and Reality. Unpublished manuscript prepared for conference on Black Women's Agenda for the Feminist

Movement in the 80's, Williams College, Williamstown, Mass., November 12–14, 1982.

Leacock, E. 1979. "Women, Development and Anthropological Facts and Fictions." In *Women in Latin America: An Anthology from Latin American Perspectives*, pp. 7–16. Riverside, Calif.: Latin American Perspectives.

Lord, S. B. 1979. "Growin' Up—Appalachian, Female, and Feminist." In *Appalachian Women: A Learning/Teaching Guide*, S. B. Lord and C. Patton-Crowder, eds., pp. 22–25. Knoxville, Tenn.: University of Tennessee.

Marable, M. 1983. *How Capitalism Underdeveloped Black America*. Boston: South End Press.

Ostrander, S. A. 1984. *Women of the Upper Class*. Philadelphia: Temple University Press.

UNDERSTANDING AND FIGHTING SEXISM: *A Call to Men*

17

Peter Blood, Alan Tuttle, and George Lakey

PART 1: UNDERSTANDING THE ENEMY: HOW SEXISM WORKS IN THE U.S.A.

What Is Sexism?

Sexism is much more than a problem with the language we use, our personal attitudes, or individual hurtful acts toward women. Sexism in our country is a complex mesh of practices, institutions, and ideas which have the overall effect of giving more power to men than to women. By "power" we mean the ability to influence important decisions—political decisions of government on every level, economic decisions (jobs, access to money, choice of priorities), and a wide variety of other life areas down to the most personal

From: *Off Their Backs . . . and on Our Own Two Feet* (Philadelphia: New Society Publishers, 1983), pp. 1–8. Reprinted by permission.

concerns, such as whether two people are going to make love on a given night or not. The word "patriarchy" is sometimes used to refer to the actual power structure built around men's domination of women. Two key areas where women are denied power are the area of jobs and the area of violence directed toward women.

Women have much less earning power in our labor market than men do. Reasons for this include the fact that much of women's labor is unwaged (housecleaning, childrearing, little services to please bosses or lovers); the low status and pay of most of the traditionally women's jobs that are waged (secretary, sales clerk, childcare, nursing home attendant); the non-union status of most women workers; and the discriminatory practices such as the recent Supreme Court decision allowing companies to exclude pregnancy from their medical insurance and sick leave benefits.

Women face a constant threat of physical violence and sexual aggression in our society. As men we are rarely aware of how pervasive this is or the powerful effect it has on women's outlook on themselves and the world. Actual rape or sadistic violence is the tip of the iceberg. Physical abuse of wives and lovers is common and rarely publicized. A majority of women have probably experienced some form of sexual abuse as children. The memory of these experiences often gets suppressed because they feel so humiliated and scared, and because adults deny repeatedly that such a thing could happen. Society is filled with messages pressuring women to provide men with sexual pleasure.

All of the above combine with differences in physical strength, voice, acculturated ways of dealing with anger, and the very concrete power men hold in other areas of life to keep many women intimidated, passive, and unable to even acknowledge their own fear openly. The rapist is the shock trooper for an overall system of unequal power.

Patriarchy is not just a power structure "out there"; it is mainly enforced by our own acceptance of its character ideals for our lives. The character ideal which is held up for men to reach toward is "masculinity." A masculine man is supposed to be tough, good at abstract reasoning, hard-working, unfeeling except for anger and sexual desire, and habitually taking the initiative. Masculinity exists only in contrast to femininity, the model for women. Feminine characteristics include cooperativeness, emotionality, patience, passivity, nurturance, and sexual appeal.

We all know that human characteristics are *not* distributed neatly between the sexes that way. A nursery school will often include girls who do abstract reasoning and get into fights and boys who cry easily. We also know that the culture does not leave them alone—the tomboy usually learns to become a lady, and the gentle boy develops armor to protect him from the jibes of his mates. They also learn that masculinity is valued in our culture more than femininity, especially when it comes to gaining power. In fact, the characteristics which are assigned to men by the patriarchy are the power-linked characteristics. In other words, by accepting masculinity as an ideal for ourselves, men buy into a system which keeps women down.

Sexism and Our Economic System

Why does sexism exist? Why is it so hard to root it out? Who really benefits from it? There is a variety of theories as to where sexism originated. Some say it started with the advent of class society; others say it preceded all other forms of oppression.

Regardless of its historic roots, it is clear that sexism today is intimately connected with our economic system, which is called "corporate capitalism."

In our society, a small group of people own and control almost all of the factories, financial institutions, networks of transport and sales of food and clothing. What this means, first of all, is that though we as men generally have more power than women do, the great majority of us have relatively little real power. Most of us are given very little chance to make the major decisions which affect our lives (for example, whether society will emphasize public transportation or private cars, how decisions are made at the factory where we work, what quality air we breathe, what is taught to our children in school). In fact, this kind of power is concentrated in the hands of a relatively small number of white, middle-aged to older men.

However much power the system has given to each of us, this power is only useful in keeping things going according to the present rules, not in changing things in any basic way. The moment one of us tries to use power conveyed by the system to make fundamental changes, we find it taken away from us by that system. (All of us do possess the power to influence the course of history and bring about fundamental changes if we work together. This power comes from a very different source: from our power to work collectively to change the world around us, by "grass roots" power.)

Corporate capitalism is supported by sexism in many ways. Perhaps the most important way is that women function as a surplus labor force, where they can be pushed in and out of employment in keeping with current needs of the economy (depression, expansion, wartime, or a period of union-busting). In effect, the prevalent attitude in this society might be: "A woman's place is in the home . . . *until she's needed in the factory.*" Women's low wages keep wages lower for all: our boss holds the implicit threat that he can replace us with lower-paid women workers if we get too uppity or demand too high wages. Job role stereotyping also helps get women to do unpleasant forms of work which men would rather not do.

There are other ways sexism helps maintain capitalism. Women's un-waged labor of reproducing and taking care of the work force is called "women's work" and taken for granted. Women's servicing of men at home keeps our feelings of alienation and frustration concerning our jobs in check, which might otherwise lead to rebellion or burnout. Men's role as sole breadwinner in many families makes them reluctant to take militant stands on safety, wages, or other issues at work. It is threatening for a man not to be filling the breadwinner role—and he knows his wife will have a very difficult time finding work that pays enough to support a family. Women and men are played off against each other in competing for scarce jobs rather than sharing the fruits of a non-competitive, non-wasteful economy. Finally, excess con-sumption is encouraged by the lifeless, unsatisfying sex roles which we get shunted into on the job and at home.

The capitalist economic-political structure works to preserve sexism through indoctrination in our schools, a constant flow of brainwashing (subtle or otherwise) in advertising, and through its control of the mass media (what news gets reported and what does not, what programs get chosen for airing . . .). It also maintains it through control of legislation (influence through money), through the policies of our large corporations, and through failure to make use of leadership positions to educate people about the ways sexism affects us and ways it can be overcome.

Sexism and capitalism are so intertwined, in fact, that we believe there is no way that sexism can be thoroughly uprooted from our society without the total remaking of our economic system. Changing over to a popularly con-trolled or socialist economy would be a great blow against sexism. Women in countries like Cuba, China, Mozambique, and the Soviet Union have made significant gains as compared with their status prior to the revolutions in those countries.

Setting up a socialist society in no way guarantees an end to sexism (as can also be seen in the persistence of sexism to one degree or another in all the above countries). The patriarchy is a power arrangement which has a life of its own independent of capitalism's indoctrination. The struggle against sexism, therefore, must be a high priority for any movement which is offering leadership in creating a new society. The style pervading socialist movements in this country and the groups which are leading socialist countries is all too often determined by the masculine conditioning of domination and competition. This conditioning needs to be struggled against much more forcefully than it has been if we are ever to achieve a world free from sexism.

Are We Men the Enemy?

Some people say that men are the enemy when it comes to fighting sexism. We do not agree; blame and guilt don't help in understanding why people function as they do or in getting them to change.

Does this mean we are not responsible for what is happening? Not at all! As men, we are all involved in the oppression women experience, and we benefit from it each day. Yet this is no reason to fix blame on ourselves as "the oppressor" (or, for that matter, to place blame on any woman for "failing to fight back"). Over many years society has forced men and women into these roles of domination and submission.

How did society do this? It is clear we were pushed into these roles when we were young children and especially vulnerable. At that time, all of us were hurt in many ways through the expectations put on our sex. These hurts came through ridicule and threats directed at us and also through having to watch others get hurt while feeling ourselves incapable (because of lack of information or strength) of stopping that hurt. This experience of powerlessness in turn has reduced our ability to see the world clearly and act accordingly. The ingrained fear from these experiences tends to lead to either of two responses: feeling powerless and playing the victim role, or turning the experience around and acting out an oppressor role.

These dynamics do not just happen between men and women, but also between races, age groups, gays and non-gays, healthy and physically challenged people, and a number of other groups. As a matter of fact, everyone in our society has probably ended up playing both of these roles at one time or another. Even the richest, most powerful man was once powerless as a child in relation to his parents. Even a poor black woman could experience some privilege in relation to a very young person or a gay person.

The point is that we were all taught very early not to go beyond the expected stereotyped behavior. The sooner we recognize the effects of this kind of conditioning on us, the sooner we can effectively change the way things happen. This may mean stopping our domination of others or ceasing to accept oppression ourselves. It is good to recognize that stepping out of the old roles usually feels uncomfortable and may well require years of painful struggle, but to give up before the process is over is to miss the rich rewards that are down the road. We can travel that road successfully if we join with others for strength and support.

Why Change?

What rewards are there for us in this process? Much of what society thinks of as being manly is really a way of hardening up so we can dominate or coerce other people. We pay a high price for this hardening, however; it means giving up much of our humanity. We men are conditioned to suppress our feelings and don't learn how to give and receive support, nurturance, and affection awarely. We are taught to take all the responsibility for a situation on our own shoulders. We are taught to have heavy expectations of accomplishment for ourselves and for others. The direct result of this is a high level of tension and anxiety; the indirect result is a high disease rate and early death.

So, as men we have a lot to gain by fighting sexism. From what we have seen and experienced, men (at least in the long run) feel relief and joy just from being freed from the roles that lead to the oppression of women.

But this in no way means that we change easily. Conditioning is far too strong, and the temptation to keep the privilege too great. Nor does it mean, as some people suggest, that "men and women are both oppressed equally by sexism." However much men are hurt or limited by sex roles in this country, the fact remains that they are *not* systematically denied power simply because of being born a certain sex, as women are. Tremendous amounts of struggle will be required—as well as lots of loving support, especially from other men—to undergo the process of change.

Racism, Ageism, and the Oppression of Lesbians and Gay Men

All forms of oppression in our society are closely connected both to each other and to our economic system. Racism, for example, has many close parallels with sexism. Racial minorities, like women, function as a "reserve labor force," shunted into unattractive jobs with little reward or decision-making power, pushed in and out of employment as benefits the system. Racism, like sexism, divides working people from other, preventing them from looking at who holds most of the power in our country. Racial minorities, like women, are thought to be unintelligent and to have less motivation to achieve and work hard than white males. Both groups are kept in place by violent intimidation and are referred to with abusive words. Both frequently get deflected from militant struggle against the oppression of their group by cooptation of a few of their leaders into the lower levels of the power structure. In addition, sexual myths and paranoia about blacks and Latinos play an especially vicious role in undergirding white people's racial fears and stereotypes.

People are just beginning to have a glimpse of what oppression based on age involves. The fact is that our society is almost totally blind to the dignity and capacities of the very young and the very old. Children are like women in being considered helpless, dependent, and cute—creatures to be cherished and taken care of, but not full human beings to be deeply respected and trusted with significant power. They experience 10–15 years of unpaid labor and brainwashing in our current form of education. Older people are looked at as children—except that they often find themselves without anyone interested in cherishing or taking care of them. For men, growing up is associated with taking on more and more of the hard masculine traits we mentioned before. Crying, acting afraid, and showing too much tenderness are all considered shameful because they are "childish" or "woman-like." ("You gotta stop that crying—don't be a sissy.")

Most of us know gay people, but usually we do not know who they are! Lesbians and gay men are so frequently hurt in this society that they usually do not feel safe to come out, even to their friends. An invisible colony of 20,000,000 people in our midst, lesbians and gay men generally work to service the status quo—even the Hollywood illusions of heterosexual romance—while their own dignity and security are denied.

People are still beaten and even killed for being homosexual in America, and the memory of the mass deaths of gays in Nazi concentration camps remains vivid. Now the "new right" is cutting back some recent gains lesbians and gay men have made in rights to jobs and housing. The fact that the same forces are opposing the Equal Rights Amendment and gay rights is a tip-off to the intimate connection between sexism and heterosexism. For one thing, gay men are mistakenly seen as taking the role of women in heterosexual relationships, and therefore not being "real men." For another, lesbians are seen as "uppity" because they act with a freedom not usually found when dependent upon men for loving.

Gay oppression is one of the ways the potential unity of all workers is prevented. It is also one of the cornerstones of the American nuclear family, which in turn is used to promote consumption and to teach sexist division of labor and sex roles. Lesbians and gay men are also exploited by being forced into ghettos and by the commercialized culture which profits from them.

Everyone is hurt by gay oppression. The fear of being considered gay limits and distorts everyone's life choices and relationships. Men are often afraid to get close to their male friends because it might imply gayness—and might even reveal a half-suspected gay dimension of themselves. An essential prop for sexism, in keeping people within their accustomed sex roles, is this fear of homosexuality, or homophobia. Because of this, women's liberation and men's liberation depend partly on gay liberation. . . .

CULTURAL AND HISTORICAL INFLUENCES ON SEXUALITY IN HISPANIC/LATIN WOMEN:

18

Implications for Psychotherapy

Oliva M. Espín

CONTEMPORARY SEXUALITY AND THE HISPANIC WOMAN

If the role of women is currently beset with contradictions in the mainstream of American society,[1] this is probably still more true for women in Hispanic groups. The honor of Latin families is strongly tied to the sexual purity of women. And the concept of honor and dignity is one of the essential distinctive marks of Hispanic culture. For example, classical Hispanic literature gives us a clue to the importance attributed to honor and to female sexual purity in the culture. La Celestina, the protagonist of an early Spanish medieval novel, illustrates the value attached to virginity and its preservation. Celestina was an old woman who earned her living in two ways: by putting young men in touch with young maidens so they could have the sexual contact that parents would never allow, and by "sewing up" ex-virgins, so that they would be considered virgins at marriage. Celestina thus made her living out of making and unmaking virgins. The fact that she ends by being punished with death further emphasizes the gravity of what she does. In the words of a famous Spanish playwright of the seventeenth century, "al Rey la hacienda y la vida se han de dar, mas no el honor; porque el honor es patrimonio del alma y el alma solo es de Dios."[2] This quotation translates literally, "to the king you give money and life, but not your honor, because honor is part of the soul, and your soul belongs only to God."

Different penalties and sanctions for the violation of cultural norms related to female sexuality are very much associated with social class. The upper classes or those seeking an improved social status tend to be more rigid

Abridged from: Carole Vance (ed.), *Pleasure and Danger* (Boston: Routledge & Kegan Paul, 1984), pp. 149–164. Reprinted by permission.

about sexuality. This of course is related to the transmission of property. In the upper classes, a man needs to know that his children are in fact his before they inherit his property. The only guarantee of his paternity is that his wife does not have sexual contact with any other man. Virginity is tremendously important in that context. However, even when property is not an issue, the only thing left to a family may be the honor of its women and as such it may be guarded jealously by both males and females. Although Hispanics in the twentieth century may not hold the same strict values—and many of them certainly cannot afford the luxury to do so—women's sexual behavior is still the expression of the family's honor. The tradition of maintaining virginity until marriage that had been emphasized among women continues to be a cultural imperative. The Virgin Mary—who was a virgin and a mother, but never a sexual being—is presented as an important role model for all Hispanic women, although Hispanic unwed mothers, who have clearly overstepped the boundaries of culturally-prescribed virginity for women, usually are accepted by their families. Married women or those living in common-law marriages are supposed to accept a double standard for sexual behavior, by which their husbands may have affairs with other women, while they themselves are expected to remain faithful to one man all of their lives. However, it is not uncommon for a Hispanic woman to have the power to decide whether or not a man is going to live with her, and she may also choose to put him out if he drinks too much or is not a good provider.[3]

In fact, Latin women experience a unique combination of power and powerlessness which is characteristic of the culture. The idea that personal problems are best discussed with women is very much part of the Hispanic culture. Women in Hispanic neighborhoods and families tend to rely on other women for their important personal and practical needs. There is a widespread belief among Latin women of all social classes that most men are undependable and are not to be trusted. At the same time, many of these women will put up with a man's abuses because having a man around is an important source of a woman's sense of self-worth. Middle-aged and elderly Hispanic women retain important roles in their families even after their sons and daughters are married. Grandmothers are ever present and highly vocal in family affairs. Older women have much more status and power than their white American counterparts, who at this age may be suffering from depression due to what has been called the "empty-nest syndrome." Many Hispanic women are providers of mental health services (which sometimes include advice about sexual problems) in an unofficial way as "curanderas," "espiritistas," or "santeras," for those people who believe in these alternative approaches to health care.[4] Some of these women play a powerful role in their communities, thanks to their reputation for being able to heal mind and body.

However, at the same time that Latin women have the opportunity to exercise their power in the areas mentioned above, they also receive constant cultural messages that they should be submissive and subservient to males in order to be seen as "good women." To suffer and be a martyr is also a characteristic of a "good woman." This emphasis on self-renunciation, combined with the importance given to sexual purity for women, has a direct bearing on the development of sexuality in Latin women. To enjoy sexual pleasure, even in marriage, may indicate lack of virtue. To shun sexual pleasure and to regard sexual behavior exclusively as an unwelcome obligation toward her husband and a necessary evil in order to have children may be seen as a manifestation of virtue. In fact, some women even express pride at their own lack of sexual pleasure or desire. Their negative attitudes toward sex are frequently reinforced by the inconsiderate behavior and demands of men.

Body image and related issues are deeply connected with sexuality for all women. Even when body-related problems may not have direct implications for sexuality, the body remains for women the main vehicle for expressing their needs. The high incidence of somatic complaints presented by low-income Hispanic women in psychotherapy might be a consequence of the emphasis on "martyrdom" and self-sacrifice, or it might be a somatic expression of needs and anxieties. More directly related to sexuality are issues of birth control, pregnancy, abortion, menopause, hysterectomy and other gynecological problems. Many of these have traditionally been discussed among women only. To be brought to the attention of a male doctor may be enormously embarrassing and distressing for some of these women. Younger Hispanic women may find themselves challenging traditional sexual mores while struggling with their own conflicts about beauty and their own embarrassment about visiting male doctors.

One of the most common and pervasive stereotypes held about Hispanics is the image of the "macho" man—an image which generally conjures up the rough, tough, swaggering men who are abusive and oppressive towards women, who in turn are seen as being exclusively submissive and long-suffering.[5]

Some authors[6] recognize that "machismo"—which is nothing but the Hispanic version of the myth of male superiority supported by most cultures—is still in existence in the Latin culture, especially among those individuals who subscribe more strongly to traditional Hispanic values. Following this tradition, Latin females are expected to be subordinated to males and to the family. Males are expected to show their manhood by behaving in a strong fashion, by demonstrating sexual prowess and by asserting their authority over women. In many cases, these traditional values may not be enacted behaviorally, but are still supported as valued assumptions concerning male and female "good" behavior. According to Aramoni,[7] himself a Mexican psychologist, "machismo" may be a reaction of Latin males to a series of social conditions, including the effort to exercise control over their ever-present, powerfully demanding, and suffering mothers and to identify with their absent fathers. Adult males continue to respect and revere their mothers, even when they may not show much respect for their wives or other women. As adolescents they may have protected their mothers from fathers' abuse or indifference. As adults they accord their mother a respect that no other woman deserves, thus following their fathers' steps. The mother herself teaches her sons to be dominant and independent in relations with other women. Other psychological and social factors may be influential in the development of "machismo." It is important to remember that not all Latin males exhibit the negative behaviors implied in the "macho" stereotype, and that even when certain individuals do, these behaviors might be a reaction to oppressive social conditions by which Hispanic men too are victimized.

Sexually, "machismo" is expressed through an emphasis on multiple, uncommitted sexual contacts which start in adolescence. In a study of adolescent rituals in Latin America, Espín[8] found that many males celebrated their adolescence by visiting prostitutes. The money to pay for this sexual initiation was usually provided by fathers, uncles or older brothers. Adolescent females, on the other hand, were offered coming-out parties, the rituals of which emphasize their virginal qualities. Somehow, a man is more "macho" if he manages to have sexual relations with a virgin; thus, fathers and brothers watch over young women for fear that other men may make them their sexual prey. These same men, however, will not hesitate to take advantage of the young women in other families. Women, in turn, are seen as capable of surrendering to men's advances, without much awareness of their own decisions on the matter. "Good women" should always say no to a sexual advance. Those who say yes are automatically assumed to be less virtuous by everyone, including the same man with whom they consent to have sex.

Needless to say, sexual understanding and communication between the sexes is practically rendered impossible by these attitudes generated by "machismo." However, not all Hispanics subscribe to this perspective and some reject it outright. In a review of the literature on studies of decision-making patterns in Mexican and Chicano families the authors concluded that "Hispanic males may behave differently from non-Hispanic men in their family and marital lives, but not in the inappropriate fashion suggested by the myth with its strong connotations of social deviance."[9] This article reviews only research on the decision-making process in married couples and, thus, other aspects of male-female relationships in the Hispanic culture are not discussed.

In the context of culturally appropriate sex-roles, mothers train their daughters to remain virgins at all cost, to cater to men's sexual needs and to play "little wives" to their father and brothers from a very early age. If a mother is sick or working outside the home and there are no adult females around, the oldest daughter, no matter how young, will be in charge of caring not only for the younger siblings, but also for the father, who would continue to expect his meals to be cooked and his clothes to be washed.

Training for appropriate heterosexuality, however, is not always assimilated by all Latin women. A seldom-mentioned fact is that, as in all cultures, there are lesbians among Hispanic women. Although emotional and physical closeness among women is encouraged by the culture, overt acknowledgment of lesbianism is even more restricted than in mainstream American society. In a study about lesbians in the Puerto Rican community, Hidalgo and Hidalgo-Christensen found that "rejection of homosexuals appears to be the dominant attitude in the Puerto Rican community."[10] Although this attitude may not seem different from that of the dominant culture, there are some important differences experienced by Latin lesbian women which are directly related to Hispanic cultural patterns. Frequent contact and a strong interdependence among family members, even in adulthood, are essential features of Hispanic family life. Leading a double life becomes more of a strain in this context. "Coming out" may jeopardize not only these strong family ties, but also the possibility of serving the Hispanic community in which the talents of all members are such an important asset. Because most lesbian women are single and self-supporting, and not encumbered by the demands of husbands and children, it can be assumed that the professional experience and educational level of Hispanic lesbians will tend to be relatively high. If this is true, professional experience and education will frequently place Hispanic lesbian women in positions of leadership or advocacy in their community. Their status and prestige, and, thus, the ability to serve their community, are threatened by the possibility of being "found out."

Most "politically aware" Latins show a remarkable lack of understanding of gay-related issues. In a recent meeting of Hispanic women in a major US city, one participant expressed the opinion that "lesbianism is a sickness we get from American women and American culture." This is, obviously, another version of the myth about the free sexuality of American women so prevalent among Hispanics. But it is also an expression of the common belief that homosexuality is chosen behavior, acquired through the bad influence of others, like drug addiction. Socialist attitudes in this respect are extremely traditional, as attitudes of the Cuban revolution towards homosexuality clearly manifest. Thus, Hispanics who consider themselves radical and committed to civil rights remain extremely traditional when it comes to gay rights. These attitudes clearly add further stress to the lives of Latin women who have a homosexual orientation and who are invested in enhancing the lives of members of their communities.

They experience oppression in three ways: as women, as Hispanics and as lesbians. This last form of oppression is in fact experienced most powerfully from inside their own culture. Most Latin women who are lesbians have to remain "closeted" among their families, their colleagues and society at large. To be "out of the closet" only in an Anglo context deprives them of essential supports from their communities and families, and, in turn, increases their invisibility in the Hispanic culture, where only the openly "butch" types are recognized as lesbians. . . .

NOTES

1. J. B. Miller, *Toward a New Psychology of Women*, Boston, Beacon, 1976.

2. Calderón de la Barca, *El Alcalde de Zalamea*.

3. S. Brown, "Love Unites Them and Hunger Separates Them: Poor Women in the Dominican Republic," in Rayna Reiter (ed.), *Toward an Anthropology of Women*, New York, Monthly Review Press, 1975, p. 322.

4. O. M. Espín, "Hispanic Female Healers in Urban Centers in the United States," unpublished manuscript, 1983.

5. V. Abad, J. Ramos, and E. Boyce, "A Model for Delivery of Mental Health Services to Spanish-Speaking Minorities," *American Journal of Orthopsychiatry*, vol. 44, no. 4, 1974, pp. 584–95.

6. E. S. Le Vine and A. M. Padilla, *Crossing Cultures in Therapy: Pluralistic Counseling for the Hispanic*, Monterey, California, Brooks/Cole, 1980.

7. A. Aramoni, "Machismo," *Psychology Today*, vol. 5, no. 8, 1982, pp 69–72.

8. O. M. Espín, "The 'Quinceañeras': A Latin American Expression of Women's Roles," unpublished paper presented at the national meeting of the Latin American Studies Association, Atlanta, 1975.

9. R. E. Cromwell and R. A. Ruiz, "The Myth of 'Macho' Dominance in Decision Making within Mexican and Chicano Families," *Hispanic Journal of Behavioral Sciences*, vol. 1, no. 4, 1979, p. 371.

10. H. Hidalgo and E. Hidalgo-Christensen, "The Puerto Rican Cultural Response to Female Homosexuality," in E. Acosta-Belén (ed.), *The Puerto Rican Woman*, New York, Praeger, 1979, p. 118.

MASCULINITIES AND ATHLETIC CAREERS

19

CAREERS

Michael Messner

The growth of women's studies and feminist gender studies has in recent years led to the emergence of a new men's studies (Brod 1987; Kimmel 1987). But just as feminist perspectives on women have been justifiably criticized for falsely universalizing the lives and issues of white, middle-class, U.S. women (Hooks 1984; Zinn, Cannon, Higginbotham, and Dill 1986), so, too, men's studies has tended to focus on the lives of relatively privileged men. As Brod (1983–1984) points out in an insightful critique of the middle-class basis and bias of the men's movement, if men's studies is to be relevant to minority and working-class men, less emphasis must be placed on personal lifestyle transformations, and more emphasis must be placed on developing a structural critique of social institutions. Although some institutional analysis has begun in men's studies, very little critical scrutiny has been focused on that very masculine institution, organized sports (Messner 1985; Sabo 1985; Sabo and Runfola 1980). Not only is the institution of sports an ideal place to study men and masculinity, careful analysis would make it impossible to ignore the realities of race and class differences.

In the early 1970s, Edwards (1971, 1973) debunked the myth that the predominance of blacks in sports to which they have access signaled an end to institutionalized racism. It is now widely accepted in sport sociology that social institutions such as the media, education, the economy, and (a more recent and controversial addition to the list) the black family itself all serve to systematically channel disproportionately large numbers of young black men into football, basketball, boxing, and baseball, where they are subsequently

From: *Gender & Society* 3 (March 1989): 71–88. Reprinted by permission of Sage Publications, Inc.

Author's note: Parts of this article were presented as papers at the American Sociological Association Annual Meeting, Chicago, in August 1987, and at the North American Society for the Sociology of Sport Annual Meeting in Edmonton, Alberta, in November 1987. I thank Maxine Baca Zinn, Bob Blauner, Bob Dunn, Pierrette Hondagneu-Sotelo, Carol Jacklin, Michael Kimmel, Judith Lorber, Don Sabo, Barrie Thorne, and Carol Warren for constructive comments on earlier versions of this article.

"stacked" into low-prestige and high-risk positions, exploited for their skills, and finally, when their bodies are used up, excreted from organized athletics at a young age with no transferable skills with which to compete in the labor market (Edwards 1984; Eitzen and Purdy 1986; Eitzen and Yetman 1977).

While there are racial differences in involvement in sports, class, age, and educational differences seem more significant. Rudman's (1986) initial analysis revealed profound differences between whites' and blacks' orientations to sports. Blacks were found to be more likely than whites to view sports favorably, to incorporate sports into their daily lives, and to be affected by the outcome of sporting events. However, when age, education, and social class were factored into the analysis, Rudman found that race did not explain whites' and blacks' different orientations. Black's affinity to sports is best explained by their tendency to be clustered disproportionately in lower-income groups.

The 1980s has ushered in what Wellman (1986, p. 43) calls a "new political linguistics of race," which emphasize cultural rather than structural causes (and solutions) to the problems faced by black communities. The advocates of the cultural perspective believe that the high value placed on sports by black communities has led to the development of unrealistic hopes in millions of black youths. They appeal to family and community to bolster other choices based upon a more rational assessment of "reality." Visible black role models in many other professions now exist, they say, and there is ample evidence which proves that sports careers are, at best, a bad gamble.

Critics of the cultural perspective have condemned it as conservative and victim blaming. But it can also be seen as a response to the view of black athletes as little more than unreflexive dupes of an all-powerful system, which ignores the importance of agency. Gruneau (1983) has argued that sports must be examined within a theory that views human beings as active subjects who are operating within historically constituted structural constraints. Gruneau's reflexive theory rejects the simplistic views of sports as either a realm of absolute oppression or an arena of absolute freedom and spontaneity. Instead, he argues, it is necessary to construct an understanding of how and why participants themselves actively make choices and construct and define meaning and a sense of identity within the institutions that they find themselves.

None of these perspectives considers the ways that gender shapes men's definitions of meaning and choices. Within the sociology of sport, gender as a process that interacts with race and class is usually ignored or taken for granted—except when it is *women* athletes who are being studied. Sociologists who are attempting to come to grips with the experiences of black men in general, and in organized sports in particular, have almost exclusively focused their analytic attention on the variable "black," while uncritically taking "men" as a given. Hare and Hare (1984), for example, view masculinity as a biologically determined tendency to act as a provider and protector that is thwarted for black men by socioeconomic and racist obstacles. Staples (1982) does view masculinity largely as a socially produced script, but he accepts this script as a given, preferring to focus on black men's blocked access to male role fulfillment. These perspectives on masculinity fail to show how the male role itself, as it interacts with a constricted structure of opportunity, can contribute to locking black men into destructive relationships and life-styles (Franklin 1984; Majors 1986).

This article will examine the relationships among male identity, race, and social class by listening to the voices of former athletes. I will first briefly describe my research. Then I will discuss the similarities and differences in the choices and experiences of men from different racial and social class backgrounds. Together, these choices and experiences help to construct what Connell (1987) calls "the gender order." Organized sports, it will be suggested, is a practice through which men's separation from and power over women is embodied and naturalized at the same time that hegemonic (white, heterosexual, professional-class) masculinity is clearly differentiated from marginalized and subordinated masculinities.

DESCRIPTION OF RESEARCH

Between 1983 and 1985, I conducted 30 open-ended, in-depth interviews with male former athletes. My purpose was to add a critical understanding of male gender identity to Levinson's (1978) conception of the "individual lifecourse"—specifically, to discover how masculinity develops and changes as a man interacts with the socially constructed world of organized sports. Most of the men I interviewed had played the U.S. "major sports"—football, basketball, baseball, track. At the time of the interview, each had been retired from playing organized sports for at least 5 years. Their ages ranged from 21 to 48, with the median, 33. Fourteen were black, 14 were white, and 2 were Hispanic. Fifteen of the 16 black and Hispanic men had come from poor or working-class families, while the majority (9 of 14) of the white men had come from middle-class or professional families. Twelve had played organized sports through high school, 11 through college, and 7 had been professional athletes. All had at some time in their lives based their identities largely on their roles as athletes and could therefore be said to have had athletic careers.

MALE IDENTITY AND ORGANIZED SPORTS

Earlier studies of masculinity and sport argued that sports socialize boys to be men (Lever 1976; Schafer 1975). Here, boys learn cultural values and behaviors, such as competition, toughness, and winning at all costs, that are culturally valued aspects of masculinity. While offering important insights, these early studies of masculinity and sports suffered from the limiting assumptions of a gender-role theory that seems to assume that boys come to their first athletic experience as blank slates onto which the values of masculinity are imprinted. This perspective oversimplifies a complex reality. In fact, young boys bring an already gendered identity to their first sports experiences, an identity that is struggling to work through the developmental task of individuation (Chodorow 1978; Gilligan 1982). Yet, as Benjamin (1988) has argued, individuation is accomplished, paradoxically, only through relationships with other people in the social world. So, although the major task of masculinity is the development of a "positional identity" that clarifies the boundaries between self and other, this separation must be accomplished through some form of connection with others. For the men in my study, the rule-bound structure of organized sports became a context in which they struggled to construct a masculine positional identity.

All of the men in this study described the emotional salience of their earliest experiences in sports in terms of relationships with other males. It was not winning and victories that seemed important at first; it was something "fun" to do with fathers, older brothers or uncles, and eventually with same-aged peers. As a man from a white, middle-class family said, "The most important thing was just being out there with the rest of the guys—being friends." A 32-year-old man from a poor Chicano family, whose mother had died when he was 9 years old, put it more succinctly:

> What I think sports did for me is it brought me into kind of an instant family. By being on a Little League team, or even just playing with kids in the neighborhood, it brought what I really wanted, which was some kind of closeness.

Though sports participation may have initially promised "some kind of closeness," by the ages of 9 or 10, the less skilled boys were already becoming alienated from—or weeded out of—the highly competitive and hierarchical system of organized sports. Those who did experience some early successes received recognition from adult males (especially fathers and older brothers) and held higher status among peers. As a result, they began to pour more and more of their energies into athletic participation. It was only after they learned that they would get recognition from other people for being a good athlete—indeed, that this attention was contingent upon *being a winner*—that performance and winning (the dominant values of organized sports) became extremely important. For some, this created pressures that served to lessen or eliminated the fun of athletic participation (Messner 1987a, 1987b).

While feminist psychoanalytic and developmental theories of masculinity are helpful in explaining boys' early attraction and motivations in organized sports, the imperatives of core gender identity do not fully determine the contours and directions of the life course. As Rubin (1985) and Levinson (1978) have pointed out, an understanding of the lives of men must take into account the processual nature of male identity as it unfolds through interaction between the internal (psychological ambivalences) and the external (social, historical, and institutional) contexts.

To examine the impact of the social contexts, I divided my sample into two comparison groups. In the first group were 10 men from higher-status backgrounds, primarily white, middle-class, and professional families. In the second group were 20 men from lower-status backgrounds, primarily minority, poor, and working-class families. While my data offered evidence for the similarity of experiences and motivations of men from poor backgrounds, independent of race, I also found anecdotal evidence of a racial dynamic that operates independently of social class. However, my sample was not large enough to separate race and class, and so I have combined them to make two status groups.

In discussing these two groups, I will focus mainly on the high school years. During this crucial period, the athletic role may become a master status for a young man, and he is beginning to make assessments and choices about his future. It is here that many young men make a major commitment to—or begin to back away from—athletic careers.

Men from Higher-Status Backgrounds

The boyhood dream of one day becoming a professional athlete—a dream shared by nearly all the men interviewed in this study—is rarely realized. The sports world is extremely hierarchical. The pyramid of sports careers narrows very rapidly as one climbs from high school, to college, to professional levels of competition (Edwards 1984; Harris and Eitzen 1978; Hill and Lowe 1978). In fact, the chances of attaining professional status in sports are approximately 4/100,000 for a white man, 2/100,000 for a black man, and 3/100,000 for a Hispanic man in the United States (Leonard and Reyman 1988). For many young athletes, their dream ends early when coaches inform them that they are not big enough, strong enough, fast enough, or skilled enough to compete at the higher levels. But six of the higher-status men I interviewed did not wait for coaches to weed them out. They made conscious decisions in high school or in college to shift their attentions elsewhere—usually toward educational and career goals. Their decision not to pursue an athletic career appeared to them in retrospect to be a rational decision based on the growing knowledge of how very slim their chances were to be successful in the sports world. For instance, a 28-year-old white graduate student said:

> By junior high I started to realize that I was a good player—maybe even one of the best in my community—but I realized that there were all these people all over the country and how few will get to play pro sports. By high school, I still dreamed of being a pro—I was a serious athlete, I played hard—but I knew it wasn't heading anywhere. I wasn't going to play pro ball.

A 32-year-old white athletic director at a small private college had been a successful college baseball player. Despite considerable attention from professional scouts, he had decided to forgo a shot at a baseball career and to enter graduate school to pursue a teaching credential. As he explained this decision:

> At the time I think I saw baseball as pissing in the wind, really. I was married, I was 22 years old with a kid. I didn't want to spend 4 or 5 years in the minors with a family. And I could see I wasn't a superstar; so it wasn't really worth it. So I went to grad school. I thought that would be better for me.

Perhaps most striking was the story of a high school student body president and top-notch student who was also "Mr. Everything" in sports. He was named captain of his basketball, baseball, and football teams and achieved All-League honors in each sport. This young white man from a middle-class family received attention from the press and praise from his community and peers for his athletic accomplishments, as well as several offers of athletic scholarships from universities. But by the time he completed high school, he had already decided to quit playing organized sports. As he said:

> I think in my own mind I kind of downgraded the stardom thing. I thought that was small potatoes. And sure, that's nice in high school and all that, but on a broad scale, I didn't think it amounted to all that much. So I decided that my goal's to be a dentist, as soon as I can.

In his sophomore year of college, the basketball coach nearly persuaded him to go out for the team, but eventually he decided against it:

> I thought, so what if I can spend two years playing basketball? I'm not going to be a basketball player forever and I might jeopardize my chances of getting into dental school if I play.

He finished college in three years, completed dental school, and now, in his mid-30s, is again the epitome of the successful American man: a professional with a family, a home, and a membership in the local country club.

How and why do so many successful male athletes from higher-status backgrounds come to view sports careers as "pissing in the wind," or as "small potatoes"? How and why do they make this early assessment and choice to shift from sports and toward educational and professional goals? The white, middle-class institutional context, with its emphasis on education and income, makes it clear to them that choices exist and that the pursuit of an athletic career is not a particularly good choice to make. Where the young male once found sports to be a convenient institution within which to construct masculine status, the postadolescent and young adult man from a higher-status background simply *transfers* these same strivings to other institutional contexts: education and careers.

For the higher-status men who had chosen to shift from athletic careers, sports remained important on two levels. First, having been a successful high school or college athlete enhances one's adult status among other men in the community —but only as a badge of masculinity that is *added* to his professional status. In fact, several men in professions chose to be interviewed in their offices, where they publicly displayed the trophies and plaques that attested to their earlier athletic accomplishments. Their high school and college athletic careers may have appeared to them as "small potatoes," but many successful men speak of their earlier status as athletes as having "opened doors" for them in their present professions and in community affairs. Similarly, Farr's (1988) research on "Good Old Boys Sociability Groups" shows how sports, as part of the glue of masculine culture, continues to facilitate "dominance bonding" among privileged men long after active sports careers end. The college-educated, career-successful men in Farr's study rarely express overtly sexist, racist, or classist attitudes; in fact, in their relationships with women, they "often engage in expressive intimacies" and "make fun of exaggerated 'machismo' " (p. 276). But though they outwardly conform more to what Pleck (1982) calls "the modern male role," their informal relationships within their sociability groups, in effect, affirm their own gender and class status by constructing and clarifying the boundaries between themselves and women and lower-status men. This dominance bonding is based largely upon ritual forms of sociability (camaraderie, competition), "the superiority of which was first affirmed in the exclusionary play activities of young boys in groups" (Farr 1988, p. 265).

In addition to contributing to dominance bonding among higher-status adult men, sports remains salient in terms of the ideology of gender relations. Most men continued to watch, talk about, and identify with sports long after their own disengagement from athletic careers. Sports as a mediated spectacle provides an important context in which traditional conceptions of masculine superiority—conceptions recently contested by women—are shored up. As a 32-year-old white professional-class man said of one of the most feared professional football players today:

> A woman can do the same job as I can do—maybe even be my boss. But I'll be *damned* if she can go out on the football field and take a hit from Ronnie Lott.

Violent sports as spectacle provide linkages among men in the project of the domination of women, while at the same time helping to construct and clarify differences among various masculinities. The statement above is a clear identification with Ronnie Lott *as a man*, and the basis of the identification is the violent male body. As Connell (1987, p. 85) argues, sports is an important organizing institution for the embodiment of masculinity. Here, men's power over women becomes naturalized and linked to the social distribution of violence. Sports, as a practice, suppresses natural (sex) similarities, constructs differences, and then, largely through the media, weaves a structure of symbol and interpretation around these differences that naturalizes them (Hargreaves 1986, p. 112). It is also significant that the man who made the above statement about Ronnie Lott was quite aware that he (and perhaps 99 percent of the rest of the U.S. male population) was probably as incapable as most women of taking a "hit" from someone like Lott and living to tell of it. For middle-class men, the "tough guys" of the culture industry—the Rambos, the Ronnie Lotts who are fearsome "hitters," who "play hurt"—are the heroes who "prove" that "we men" are superior to women. At the same time, they play the role of the "primitive other," against whom higher-status men define themselves as "modern" and "civilized."

Sports, then, is important from boyhood through adulthood for men from higher-status backgrounds. But it is significant that by adolescence and early adulthood, most of these young men have concluded that sports *careers* are not for them. Their middle-class cultural environment encourages them to decide to shift their masculine strivings in more "rational" directions: education and nonsports careers. Yet their previous sports participation continues to be very important to them in terms of constructing and validating their status within privileged male peer groups and within their chosen professional careers. And organized sports, as a public spectacle, is a crucial locus around which ideologies of male superiority over women, as well as higher-status men's superiority over lower-status men, are constructed and naturalized.

Men from Lower-Status Backgrounds

For the lower-status young men in this study, success in sports was not an added proof of masculinity; it was often their only hope of achieving public masculine status. A 34-year-old black bus driver who had been a star athlete in three sports in high school had neither the grades nor the money to attend college, so he accepted an offer from the U.S. Marine Corps to play on their baseball team. He ended up in Vietnam, where a grenade blew four fingers off his pitching hand. In retrospect, he believed that his youthful focus on sports stardom and his concomitant lack of effort in academics made sense:

> You can go anywhere with athletics—you don't have to have brains. I mean, I didn't feel like I was gonna go out there and be a computer expert, or something that was gonna make a lot of money. The only thing I could do and live comfortably would be to play sports—just to get a contract—doesn't matter if you play second or third team in the pros, you're gonna make big bucks. That's all I wanted, a confirmed livelihood at the end of my ventures, and the only way I could do it would be through sports. So I tried. It failed, but that's what I tried.

Similar, and even more tragic, is the story of a 34-year-old black man who is now serving a life term in prison. After a career-ending knee injury at the age of 20 abruptly ended what had appeared to be a certain road to professional football fame and fortune, he decided that he "could still be rich and famous" by robbing a bank. During his high school and college years, he said, he was nearly illiterate:

> I'd hardly ever go to classes and they'd give me Cs. My coaches taught some of the classes. And I felt, "So what? They *owe* me that! I'm an *athlete!* I thought that was what I was born to do—to play sports—and everybody understood that.

Are lower-status boys and young men simply duped into putting all their eggs into one basket? My research suggested that there was more than "hope for the future" operating here. There were also immediate psychological reasons that they chose to pursue athletic careers. By the high school years, class and ethnic inequalities had become glaringly obvious, especially for those who attended socioeconomically heterogeneous schools. Cars, nice clothes, and other signs of status were often unavailable to these young men, and this contributed to a situation in which sports took on an expanded importance for them in terms of constructing masculine identities and status. A white, 36-year-old man from a poor, single-parent family who later played professional baseball had been acutely aware of his low-class status in his high school:

> I had one pair of jeans, and I wore them every day. I was always afraid of what people thought of me—that this guy doesn't have anything, that he's wearing the same Levi's all the time, he's having to work in the cafeteria for his lunch. What's going on? I think that's what made me so shy. . . . But boy, when I got into sports, I let it all hang out—[laughs]—and maybe that's why I became so good, because I was frustrated, and when I got into that element, they gave me my uniform in football, basketball, and baseball, and I didn't have to worry about how I looked, because then it was *me* who was coming out, and not my clothes or whatever. And I think that was the drive.

Similarly, a 41-year-old black man who had a 10-year professional football career described his insecurities as one of the few poor blacks in a mostly white, middle-class school and his belief that sports was the one arena in which he could be judged solely on his merit:

> I came from a poor family, and I was very sensitive about that in those days. When people would say things like "Look at him—he has dirty pants on," I'd think about it for a week. [But] I'd put my pants on and I'd go out on the football field with the intention that I'm gonna do a job. And if that calls on me to hurt you, I'm gonna do it. It's as simple as that. I demand respect just like everybody else.

"Respect" was what I heard over and over when talking with the men from lower-status backgrounds, especially black men. I interpret this type of respect to be a crystallization of the masculine quest for recognition through public achievement, unfolding within a system of structured constraints due to class and race inequities. The institutional context of education (sometimes with the collusion of teachers and coaches) and the constricted structure of opportunity in the economy made the pursuit of athletic careers appear to be the most rational choice to these young men.

The same is not true of young lower-status women. Dunkle (1985) points out that from junior high school through adulthood, young black men are far more likely to place high value on sports than are young black women, who are more likely to value academic achievement. There appears to be a gender dynamic operating in adolescent male peer groups that contributes toward their valuing sports more highly than education. Franklin (1986, p. 161) has argued that many of the normative values of the black male peer group (little respect for nonaggressive solutions to disputes, contempt for nonmaterial culture) contribute to the constriction of black men's views of desirable social positions, especially through education. In my study, a 42-year-old black man who did succeed in beating the odds by using his athletic scholarship to get a college degree and eventually becoming a successful professional said:

> By junior high, you either got identified as an athlete, a thug, or a book-worm. It's very important to be seen as somebody who's capable in some area. And you *don't* want to be identified as a bookworm. I was very good with books, but I was kind of covert about it. I was a closet bookworm. But with sports, I was *somebody;* so I worked very hard at it.

For most young men from lower-status backgrounds, the poor quality of their schools, the attitudes of teachers and coaches, as well as the antieducation environment within their own male peer groups, made it extremely unlikely that they would be able to succeed as students. Sports, therefore, became *the* arena in which they attempted to "show their stuff." For these lower-status men, as Baca Zinn (1982) and Majors (1986) argued in their respective studies of chicano men and black men, when institutional resources that signify masculine status and control are absent, physical presence, personal style, and expressiveness take on increased importance. What Majors (1986, p. 6) calls "cool pose" is black men's expressive, often aggressive, assertion of masculin-ity. This self-assertion often takes place within a social context in which the young man is quite aware of existing social inequities. As the black bus driver, referred to above, said of his high school years:

> See, the rich people use their money to do what they want to do. I use my ability. If you wanted to be around me, if you wanted to learn something about sports, I'd teach you. But you're gonna take me to lunch. You're gonna let me use your car. See what I'm saying? In high school I'd go where I wanted to go. I didn't have to be educated. I was well-respected. I'd go some-where, and they'd say, "Hey, that's Mitch Harris,[1] yeah, that's a bad son of a bitch!'

Majors (1986) argues that although "cool pose" represents a creative survival technique within a hostile environment, the most likely long-term effect of this masculine posturing is educational and occupational dead ends. As a result, we can conclude, lower-status men's personal and peer-group responses to a constricted structure of opportunity—responses that are rooted, in part, in the developmental insecurities and ambivalences of mas-culinity—serve to lock many of these young men into limiting activities such as sports.

SUMMARY AND CONCLUSIONS

This research has suggested that within a social context that is stratified by social class and by race, the choice to pursue—or not to pursue—an athletic career is explicable as an individual's rational assessment of the available means to achieve a respected masculine identity. For nearly all of the men from lower-status backgrounds, the status and respect that they received through sports was temporary—it did not translate into upward mobility. Nonetheless, a strategy of discouraging young black boys and men from involvement in sports is probably doomed to fail, since it ignores the continued existence of structural constraints. Despite the increased number of black role models in nonsports professions, employment opportunities for young black males have actually deteriorated in the 1980s (Wilson and Neckerman 1986), and nonathletic opportunities in higher education have also declined. While blacks constitute 14 percent of the college-aged (18–24 years) U.S. population, as a proportion of students in four-year colleges and universities, they have dropped to 8 percent. In contrast, by 1985, black men constituted 49 percent of all college basketball players and 61 percent of basketball players in institutions that grant athletic scholarships (Berghorn et al., 1988). For young black men, then, organized sports appears to be more likely to get them to college than their own efforts in nonathletic activities.

But it would be a mistake to conclude that we simply need to breed socioeconomic conditions that make it possible for poor and minority men to mimic the "rational choices" of white, middle-class men. If we are to build an appropriate understanding of the lives of all men, we must critically analyze white middle-class masculinity, rather than uncritically taking it as a normative standard. To fail to do this would be to ignore the ways in which organized sports serves to construct and legitimate gender differences and inequalities among men and women.

Feminist scholars have demonstrated that organized sports gives men from all backgrounds a means of status enhancement that is not available to young women. Sports thus serve the interests of all men in helping to construct and legitimize their control of public life and their domination of women (Bryson 1987; Hall 1987; Theberge 1987). Yet concrete studies are suggesting that men's experiences within sports are not all of a piece. Brian Pronger's (1990) research suggests that gay men approach sports differently than straight men do, with a sense of "irony." And my research suggests that although sports are important for men from both higher- and lower-status backgrounds, there are crucial differences. In fact, it appears that the meaning that most men give to their athletic strivings has more to do with competing for status among men than it has to do with proving superiority over women. How can we explain this seeming contradiction between the feminist claim that sports links all men in the domination of women and the research findings that different groups of men relate to sports in very different ways?

The answer to this question lies in developing a means of conceptualizing the interrelationships between varying forms of domination and subordination. Marxist scholars of sports often falsely collapse everything into a class analysis; radical feminists often see gender domination as universally fundamental. Concrete examinations of sports, however, reveal complex and multilayered systems of inequality: Racial, class, gender, sexual preference, and age dynamics are all salient features of the athletic context. In examining this reality, Connell's (1987) concept of the "gender order" is useful. The gender order is a dynamic process that is constantly in a state of play. Moving beyond static gender-role theory and reductionist concepts of patriarchy that view men as an undifferentiated group which oppresses women, Connell argues that at any given historical moment, there are competing masculinities—some hegemonic, some marginalized, some stigmatized. Hegemonic masculinity (that definition of masculinity which is culturally ascendant) is constructed in relation to various subordinated masculinities as well as in relation to femininities. The project of male domination of women may tie all men together, but men share very unequally in the fruits of this domination.

These are key insights in examining the contemporary meaning of sports. Utilizing the concept of the gender order, we can begin to conceptualize how hierarchies of race, class, age, and sexual preference among men help to construct and legitimize men's overall power and privilege over women. And how, for some black, working-class, or gay men, the false promise of sharing in the fruits of hegemonic masculinity often ties them into their marginalized and subordinate statuses within hierarchies of intermale dominance. For instance, black men's development of what Majors (1986) calls "cool pose" within sports can be interpreted as an example of creative resistance to one form of social domination (racism); yet it also demonstrates the limits of an agency that adopts other forms of social domination (masculinity) as its vehicle. As Majors (1990) points out:

> Cool Pose demonstrates black males' potential to transcend oppressive conditions in order to express themselves *as men.* [Yet] it ultimately does not put black males in a position to live and work in more egalitarian ways with women, nor does it directly challenge male hierarchies.

Indeed, as Connell's (1990) analysis of an Australian "Iron Man" shows, the commercially successful, publicly acclaimed athlete may embody all that is valued in present cultural conceptions of hegemonic masculinity—physical strength, commercial success, supposed heterosexual virility. Yet higher-status men, while they admire the public image of the successful athlete, may also look down on him as a narrow, even atavistic, example of masculinity. For these higher-status men, their earlier sports successes are often status enhancing and serve to link them with other men in ways that continue to exclude women. Their decisions not to pursue athletic careers are equally important signs of their status vis-à-vis other men. Future examinations of the contemporary meaning and importance of sports to men might take as a fruitful point of departure that athletic participation, and sports as public spectacle serve to provide linkages among men in the project of the domination of women, while at the same time helping to construct and clarify differences and hierarchies among various masculinities.

NOTE

1. "Mitch Harris" is a pseudonym.

REFERENCES

Benjamin, J. 1988. *The Bonds of Love: Psychoanalysis, Feminism, and the Problem of Domination.* New York: Pantheon.

Berghorn, F. J. et al. 1988. "Racial Participation in Men's and Women's Intercollegiate Basketball: Continuity and Change, 1958–1985." *Sociology of Sport Journal* 5:107–24.

Brod, H. 1983–84. "Work Clothes and Leisure Suits: The Class Basis and Bias of the Men's Movement." *M: Gentle Men for Gender Justice* 11:10–12, 38–40.

Brod, H. (ed.). 1987. *The Making of Masculinities: The New Men's Studies.* Winchester, MA: Allen & Unwin.

Bryson, L. 1987. "Sport and the Maintenance of Masculine Hegemony." *Women's Studies International Forum* 10:349–60.

Chodorow, N. 1978. *The Reproduction of Mothering.* Berkeley: University of California Press.

Connell, R. W. 1987. *Gender and Power.* Stanford, CA: Stanford University Press.

———. 1990. "An Iron Man: The Body and Some Contradictions of Hegemonic Masculinity." In *Sport, Men, and the Gender Order: Critical Feminist Perspectives,* edited by M. A. Messner and D. S. Sabo. Champaign, IL: Human Kinetics.

Dunkle, M. 1985. "Minority and Low-Income Girls and Young Women in Athletics." *Equal Play* 5(Spring-Summer):12–13.

Duquin, M. 1984 "Power and Authority: Moral Consensus and Conformity in Sport." *International Review for Sociology of Sport* 19:295–304.

Edwards, H. 1971. "The Myth of the Racially Superior Athlete." *The Black Scholar* 3(November).

———. 1973. *The Sociology of Sport*. Homewood, IL: Dorsey.

———. 1984. "The Collegiate Athletic Arms Race: Origins and Implications of the 'Rule 48' Controversy." *Journal of Sport and Social Issues* 8:4–22.

Eitzen, D. S. and D. A. Purdy, 1986. "The Academic Preparation and Achievement of Black and White College Athletes." *Journal of Sport and Social Issues* 10:15–29.

Eitzen, D. S. and N. B. Yetman. 1977. "Immune From Racism?" *Civil Rights Digest* 9:3–13.

Farr, K. A. 1988. "Dominance Bonding Through the Good Old Boys Sociability Group." *Sex Roles* 18:259–77.

Franklin, C. W. II. 1984. *The Changing Definition of Masculinity*. New York: Plenum.

———. 1986. "Surviving the Institutional Decimation of Black Males: Causes, Consequences, and Intervention." Pp. 155–70 in *The Making of Masculinities: The New Men's Studies*, edited by H. Brod. Winchester, MA: Allen & Unwin.

Gilligan, C. 1982. *In a Different Voice: Psychological Theory and Women's Development*. Cambridge, MA: Harvard University Press.

Gruneau, R. 1983. *Class, Sports, and Social Development*. Amherst: University of Massachusetts Press.

Hall, M. A. (ed.). 1987. "The Gendering of Sport, Leisure, and Physical Education." *Women's Studies International Forum* 10:361–474.

Hare, N. and J. Hare. 1984. *The Endangered Black Family: Coping With the Unisexualization and Coming Extinction of the Black Race*. San Francisco, CA: Black Think Tank.

Hargreaves, J. A. 1986. "Where's the Virtue? Where's the Grace? A Discussion of the Social Production of Gender Through Sport." *Theory, Culture and Society* 3:109–21.

Harris, D. S. and D. S. Eitzen. 1978. "The Consequences of Failure in Sport." *Urban Life* 7:177–88.

Hill, P. and B. Lowe. 1978. "The Inevitable Metathesis of the Retiring Athlete." *International Review of Sport Sociology* 9:5–29.

Hooks, B. 1984. *Feminist Theory: From Margin to Center*. Boston: South End Press.

Kimmel, M. S. (ed.). 1987. *Changing Men: New Directions in Research on Men and Masculinity*. Newbury Park, CA: Sage.

Leonard, W. M. II and J. M. Reyman. 1988. "The Odds of Attaining Professional Athlete Status: Refining the Computations." *Sociology of Sport Journal* 5:162–69.

Lever, J. 1976. "Sex Differences in the Games Children Play." *Social Problems* 23: 478–87.

Levinson, D. J. 1978. *The Seasons of a Man's Life*. New York: Ballantine.

Majors, R. 1986. "Cool Pose: The Proud Signature of Black Survival." *Changing Men: Issues in Gender, Sex, and Politics* 17:5–6.

———. 1990. "Cool Pose: Black Masculinity in Sports." In *Sport, Men, and the Gender Order: Critical Feminist Perspectives*, edited by M. A. Messner and D. S. Sabo. Champaign, IL: Human Kinetics.

Messner, M. 1985. "The Changing Meaning of Male Identity in the Lifecourse of the Athlete." *Arena Review* 9:31–60.

———. 1987a. "The Meaning of Success: The Athletic Experience and the Development of Male Identity." Pp. 193–209 in *The Making of Masculinities: The New Men's Studies*, edited by H. Brod. Winchester, MA: Allen & Unwin.

———. 1987b. "The Life of a Man's Seasons: Male Identity in the Lifecourse of the Athlete." Pp. 53–67 in *Changing Men: New Directions in Research on Men and Masculinity*, edited by M. S. Kimmel. Newbury Park, CA: Sage.

Pleck, J. H. 1982. *The Myth of Masculinity*. Cambridge: MIT Press.

Pronger, B. 1990. "Gay Jocks: A Phenomenology of Gay Men in Athletics." In *Sport, Men, and the Gender Order: Critical Feminist Perspectives*, edited by M. A. Messner and D. S. Sabo. Champaign, IL: Human Kinetics.

Rubin, L. B. 1985. *Just Friends: The Role of Friendship in Our Lives*. New York: Harper & Row.

Rudman, W. J. 1986. "The Sport Mystique in Black Culture." *Sociology of Sport Journal* 3:305–19.

Sabo, D. 1985. "Sport, Patriarchy, and Male Identity: New Questions About Men and Sport." *Arena Review* 9:1–30.

Sabo, D. and R. Runfola (eds.). 1980. *Jocks: Sports and Male Identity*. Englewood Cliffs, NJ: Prentice-Hall.

Schafer, W. E. 1975. "Sport and Male Sex Role Socialization." *Sport Sociology Bulletin* 4:17–54.

Staples, R. 1982. *Black Masculinity*. San Francisco, CA: Black Scholar Press.

Theberge, N. 1987. "Sport and Women's Empowerment." *Women's Studies International Forum* 10:387–93.

Wellman, D. 1986. "The New Political Linguistics of Race." *Socialist Review* 87/88:43–62.

Wilson, W. J. and K. M. Neckerman. 1986. "Poverty and Family Structure: The Widening Gap Between Evidence and Public Policy Issues." Pp. 232–59 in *Fighting Poverty*, edited by S. H. Danzinger and D. H. Weinberg. Cambridge, MA: Harvard University Press.

Zinn, M. Baca. 1982. "Chicano Men and Masculinity." *Journal of Ethnic Studies* 10:29–44.

Zinn, M. Baca, L. Weber Cannon, E. Higginbotham, and B. Thornton Dill. 1986. "The Costs of Exclusionary Practices in Women's Studies." *Signs: Journal of Women in Culture and Society* 11:290–303.

ASIAN AMERICAN WOMEN: NOT FOR SALE

20

Tracy Lai

Asian American women are not for sale. We will not be bought off, materially or otherwise. We say this to the white men who use the mail-order bride catalogues, hoping to buy an obedient Asian wife. But we also say this to anyone who participates in the long history of stereotyping Asian peoples and cultures as inferior and exotic. Stereotypes dehumanize people and turn them into objects to be manipulated.

It is a struggle to be an Asian in America. Historically, Asians have been denied political, economic and social equality in America. The very term

From: Jo Whitehorse Cochran, Donna Langston, and Carolyn Woodward (eds.), *Changing Our Power: An Introduction to Women's Studies* (Dubuque, Iowa: Kendall-Hunt, 1988), pp. 120–127. Reprinted by permission.

"Asian American" carries a political assertion that Asians have been and continue to be a legitimate and integral part of American society. We are not forever foreign with an identity attached only to an Asian country. The Asian American movement has its origins in the social uprising of the 1960s and '70s, inspired by the black liberation movement. Chinese Americans, Japanese Americans, Pilipino Americans and Korean Americans united in recognition of a common history of oppression and common goals of community empowerment and pride. Asian American women played a leading role, drawing from the strength of their Vietnamese sisters in the National Liberation Front. The racist war abroad in Vietnam had its counterpart back home. Asian American communities fought the enemy at home, raising such issues as bilingual-bicultural education, ethnic studies, and low-income housing. Today, that quest for equality and political power continues. And Asian American women continue to be an important part of that struggle. The urgency of this struggle is reflected in the rising incidence of anti-Asian violence. *Pacific Citizen*, newspaper of the Japanese American Citizens League, reported the tragic death in February, 1984, of Ly Yung Cheung, a seamstress in New York's Chinatown. She was pushed into the path of an oncoming subway train and was decapitated. Her attacker, John Cardinale, reportedly shouted, "we're even" and later based his defense on a "psychotic phobia about Orientals."

What makes this struggle even more complicated is the die-hard myth that Asians have made it. We are told we have overcome our oppression, and that therefore we are the model minority. *Model* refers to the cherished dictum of capitalism that "pulling hard on your bootstraps" brings due rewards. The lesson drawn is that if you work hard enough, you will succeed—and if you don't succeed, you must not be working hard enough. High-profile Asian American women such as Connie Chung, a national television newscaster with a six-figure salary, are promoted as examples of Asian American success stories. But such examples, while certainly remarkable, do little to illuminate the actual conditions of the majority of Asian Americans. Such examples conceal the more typical Asian American experience of unemployment, underemployment and struggle to survive.

The model minority myth thus classically scapegoats Asian Americans. It labels us in a way that dismisses the real problems that many do face, while at the same time pitting Asians against other oppressed people of color. The fact that Asian Americans lack political representation, power and community control conveniently disappears. Model minority labelling has also given rise to an insidious cultural hierarchy. The concept of cultural deprivation implies that black, Latino, and American Indian cultures lack the cultural reinforcements that lead to successful achievement in education and career advancement, and hence to higher socioeconomic levels. For example, Asians are claimed to value education more than other minorities and to have special intellectual affinities for math and science. In fact, this is a racist rationale implying the intellectual inferiority of other minorities, while ignoring important historical and class differences in backgrounds. The cultural deprivation and model minority analyses also fail to examine capitalism as an economic system that thrives on exploitation by class, sex and race. The lack of success of other minority groups and women of all races is deliberate and necessary under capitalism. Profits for capitalism come from the low wages justified in sexist and racist terms.

A MULTIFACETED COMMUNITY

The forces shaping the experience of Asian American women come out of the historical policies of the U.S. toward Asians. These policies were largely aimed at using and discarding Asians as a temporary, cheap labor pool. Thus, young Asian men were desirable while Asian women were not, especially since women would bear children who could legally claim citizenship rights in the United States. Asian Americans are united by our oppression. The racist claim that all Asians look alike could more accurately be stated, "treat all Asians as if they were alike." We are denied respect for our cultural identities, and in the American eye, Asia and the Pacific merge into a single cultural entity. No matter how many generations we have lived in America, we are assumed to be foreigners. The 1980 Census counted more than 20 separate Asian and Pacific nationalities in the United States. The total number of Asian Americans is approximately 3.7 million, or 1.6 percent of the population, mostly concentrated in the western United States. The largest nationality groups, in decreasing order, are Chinese, Pilipino, Japanese, Asian Indian, Korean, and Vietnamese. Others include Hmong, Laotian, (native) Hawaiian, Samoan, Guamanian, Marshallese, and Micronesian. Each of these nationalities has a unique history and culture. However, common to all has been the history of U.S. intervention. Beginning in the nineteenth century, the U.S. followed Britain's example, forcing China and then Japan to open their doors to trade and immigration. Eventually, the U.S. sought to dominate the Pacific and Asia for trade and military purposes. As a consequence, the U.S. annexed, occupied or otherwise dominated Hawaii, the Micronesian Islands, the Philippines, South Korea, Vietnam, and Kampuchea.

Immigration of Asian and Pacific people has been heavily shaped by the nature of U.S. involvement in their countries. Today, the highest rate of immigration for Asians is from South Korea and the Philippines, two countries that are heavily dominated by U.S. capital and are occupied by strategic U.S.

military bases. According to the *Seattle Times* (November 15, 1983), the U.S. maintains 38,882 military personnel in South Korea, 15,123 in the Philippines, 48,496 in Japan, 8,959 in Guam, and 23,214 at sea near Asia. The U.S. military bases have a devastating impact on the local Asian women, one that spills over to Asian American women as American military men bring back stereotypes and expectations of conquest. For instance, U.S. bases generate a huge prostitution business, reinforcing the stereotype that Asian women seek fulfillment through serving men.

Historically, the U.S. has also maintained discriminatory immigration policies explicitly aimed at controlling and eliminating the Asian population in the United States. The first wave of Chinese immigrants arrived in the 1850s, but by 1882, an organized movement of trade unions and opportunistic politicians secured the Chinese Exclusion Act which prohibited immigration of Chinese laborers and their wives. Thus, families were curtailed, wives effectively abandoned in China, and an entire generation of Chinese "bachelors" were trapped in the United States. Violent killings and expulsions followed in the wake of this legislation, such as the 1885–86 expulsions of the Chinese communities from Tacoma and Seattle, Washington. The Chinese were wanted for their labor but they were considered undesirable and unassimilable for settlement. The Chinese and, later, other Asians were accused of stealing white workers' jobs and lowering the standard of living. In fact, Asians performed work that white workers refused to do, and Asians had to be recruited to fill the labor shortage of the westward expansion. Their labor laid the foundation for the industrial and agricultural wealth of the West today.

Japanese, Korean and Pilipino workers followed in successive waves, filling one another's footsteps in low-paying, low-status jobs. In turn, each faced similarly hostile accusations and blame for downturns in the economy. Recruited for the sugar plantations in the 1800s, the Japanese immigrated to Hawaii, and subsequently to the mainland. The anti-Chinese movement reorganized itself as the Asiatic Exclusion League [i]n 1905, dedicated to the preservation of the Caucasian race upon American soil. In 1924 the League successfully passed the National Origins Act which barred immigration of all Asians. Only the Pilipinos remained problematic. Pilipinos were considered nationals, since the U.S. had seized the Philippines during the Spanish-American War of 1898. As nationals, they were exempt from exclusionary immigration laws. After 1924, Pilipinos were a primary source of labor and, as their numbers increased, so did white hostility. In 1929 and 1930, anti-Pilipino riots erupted all along the west coast. The Tydings-McDuffie Act of 1934 ostensibly granted independence to the Philippines but its real purpose was to limit the immigration quota of Pilipinos to 50 per year.

In many ways, these exclusionary laws were aimed at Asian women to prevent the development of families and communities. By keeping Asian women from immigrating, and by passing anti-miscegenation laws, it was hoped that the largely male Asian labor force would eventually die out. A common theme in the anti-Asian propaganda threatened destruction of America through an invasion of the "yellow hordes" or the "yellow peril." Asian American women were described as breeding like rats. This stereotype continues into the present in the form of the "Oriental Beauty" who has extraordinary sexual powers. To raise families and to build communities under such conditions become acts of resistance.

A more recent example of U.S. foreign policy impacting Asian Americans is the resettlement in the United States of 760,854 Southeast Asians between 1975–1985. Over half are Vietnamese; the rest are nearly evenly divided between Laotians and Kampucheans. They are all refugees created by the U.S. imperialist war in Southeast Asia, which raged from the 1950s to 1975. These newer Asian Americans have borne the brunt of the anti-Asian violence, as well as a specifically anti-refugee/anti-Southeast Asian hostility. Refugee women are especially vulnerable to attacks such as robbery, rape and intimidation. The perpetrators seem to believe that these attacks are acceptable, even deserved, because the U.S. lost the war in Vietnam, and war can now be made on its victims/refugees. Refugee women are perceived as likely targets, easier to physically overpower and intimidate. Because refugees are unfamiliar with American behavior, language and laws, it is difficult for them to fight back. At the same time, the pressure to assimilate falls heavily on the women, even as the community's traditional values and roles are fundamentally undermined and their children become strangers to them.

Historically, the tendency has been to reject and exclude Asians from participating fully in American society. Besides the exclusionary immigration laws, in many states, Asians could not be naturalized, vote, own property, or marry persons of other races. Their lives and jobs were restricted in every way. Although most of the discriminatory laws have eventually changed, deep-rooted stereotypes and hostility towards Asians have not. Throughout there has been a clear pattern of violence used to intimidate and eliminate Asians. Asians, like other minorities, have been expendable: their lives have not been valued as highly as white lives. Burned into Asian American consciousness is the violent uprooting of more than 110,000 Japanese who were interned in American concentration camps during World War II. Western Defense Commander General John L. DeWitt declared that "the Japanese race is an enemy race," thus providing the racist rationale that all Japanese on the west coast must be locked up as a military necessity (see notes). They were marched away at gunpoint and imprisoned behind barbed wire, arbitrarily and illegally stripped of all civil rights. They were stripped of their dignity and pride as a people and of their dreams. Most lost their businesses, homes and possessions, an estimated value of as much as $400 million (Weglyn, p. 276). Japanese American women fiercely resisted these attacks on family and community integrity, and the demoralization and shame. They turned the prisons into homes and transformed the anger into the will to survive. Today, the camps remain a warning that the old anti-Asian hysteria could strike at any time; you are not safe behind the yellow face.

ASIAN AMERICAN WOMEN: DANGERS WITHIN AND WITHOUT

We are triply oppressed: as Asian Americans, as Asian American women, and as Asian American women workers. Racism has been and continues to be a primary force in shaping our oppression as women and as workers. The model minority stereotype has ominous overtones when applied to Asian American women. Asian American women are described as being desirable because they are cute (as in doll-like), quiet rather than militant, and unassuming rather than assertive. In a word, non-threatening. This is the image being sold as a commodity on the front page of the *Wall Street Journal*, January 25, 1984, headlined: "American Men Find Asian Brides Fill the Unliberated Bill— Mailorder Firms Help Them Look for the Ideal Women They Didn't Find at Home."

There are about 50 mailorder bride services in the U.S., carrying names such as "Cherry Blossom" and "Love Overseas." For a fee, men receive photo catalogs of Asian women, primarily from poor families in Malaysia and the Philippines. Descriptions of the women include statements such as "They love to do things to make their husbands happy," and "Most, if not all, are very feminine, loyal, loving—and virgins!" (as quoted in *Pacific Citizen*). The men who use these services are often middle-aged or older, disillusioned and divorced. Many have served in the U.S. military overseas in Asia. They blame previous marriage failures on the women's liberation movement. The mail order services claim to sell unliberated women who will supposedly be satisfied homemakers and be subservient to their husbands. The reality is that this market is a by-product of the U.S. military and economic domination in Asia. The mail order phenomenon is a threat not only to Asian and Asian American women, but to all women. It promotes a degrading view of women's roles and the acceptability of selling women.

The stereotypes also pay off in the form of inflated profits extracted by superexploiting Asian American women workers. Businesses want docile, subservient workers who will not complain, file grievances, or organize unions. Many businesses purposely seek immigrant workers with limited English skills as further insurance against backtalk. Asian American women are also stereotyped as having special dexterity and endurance for routine, thus making them fit for assembly work of various types. They are thought to be "loyal, diligent and attentive to detail," again good qualities for subordinates, but certainly not for supervisors. Asian American women continue to be hired mainly in low-profile, low-status, low-paying occupations, such as clerical and service work. Asian American families tend to have multiple wage earners, to support larger, often extended, families, and to live in urban areas with a relatively high cost of living. These factors skew the Asian American family median income upwards. This higher figure has been used to suggest wrongly that Asian American families are as or more successful than white families. Comparisons of median income levels within specific cities (instead of using national averages) reveal that Asian Americans, like other minorities, consistently earn less than whites.

The force of history and the conditions of our lives demand many battles, but Asian American women must also simultaneously wage an inner struggle with feudal and religious cultural baggage. In Asian cultures that have been heavily influenced by Confucianism, women are regarded as secondary to men, existing for their service. The Spanish imposed Catholicism on the Philippines with similar results. While the Asian experience in America has modified some of these ideas, every wave of immigration tends to revive the old cultures. Asian American women must be able to reject negative traditions without feeling like they are rejecting their whole Asian American identity. Assimilation appears to demand this same rejection, but it is from the standpoint of shame and self-hatred. No culture is static, and this struggle to consciously develop and redefine the best in Asian American culture is based on pride and love of our people.

Writers Merle Woo and Kitty Tsui have eloquently articulated this many-fronted struggle, becoming a voice for other Asian American lesbians. As lesbians, they have faced a painful rejection from the Asian American community. In "Letter to Ma," Merle directly addresses homophobia in the community: "If my reaction to being a Yellow Woman is different than yours was, please know that that is not a judgment on you, a criticism or denial of you, your worth" (*Bridge*, p. 146). Merle explains that being a Yellow Feminist does not mean " 'separatism,' either by cutting myself off from non-Asians or men . . . it means changing the economic class system and psychological forces (sexism, racism, and homophobia) that really hurt all of us" (p. 142). Kitty describes herself as a warrior who grapples with those same three many-headed demons. In "The Words of A Woman Who Breathes Fire," she affirms: "I am a woman who loves women, / I am a woman who loves myself'' (p. 52). Self-affirmation as a source of boldness and vision becomes a strength for Asian American women, lesbian and straight.

Writers/activists Sasha Hohri, Miya Iwataki and Janice Mirikitani are a few more of the unsung Asian American women continuing the strong tradition of political activism and organizing. Their issues range from redress/reparations for the Japanese interned during World War II to racist violence against Asians and the Rainbow Coalition for political power. They continue in the spirit of earlier Korean and Pilipino women who organized and continue to organize in the U.S. for independence in their homelands. A Japanese American woman, Mitsuye Endo, had partial success in the Supreme Court in 1944, challenging the internment of concededly loyal American citizens (Weglyn, p. 227). More recently, some of the largest labor rallies and significant employer concessions have been won by striking Chinese American garment workers. In 1982, 10,000 Chinese American women garment workers rallied in New York, winning a union contract that addressed their substandard working conditions. In 1986, following the shutdown of P & L Sportswear, 300 Chinese American women garment workers forced the city of Boston and the state of Massachusetts to implement the required retraining.

But while the Chinese American community is celebrating these victories, the women's movement has yet to recognize the significance of this achievement. Asian American women are trying to organize one of the least organized sectors of labor. They are fighting for basic working conditions denied to them precisely because they are Asian American women. Asian American women are often most actively involved in their communities and workplaces because those conditions directly determine their future. If we do not fight our own battles, who will? In *East Wind: Focus on Asian Women*, Sasha Hohri and Sadie Lum analyze Asian American women's oppression as intrinsically linked to class and race issues. We cannot separate ourselves from any one part. Our liberation is linked to that of our communities and ultimately, to that of our whole society. Liberation requires revolution.

As yet, feminism has not provided sufficient analysis and direction to the basic struggle of survival facing Asian Americans in this country. Feminism appears to have a more limited agenda, one concerned primarily with women's oppression. However, women's oppression is irresolvable in a society which is inherently unequal. A capitalist society means that a few will profit while the majority will not. Feminism must deal with the structure of capitalism and its exploitation of people by race and class, as well as the way this exploitation parallels and compounds women's oppression. As feminists broaden their perspective on what issues are of priority to women of all colors, more unity can be forged with Asian American and other sisters of color who are moving ahead, organizing and surviving. We cannot choose to stop struggling. We can only choose how we work together.

NOTES

"Pilipino"; Filipino is the anglicized form and symbolizes the colonization and domination of the Philippines by foreign powers such as the United States. In Tagalog, the national language of the Philippines, the word is pronounced with a "p" sound, hence "Pilipino."

General DeWitt's statement is part of his February 1942 recommendation to Secretary Stimson on exclusion of the Japanese, as quoted in *Personal Justice Denied*, p. 6.

REFERENCES

"American Men Find Asian Brides Fill the Unliberated Bill," Raymond A. Joseph, *Wall Street Journal*, January 25/84, p. 1, 22.

"Chinese Garment Workers Shake Up New York" August 20/82 and "Chinese Garment Workers Win Retraining in Boston" September 12/86 in *Unity*, Unity Publications: Oakland, California.

East Wind: Politicians and Culture of Asians in the U.S. Focus: Asian Women, V. 2 N. 1, Spring/Summer 1983, Getting Together Publications: Oakland, California.

"JACL Report on Asian Bride Catalogs," *Pacific Citizen*, February 22/85, p. 10–11.

"Letter to Ma," Merle Woo, in *This Bridge Called My Back*, Cherríe Moraga and Gloria Anzaldúa, editors, Persephone Press: Watertown, Massachusetts, 1981.

Personal Justice Denied, Report of the Commission on Wartime Relocation and Internment of Civilians, U.S. Government Printing Office, Washington, D.C., 1982.

Recent Activities Against Citizens and Residents of Asian Descent, U.S. Commission on Civil Rights, Clearinghouse Publication No. 88.

With Silk Wings, Elaine H. Kim with Janice Otani, Asian Women United of California, 1983.

The Words of a Woman Who Breathes Fire, Kitty Tsui, Spinsters, Ink: Argyle, New York, 1983.

Years of Infamy, Michi Weglyn, William Morrow and Co.: New York, New York, 1976.

III

Rethinking Institutions

Social institutions exert a powerful influence on our everyday lives. The type of work people in the United States do, our families, our schooling, the beliefs we encounter about ourselves, and our treatment by institutions of social control shape our varying experiences with and perceptions of race, class, and gender. Despite their importance, social institutions are often presented as entities far removed from systems of race, class, and gender rather than as fundamental conduits for oppression. We often see individuals and not institutions as possessing race, class, and gender identities.

Centering our analysis on the experiences of historically marginalized groups gives us new insights about the connections among social institutions and systems of race, class, and gender. The six sections in Part Three examine how race, class, and gender shape the organization of social institutions and how different groups experience these three factors.

"Work and Economic Transformation" opens with D. Stanley Eitzen and Maxine Baca Zinn's analysis of how structural transformations in the economy have dramatically transformed domestic and global markets. New technologies, global economic interdependence, capital flight, and the growth of the service sector represent new opportunities for individuals positioned to benefit from these changes. Economic transformation holds different meaning for African-Americans, Latinos, large numbers of women, and other historically marginalized groups. Elizabeth Higginbotham illustrates how past discrimination in the labor market and other institutional structures continues to influence the economic position of women of color. Deborah Woo refutes a recurring claim that current economic changes are allowing Asian Americans, an alleged "model minority," somehow to escape racial discrimination. Robyn Stone's examination of poverty among the elderly reveals significant gender differences that accompany structural transformations.

Families are another primary social institution profoundly influenced by systems of race, class, and gender. Bonnie Thornton Dill's historical analysis of racial/ethnic women and their families examines diverse patterns of family organization directly influenced by a group's placement in the larger political economy. Through research on elderly Puerto Rican women's active participation in shaping viable family networks, Audre Lorde's insightful view of lesbian mothers and their sons, and the voices of poor women dealing with mothering in conjunction with the social welfare system, we see how individuals have different family experiences due to their place in race, class, and gender hierarchies. The resulting diversity diffuses the widespread notion that the normative family is white, middle class, with children, organized around a heterosexual married couple, preferably contains a nonworking wife, and needs little support from relatives or neighbors. As the experiences of African-Americans, Latinos, lesbians, Asian Americans, and others reveal, this so-called normal family actually represents a minority perspective.

"Identity and the Life Cycle" explores how institutional expressions of beliefs about race, class, and gender affect individual experiences and consciousness at different points in life. Age is a social category similar to race, class, and gender, with its own structures of inequality, supported by ideologies concerning appropriate behaviors for individuals of varying ages. Like social institutions, age provides different opportunities based on race, class, and gender. For example, Jewelle Taylor Gibbs chronicles young African-American men's political and economic vulnerability, a situation exacerbated by their age. While youth places Black men at greater risk, middle age can lead to more positive experiences for lesbians suggests Martha Kirkpatrick. Age is also a state of becoming, a dynamic process whereby individuals grapple with ideologies of race, class, and gender differently depending on where they are in the life cycle. In his analysis of racial identity among Puerto Rican youth, Samuel Betances contends that racial identity is not absolute and that adolescence is one important period of life where race is socially constructed. Sucheng Chan's narrative provides a powerful glimpse of how one individual negotiated the ideological terrain of race, class, and gender at different times in her life. Chan's narrative not only taps dimensions of age but also does so from the perspective of a physically challenged individual. And Emily Warn's account of her struggle to reconcile her Jewish faith with her feminism shows how creating identity often involves redefining and challenging expectations imposed on us.

In "Ideology and Belief Systems" we see how dominant ideologies about race, class, and gender and ideologies of resistance developed by subordinated groups gain institutional expression in language, the media, humor, and music. People with the power to define reality create dominant ideologies reflecting their own interests, as Gloria Steinem reminds us in "If Men Could Menstruate." These ideologies shape all social institutions, especially those central to reinforcing beliefs. For example, cultural beliefs about African-Americans permeate our media ("TV's Black World Turns—But Stays Unreal") and our vocabulary ("On Language and Race"). Evelynn Hammonds's article on AIDS examines not only differential health care based on group membership but also how the very definitions of health and disease themselves vary by race, class, and gender. However, exposure to dominant ideologies does not mean that historically marginalized groups mindlessly accept such belief systems. Vine Deloria's exploration of Indian humor and Felix Padilla's analysis of salsa music demonstrate how access to alternative belief systems allow Native Americans and Latinos to resist powerful dominant ideologies.

The interdependence of race, class, and gender in structuring social institutions, the importance of ideology and belief systems in maintaining and challenging institutions, and the ways that individuals negotiate these systems converge in our experiences with education. Roslyn Mickelson and Stephen Samuel Smith's analysis of the limitations of educational reforms in reducing social inequality explores how schools promote inequalities of race, class, and gender. We can see the interplay between school policies that perpetuate existing hierarchies, such as credential inflation, and belief systems about race, class, and gender that are embedded in the so-called hidden curriculum. Students encounter these structures and belief systems while young, when identity takes on major importance. Schools thus become key sites where inequalities of race, class, and gender are fostered and resisted. Gaye Williams and Olivia Castellano offer compelling narratives about how African-American and Latino women experience their schooling, yet manage to cope and often excel. Both women identify their struggle for a self-defined consciousness as fundamental to their survival. In her demand that education "take women students seriously," Adrienne Rich analyzes the gendered nature of the hidden curriculum.

To function, systems of race, class, and gender rely on institutional policies and belief systems concerning work, family, and education. Interwoven throughout these and other social institutions is the implicit question of how social institutions remain stable when they are challenged. Violent acts, the threat of violence, and more generalized policies based on the use of force find organizational homes in designated institutions of social control—primarily the police, the military, and the criminal justice system. But violence simultaneously pervades a range of other social institutions. Male violence against women and children whether physical, emotional, or sexual, in families of all social classes and racial/ethnic compositions contradicts dominant beliefs that the home is a place of tranquility and love. Sexual harassment on the job as a dimension of social control belies the belief that men and women encounter a similar work environment. In the media, depicting rape as pleasurable to women, and portraying violence against Native Americans, Asian Americans, and African-Americans in numerous movies as justified contributes to a generalized belief system condoning violence. Thus, violence is simultaneously concentrated and diffuse; some social institutions are known for their use of force, while others are less peaceful than they appear. It is important to see violence not as acts of individual social deviance but as a component of social institutions.

One prominent theme in the readings in "Violence and Social Control" concerns the links between individual acts of violence and more routinized, systemic violence. Rape, for example, appears to be a private act. But as Patricia Yancey Martin and Robert Hummer compellingly explore in "Fraternities and Rape on Campus," rapes occur as part of a generalized climate condoning violence against women. Lynching African-American men may have seemed to be the random acts of unruly mobs, yet, as Jacquelyn Dowd Hall argues in her essay, the lack of arrest, prosecution, and convictions of those who lynched human beings is powerful testament to public endorsement of these seemingly individual acts of violence. Although violence may be experienced individually, it occurs in specific organizational and institutional contexts.

Race, class, and gender are fundamental determinants of organizational policies that foster social control. As Mary Frances Berry and John Blassingame point out, African-American men's experiences with the criminal justice system exemplify the differential treatment that individuals receive based on race, class, and gender. Similarly, Hall's historical analysis of the specific forms of assault against African-American men and women—lynching and institutionalized rape—explores the complex interconnections among race, class, and gender in making African-American women and men vulnerable to racial violence in gender specific ways.

Investigating violence and social control also reveals the interconnected nature of dominant ideologies of masculinity, the individualized and systemic forms of violence they justify, and the mechanisms of social control that support masculinity. "More Power Than We Want: Masculine Sexuality and Violence" by Bruce Kokopeli and George Lakey investigates these links and elaborates on Martin and Hummer's discussion of the connection between masculine identity and campus rape and Hall's analysis of lynching and white masculinity. Although we include no articles on violence against gays and lesbians, homophobic violence and violence against women are both ways of enforcing interlocking belief systems concerning heterosexism and masculinity. Violence based on race, gender, and heterosexism are part of one system of social control: All of these types of violence aim to reinforce systems of privilege.

Moving historically marginalized groups to the center of analysis clarifies the importance of social institutions as links between individual experience and larger structures of race, class, and gender. Social institutions such as the family and school become powerful channels for societal penalties and privileges. Studying social institutions shows us how race, class, and gender oppression rest on a network of interconnected social institutions. Moreover, examining social institutions reveals that everyone's life is framed by inequalities of race, class, and gender. African-Americans and other racial/ethnic groups are not the sole recipients of differential treatment by race; racial politics also encompass the experiences of whites. Women and men are both affected by gender, and the lives of the poor and their more affluent counterparts are intimately intertwined. By seeing that we are all part of one historically created system that finds structural form in interconnected social institutions, we gain greater insight about the actual and potential shape of our own lives.

Work and Economic Transformation

STRUCTURAL TRANSFORMATION AND SYSTEMS OF INEQUALITY

21

D. Stanley Eitzen and Maxine Baca Zinn

The technological and economically based reorganization of society has created wide disparities in the distribution of economic resources. All people in the United States are affected by the economic changes. The magnitude of structural transformation, however, is different throughout society. The old inequalities of class, race, and gender are thriving. New and subtle forms of discrimination are becoming prevalent throughout society as the economic base shifts and settles.

Four factors are at work here: new technologies, global economic inter-dependence, capital flight, and the dominance of the information and service sectors over basic manufacturing industries. Together these factors have reinforced the unequal placement of individuals and families in the larger society. They have deepened patterns of social inequality, and they have formed new patterns of domination in which the affluent control the poor, whites control people of color, and men control women.

The disproportionate effects of economic and industrial change are most visible in three trends: (1) structural unemployment, (2) the changing

From: D. Stanley Eitzen and Maxine Baca Zinn (eds.), *The Reshaping of America: Social Consequences of the Changing Economy* (Englewood Cliffs, N.J.: Prentice-Hall), 1989, © 1989, pp. 131–143. Reprinted by permission.

distribution and organization of jobs, and (3) the low income-generating capacity of jobs. The first two trends have their most obvious effects on the changing class structure and the new racial order, while the second and third trends have particular ramifications for women and for gender relations. Still, all three trends have significant consequences for the hierarchies of class, race, and gender.

CLASS

Two major developments stand out when we look at the emerging class structure. The first is the growing gap between the rich and the poor since 1970. The second is the decline of the middle class.

The distribution of income is very unequal and widening. From 1970 to 1986, the income share of the highest quintile rose from 43.3 to 46.1 percent, while the bottom one fifth fell from 4.1 percent to 3.8 percent of all income (Pear 1987). The growing disparity in income and wealth is directly related to the changing job structure as the economy shifts from manufacturing to service.

Many Americans have experienced a sharp slowdown of income growth. This has caused a shrinkage of the middle class that is related in large measure to the erosion of middle-income jobs and the emergence of a bipolar wage structure in high tech and service work. The middle portion of the workforce fell from 52.3 percent of the population in 1978 to 44.3 in 1986 (Rose 1986:9). To be fair, demographic conditions as well as labor market forces are responsible for middle class decline. Nevertheless, the current period is the first in American history where the rate of downward mobility exceeds the rate of upward mobility. Home ownership illustrates how the middle class is losing ground. The percentage of families owning their homes has declined each year in the 1980s (American Demographics 1986). Furthermore, changes have occurred in the population with a middle-class life style. As Barbara Ehrenreich has observed: "Middle class is a matter of status as well as income and is signaled by subtler cues: how we live, what we spend our money on, what expectations we have for the future. Since the post-war period, middle class status has been defined by home ownership, college education (at least for the children), and the ability to afford such amenities as a second car and family vacations" (Ehrenreich 1986:50). Using this colloquial understanding of "middle class," it is clear that fewer Americans will achieve this status because many of the old avenues to social mobility no longer exist in the new society.

RACE

Technology and the changing distribution of jobs are having devastating effects on minority communities across America. The employment status of minorities is falling in all regions. It is worse however, in areas of industrial decline. The labor market status of whites has also been lowered in these areas, but the level of racial inequality has increased to scandalous levels. "In cities such as Detroit, Buffalo, Chicago, and Cleveland, the gap between the labor market position of blacks, especially black males, and whites probably exceeds the highest levels that ever existed in the most racist of the South's cities" (Swinton 1987:68). Racial inequality is partly a class issue. Prominent sociologist William J. Wilson has argued that the long-term removal of job opportunities for minority skilled and semiskilled workers is the force most responsible for the growth of the Black underclass in America's inner cities (Wilson 1987). Furthermore, the racial underclass is expanding to include Hispanics whose poverty rate now exceeds that of Blacks and who are expected, shortly after the turn of the century, to surpass Blacks as the largest racial-minority group.

Hispanics and Blacks have suffered disproportionately from industrial job loss and declining manufacturing employment. Their concentration in industries that have deteriorated in recent years is well documented. . . . By every measure including employment rates, occupational standing, and wage rates, the labor market status of racial minorities has deteriorated relative to whites. While the official unemployment rate for March 1987 was 6.5 percent, the rate for Blacks was 13.9 percent and 9 percent for Hispanics. These government rates, of course, are misleading because they count as employed those 5.5 million who work part time because they cannot find full-time jobs, and they do not count as unemployed the 1.17 million discouraged workers who have given up their search for work (Hershey 1987).

GENDER

Women and men are affected differently by the transformation of the economy from its manufacturing base to a base in service and high technology. Industrial jobs, traditionally filled by men, are being replaced with service jobs that are increasingly filled by women. Since 1980, women have taken 80 percent of the new jobs created in the economy. If this pace continues, women will make up most of the work force by the turn of the century (Hacker 1986:26). Unlike other forms of inequality, sexism in American society has not become more intense as a result of economic transformations. Instead, sexism has taken new forms as women are propelled into the labor market. Women have continued to move from the private sphere (family) to public arenas, but they have done so under conditions of labor market discrimination that have always plagued women. . . . Today, the "typical" job is a non-union, service sector, low-paying job occupied by a woman. Despite the growing feminization of the work force, male domination has been more firmly entrenched in the social organization of work. The rise of the contingent work force (including part-time work, temporary agencies, and subcontracted work) offers many advantages to employers but at considerable cost to women workers. Technological innovations in the workplace offer women dubious gains:

> In any number of cases, the outcome is more work opportunities for women, even if that work is less skilled, less autonomous and less rewarding . . . for many other women, new office machines have made them develop greater skills even if the jobs they use them for have become more rather than less fragmented and alienated and are no better than they were in the first place. What was once professional-level work—typically reserved for men—is often eliminated, and the residue or more routine tasks is added to the responsibilities of clerical workers who are, of course, women. The new technologies may develop more skills, but they also introduce clear monitoring and a stepped-up work pace. (Smith 1987:6)

The full impact of economic restructuring on women must take into account the low wage levels and the limited opportunities for advancement that characterize their work in the new economy.

NEW INTERSECTIONS OF CLASS, RACE, AND GENDER

The hierarchies of class, race, and gender are simultaneous and interlocking systems. For this reason, they frequently operate with and through each other to produce social inequality. Not only are many existing inequalities being exacerbated by the structural transformation of the economy, but the combined efforts of class, race, and gender are producing new kinds of subordination and exclusion throughout society and especially in the workplace. For example, the removal of manufacturing jobs has severely increased Black and Hispanic male job loss. Just how much of this is due to class and how much is due to race remains an important question.

In contrast, many women of color have found their work opportunities expanded, albeit in marginal work settings in service jobs and high-tech jobs. Does such growth offer traditionally oppressed race/gender groups new mobility opportunities or does the expansion of new kinds of work reproduce existing forms of inequality? The impact of economic restructuring on race and gender varies considerably. In some cases, it generates no jobs at all and displaces minority women workers. In other cases, minority women benefit by the creation of new jobs. Third world immigrant women provide the bulk of high-tech productive labor force in Silicon Valley. Yet a growing "underclass" in high tech consists of low-paid immigrant women from Mexico, Vietnam, Korea, and the Philippines. These examples reveal new labor systems as well as new forms of racial control based on class, race, and gender. . . .

REFERENCES

American Demographics. 1986. "The Affordable Dream." *American Demographics* (July):12, 14.

Ehrenreich, Barbara. 1986. "Is the Middle Class Doomed?" *The New York Times Magazine* (Sept. 7):44, 50, 54, 62, 64.

Hacker, Andrew. 1986. "Women at Work," *New York Review of Books* 33(13) (August 14):26–32.

Hershey, Robert D. 1987. "Jobless Rate Down but Growth of Jobs Also Falls." *The New York Times* (April 4):7.

Moberg, David. 1986. "Middle Class May Be Losing the Economic War of Attrition." *In These Times* (Nov. 12, 16).

Pear, Robert. 1987. "Poverty Rate Dips as the Median Family Income Rises." *The New York Times* (July 31):8.

Rose, Stephen J. 1986. *The American Profile Poster.* New York: Pantheon.

Smith, Joan. 1987. "Terminal Illnesses," *The Women's Review of Books* IV, 7 (April):6–7.

Swinton, David. 1987. "Economic Status of Blacks 1986." *The State of Black America 1987.* New York: National Urban League (Jan.):49–73.

Wilson, William J. 1987. *The Truly Disadvantaged.* Chicago: University of Chicago Press.

WE WERE NEVER ON A PEDESTAL:

22

Women of Color Continue to Struggle
with Poverty, Racism, and Sexism

Elizabeth Higginbotham

When I came out of high school, I thought I was going to get a good job. I tried looking in many places, but the big companies downtown just took my application and I never heard from them. I was able to get a job at a small office in the midtown area. I am the secretary for many people. At first, I was excited about making $120 per week. But I quickly discovered that after Social Security, taxes, and my health insurance were taken out, I was left with very little. It was hard to make it from one payday to the next. I've been there seven years now. I really cannot find another job. This place is sort of comfortable. They know me and they know my work. I even get small raises and occasional bonuses when we have a good season. They were very good about letting me work less when my daughter was first born. But I would really like to do the same type of work and just make more money.

Anna Rivera has a high school diploma and works as a clerk-typist for a small firm in an Eastern city. When she began working, she felt lucky to find a job. Many of her female Puerto Rican friends were less successful in their efforts and could not find clerical work. They followed their mothers into the garment factories. So there was much celebration in Anna's family when she got a white-collar job. She made more money than her father, who washed dishes for a major hotel in the city. And her job was far more regular than the garment factory work her mother did. Initially, her weekly wages sounded very good. She even got two weeks paid vacation each year and sick pay. Yet, over time, Anna and her family came to question the "goodness" of her job.

When she was twenty-two Anna married José, who works as an operative in a small factory. And when she was twenty-three, their daughter, Iris, was born. Both Anna and José are employed full-time and her sister, Nilsa, watches Iris. Anna gives her sister a little money for helping her with child care. She would like to give her more but cannot. She and José are perplexed by their persistent poverty. They have more education than their own parents. They

From: Rochelle Lefkowitz and Ann Withorn (eds.), *For Crying Out Loud: Women and Poverty in the United States* (New York: Pilgrim Press, 1986), pp. 99–110. Reprinted by permission.

have mastered English and hold regular jobs. Yet, they cannot save enough money to leave their tiny apartment. They have already given up the dream of owning their own home but would just like a little more room for their family. Limited job mobility plagues their lives. They, like many of their friends, are keenly aware that racism continues to be a major limit on their lives, just as it was for their parents, but the nature of the restrictions has changed.

There are many young women of color who share Anna's plight. Even though they have worked to make a "better life," they still find themselves well acquainted with inadequate housing, poor health-care facilities, and jobs that are not leading them anywhere. Afro-American, Latina, Asian American, and Native American women have never been on a pedestal. Thus, they are not suffering the shocks of the fall. Instead, they are choking on the bitterness of despair because their many efforts have not resulted in significant changes in their lives.

It is very common for Afro-American, Latina, Asian American, and Native American women to complete high school and to avoid adolescent pregnancy, single parenthood, and welfare. Yet these young women still find themselves either in poverty or near poverty. Gender, race, and class oppression make it particularly difficult for women of color who are raised in poor families to climb out of poverty. This essay focuses on work for women of color and briefly addresses three major issues, which are rarely given attention, but which contribute to the persistence of their poverty. First, is their history in the labor market. Women of color share a legacy of racial oppression with other members of their racial-ethnic group. Second, race and sex discrimination have kept women of color at the bottom of the occupational ladder. Therefore, their high rates of labor-force participation have been ineffective in bringing them out of poverty. And finally, the past few decades have seen women of color enter new occupations around the nation. This progress is celebrated in many spheres, but questions remain about the significance of employment shifts for the economic well-being of women of color.

A HISTORY OF EXPLOITATION

People of color were brought to the United States to work. There was little attention to other aspects of their lives, such as family life, education, culture, political rights, and so forth. Instead, the racism of the eighteenth and especially the nineteenth centuries denied them their rights and justified the exploitation of their labor. Therefore, while work in the nineteenth century was frequently organized in ways that jeopardized white working-class life, this was always true for working-class Afro-Americans, Chinese immigrants, Japanese immigrants, Mexican Americans, and Native American Indians.[1]

Concerned only with the labor power of people of color, white landowners and employers showed only a minimal interest in their lives outside the fields, factories, kitchens, mines, canneries, and railroad yards. Frequently the harsh working conditions made family and community life precarious. Women of color were forced into market work, along with their men. This employment complicated their tasks of caring for children and the home. Frequently, they could only tend to their own children after they had worked long hours in the labor market.[2]

This point is easily illustrated in the case of slavery, where creating profits for the owners took priority over the survival of any individual slave or slave family. Angela Davis identified what this meant for Black slave women. "The slave system defined Black people as chattel. Since women, no less than men, were viewed as profitable labor units, they might as well have been genderless as far as the slaveholders were concerned. In the words of scholar Kenneth Stammp 'the slave woman was first a full-time worker, and only incidentally a wife, mother and homemaker.' "[3]

It was under such harsh conditions that Afro-American people had to persist in building and maintaining family life. Other people of color share a heritage of labor exploitation and the task of maintaining family life without institutional supports. For example, there was no "family wage" for Black, Latino, and Asian men, while this privilege was extended to native-born white males and many white immigrants. Such efforts, which supported patriarchal families and afforded white women a level of protection, were routinely denied to people of color.[4]

Chinese immigrants, who constructed railroad lines and developed agricultural areas in the late nineteenth century, also faced oppressive working conditions and low wages. Federal legislation prohibited these laborers from bringing their wives to join them. They were explicitly given the message that their families were not permitted to flourish on American soil.[5]

This legacy is also shared by Mexican Americans, who suffered horrible living and working conditions to open the mines of the Southwest. Their work necessitated either separation from their families or bringing them along to live in isolated mining communities.[6] In each instance, like slavery for Afro-Americans, men were either unavailable or unable to protect and provide for the family. This situation had a direct impact on the roles of females. Women not only had to bear and raise children and care for the home, they also had to contribute directly to the economic support of the family.

Like other working-class daughters in the nineteenth century, women of color frequently had to take paid employment to bring wages into the household. Yet, they entered a labor market where they faced both gender and racial restrictions. For example, when the structure of Southern agriculture in the late nineteenth century jeopardized the survival of sharecropping Black families, it was the women, frequently daughters, who were released from farm work to sell their labor. The only positions open to them were in household work, which paid low wages.[7] Regardless of whether they stayed in the South or migrated to the North, they were routinely denied factory work, and had to do domestic work to supplement their families' income.[8] These women discovered through their personal experiences that the labor market was a limited one for women and a more restrictive one for women of color.

The same discovery was made by nineteenth-century Mexican American women in California, who watched their husbands' livelihoods disappear. Like their Afro-American counterparts, they sought paid employment but could find work only in laundries, canneries, other people's houses, and in the fields as migrant laborers.[9] The small population of Chinese immigrant women found new employment options outside of the "Chinatowns" around the nation, but they were able to find employment only in garment factories and other low-wage manufacturing jobs. A high percentage of Japanese immigrant women, who entered this country in the early twentieth century, were household workers.[10]

Women of color learned that race and sex discrimination were to be parts of their lives. Industrialization in the late nineteenth and early twentieth centuries created new employment opportunities for women. But these jobs were limited to native-born white women. Later clerical, sales, teaching, and social work positions would be expanded to incorporate the daughters of white immigrant families. Meanwhile, women of color were still overwhelmingly found in private household work, farm labor, laundries, canneries, and the lowest of manufacturing jobs.

Job ceilings and various types of racial barriers operated well into the twentieth century to keep Afro-American, Latina, Asian American, and Native American Indian women out of "traditional white women's jobs." Prior to the 1960s, it frequently took a college education to make significant gains in the labor market. And few families had the resources to enable their daughters to attain higher education.[11] Women of color with various levels of high school education found that many segments of the labor market were still hostile to them. It would take more than their own individual efforts at improvement to challenge the blatant discrimination in the labor market. Their wages were essential to the economic survival of their families, but even with both spouses employed full-time, people of color in working-class occupations had difficulties escaping poverty.

THE CONTEMPORARY SCENE

In the last decade, each racial or ethnic community has become more stratified. Blacks, Latinos, Asian Americans, and Native Americans with college
and advanced degrees have been able to move into the middle class, but other
members of their communities have been untouched by these advance-
ments.[12] After major campaigns to encourage racial and ethnic youth to stay
in school and get a high school diploma, the labor market has not fulfilled
its end of the bargain.[13] Racial discrimination is still quite pronounced, and
at this time of dramatic economic shifts, race is a key factor in the process
of who stays middle class, who becomes middle class, who remains stably
employed in the working class, who falls through the cracks, and who is not
able to get out of poverty.

As deindustrialization proceeds in the Northwest and Midwest, and the
nonunionized industrialization of the Sun Belt and Third World nations
continues, it is evident that the working class suffers. But just as in the past,
people of color are particularly jeopardized. After decades of struggle, Black
and Latino men and women had made real employment gains in heavy,
unionized industries, and their families were beginning to appreciate a margin
of security. But these sectors are currently in decline, especially steel, automo-
biles, and rubber. Families that have crawled out of poverty on unionized
wages are now losing their edge as their jobs disappear.

Women of color, who traditionally have been called upon to enter
paid employment on behalf of their families, continue to do so. In the last
two decades, many have found new areas of employment, especially clerical and sales positions, but many of their sisters are still found in private
household work, factory work, and the service industries. All of these jobs
are only minimally rewarding financially. Thus, families who have lost the
security of employment in heavy industry have watched their economic
positions deteriorate. The contributions of women employed in low-wage
sectors have become even more critical to the survival of their families.
This is the scenario that is enacted weekly around the nation. Too often
scholars only focus on the difficulties of deindustrialization for white
working-class families, but Black and Latino working-class families who
had just begun to "make it" are also now living on the "edge" again.

. . . Data support the contention that men are poor as a result of unemployment, while women are poor because of the type of work they do.[14] . . .
A high percentage of women are found in near poverty (between $6,700 and
$9,999). Many are caught in nonunionized work settings and forced to exist
on minimum wage; thus their earnings push them just over the poverty line.
While a significant number of women are clustered in this wage bracket, there

are clear ethnic differences. Hispanic women are more likely to be found at this wage level than are Black or white women. Poverty is even more exaggerated for working Hispanic women than the figures reflect. Many Latinas work in the garment industry and other factories where work is seasonal. Thus, annually they face periods of unemployment.

. . . Being employed full-time, year-round is not a guarantee that you will not be poor, if you are a Black or Hispanic male or a woman of any color. The data show that only 11.2 percent of white males who are employed year-round in full-time positions make under $10,000 per year, leaving them either in poverty or near poverty. Yet, 20 percent of Black males, 21.2 percent of Hispanic males, 27 percent of white females, 30.7 percent of Black females, and 40.1 percent of Hispanic females do not earn more than $10,000 per year for their labor.[15]

. . . Women are still heavily represented in clerical jobs (along with other administrative support positions) and sales jobs, and people of color are still more likely to be found in certain occupations. Increasingly, women are entering professions. In 1982, 15.9 percent of employed white women and 12.6 percent of employed Black women were in professional specialities. Yet, the majority of professional Black women are found in traditionally female occupations, especially teaching, library work, nursing, and social work, and they are overwhelmingly employed in the public sector.[16] Hispanic women have made fewer gains in this area. What is troubling with respect to this occupational distribution is the large numbers of women of color in service and factory work. Julianne Malveaux suggests that Black women have moved out of private household work into occupations that offer only a slightly better standard of living.[17] . . .

We know that operative positions are jeopardized by the economy. Service work tends to be paid either a minimum wage or slightly above it. This includes service work organized in traditional ways, like hospital and hotel work and occupations influenced by technology, particularly in the fast-food industries. While these are growing sectors they provide barely livable wages and do not foster full participation in the mainstream. The tight economy and discriminatory barriers have operated to keep people of color in this tiny corner of the labor market, where they continue to struggle against the odds to make a living and raise their families.

An examination of current employment for women of color reveals a decline in private household workers and an increase in women of color entering traditionally white female occupations. Today, Afro-American women who could only clean and cook for affluent white families watch their grandchildren while their daughters go to work in clean offices.

Puerto Rican women who could find jobs only in the low-wage garment industry, are proud of their daughters, who now work in fashionable department stores. People can see the progress, but they are also aware of the ways that racism, class, and gender continue to limit employment options.

A history of labor exploitation and limited access to jobs continue to hamper the efforts of women of color to improve their occupational positions. Economic circumstances still force them into the labor market to assist their families. As daughters, wives, or mothers, their wages are critical to the economic well-being of their families. People of color find many aspects of the new poverty to be familiar to them. Their experiences indicate the need systematically to address the nature of racial discrimination in current educational and employment settings. Without an agenda that acknowledges these factors, there will be few significant changes in the lives of people of color. Anna's daughter and the daughters of other working women of color are likely to find that the labor market is also hostile to them. They are destined to face barriers in schools and on the job, which steer them toward low wages and dead-end jobs. Thus, the contemporary attention to poverty must seriously address differences in women's situations that are rooted in race and class and also examine the factors that persist in keeping certain segments of the male population in or near poverty.

NOTES

1. Few people are familiar with the history of people of color. Yet, an appreciation of their experiences in this nation is critical for grasping the complications and multiple roles of women of color.

2. Elizabeth Higginbotham, "Laid Bare by the System: Work and Survival for Black and Hispanic Women," in *Class, Race, and Sex: The Dynamics of Control*, ed. Amy Swerdlow and Hanna Lessinger (Boston: G. K. Hall, 1983), pp. 200–15.

3. Angela Davis, *Women, Race, and Class* (New York: Random House, 1981), p. 5.

4. Bonnie Thornton Dill, "Our Mothers' Grief: Racial-Ethnic Women and the Maintenance of Families" (Research paper no. 4, Memphis State University, Center for Research on Women, 1986).

5. Maxine Hong Kingston, *Chinamen* (New York: Knopf, 1980); and Victor G. Nee and Brett De Bary Nee, *Longtime Californ': A Documentary Study of an American Chinatown* (New York: Pantheon, 1972).

6. Mario Barrera, *Race and Class in the Southwest* (South Bend, Ind.: University of Notre Dame Press, 1979).

7. Jacqueline Jones, *Labor of Love, Labor of Sorrow* (New York: Basic Books, 1985).

8. For more about this, see Elizabeth Clark-Lewis, "This Work Had A' End: The Transition from Live-in to Day Work" (Working paper no. 2: Southern Women: The Intersection of Race, Class, and Gender, Memphis State University, Center for Research on Women, 1985); David Katzman, *Seven Days a Week: Women and Domestic Service in Industrial America* (New York: Oxford University Press, 1978); Julia Kirk Blackwelder, "Women in the Work Force: Atlanta, New Orleans, and San Antonio, 1930–1940," *Journal of Urban History* 4, no. 3 (May 1978): 331–58; Alice Kessler-Harris, *Out to Work* (New York: Oxford University Press, 1982).

9. Barrera, *Race and Class in the Southwest*; and Albert Camarillo, *Chicanos in a Changing Society* (Cambridge, Mass.: Harvard University Press, 1979).

10. Evelyn Nakano Glenn, "The Dialectics of Wage Work: Japanese American Women and Domestic Service, 1905–1940," *Feminist Studies* 6 (Fall 1983): 432–71.

11. Elizabeth Higginbotham, "Employment for Professional Black Women in the Twentieth Century" (Research paper no. 3, Memphis State University, Center for Research on Women, 1985).

12. Barrera, *Race and Class in the Southwest*; and William J. Wilson, *The Declining Significance of Race* (Chicago: University of Chicago Press, 1978).

13. Dorothy Newman et al., *Protest, Politics, and Prosperity* (New York: Pantheon, 1978).

14. Karin Stallard, Barbara Ehrenreich, and Holly Sklar, *Poverty in the American Dream* (Boston: South End Press, 1983).

15. These data do not even begin to present a full appreciation of the extent of poverty, since these figures are for those people who have secured full-time employment. It is well known that there are high percentages of unemployment in racial-ethnic communities. Existence is often more precarious for those who experience short- and long-term unemployment. See Bettylou Valentine, *Hustling and Other Hard Work* (New York: Free Press, 1978).

16. Higginbotham, "Employment for Professional Black Women."

17. Julianne Malveaux, "The Status of Women of Color in the Economy: The Legacy of Being Other" (Paper presented at the National Conference on Women: "The Economy and Public Policy," Washington, D.C. June 19–20, 1984).

THE GAP BETWEEN STRIVING AND ACHIEVING: *The Case of Asian American Women*

23

Deborah Woo

Much academic research on Asian Americans tends to underscore their success, a success which is attributed almost always to a cultural emphasis on education, hard work, and thrift. Less familiar is the story of potential not fully realized. For example, despite the appearance of being successful and highly educated, Asian American women do not necessarily gain the kind of recognition or rewards they deserve.

The story of unfulfilled dreams remains unwritten for many Asian Americans. It is specifically this story about the gap between striving and achieving that I am concerned with here. Conventional wisdom obscures the discrepancy by looking primarily at whether society is adequately rewarding individuals. By comparing how minorities as disadvantaged groups are doing relative to each other, the tendency is to view Asian Americans as a "model minority." This practice programs us to ignore structural barriers and inequities and to insist that any problems are simply due to different cultural values or failure of individual effort.

Myths about the Asian American community derive from many sources. All ethnic groups develop their own cultural myths. Sometimes, however, they create myths out of historical necessity, as a matter of subterfuge and survival. Chinese Americans, for example, were motivated to create new myths because institutional opportunities were closed off to them. Succeeding in America meant they had to invent fake aspects of an "Oriental culture," which became the beginning of the Chinatown tourist industry.

What has been referred to as the "model minority myth," however, essentially originated from without. The idea that Asian Americans have been a successful group has been a popular news media theme for the last twenty years. It has become a basis for cutbacks in governmental support for all ethnic

minorities—for Asian Americans because they apparently are already successful as a group; for other ethnic minorities because they are presumably not
working as hard as Asian Americans or they would not need assistance. Critics
of this view argue that the portrayal of Asian Americans as socially and
economically successful ignores fundamental inequities. That is, the question
"Why have Asians been successful vis-à-vis other minorities?" has been asked
at the expense of another equally important question: "What has kept Asians
from *fully* reaping the fruits of their education and hard work?"

The achievements of Asian Americans are part reality, part myth. Part of
the reality is that a highly visible group of Asian Americans are college-
educated, occupationally well-situated, and earning relatively high incomes.
The myth, however, is that hard work reaps commensurate rewards. This essay
documents the gap between the level of education and subsequent occupational or income gains.

THE ROOTS AND CONTOURS OF THE "MODEL MINORITY" CONCEPT

Since World War II, social researchers and news media personnel have been
quick to assert that Asian Americans excel over other ethnic groups in terms
of earnings, education, and occupation. Asian Americans are said to save more,
study more, work more, and so achieve more. The reason given: a cultural
emphasis on education and hard work. Implicit in this view is a social judgment
and moral injunction: if Asian Americans can make it on their own, why can't
other minorities?

While the story of Asian American women workers is only beginning to
be pieced together, the success theme is already being sung. The image prevails
that despite cultural and racial oppression, they are somehow rapidly assimilating into the mainstream. As workers, they participate in the labor force at
rates higher than all others, including Anglo women. Those Asian American
women who pursue higher education surpass other women, and even men, in
this respect. Moreover, they have acquired a reputation for not only being
conscientious and industrious but docile, compliant, and uncomplaining as
well.

In the last few decades American women in general have been demanding
"equal pay for equal work," the legitimation of housework as work that needs
to be recompensed, and greater representation in the professional fields.
These demands, however, have not usually come from Asian American
women. From the perspective of those in power, this reluctance to complain
is another feature of the "model minority." But for those who seek to uncover

employment abuses, the unwillingness to talk about problems on the job is itself a problem. The garment industry, for example, is a major area of exploitation, yet it is also one that is difficult to investigate and control. In a 1983 report on the Concentrated Employment Program of the California Department of Industrial Relations, it was noted:

> The major problem for investigators in San Francisco is that the Chinese community is very close-knit, and employers and employees cooperate in refusing to speak to investigators. In two years of enforcing the Garment Registration Act, the CEP has never received a complaint from an Asian employee. The few complaints received have been from Anglo or Latin workers.[1]

While many have argued vociferously either for or against the model minority concept, Asian Americans in general have been ambivalent in this regard. Asian Americans experience pride in achievement born of hard work and self-sacrifice, but at the same time, they resist the implication that all is well. Data provided here indicate that Asian Americans have not been successful in terms of benefitting fully, (i.e., monetarily), from their education. It is a myth that Asian Americans have proven the American Dream. How does this myth develop?

The Working Consumer: Income and Cost of Living

One striking feature about Asian Americans is that they are geographically concentrated in areas where both income and cost of living are very high. In 1970, 80 percent of the total Asian American population resided in five states—California, Hawaii, Illinois, New York, and Washington. Furthermore, 59 percent of Chinese, Filipino, and Japanese Americans were concentrated in only 5 of the 243 Standard Metropolitan Statistical Areas (SMSA) in the United States—Chicago, Honolulu, Los Angeles/Long Beach, New York, and San Francisco/Oakland.[2] The 1980 census shows that immigration during the intervening decade has not only produced dramatic increases, especially in the Filipino and Chinese populations, but has also continued the overwhelming tendency for these groups to concentrate in the same geographical areas, especially those in California.[3] Interestingly enough, the very existence of large Asian communities in the West has stimulated among more recent refugee populations what is now officially referred to as "secondary migration," that is, the movement of refugees away from their sponsoring communities (usually places where there was no sizeable Asian population prior to their own arrival) to those areas where there are well-established Asian communities.[4]

This residential pattern means that while Asian Americans may earn more by living in high-income areas, they also pay more as consumers. The additional earning power gained from living in San Francisco or Los Angeles, say, is absorbed by the high cost of living in such cities. National income averages which compare the income of Asian American women with that of the more broadly dispersed Anglo women systematically distort the picture. Indeed, if we compare women within the same area, Asian American women are frequently less well-off than Anglo American females, and the difference between women pales when compared with Anglo males, whose mean income is much higher than that of any group of women.[5]

When we consider the large immigrant Asian population and the language barriers that restrict women to menial or entry-level jobs, we are talking about a group that not only earns minimum wage or less, but one whose purchasing power is substantially undermined by living in metropolitan areas of states where the cost of living is unusually high.

Another striking pattern about Asian American female employment is the high rate of labor force participation. Asian American women are more likely than Anglo American women to work full time and year round. The model minority interpretation tends to assume that mere high labor force participation is a sign of successful employment. One important factor motivating minority women to enter the work force, however, is the need to supplement family resources. For Anglo American women some of the necessity for working is partly offset by the fact that they often share in the higher incomes of Anglo males, who tend not only to earn more than all other groups but, as noted earlier, also tend to receive higher returns on their education. Moreover, once regional variation is adjusted for, Filipino and Chinese Americans had a median annual income equivalent to black males in four mainland SMSAs—Chicago, Los Angeles/Long Beach, New York, San Francisco/Oakland.[6] Census statistics point to the relatively lower earning capacity of Asian males compared to Anglo males, suggesting that Asian American women enter the work force to help compensate for this inequality. Thus, the mere fact of high employment must be read cautiously and analyzed within a larger context.

The Different Faces of Immigration

Over the last decade immigration has expanded the Chinese population by 85.3 percent, making it the largest Asian group in the country at 806,027, and has swelled the Filipino population by 125.8 percent, making it the second largest at 774,640. Hence at present the majority of Chinese American and Filipino American women are foreign-born. In addition the Asian American "success story" is misleading in part because of a select group of these immigrants: foreign-educated professionals.

Since 1965 U.S. immigration laws have given priority to seven categories of individuals. Two of the seven allow admittance of people with special occupational skills or services needed in the United States. Four categories facilitate family reunification, and the last applies only to refugees. While occupation is estimated to account for no more than 20 percent of all visas, professionals are not precluded from entering under other preference categories. Yet this select group is frequently offered as evidence of the upward mobility possible in America when Asian Americans who are born and raised in the United States are far less likely to reach the doctoral level in their education. Over two-thirds of Asians with doctorates in the United States are trained and educated abroad.[7]

Also overlooked in some analyses is a great deal of downward mobility among the foreign-born. For example, while foreign-educated health professionals are given preferential status for entry into this country, restrictive licensing requirements deny them the opportunity to practice or utilize their special skills. They are told that their educational credentials, experience, and certifications are inadequate. Consequently, for many the only alternatives are menial labor or unemployment.[8] Other highly educated immigrants become owner/managers of Asian businesses, which also suggests downward mobility and an inability to find jobs in their field of expertise.

"Professional" Obscures More Than It Reveals

Another major reason for the perception of "model minority" is that the census categories implying success, "professional-managerial" or "executive, administrative, managerial," frequently camouflage important inconsistencies with this image of success. As managers, Asian Americans, usually male, are concentrated in certain occupations. They tend to be self-employed in small-scale wholesale and retail trade and manufacturing. They are rarely buyers, sales managers, administrators, or salaried managers in large-scale retail trade, communications, or public utilities. Among foreign-born Asian women, executive-managerial status is limited primarily to auditors and accountants.[9]

In general, Asian American women with a college education are concentrated in narrow and select, usually less prestigious, rungs of the "professional-managerial" class. In 1970, 27 percent of native-born Japanese women were either elementary or secondary school teachers. Registered nurses made up the next largest group. Foreign-born Filipino women found this to be their single most important area of employment, with 19 percent being nurses.

They were least represented in the more prestigious professions—physicians, judges, dentists, law professors, and lawyers.[10] In 1980 foreign-born Asian women with four or more years of college were most likely to find jobs in administrative support or clerical occupations.

Self-Help Through "Taking Care of One's Own"

Much of what is considered ideal or model behavior in American society is based on Anglo-Saxon, Protestant values. Chief among them is an ethic of individual self-help, of doing without outside assistance or governmental support. On the other hand, Asian Americans have historically relied to a large extent on family or community resources. Their tightly-knit communities tend to be fairly closed to the outside world, even when under economic hardship. Many below the poverty level do not receive any form of public assistance.[11] Even if we include social security benefits as a form of supplementary income, the proportion of Asian Americans who use them is again very low, much lower than that for Anglo Americans.[12] Asian American families, in fact, are more likely than Anglo American families to bear economic hardships on their own.

While Asian Americans appear to have been self-sufficient as communities, we need to ask, at what personal cost? Moreover, have they as a group reaped rewards commensurate with their efforts? The following section presents data which document that while Asian American women may be motivated to achieve through education, monetary returns for them are less than for other groups.

THE NATURE OF INEQUALITY

The decision to use white males as the predominant reference group within the United States is a politically charged issue. When women raise and push the issue of "comparable worth," of "equal pay for equal work," they argue that women frequently do work equivalent to men's, but are paid far less for it.

The same argument can be made for Asian American women, and the evidence of inequality is staggering. For example, after adjustments are made for occupational prestige, age, education, weeks worked, hours worked each week, and state of residence in 1975, Chinese American women could be expected to earn only 70 percent of the majority male income. Even among the college-educated, Chinese American women fared least well, making only 42 percent of what majority males earned. As we noted earlier, the mean income of all women, Anglo and Asian, was far below that of Anglo males in 1970 and 1980. This was true for both native-born and foreign-born Asians. In 1970 Anglo women earned only 54 percent of what their male counterparts did. Native-born Asian American women, depending on the particular ethnic group, earned anywhere from 49 to 57 percent of what Anglo males earned. In 1980, this inequity persisted.

Another way of thinking about comparable worth is not to focus only on what individuals do on the job, but on what they bring to the job as well. Because formal education is one measure of merit in American society and because it is most frequently perceived as the means to upward mobility, we would expect greater education to have greater payoffs.

Asian American women tend to be extraordinarily successful in terms of attaining higher education. Filipino American women have the highest college completion rate of all women and graduate at a rate 50 percent greater than that of majority males. Chinese American and Japanese American women follow closely behind, exceeding both the majority male and female rate of college completion.[13] Higher levels of education, however, bring lower returns for Asian American women than they do for other groups.

While education enhances earnings capability, the return on education for Asian American women is not as great as that for other women, and is well below parity with white males. Data on Asian American women in the five SMSAs where they are concentrated bear this out.[14] In 1980 all these women fell far behind Anglo males in what they earned in relation to their college education. Between 8 and 16 percent of native-born women earned $21,200 compared to 50 percent of Anglo males. Similar patterns were found among college-educated foreign-born women.

The fact that Asian American women do not reap the income benefits one might expect given their high levels of educational achievement raises questions about the reasons for such inequality. To what extent is this discrepancy based on outright discrimination? On self-imposed limitations related to cultural modesty? The absence of certain social or interpersonal skills required for upper managerial positions? Or institutional factors beyond their control? It is beyond the scope of this paper to address such concerns. However, the fact of inequality is itself noteworthy and poorly appreciated.

In general, Asian American women usually are overrepresented in clerical or administrative support jobs. While there is a somewhat greater tendency for foreign-born college-educated Asian women to find clerical-related jobs, both native- and foreign-born women have learned that clerical work is the area where they are most easily employed. In fact, in 1970 a third of native-born Chinese women were doing clerical work. A decade later Filipino women were concentrated there. In addition Asian American women tend to be overrepresented as cashiers, file clerks, office machine operators, and typists. They are less likely to get jobs as secretaries or receptionists. The former occupations not only carry less prestige but generally have "little or no decision-making authority, low mobility and low public contact."[15]

In short, education may improve one's chances for success, but it cannot promise the American Dream. For Asian American women education seems to serve less as an opportunity for upward mobility than as a protection against jobs as service or assembly workers, or as machine operatives—all areas where foreign-born Asian women are far more likely to find themselves.

CONCLUSION

In this essay I have attempted to direct our attention on the gap between achievement and reward, specifically the failure to reward monetarily those who have demonstrated competence. Asian American women, like Asian American men, have been touted as "model minorities," praised for their outstanding achievements. The concept of model minority, however, obscures the fact that one's accomplishments are not adequately recognized in terms of commensurate income or choice of occupation. By focusing on the achievements of one minority in relation to another, our attention is diverted from larger institutional and historical factors which influence a group's success. Each ethnic group has a different history, and a simplistic method of modeling which assumes the experience of all immigrants is the same ignores the sociostructural context in which a certain kind of achievement occurred. For example, World War II enabled many Asian Americans who were technically trained and highly educated to move into lucrative war-related industries.[16] More recently, Korean immigrants during the 1960s were able to capitalize on the fast-growing demand for wigs in the United States. It was not simply cultural ingenuity or individual hard work which made them successful in this enterprise, but the fact that Korean immigrants were in the unique position of being able to import cheap hair products from their mother country.[17]

Just as there are structural opportunities, so there are structural barriers. However, the persistent emphasis in American society on individual effort deflects attention away from such barriers and creates self-doubt among those who have not "made it." The myth that Asian Americans have succeeded as a group, when in actuality there are serious discrepancies between effort and achievement, and between achievement and reward, adds still further to this self-doubt.

While others have also pointed out the myth of the model minority, I want to add that myths do have social functions. It would be a mistake to dismiss the model minority concept as merely a myth. Asian Americans are—however inappropriately—thrust into the role of being models for other minorities.

A closer look at the images associated with Asians as a model minority group suggests competing or contradictory themes. One image is that Asian Americans exemplify a competitive spirit enabling them to overcome structural barriers through perseverance and ingenuity. On the other hand, they are also seen as complacent, content with their social lot, and expecting little in the way of outside help. A third image is that Asian Americans are experts at assimilation, demonstrating that this society still functions as a melting pot. Their values are sometimes equated with white, middle-class, Protestant values of hard work, determination, and thrift. Opposing this image, however, is still another, namely that Asian Americans have succeeded because they possess cultural values unique to them as a group—their family-centeredness and long tradition of reverence for scholarly achievement, for example.

Perhaps, then, this is why so many readily accept the myth, whose tenacity is due to its being vague and broad enough to appeal to a variety of different groups. Yet to the extent that the myth is based on misconceptions, we are called upon to reexamine it more closely in an effort to narrow the gap between striving and achieving.[18]

1. Ted Bell, "Quiet Loyalty Keeps Shops Running," *Sacramento Bee*, 11 February 1985.

2. Amado Y. Cabezas and Pauline L. Fong, "Employment Status of Asian-Pacific Women" (Background paper; San Francisco: ASIAN, Inc., 1976).

3. U.S. Bureau of the Census, *Race of the Population by States* (Washington, D.C., 1980). According to the census, 40 percent of all Chinese in America live in California, as well as 46 percent of all Filipinos, and 37 percent of all Japanese. New York ranks second for the number of Chinese residing there, and Hawaii is the second most populated state for Filipinos and Japanese.

4. Tricia Knoll, *Becoming Americans: Asian Sojourners, Immigrants, and Refugees in the Western United States* (Portland, Oreg.: Coast to Coast Books, 1982), 152.

5. U.S. Commission on Civil Rights, *Social Indicators of Equality for Minorities and Women* (Washington, D.C., 1978), 24, 50, 54, 58, 62.

6. David M. Moulton, "The Socioeconomic Status of Asian American Families in Five Major SMSAs" (Paper prepared for the Conference of Pacific and Asian American

Families and HEW-related Issues, San Francisco, 1978). No comparative data were available on blacks for the fifth SMSA, Honolulu.

7. James E. Blackwell, *Mainstreaming Outsiders* (New York: General Hall, Inc., 1981), 306; and Commission on Civil Rights, *Social Indicators*, 9.

8. California Advisory Committee, "A Dream Unfulfilled: Korean and Pilipino Health Professionals in California" (Report prepared for submission to U.S. Commission on Civil Rights, May 1975), iii.

9. See Amado Y. Cabezas, "A View of Poor Linkages between Education, Occupation and Earnings for Asian Americans" (Paper presented at the Third National Forum on Education and Work, San Francisco, 1977), 17; and Census of Population, PUS, 1980.

10. Census of the Population, PUS, 1970, 1980.

11. A 1977 report on California families showed that an average of 9.3 percent of Japanese, Chinese, and Filipino families were below the poverty level, but that only 5.4 percent of these families received public assistance. The corresponding figures for Anglos were 6.3 percent and 5.9 percent. From Harold T. Yee, "The General Level of Well-Being of Asian Americans" (Paper presented to U.S. government officials in partial response to Justice Department amicus).

12. Moulton, "Socioeconomic Status," 70–71.

13. Commission on Civil Rights, *Social Indicators*, 54.

14. The few exceptions occur in Honolulu with women who had more than a high school education and in Chicago with women who had a high school education or three years of college. Even those women fared poorly when compared to men, however.

15. Bob H. Suzuki, "Education and the Socialization of Asian Americans: A Revisionist Analysis of the 'Model Minority' Thesis," *Amerasia Journal* 4:2 (1977): 43. See also Fong and Cabezas, "Economic and Employment Status," 48–49; and Commission on Civil Rights, *Social Indicators*, 97–98.

16. U.S. Commission on Civil Rights, "Education Issues" in *Civil Rights Issues of Asian and Pacific Americans: Myths and Realities* (Washington, D.C., 1979), 370–376. This material was presented by Ling-chi Wang, University of California, Berkeley.

17. Illsoo Kim, *New Urban Immigrants: The Korean Community in New York* (Princeton, N.J.: Princeton University Press, 1981).

18. For further discussion of the model minority myth and interpretation of census data, see Deborah Woo, "The Socioeconomic Status of Asian American Women in the Labor Force: An Alternative View," *Sociological Perspectives* 28:3 (July 1985): 307–338.

THE FEMINIZATION OF POVERTY AMONG THE ELDERLY

24

Robyn I. Stone

Poverty rates among the elderly population have declined during the past decade. National statistics indicate that there has been a strong growth in after-tax income for the elderly as a group, including those with relatively low incomes. Furthermore, in 1982, for the first time since the official poverty index was introduced, a smaller proportion of the elderly than the nonelderly lived in poverty.

Evidence of improvement in the economic status of the elderly population has led to increased concern over the "graying of the budget," particularly with respect to the allocation of resources between the young and the old. In a provocative presidential address to the Population Association of America, Samuel H. Preston argued that benefits to the politically powerful elderly have expanded during the 1980s while the increasing subpopulation of poor children in America is faced with cutbacks in important public programs. He called for a reordering of priorities and a reallocation of resources toward the youth of this country.[1]

While the economic conditions of the elderly as a group have improved in recent years, pockets of poverty still prevail among this heterogeneous population. A number of researchers have argued that there has been a "feminization of poverty" among the elderly,[2] a phrase coined in the late 1970s in reference to those societal processes through which poverty is concentrated among younger women and children.[3] This article will demonstrate that poverty among the elderly also is concentrated among women. . . .

MEASURING POVERTY

There is continuing controversy over the definition and measurement of poverty. This paper uses the official poverty index computed by the U.S. Bureau of the Census which in 1986 was $5,255 for elderly individuals and $6,630 for elderly couples. This index, however, excludes the near poor, that

From: *Women's Studies Quarterly* 17 (Spring/Summer 1989): 20–34. Copyright © 1989 by Robyn I. Stone. Reprinted by permission.

is, those who live below 125 percent of the poverty line. Elderly persons with incomes between the poverty line and twice that level are particularly vulnerable because they are at high risk of dropping through the so-called "safety nets" of public programs.[4] They typically have too much income to qualify for such programs as Supplemental Security Income, Medicaid, or food stamps, even though their economically disadvantaged status often makes it difficult for them to purchase even the basic necessities.

In recent years the official poverty index, an absolute measure of money income, has been criticized for its failure to consider poverty as a relative concept. Researchers have attempted to estimate a measure of the relative economic status of the elderly population by adjusting for taxes, asset holdings, and household composition.[5] Using data on consumption expenditures in 1973, this study concluded that after the aforementioned adjustments, the average income of the elderly was roughly equal to the average income of the nonelderly.

There has been continuing debate over the past few years concerning the utility of including cash transfers and in-kind benefits as measures of economic status. Some poverty analysts estimate that the inclusion of all in-kind benefits received by the elderly (e.g., Medicare, Medicaid, food stamps) would lower the poverty rate to between 2 and 3 percent.[6] Others have warned that the value of health care benefits from Medicare and Medicaid should not be included in the formula unless the poverty threshold is substantially raised.[7] They argue that the receipt of Medicaid and Medicare benefits does not reduce the need for other income to meet basic food and housing requirements. Furthermore, the elderly spent over 15 percent of their income on health care in 1985—an average of $1,660 per person.[8] If the poverty threshold were revised to adjust for these out-of-pocket health care costs, it is likely that the poverty rate among the elderly would increase dramatically.

Further, while it is not within the purview of this paper to examine the voluminous literature on the definition and measurement of poverty, some have argued that poverty must be more broadly defined as lack of access to the whole array of resources that allow participation in society—not just income, but basic services, decision-making power, and dignity.[9]

FEMINIZATION OF POVERTY: THE EVIDENCE

With these caveats in mind, let us proceed with a brief examination of the gender gap in poverty among the elderly population. The differential is evident both in terms of changes in poverty over time and current poverty rates of men and women. While the rates of poverty for both genders

Table 1 Percent of Persons Aged 65 and over Living Below the Poverty Level[a] in 1986 by Race and Hispanic Origin

	Total	White	Black	Hispanic[b]
Male	8.5	6.9	24.2	18.8
Female	15.2	13.3	35.5	25.2
Both Sexes	12.4	10.7	31.0	22.5

[a]The poverty threshold for unrelated individuals in 1986 was $5,255; for couples the threshold was $6,630.

[b]Persons of Hispanic origin may be of any race.

Source: U.S. Department of Commerce, Bureau of the Census, "Money Income and Poverty Status of Families and Persons in the United States: 1986." Current Population Reports, Series P-60, No. 157, Table 18 (Washington, D.C., 1987).

decreased over the past three decades, poverty rates fell more slowly among females than among males.[10] Today women constitute 72.4 percent of the elderly poor although they account for only 58.7 percent of all elderly. Approximately 2.5 million women or 15.2 percent of noninstitutionalized women aged sixty-five years or over live below the poverty threshold compared with only 8.5 percent of elderly men (Table 1). The poverty rate for women aged eighty-five years and over is 19.7 percent, a figure that approximates the poverty rate of children under age eighteen.

Widowhood and the Gender Gap

Differences in the marital status of elderly women and men help to explain why the elderly poor are disproportionately female. Women aged sixty-five and over are almost three times as likely as elderly males to be widowed due to the convergence of greater longevity (females' life expectancy at age sixty-five is 4.3 years longer than males'), the tendency among women to marry men older than themselves, and lower rates of remarriage among widows. Because widowhood is linked with lower incomes[11] and elderly females are more likely to be widowed, the poor elderly population is disproportionately female. Widowhood, however, also has an independent effect on the gender differential in poverty rates—21.3 percent of widowed elderly females live below the poverty line compared with 14.7 percent of widowers.[12]

Cross-sectional data provide only a snapshot view of women in the midst of a spell of poverty. Findings from a recent longitudinal analysis of the dynamics of poverty among the elderly indicate that poverty rates rise sharply with widowhood.[13] Furthermore, the risk of experiencing at least one spell of poverty over a ten-year period is greater than is suggested by single-period rates. For widows the ten-year risk of being impoverished is 30 percent higher than the peak annual poverty rate.

Living Arrangements and the Gender Gap

Elderly women also are almost three times as likely as elderly men to be living alone, a phenomenon that results in large part from higher rates of widowhood. Living alone is associated with higher poverty rates, primarily because those sharing households receive the economic benefits of combined family incomes. Gender also appears to have an independent effect on the likelihood of being poor. A larger proportion of elderly women living alone (26.8 percent) are impoverished than of elderly men with the same living arrangement (19.2 percent).[14]

The growing propensity for elderly women to live alone has had a significant effect on the change in the economic status of this subpopulation as well as on poverty rates at one point in time. A recent study found that the measured decline in poverty for noninstitutionalized older women from 52 percent in 1950 to 16.1 percent in 1980 would have been larger (to 13.3 percent) if living arrangement patterns had not changed the way they did during that thirty-year period.[15] The findings suggest that part of the reason for the slower decrease in female poverty rates compared to those of men was the diminishing propensity for elderly women to share households with relatives other than husbands and the consequent increase in the proportion who chose to live alone.

Institutionalized Females: The Invisible Poor

Reported poverty statistics usually refer to the civilian noninstitutionalized population. However, many elderly women residing in institutions also are impoverished. Although no data currently are available on the economic status of this important subgroup of elderly individuals, national estimates recently published from the 1985 National Nursing Home Survey (NNHS) provide some clues. Study findings indicate that approximately 982,000 elderly women or 6 percent of the female elderly population reside in nursing homes.[16] Elderly women are twice as likely as elderly men to be institutionalized. This is particularly true for the oldest-old; one in four women aged eighty-five years or over resides in a nursing home compared to one in seven men in this age group.

A gross measure of economic status of the current institutionalized population is the primary source of payment for nursing home care during the month of admission. According to the NNHS, approximately 42 percent of elderly female nursing home residents relied primarily on Medicaid at the time of admission compared to only 36 percent of male residents. Furthermore, many residents who are not originally dependent upon Medicaid report primary reliance on this public program at the month of discharge.[17] The figure ranges from 11 to 22 percent depending upon the duration of the nursing home stay. These findings suggest that a large proportion of elderly female nursing home residents are impoverished either at the outset of institutionalization or sometime during the nursing home stay.

In sum, the evidence indicates that the elderly poor population is disproportionately female due, in large part, to their higher rates of widowhood, living alone, and institutionalization. These conditions, however, do not explain why men with the same marital status and living arrangement are not as likely to be impoverished. The following discussion explores some of the reasons for the feminization of poverty in old age.

REASONS FOR THE FEMINIZATION OF POVERTY AMONG THE ELDERLY

In order to understand why women are more likely than men to be poor in old age, it is important to recognize that the economic status of elderly persons depends upon their lifelong marital and family obligations and their employment history. Paternalistic customs and laws that encouraged female dependency, the division of labor between genders with women as primary caregivers, and labor market discrimination are important determinants of gender differences in poverty among the elderly.

Female Dependence

At the root of the feminization of poverty is the history of economic dependence of women on men in this society. According to British common law, which served as the basis for American practices and policies, a married couple was treated as a single person with the husband assuming all legal and economic responsibilities. Custody of children and earnings belonged to the father. The nineteenth-century female was not allowed to testify in court, to hold property, or to establish a business.[18] In fact, during the latter part of the nineteenth century, a woman's idleness was a measure of her husband's status.[19]

Although a significant proportion of women has always worked,[20] the widespread belief in female dependence has had a profound effect on the design of policies that influence the economic status of elderly women. The Social Security program has played a significant role in reducing the poverty rate of older Americans.[21] Nevertheless, this program has major gaps in benefits for certain subgroups of elderly women. While a thorough discussion of inequities in Social Security is beyond the scope of this article, the major point to be made here is that this program was predicated on the assumption that workers are males in stable, nuclear family relationships with wives as dependents. Homemaking wives of working husbands receive a dependent benefit from Social Security. Since the early 1950s, however, there has been an increasing trend toward female labor force participation and dual-earner couples. Current Social Security provisions cause inequities between one- and two-earner couples. Specifically, dual-earner couples tend to receive lower benefits than one-earner couples with the same total earnings. Consequently the surviving spouse of a dual-earner couple generally receives less than the surviving spouse of a one-earner couple with the same earnings record. Because women are more likely than men to be widowed, this policy differentially affects women.

The Social Security program's spousal benefits also are based on the premise that marriage will end in death, not divorce. A divorced woman is eligible for the dependent benefit based on the ex-spouse's work history only if the marriage lasted at least ten years and she has not remarried.

Private pension policies also contain gender inequities. Until 1983, pension plans were allowed to pay female retirees at lower rates based upon their greater life expectancy. A 1983 Supreme Court decision finally required equal payments to female pensioners.[22] Many women who outlive their husbands do not receive private pension benefits when they are widowed because husbands have failed to elect survivorship coverage for their spouses. Mandatory provisions for private pensions are just beginning to address this problem.

In sum, the institutionalization of the economic dependence of women on men fostered policies that contribute to the economically disadvantaged position of many elderly women. According to one report on the status of women, many are "only one man away from poverty."[23]

Family and Work History

The family and work history of individuals during the years before they reach sixty-five strongly influences their economic status in old age. These patterns determine both the assets accrued before retirement and the benefits received after age sixty-five. The division of labor between genders, which assigns primary family responsibilities to the woman of the household, and labor market discrimination, which limits employment choices, contribute to the impoverishment of many elderly women.

The Division of Labor Between Genders

While it is not within the purview of this article to explore the origins of the division of labor between genders, it is important to recognize that the primary female role of homemaker and caregiver has a profound influence on a woman's economic position in old age. This unpaid labor is not assigned any value in terms of the financial resources one obtains over a lifetime or the public and private pension benefits one receives after age sixty-five. As previously noted, women who are career homemakers are dependent upon their husbands' economic status with potentially devastating financial consequences for those who become widowed or divorced.

Many women who do work for pay exhibit interrupted work patterns including mid-life career entry, intermittent employment throughout the work cycle, and frequent job changes.[24] Erratic work history is most often the consequence of childbearing and child rearing, which cause many women to delay or interrupt their work careers. This "in and out" pattern decreases a woman's opportunity to become vested in a pension plan and ensures lower wages upon which retirement income is based.[25]

The division of labor with regard to caregiving does not stop with child rearing but continues throughout the life cycle. Just as women are beginning to anticipate the empty nest, many are faced with the responsibility of caring for disabled husbands, parents, and other adult family members.[26] A large proportion also must deal with the competing demands of employment and elder care, which may contribute further to the disadvantaged economic position of many elderly women. A national survey of informal caregivers to disabled elders found that 14 percent of wives caring for disabled husbands and 12 percent of daughters caring for disabled parents quit their jobs to assume caregiver responsibilities.[27] Approximately 39.4 percent of the daughters who worked during the caregiver experience rearranged their schedules, 22.8 percent cut back on hours, and 24.8 percent took time off without pay. Among those who used unpaid leave, one-fifth had been off the job for more than five days during their last episode of work accommodation.

Researchers examining the effects of child rearing on the economic status of elderly women found that each child reduces a woman's chances of pension coverage by 2 percent and decreases annual retirement income by $94.[28] The potential loss in earnings and pension benefits associated with elder care also warrants investigation.

Labor Market Discrimination

Gender discrimination in the labor market also contributes to poverty among elderly women. A number of theories have been proposed to explain this phenomenon ranging from individual employer discrimination, employee choice, and the structural approach of the dual labor market to a combination of these perspectives. Women are overrepresented in industries and occupations characterized by relatively low earnings, few fringe benefits, poor working conditions, and little job security.

Low earnings and pension coverage increase the risk of impoverishment among female retirees relative to men. Approximately 42 percent of married couples, 32 percent of unmarried men, but only 22 percent of unmarried women receive private pension income.[29] Moreover, even when older women accrue pension benefits, their income from private plans tends to be lower than that of their male peers. In 1982, for example, the median private pension income was $2,980 for male retirees compared to $1,520 for older women.[30] An analysis of retirement incomes among unmarried men and women participating in the Social Security Administration's Longitudinal Retirement History Study found that having one or more private pensions exerts a strong influence on retirement income among female retirees.[31] However, even location in the primary industrial sector increased a woman's retirement income by only $275 while her male counterpart enjoyed a $395 increase.

Spousal Impoverishment

Many elderly women are impoverished when their disabled husbands are institutionalized. Medicaid has become the largest insurer for long-term care provided in a nursing home but comes with a heavy price tag for the disabled elder and his or her spouse. In order to become eligible for Medicaid coverage, persons must either be poor or "spend down" their income to the level established by a particular state Medicaid program.

Most states consider the income and/or the assets of the noninstitutionalized spouse to be available to the institutionalized spouse to pay for long-term care services, a process referred to as "deeming of resources."[32] Although there are five deeming methods currently used by state programs, ranging from deeming all of a spouse's income and assets for the entire nursing home stay (e.g., Nebraska) to no deeming of assets (e.g., Michigan), many spouses become impoverished before their institutionalized partners are covered by Medicaid.

According to the findings from a recent report that developed estimates of the long-term care-related financial risk faced by the elderly, 56 percent of the spouses would have to spend down their income after the disabled spouse had spent only one-half year in the nursing home.[33] When both income and assets are considered, approximately 34 percent of the community-residing spouses would be impoverished within one-half year and 46 percent would spend down to the poverty level by the end of the year. A preliminary state analysis included in this study indicates that considering income only, between 15 and 59 percent of the noninstitutionalized spouses would be impoverished after only thirteen weeks of a disabled spouse's placement in a nursing home. When assets are included, the rates range from 9 to 13 percent depending upon the state deeming policy. Because women live longer and tend to marry men older than themselves, they are more likely than men to have institutionalized spouses. Spousal impoverishment resulting from Medicaid policies therefore affects many more women than men.

Current and Proposed Policy Initiatives

In recent years, policymakers have begun to alter some of the provisions in employment and retirement legislation that have contributed to the gender gap in poverty among the elderly population. For example, the Retirement Equity Act of 1984 requires the consent of the dependent spouse before pension survivor benefits can be waived by a worker and allows employees to take time off from work without losing pension credit for earlier work history.

The Economic Equity Act of 1986 (which was incorporated into the Tax Reform Act of 1986 and goes into effect in 1989) lowers the years of service required for vesting of private pensions from ten to five years for most employees. This legislation also requires employers to extend private pension coverage to more employees, a change designed to benefit lower-paid workers. In addition, this act restricts the degree to which employers can integrate Social Security and private pension benefits—that is, reduce private pension benefits as Social Security benefits increase. Counting the higher of the two benefits tended to wipe out private pensions for many employees, and for lower-wage earners in particular. According to the provisions of this legislation, employers must leave at least one-half the private pension benefit when integrating private and public plans.

The proposed 1988 Economic Equity Act would abolish integration of Social Security and private pension benefits altogether and would require private pension plans to award credits to part-time workers, the majority of whom are female. This initiative also would extend five-year vesting rights to all pension plans. None of these initiatives, however, addresses the problem of lack of portability of pension benefits, an omission that penalizes many women who have made frequent job changes.

With respect to public pension policy, one strategy being explored to redress the current provision in Social Security that penalizes the survivor of a dual-earner couple is to base the survivor's benefit on the couple's combined earnings during the marriage. Similarly, the Social Security earnings credits received during the years of marriage would be aggregated and split equally in the event of a divorce. Although the earnings sharing concept has been the subject of much debate and would require a wide variety of provisions to address the problems of potential losers, this strategy would help to ensure a more adequate income for widowed and divorced retirees.[34] Canada implemented a voluntary program of earnings sharing in 1978 and found that very few individuals were using this option. The Canadian experience suggests that the program should be mandatory and automatic.[35]

The U.S. Senate's proposed Medicare Catastrophic Loss Prevention Act of 1987 and the U.S. House of Representatives' Medicare Catastrophic Protection Act of 1987 both contain provisions to mitigate against impoverishment of a spouse in cases where the married partner is institutionalized. The House bill allows the community-residing spouse to keep up to $925 of her or his monthly income; the Senate's ceiling is $750 per month. According to both bills, the couple's assets are divided and the noninstitutionalized spouse is allowed to keep at least $12,000 with a ceiling of $48,000.

The proposed Family and Medical Leave Act of 1987 mandates employers to grant maternity/paternity leave without pay. This proposal also requires that employers allow workers to take time off without pay to care for a disabled child, spouse, or parent. This legislative initiative would help female workers to maintain their earnings credits during work periods interrupted by caregiver responsibilities.

CONCLUSION

This article has examined the gender gap in poverty among the elderly population and has explored several reasons why women are poorer than men in old age. Part of the feminization of poverty is associated with higher female rates of widowhood, living alone, and nursing home residence. However, even these factors fail to account for the differential in poverty among women and men aged sixty-five and over.

The feminization of poverty among the elderly is rooted in a history of economic dependence of women on men in this society. This dependence fostered policies that have contributed to the impoverished status of many elderly females who find themselves widowed or divorced.

Preretirement work and family history play an important role in determining a woman's economic situation in old age. The overrepresentation of women in certain industries and occupations is linked to lower earnings and little access to private pensions. Further, the major female role of caregiver to children, disabled husbands, and parents causes many women to delay or interrupt their work careers. This interruption further reduces their earning power and access to public and private pension benefits. Another threat to the economic security of many elderly wives is the risk of spousal impoverishment, which is associated with the placement of a disabled husband in a nursing home.

A report issued by the Women's Research and Education Institute suggests that the elderly women of the future should be better off financially because they are staying in the labor force to a much greater extent than did their mothers and grandmothers.[36] Experiments with alternative work options (e.g., job sharing, flextime, employer-based day care) are making it easier for women to maintain jobs and to care for families. Furthermore, movement of women into more highly paid occupations with better employee benefits should bring them into retirement with more income protection. To the extent that the wages and salaries of female-dominated jobs are adjusted upward (in response to pay equity or comparable worth legislation) women in these occupations also may see their earnings translated into higher Social Security and private pension benefits.

Others are not as optimistic. Although some working women have moved into fields dominated by men, the gender division of labor remains firm. Projections from a recent report sponsored by the Commonwealth Fund Commission (CFC) on Elderly Persons Living Alone suggest that male poverty will drop sharply by the year 2020 while women will experience little improvement.[37] Part of this differential is attributed to the demographic boom of the very old. Between 1980 and 2050, the proportion of the population aged eighty-five years and over is expected to increase from 1 percent to over 5 percent of the total population and from 9 percent to 24 percent of population aged sixty-five and over. The majority will be women living alone in poverty. Thus, by the year 2020, the CFC report suggests that poverty among the elderly population will be almost exclusively a problem of elderly women living alone.

Whatever the future of the gender gap in poverty among the elderly, this gap should be placed in perspective. Racial differences in poverty surpass the gender differences discussed in this paper. The poverty rate among black men in 1986, for example, was 11 percentage points higher than the rate for white women (Table 1).[38] Moreover, elderly Hispanic females were twice as likely as aged white females to live in poverty; black females aged sixty-five and over were almost three times as likely as their white age peers to be impoverished.

Several feminist writers have argued that poverty did not become a women's issue until large numbers of white middle-class women began to fall below the poverty threshold due to rising divorce, separation, and teenage pregnancy rates.[39] It has been suggested that "as the white women's movement takes up the slogan of the 'feminization of poverty' to advocate government programs and social services on behalf of women, it is essential to keep in mind which women are being impoverished, in what ways, and for what reasons."[40] We need to focus more attention on the racial gap in poverty rates among the elderly population and the feminization of poverty among minorities.

NOTES

1. S. Preston, "Children and the Elderly in the U.S.," *Scientific American* 251 (1984): 44–49.

2. B. Ehrenreich and F. F. Piven, "The Feminization of Poverty," *Dissent* 2 (1984): 162–70; M. Minkler and R. Stone, "The Feminization of Poverty and Older Women," *The Gerontologist* 25 (1985): 351–57; J. L. Warlick, "Why Is Poverty after 65 a Woman's Problem?" *Journal of Gerontology* 40 (1983): 751–57.

3. D. Pearce, "The Feminization of Poverty: Women, Work and Welfare," *Urban and Social Change Review* 11 (1978): 28–36.

4. T. Smeeding, "Non-money Income and the Elderly: The Case of the 'Tweeners,' " Institute for Poverty Research, Discussion Paper No. 759–84, University of Wisconsin-Madison, 1984.

5. S. Danziger et al., "Income Transfers and the Economic Status of the Elderly," in *Economic Transfers in the United States*, ed. M. Moon (Chicago: University of Chicago Press, 1984).

6. U.S. Bureau of the Census, "Estimates of Poverty Including the Value of Noncash Benefits." Technical Paper No. 52 (Washington, D.C.: Government Printing Office, 1984).

7. M. Moon, "Poverty among Elderly Women and Minorities" (Discussion paper, The Urban Institute, Washington, D.C., 1985).

8. U.S. House of Representatives, Select Committee on Aging, *America's Elderly at Risk*, 99th Cong. (Washington, D.C.: Government Printing Office, 1985).

9. H. Scott, *Working Your Way to the Bottom: The Feminization of Poverty* (London: Pandora Press, 1984); K. B. Griffin, *International Inequality and National Poverty* (New York: Holmes and Meier, 1978).

10. C. Ross, S. Danzinger, and E. Smolensky, "The Level and Trend in Poverty in the United States, 1939–1979," *Demography* 24 (1987).

11. A. M. O'Rand, "Women," in *Handbook of the Aged in the United States*, ed. E. Palmore (Westport, Conn.: Greenwood Press, 1985); T. Tissue and J. F. McCoy, "Income and Living Arrangements among Poor Aged Singles," *Social Security Bulletin* 44 (1981): 3–13.

12. U.S. Bureau of the Census, "Poverty in the United States 1985." *Current Population Reports.* Series P-60, No. 158. (Washington, D.C.: Government Printing Office, 1986).

13. K. C. Holden, R. V. Burkhauser, and D. A. Myers, "Income Transitions at Older Stages of Life: The Dynamics of Poverty," *Gerontologist* 26 (1986): 292–97.

14. U.S. Bureau of the Census, "Poverty in the U.S."

15. K. C. Holden, "Poverty and Living Arrangements among Older Women: Are Changes in Economic Well-being Underestimated?" *Journal of Gerontology* 43 (1988): 522–27.

16. E. Hing, "Use of Nursing Homes by the Elderly: Preliminary Data from the 1985 National Nursing Home Survey," Advance Data from Vital and Health Statistics, No. 135, Department of Health and Human Services Pub. No. (PHS) 87–1250 (Hyattsville, Md.: Public Health Service, 1987).

17. E. S. Sckscenski, "Discharges from Nursing Homes: Preliminary Data from the 1985 National Nursing Home Survey," Advance Data from Vital and Health Statistics, No. 142, Department of Health and Human Services Pub. No. (PHS) 87–1250 (Hyattsville, Md.: Public Health Service, 1987).

18. H. Z. Lopata, "Economic Support of Women and Children," in *Aging*, ed. A. Kolker and P. I. Ahmed (New York: Elsevier Biomedical, 1982).

19. V. Klein, "The Historical Background," in *Women: A Feminist Perspective*, 3d. ed., ed. J. Freeman (Palo Alto, Calif.: Mayfield, 1984).

20. A. Kessler-Harris, *Out to Work* (New York: Oxford University Press, 1982).

21. A. Blaustein, *The American Promise* (New Brunswick, N.J.: Transaction Books, 1982).

22. C. L. Estes, L. Gerard, and A. Clark, "Women and the Economics of Aging," *International Journal of Health Services* 14 (1984): 55–68.

23. Friends of the San Francisco Commission on the Status of Women, *Women News* (San Francisco, 1980).

24. L. C. Chenoweth and E. Maret, "The Career Patterns of Mature American Women," *Sociology of Work and Occupation* 7 (1980): 222–51.

25. A. M. O'Rand and J. C. Henretta, "Midlife Work History and the Retirement Income of the Aged in the United States," in *Women's Retirement: Policy Implications of Recent Research*, ed. M. Szinovacz (Beverly Hills: Sage Pub., 1982).

26. E. M. Brody, "Parent Care as a Normative Family Stress," *The Gerontologist* 25 (1985): 19–29; R. Stone, G. L. Cafferata, and J. Sangl, "Caregivers of the Frail Elderly: A National Profile," *The Gerontologist* 27 (1987): 616–26.

27. Stone et al., "Caregivers."

28. A. M. O'Rand and R. Landerman, "Early Family Role Effects on Women's and Men's Retirement Income Status," *Research on Aging* (1984).

29. Women's Studies Program at George Washington University and the Women's Research and Education Institute of the Congressional Caucus for Women's Issues, *Older Women: The Economics of Aging* (Washington, D.C., 1981).

30. S. Grad, "Incomes of the Aged and Nonaged, 1950–82," *Social Security Bulletin* 47 (1984): 3–17.

31. O'Rand and Landerman, "Early Family Role."

32. ICF Incorporated, *The Effects of Variations in Medicaid Programs on Older Women* (Washington, D.C.: American Association of Retired Persons, 1986).

33. U.S. House of Representatives, Select Committee on Aging, *Long Term Care and Personal Impoverishment: Seven in Ten Elderly Living Alone Are at Risk.* Committee Pub. No. 100–631 (Washington, D.C.: Government Printing Office, 1987).

34. S. J. Rix, *Older Women: The Economics of Aging* (Washington, D.C.: Women's Research and Education Institute of the Congressional Caucus for Women's Issues, 1984).

35. M. B. Tracy, "Credit-splitting and Private Pension Awards in Divorce: A Case Study of British Columbia," *Research on Aging* 9 (1987).

36. Rix, *Older Women.*

37. Commonwealth Fund Commission on Elderly People Living Alone, *Old, Alone and Poor: A Plan for Reducing Poverty among Elderly People Living Alone* (New York: The Commonwealth Fund, 1987).

38. U.S. Bureau of the Census, "Poverty in the U.S."

39. Ehrenreich and Piven, "Feminization of Poverty"; P. Palmer, " 'The Racial Feminization of Poverty': Women of Color as Portents of the Future for All Women," *Women's Studies Quarterly* 11, No. 3 (1983): 4–6.

40. Palmer, " 'Racial Feminization of Poverty.' "

Families

OUR MOTHERS' GRIEF: *Racial Ethnic*   **25**
Women and the Maintenance of Families

Bonnie Thornton Dill

REPRODUCTIVE LABOR[1] FOR WHITE WOMEN IN EARLY AMERICA

In eighteenth- and nineteenth-century America, the lives of white[2] women in the United States were circumscribed within a legal and social system based on patriarchal authority. This authority took two forms: public and private. The social, legal, and economic position of women in this society was controlled through the private aspects of patriarchy and defined in terms of their relationship to families headed by men. The society was structured to confine white wives to reproductive labor within the domestic sphere. At the same time the formation, preservation and protection of families among white settlers was seen as crucial to the growth and development of American society. Building, maintaining, and supporting families was a concern of the State and of those organizations that prefigured the State. Thus, while white women had few legal rights as women, they were protected through public forms of patriarchy that acknowledged and supported their family roles of wives, mothers, and daughters because they were vital instruments for building American society.

From: *Journal of Family History* 13 (1988): 415–431. Reprinted by permission.

The groundwork for public support of women's family roles was laid during the colonial period. As early as 1619, the London Company began planning for the importation of single women into the colonies to marry colonists, form families, and provide for a permanent settlement. The objective was to make the men "more settled and less moveable . . . instability would breed a dissolution, and so an overthrow of the Plantation" (cited in Spruill 1972, p. 8).

In accordance with this recognition of the importance of families, the London Company provided the economic basis necessary for the development of the family as a viable and essential institution within the nascent social structure of the colonies. Shares of land were allotted for both husbands and wives in recognition of the fact that "in a new plantation it is not known whether men or women be the most necessary" (cited in Spruill 1972, p. 9).

This pattern of providing an economic base designed to attract, promote and maintain families was followed in the other colonial settlements. Lord Baltimore of Maryland ". . . offered to each adventurer a hundred acres for himself, a hundred for his wife, fifty for each child, a hundred for each man servant, and sixty for a woman servant. Women heads of families were treated just as men" (Spruill 1972, p. 11).

In Georgia, which appealed to poorer classes for settlers more than did Virginia or Maryland, ". . . among the advantages they offered men to emigrate was the gainful employment of their wives and children" (Spruill 1972, p. 16).

In colonial America, white women were seen as vital contributors to the stabilization and growth of society. They were therefore accorded some legal and economic recognition through a patriarchal family structure.

> While colonial life remained hard, . . . American women married earlier [than European women], were less restricted by dowries, and often had legal protection for themselves and their children in antenuptial contracts (Kennedy 1979, p. 7).

Throughout the colonial period, women's reproductive labor in the family was an integral part of the daily operation of small-scale family farms or artisan's shops. According to Kessler-Harris (1981), a gender-based division of labor was common, but not rigid. The participation of women in work that was essential to family survival reinforced the importance of their contributions to both the protection of the family and the growth of society.

Between the end of the eighteenth and mid-nineteenth century, what is labeled the "modern American family" developed. The growth of industrialization and an urban middle class, along with the accumulation of agrarian wealth among Southern planters, had two results that are particularly pertinent to this discussion. First, class differentiation increased and sharpened, and with it, distinctions in the content and nature of women's family lives. Second, the organization of industrial labor resulted in the separation of home and family and the assignment to women of a separate sphere of activity focused on childcare and home maintenance. Whereas men's activities became increasingly focused upon the industrial competitive sphere of work, "women's activities were increasingly confined to the care of children, the nurturing of the husband, and the physical maintenance of the home" (Degler 1980, p. 26).

This separate sphere of domesticity and piety became both an ideal for all white women as well as a source of important distinctions between them. As Matthei (1982) points out, tied to the notion of wife as homemaker is a definition of masculinity in which the husband's successful role performance was measured by his ability to keep his wife in the homemaker role. The entry of white women into the labor force came to be linked with the husband's assumed inability to fulfill his provider role.

For wealthy and middle-class women, the growth of the domestic sphere offered a potential for creative development as homemakers and mothers. Given ample financial support from their husband's earnings, some of these women were able to concentrate their energies on the development and elaboration of the more intangible elements of this separate sphere. They were also able to hire other women to perform the daily tasks such as cleaning, laundry, cooking, and ironing. Kessler-Harris cautions, however, that the separation of productive labor from the home did not seriously diminish the amount of physical drudgery associated with housework, even for middle-class women.

> It did relegate the continuing hard work to second place, transforming the public image of the household by the 1820s and 1830s from a place where productive labor was performed to one whose main goals were the preservation of virtue and morality . . . Many of the "well-run" homes of the pre–Civil War period seem to have been the dwelling of overworked women. Short of household help, without modern conveniences, and frequently pregnant, these women complained bitterly of their harsh existence (Kessler-Harris 1981, p. 39).

In effect, household labor was transformed from economic productivity done by members of the family group to home maintenance; childcare and moral uplift done by an isolated woman who perhaps supervised some servants.

Working-class white women experienced this same transformation but their families' acceptance of the domestic code meant that their labor in the home intensified. Given the meager earnings of working-class men, working-class families had to develop alternative strategies to both survive and keep the wives at home. The result was that working-class women's reproductive labor increased to fill the gap between family need and family income. Women increased their own production of household goods through things such as canning and sewing; and by developing other sources of income, including boarders and homework. A final and very important source of other income was wages earned by the participation of sons and daughters in the labor force. In fact, Matthei argues that "the domestic homemaking of married women was supported by the labors of their daughters" (1982, p. 130).

The question arises: Why did white working-class families sacrifice other aspects of this nineteenth-century notion of family, such as privacy and the protection of children, to keep wives as homemakers within the home? Zaretsky (1978) provides a possible answer.

> The Victorian emphasis on the sanctity of the family and on the autonomy of women within the family marked an advance for women of all classes over the interdependent but male dominated subsistence farm of the 18th century . . . most of women's adult life was taken up with childrearing. As a result, a special respect for her place within the home, and particularly for her childrearing activities was appreciated by working class women (p. 211).

Another way in which white women's family roles were socially acknowledged and protected was through the existence of a separate sphere for women. The code of domesticity, attainable for affluent women, became an ideal toward which nonaffluent women aspired. Notwithstanding the personal constraints placed on women's development, the notion of separate spheres promoted the growth and stability of family life among the white middle class and became the basis for working-class men's efforts to achieve a family wage, so that they could keep their wives at home. Also, women gained a distinct sphere of authority and expertise that yielded them special recognition.

During the eighteenth and nineteenth centuries, American society accorded considerable importance to the development and sustenance of European immigrant families. As primary laborers in the reproduction and maintenance of family life, women were acknowledged and accorded the privileges and protections deemed socially appropriate to their family roles. This argument acknowledges the fact that the family structure denied these women many rights and privileges and seriously constrained their individual growth and development. Because women gained social recognition primarily through their membership in families, their personal rights were few and privileges were subject to the will of the male head of the household. Nevertheless, the recognition of women's reproductive labor as an essential building block of the family, combined with a view of the family as the cornerstone of the nation, distinguished the experiences of the white, dominant culture from those of racial ethnics.

Thus, in its founding, American society initiated legal, economic, and social practices designed to promote the growth of family life among European colonists. The reception colonial families found in the United States contrasts sharply with the lack of attention given to the families of racial-ethnics. Although the presence of racial-ethnics was equally as important for the growth of the nation, their political, economic, legal, and social status was quite different.

REPRODUCTIVE LABOR AMONG RACIAL-ETHNICS IN EARLY AMERICA

Unlike white women, racial-ethnic women experienced the oppressions of a patriarchal society but were denied the protections and buffering of a patriarchal family. Their families suffered as a direct result of the organization of the labor systems in which they participated.

Racial-ethnics were brought to this country to meet the need for a cheap and exploitable labor force. Little attention was given to their family and community life except as it related to their economic productivity. Labor, and not the existence or maintenance of families, was the critical aspect of their role in building the nation. Thus they were denied the social structural supports necessary to make *their* families a vital element in the social order. Family membership was not a key means of access to participation in the wider society. The lack of social, legal, and economic support for racial-ethnic families intensified and extended women's reproductive labor, created tensions and strains in family relationships, and set the stage for a variety of creative and adaptive forms of resistance.

AFRICAN-AMERICAN SLAVES

Among students of slavery, there has been considerable debate over the relative "harshness" of American slavery, and the degree to which slaves were permitted or encouraged to form families. It is generally acknowledged that many slaveowners found it economically advantageous to encourage family formation as a way of reproducing and perpetuating the slave labor force. This became increasingly true after 1807 when the importation of African slaves was explicitly prohibited. The existence of these families and many aspects of their functioning, however, were directly controlled by the master. In other words, slaves married and formed families but these groupings were completely subject to the master's decision to let them remain intact. One study has estimated that about 32% of all recorded slave marriages were disrupted by sale, about 45% by death of a spouse, about 10% by choice, with the remaining 13% not disrupted at all (Blassingame 1972, pp. 90–92). African slaves thus quickly learned that they had a limited degree of control over the formation and maintenance of their marriages and could not be assured of keeping their children with them. The threat of disruption was perhaps the most direct and pervasive cultural assault[3] on families that slaves encountered. Yet there were a number of other aspects of the slave system which reinforced the precariousness of slave family life.

In contrast to some African traditions and the Euro-American patterns of the period, slave men were not the main provider or authority figure in the family. The mother-child tie was basic and of greatest interest to the slave-owner because it was critical in the reproduction of the labor force.

In addition to the lack of authority and economic autonomy experienced by the husband-father in the slave family, use of the rape of women slaves as a weapon of terror and control further undermined the integrity of the slave family.

> It would be a mistake to regard the institutionalized pattern of rape during slavery as an expression of white men's sexual urges, otherwise stifled by the spector of the white womanhood's chastity . . . Rape was a weapon of domination, a weapon of repression, whose covert goal was to extinguish slave women's will to resist, and in the process, to demoralize their men (Davis 1981, pp. 23–24).

The slave family, therefore, was at the heart of a peculiar tension in the master-slave relationship. On the one hand, slaveowners sought to encourage familial ties among slaves because, as Matthei (1982) states: ". . . these provided the basis of the development of the slave into a self-conscious socialized human being" (p. 81). They also hoped and believed that this socialization process would help children learn to accept their place in society as slaves. Yet the master's need to control and intervene in the familial life of the slaves is indicative of the other side of this tension. Family ties had the potential for becoming a competing and more potent source of allegiance than the slave-master himself. Also, kin were as likely to socialize children in forms of resistance as in acts of compliance.

It was within this context of surveillance, assault, and ambivalence that slave women's reproductive labor took place. She and her menfolk had the task of preserving the human and family ties that could ultimately give them a reason for living. They had to socialize their children to believe in the possibility of a life in which they were not enslaved. The slave woman's labor on behalf of the family was, as Davis (1971) has pointed out, the only labor the slave engaged in that could not be directly appropriated by the slaveowner for his own profit. Yet, its indirect appropriation, as labor crucial to the reproduction of the slaveowner's labor force, was the source of strong ambivalence for many slave women. Whereas some mothers murdered their babies to keep them from being slaves, many sought within the family sphere a degree of autonomy and creativity denied them in other realms of the society. The maintenance of a distinct African-American culture is testimony to the ways in which slaves maintained a degree of cultural autonomy and resisted the creation of a slave family that only served the needs of the master.

Gutman (1976) provides evidence of the ways in which slaves expressed a unique Afro-American culture through their family practices. He provides data on naming patterns and kinship ties among slaves that flies in the face of the dominant ideology of the period. That ideology argued that slaves were immoral and had little concern for or appreciation of family life.

Yet Gutman demonstrated that within a system which denied the father authority over his family, slave boys were frequently named after their fathers, and many children were named after blood relatives as a way of maintaining family ties. Gutman also suggested that after emancipation a number of slaves took the names of former owners in order to reestablish family ties that had been disrupted earlier. On plantation after plantation, Gutman found considerable evidence of the building and maintenance of extensive kinship ties among slaves. In instances where slave families had been disrupted, slaves in new communities reconstituted the kinds of family and kin ties that came to characterize black family life throughout the South. These patterns included, but were not limited to, a belief in the importance of marriage as a long-term commitment, rules of exogamy that included marriage between first cousins, and acceptance of women who had children outside of marriage. Kinship networks were an important source of resistance to the organization of labor that treated the individual slave, and not the family, as the unit of labor (Caulfield 1974).

Another interesting indicator of the slaves' maintenance of some degree of cultural autonomy has been pointed out by Wright (1981) in her discussion of slave housing. Until the early 1800s, slaves were often permitted to build their housing according to their own design and taste. During that period, housing built in an African style was quite common in the slave quarters. By

1830, however, slaveowners had begun to control the design and arrangement of slave housing and had introduced a degree of conformity and regularity to it that left little room for the slave's personalization of the home. Nevertheless, slaves did use some of their own techniques in construction and often hid it from their masters.

> Even the floors, which usually consisted of only tamped earth, were evidence of a hidden African tradition: slaves cooked clay over a fire, mixing in ox blood or cow dung, and then poured it in place to make hard dirt floors almost like asphalt . . . In slave houses, in contrast to other crafts, these signs of skill and tradition would then be covered over (Wright 1981, p. 48).

Housing is important in discussions of family because its design reflects sociocultural attitudes about family life. The housing that slaveowners provided for their slaves reflected a view of Black family life consistent with the stereotypes of the period. While the existence of slave families was acknowledged, it certainly was not nurtured. Thus, cabins were crowded, often containing more than one family, and there were no provisions for privacy. Slaves had to create their own.

> Slave couples hung up old clothes or quilts to establish boundaries; others built more substantial partitions from scrap wood. Parents sought to establish sexual privacy from children. A few ex-slaves described modified trundle beds designed to hide parental lovemaking . . . Even in one room cabins, sexual segregation was carefully organized (Wright 1981, p. 50).

Perhaps most critical in developing an understanding of slave women's reproductive labor is the gender-based division of labor in the domestic sphere. The organization of slave labor enforced considerable equality among men and women. The ways in which equality in the labor force was translated into the family sphere is somewhat speculative. Davis (1981), for example, suggests that egalitarianism between males and females was a direct result of slavery when she says:

> Within the confines of their family and community life, therefore, Black people managed to accomplish a magnificent feat. They transformed that negative equality which emanated from the equal oppression they suffered as slaves into a positive quality: the egalitarianism characterizing their social relations (p. 18).

It is likely, however, that this transformation was far less direct than Davis implies. We know, for example, that slave women experienced what has recently been called the "double day" before most other women in this society. Slave narratives (Jones 1985; White 1985; Blassingame 1977) reveal that women had primary responsibility for their family's domestic chores. They cooked (although on some plantations meals were prepared for all of the slaves), sewed, cared for their children, and cleaned house, all after completing a full day of labor for the master. Blassingame (1972) and others have pointed out that slave men engaged in hunting, trapping, perhaps some gardening, and furniture making as ways of contributing to the maintenance of their families. Clearly, a gender-based division of labor did exist within the family and it appears that women bore the larger share of the burden for housekeeping and child care.

By contrast to white families of the period, however, the division of labor in the domestic sphere was neither reinforced in the relationship of slave women to work nor in the social institutions of the slave community. The gender-based division of labor among the slaves existed within a social system that treated men and women as almost equal, independent units of labor.[4] Thus Matthei (1982) is probably correct in concluding that:

> Whereas . . . the white homemaker interacted with the public sphere through her husband, and had her work life determined by him, the enslaved Afro-American homemaker was directly subordinated to and determined by her owner . . . The equal enslavement of husband and wife gave the slave marriage a curious kind of equality, an equality of oppression (p. 94).

Black men were denied the male resources of a patriarchal society and therefore were unable to turn gender distinctions into female subordination, even if that had been their desire. Black women, on the other hand, were denied support and protection for their roles as mothers and wives and thus had to modify and structure those roles around the demands of their labor. Thus, reproductive labor for slave women was intensified in several ways: by the demands of slave labor that forced them into the double-day of work; by the desire and need to maintain family ties in the face of a system that gave them only limited recognition; by the stresses of building a family with men who were denied the standard social privileges of manhood; and by the struggle to raise children who could survive in a hostile environment.

This intensification of reproductive labor made networks of kin and quasi-kin important instruments in carrying out the reproductive tasks of the slave community. Given an African cultural heritage where kinship ties formed the basis of social relations, it is not at all surprising that African American slaves developed an extensive system of kinship ties and obligations (Gutman 1976; Sudarkasa 1981). Research on Black families in slavery provides considerable documentation of participation of extended kin in childrearing, childbirth, and other domestic, social, and economic activities (Gutman 1976; Blassingame 1972; Genovese 1974).

After slavery, these ties continued to be an important factor linking individual household units in a variety of domestic activities. While kinship ties were also important among native-born whites and European immigrants, Gutman (1976) has suggested that these ties:

> were comparatively more important to Afro-Americans than to lower-class native white and immigrant Americans, the result of their distinctive low economic status, a condition that denied them the advantages of an extensive associational life beyond the kin group and the advantages and disadvantages resulting from mobility opportunities (p. 213).

His argument is reaffirmed by research on Afro-American families after slavery (Shimkin et al. 1978; Aschenbrenner 1975; Davis 1981; Stack 1974). Sudarkasa (1981) takes this argument one step further and links this pattern to the African cultural heritage.

> historical realities require that the derivation of this aspect of Black family organization be traced to its African antecedents. Such a view does not deny the adaptive significance of consanguineal (kin) networks. In fact, it helps to clarify why these networks had the flexibility they had and why, they, rather than conjugal relationships came to be the stabilizing factor in Black families (p. 49).

With individual households, the gender-based division of labor experienced some important shifts during emancipation. In their first real opportunity to establish family life beyond the controls and constraints imposed by a slavemaster, family life among Black sharecroppers changed radically. Most women, at least those who were wives and daughters of able-bodied men, withdrew from field labor and concentrated on their domestic duties in the home. Husbands took primary responsibility for the fieldwork and for relations with the owners, such as signing contracts on behalf of the family. Black women were severely criticized by whites for removing themselves from field labor because they were seen to be aspiring to a model of womanhood that was considered inappropriate for them. This reorganization of female labor, however, represented an attempt on the part of Blacks to protect women from some of the abuses of the slave system and to thus secure their family life. It was more likely a response to the particular set of circumstances that the newly freed slaves faced than a reaction to the lives of their former masters. Jones (1985) argues that these patterns were "particularly significant" because at a time when industrial development was introducing a labor system that divided male and female labor, the freed black family was establishing a pattern of joint work and complementary tasks between males and females that was reminiscent of the preindustrial American families. Unfortunately, these former slaves had to do this without the institutional supports that white farm families had in the midst of a sharecropping system that deprived them of economic independence.

CHINESE SOJOURNERS

An increase in the African slave population was a desired goal. Therefore, Africans were permitted and even encouraged at times to form families subject to the authority and whim of the master. By sharp contrast, Chinese people were explicitly denied the right to form families in the United States through both law and social practice. Although male laborers began coming to the United States in sizable numbers in the middle of the nineteenth century, it was more than a century before an appreciable number of children of Chinese parents were born in America. Tom, a respondent in Nee and Nee's (1973) book, *Longtime Californ'* says: "One thing about Chinese men in America was you had to be either a merchant or a big gambler, have lot of side money to have a family here. A working man, an ordinary man, just can't!" (p. 80).

Working in the United States was a means of gaining support for one's family with an end of obtaining sufficient capital to return to China and purchase land. The practice of sojourning was reinforced by laws preventing Chinese laborers from becoming citizens, and by restrictions on their entry into this country. Chinese laborers who arrived before 1882 could not bring their wives and were prevented by law from marrying whites. Thus, it is likely that the number of Chinese-American families might have been negligible had it not been for two things: the San Francisco earthquake and fire in 1906, which destroyed all municipal records; and the ingenuity and persistence of the Chinese people who used the opportunity created by the earthquake to increase their numbers in the United States. Since relatives of citizens were permitted entry, American born Chinese (real and claimed) would visit China, report the birth of a son, and thus create an entry slot. Years later the slot could be used by a relative or purchased. The purchasers were called "paper sons." Paper sons became a major mechanism for increasing the Chinese population, but it was a slow process and the sojourner community remained predominantly male for decades.

The high concentration of males in the Chinese community before 1920 resulted in a split household form of family. As Glenn observes:

> In the split household family, production is separated from other functions and is carried out by a member living far from the rest of the household. The rest—consumption, reproduction and socialization—are carried out by the wife and other relatives from the home village . . . The split household form makes possible maximum exploitation of the workers . . . The labor of prime-age male workers can be bought relatively cheaply, since the cost of reproduction and family maintenance is borne partially by unpaid subsistence work of women and old people in the home village (Glenn 1981, pp. 14–15).

The women who were in the United States during this period consisted of a small number who were wives and daughters of merchants and a larger percentage who were prostitutes. Hirata (1979) has suggested that Chinese prostitution was an important element in helping to maintain the split-household family. In conjunction with laws prohibiting intermarriage, Chinese prostitution helped men avoid long-term relationships with women in the United States and ensured that the bulk of their meager earnings would continue to support the family at home.

The reproductive labor of Chinese women, therefore, took on two dimensions primarily because of the split-household family form. Wives who remained in China were forced to raise children and care for in-laws on the meager remittances of their sojourning husband. Although we know few details about their lives, it is clear that the everyday work of bearing and maintaining children and a household fell entirely on their shoulders. Those women who immigrated and worked as prostitutes performed the more nurturant aspects of reproductive labor, that is, providing emotional and sexual companionship for men who were far from home. Yet their role as prostitute was more likely a means of supporting their families at home in China than a chosen vocation.

The Chinese family system during the nineteenth century was a patriarchal one wherein girls had little value. In fact, they were considered only temporary members of their father's family because when they married, they became members of their husband's families. They also had little social value: girls were sold by some poor parents to work as prostitutes, concubines, or servants. This saved the family the expense of raising them, and their earnings also became a source of family income. For most girls, however, marriages were arranged and families sought useful connections through this process.

With the development of a sojourning pattern in the United States, some Chinese women in those regions of China where this pattern was more prevalent would be sold to become prostitutes in the United States. Most, however, were married off to men whom they saw only once or twice in the 20- or 30-year period during which he was sojourning in the United States. Her status as wife ensured that a portion of the meager wages he earned would be returned to his family in China. This arrangement required considerable sacrifice and adjustment on the part of wives who remained in China and those who joined their husbands after a long separation.

Kingston (1977) tells the story of the unhappy meeting of her aunt, Moon Orchid, with her husband from whom she had been separated for 30 years.

> For thirty years she had been receiving money from him from America. But she had never told him that she wanted to come to the United States. She waited for him to suggest it, but he never did (p. 144).

His response to her when she arrived unexpectedly was to say:

> "Look at her. She'd never fit into an American household. I have important American guests who come inside my house to eat." He turned to Moon Orchid, "You can't talk to them. You can barely talk to me." Moon Orchid was so ashamed, she held her hands over her face. She wished she could also hide her dappled hands (p. 178).

Despite these handicaps, Chinese people collaborated to establish the opportunity to form families and settle in the United States. In some cases it took as long as three generations for a child to be born on United States soil.

> In one typical history, related by a 21 year old college student, great-grandfather arrived in the States in the 1890s as a "paper son" and worked for about 20 years as a laborer. He then sent for the grandfather, who worked alongside greatgrandfather in a small business for several years. Greatgrandfather subsequently returned to China, leaving grandfather to run the business and send remittance. In the 1940s, grandfather sent for father; up to this point, none of the wives had left China. Finally, in the late 1950s father returned to China and brought his wife back with him. Thus, after nearly 70 years, the first child was born in the United States (Glenn 1981, p. 14).

CHICANOS

Africans were uprooted from their native lands and encouraged to have families in order to increase the slave labor force. Chinese people were immigrant laborers whose "permanent" presence in the country was denied. By contrast, Mexican-Americans were colonized and their traditional family life was disrupted by war and the imposition of a new set of laws and conditions of labor. The hardships faced by Chicano families, therefore, were the result of the United States colonization of the indigenous Mexican population, accompanied by the beginnings of industrial development in the region. The treaty of Guadalupe Hidalgo, signed in 1848, granted American citizenship to Mexicans living in what is now called the Southwest. The American takeover, however, resulted in the gradual displacement of Mexicans from the land and their incorporation into a colonial labor force (Barrera 1979). In addition, Mexicans who immigrated into the United States after 1848 were also absorbed into the labor force.

Whether natives of Northern Mexico (which became the United States after 1848) or immigrants from Southern Mexico, Chicanos were a largely peasant population whose lives were defined by a feudal economy and a daily struggle on the land for economic survival. Patriarchal families were important instruments of community life and nuclear family units were linked together through an elaborate system of kinship and godparenting. Traditional life was characterized by hard work and a fairly distinct pattern of sex-role segregation.

> Most Mexican women were valued for their household qualities, men by their ability to work and to provide for a family. Children were taught to get up early, to contribute to the family's labor to prepare themselves for adult life . . . Such a life demanded discipline, authority, deference—values that cemented the working of a family surrounded and shaped by the requirements of Mexico's distinctive historical pattern of agricultural development, especially its pervasive debt peonage (Saragoza 1983, p. 8).

As the primary caretakers of hearth and home in a rural environment, *Las Chicanas* labor made a vital and important contribution to family survival. A description of women's reproductive labor in the early twentieth century can be used to gain insight into the work of the nineteenth-century rural women.

> For country women, work was seldom a salaried job. More often it was the work of growing and preparing food, of making adobes and plastering houses with mud, or making their children's clothes for school and teaching them the hymns and prayers of the church, or delivering babies and treating sicknesses with herbs and patience. In almost every town there were one or two women who, in addition to working in their own homes, served other families in the community as *curanderas* (healers), *parteras* (midwives), and schoolteachers (Elasser 1980, p. 10).

Although some scholars have argued that family rituals and community life showed little change before World War I (Saragoza 1983), the American conquest of Mexican lands, the introduction of a new system of labor, the loss of Mexican-owned land through the inability to document ownership, plus the transient nature of most of the jobs in which Chicanos were employed, resulted in the gradual erosion of this pastoral way of life. Families were uprooted as the economic basis for family life changed. Some immigrated from

Mexico in search of a better standard of living and worked in the mines and railroads. Others who were native to the Southwest faced a job market that no longer required their skills and moved into mining, railroad, and agricultural labor in search of a means of earning a living. According to Camarillo (1979), the influx of Anglo[5] capital into the pastoral economy of Santa Barbara rendered obsolete the skills of many Chicano males who had worked as ranchhands and farmers prior to the urbanization of that economy. While some women and children accompanied their husbands to the railroad and mine camps, they often did so despite prohibitions against it. Initially many of these camps discouraged or prohibited family settlement.

The American period (post-1848) was characterized by considerable transiency for the Chicano population. Its impact on families is seen in the growth of female-headed households, which was reflected in the data as early as 1860. Griswold del Castillo (1979) found a sharp increase in female-headed households in Los Angeles, from a low of 13% in 1844 to 31% in 1880. Camarillo (1979, p. 120) documents a similar increase in Santa Barbara from 15% in 1844 to 30% by 1880. These increases appear to be due not so much to divorce, which was infrequent in this Catholic population, but to widowhood and temporary abandonment in search of work. Given the hazardous nature of work in the mines and railroad camps, the death of a husband, father or son who was laboring in these sites was not uncommon. Griswold del Castillo (1979) reports a higher death rate among men than women in Los Angeles. The rise in female-headed households, therefore, reflects the instabilities and insecurities introduced into women's lives as a result of the changing social organization of work.

One outcome, the increasing participation of women and children in the labor force was primarily a response to economic factors that required the modification of traditional values. According to Louisa Vigil, who was born in 1890:

> The women didn't work at that time. The man was supposed to marry that girl and take [care] of her . . . Your grandpa never did let me work for nobody. He always had to work, and we never did have really bad times (Elasser 1980, p. 14).

Señora Vigil's comments are reinforced in Garcia's (1980) study of El Paso. In the 393 households he examined in the 1900 census, he found 17.1% of the women to be employed. The majority of this group were daughters, mothers with no husbands, and single women. In the cases of Los Angeles and Santa Barbara, where there were even greater work opportunities for women than in El Paso, wives who were heads of household worked in seasonal and part-time jobs and lived from the earnings of children and relatives in an effort to maintain traditional female roles.

Slowly, entire families were encouraged to go to railroad workcamps and were eventually incorporated into the agricultural labor market. This was a response both to the extremely low wages paid to Chicano laborers and to the preferences of employers who saw family labor as a way of stabilizing the workforce. For Chicanos, engaging all family members in agricultural work was a means of increasing their earnings to a level close to subsistence for the entire group and of keeping the family unit together. Camarillo (1979, p. 93) provides a picture of the interplay of work, family, and migration in the Santa Barbara area in the following observation:

> The time of year when women and children were employed in the fruit cannery and participated in the almond and olive harvests coincided with the seasons when the men were most likely to be engaged in seasonal migratory work. There were seasons, however, especially in the early summer when the entire family migrated from the city to pick fruit. This type of family seasonal harvest was evident in Santa Barbara by the 1890s. As walnuts replaced almonds and as the fruit industry expanded, Chicano family labor became essential.

This arrangement, while bringing families together, did not decrease the hardships that Chicanas had to confront in raising their families. We may infer something about the rigors of that life from Jesse Lopez de la Cruz's description of the workday of migrant farm laborers in the 1940s. Work conditions in the 1890s were as difficult, if not worse.

> We always went where the women and men were going to work, because if it were just the men working it wasn't worth going out there because we wouldn't earn enough to support a family . . . We would start around 6:30 a.m. and work for four or five hours, then walk home and eat and rest until about three-thirty in the afternoon when it cooled off. We would go back and work until we couldn't see. Then I'd clean up the kitchen. I was doing the housework and working out in the fields and taking care of two children (quoted in Goldman 1981, pp. 119–120).

In the towns, women's reproductive labor was intensified by the congested and unsanitary conditions of the *barrios* in which they lived. Garcia (1980) described the following conditions in El Paso:

> Mexican women had to haul water for washing and cooking from the river or public water pipes. To feed their families, they had to spend time marketing, often in Cuidad Juarez across the border, as well as long, hot hours

cooking meals and coping with the burden of desert sand both inside and outside their homes. Besides the problem of raising children, unsanitary living
conditions forced Mexican mothers to deal with disease and illness in their
families. Diphtheria, tuberculosis, typhus and influenza were never too far
away. Some diseases could be directly traced to inferior city services . . . As a
result, Mexican mothers had to devote much energy to caring for sick children, many of whom died (pp. 320–321).

While the extended family has remained an important element of Chicano
life, it was eroded in the American period in several ways. Griswold del Castillo
(1979), for example, points out that in 1845 about 71% of Angelenos lived in
extended families and that by 1880, fewer than half did. This decrease in
extended families appears to be a response to the changed economic conditions
and to the instabilities generated by the new sociopolitical structure. Additionally, the imposition of American law and custom ignored and ultimately
undermined some aspects of the extended family. The extended family in
traditional Mexican life consisted of an important set of familial, religious, and
community obligations. Women, while valued primarily for their domesticity,
had certain legal and property rights that acknowledged the importance of
their work, their families of origin and their children. In California, for
example:

Equal ownership of property between husband and wife had been one
of the mainstays of the Spanish and Mexican family systems. Community-
property laws were written into the civil codes with the intention of strengthening the economic controls of the wife and her relatives. The American
government incorporated these Mexican laws into the state constitution, but
later court decisions interpreted these statutes so as to undermine the wife's
economic rights. In 1861, the legislature passed a law that allowed the de-
ceased wife's property to revert to her husband. Previously it had been inherited by her children and relatives if she died without a will (Griswold del
Castillo 1979, p. 69).

The impact of this and other similar court rulings was to "strengthen the
property rights of the husband at the expense of his wife and children"
(Griswold del Castillo 1979, p. 69).

In the face of the legal, social, and economic changes that occurred during
the American period, Chicanas were forced to cope with a series of dislocations
in traditional life. They were caught between conflicting pressures to maintain
traditional women's roles and family customs and the need to participate in
the economic support of their families by working outside the home. During
this period the preservation of some traditional customs became an important
force for resisting complete disarray.

According to Saragoza (1983), transiency, the effects of racism, and segregation, and proximity to Mexico aided in the maintenance of traditional family practices. Garcia has suggested that women were the guardians of Mexican cultural traditions within the family. He cites the work of anthropologist Manuel Gamio, who identified the retention of many Mexican customs among Chicanos in settlements around the United States in the early 1900s.

> These included folklore, songs and ballads, birthday celebrations, saints' day, baptism, weddings, and funerals in the traditional style. Because of poverty, a lack of physicians in the barrios, and adherence to traditional customs, Mexicans continued to use medicinal herbs. Gamio also identified the maintenance of a number of oral traditions, and Mexican style cooking (Garcia 1980, p. 322).

Of vital importance to the integrity of traditional culture was the perpetuation of the Spanish language. Factors that aided in the maintenance of other aspects of Mexican culture also helped in sustaining the language. However, entry into English-language public schools introduced the children and their families to systematic efforts to erase their native tongue. Griswold del Castillo reports that in the early 1880s there was considerable pressure against the speaker of Spanish in the public school. He also found that some Chicano parents responded to this kind of discrimination by helping support independent bilingual schools. These efforts, however, were short-lived.

Another key factor in conserving Chicano culture was the extended family network, particularly the system of *compadrazgo* or godparenting. Although the full extent of the impact of the American period on the Chicano extended family is not known, it is generally acknowledged that this family system, though lacking many legal and social sanctions, played an important role in the preservation of the Mexican community (Camarillo 1979, p. 13). In Mexican society, godparents were an important way of linking family and community through respected friends or authorities. Named at the important rites of passage in a child's life, such as birth, confirmation, first communion, and marriage, *compadrazgo* created a moral obligation for godparents to act as guardians, to provide financial assistance in times of need, and to substitute in case of the death of a parent. Camarillo (1979) points out that in traditional society these bonds cut across class and racial lines.

> The rites of baptism established kinship networks between rich and poor—between Spanish, mestizo and Indian—and often carried with them political loyalty and economic-occupational ties. The leading California patriarchs in the pueblo played important roles in the compadrazgo network. They sponsored dozens of children for their workers or poor relatives. The kindness

of the *padrino* and *madrina* was repaid with respect and support from the *pobladores* (pp. 12–13).

The extended family network—which included godparents—expanded the support groups for women who were widowed or temporarily abandoned and for those who were in seasonal, part- or full-time work. It suggests, therefore, the potential for an exchange of services among poor people whose income did not provide the basis for family subsistence. Griswold del Castillo (1980) argues that family organization influenced literacy rates and socioeconomic mobility among Chicanos in Los Angeles between 1850 and 1880. His data suggest that children in extended families (defined as those with at least one relative living in a nuclear family household) had higher literacy rates than those in nuclear families. He also argues that those in larger families fared better economically, and experienced less downward mobility. The data here are too limited to generalize to the Chicano experience as a whole but they do reinforce the actual and potential importance of this family form to the continued cultural autonomy of the Chicano community.

CONCLUSION: OUR MOTHERS' GRIEF

Reproductive labor for Afro-American, Chinese-American, and Mexican-American women in the nineteenth century centered on the struggle to maintain family units in the face of a variety of cultural assaults. Treated primarily as individual units of labor rather than as members of family groups, these women labored to maintain, sustain, stabilize, and reproduce their families while working in both the public (productive) and private (reproductive) spheres. Thus, the concept of reproductive labor, when applied to women of color, must be modified to account for the fact that labor in the productive sphere was required to achieve even minimal levels of family subsistence. Long after industrialization had begun to reshape family roles among middle-class white families, driving white women into a cult of domesticity, women of color were coping with an extended day. This day included subsistence labor outside the family and domestic labor within the family. For slaves, domestics, migrant farm laborers, seasonal factory-workers, and prostitutes, the distinctions between labor that reproduced family life and which economically sustained it were minimized. The expanded workday was one of the primary ways in which reproductive labor increased.

Racial-ethnic families were sustained and maintained in the face of various forms of disruption. Yet they and their families paid a high price in the process.

High rates of infant mortality, a shortened life span, the early onset of crippling and debilitating disease provided some insight into the costs of survival.

The poor quality of housing and the neglect of communities further increased reproductive labor. Not only did racial-ethnic women work hard outside the home for a mere subsistence, they worked very hard inside the home to achieve even minimal standards of privacy and cleanliness. They were continually faced with disease and illness that directly resulted from the absence of basic sanitation. The fact that some African women murdered their children to prevent them from becoming slaves is an indication of the emotional strain associated with bearing and raising children while participating in the colonial labor system.

We have uncovered little information about the use of birth control, the prevalence of infanticide, or the motivations that may have generated these or other behaviors. We can surmise, however, that no matter how much children were accepted, loved, or valued among any of these groups of people, their futures in a colonial labor system were a source of grief for their mothers. For those children who were born, the task of keeping them alive, of helping them to understand and participate in a system that exploited them, and the challenge of maintaining a measure—no matter how small—of cultural integrity, intensified reproductive labor.

Being a racial-ethnic woman in nineteenth century American society meant having extra work both inside and outside the home. It meant having a contradictory relationship to the norms and values about women that were being generated in the dominant white culture. As pointed out earlier, the notion of separate spheres of male and female labor had contradictory outcomes for the nineteenth-century whites. It was the basis for the confinement of women to the household and for much of the protective legislation that subsequently developed. At the same time, it sustained white families by providing social acknowledgment and support to women in the performance of their family roles. For racial-ethnic women, however, the notion of separate spheres served to reinforce their subordinate status and became, in effect, another assault. As they increased their work outside the home, they were forced into a productive labor sphere that was organized for men and "desperate" women who were so unfortunate or immoral that they could not confine their work to the domestic sphere. In the productive sphere, racial-ethnic women faced exploitative jobs and depressed wages. In the reproductive sphere, however, they were denied the opportunity to embrace the dominant ideological definition of "good" wife or mother. In essence, they were faced with a double-bind situation, one that required their participation in the labor force to sustain family life but damned them as women, wives, and mothers because they did not confine their labor to the home. Thus, the conflict between ideology and reality in the lives of racial-ethnic women during the nineteenth century sets the stage for stereotypes, issues of self-esteem, and conflicts around gender-role prescriptions that surface more fully in the twentieth century. Further, the tensions and conflicts that characterized their lives during this period provided the impulse for community activism to jointly address the inequities, which they and their children and families faced.

ACKNOWLEDGMENTS

The research in this study is the result of the author's participation in a larger collaborative project examining family, community, and work lives of racial-ethnic women in the United States. The author is deeply indebted to the scholarship and creativity of members of the group in the development of this study. Appreciation is extended to Elizabeth Higginbotham, Cheryl Townsend Gilkes, Evelyn Nakano Glenn, and Ruth Zambrana (members of the original working group), and to the Ford Foundation for a grant that supported in part the work of this study.

NOTES

1. The term *reproductive labor* is used to refer to all of the work of women in the home. This includes but is not limited to: the buying and preparation of food and clothing, provision of emotional support and nurturance for all family members, bearing children, and planning, organizing, and carrying out a wide variety of tasks associated with their socialization. All of these activities are necessary for the growth of patriarchal capitalism because they maintain, sustain, stabilize, and *reproduce* (both biologically and socially) the labor force.

2. The term *white* is a global construct used to characterize peoples of European descent who migrated to and helped colonize America. In the seventeenth century, most of these immigrants were from the British Isles. However, during the time period covered by this article, European immigrants became increasingly diverse. It is a limitation of this article that time and space does not permit a fuller discussion of the variations in the white European immigrant experience. For the purposes of the argument made herein and of the contrast it seeks to draw between the experiences of mainstream (European) cultural groups and that of racial/ethnic minorities, the differences among European settlers are joined and the broad similarities emphasized.

3. Cultural assaults, according to Caulfield (1974) are benign and systematic attacks on the institutions and forms of social organization that are fundamental to the maintenance and flourishing of a group's culture.

4. Recent research suggests that there were some tasks that were primarily assigned to males and some others to females. Whereas some gender-role distinctions with regard to work may have existed on some plantations, it is clear that slave women were not exempt from strenuous physical labor.

5. This term is used to refer to white Americans of European ancestry.

REFERENCES

Aschenbrenner, Joyce. 1975. *Lifelines: Black Families in Chicago.* New York, NY: Holt, Rinehart, and Winston.

Barrera, Mario. 1979. *Race and Class in the Southwest.* South Bend, IN: Notre Dame University Press.

Blassingame, John. 1972. *The Slave Community: Plantation Life in the Antebellum South.* New York: Oxford University Press.

———. 1977. *Slave Testimony: Two Centuries of Letters, Speeches, Interviews, and Autobiographies.* Baton Rouge, LA: Louisiana State University Press.

Camarillo, Albert. 1979. *Chicanos in a Changing Society.* Cambridge, MA: Harvard University Press.

Caulfield, Mina Davis. 1974. "Imperialism, The Family, and Cultures of Resistance." *Socialist Review* 4(2)(October): 67–85.

Davis, Angela. 1971. "The Black Woman's Role in the Community of Slaves." *Black Scholar* 3(4)(December): 2–15.

———. 1981. *Women, Race and Class.* New York: Random House.

Degler, Carl. 1980. *At Odds.* New York: Oxford University Press.

Elasser, Nan Kyle MacKenzie, and Yvonne Tixier Y. Vigil. 1980. *Las Mujeres.* New York: The Feminist Press.

Garcia, Mario T. 1980. "The Chicano in American History: The Mexican Women of El Paso, 1880–1920—A Case Study." *Pacific Historical Review* 49(2)(May): 315–358.

Genovese, Eugene D. and Elinor Miller, eds. 1974. *Plantation, Town, and County: Essays on the Local History of American Slave Society.* Urbana: University of Illinois Press.

Glenn, Evelyn Nakano. 1981. "Family Strategies of Chinese-Americans: An Institutional Analysis." Paper presented at the Society for the Study of Social Problems Annual Meetings.

Goldman, Marion S. 1981. *Gold Diggers and Silver Miners.* Ann Arbor: The University of Michigan Press.

Griswold del Castillo, Richard. 1979. *The Los Angeles Barrio: 1850–1890.* Los Angeles: The University of California Press.

Gutman, Herbert. 1976. *The Black Family in Slavery and Freedom: 1750–1925.* New York: Pantheon.

Hirata, Lucie Cheng. 1979. "Free, Indentured, Enslaved: Chinese Prostitutes in Nineteenth-Century America." *Signs* 5 (Autumn): 3–29.

Jones, Jacqueline. 1985. *Labor of Love, Labor of Sorrow.* New York: Basic Books.

Kennedy, Susan Estabrook. 1979. *If All We Did Was to Weep at Home: A History of White Working-Class Women in America.* Bloomington: Indiana University Press.

Kessler-Harris, Alice. 1981. *Women Have Always Worked.* Old Westbury: The Feminist Press.

———. 1982. *Out to Work.* New York: Oxford University Press.

Kingston, Maxine Hong. 1977. *The Woman Warrior.* Vintage Books.

Matthei, Julie. 1982. *An Economic History of Women in America.* New York: Schocken Books.

Nee, Victor G., and Brett de Bary Nee. 1973. *Longtime Californ'.* New York: Pantheon Books.

Saragoza, Alex M. 1983. "The Conceptualization of the History of the Chicano Family: Work, Family, and Migration in Chicanos." Research Proceedings of the Symposium on Chicano Research and Public Policy. Stanford, CA: Stanford University, Center for Chicano Research.

Shimkin, Demetri, E. M. Shimkin, and D. A. Frate, eds. 1978. *The Extended Family in Black Societies.* The Hague: Mouton.

Spruill, Julia Cherry. 1972. *Women's Life and Work in the Southern Colonies.* New York: W. W. Norton and Company (First published in 1938, University of North Carolina Press).

Stack, Carol S. 1974. *All Our Kin: Strategies for Survival in a Black Community.* Harper and Row.

Sudarkasa, Niara. 1981. "Interpreting the African Heritage in Afro-American Family Organization." Pp. 37–53 in *Black Families,* edited by Harriette Pipes McAdoo. Beverly Hills, CA: Sage Publications.

White, Deborah Gray. 1985. *Ar'n't I a Woman?: Female Slaves in the Plantation South.* New York: W. W. Norton.

Wright, Gwendolyn. 1981. *Building the Dream: A Social History of Housing in America.* New York: Pantheon Books.

Zaretsky, Eli. 1978. "The Effects of the Economic Crisis on the Family." Pp. 209–218 in *U.S. Capitalism in Crisis,* edited by Crisis Reader Editorial Collective. New York: Union of Radical Political Economists.

PUERTO RICAN ELDERLY WOMEN:
Shared Meanings and Informal Supportive Networks

26

Melba Sánchez-Ayéndez

INTRODUCTION

Studies of older adults' support systems have seldom taken into account how values within a specific cultural context affect expectations of support and patterns of assistance in social networks. Such networks and supportive relations have a cultural dimension reflecting a system of shared meanings. These meanings affect social interaction and the expectations people have of their relationships with others.

Ethnicity and gender affect a person's adjustment to old age. Although sharing a "minority" position produces similar consequences among members of different ethnic minority groups, the groups' diversity lies in their distinctive systems of shared meanings. Studies of older adults in ethnic minority groups have rarely focused on the cultural contents of ethnicity affecting the aging process, particularly of women (Barth 1969). Cultural value orientations are central to understanding how minority elders approach

From: Johnnetta Cole (ed.), *All-American Women: Lines That Divide, Ties That Bind* (New York: Free Press, 1986), pp. 172–186. Copyright © 1986 The Free Press. Reprinted by permission.

growing old and how they meet the physical and emotional changes associated with aging.

This article describes the interplay between values and behavior in family and community of a group of older Puerto Rican women living on low incomes in Boston.[1] It explores how values emphasizing family interdependence and different roles of women and men shape the women's expectations, behavior, and supportive familial and community networks.

BEING A WOMAN IS DIFFERENT FROM BEING A MAN

The women interviewed believe in a dual standard of conduct for men and women. This dual standard is apparent in different attributes assigned to women and men, roles expected of them, and authority exercised by them.

The principal role of men in the family is viewed as that of provider; their main responsibility is economic in nature. Although fathers are expected to be affectionate with their children, child care is not seen to be a man's responsibility. Men are not envisioned within the domestic sphere.

The "ideal" man must be the protector of the family, able to control his emotions and be self-sufficient. Men enjoy more freedom in the public world than do women. From the women's perspective, the ideal of maleness is linked to the concept of *machismo*. This concept assumes men have a stronger sexual drive than women, a need to prove virility by the conquest of women, a dominant position in relation to females, and a belligerent attitude when confronted by male peers.

The women see themselves as subordinate to men and recognize the preeminence of male authority. They believe women ought to be patient and largely forbearing in their relations with men, particularly male family members. Patience and forbearance, however, are not confused with passivity or total submissiveness. The elderly Puerto Rican women do not conceive of themselves or other women as "resigned females" but as dynamic beings, continually devising strategies to improve everyday situations within and outside the household.

Rosa Mendoza,[2] now sixty-five, feels no regrets for having decided at thirty years of age and after nine years of marriage not to put up with her husband's heavy drinking any longer. She moved out of her house and went to live with her mother.

> I was patient for many years. I put up with his drunkenness and worked hard to earn money. One day I decided I'd be better off without him. One thing is to be patient, and another to be a complete fool. So I moved out.

Although conscious of their subordinate status to their husbands, wives are also aware of their power and the demands they can make. Ana Fuentes recalls when her husband had a mistress. Ana was thirty-eight.

> I knew he had a mistress in a nearby town. I was patient for a long time, hoping it would end. Most men, sooner or later, have a mistress somewhere. But when it didn't end after quite a time and everyone in the neighborhood knew about it, I said "I am fed up!" He came home one evening and the things I told him! I even said I'd go to that woman's house and beat her if I had to. . . . He knew I was not bluffing; that this was not just another argument. He tried to answer back and I didn't let him. He remained silent. . . . And you know what? He stopped seeing her! A woman can endure many things for a long time, but the time comes when she has to defend her rights.

These older Puerto Rican women perceive the home as the center around which the female world revolves. Home is the woman's domain; women generally make decisions about household maintenance and men seldom intervene.

Family relations are considered part of the domestic sphere and therefore a female responsibility. The women believe that success in marriage depends on the woman's ability to "make the marriage work."

> A marriage lasts as long as the woman decides it will last. It is us who make a marriage work, who put up with things, who try to make ends meet, who yield.

The norm of female subordination is evident in the view that marriage will last as long as the woman "puts up with things" and deals with marriage from her subordinate status. Good relations with affinal kin are also a woman's responsibility. They are perceived as relations between the wife's domestic unit and other women's domestic units.

Motherhood

Motherhood is seen by these older Puerto Rican women as the central role of women. Their concept of motherhood is based on the female capacity to bear children and on the notion of *marianismo*, which presents the Virgin Mary as a role model (Stevens 1973). *Marianismo* presupposes that it is through motherhood that a woman realizes herself and derives her life's greatest satisfactions.

A woman's reproductive role is viewed as leading her toward more commitment to and a better understanding of her children than is shown by the father. One of the women emphasized this view:

> It is easier for a man to leave his children and form a new home with another woman, or not to be as forgiving of children as a mother is. They will

never know what it is like to carry a child inside, feel it growing, and then bring that child into the world. This is why a mother is always willing to forgive and make sacrifices. That creature is part of you; it nourished from you and came from within you. But it is not so for men. To them, a child is a being they receive once it is born. The attachment can never be the same.

The view that childrearing is their main responsibility in life comes from this conceptualization of the mother-child bond. For the older women, raising children means more than looking after the needs of offspring. It involves being able to offer them every possible opportunity for a better life, during childhood or adulthood, even if this requires personal sacrifices.

As mother and head of the domestic domain, a woman is also responsible for establishing the bases for close and good relations among her children. From childhood through adulthood, the creation and maintenance of family unity among offspring is considered another female responsibility.

FAMILY UNITY AND INTERDEPENDENCE

Family Unity

Ideal family relations are seen as based on two interrelated themes, family unity and family interdependence. Family unity refers to the desirability of close and intimate kin ties, with members getting along well and keeping in frequent contact despite dispersal.

Celebration of holidays and special occasions are seen as opportunities for kin to be together and strengthen family ties. Family members, particularly grandparents, adult children, and grandchildren, are often reunited at Christmas, New Year's, Mother's and Father's days, Easter, and Thanksgiving. Special celebrations like weddings, baptisms, first communions, birthdays, graduations, and funerals occasion reunions with other family members. Whether to celebrate happy or sad events, the older women encourage family gatherings as a way of strengthening kinship ties and fostering family continuity.

The value the women place on family unity is also evident in their desire for frequent interaction with kin members. Visits and telephone calls demonstrate a caring attitude by family members which cements family unity.

Family unity is viewed as contributing to the strengthening of family interdependence. Many of the older women repeat a proverb when referring to family unity: *En la unión está la fuerza.* ("In union there is strength.") They believe that the greater the degree of unity in the family, the greater the emphasis family members will place on interdependence and familial obligation.

Family Interdependence

Despite adaptation to life in a culturally different society, Puerto Rican families in the United States are still defined by strong norms of reciprocity among family members, especially those in the immediate kinship group (Cantor 1979; Carrasquillo 1982; Delgado 1981; Donaldson and Martínez 1980; Sánchez-Ayéndez 1984). Interdependence within the Puerto Rican symbolic framework "fits an orientation to life that stresses that the individual is not capable of doing everything and doing it well. Therefore, he should rely on others for assistance" (Bastida 1979: 70). Individualism and self-reliance assume a different meaning from the one prevailing in the dominant U.S. cultural tradition. Individuals in Puerto Rican families will expect and ask for assistance from certain people in their social networks without any derogatory implications for self-esteem.

Family interdependence is a value to which these older Puerto Rican women strongly adhere. It influences patterns of mutual assistance with their children as well as expectations of support. The older women expect to be taken care of during old age by their adult children. The notion of filial duty ensues from the value orientation of interdependence. Adult children are understood to have a responsibility toward their aged parents in exchange for the functions that parents performed for them throughout their upbringing. Expected reciprocity from offspring is intertwined with the concept of filial love and the nature of the parent-child relationship.

Parental duties of childrearing are perceived as inherent in the "parent" role and also lay the basis for long-term reciprocity with children, particularly during old age. The centrality that motherhood has in the lives of the older women contributes to creating great expectations among them of reciprocity from children. More elderly women than men verbalize disappointment when one of their children does not participate in the expected interdependence ties. Disappointment is unlikely to arise when an adult child cannot help due to financial or personal reasons. However, it is bound to arise when a child chooses not to assist the older parent for other reasons.

These older Puerto Rican women stress that good offspring ought to help their parents, contingent upon available resources. Statements such as the following are common:

> Of course I go to my children when I have a problem! To whom would I turn? I raised them and worked very hard to give them the little I could. Now that I am old, they try to help me in whatever they can. . . . Good offspring should help their aged parents as much as they are able to.

Interdependence for Puerto Rican older parents also means helping their children and grandchildren. Many times they provide help when it is not explicitly requested. They are happy when they can perform supportive tasks for their children's families. The child who needs help, no matter how old, is not judged as dependent or a failure.

Reciprocity is not based on strictly equal exchanges. Due to the rapid pace of life, lack of financial resources, or personal problems, adult children are not always able to provide the care the elder parent needs. Many times, the older adults provide their families with more financial and instrumental assistance than their children are able to provide them. Of utmost importance to the older women is not that their children be able to help all the time, but that they visit or call frequently. They place more emphasis on emotional support from their offspring than on any other form of support.

Gloria Santos, for example, has a son and a daughter. While they do not live in the same state as their mother, they each send her fifty to seventy dollars every month. Yet, she is disappointed with her children and explains why:

> They both have good salaries but call me only once or twice a month. I hardly know my grandchildren. All I ask from them is that they be closer to me, that they visit and call me more often. They only visit me once a year and only for one or two days. I've told my daughter that instead of sending me money she could call me more often. I was a good mother and worked hard in order for them to get a good education and have everything. All I expected from them was to show me they care, that they love me.

The importance that the older women attach to family interdependence does not imply that they constantly require assistance from children or that they do not value their independence. They prefer to live in their own households rather than with their adult children. They also try to solve as many problems as possible by themselves. But when support is needed, the adult children are expected to assist the aged parent to the degree they are able. This does not engender conflict or lowered self-esteem for the aged adult. Conflict and dissatisfaction are caused when adult children do not offer any support at all.

SEX ROLES AND FAMILIAL SUPPORTIVE NETWORKS

The family is the predominant source of support for most of these older women, providing instrumental and emotional support in daily life as well as assistance during health crises or times of need. Adult children play a central role in providing familial support to old parents. For married women, husbands are also an important component of their support system. At the same time, most of the older women still perform functional roles for their families.

Support from Adult Children

The support and helpfulness expected from offspring is related to perceptions of the difference between men and women. Older women seek different types of assistance from daughters than from sons. Daughters are perceived as being inherently better able to understand their mothers due to their shared status and qualities as women; they are also considered more reliable. Sons are not expected to help as much as daughters or in the same way. When a daughter does not fulfill the obligations expected of her, complaints are more bitter than if the same were true of a son: "Men are different; they do not feel as we feel. But she is a woman; she should know better." Daughters are also expected to visit and/or call more frequently than are sons. As women are linked closely to the domestic domain, they are held responsible for the care of family relations.

Motherhood is perceived as creating an emotional bond among women. When daughters become mothers, the older women anticipate stronger ties and more support from them.

> Once a daughter experiences motherhood, she understands the suffering and hardships you underwent for her. Sons will never be able to understand this.
>
> My daughter always helped me. But when she became a mother for the first time, she grew much closer to me. It was then when she was able to understand how much a mother can love.

Most of the older women go to a daughter first when confronted by an emotional problem. Daughters are felt to be more patient and better able to understand them as women. It is not that older women never discuss their emotional problems with their sons, but they prefer to discuss them with their daughters. For example, Juana Rivera has two sons who live in the same city as she and a daughter who resides in Puerto Rico. She and her sons get along well and see each other often. The sons stop by their mother's house every day after work, talk about daily happenings, and assist her with some tasks. However, when a physical exam revealed a breast tumor thought to be malignant, it was to her daughter in Puerto Rico that the old woman expressed her worries. She recalls that time of crisis:

> Eddie was with me when the doctor told me of the possibility of a tumor. I was brave. I didn't want him to see me upset. They [sons] get nervous when I

get upset or cry. . . . That evening I called my daughter and talked to her. . . .
She was very understanding and comforted me. I can always depend on her
to understand me. She is the person who better understands me. My sons are
also understanding, but she is a woman and understands more.

Although adult children are sources of assistance during the illnesses
of their mothers, it is generally daughters from whom more is expected.
Quite often daughters take their sick parents into their homes or stay
overnight in the parental household in order to provide better care. Sons,
as well as daughters, take the aged parent to the hospital or doctors' offices
and buy medicines if necessary. However, it is more often daughters who
check on their parents, provide care, and perform household chores when
the parent is sick.

When the old women have been hospitalized, adult children living nearby
tend to visit the hospital daily. Daughters and daughters-in-law sometimes
cook special meals for the sick parent and bring the meals to the hospital. Quite
often, adult children living in other states or in Puerto Rico come to help care
for the aged parent or be present at the time of an operation. When Juana
Rivera had exploratory surgery on her breast, her daughter came from Puerto
Rico and stayed with her mother throughout the convalescence. Similarly,
when Ana Toledo suffered a stroke and remained unconscious for four days,
three of her six children residing in other states came to be with her and their
siblings. After her release from the hospital, a daughter from New Jersey
stayed at her mother's house for a week. When she left, the children who live
near the old woman took turns looking after her.

Most adult children are also helpful in assisting with chores of daily living.
At times, offspring take their widowed mothers grocery shopping. Other
times, the older women give their children money to do the shopping for them.
Daughters are more often asked to do these favors and to also buy personal
care items and clothes for their mothers. Some adult offspring also assist by
depositing Social Security checks, checking post office boxes, and buying
money orders.

Support from Elderly Mothers

The Puerto Rican older women play an active role in providing assistance to
their adult children. Gender affects the frequency of emotional support
offered as well as the dynamics of the support. The older women offer advice
more often to daughters than to sons on matters related to childrearing. And
the approach used differs according to the children's gender. For example, one
older woman stated,

> I never ask my son openly what is wrong with him. I do not want him to think that I believe he needs help to solve his problems; he is a man. . . . Yet, as a mother I worry. It is my duty to listen and offer him advice. With my daughter it is different; I can be more direct. She doesn't have to prove to me that she is self-sufficient.

Another woman expressed similar views:

> Of course I give advice to my sons! When they have had problems with their wives, their children, even among themselves, I listen to them, and tell them what I think. But with my daughters I am more open. You see, if I ask one of my sons what is wrong and he doesn't want to tell me, I don't insist too much; I'll ask later, maybe in a different way; and they will tell me sooner or later. With my daughters, if they don't want to tell me, I insist. They know I am a mother and a woman like them and that I can understand.

Older mothers perceive sons and daughters as in equal need of support. Daughters, however, are understood to face additional problems in areas such as conjugal relations, childrearing, and sexual harassment, due to their status as women.

Emotional support to daughters-in-law is also offered, particularly when they are encountering marriage or childrearing problems. Josefina Montes explains the active role she played in comforting her daughter-in-law, whose husband was having an extramarital affair:

> I told her not to give up, that she had to defend what was hers. I always listened to her and tried to offer some comfort. . . . When my son would come to my home to visit I would ask him "What is wrong with you? Don't you realize what a good mother and wife that woman is?" . . . I made it my business that he did not forget the exceptional woman she is. . . . I told him I didn't want to ever see him with the other one and not to mention her name in front of me. . . . I was on his case for almost two years. . . . All the time I told her to be patient. . . . It took time but he finally broke up with the other one.

When relations between mother and daughters-in-law are not friendly, support is not usually present. Eulalia Valle says that when her son left his wife and children to move in with another woman, there was not much she could do for her daughter-in-law.

> There was not much I could do. What could I tell him? I couldn't say she was nice to me. . . . Once I tried to make him see how much she was hurting and he replied: "Don't defend her. She has never been fond of you and you know it." What could I reply to that? All I said was, "That's true but, still, she must be very hurt." But there was nothing positive to say about her!

Monetary assistance generally flows from the older parent to the adult children, although few old people are able to offer substantial financial help. Direct monetary assistance, rarely exceeding fifty dollars, is less frequent than gift-giving. Gift-giving usually takes the form of monetary contributions for specific articles needed by their children or children's families. In this way the older people contribute indirectly to the maintenance of their children's families.

The older women also play an active role in the observance of special family occasions and holidays. On the days preceding the celebration, they are busy cooking traditional Puerto Rican foods. It is expected that those in good health will participate in the preparation of foods. This is especially true on Christmas and Easter when traditional foods are an essential component of the celebrations.

Cooking for offspring is also a part of everyday life. In many of the households, meals prepared in the Puerto Rican tradition are cooked daily "in case children or grandchildren come by." Josefina Montes, for example, cooks a large quantity of food every day for herself, her husband, and their adult children and grandchildren. Her daughters come by after work to visit and pick up their youngest children, who stay with grandparents after school. The youngest daughter eats dinner at her parents' home. The oldest takes enough food home to serve her family. Doña[3] Josefina's sons frequently drop by after work or during lunch and she always insists that they eat something.

The older women also provide assistance to their children during health crises. When Juana Rivera's son was hospitalized for a hernia operation, she visited the hospital every day, occasionally bringing food she had prepared for him. When her son was released, Doña Juana stayed in his household throughout his convalescence, caring for him while her daughter-in-law went off to work.

The aged women also assist their children by taking care of grandchildren. Grandchildren go to their grandmother's house after school and stay until their parents stop by after work. If the children are not old enough to walk home by themselves, the grandparent waits for them at school and brings them home. The women also take care of their grandchildren when they are not old enough to attend school or are sick. They see their role as grandmothers as a continuation or reenactment of their role as mothers and childrearers.

The women, despite old age, have a place in the functional structure of their families. The older women's assistance is an important contribution to their children's households and also helps validate the women's sense of their importance and helpfulness.

Mutual Assistance in Elderly Couples

Different conceptions of women and men influence interdependence between husband and wife as well as their daily tasks. Older married women are responsible for domestic tasks and perform household chores. They also take care of grandchildren, grocery shopping, and maintaining family relations. Older married men have among their chores depositing Social Security checks, going to the post office, and buying money orders. Although they stay in the house for long periods, the men go out into the community more often than do their wives. They usually stop at the *bodegas*,[4] which serve as a place for socializing and exchange of information, to buy items needed at home and newspapers from Puerto Rico.

Most married couples have a distinctive newspaper reading pattern. The husband comments on the news to his wife as he reads or after he has finished. Sometimes, after her husband finishes reading and commenting on the news, the older woman reads about it herself. Husbands also inform their wives of ongoing neighborhood events learned on their daily stops at the *bodegas*. Wives, on the other hand, inform husbands of familial events learned through their daily telephone conversations and visits from children and other kin members.

The older couple escort each other to service-providing agencies, even though they are usually accompanied by an adult child, adolescent grandchild, or social worker serving as translator. An older man still perceives himself in the role of "family protector" by escorting the women in his family, particularly his wife.

Older husbands and wives provide each other with emotional assistance. They are daily companions and serve as primary sources of confidence for each other, most often sharing children's and grandchildren's problems, health concerns, or financial worries. The couple do not always agree on solutions or approaches for assisting children when sharing their worries about offspring. Many times the woman serves as a mediator in communicating her husband's problems to adult children. The men tend to keep their problems, particularly financial and emotional ones, to themselves or tell their wives but not their children. This behavior rests upon the notion of men as financially responsible for the family, more self-sufficient, and less emotional than women.

Among the older couples, the husband or wife is generally the principal caregiver during the health crises of their spouse. Carmen Ruiz, for example, suffers from chronic anemia and tires easily. Her husband used to be a cook and has taken responsibility for cooking meals and looking after the household. When Providencia Cruz's husband was hospitalized she spent many hours each day at the hospital, wanting to be certain he was comfortable. She brought meals she had cooked for him, arranged his pillows, rubbed him with bay leaf rubbing alcohol, or watched him as he slept. When he was convalescing at home, she was his principal caregiver. Doña Providencia suffers from osteoarthritis and gastric acidity. When she is in pain and spends the day in bed, her husband provides most of the assistance she needs. He goes to the drugstore to buy medicine or ingredients used in folk remedies. He knows how to prepare the mint and chamomile teas she drinks when not feeling well. He also rubs her legs and hands with ointments when the arthritic pain is more intense than usual. Furthermore, during the days that Doña Providencia's ailments last, he performs most of the household chores.

While both spouses live, the couple manages many of their problems on their own. Assistance from other family members with daily chores or help during an illness is less frequent when the woman still lives with her husband than when she lives alone. However, if one or both spouses is ill, help from adult children is more common.

FRIENDS AND NEIGHBORS AS COMMUNITY SOURCES OF SUPPORT

Friends and neighbors form part of the older women's support network. However, the women differentiate between "neighbors" and "friends." Neighbors, unlike kin and friends, are not an essential component of the network which provides emotional support. They may or may not become friends. Supportive relations with friends involve being instrumental helpers, companions, and confidants. Neighbors are involved only in instrumental help.

Neighbors as Sources of Support

Contact with neighbors takes the form of greetings, occasional visits, and exchanges of food, all of which help to build the basis for reciprocity when and if the need arises. The establishment and maintenance of good relations with neighbors is considered to be important since neighbors are potentially helpful during emergencies or unexpected events. Views such as the following are common: "It is good to get acquainted with your neighbors; you never know when you might need them."

Josefina Rosario, a widow, has lived next door to an older Puerto Rican couple for three years. Exchange of food and occasional visits are part of her interaction with them. Her neighbor's husband, in his mid-sixties, occasionally runs errands for Doña Josefina, who suffers from rheumatoid arthritis and needs a walker to move around. If she runs out of a specific food item, he goes to the grocery store for her. Other times, he buys stamps, mails letters, or goes to the drugstore to pick up some medicines for her. Although Doña Josefina cannot reciprocate in the same way, she repays her neighbors by visiting every other week and exchanging food. Her neighbors tell her she is to call them day or night if she ever feels sick. Although glad to have such "good neighbors" as she call them, she stresses she does not consider them friends and therefore does not confide her personal problems to them.

Supportive Relationships Among Friends

Although friends perform instrumental tasks, the older women believe that a good friend's most important quality is being able to provide emotional support. A friend is someone willing to help during the "good" and "bad" times, and is trustworthy and reserved. Problems may be shared with a friend with the certainty that confidences will not be betrayed. A friend provides emotional support not only during a crisis or problem, but in everyday life. Friends are companions, visiting and/or calling on a regular basis.

Friendship for this group of women is determined along gender lines. They tend to be careful about men. Relationships with males outside the immediate familial group are usually kept at a formal level. Mistrust of men is based upon the women's notion of *machismo*. Since men are conceived of as having a stronger sexual drive, the women are wary of the possibility of sexual advances, either physical or verbal. None of the women regards a male as a confidant friend. Many even emphasize the word *amiga* ("female friend") instead of *amigo* ("male friend"). Remarks such as the following are common:

> I've never had an *amigo*. Men cannot be trusted too much. They might misunderstand your motives and some even try to make a pass at you.

The few times the women refer to a male as a friend they use the term *amigo de la familia* ("friend of the family"). This expression conveys that the friendly relations are not solely between the woman and the man. The expression is generally used to refer to a close friend of the husband. *Amigos de la familia* may perform instrumental tasks, be present at family gatherings and unhappy events, or drop by to chat with the respondent's husband during the day. However, relations are not based on male-female relationships.

Age similarity is another factor that seems to affect selection of friends. The friendship networks of the older women are mainly composed of people sixty years of age and older. Friends who fill the role of confidant are generally women of a similar age. The women believe that younger generations, generally, have little interest in the elders. They also state that people their own age are better able to understand their problems because they share many of the same difficulties and worries.

Friends often serve as escorts, particularly in the case of women who live alone. Those who know some English serve as translators on some occasions. Close friends also help illiterate friends by reading and writing letters.

Most of the support friends provide one another is of an emotional nature, which involves sharing personal problems. Close friends entrust one another with family and health problems. This exchange occurs when friends either visit or call each other on the telephone. A pattern commonly observed between dyads of friends is daily calls. Many women who live alone usually call the friend during the morning hours, to make sure she is all right and to find out how she is feeling.

Another aspect of the emotional support the older women provide one another is daily companionship, occurring more often among those who live alone. For example, Hilda Montes and Rosa Mendoza sit together from 1:00 to 3:00 in the afternoon to watch soap operas and talk about family events, neighborhood happenings, and household management. At 3:00 P.M., whoever is at the other's apartment leaves because their grandchildren usually arrive from school around 4:00 P.M.

Friends are also supportive during health crises. If they cannot come to visit, they inquire daily about their friend's health by telephone. When their health permits, some friends perform menial household chores and always bring food for the sick person. If the occasion requires it, they prepare and/or administer home remedies. Friends, in this sense, alleviate the stress adult children often feel in assisting their aged mothers, particularly those who live by themselves. Friends take turns among themselves or with kin in taking care of the ill during the daytime. Children generally stay throughout the night.

Exchange ties with female friends include instrumental support, companionship, and problem sharing. Friends, particularly age cohorts, play an important role in the emotional well-being of the elders.

The relevance of culture to experience of old age is seen in the influence of value orientations on the expectations these Puerto Rican women have of themselves and those in their informal supportive networks. The way a group's cultural tradition defines and interprets relationships influences how elders use their networks to secure the support needed in old age. At the same time, the extent to which reality fits culturally-based expectations will contribute, to a large extent, to elders' sense of well-being.

NOTES

1. The article is based on a nineteen-month ethnographic study. The research was supported by the Danforth Foundation; Sigma Xi; the Scientific Research Society; and the Delta Kappa Gamma Society International.

2. All names are fictitious.

3. The deference term *Doña* followed by the woman's first name is a common way by which to address elderly Puerto Rican women and the one preferred by those who participated in the study.

4. Neighborhood grocery stores, generally owned by Puerto Ricans or other Hispanics, where ethnic foods can be purchased.

REFERENCES CITED

Barth, F. 1969. Introduction to *Ethnic Groups and Boundaries*, F. Barth, ed. Boston: Little, Brown.

Bastida, E. 1979. "Family Integration and Adjustment to Aging Among Hispanic American Elderly." Ph.D. dissertation, University of Kansas.

Cantor, M. H. 1979. "The Informal Support System of New York's Inner City Elderly: Is Ethnicity a Factor?" In *Ethnicity and Aging*, D. L. Gelfand and A. J. Kutzik, eds. New York: Springer.

Carrasquillo, H. 1982. "Perceived Social Reciprocity and Self-Esteem Among Elderly Barrio Antillean Hispanics and Their Familial Informal Networks." Ph.D. dissertation, Syracuse University.

Delgado, M. 1981. "Hispanic Elderly and Natural Support Systems: A Special Focus on Puerto Ricans." Paper presented at the Scientific Meeting of the Boston Society for Gerontological Psychiatry, November, Boston, Mass.

Donaldson, E. and E. Martínez. 1980. "The Hispanic Elderly of East Harlem." *Aging* 305–306: 6–11.

Sánchez-Ayéndez, M. 1984. "Puerto Rican Elderly Women: Aging in an Ethnic Minority Group in the United States." Ph.D. dissertation, University of Massachusetts at Amherst.

Stevens, E. P. 1973. "Marianismo: The Other Face of Machismo in Latin America." In *Female and Male in Latin America*, A. Pescatello, ed. Pittsburgh: University of Pittsburgh Press.

MAN CHILD: *A Black Lesbian Feminist's Response*

27

Audre Lorde

This article is not a theoretical discussion of Lesbian Mothers and their Sons, nor a how-to article. It is an attempt to scrutinize and share some pieces of that common history belonging to my son and me. I have two children: a fifteen-and-a-half-year-old daughter Beth, and a fourteen-year-old son Jonathan. This is the way it was/is with me and Jonathan, and I leave the theory to another time and person. This is one woman's telling.

I have no golden message about the raising of sons for other lesbian mothers, no secret to transpose your questions into certain light. I have my own ways of rewording those same questions, hoping we will all come to speak those questions and pieces of our lives we need to share. We are women making contact within ourselves and with each other across the restrictions of a printed page, bent upon the use of our own/one another's knowledges.

The truest direction comes from inside. I give the most strength to my children by being willing to look within myself, and by being honest with them about what I find there, without expecting a response beyond their years. In this way they begin to learn to look beyond their own fears.

All our children are outriders for a queendom not yet assured.

My adolescent son's growing sexuality is a conscious dynamic between Jonathan and me. It would be presumptuous of me to discuss Jonathan's sexuality here, except to state my belief that whomever he chooses to explore this area with, his choices will be nonoppressive, joyful, and deeply felt from within, places of growth.

One of the difficulties in writing this piece has been temporal; this is the summer when Jonathan is becoming a man, physically. And our sons must become men—such men as we hope our daughters, born and unborn, will be pleased to live among. Our sons will not grow into women. Their way is more difficult than that of our daughters, for they must move away from us, without

From: Audre Lorde, *Sister Outsider* (Freedom, CA: Crossing Press, 1984), pp. 72–80. First published in *Conditions: Four* (1979). Reprinted by permission.

us. Hopefully, our sons have what they have learned from us, and a howness to forge it into their own image.

Our daughters have us, for measure or rebellion or outline or dream; but the sons of lesbians have to make their own definitions of self as men. This is both power and vulnerability. The sons of lesbians have the advantage of our blueprints for survival, but they must take what we know and transpose it into their own maleness. May the goddess be kind to my son, Jonathan.

Recently I have met young Black men about whom I am pleased to say that their future and their visions, as well as their concerns within the present, intersect more closely with Jonathan's than do my own. I have shared vision with these men as well as temporal strategies for our survivals and I appreciate the spaces in which we could sit down together. Some of these men I met at the First Annual Conference of Third World Lesbians and Gays held in Washington D.C. in October, 1979. I have met others in different places and do not know how they identify themselves sexually. Some of these men are raising families alone. Some have adopted sons. They are Black men who dream and who act and who own their feelings, questioning. It is heartening to know our sons do not step out alone.

When Jonathan makes me angriest, I always say he is bringing out the testosterone in me. What I mean is that he is representing some piece of myself as a woman that I am reluctant to acknowledge or explore. For instance, what does "acting like a man" mean? For me, what I reject? For Jonathan, what he is trying to redefine?

Raising Black children—female and male— in the mouth of a racist, sexist, suicidal dragon is perilous and chancy. If they cannot love and resist at the same time, they will probably not survive. And in order to survive they must let go. This is what mothers teach—love, survival—that is, self-definition and letting go. For each of these, the ability to feel strongly and to recognize those feelings is central: how to feel love, how to neither discount fear nor be overwhelmed by it, how to enjoy feeling deeply.

I wish to raise a Black man who will not be destroyed by, nor settle for, those corruptions called *power* by the white fathers who mean his destruction as surely as they mean mine. I wish to raise a Black man who will recognize that the legitimate objects of his hostility are not women, but the particulars of a structure that programs him to fear and despise women as well as his own Black self.

For me, this task begins with teaching my son that I do not exist to do his feeling for him.

Men who are afraid to feel must keep women around to do their feeling for them while dismissing us for the same supposedly "inferior" capacity to feel deeply. But in this way also, men deny themselves their own essential humanity, becoming trapped in dependency and fear.

As a Black woman committed to a liveable future, and as a mother loving and raising a boy who will become a man, I must examine all my possibilities of being within such a destructive system.

Jonathan was three-and-one-half when Frances, my lover, and I met; he was seven when we all began to live together permanently. From the start, Frances' and my insistence that there be no secrets in our household about the fact that we were lesbians has been the source of problems and strengths for both children. In the beginning, this insistence grew out of the knowledge, on both our parts, that whatever was hidden out of fear could always be used either against the children or ourselves—one imperfect but useful argument for honesty. The knowledge of fear can help make us free.

> for the embattled
> there is no place
> that cannot be
> home
> nor is.*

For survival, Black children in america must be raised to be warriors. For survival, they must also be raised to recognize the enemy's many faces. Black children of lesbian couples have an advantage because they learn, very early, that oppression comes in many different forms, none of which have anything to do with their own worth.

To help give me perspective, I remember that for years, in the namecalling at school, boys shouted at Jonathan not—"your mother's a lesbian"—but rather—"your mother's a nigger."

When Jonathan was eight years old and in the third grade we moved, and he went to a new school where his life was hellish as a new boy on the block. He did not like to play rough games. He did not like to fight. He did not like to stone dogs. And all this marked him early on as an easy target.

When he came in crying one afternoon, I heard from Beth how the corner bullies were making Jonathan wipe their shoes on the way home whenever Beth wasn't there to fight them off. And when I heard that the ringleader was a little boy in Jonathan's class his own size, an interesting and very disturbing thing happened to me.

My fury at my own long-ago impotence, and my present pain at his suffering, made me start to forget all that I knew about violence and fear, and

---

*From "School Note" in *The Black Unicorn* (W.W. Norton and Company, New York, 1978), p. 55.

blaming the victim, I started to hiss at the weeping child. "The next time you come in here crying . . . ," and I suddenly caught myself in horror.

This is the way we allow the destruction of our sons to begin—in the name of protection and to ease our own pain. *My* son get beaten up? I was about to demand that he buy that first lesson in the corruption of power, that might makes right. I could hear myself beginning to perpetuate the age-old distortions about what strength and bravery really are.

And no, Jonathan didn't have to fight if he didn't want to, but somehow he did have to feel better about not fighting. An old horror rolled over me of being the fat kid who ran away, terrified of getting her glasses broken.

About that time a very wise woman said to me, "Have you ever told Jonathan that once you used to be afraid, too?"

The idea seemed far-out to me at the time, but the next time he came in crying and sweaty from having run away again, I could see that he felt shamed at having failed me, or some image he and I had created in his head of mother/woman. This image of woman being able to handle it all was bolstered by the fact that he lived in a household with three strong women, his lesbian parents and his forthright older sister. At home, for Jonathan, power was clearly female.

And because our society teaches us to think in an either/or mode—kill or be killed, dominate or be dominated—this meant that he must either surpass or be lacking. I could see the implications of this line of thought. Consider the two western classic myth/models of mother/son relationships: Jocasta/Oedipus, the son who fucks his mother, and Clytemnestra/Orestes, the son who kills his mother.

It all felt connected to me.

I sat down on the hallway steps and took Jonathan on my lap and wiped his tears. "Did I ever tell you about how I used to be afraid when I was your age?"

I will never forget the look on that little boy's face as I told him the tale of my glasses and my after-school fights. It was a look of relief and total disbelief, all rolled into one.

It is as hard for our children to believe that we are not omnipotent as it is for us to know it, as parents. But that knowledge is necessary as the first step in the reassessment of power as something other than might, age, privilege, or the lack of fear. It is an important step for a boy, whose societal destruction begins when he is forced to believe that he can only be strong if he doesn't feel, or if he wins.

I thought about all this one year later when Beth and Jonathan, ten and nine, were asked by an interviewer how they thought they had been affected by being children of a feminist.

Jonathan said that he didn't think there was too much in feminism for boys, although it certainly was good to be able to cry if he felt like it and not to have to play football if he didn't want to. I think of this sometimes now when I see him practicing for his Brown Belt in Tai Kwon Do.

The strongest lesson I can teach my son is the same lesson I teach my daughter: how to be who he wishes to be for himself. And the best way I can do this is to be who I am and hope that he will learn from this not how to be me, which is not possible, but how to be himself. And this means how to move to that voice from within himself, rather than to those raucous, persuasive, or threatening voices from outside, pressuring him to be what the world wants him to be.

And that is hard enough.

Jonathan is learning to find within himself some of the different faces of courage and strength, whatever he chooses to call them. Two years ago, when Jonathan was twelve and in the seventh grade, one of his friends at school who had been to the house persisted in calling Frances "the maid." When Jonathan corrected him, the boy then referred to her as "the cleaning woman." Finally Jonathan said, simply, "Frances is not the cleaning women, she's my mother's lover." Interestingly enough, it is the teachers at this school who still have not recovered from his openness.

Frances and I were considering attending a Lesbian/Feminist conference this summer, when we were notified that no boys over ten were allowed. This presented logistic as well as philosophical problems for us, and we sent the following letter:

> Sisters:
> Ten years as an interracial lesbian couple has taught us both the dangers of an oversimplified approach to the nature and solutions of any oppression, as well as the danger inherent in an incomplete vision.
> Our thirteen-year-old son represents as much hope for our future world as does our fifteen-year-old daughter, and we are not willing to abandon him to the killing streets of New York City while we journey west to help form a Lesbian-Feminist vision of the future world in which we can all survive and flourish. I hope we can continue this dialogue in the near future, as I feel it is important to our vision and our survival.

The question of separatism is by no means simple. I am thankful that one of my children is male, since that helps to keep me honest. Every line I write shrieks there are no easy solutions.

I grew up in largely female environments, and I know how crucial that has been to my own development. I feel the want and need often for the society of women, exclusively. I recognize that our own spaces are essential for developing and recharging.

As a Black woman, I find it necessary to withdraw into all-Black groups at times for exactly the same reasons—differences in stages of development and differences in levels of interaction. Frequently, when speaking with men and white women, I am reminded of how difficult and time-consuming it is to have to reinvent the pencil every time you want to send a message.

But this does not mean that my responsibility for my son's education stops at age ten, any more than it does for my daughter's. However, for each of them, that responsibility does grow less and less as they become more woman and man.

Both Beth and Jonathan need to know what they can share and what they cannot, how they are joined and how they are not. And Frances and I, as grown women and lesbians coming more and more into our power, need to relearn the experience that difference does not have to be threatening.

When I envision the future, I think of the world I crave for my daughters and my sons. It is thinking for survival of the species—thinking for life.

Most likely there will always be women who move with women, women who live with men, men who choose men. I work for a time when women with women, women with men, men with men, all share the work of a world that does not barter bread or self for obedience, nor beauty, nor love. And in that world we will raise our children free to choose how best to fulfill themselves. For we are jointly responsible for the care and raising of the young, since *that* they be raised is a function, ultimately, of the species.

Within that tripartite pattern of relating/existence, the raising of the young will be the joint responsibility of all adults who choose to be associated with children. Obviously, the children raised within each of these three relationships will be different, lending a special savor to that eternal inquiry into how best can we live our lives.

Jonathan was three-and-a-half when Frances and I met. He is now fourteen years old. I feel the living perspective that having lesbian parents has brought to Jonathan is a valuable addition to his human sensitivity.

Jonathan has had the advantage of growing up within a nonsexist relationship, one in which this society's pseudonatural assumptions of ruler/ruled are being challenged. And this is not only because Frances and I are lesbians, for unfortunately there are some lesbians who are still locked into patriarchal patterns of unequal power relationships.

These assumptions of power relationships are being questioned because Frances and I, often painfully and with varying degrees of success, attempt to evaluate and measure over and over again our feelings concerning power, our own and others'. And we explore with care those areas concerning how it is used and expressed between us and between us and the children, openly and otherwise. A good part of our biweekly family meetings are devoted to this exploration.

As parents, Frances and I have given Jonathan our love, our openness, and our dreams to help form his visions. Most importantly, as the son of lesbians, he has had an invaluable model—not only of a relationship—but of relating.

Jonathan is fourteen now. In talking over this paper with him and asking his permission to share some pieces of his life, I asked Jonathan what he felt were the strongest negative and the strongest positive aspects for him in having grown up with lesbian parents.

He said the strongest benefit he felt he had gained was that he knew a lot more about people than most other kids his age that he knew, and that he did not have a lot of the hang-ups that some other boys did about men and women.

And the most negative aspect he felt, Jonathan said, was the ridicule he got from some kids with straight parents.

"You mean, from your peers?" I said.

"Oh no," he answered promptly. "My peers know better. I mean other kids."

REPORTS FROM THE FRONT: **28**

Welfare Mothers up in Arms

Diane Dujon, Judy Gradford, and Dottie Stevens

Women on welfare know they are in constant battle to provide for themselves and their children. Their "enemies" are multiple, often including husbands, the welfare bureaucracy, and the attitudes of the general public. In this essay representatives from a group of welfare recipients in the Boston area who have organized into a welfare-rights group called ARMS (Advocacy for Resources for Modern Survival) describe some of the skirmishes they face every day.*

From: Rochelle Lefkowitz and Ann Withorn (eds.), *For Crying Out Loud: Women and Poverty in the United States* (New York: Pilgrim Press, 1986), pp. 211–219. Reprinted by permission.

*In addition to the three authors, several other members of the ARMS collective should be mentioned for their contributions to the larger unpublished paper from which this essay is taken, "Welfare Mothers up in Arms." They are Angela Hannon, Marion Graham, Jeannie MacKenzie, Carolyn Turner, and Hope Habtemarian. The cited quotations in this essay are taken from interviews with various ARMS members.

OUR LIVES NO LONGER BELONG TO US

One of my sons was diagnosed as having a high lead level in his blood. The Welfare Department placed my son under protective services and told me that I would have to find another place to live or they would put my son into a foster home. With six children on a welfare budget, it's not easy to find an apartment. And I had to find one within thirty days! To keep the state from taking my son, I was forced to move into the first available housing I could find.

Since I was an emergency case and eligible for a housing subsidy, my name was placed at the top of the list. I had to take the first available unit offered by the Housing Authority. The offer: a brand new town-house-type apartment *fifty miles away* in a white, middle-class suburb!

I knew this move would devastate my family because we would be so far away from our relatives and friends. When you're poor, you have to depend on your family and friends to help you through when you don't have the money to help yourself. At least two or three times every month I take my children to my mother's house to eat. How would we ever be able to get to her house from fifty miles away?

I also knew that my neighbors would not welcome me and my children: a black single woman with six children. I imagined the sneers of the merchants as I paid for my groceries with food stamps and the grunts of the doctors as I pulled out my Medicaid card.

I thought about the problems of transportation that were sure to crop up. How would I get my children to school? What if they got sick; how far was the nearest hospital? I envisioned the seven of us walking for miles with grocery bags. In short, I felt no relief at having found a nice clean apartment within the allotted time, but my back was against the wall. I could not refuse or my son would be put into foster care.

We now live in a totally hostile environment severed from our family and friends. And although we live in a physically beautiful development, life for us is hard. A poor family with no transportation is lost in the suburbs. We are as isolated as if we lived on a remote island in the Pacific.

Situations like the one described by this woman show how our lives no longer belong to us. We have, in effect, married the state. To comply with the conditions of our recipient status, we cannot make any personal decisions ourselves. We must consult the Welfare Department first, and the final decision is theirs. The state is a domineering, chauvinistic spouse.

Politicians often boast or complain about the many services and benefits welfare recipients receive. For us, these services and benefits are the bait that the predatory department uses to entrap us and our families. Like the wiley fox, we are driven by hunger to the trap. We must carefully trip the trap, retrieve the bait, and escape, hopefully unscathed. Also similar to the fox, our incompetence can lead to starvation, disease, and death for ourselves and our families.

This may seem an unlikely analogy to some; but the Welfare Department, in its *eagerness* to help us constantly adopts policies that put us in catch-22 situations. We are continuously in a dilemma over whether we should seek the help we desperately need or not. The purportedly "free" social services that are available to us extort a usurer's fee in mental and physical anguish. So, although there are several services available, we are often unable or reluctant to receive them. Below we describe some of the catch-22's that constitute mental cruelty for us.

CATCH-22: A LOW BUDGET

The first catch-22 we encounter is living under the conditions set up by the state for recipients. Under penalty of law we are required adequately to house, clothe, feed, and otherwise care for our children on a budget that is two thirds of the amount considered to be at the poverty line. If we fail to fulfill our obligation in the opinion of friends, strangers, neighbors, relatives, enemies, or representatives of the Welfare Department, the state can and *will* take our children from our homes. Anyone can call the department anonymously and report that we are neglecting or abusing our children. With no further questions, the state initiates an investigation, which further jeopardizes our family stability. While it is necessary for the state to protect children from abuse and neglect, a large portion of the investigations are based on unfounded allegations for which no one can be held accountable. It is no easy task to fulfill the basic obligation of surviving on welfare, because we often pay as much as 85 to 95 percent of our income for rent and utilities.

On the other hand, there is no reward for a job well done. If we manage to clothe, feed, and house our children, the risk is the same: at the least, biting remarks from people in public, and at the most, an investigation of fraud.

We are constantly under public scrutiny. We are made to feel uncomfortable if we wear jewelry, or buy a nice blouse, or own a warm coat. It's as if we're not supposed to have families or friends who love us and might give us a birthday or Christmas present. Absolutely no thought is given to the fact that we may have had a life before welfare! Heaven forbid that anyone should honor the great job we must do as shoppers!

There are a few legal ways in which welfare mothers can supplement their monthly grant. Some of these supports are available upon eligibility for Aid to Families with Dependent Children (AFDC); others, termed "social services," have additional individual eligibility requirements. Each has its quota of catch-22's:

CATCH-22: EMERGENCY ASSISTANCE

I was $300 in arrears with my electric bill. The electric company sent me several reminders, but I didn't have the money to pay my bill. It made me very nervous. It was winter, and although I had oil, if my electricity were turned off, my pilot light would go out and my children would be cold.

I took my bill and the warning notices to my social worker at the Welfare Department. She told me that I could receive up to $500 of Emergency Assistance per year, but that only one such grant could be made in any twelve-month period. However, I could not receive any Emergency Assistance until I received a 'shut-off' notice. She further explained that I should wait because if I received the $300 EA grant, I could not get the additional $200 to which I was entitled that year. I would have to wait twelve months before I could be eligible for another grant. I really wasn't interested in getting all I could, I just wanted to be able to sleep at night; but since I didn't have a shut-off notice, I had no choice but to wait.

I received a shut-off notice when my bill was about $400. I applied for, and received, the EA grant.

The very next year, I was in a similar situation. I again attempted to wait for the shut-off notice. One day I received a notice from the electric company stating that I was scheduled for a "field collection." My social worker reminded me that EA can only be awarded upon my receipt of a shut-off notice. Even though the notice stated that my service would be "interrupted" if I failed to honor the collector, it did not have the specific words *shut off* and, therefore, I was ineligible for EA. I couldn't believe what she was telling me! To become eligible, I had to go to the electric company to ask them to stamp "shut off" on my bill. I was angry that I was being forced to humiliate myself by revealing my personal business to the electric company representative.

CATCH-22: MEDICAID

Medicaid is the most treasured benefit to families who must depend on AFDC, but it, too, falls short of the expectations of beneficiaries. Doctors, hospitals, druggists, and other health providers often refuse to accept Medicaid patients. The amount of paper work that is required for each and every patient is tedious and time-consuming. Medicaid also sets limits on the type and amount of treatments it will cover.

Every trip to the doctor is a grueling, costly, and time-consuming event. First, we must search for a doctor or medical facility that will accept Medicaid. If we are lucky enough to have a neighborhood health center nearby, we will often go to the clinic. In either situation, we usually have to wait for hours to receive the medical attention we need. Doctors often remark about the amount of paperwork that is required by the state and the fact that they often have to wait six to eight months to obtain their fees from the state. It is exceedingly distressing to be sick and to have to hear about the doctor's problems.

> I had periodontal disease once. The dentist explained that an infection had settled under my gums and he would have to cut my gums and scrape the infection away. Since I was on Medicaid, I was required to wait until Medicaid approved the dental procedure.
>
> After several weeks, the approval arrived. My dentist informed me that although Medicaid approved the procedure, the amount approved was too low to allow him to use gas as was customary. I had a choice: either I could pay him the difference, and *enjoy* a painless procedure; or I could have the procedure done for the cost Medicaid allotted and he could use novocaine, which would be at least moderately painful.
>
> I didn't have the money to pay the difference, but I knew that if I delayed the operation I stood a good chance of losing my teeth. I decided to brave the novocaine.
>
> The dentist had to cut deep into my gums and the novocaine did nothing for the pain below the surface. I tried hard to be still and keep my mouth open wide, but I was in agony with the pain. The procedure took four hours and required sixty-four stitches and forty-seven injections of novocaine!

CATCH-22: FOOD STAMPS

Food Stamps are a symbol of the government's benevolence. Rather than increase the amount of the welfare budget so that we can afford to buy more food, the government *supplements* our budgets with food stamps. As the name suggests, food is all that can be purchased with them. And not much food at that. Households receiving the maximum amount of food stamps receive an average of forty cents per meal per person. All other commodities, such as soap, detergent, toilet paper, diapers, etc., must be separated at the time of purchase. Food, by anyone's definition, is a necessity for sustaining life. Why, then, do we feel as if food is a luxury?

Contrary to public opinion, we pay for these food stamps at a cost significantly higher than a cup of coffee per meal. We pay with the anguish of wondering how we are going to maintain healthy children on $1.20 per day. Food stamps last an average of ten days, depending on the supply of staples (flour, sugar, cereal, salt, spaghetti, etc.) we have on hand; the rest of the month we struggle to keep up with the milk, eggs, juice, fruits, vegetables, and bread so vital to good health. The last two weeks we are challenged to use our imaginations to ensure that our children receive the best nutrition possible. For those of us who are lucky enough to be able to commit "fraud" through friends and relatives, it's a little easier; but for many of us it's often an impossible task!

> The way the food stamp budget is calculated, it's as if our diet is supposed to shrink in the summer. Our fuel costs are counted as an expense in the winter, so we receive more food stamps in the winter and less in the summer. This budget policy is ludicrous because most of our fuel costs in the winter are paid with Fuel Assistance.
>
> I had trouble one time receiving my food stamps. Every month I would have to commute to the next town where my welfare office was located to report that I had not received my food stamps. Each time I was interrogated by the food stamps worker about whether I had cashed my food stamps and was trying to get some more under false pretenses. I had to sign a sworn statement to the effect that I had not received my food stamps before they could issue replacement stamps.
>
> I finally decided that rather than go through the hassle and expense of picking up my food stamps from the welfare office each month, I would purchase a post office box. When I went to inform my worker of my box number, I was told that food stamps could not be sent to a post office box. This policy was supposed to deter fraud. I was forced to continue to pick up my stamps from the welfare office each month.

Food stamp redemption centers are generally located in areas that are virtually inaccessible to those of us without cars. Much of the money we are supposed to be saving with food stamps is spent on transportation to the centers.

> My food stamps usually come on the due date, but my welfare check is often late. This creates a problem for me because I always need the food, but with no cash money it is almost impossible to do the shopping I need to do the first time. I have to make at least two trips to the supermarket: the first trip for food only with the food stamps and the second, when my check comes, to buy soap, cleaning products, etc. Two trips to the store doubles the amount of transportation expenses, too.

CATCH-22: WELFARE FRAUD

Fraud within the welfare system might also be called "devising a way to survive." The federal and state laws call it fraud if a welfare recipient uses up her allotment for any reason and seeks assistance from a friend, relative, or acquaintance (be it ten cents or $10). If she does not report this money to the welfare office, she is technically considered to be defrauding the Welfare Department. Such unrealistic definitions leave all of us vulnerable to fraud and make it difficult to separate honest need from intentional deception.

According to the narrow, unrealistic guidelines of the state and federal government, most or all welfare recipients could be accused of having committed fraud at some time during their ordeal with the welfare system, even though they would not have meant to defraud anyone. We are stuck in a system that inadequately provides for us and that even the social workers know, depends upon our having a "little help from our friends." However, if we are caught doing what we all have to do to survive, we may even be made into an "example" and used to discredit the difficulties faced by women on welfare.

We are poor because we do not receive enough money from the Welfare Department to live decently. If we lack family or friends, we may feel forced to find ways to get a little extra money for our families. Many who have been discovered working to buy Christmas presents, for example, have been brought to court by the Welfare Department and either fined, jailed, or made to pay back all monies received while working.

Although there seems to be large-scale vendor fraud among those who supply Medicaid services, it is seldom investigated or taken to court. While we are hounded for minor infractions, little is done to the unscrupulous doctors, dentists, druggists, nursing-home operators, and others in the health field who blatantly commit welfare fraud as a regular practice. Because of their "respectability" in the community, these providers are in a position to bill Medicaid for services never rendered, and they do so with some regularity. When these abuses are publicized, public outcry is minimal and fleeting at best. It is so much easier to blame "those people."

Even in the event of discovery by a Medicaid "fraud squad," the welfare recipient, rather than the health professional suspected of illegally using the system, often becomes the target of their investigation.

> I was ordered by our Medicaid fraud squad to appear at my local welfare office within the week. A dentist who had done surgery on my mouth for a periodontal disease was under suspicion of committing fraud.
>
> I arrived at the office not knowing what to expect. Two men who resembled G-Men arrived and hustled me into a cubicle and began interrogating me. Not being satisfied with my answers, they proceeded to look into my mouth at every tooth in my head to prove I had fillings where they were not supposed to be, according to the computer printout they were studying. They also wanted me to account for every filling, extraction, check-up, and cleaning of my three children, which had been done by the same dentist. This took me another week.
>
> I was treated as if I was guilty of something. When you are on welfare, no one cares about your feelings—they don't count.

The welfare system, in reality, has been set up to promote fraud as a means of survival. They *know* we can't live on budgets "below the poverty line." With a more reasonable system of providing financial assistance, there would be less "fraud" because people on welfare would be less desperate. But as it is, women are punished for being on welfare and pushed into impossible binds.

ENOUGH ALREADY

Families who must rely on the welfare system to survive are constantly torn to pieces by the bureaucratic policies that supply the services they need. Each benefit comes with its own rules and regulations, which must be followed if recipients are to remain eligible. The policies are designed separately, with little regard to policies of other agencies, so we are continuously in compromising positions.

Welfare policies are written in "still life." Like the prepackaged vegetables in the supermarkets, they look fine on the surface: but turn them over and look beneath the surface and you may see rotten spots. Living, breathing people need policies that allow for individuality and flexibility. No two families are alike or have the same needs. We should not be lumped together and threatened with extinction if we complain. Women who are already in crises do not need the added stress of conflicting policies among the services that are ours by right. We are strong, capable, and often wise beyond our years. We demand that we be allowed to have some control over our own lives. No governor, president, general, or legislator should be able to dictate to us where we live, what we eat, or where, or even, whether we should work outside the home when we are already taking care of our children.

Identity and the Life Cycle

YOUNG BLACK MALES IN AMERICA:

29

Endangered, Embittered, and Embattled

Jewelle Taylor Gibbs

I am an invisible man. . . . I am a man of substance, of flesh and bone, fiber and liquids—and I might even be said to possess a mind. I am invisible, understand, simply because people refuse to see me. . . . When they approach me, they see only my surroundings, themselves, or figments of their imagination—indeed, everything and anything except me.

Ralph Ellison in *Invisible Man* (New York: Random House, 1972).

An endangered species is, according to Webster, "a class of individuals having common attributes and designated by a common name . . . [which is] in danger or peril of probable harm or loss." This description applies in a metaphorical sense, to the current status of young black males in contemporary American society. They have been miseducated by the educational system, mishandled by the criminal justice system, mislabeled by the mental health system, and mistreated by the social welfare system. All the major institutions of American society have failed to respond appropriately and effectively to their multiple needs and problems. As a result, they have become—in an unenviable and unconscionable sense—rejects of our affluent society and misfits in their own communities (Gibbs, 1984).

From: Jewelle Taylor Gibbs, *Young, Black and Male in America* (Dover, Mass.: Auburn, 1988). Reprinted by permission of Greenwood Publishing Group, Inc.

Who are these black youth who are increasingly subjected to the belated scrutiny of social scientists, educators, policymakers, and the mass media? They are black males in the 15–24-year-old age group who live predominantly in urban inner-city neighborhoods but can also be found in rural areas, working-class suburbs, and small towns all over America. They are the teenagers and young adults from families at the lower end of the socioeconomic spectrum, many of whom are welfare-dependent and live below the poverty line. They are the black youth who are seen when one drives through inner-city ghetto neighborhoods, hanging out on dimly lit street corners, playing basketball on littered school lots, selling dope in darkened alleys, and "rapping" in front of pool halls and bars. The media refer to them by a variety of labels: "dropouts," "delinquents," "dope addicts," "street-smart dudes," "welfare pimps," and, even more pejoratively, as members of the "underclass." They refer to themselves as "home boys," "hardheads," "bloods," and "soul brothers." Labels are powerful clues to the ways in which groups are perceived, valued, and treated, but labels cannot convey the feelings of frustration, humiliation, and anger of these black youth who experience daily doses of failure, rejection, and discrimination. From the brutal lynching of Emmett Till in Mississippi in 1955 to the "justifiable" police killing of Michael Stewart on a New York City subway in 1983, young black males in America have been the primary victims of mob violence, police brutality, legal executions, and ghetto homicide.

Black males are portrayed by the mass media in a limited number of roles, most of them deviant, dangerous, and dysfunctional. This constant barrage of predominantly disturbing images inevitably contributes to the public's negative stereotypes of black men, particularly of those who are perceived as young, hostile, and impulsive. Even the presumably positive images of blacks as athletes and entertainers project them as animal-like or childlike in their aggressiveness, sensuality, "natural rhythm," and uninhibited expressiveness. Clearly, the message says: If they entertain you, enjoy them (at a safe distance); if they serve you, patronize them (and don't forget to leave a tip); if they threaten you, avoid them (don't ride on the subway). Thus, young black males are stereotyped by the five "d's": dumb, deprived, dangerous, deviant, and disturbed. There is no room in this picture for comprehension, caring, or compassion of the plight of these young black men.

A few vignettes illustrate the impact of these stereotypes on community attitudes and behaviors toward this group:

- Just five days before Christmas 1986, three young black men (ages 19, 23, and 37) stopped at a pizza parlor to call for help when their car broke down in the predominantly white neighborhood of Howard Beach, Queens.

While there, they ordered pizza and chatted briefly with the counterman, but became apprehensive when a crowd of white youth gathered outside and began chanting: "Niggers, go home." As they left the restaurant, they were beaten and chased by the angry youth in various directions. One of the black youth, 23-year-old Michael Griffith, after pleading to an onlooker for help, ran onto the nearby freeway to escape his assailants and was killed by an oncoming car. Subsequently, four white teenagers, none older than 18, were arrested and charged with manslaughter. In their defense, neighbors were quoted as saying that they were "just average boys from respectable families," and that they probably thought that the three black men were "up to no good."

- In October 1986, the *Washington Post* inaugurated a new Sunday magazine section with a feature story on the problems of operating small businesses in the downtown areas of the capital city, where merchants customarily installed bars on their windows and frequently refused to open their doors to young black males whom they viewed as potential assailants. Although the *Post* was heavily criticized by local black leaders for this inflammatory article, the paper was only revealing a practice that is common in central city shopping areas of New York, Chicago, Los Angeles, and many others.

- The sheriff of Jefferson Parish, Louisiana, a predominantly white suburb of New Orleans, called a news conference on December 2, 1986 to announce that his deputies would henceforth arrest any young black males seen in the residential areas of his community after dark. When civil rights groups objected to this policy, the sheriff defended his position on the grounds that most of the crime in the New Orleans area was committed by young black men and, therefore, it seemed perfectly reasonable and justifiable to arrest anyone fitting that description, as a preventive measure.

- In Liberty City, Florida, a riot broke out in the predominantly black area after a young black male died in police custody in May 1980. The police claimed that his death was an accident, but witnesses swore that he had been subdued with a choke hold and brutally beaten by the police. This incident was one of a series of confrontations between blacks and the local police, with black males consistently complaining of police brutality and discrimination.

- In December 1984, a young black man approached a white man riding on a New York City subway, asking him for five dollars. Three of the black youth's friends sitting nearby were watching, perhaps planning to join in the panhandling, as the white man pulled out a gun and shot all four of them. One youth is paralyzed for life, but Bernhard Goetz, a 37-year-old electrical engineer, was hailed as a hero by many New Yorkers and was treated as a celebrity by the mass media. In his defense, Goetz's lawyer claimed that he felt his life was threatened because of the "gleam in their eyes." Nearly two and a half years later, in June 1987, a jury of his peers found him "not guilty" of attempted murder and assault.

In 1985 there were 8.5 million black youth in the 10–24-year-old age range, with nearly 3 million each in the 15–19 and 20–24-year-old age groups. Black males accounted for nearly 3 million in the 15–24 category, or 50 percent of the total group. Since nearly half of the total black population is composed of children and youth, the median age for blacks is 25.8 years compared to a median age of 31.8 for whites (U.S. Census Bureau, 1987). Thus, any social and economic problems in the black community will have a disproportionate impact on black youth under the age of 25, and more particularly on the additional unenumerated black males (Gibbs, 1985).

Nearly half (42.7 percent) of black youth under 18 live in families who are below the poverty line, while two-thirds (67.1 percent) of those living in female-headed families are classified as poor. Two of every five (42 percent) black youth live in female-headed families (U.S. Census Bureau, 1987). Clearly, this type of family structure tends to have a negative impact on the economic status and opportunities for all black youth, and it may have particularly negative effects on black males (CDF, 1986c).

Children in black female-headed families are five times as likely to be welfare-dependent than those in intact black families. Thus, males in female-headed families are not only reared without fathers as role models, but are also reared in families triply stigmatized by being black, single-parent, and on welfare. Furthermore, youth in these families are more likely to live in substandard housing, to attend inferior schools, to have inadequate health and dental care, to have higher rates of chronic illnesses, to have more behavioral problems, and to live in deteriorating neighborhoods with high crime rates, poor services, and inadequate public transportation (CDF, 1985a and 1986a).

Even for those black youth who live in intact nuclear families, economic stability and quality of life are much less predictable and permanent than for comparable white youth (CDF, 1985b). For such youth, total family income is more likely to depend on both parents working, but their fathers are 2.5 times more likely than adult white males to be unemployed. Both parents are more likely than parents of white youth to be employed in lower-status, lower-income jobs in the white-collar, blue-collar, and unskilled sectors of the economy. In 1986, the median black family income of $17,604 was only 57 percent of white family income of $30,809, a decrease from 61 percent in 1970. Thus, it is an illusion that the gap between black and white family income has narrowed in the past 15 years. In fact, black family income is lower than it was in 1978, and its modest gains since 1980 remain heavily dependent on two parents working, a stable economy, and the security of government employment (U.S. Census Bureau, 1987).

Just as the modest economic gains experienced by the black family in the late 1960s and early 1970s have largely been offset by the increasing rate of poverty among single-parent families, black youth have also lost ground on five out of six social indicators. What is particularly dramatic and demoralizing is that, while all other groups (including women and recent immigrants) have made progress since 1960 in all of these areas, young black males in particular are now more likely than they were in 1960 to be unemployed, to be addicted to drugs, to be involved in the criminal justice system, to be unwed fathers, and to die from homicide or suicide. The educational statistics indicate a reduction in high school drop-out rates among black males during this period, but this improved high school completion rate has been offset by a decline in the college enrollment rates of black high school graduates and a continuing high rate of illiteracy among 18–21-year-old black youth, both of which are more characteristic of black males. . . .

CONTRIBUTING FACTORS TO THE DETERIORATING STATUS OF YOUNG BLACK MALES

Four major sets of factors can account for this downward spiral of black youth, and particularly black males, since 1960: historical, sociocultural, economic, and political. These factors are briefly discussed below.

Historical Factors

Black youth today are the ultimate victims of a legacy of nearly 250 years of slavery, 100 years of legally enforced segregation, and decades of racial discrimination and prejudice in every facet of American life. Countless authors have documented the brutality of slavery, the cruelty of segregation, and the injustice of discrimination. Generations of blacks have endured inferior schools, substandard housing, menial jobs, and the indignities of poverty. Yet, through all of these travails, each generation of blacks made some progress and believed that their children would eventually merge into the mainstream of American society. These beliefs were infused with new life by the New Deal programs of the 1930s, nurtured by the economic opportunities of World War II, and fostered by the postwar policies of the Truman administration. By 1960, many blacks were optimistic that "Jim Crow" was in a terminal stage, that opportunities were increasing for minorities, and that black youth would finally be able to share in the American dream. No one could have anticipated that the tremendous civil rights and economic gains of the 1960s would have been seriously eroded and ideologically challenged by the mid-1980s, leaving black youth in a worse economic and social situation than they had experienced since before President John F. Kennedy initiated his New Frontier.

The past two and one-half decades since 1960 have been one of the most turbulent periods in American history, encompassing the rise of the civil rights movement, the urban riots, the women's movement, the Vietnam War, the war on poverty, and major political and economic changes in the society. The era began with a liberal Democratic administration committed to increasing opportunities for minorities, but it has gradually evolved into a conservative Republican administration which has aggressively dismantled or diluted many of the most effective civil rights and social welfare programs.

Black youth, who lived through a period of heightened expectations and increased opportunities in the 1960s and early 1970s, began to see their dreams of major social change gradually fade as the economy stopped expanding and other groups (e.g., women, immigrants) began competing for the same limited resources. While much of the civil rights legislation and many of the antipoverty programs primarily benefited working and middle-class blacks (who were in a better position to take advantage of them), the unanticipated effect of these changes was to create a wide gap between middle-class and poor blacks. Middle-class blacks moved out of the inner cities into integrated urban and suburban areas, leaving poor blacks behind in blighted neighborhoods without effective leadership, successful role models, or the supportive institutions and social networks that provided social stability, economic diversity, and traditional values to the community (see Clark, 1965; Glasgow, 1981). Thus, with increased isolation from the black middle class and alienation from the white community, black inner-city ghettos have gradually become "welfare reservations" where black youth have few, if any, positive role models; where they lack access to high-quality educational, recreational, and cultural facilities; where they do not have job opportunities or adequate transportation to locate jobs; and where they are confronted daily with adult role models who are openly involved in drugs, prostitution, gambling, and other forms of deviant behavior.

Sociocultural Factors

These recent historical and demographic developments have undoubtedly contributed to sociocultural changes in the black community. As the black middle class has drifted away from the inner cities, it has left a vacuum not only in terms of leadership but also in terms of values and resources. For example, in these transformed ghettos, the black church, which had formerly been the center of activity in the black community, has lost much of its central function as a monitor of norms and values. The power of political organizations has been diminished, as their constituencies no longer include the better educated and wealthier blacks who are more likely to participate actively in the political process. In cities with shrinking tax bases, civic and social organizations have fewer resources to improve neighborhoods, initiate youth programs, or provide incentives to attract external sources of support.

With the breakdown or weakening of these traditional institutions within inner-city communities, there has been a parallel breakdown of the traditional black community values of the importance of family, religion, education, self-improvement, and social cohesion through extensive social support networks. Many blacks in inner cities no longer seem to feel connected to each other, responsible for each other, or concerned about each other. Rather than a sense of shared community and a common purpose, which once characterized black neighborhoods, these inner cities now reflect a sense of hopelessness, alienation, and frustration. It is exactly this kind of frustration that exploded in the urban riots of the 1960s from Watts, California, to Detroit, Michigan, to Washington, D.C.

It is also this kind of frustration that erupts into urban crime and violence, family violence, and self-destructive violence. Thus, we see situations in which young black men sell drugs openly on major thoroughfares without fear of apprehension; teenage girls have multiple out-of-wedlock pregnancies without fear of ostracism; youthful gangs terrorize neighborhoods without fear of retaliation; and young teenagers loiter aimlessly at night on street corners without fear of reprobation.

The poverty and the powerlessness of black youth are inextricably linked to the safety and security of the rest of the society, since the frustration-bred violence will ultimately spill over the invisible walls of the ghetto. The violence which young black males now direct mainly against the black community (black-on-black crime), against relatives and friends (homicide), and against themselves (suicide), will inevitably erupt and spread throughout urban and suburban America, leaving behind damage, destruction, and distrust in its wake. In anxious anticipation of this rising tide of black rage, urban dwellers now put bars on their doors and windows, shopkeepers turn their stores into fortresses, and politicians build new prisons. The causes of these antisocial behaviors are ignored, denied, or blamed on the black youth, who are written off as being intellectually deficient, culturally deprived, and pathologically deviant. Short-term remedies are devised for the consequences of their behaviors, with little understanding that these band-aid solutions are very temporary, very perishable, and very ineffective to cure the underlying causes of frustration and anger in these black youth.

Economic Factors

The post–World War II economic revolution in the United States is the third major factor contributing to the problems of black youth. Two parallel developments created chronic unemployment among black males, both young and old: the structural change in the economy from a predominantly manufacturing and industrial base to a predominantly high-technology and service base, and the movement of these newer jobs from the central cities to the suburbs and peripheral areas (Kasarda, 1985; Sum, Harrington, and Goedicke, 1987). Black youth did not have the skills to compete in the new industries; nor did they have the transportation to follow the jobs to the suburbs. As these jobs moved away from the central cities to the suburbs and exurbs, new services were developed to supply the needs of employers in these industrial and technical companies. These new employment opportunities were increasingly filled by white women and young immigrant workers. After the urban riots of the 1960s, many of the "Mom-and-Pop" stores were forced to close or moved away from the inner cities, removing another source of employment for black youth. As these convenience stores have gradually been replaced, the new owners are predominantly Asian, Hispanic, and Middle-Eastern immigrants who tend to employ family members rather than black youth from the community. Some black leaders have accused these immigrant shopkeepers of commercial exploitation of the black community without returning any economic benefits to the community by hiring black youth.

Black youth, who once had the monopoly on menial service and domestic jobs in restaurants, airports, and department stores, are increasingly being displaced by Asian and Hispanic youth. Although there is some controversy about the displacement theory, statistics indicate that black youth employment rates have decreased as the employment rates of other nonwhite youth have increased. In any case, whether the competition for jobs between black and immigrant youth is perceived or actual, interethnic tensions have increased between blacks and these other minority groups in many urban areas. However, some employers have suggested that immigrant youth are more cooperative, less aggressive, and willing to work for lower wages than black youth. In their analysis of the employment problems of poor youth in America, Sum and his colleagues (1987) conclude that "it is poor black teens who were experiencing the most severe employment problems in March 1985 in both an absolute sense and relative to whites and Hispanics in similar family income positions" (p. 217). Clearly, there are some "noneconomic" factors operating in the severe employment problems of young black males—problems which reflect discriminatory hiring practices as much as they reflect economic and technological changes. . . .

Political Factors

The fourth major factor which has exacerbated already existing problems for black youth is the conservative political climate in this country, which began with the election of Richard Nixon in 1968 and has been strongly reinforced by the Reagan administration. Many political analysts interpret this growing conservatism as a backlash to the antipoverty programs and affirmative action policies of the Johnson and Carter administrations, a not-so-subtle protest of the "middle-American majority" to the civil rights and economic gains of minority groups (Omi and Winant, 1986). Threatened with the loss of their special status, these "middle Americans" have been manipulated by politicians and lobbyists for their own self-serving goals. Framing their rationale in neoconservative dogma, these policymakers have shifted the emphasis from the goal of providing all citizens with a decent standard of living through federally subsidized health and welfare programs to the need to blame the poor and disadvantaged for their perceived lack of motivation, their "dysfunctional" family systems, and their dependency on welfare programs. By shifting the focus from society's responsibility for its most vulnerable citizens to an emphasis on the so-called "social pathology" of minority youth and their families, advocates of this view (such as Murray, 1984) have quite deliberately and effectively transformed the national debate from a proactive emphasis on policies of prevention and early intervention to a reactive emphasis on retrogressive policies and punitive programs. As a result, politicians who support cuts in social programs aimed primarily at disadvantaged and minority families have found increasing favor with the voters in the past 20 years; thus programs with a direct impact on black youth, such as CETA, the Job Corps, federally subsidized loans for college, and youth employment programs, all have been severely cut back or eliminated.

The impact of these political and economic changes has resulted in direct negative consequences of fewer educational and employment opportunities for young black males. It has also affected their perceptions of opportunity and their access to the American dream of social and economic mobility. Several national surveys and opinion polls have shown that black families believe they are worse off economically and politically in the 1980s than they were in the 1970s. Consequently, black youth have responded by withdrawing from the labor market, reducing their applications to four-year colleges, and increasing their involvement in self-destruction and deviant behavior. . . . Peak suicide rates of black youth are also correlated with periods of political conservatism in the past two decades. Thus, there is a reciprocal relationship between the political backlash against minority gains and the social indicators for black youth; that is, these youth respond in a *rational manner* to perceived prejudice and socioeconomic barriers to their mobility by dropping out of the labor market and choosing not to attend college. This reciprocal relationship suggests a self-fulfilling prophecy, which could be reversed if policies and programs were to change. . . .

REFERENCES

CDF. See Children's Defense Fund.

Census Bureau. See U.S. Bureau of the Census.

Centers for Disease Control (1986a). Acquired immunodeficiency syndrome (AIDS) among blacks and Hispanics—United States. *Morbidity and Mortality Weekly Report* 35: 656–58.

———. (1986b). Update—Acquired immunodeficiency syndrome—United States. *Morbidity and Mortality Weekly Report* 35: 757–65.

Children's Defense Fund. (1985a). *A children's defense budget.* Washington, D.C.: CDF.

———. (1985b). *Black and white children in America.* Washington, D.C.: CDF.

———. (1986a). *A children's defense budget.* Washington, D.C.: CDF.

———. (1986b). *Building health programs for teenagers.* Washington, D.C.: CDF.

———. (1986c). *Declining earnings of young men: Their relation to poverty, teen pregnancy and family formation.* Washington, D.C.: CDF.

———. (1986d). *Welfare and teen pregnancy: What do we know? What do we do?* Washington, D.C.: CDF.

Clark, K. B. (1965). *Dark ghetto: Dilemmas of social power.* New York: Harper & Row.

Gibbs, J. T. (1984). Black adolescents and youth: An endangered species. *American Journal of Orthopsychiatry* 54: 6–21.

———. (1985). Young black males: An endangered species. Invited lecture at Annual Civil Rights Institute, NAACP Legal Defense and Educational Fund, Inc., New York (May).

———. (1986). Psychosocial correlates of sexual attitudes and behaviors in urban early adolescent females: Implications for intervention. *Journal of Social Work and Human Sexuality* 5: 81–97.

Glasgow, D. (1981). *The black underclass.* New York: Vintage Books.

Kasarda, J. (1985). Urban change and minority opportunities. In *The new urban reality,* edited by P. E. Peterson. Washington, D.C.: The Brookings Institute.

Murray, C. (1984). *Losing ground: American social policy 1950–1980.* New York: Basic Books.

Omi, M., and Winant, H. (1986). *Racial formation in the United States: From the 1960s to the 1980s.* New York: Routledge & Kegan.

Sum, A., Harrington, P., and Goedicke, W. (1987). One-fifth of the nation's teenagers: Employment problems of poor youth in America, 1981–1985. *Youth and Society* 18: 195–237.

U.S. Bureau of the Census. (1981). School enrollment: Social and economic characteristics of students, 1980 (advance report). *Current population reports*, ser. P-20. Washington, D.C.

———. (1987). *Statistical abstract of the United States, 1987.* 107th ed. Washington, D.C.: U.S. Government Printing Office.

———. (1987). *Money income and poverty status of families and persons in the United States: 1986. Current population reports*, ser. P-60, 157. Washington, D.C.

RACE AND THE SEARCH FOR IDENTITY   **30**

Samuel Betances

Puerto Ricans are sometimes white, they are sometimes black, and they are sometimes Puerto Ricans—and so they are quite often confused. This holds particularly true for the second generation Puerto Ricans in the U.S. mainland. The single most crucial issue burning deep in the souls of many young, second generation Puerto Ricans in the United States is that of the wider identity—the search for ethnicity.

Puerto Rican youth in America in search of their ethnic identity have often faced the stark reality of having to relate to critical issues solely on the basis of black and white. In other words, it becomes impossible simply to be "Puerto

From: Maria Teresa Babin and Stan Steiner (eds.), *Borinquen: An Anthology of Puerto Rican Literature* (New York: Vintage, 1974), pp. 425–438. Reprinted by permission.

Rican" or "Latin" or a "Third World type" or "Spanish" in a society that demands categories based on black and white.

To a large degree, Puerto Rican youth who come from a racially mixed background believe that in America they can choose whether they want to be black or white. Some have decided not to suffer the plight of becoming black. It is hard for them to be Puerto Rican without becoming black as well, the assumption being that one can choose with which group to relate.

Erik Erikson suggests that Negro creative writers are in a battle to reconquer for their people a "surrendered identity." He states:

> I like this term because it does not assume total absence, as many contemporary writers do—something to be searched for and found, to be granted or given, to be created or fabricated—but something to be recovered. This must be emphasized because what is latent can become a living actuality, and thus a bridge from past to future.[1]

If what Erikson says is true, then the Puerto Rican adolescent's search for a wider identity becomes even more complicated in the light of some historical facts that are uniquely Puerto Rican.

Puerto Rico at present has no definite political status. The island is neither a state of the union, nor is it an independent nation. It is no more than a "perfume colony," as a critic of the present system has described it. Puerto Ricans are considered "Americans" by their Latin American cousins and "Latins" by the Americans. They have never been in control of their island and during a period of nineteen years, between 1898 and 1917, were citizens of no country.[2]

Dr. Román López Tames, a careful student of the Puerto Rican experience, has noted that there is insecurity in the island. Puerto Ricans are forever asking themselves, "What am I?" ("Que soy?"), and "What are we?" ("Que somos?"). He notes that "for the North Americans the island is hispanic, this is to say, strange sister to what they call Latin American." But on the other hand, "Latin American countries without having a very concrete notion about the island, quite frequently reject her considering her North Americanized, lost to the great family."[3] Puerto Rico has been likened by Dr. López Tames to the plight of the bat who is rejected by birds and by rodents, belonging to neither family in any concrete way, who is condemned to live a solitary life between the two worlds, misunderstood by both.

To some degree, the seeds of insecurity toward ethnicity are already planted in the minds of first generation Puerto Ricans. Thus, a youngster who has parents who have some doubt as to their own identity has to face new problems which indicate further that he is neither black nor white. He is neither American nor Latin American. He comes from an island which is neither a state nor a nation. Is it possible for Puerto Ricans to find their "surrendered identity"? Or is it not a fact that to some degree the historical experience indicates that there is nothing there which is latent, nothing that can come alive, nothing that can serve as a bridge from the past to the future, since Puerto Rico, as a geographical entity, has been molded in an experience of dependency, first to Spain and then to the United States?

Confusion, ambivalency, and contradictions are present in the lives of Puerto Rican adolescents as they relate to the issue of race and color. Some Puerto Ricans learn English very quickly and refuse to speak Spanish in hopes of finding acceptance in the larger society. Others who are dark-skinned deliberately keep their Spanish, lest they be mistaken for American Negroes. Still others will hide their dark-skinned grandmother in the kitchen while introducing their potential spouses to their lighter-skinned parents.[4] The more successful the Puerto Rican, the more "European-looking" his wife tends to be. It's an interesting commentary that the first book [5] out of East Harlem, *Down These Mean Streets*, based on the second generation experience, was written by Piri Thomas, a Puerto Rican who is very concerned with the crucial issue of identity. One chapter in his book is entitled, "How to be a Negro Without Really Trying." Others are, "Hung up Between Two Sticks" and "Brothers Under the Skin."

The migrant Puerto Rican, whose children are the focus of this paper, have brought with them certain experiences and outlooks on the issue of race and color that have influenced to some degree the lives of their children. The first generation grew up on an island which historically has experienced "whiteness" as a positive value and "blackness" as a negative one. "White is right," in Puerto Rico, too. While blackness may not be as negative as in America, it is still negative enough to be a source of embarrassment in many instances of Puerto Rican life.

Puerto Rico has a problem of color; America has a problem of race.[6] That is the critical difference between discrimination in Puerto Rico and in the U.S. mainland.

Discrimination in Puerto Rico is based on color. As such, color is a physical characteristic which can be altered and/or changed in several generations. Marrying someone lighter-skinned than oneself immediately alters the way in which the offspring of such a union would be described. A Negro–Puerto Rican who marries a non-Negro–Puerto Rican will have children which will be described as non-Negro.

If the pattern is continued through several generations, a Negro Puerto Rican can live to see his "white" great-grandchildren. The negative physical element, color, can be eliminated or be made to play a less embarrassing role in the lives of those who seek to make things "better for their children."[7]

Not so in America where discrimination is based on the concept of race. It has to do with a deep-seated conviction about one group being superior to another. In the United States, the element of racial inequality is prevalent. Racism has to do with the issue of the "purity of the blood," a kind of changeless, hereditary disease or blessing which is transmitted from parent to offspring. In America many gain their sense of being and power from their membership in the "superior" white race. The most deprived white man can think of himself as "better than any Nigger." It doesn't really matter what his position or educational background may be: "No matter how you dress him up, a Nigger is a Nigger," a racist will tell you.

To be black in America is such a serious handicap that a person with "one drop" of Negro blood is considered Negro. Negro blood is a kind of reverse and negative "black power," which haunts a person reminding him that he is inferior—at best, a mere shadow of a white figure. Such are the "deep-seated, anxiety-rooted, sado-masochistic drives"[8] which account for much of the racial problems in America. Is it any wonder that in the United States intermarriage is considered the unpardonable social sin?

Puerto Rican discrimination based on color as opposed to race can be labeled as a "milder" type of discrimination. It has, nevertheless, influenced the outlook of the people, including those who journeyed to the mainland with notions that blackness is a negative aspect in a person's life and whiteness is a positive value.

So that the non-Negroid Puerto Rican may look upon his darker skinned counterpart as a person with certain drawbacks, a descendant of slaves whose physical features, texture of hair and/or color of the skin may leave something to be desired. He is not necessarily someone to hate, to control, or to fear, but perhaps to avoid in certain social contexts.

And it is not always a matter of color that determines desirability in certain social contexts. Negroid features: full lips, kinky hair ("pelo malo") may play a much more crucial role in terms of desirability over light complexion in Puerto Rico. A man with "good" hair, but dark skin ("un trigueño de pelo bueno") may be more desirable than a light-skinned but kinky-haired individual. Color gives way to other physical characteristics at times. Distinction, however, may not be made verbally, so that when individuals refer to a person of "color," they may be really referring to "Negroid" features as opposed to complexion—although they may still relate to the question as one of "color."

Puerto Ricans believe that "trigueñas" or "morenas" (women of dark complexion) make better lovers than those who are non-dark. The belief that color plays a positive role in sex is somewhat different than the racist connotations found in such belief in America. One observer has noted, "this is not the expression of a neurotic fear of sexual insufficiency but an accepted and openly stated commonplace."[9]

Alex Rodríguez, a Puerto Rican spokesman in the city of Boston and past director of the Cooper Community Center in Lower Roxbury, was recently interviewed in the *Boston Globe* on the role of color and race in Puerto Rican life. Rodríguez noted that most Puerto Ricans, while identifying themselves as non-white, quickly learned the advantages of being "white" in a racist society. He suggests that in Puerto Rico, blackness is thought of as a beautiful trait. He used the following examples: "One of the most affectionate terms in Spanish is 'negra,' which means Dear or Darling, but literally translated means 'black one.'"

Rodríguez's example is used quite frequently by people of Latin America who would imply racial equality by citing it. The term "negrita" *does* imply intimacy and affection in the usage that Rodríguez gave it. But there is some difference between "intimacy" and "affection" with "equality" which should be considered. A Peruvian newspaper quoted Velarge who held to the same interpretation on this matter as Alex Rodríguez. Pitt-Rivers brings focus to that difference:

> The implication of racial equality that he drew from his examples invites precision. Such terms do not find way into such context because they are flattering in formal usage, but because they are not. Intimacy is opposed to respect; because these terms are disrespectful, they are used to establish or stress a relationship where no respect is due. The word "Nigger" is used in this way among Negroes in the United States, but only among Negroes. Color has, in fact, the same kind of class connotation in the Negro community as in Latin America: pale-skinned means upper class. Hence, Nigger, in this context dark-skinned or lower class, implies a relationship that is free of obligation of mutual respect.[10]

It is true that Puerto Rico has never had a race riot. But the assertion made by Puerto Rican spokesmen[11] that all is well in this matter of race and color in the island, or that Puerto Rico is one thousand years ahead of America on this issue is misleading. The fact that there is discrimination against those who would embrace the "Afro-Antillean cultured tradition" or those who are dark-skinned, certainly enough discrimination to make those who are black wish that they were not, indicates all is not well in Puerto Rico.

Those who damned the United States race riots and point to the superior culture which does not have race riots in Puerto Rico, have not been as zealous in explaining the problem of color that does exist in the island. As a result many citizens on the mainland, including such noted sociologists as Nathan Glazer,[12] believe the problem to be less serious than in reality.

The point being suggested here is that the problem of color is serious enough in Puerto Rican life to complicate further the second generation's search for ethnicity in the mainland. As the second generation looks toward the island and toward their homes, they don't find a people who have solved the problem of black and white. Instead they find further reasons for added anxiety, confusion, and feelings of uncertainty. Pointing out that Puerto Rico does not have race riots does not solve the problem of a youngster who must not only deal with a world outside of his home which is unsympathetic and at times cruel, but he also must confront his family and Puerto Rican neighbors who for reasons all their own seem to be making efforts toward concealment of color.

In the early part of 1970, sixty young second-generation Puerto Ricans were interviewed concerning this issue of race and color as it affected their search for ethnicity in the U.S. mainland. Thirty of the youth resided in the South Bronx in New York City; fifteen of them resided in the Division Street area of Chicago's Northwest Side; and fifteen lived in the South End of Boston. Their response to the questionnaire and their willingness to have their answers taped when requested, provided perspective in attempting to understand this very crucial issue. A close look at their responses indicates the problem to be much more complicated than previously imagined.

One young Puerto Rican in Boston, when asked how she was perceived by other people in a downtown store or in a crowded bus or walking through the busy streets of Boston, answered that most people would consider her "white." She quickly added, "an Eastern European type or Italian."

When asked how she described herself—"say that you were applying for a job and you had to fill out a blank which demanded some definition on your part"—she said, "Negro." Why? She explained that people on the streets tend to look at her very superficially. Since she has a light complexion and long, black hair, she could "pass" in that kind of situation. However, when applying for a job, she explained, employers tend to take a second look, even a third look, especially if the job requires one to be visible, like office work. By filling the blank "Negro," she felt the employer would probably say to himself that she was not really black. But he would probably be happy to hire such a nice, light-skinned, safe Negro.

On the other hand, if she filled in the blank "White," the employer would probably think her dishonest since she was not really white. He probably would not forgive her for trying to "pass." The chances of his objecting to one's describing oneself "Negro" are less than the other way around.

Here is the case of a nineteen-year-old Puerto Rican youth trying desperately to psyche out the society in which she lives, anticipating the moods of people she somehow must not offend if she is to make it in racially tense

America in the 1970s. It is difficult to ascertain just what psychological price she and many like her are paying in their attempt to survive without arousing people's prejudices.

Several youths, when asked whether they thought people in America were prejudiced towards them because they were Puerto Ricans, answered, "no." They explained that prejudice stemmed from the fact of their dark skin color. Somehow in their minds they had carefully separated their skin color from their Puerto Ricanness.

Answering another question, this time on the issue of intermarriage between American Negroes and Puerto Ricans, one of the interviewees from New York answered:

> Puerto Ricans are on the bottom of the social ladder in this country; blacks are even worse off. Blacks should not marry Puerto Ricans since two wrongs don't make a right!

While most of those interviewed said that when it comes to marriage it should really be up to the people involved, it would appear that the "two wrongs don't make a right" answer is closer to the feeling of those questioned. Deeper probing indicated that while most of them "prefer" not to marry American Negroes, they would not voice "opposition" to such marriages.

The question of intermarriage is a very difficult one for Puerto Rican youth to answer. Admitting that one has reservations, or voicing opposition to marriage with American Negroes, is in effect, admission of prejudice based on cultural and color differences. To agree even in principle with a stance against Negroes having a choice on who should be their potential spouses is to undermine the Puerto Rican position. If it is possible for a Puerto Rican to be prejudiced against Negroes in America, then it is possible for American-Anglos to be prejudiced towards Puerto Ricans, for similar reasons. This the second generation does not want.

What makes it difficult, then, is the fact that Puerto Ricans *do* express preference in regard to skin color. Deep inside they know that Americans have "legitimate" reasons for prejudice toward Puerto Ricans since they have, perhaps themselves, reasons why they discriminate against blacks. The feelings of insecurity are there.

Interestingly enough, second generation Puerto Ricans believe that even marrying a darker Puerto Rican than oneself is not desirable. Most of the youth simply stated that they expected to marry someone lighter-skinned, but not darker than themselves. Most of them know of Puerto Rican neighbors or had parents or relatives who would oppose their children marrying anyone, whether American Negro or Puerto Rican, who happened to be darker than they were, who could be described as "real black."

In the area of mutual cooperation with American Negroes in pursuit of better wages and against social discrimination most Puerto Rican youth answered affirmatively. One youth in the Bronx voiced the opinion by stating that while Negroes experienced 100% prejudice, Puerto Ricans experienced about 99% prejudice; so they should work together. Five young Puerto Ricans in Chicago who had actually worked together in an organization with blacks were a little more cautious on the matter. They wanted to know what "together" meant. One young man in Chicago simply said that as long as there is a "fifty-fifty" cooperation at the top of such an organization that is all right, but not otherwise.

One response was somewhat bitter; a young man who obviously had some experience in black endeavors snapped at the question by saying:

> When blacks need an extra pair of feet to march, they welcome the Puerto Rican cooperation. When they need an extra voice to shout against injustice, they welcome Puerto Rican cooperation. When they need another head to bleed in the struggle, cooperation is welcomed from their "Latin brothers." But when, as a result of the shouting, the marching, and the bloody head, there is an extra pocket to fill, the Puerto Ricans are suddenly not black enough.

When asked if Puerto Ricans should work with white Anglos in the same way that they would work with Negroes, most of them said, "yes." As one Puerto Rican put it, "Puerto Ricans should work with blacks and whites. The blacks have the power (aggressiveness) and the whites have the money; by working with both groups we can come out on top."

Another dimension in the trials of young Puerto Ricans' search for identity and ethnicity is the issue of just how black can a Puerto Rican become? Afro-American youth see their ultimate unity revolving around the issue of "blackness." The cry is "I am black and beautiful." Puerto Ricans who participate in all black meetings find themselves apprehensive when the anti-white rhetoric reminds them that the "white devil" is just as much a part of his experience as the heritage and concern which make it possible for him to be allowed into such organizations. As Piri Thomas puts it, "It wasn't right to be ashamed of what one was. It was like hating Momma for the color she was and Poppa for the color he wasn't."[13]

If one can be a "Negro" without really trying as Thomas would suggest,[14] then it is quite another matter to be "black." The politics of race in the black movement at times make a distinction between those who are described as "colored," those who are described as "Negroes," and those who are "black."

If the society at large determines that racially mixed Puerto Ricans are Negro (using the "one drop" formula), where will the black movement place them? Can Puerto Ricans ever be "black" enough for such groups and still be Puerto Rican?

Puerto Ricans in Chicago, those who had some experience in black organizations, complained that the "black power" movement is too obsessed with "blackness" and not enough with "power," thereby writing off some potential energy from Puerto Ricans who up to that time wanted to embrace their African heritage.

Most Puerto Rican youth interviewed expressed pessimism about their ability to resolve the issue of race and color and identity in their own lives. They have felt that for too long they have been in the middle of blacks and whites receiving the worst from both sides. They were relieved to learn that other Puerto Rican youth were having similar problems over the issue of identity. Some were also glad to hear that an adult, the interviewer, was having a difficult time as well; that while the problem has not been resolved one can still function and have self-respect. Perhaps that in itself is a very important beginning at resolving the destructive trauma which creates so much confusion in the lives of second generation Puerto Rican adolescents.

It's a good feeling to know that one is not alone when facing critical problems. If more Puerto Rican adults would but share some of their ambivalency and their confusion and end "the conspiracy of silence," it could lead more second generation Puerto Ricans to the conclusion that given the historical experience of Puerto Ricans in the island and in the "barrios" in the mainland, confusion and ambivalency may not be abnormal as all that.

At a time when the governor of Puerto Rico is desperately trying to coin the phrase, "Puerto Rico is our fatherland, but the United States is our nation," confusion and ambivalency may indeed not be as abnormal as all that!

NOTES

1. Erik H. Erikson, *Identity, Youth and Crisis* (New York, W. W. Norton and Company, Inc., 1968), p. 297. The phrase "surrendered identity" was borrowed by Erikson from Van Woodward.

2. The U. S. Government declared the residents of Puerto Rico citizens on the eve of the First World War, in 1917.

3. Román López Tames, *El Estado Libre Asociado de Puerto Rico* (Oviedo: Publicaciones del Instituo Jurídico, 1965), pp. 14, 15.

4. Fortunato Vizcarrondo popularized the problem in his famous poem, "Y tu agüela, donde ejta?" Literally translated, it means, "And your grandmother, where is she?"

5. While Jesús Colón's book, *A Puerto Rican in New York: And Other Sketches*, was published in 1961, several years before *Down These Mean Streets*, the treatment he gives his sketches suggests more of a first generation view of New York City rather than a second generation approach. Colón's formative years were spent in Puerto Rico; see pages 11 to 15 of his book.

6. Eric Williams, "Race Relations in Puerto Rico and the Virgin Islands," *Foreign Affairs* (1945, Vol. 23: 308). As quoted in Renzo Sereno's *Psychiatry*, "Cryptomelanism: A Study of Color Relations and Personal Insecurity in Puerto Rico," Vol. X, 1947, p. 264.

7. "Color is an ingredient, not a determinant of class. It can, therefore, be traded for other ingredients. It is something that can be altered in the individual life, but it is something that can be put right in the next generation." Julian Pitt-Rivers, "Race, Color and Class in Central America and the Andes," *Daedalus: Journal of the American Academy of Arts and Sciences* (Cambridge, Mass., Spring 1967), Vol. 96, p. 556.

8. Pitt-Rivers, *op. cit.*, p. 547.

9. *Ibid.*, p. 550.

10. Joseph Monserrat is guilty of this one-sided type of analysis. See his report, "School Integration: A Puerto Rican View" (New York, The Commonwealth of Puerto Rico, 1966), p. 5.

11. Gordon K. Lewis, *Puerto Rico: Freedom and Power in the Caribbean* (New York, Harper & Row, 1963), p. 286.

12. For example, Nathan Glazer writes in his book: "The Puerto Rican introduced into the city a group that is intermediate in color, neither all white nor all dark, but having some of each, and a large number that show the physical characteristics of both groups. (They) carry new attitudes toward color—and attitudes that may be corrupted by continental color prejudice but it is more likely, since this is in harmony with terms that are making all nations of a single world community, that the Puerto Rican attitude to color, or something like it, will become the New York attitude." *Beyond the Melting Pot* (Cambridge, Ma., M.I.T. Press, 1963), p. 132.

13. Piri Thomas, *Down These Mean Streets* (New York, Signet Books, The New American Library, Inc., 1967), p. 122.

14. *Ibid.*, pp. 124–126.

MIDDLE AGE AND THE LESBIAN EXPERIENCE

31

Martha Kirkpatrick

As a psychotherapist I have noticed an impressive increase in articles and presentations on middle age, adult development or life-span issues in recent years. As an aging woman, I too, have grown more aware of the problems of middle age, my own and those of my friends and patients. Inevitably many factors influence how one ages, physically and psychologically, and how one manages the benefits and losses of this period in life. This article attempts to consider the interaction of middle age and lesbianism from several perspectives, and to consider the problems and benefits of lesbian middle age as compared to those of the middle age of heterosexual women.

MOTHERHOOD AT MIDLIFE

Lesbians, like heterosexual women, are a diverse group. We might assume the effect of middle age on most lesbians to be different from that on most heterosexual women because reproduction and child rearing have not structured the phases of their adult lives. However, studies of the lesbian population reveal that twenty-five to thirty-five percent have been married and at least half of these have children (Saghir and Robins, 1973; Bell and Weinberg, 1978). For those women, as for most heterosexual women, the phases of adult life have been organized largely around their children's needs.

Middle-aged lesbian mothers with adolescent children suffer the burdens and fears common to all parents at that time. They are additionally burdened by the fear that their children will turn against them because of their sexual orientation. The adolescents' need to conform to peer attitudes, their fear of embarrassment or ridicule, as well as their concern over their own sexuality,

From: *Women's Studies Quarterly* 17 (Spring/Summer 1989): 87–96. Abridged from Martha Kirkpatrick, M.D., "Lesbians: A Different Middle Age?" in *The Middle Years: New Psychoanalytic Perspectives*, edited by John M. Oldham, M.D., and Robert S. Liebert, M.D. Copyright © by Yale University. Used by permission.

make lesbian mothers an easy target for hostility and devaluation, especially by sons. The need of adolescents to devalue parents in the struggle to consolidate a separate self is familiar to us all. Ethnic origin, foreign accent, age, physical disabilities, or of features aging, such as hair style or taste in music or clothes, all are evidence to our children of our defective natures. If society's ongoing devaluation and discrimination against lesbians have undermined the lesbian mother's self-esteem, this period may be especially frightening and painful for her.

DISCOVERING LESBIANISM IN MIDDLE AGE

A different group of lesbians who are mothers may be found in a seemingly new segment of the older lesbian population. These are women who, after twenty to thirty years of marriage and with child raising completed, leave their husbands and establish enduring lesbian partnerships. Philip Blumstein and Pepper Schwartz engagingly describe one such couple in their large study, *The American Couple* (1983). Two women in their mid-fifties, both grandmothers with long marriages, met through a personal ad one woman had placed in a women's magazine. Both described long years of loneliness and emptiness in their marriages. Both felt they had paid their dues to society and now longed for an intimacy they had not found in their marriages. For these women the new experience of being touched lovingly by another woman was deeply gratifying, but a new or better sexual experience was neither the motivating force nor the binding experience. To quote from the Blumstein and Schwartz interview: "The thing that is important is the to-getherness of our heads and the side-by-sideness of our bodies; the sex is just a side issue . . . an outgrowth of tenderness" (453). Christenson and Johnson (1973) surveyed seventy-one never-married women over fifty. Eleven percent were lesbians and most of these had had lesbian experiences in their youth, had adopted heterosexual behavior, and then returned to lesbian relationships. That women might lead long, apparently successful heterosexual lives and then turn to homosexuality in midlife seems hard to explain by current theories of adult development.

For the couple described above, it was the courageous fulfillment of a life-long dream, a different childhood dream than their lives had enacted. Barbara Ponce (1980) in her study of lesbian identity found married women without any homosexual experience identifying themselves as lesbians because of their fantasies and their recognized but inhibited longings. Some of these women may choose to act on their desires as part of the re-evaluation process of middle age; they establish lesbian relationships despite the loss of the heterosexual support system and the incredulity and/or disapproval of families and friends. The costs and benefits of such a decision cannot be known in advance. As with many behavioral changes, this one might represent a healthy effort to integrate a valuable but previously abandoned part of the self, or it could represent the loss of ego integration and a retreat to a limited and child-like relationship.

I was recently consulted by a dentist in her mid-fifties. She had always been shy, slow to make friends, and slow to complain or demand anything of those she made. She had married shortly after college with the hope of establishing a family. Three children were born during the first seven years of the marriage. She found herself inexplicably depressed when her youngest child was two, and entered a five-year analysis with an experienced female analyst. She reported being terrified throughout the analysis of revealing something which would be used to point out how bad she really was. The source of this expectation was never uncovered, though she found great comfort in what she perceived as the analyst's genuine interest in her and patience with her inhibitions. She felt deeply grateful and experienced a sense of great love for the analyst, which she carefully concealed. The analysis terminated and life went on in its shy and lonely way.

During the children's late adolescence, she underwent a mastectomy. Faced with morbidity and mortality and the realization that her husband's presence did not comfort her, she separated from him. She cared for her children until they left for college and discovered pride in her competence to manage her own life for the first time. Four years after the mastectomy and separation she began planning breast reconstruction, largely because she found herself in love with another woman, a colleague older than herself, a revival of her secret feelings for her analyst. She believed for a while that her sexual longing was reciprocated and this gave her a new sense of worthiness and lovability. She got contact lenses and a permanent and began dressing in a more stylish and attractive fashion. Her new image of herself as a lovable and feminine woman led to the breast reconstruction. She subsequently realized that her affection was not returned but despite the sadness this caused, she maintained her pride in her reconstructed self. She is much less shy and has enlarged her circle of friends with a new hope that she may yet experience an intimate loving relationship.

Thus, middle age for some heterosexual women opens the possibility of finding a new intimacy with a woman, an important option considering the diminished availability of male partners at later ages. For other lesbians it may be the time to find or return to heterosexual relationships. One such story is reported in Blumstein and Schwartz. In my clinical experience this wish to become comfortably heterosexual is experienced more regularly by young lesbian women, frightened about their future as lesbians, unsure of the cost of social stigma, and faced with the potential loss of motherhood. This provides a motivation not commonly found in middle-aged lesbians. In actuality, the midlife lesbian may have little reason to envy her heterosexual sister's life.

LESS DREAD OF AGING FOR LESBIANS

A number of features of life-long lesbian orientation may contribute to the more sanguine approach to aging of many lesbians. While women have lower incomes than men, and lesbians have not shared in a husband's income, surveys usually find lesbians better educated and in higher paid jobs than heterosexual women (Bell and Weinberg, 1979). If they have no children, their time and energy have been directed toward building careers, and the money they have made has been used to enhance their own lives. Furthermore, it is expected in lesbian relationships that each partner works. Supporting one's self and managing one's own affairs are not new nor to be feared if one is left alone in later middle age. The stigma of middle age also has less sting for those who have coped with stigma throughout life. They have learned that a satisfying life is possible without society's approval. Saghir and Robins's (1973) study found lesbians to be more involved in leisure time activities, artistic pursuits, and individual sports than heterosexual women, and thus connected to more sources of personal satisfaction. Lesbians tend to have close networks of friends that may substitute for estranged family members. These networks do not depend on couple status. Raphael and Robinson's (1984) survey of twenty lesbians over fifty found no evidence for the myth of lonely isolated lives of older lesbians. Strong friendship ties provided support and correlated positively with high self-esteem. Bell and Weinberg's (1978) survey of 385 lesbians, for example, showed that the stereotype of the lonely, isolated, bitter homosexual fits only a small group of homosexuals whose personality structure impairs their capacity for social and intimate connections. It was this personality problem and not homosexuality that led to isolation and suffering. In fact, coupled lesbians were very like coupled heterosexual women, except that the lesbians had fewer complaints of loneliness.

Like her heterosexual counterpart, most lesbians at middle age have a partner and expect to grow old together (Saghir and Robins, 1973: 311–12). Heterosexual women are often younger than their husbands. With a longer life expectancy than their mates, these women may be widows for a considerable period of their lives. Heterosexual remarriage or sexual partnership are often hard to find for older women. On the other hand, lesbian couples are on the same life-expectancy curve and if a partner is lost the pool of same-age mates remains. Since the greatest motivator for a man to begin a new relationship is the physical appearance of the woman, middle-aged women face the future with a fear of losing the ability to attract (or maintain) a heterosexual partnership. Lesbians, like other women, place less emphasis on youth and/or beauty in their partners, and thus they are generally less threatened by the changes age brings in their own appearance. A curious study of personal ads undertaken by Mary Riege Laner (1978) found that ninety-eight percent of lesbian advertisers stated their age compared to seventy-six of heterosexual women. Also, far fewer lesbians restricted the age for the respondent than did heterosexual women. Raphael and Robinson (1984) found that lesbians over fifty preferred partners of the same age.

Differences Between Older Lesbian and Heterosexual Couples Sexuality

Lillian Rubin's sensitive book, *Women of a Certain Age* (1979), tells us that the sexual lives of many married women become freer, more flexible, and more satisfying at middle age. With the children gone, mother is less tired, there may be no fear of unwanted pregnancy, and the capacity to respond increases. Midlife releases possibilities for new forms of creativity, as well as making old forms more pleasurable as fears and superego rigidities give way against increased desires for personal gratification. At the same time in life the male partner is likely to be less interested sexually, especially if he is worried about possible erectile failures. This imbalance in sexual response does not weigh on lesbian couples. Raphael and Robinson (1984) discovered that many of their sample of lesbians over fifty had a continuing interest in a sexual life and, unlike heterosexual older women, they looked forward to having sexual partners in their later years. While many lesbian couples remain sexually active into old age, Blumstein and Schwartz and others have found the frequency of sexual relations to be less in lesbian couples than in any other couples, even at young ages. However, physical affection and nongenital contact are highly prized and in later years physical intimacy continues to be sought and expressed independent of a need for genital experience. The qualities of mutual understanding, expression of feelings, sensitivity toward others, and mutual nurturing are rated by lesbians as more important to a relationship than sexual excitement. Furthermore, despite a lower frequency of sexual relations, lesbians report greater satisfaction with the sexual aspect of their relationship than other couples, according to Blumstein and Schwartz.

Termination of the Couple Relationship

Nevertheless, lesbian couples, like heterosexual couples, may break up in middle age with the approach of life's end, the fear of missing something more exciting, and the desire for a last chance for the fulfillment of great expectations. In my experience as a psychotherapist trying to help individual women, some heterosexual and some lesbians, going through separations in middle age, I have noticed both similarities of loss, pain, and anger, and differences in the problems faced by lesbians and heterosexual women. These differences lie in each group's relationship to the larger community, to their social network, and in the experience of being coupled.

The lesbian couple's relationship to both the lesbian group and the mainstream community is a complicated one. The relationship to the larger community provides none of the supportive rituals or rules that surround and sustain heterosexual marriages. The couple may keep their relationship a secret for fear of job loss or censure by coworkers. Colleagues may neither acknowledge the couple as a unit nor provide comfort if the relationship is severed. For some lesbians, retirement age may remove the strain of leading a double life; middle age may provide relief from the social pressure to date men, but the larger community still may oppose the couple's bond and applaud a breakup. The lesbian community on the other hand, while acknowledging the couple, poses a threat as well. Susan Krieger, in the excellent article "Lesbian Identity and Community" (1982), states: "The lesbian community, like many stigmatized minority groups, offers the individual lesbian a sense of self, especially in that it commands recognition of a distinctly lesbian sensibility, unusual in the value it places on intimacy between women, but it also conflicts with efforts to enhance individuality and to recognize and benefit from internal deviance." The lesbian community demands loyalty and conformity to group standards. For women who are enmeshed in this community there may be serious tension between the demands of the community and the demands of the couple relationship. Unlike heterosexual separations, lesbian ex-lovers tend to remain friends; thus the community stays intact. Blumstein and Schwartz report that lesbian couples who were actively engaged in the lesbian community were more likely to break up than those who were not. In the heterosexual woman's world the breakup of a marriage, especially in middle age, means not only a sixty-eight percent lowering of her standard of living, frequently the loss of the family home, loss of credit, loss of membership in social organizations, such as a country club or faculty club, and loss of a sexual partner, but also the loss of the supportive network of married women friends. This comes as a shock and deep disappointment to many women who find themselves isolated and ignored when they most need comfort and support. The world of married couples is elite, chauvinistic, and has no room for dropouts. The profound sense of betrayal by old and trusted friends is often the most painful loss for divorced women. The lesbian community responds very differently to the breakup of a couple. While some choosing of sides may result in lessening the closeness of some friendships, the community tends to rush to the aid of the separated members and provide comfort and participation in the search for new relationships.

SPECIAL PROBLEMS OF LESBIAN PARTNERSHIPS

The search for intimacy is a major theme in many, if not most, women's lives. In fact, I think of intimacy as the major organizer of women's identity. This search for intimacy seems to be an even greater imperative in the lives of lesbians. The importance of intimacy is shared by both partners in a lesbian relationship and by others in the lesbian community. This fuels and helps maintain the supportive network of friendships enjoyed by many older lesbians (Wolf, 1978).

Lesbian and heterosexual relationships present distinctly different short-comings. While complaints of loneliness, emotional distance, and lack of communication and understanding are frequent in heterosexual women's history, lesbian couples suffer from excessive intensity, lack of privacy, and a strong tendency for psychological fusion with concomitant loss of the sense of one's separate feelings and an inability to express or tolerate differences. The requirement of sensitive mutual understanding may inhibit healthy aggression and tend toward a suffocating exclusivity. It is clear that similar characteristics in heterosexual couples might be described in admiring rather than pejorative terms: "They are so close . . . they've never been apart in thirty years of marriage . . . the perfect helpmate, my better half." Consider, for example, the closing lines of a Victorian poem quoted by Ehrenreich and English in their book, *For Her Own Good: 150 Years of the Experts' Advice to Women*. Extolling the ideal woman's development the poem terminates with:

> *There's nothing left of what she was;*
> *Back to the babe the woman dies,*
> *And all the wisdom that she has*
> *Is to love him for being wise.*

This idealization of merger, with its loss of boundaries between self and partner (not less of ego boundaries between ego, id, and super ego), continues to be a millstone around women's necks, lesbian or heterosexual, interfering with individualization. Despite the fact that they have survived without men and that they value women, lesbians are not protected from merger in their relationships. For some women an intense indentification with their fathers, or with male values of independence, competence, and courage, may have arisen partly to protect them against a pull toward merger with their mothers. In many lesbian relationships similarities are over-valued and differences diminished and often feared as divisive. The lack of differentiation in sociali-zation for sex roles as well as the actual role expectations of compliance and nurturance make the struggle toward individuation conflicted and guilt rid-den. Two women moving urgently toward each other for intimacy, with their nesting "instincts" outstretched, can create a mutual prison. Occasionally such a merger is patently obvious, as when the women dress alike, have the same hair style, finish each other's sentences, and share experience. Personal space or differences are feared and experienced as abandonment or hostility. To want privacy suggests to such women a lack of love and is a source of guilt.

THE IMPACT OF CHILDLESSNESS

Homosexual women were once thought to be uninterested in motherhood. We know now that the desire for children has many roots and does not originate in the resolution of the oedipal configuration. It is not the desire for a baby, but the discovery and wish for the father's participation that originates during that process. The longing of lesbians for children has been made manifest in recent years now that "single" motherhood is more acceptable and available through artificial insemination. Older lesbians for whom mother-hood was not a possibility, like other women who elected to be childless or were infertile, usually come to terms with this issue before middle age. Curiously enough, depression following hysterectomy or the onset of meno-pause is less likely to occur in childless women than in mothers. Having invested much of her energy in motherhood seems to make a woman more vulnerable to a pathological experience of loss at this time.

ILLNESS AND LIFE EXPECTANCY

Medical problems, particularly gynecological problems, however, may be ignored by middle-aged lesbians due to apprehension about revealing their sexual preference or being embarrassed by questions about birth control or intercourse. Lesbians in this age group are also at a disadvantage in tending to the health needs of their partners. "Family only" visiting rules prevent them and their partners from caring for each other and taking responsibility for necessary decisions. Estate planning is fraught with uncertainties that a lover can receive what her partner wishes to give without legal barriers (Adelman, 1986: 219–56). The support of a nonjudgmental therapist may assist in reaching creative solutions to these middle age problems.

As women's life expectancy increases, middle age occupies a greater percentage of our lives and more of our investigative energy. Being there, I'm glad it does. For lesbian women as for others, it can be a time of discovery of new creative potential, especially if the sense of having weathered life's slings and arrows supports one's adult confidence and the integration of adult understanding and promises to enrich the future. Neither homosexuality nor heterosexuality can guarantee a positive middle age experience, but it seems clear that lesbians have some advantages in dealing with the problems of middle age.

REFERENCES

Adelman, M. 1986. *Long Time Passing: Lives of Older Lesbians*. Boston: Alyson Publications.

Bell, A. and Weinberg, M. 1978. *Homosexualities: A Study of Diversity among Men and Women*. New York: Simon & Schuster.

Blumstein, P. and Schwartz, P. 1983. *American Couples*. New York: William Morrow.

Christenson, B. and Johnson, A. 1973. Sexual patterns in a group of older never married women. *Journal of Geriatric Psychiatry* 6: 680–89.

Ehrenreich, B. and English, D. 1978. *For Her Own Good: 150 Years of the Experts' Advice to Women*. Garden City, N.Y.: Anchor Press.

Kinsey, A., Pomeroy, W., Martin, C. and Gebhard, P. 1953. *Sexual Behavior in the Human Female*. Philadelphia: W. B. Saunders.

Kirkpatrick, M., Smith, C. and Roy, R. 1981. Lesbian mothers and their children. *American Journal of Orthopsychiatry* 51: 545–51.

Krieger, S. 1982. Lesbian identity and community. *Signs* 8: 91–108.

Laner, M. 1978. Media mating II: "Personals" advertisements of lesbian women. *Journal of Homosexuality* 4: 41–61.

Ponce, B. 1980. Lesbians and their worlds. In *Homosexual Behavior: A Modern Reappraisal*, ed. Judd Marmor. New York: Basic Books, 157–75.

Raphael, S. and Robinson, M. 1984. The older lesbian: love relationships and friendship patterns. In *Women Identified Women*, eds. Trudy Darty and Sandee Potter. Palo Alto: Mayfield Publishing, 67–82.

Rubin, L. 1981. *Women of a Certain Age: The Midlife Search for Self.* New York: Harper & Row.

Saghir, M. and Robins, E. 1973. *Male and Female Homosexuality: A Comprehensive Investigation.* Baltimore: Wilkins & Wilkins.

Wolf, D. 1978. Close friendship patterns of older lesbians. Presented at Gerontological Society Meeting, Dallas: November, 1978. Reported in Raphael and Robinson.

YOU'RE SHORT, BESIDES!   32

Sucheng Chan

When asked to write about being a physically handicapped Asian American woman, I considered it an insult. After all, my accomplishments are many, yet I was not asked to write about any of them. Is being handicapped the most salient feature about me? The fact that it might be in the eyes of others made me decide to write the essay as requested. I realized that the way I think about myself may differ considerably from the way others perceive me. And maybe that's what being physically handicapped is all about.

I was stricken simultaneously with pneumonia and polio at the age of four. Uncertain whether I had polio of the lungs, seven of the eight doctors who attended me—all practitioners of Western medicine—told my parents they should not feel optimistic about my survival. A Chinese fortune teller my mother consulted also gave a grim prognosis, but for an entirely different reason: I had been stricken because my name was offensive to the gods. My grandmother had named me "grandchild of wisdom," a name that the fortune teller said was too presumptuous for a girl. So he advised my parents to change

From: Asian Women United of California (eds.), *Making Waves: An Anthology of Writings By and About Asian American Women* (Boston: Beacon Press, 1989), pp. 265–272. Copyright © 1989 by Asian Women United. Reprinted by permission.

my name to "chaste virgin." All these pessimistic predictions notwithstanding, I hung onto life, if only by a thread. For three years, my body was periodically pierced with electric shocks as the muscles of my legs atrophied. Before my illness, I had been an active, rambunctious, precocious, and very curious child. Being confined to bed was thus a mental agony as great as my physical pain. Living in war-torn China, I received little medical attention; physical therapy was unheard of. But I was determined to walk. So one day, when I was six or seven, I instructed my mother to set up two rows of chairs to face each other so that I could use them as I would parallel bars. I attempted to walk by holding my body up and moving it forward with my arms while dragging my legs along behind. Each time I fell, my mother gasped, but I badgered her until she let me try again. After four nonambulatory years, I finally walked once more by pressing my hands against my thighs so my knees wouldn't buckle.

My father had been away from home during most of those years because of the war. When he returned, I had to confront the guilt he felt about my condition. In many East Asian cultures, there is a strong folk belief that a person's physical state in this life is a reflection of how morally or sinfully he or she lived in previous lives. Furthermore, because of the tendency to view the family as a single unit, it is believed that the fate of one member can be caused by the behavior of another. Some of my father's relatives told him that my illness had doubtless been caused by the wild carousing he did in his youth. A well-meaning but somewhat simple man, my father believed them.

Throughout my childhood, he sometimes apologized to me for having to suffer retribution for his former bad behavior. This upset me; it was bad enough that I had to deal with the anguish of not being able to walk, but to have to assuage his guilt as well was a real burden! In other ways, my father was very good to me. He took me out often, carrying me on his shoulders or back, to give me fresh air and sunshine. He did this until I was too large and heavy for him to carry. And ever since I can remember, he has told me that I am pretty.

After getting over her anxieties about my constant falls, my mother decided to send me to school. I had already learned to read some words of Chinese at the age of three by asking my parents to teach me the sounds and meaning of various characters in the daily newspaper. But between the ages of four and eight, I received no education since just staying alive was a full-time job. Much to her chagrin, my mother found no school in Shanghai, where we lived at the time, which would accept me as a student. Finally, as a last resort, she approached the American School which agreed to enroll me only if my family kept an *amah* (a servant who takes care of children) by my side at all times. The tuition at the school was twenty U.S. dollars per month—a huge sum of money during those years of runaway inflation in China—and payable only in U.S. dollars. My family afforded the high cost of tuition and the expense of employing a full-time *amah* for less than a year.

We left China as the Communist forces swept across the country in victory. We found an apartment in Hong Kong across the street from a school run by Seventh-Day Adventists. By that time I could walk a little, so the principal was persuaded to accept me. An *amah* now had to take care of me only during recess when my classmates might easily knock me over as they ran about the playground.

After a year and a half in Hong Kong, we moved to Malaysia, where my father's family had lived for four generations. There I learned to swim in the lovely warm waters of the tropics and fell in love with the sea. On land I was a cripple; in the ocean I could move with the grace of a fish. I liked the freedom of being in the water so much that many years later, when I was a graduate student in Hawaii, I became greatly enamored with a man just because he called me a "Polynesian water nymph."

As my overall health improved, my mother became less anxious about all aspects of my life. She did everything possible to enable me to lead as normal a life as possible. I remember how once some of her colleagues in the high school where she taught criticized her for letting me wear short skirts. They felt my legs should not be exposed to public view. My mother's response was, "All girls her age wear short skirts, so why shouldn't she?"

The years in Malaysia were the happiest of my childhood, even though I was constantly fending off children who ran after me calling, "*Baikah! Baikah!*" ("Cripple! Cripple!" in the Hokkien dialect commonly spoken in Malaysia). The taunts of children mattered little because I was a star pupil. I won one award after another for general scholarship as well as for art and public speaking. Whenever the school had important visitors my teacher always called on me to recite in front of the class.

A significant event that marked me indelibly occurred when I was twelve. That year my school held a music recital and I was one of the students chosen to play the piano. I managed to get up the steps to the stage without any problem, but as I walked across the stage, I fell. Out of the audience, a voice said loudly and clearly, "Ayah! A *baikah* shouldn't be allowed to perform in public." I got up before anyone could get on stage to help me and, with tears streaming uncontrollably down my face, I rushed to the piano and began to play. Beethoven's "Für Elise" had never been played so fiendishly fast before or since, but I managed to finish the whole piece. That I managed to do so made me feel really strong. I never again feared ridicule.

In later years I was reminded of this experience from time to time. During my fourth year as an assistant professor at the University of California at Berkeley, I won a distinguished teaching award. Some weeks later I ran into a former professor who congratulated me enthusiastically. But I said to him, "You know what? I became a distinguished teacher by *limping* across the stage of Dwinelle 155!" (Dwinelle 155 is a large, cold classroom that most colleagues of mine hate to teach in.) I was rude not because I lacked graciousness but because this man, who had told me that my dissertation was the finest piece of work he had read in fifteen years, had nevertheless advised me to eschew a teaching career.

"Why?" I asked.

"Your leg . . ." he responded.

"What about my leg?" I said, puzzled.

"Well, how would you feel standing in front of a large lecture class?"

"If it makes any difference, I want you to know I've won a number of speech contests in my life, and I am not the least bit self-conscious about speaking in front of large audiences. . . . Look, why don't you write me a letter of recommendation to tell people how brilliant I am, and let *me* worry about my leg!"

This incident is worth recounting only because it illustrates a dilemma that handicapped persons face frequently: those who care about us sometimes get so protective that they unwittingly limit our growth. This former professor of mine had been one of my greatest supporters for two decades. Time after time, he had written glowing letters of recommendation on my behalf. He had spoken as he did because he thought he had my best interests at heart; he thought that if I got a desk job rather than one that required me to be a visible, public person, I would be spared the misery of being stared at.

Americans, for the most part, do not believe as Asians do that physically handicapped persons are morally flawed. But they are equally inept at interacting with those of us who are not able-bodied. Cultural differences in the perception and treatment of handicapped people are most clearly expressed by adults. Children, regardless of where they are, tend to be openly curious about people who do not look "normal." Adults in Asia have no hesitation in asking visibly handicapped people what is wrong with them, often expressing their sympathy with looks of pity, whereas adults in the United States try desperately to be polite by pretending not to notice.

One interesting response I often elicited from people in Asia but have never encountered in America is the attempt to link my physical condition to the state of my soul. Many a time while living and traveling in Asia people would ask me what religion I belonged to. I would tell them that my mother is a devout Buddhist, that my father was baptized a Catholic but has never practiced Catholicism, and that I am an agnostic. Upon hearing this, people would try strenuously to convert me to their religion so that whichever God they believed in could bless me. If I would only attend this church or that

temple regularly, they urged, I would surely get cured. Catholics and Bud-
dhists alike have pressed religious medallions into my palm, telling me if I
would wear these, the relevant deity or saint would make me well. Once while
visiting the tomb of Muhammad Ali Jinnah in Karachi, Pakistan, an old
Muslim, after finishing his evening prayers, spotted me, gestured toward my
legs, raised his arms heavenward, and began a new round of prayers, apparently
on my behalf.

In the United States adults who try to act "civilized" towards handicapped
people by pretending they don't notice anything unusual sometimes end up
ignoring handicapped people completely. In the first few months I lived in this
country, I was struck by the fact that whenever children asked me what was
the matter with my leg, their adult companions would hurriedly shush them
up, furtively look at me, mumble apologies, and rush their children away. After
a few months of such encounters, I decided it was my responsibility to educate
these people. So I would say to the flustered adults, "It's okay, let the kid ask."
Turning to the child, I would say, "When I was a little girl, no bigger than
you are, I became sick with something called polio. The muscles in my leg
shrank up and I couldn't walk very well. You're much luckier than I am because
now you can get a vaccine to make sure you never get my disease. So don't cry
when your mommy takes you to get a polio vaccine, okay?" Some adults and
their little companions I talked to this way were glad to be rescued from
embarrassment; others thought I was strange.

Americans have another way of covering up their uneasiness: they become
jovially patronizing. Sometimes when people spot my crutch, they ask if I've
had a skiing accident. When I answer that unfortunately it is something less
glamorous than that, they say, "I bet you *could* ski if you put your mind to it!"
Alternately, at parties where people dance, men who ask me to dance with
them get almost belligerent when I decline their invitation. They say, "Of
course you can dance if you *want* to!" Some have given me pep talks about
how if I would only develop the right mental attitude, I would have more fun
in life.

Different cultural attitudes toward handicapped persons came out clearly
during my wedding. My father-in-law, as solid a representative of middle
America as could be found, had no qualms about objecting to the marriage on
racial grounds, but he could bring himself to comment on my handicap only
indirectly. He wondered why his son, who had dated numerous high school
and college beauty queens, couldn't marry one of them instead of me. My
mother-in-law, a devout Christian, did not share her husband's prejudices, but
she worried aloud about whether I could have children. Some Chinese friends
of my parents, on the other hand, said that I was lucky to have found such a
noble man, one who would marry me despite my handicap. I, for my part,

appeared in church in a white lace wedding dress I had designed and made myself—a miniskirt!

How Asian Americans treat me with respect to my handicap tells me a great deal about their degree of acculturation. Recent immigrants behave just like Asians in Asia; those who have been here longer or who grew up in the United States behave more like their white counterparts. I have not encountered any distinctly Asian American pattern of response. What makes the experience of Asian American handicapped people unique is the duality of responses we elicit.

Regardless of racial or cultural background, most handicapped people have to learn to find a balance between the desire to attain physical independence and the need to take care of ourselves by not overtaxing our bodies. In my case, I've had to learn to accept the fact that leading an active life has its price. Between the ages of eight and eighteen, I walked without using crutches or braces but the effort caused my right leg to become badly misaligned. Soon after I came to the United States, I had a series of operations to straighten out the bones of my right leg; afterwards though my leg looked straighter and presumably better, I could no longer walk on my own. Initially my doctors fitted me with a brace, but I found wearing one cumbersome and soon gave it up. I could move around much more easily—and more important, faster—by using one crutch. One orthopedist after another warned me that using a single crutch was a bad practice. They were right. Over the years my spine developed a double-S curve and for the last twenty years I have suffered from severe, chronic back pains, which neither conventional physical therapy nor a lighter work load can eliminate.

The only thing that helps my backaches is a good massage, but the soothing effect lasts no more than a day or two. Massages are expensive, especially when one needs them three times a week. So I found a job that pays better, but at which I have to work longer hours, consequently increasing the physical strain on my body—a sort of vicious circle. When I was in my thirties, my doctors told me that if I kept leading the strenuous life I did, I would be in a wheelchair by the time I was forty. They were right on target: I bought myself a wheelchair when I was forty-one. But being the incorrigible character that I am, I use it only when I am *not* in a hurry!

It is a good thing, however, that I am too busy to think much about my handicap or my backaches because pain can physically debilitate as well as cause depression. And there are days when my spirits get rather low. What has helped me is realizing that being handicapped is akin to growing old at an accelerated rate. The contradiction I experience is that often my mind races along as though I'm only twenty while my body feels about sixty. But fifteen or twenty years hence, unlike my peers who will have to cope with aging for the first time, I shall be full of cheer because I will have already fought, and I hope won, that battle long ago.

Beyond learning how to be physically independent and, for some of us, living with chronic pain or other kinds of discomfort, the most difficult thing a handicapped person has to deal with, especially during puberty and early adulthood, is relating to potential sexual partners. Because American culture places so much emphasis on physical attractiveness, a person with a shriveled limb, or a tilt to the head, or the inability to speak clearly, experiences great uncertainty—indeed trauma—when interacting with someone to whom he or she is attracted. My problem was that I was not only physically handicapped, small, and short, but worse, I also wore glasses and was smarter than all the boys I knew! Alas, an insurmountable combination. Yet somehow I have managed to have intimate relationships, all of them with extraordinary men. Not surprisingly, there have also been countless men who broke my heart—men who enjoyed my company "as a friend," but who never found the courage to date or make love with me, although I am sure my experience in this regard is no different from that of many able-bodied persons.

The day came when my backaches got in the way of having an active sex life. Surprisingly that development was liberating because I stopped worrying about being attractive to men. No matter how headstrong I had been, I, like most women of my generation, had had the desire to be alluring to men ingrained into me. And that longing had always worked like a brake on my behavior. When what men think of me ceased to be compelling, I gained greater freedom to be myself.

I've often wondered if I would have been a different person had I not been physically handicapped. I really don't know, though there is no question that being handicapped has marked me. But at the same time I usually do not *feel* handicapped—and consequently, I do not *act* handicapped. People are therefore less likely to treat me as a handicapped person. There is no doubt, however, that the lives of my parents, sister, husband, other family members, and some close friends have been affected by my physical condition. They have had to learn not to hide me away at home, not to feel embarrassed by how I look or react to people who say silly things to me, and not to resent me for the extra demands my condition makes on them. Perhaps the hardest thing for those who live with handicapped people is to know when and how to offer help. There are no guidelines applicable to all situations. My advice is, when in doubt, ask, but ask, in a way that does not smack of pity or embarrassment. Most important, please don't talk to us as though we are children.

So, has being physically handicapped been a handicap? It all depends on one's attitude. Some years ago, I told a friend that I had once said to an affirmative action compliance officer (somewhat sardonically since I do not

believe in the head count approach to affirmative action) that the institution which employs me is triply lucky because it can count me as nonwhite, female and handicapped. He responded, "Why don't you tell them to count you four times? . . . Remember, you're short, besides!"

ESTHER'S STORY   33

Emily Warn

I grew up in a Jewish community in Detroit. On Succoth—the Jewish holiday commemorating the forty years the Jews spent in the desert—I used to look up at the stars through the cedar boughs of the succoh, a three-sided temporary wood hut, built outside on the driveway and connected to the kitchen through a side door. I liked to think about how those stars were the same stars that shone in a wide arc over the desert 5,000 years ago. As a young girl, each holiday and every shabbas (Sabbath) when we said the blessings first over the wine and then the challa (egg bread), I believed I held my part of the long note that stretched from the past to the future, as if we Jews had inhaled one infinite breath of God's and were singing back to him a limitless song, or shofar cry.

At thirteen I was banished because I was a young girl becoming a woman. No longer could I sit by my grandfather in Shul (synagogue), or wrap myself in his shawl. No longer could I ask one of the four questions at Pesach (Passover). Although the change was dramatic and abrupt, the rabbis had long prepared me for it. My role was to bear the pain of labor, to serve my grandfather, husband, brother or son. I accepted without question because I was a child, and more importantly, because I *believed* with all my heart and intellect in the strength and mystery of a God whose tribe of people had survived over five thousand years because they studied and interpreted the laws and stories of the Torah.

From: Jo Whitehorse Cochran, Donna Langston, and Carolyn Woodward (eds.), *Changing Our Power: An Introduction to Women's Studies* (Dubuque, Iowa: Kendall-Hunt, 1988). Reprinted by permission.

The rabbis showed me how to take my place in that continuous line when they taught me how to read the Hebrew of the Torah, how to pray, and how the Jews had managed to survive through the countless pogroms aimed at ending the Jewish people. Three days a week, from the age of seven on, I would trudge from the public school to our synagogue. The rabbis extracted one lesson from every Torah story and holiday: our survival depended on our identifying ourselves as Jews. In a way, to be a practicing Jew is the very definition of identity: the fact of remaining the same even under varying conditions. Or as Elie Wiesel writes: "To be a Jew meant to live with memory. To be a Jew meant creating links, a network of continuity."[1] For me to be a Jew meant to hunger for more knowledge about my history and identity.

How much I wanted to follow in the footsteps of the scholars and rabbis before me. How I watched with envy as my male cousins and my brother were Bar Mitzvahed. How I wished I could walk up to the podium, on my head a yalmulka (skull cap), a reminder of the God above, and on my shoulders a prayer shawl like those of my grandfather, uncles, rabbi and cantor, who would surround me as I sang the story from the Torah designated to be read that Shabbas in shul. How proud I would feel as I participated in a custom commonly shared by every male Jew in every part of the world at every time in history. I would become part of the larger community of Jews, which was the other lesson that the rabbis hammered home: there is no such thing as a Jew alone. To identify oneself as a Jew is to know that one's individual consciousness is transcended by a historical and communal consciousness. In fact, the very concept of Jewish enlightenment—the moment when the Messiah will come—was linked to community. If every Jew, in every part of the world, observed the Sabbath, the Messiah would come. If all Jews proclaimed our Jewish identity, we would be refusing to resemble the cultures of which we were a part. Diaspora, the condition of Jewish exile that began when the Jews were expelled from Babylon, would cease to exist; the Messiah would come.

Instead, when I turned thirteen, I could only watch and listen to my cousins' or brother's trembling voices from the women's side of the synagogue, a separate section where we were shielded by a screen from the eyes of the men. A boy's passage to adulthood was marked by ceremony and celebration; a girl's passage into the invisibility of womanhood was marked by silence. The woman's role, including the role of motherhood, was defined by men. Very orthodox Jewish men held women almost in contempt. When they walked into rooms, they crossed their arms because

---

1. Elie Wiesel, *A Jew Today* (New York: Random House, 1978), p. 6.

they considered it sinful to shake the hand of a woman. According to these ultra-orthodox men, a married woman must shave off her hair and replace it with a wig, and wear long-sleeved dresses that rise no higher than six inches above the shoe tops so that she will attract no men except her husband. Each morning, orthodox men include in their prayers a blessing that thanks the Lord for letting them be men and not women. The women thank the Lord for letting them bear the pain of labor.

My early schooling by the rabbis left me confused and sad. They had instilled in me a love of learning, especially of reading the Torah and deciphering its meaning; yet at the same time they had asked me to accept the Torah's commandment that when I became a woman, I would be expelled from the joyous circle of scholars. In retrospect, I can see that my sense of identity as a Jew was enriched by the rabbis' teachings, and yet I also felt a great disappointment at not being able to follow the holiest path in Judaism, to be a Torah scholar. The following story illustrates the rabbis' mixed messages. As a girl I longed to lead the prayers in Hebrew School, a function normally reserved for boys. One day, when I was still a young girl, the rabbi gave me the opportunity. Every day the rabbis checked to make sure each boy wore a yalmulka, or skull cap, and a pair of tzitzis, a white, cotton undershirt which had a tassle at each corner to symbolize the four corners of the world where the Jews of Diaspora had been scattered. One day, not one boy had remembered to wear them. The rabbi chose me, the girl who read Hebrew the best, to be the cantor. I felt proud that the rabbi had acknowledged my talent, but ashamed that he had used it to humiliate the boys.

When I reached womanhood, I was given a painful choice: to assume an assigned role that was demeaning, or reject Judaism. Ultimately, I decided that the pain of exclusion from dwelling in the mystery felt greater than the loss I would feel upon leaving. I turned my back on Judaism and joined the secular world.

For fifteen years, I cut myself off from the Judaism of my past. When I met another Jewish person we would often compare backgrounds: Were you raised Orthodox, Conservative or Reform? Were you raised in a Jewish community like me, or in a town that only had a few Jewish families? Most of the Jews I met had not been raised in an orthodox family. As a consequence, they did not feel compelled to reject Judaism; in fact many of them were busy embracing their new "Jewishness." Friends I knew joined Jewish Progressive organizations, or held holiday Seders, or celebrated Hanuka. I could not participate, because I knew if my friends examined the original meaning of these holidays and ceremonies, they would find that they excluded women. I watched with anger and envy at the ease with which they proclaimed the importance of identifying oneself as a Jew.

A single event two years ago led me back to the fold. On Christmas Eve in Seattle in 1986, a man, influenced by right-wing ideology, murdered a family whom I knew because he mistakenly thought they were Jewish and communist. The unimaginable brutality of the crime triggered a flood of Holocaust stories that rabbis had told me as a child. As a child I had simply absorbed all the gruesome details without feeling morally outraged, because, as a child, I had not yet developed that sensibility. I learned that during World War II in Europe the Nazis murdered six million Jews, that entire Jewish communities, the stepping stones of the larger Eastern European Jewry, were annihilated. I was born eight years after the American GIs liberated the concentration camps. The tattooed blue numbers on the forearms of several of my friends' grandparents were proof that the grotesque stories of the rabbis were true: lampshades were made from Jewish skin, scientific tests were conducted on Jews as if they were laboratory rats, a constant stream of smoke had risen from the human gas chambers at Auschwitz and Burkenvald. And now, forty years later, close friends of mine were brutally murdered by a man who thought they deserved to die because they were Jews. Now that I was an adult and knew what it meant to be morally outraged, I could not and did not know how to incorporate the horrible fact of their deaths into my life. What I did know was that in the eyes of the world I was a Jew whether I called myself one or not.

I faced, although on an infinitesimally smaller scale, the same questions that the victims and survivors of the Holocaust faced: If a human being had perpetrated such an inconceivably evil crime, how was it possible to believe in a just God, or in the sanctity of the human heart? What reason could there be to struggle to live a meaningful life if it could be taken from me at any minute because I was a Jew? If identifying oneself as a Jew was so dangerous, wouldn't it, as many Holocaust survivors decided, be better to refuse to acknowledge their Judaism, to become invisible?

I turned to Holocaust literature for guidance, and in the diary of Esther Hillesum, I found an answer.[2] Like Anne Frank, Hillesum lived in Amsterdam during the time of its Nazi occupation. Her diary records her struggle to define herself as a woman, and also records the increasingly harsh conditions imposed on Amsterdam's Jewish population. Her search to find herself and her refusal to be conquered by the enemy became the same struggle. She realized that if one believes in the sanctity and joy of human life, then one refuses to believe the enemy's versions of oneself. Even if one has to die, one can die praising life and thus resist being brought down to the enemy's level. I further

---

2. Esther Hillesum, *An Interrupted Life* (New York: Simon and Schuster, 1985).

understood that if one proclaims one's Jewish identity, then one is linking oneself to all Jews, past, present, and future. This identification strengthens the chain and nullifies the belief that death is final. If I make that same choice, if I identify part of my essential, inviolable self as Jewish, then I am refusing to believe in death because I am continuing the long line of people who have named themselves Jews.

Several years before my friends' murders, I had begun to write about a fictional character named Esther. As I began reading about Judaism, I realized that Esther was *the* Esther of the Torah, a woman who saved her people by selecting the critical time to reveal her Jewish identity. By making her live again in my poems, I was continuing one of the stories of Jewish history. Therefore, my book *The Book of Esther* tells the story of my return to Judaism, because in it I reclaim my right to interpret a sacred book of the Torah.

When I started writing about Esther, all I knew about her was her name and that she was an outsider, someone who lives and survives on the fringes of a society that excludes her, and in some cases, tries to silence her. Slowly, I began gathering evidence that there were many Esthers, and that perhaps the Esther in the Torah was the mother goddess Ishtar who was worshipped in the same region of the world and during the same time that the Torah story takes place. Esther sounds phonetically very similar to Ishtar. In addition, the Hebrew God's name is never mentioned in the Torah's story. The traditional interpretation of this absence is that Jews were meant to celebrate Purim, the spring holiday when Esther's story is re-told, in a joyous and often comic manner. Yet perhaps the Jews have usurped the story. After all, the Torah story opens with a description of Queen Vashti's humiliation, arousing an urge to avenge her that the story never satisfies. My poems are attempts to re-define Esther and myself as a woman who discovers her true and essential self by listening to her own interpretations of the old stories rather than to the traditional, often mistaken interpretations of men.

Before I could begin defining myself, I had to separate myself painfully from the patriarchal religion of my childhood. To do that I had to examine the assumptions about women which had molded me, so that I could identify those parts of my Jewish identity I wanted to embrace, those parts that I believed stretched far into the past and future. With *The Book of Esther* I take my place beside my grandfather in front of the congregation; only now the congregation includes women singing praises of the difficult, but often sweet struggle for a Jewish self.

Ideology and Belief Systems

IF MEN COULD MENSTRUATE—

34

Gloria Steinem

A white minority of the world has spent centuries conning us into thinking that a white skin makes people superior—even though the only thing it really does is make them more subject to ultraviolet rays and to wrinkles. Male human beings have built whole cultures around the idea that penis-envy is "natural" to women—though having such an unprotected organ might be said to make men vulnerable, and the power to give birth makes womb-envy at least as logical.

In short, the characteristics of the powerful, whatever they may be, are thought to be better than the characteristics of the powerless—and logic has nothing to do with it.

What would happen, for instance, if suddenly, magically, men could menstruate and women could not?

The answer is clear—menstruation would become an enviable, boast-worthy, masculine event:

Men would brag about how long and how much.

Boys would mark the onset of menses, that longed-for proof of manhood, with religious ritual and stag parties.

Congress would fund a National Institute of Dysmenorrhea to help stamp out monthly discomforts.

From: *Ms.* VII (October 1978): 110. © Gloria Steinem. Reprinted by permission.

Sanitary supplies would be federally funded and free. (Of course, some men would still pay for the prestige of commercial brands such as John Wayne Tampons, Muhammad Ali's Rope-a-dope Pads, Joe Namath Jock Shields— "For Those Light Bachelor Days," and Robert "Baretta" Blake Maxi-Pads.)

Military men, right-wing politicians, and religious fundamentalists would cite menstruation ("*men*-struation") as proof that only men could serve in the Army ("you have to give blood to take blood"), occupy political office ("can women be aggressive without that steadfast cycle governed by the planet Mars?"), be priests and ministers ("how could a woman give her blood for our sins?"), or rabbis ("without the monthly loss of impurities, women remain unclean").

Male radicals, left-wing politicians, and mystics, however, would insist that women are equal, just different; and that any woman could enter their ranks if only she were willing to self-inflict a major wound every month ("you *must* give blood for the revolution"), recognize the preeminence of menstrual issues, or subordinate her selfness to all men in the Cycle of Enlightenment.

Street guys would brag ("I'm a three-pad man") or answer praise from a buddy ("Man, you lookin' *good!*") by giving fives and saying, "Yeah, man, I'm on the rag!"

TV shows would treat the subject at length. ("Happy Days": Richie and Potsie try to convince Fonzie that he is still "The Fonz," though he has missed two periods in a row.) So would newspapers. (SHARK SCARE THREAT-ENS MENSTRUATING MEN. JUDGE CITES MONTHLY STRESS IN PARDONING RAPIST.) And movies. (Newman and Redford in "Blood Brothers"!)

Men would convince women that intercourse was *more* pleasurable at "that time of the month." Lesbians would be said to fear blood and therefore life itself—though probably only because they needed a good menstruating man.

Of course, male intellectuals would offer the most moral and logical arguments. How could a woman master any discipline that demanded a sense of time, space, mathematics, or measurement, for instance, without that in-built gift for measuring the cycles of the moon and planets—and thus for measuring anything at all? In the rarefied fields of philosophy and religion, could women compensate for missing the rhythm of the universe? Or for their lack of symbolic death-and-resurrection every month?

Liberal males in every field would try to be kind: the fact that "these people" have no gift of measuring life or connecting to the universe, the liberals would explain, should be punishment enough.

And how would women be trained to react? One can imagine traditional women agreeing to all these arguments with a staunch and smiling masochism.

("The ERA would force housewives to wound themselves every month": Phyllis Shlafley. "Your husband's blood is as sacred as that of Jesus—and so sexy, too!": Marabel Morgan.) Reformers and Queen Bees would try to imitate men, and *pretend* to have a monthly cycle. All feminists would explain endlessly that men, too, needed to be liberated from the false idea of Martian aggressiveness, just as women needed to escape the bonds of menses-envy. Radical feminists would add that the oppression of the nonmenstrual was the pattern for all other oppressions. ("Vampires were our first freedom fighters!") Cultural feminists would develop a bloodless imagery in art and literature. Socialist feminists would insist that only under capitalism would men be able to monopolize menstrual blood. . . .

In fact, if men could menstruate, the power justifications could probably go on forever.

If we let them.

<hr />

TV'S BLACK WORLD TURNS—BUT STAYS UNREAL

35

Henry Louis Gates Jr.

There is a telling moment in the 1986 film "Soul Man" when a young man explains to a friend why he has decided to down a bottle of tanning pills and turn himself black. The friend is skeptical: What's it actually going to be like, being black?

"It's gonna be great," the hero assures him. "These are the 80's, man. This is the 'Cosby' decade. America *loves* black people."

Alas, he soon discovers the gulf that separates the images of black people he sees on television and the reality that blacks experience every day.

Even black Americans sometimes need to be reminded about the deceptiveness of television. Blacks retain their fascination with black characters on TV: Many of us buy Jet magazine primarily to read its weekly television feature, which lists *every* black character (major or minor) to be seen on the screen that week. Yet our fixation with the presence of black characters on TV has blinded us to an important fact that "Cosby," which began in 1984, and its offshoots over the years demonstrate convincingly: There is very little connection between the social status of black Americans and the fabricated images of black people that Americans consume each day. Moreover, the representation of blacks on TV is a very poor index to our social advancement or political progress.

But the young man is right about one thing: This is the "Cosby" decade. The show's unprecedented success in depicting the lives of affluent blacks has exercised a profound influence on television in the last half of the 80's. And, judging from the premiere of this season's new black series—"Family Matters," "Homeroom" and "Snoops," as well as "Generations," an interracial soap opera—"Cosby's" success has led to the flow of TV sitcoms that feature the black middle class, each of which takes its lead from the "Cosby" show.

Historically blacks have always worried aloud about the image that white Americans harbor of us, first because we have never had control of those images and, second, because the greater number of those images have been negative. And given television's immediacy, and its capacity to reach so many viewers so quickly, blacks, at least since "Amos 'n' Andy" back in the early 50's, have been especially concerned with our images on the screen. I can remember as a child sitting upstairs in my bedroom and hearing my mother shout at the top of her voice that someone *"colored . . . colored!"* was on TV and that we had all better come downstairs at once. And, without fail, we did, sitting in front of our TV, nervous, full of expectation and dread, praying that our home girl or boy would not let the race down.

"WHITE" MONEY VS. "COLORED" MONEY

Later, when American society could not successfully achieve the social reformation it sought in the 60's through the Great Society, television solved the problem simply by inventing symbols of that transformation in the 80's, whether it was Cliff Huxtable—whom we might think of as the grandson of Alexander Scott (played by Mr. Cosby in "I Spy," 1965–68)—or Benson (1979–86), the butler who transforms himself into a lieutenant governor.

Today, blacks are doing much better on TV than they are in real life, an irony underscored by the use of black public figures (Mr. Cosby, Michael Jackson, Michael Jordan, Bobby Ferrin) as spokesmen for major businesses. When Mr. Cosby, deadpan, faces the camera squarely and says, "E. F. Hutton.

Because it's my money," the line blurs between Cliff Huxtable's successful career and Mr. Cosby.

This helps to explain why "Cosby" makes some people uncomfortable. As the dominant representation of blacks on TV, it suggests that blacks are solely responsible for their social conditions, with no acknowledgment of the severely constricted life opportunities that most black people face. What's troubling about the phenomenal success of "Cosby," then, is what was troubling about the earlier popularity of "Amos 'n' Andy": it's not the representation itself (Cliff Huxtable, a child of college-educated parents, is altogether believable), but the role it begins to play in our culture, the status it takes on as being, well, truly representative.

As long as *all* blacks were represented in demeaning or peripheral roles, it was possible to believe that American racism was, as it were, indiscriminate. The social vision of "Cosby," however, reflecting the minuscule integration of blacks into the upper middle class (having "white money," my mother used to say, rather than "colored" money) reassuringly throws the blame for black poverty back onto the impoverished.

This is the subliminal message of America's weekly dinner date with the Huxtables, played out to a lesser extent in other weekly TV encounters with middle-class black families, such as "227," "A Different World," "Amen" (Sherman Helmsley is a lawyer), and with isolated black individuals, such as the dashing Blair Underwood on "L. A. Law" and Philip Michael Thomas on "Miami Vice." One principal reason for the failure of Flip Wilson's "Charlie & Company" was the ambiguity of his class status; Wilson's character, Charlie Richmond, was an office worker at the Department of Highways, his wife (Gladys Knight) a schoolteacher. Wilson once joked, acidly, that he was the star of the black version of "The Cosby Show," which may have been true in ways that he did not intend.

THE GREAT "AMOS 'N' ANDY" DEBATE

In 1933, Sterling Brown, the great black poet and critic, divided the full range of black character types in American literature into seven categories: the contented slave; the wretched freeman; the comic Negro; the brute Negro; the tragic mulatto; the local color Negro; and the exotic primitive. It was only one small step to associate our public negative image in the American mind with the public negative social roles that we were assigned and to which we were largely confined. "If only they could be exposed to the *best* of the race," the sentiment went, "then they would see that we were normal human beings and treat us better."

Such a burdensome role for the black image led, inevitably, to careful monitoring and, ultimately, to censorship of our representations in literature, film, radio and later television. The historian W. E. B. Du Bois summarized this line of thinking among blacks: "We want," he said in 1925, "everything that is said about us to tell of the best and highest and noblest in us. We insist that our Art and Propaganda be one. We fear that the evil in us will be called racial while in others it is viewed as individual. We fear that our shortcomings are not merely human but foreshadowings and threatenings of disaster and failure." And the genre about which we were most sensitive, Du Bois wrote, was comedy. "The more highly trained we become," he wrote in 1921, "the less we can laugh at Negro comedy."

One of my favorite pastimes is screening episodes of "Amos 'n' Andy" for black friends who think that the series was both socially offensive and politically detrimental. After a few minutes, even hard-liners have difficulty restraining their laughter. "It's still racist," is one typical comment, "but it was funny."

The performance of those great black actors—Tim Moore, Spencer Williams and Ernestine Wade—transformed racist stereotypes into authentic black humor. The dilemma of "Amos 'n' Andy," however, was that these were the *only* images of blacks that Americans could see on TV. The political consequences for the early civil rights movement were thought to be threatening. The N.A.A.C.P. helped to have the series killed.

What lies behind these sorts of arguments is a belief that social policies affecting black Americans were largely determined by our popular images in the media. But the success of the "Cosby" show has put the lie to that myth: "Cosby" exposes more white Americans than ever before to the most nobly idealized blacks in the history of entertainment, yet social and economic conditions for the average black American have not been bleaker in a very long time.

To make matters worse, "Cosby" is also one of the most popular shows in apartheid South Africa, underscoring the fact that the relationship between how whites treat us and their exposure to "the best" in us is far from straightforward. (One can hear the Afrikaaner speaking to his black servants: "When you people are like Cliff and Clare, *then* we will abandon apartheid.")

There are probably as many reasons to like the "Cosby" show as there are devoted viewers—and there are millions of them. I happen to like it because my daughters (ages 9 and 7) like it, and I enjoy watching them watch themselves in the depictions of middle-class black kids, worrying about school, sibling rivalries and family tradition. But I also like "Cosby" because its very success has forced us to rethink completely the relation between black social progress and the images of blacks that American society fabricates, projects and digests.

But the "Cosby" vision of upper-middle-class blacks and their families is comparatively recent. And while it may have constituted the dominant image of blacks for the last five years, it is a direct reaction against the lower-class ghetto comedies of the 70's, such as "Sanford and Son" (1972–77), "Good Times" (1974–79), "That's My Mama" (1974–75) and "What's Happening!!" (1976–79). The latter three were single-mother-dominated sitcoms. Although "Good Times" began with a nuclear family, John Amos—who had succeeded marvelously in transforming the genre of the black maternal household—was soon killed off, enabling the show to conform to the stereotype of a fatherless black family.

Even "The Jeffersons" (1975–85) conforms to this mold. George and Louise began their TV existence as Archie Bunker's working-class neighbors, saved their pennies, then "moved on up," as the theme song says, to Manhattan's East Side. "The Jeffersons" also served as a bridge between sitcoms depicting the ghetto and those portraying the new black upper class.

In fact, in the history of black images on television, character types have distinct pasts and, as is also the case with white shows, series seem both to lead to other series and to spring from metaphorical ancestors.

PURE STREET IN A BROOKS BROTHERS SUIT

Let's track the evolution of the "Cosby" type on television. While social engineering is easier on the little screen than in the big city, Sterling Brown's list of black stereotypes in American literature proves quite serviceable as a guide to the images TV has purveyed for the last two decades. Were we writing a new sitcom using these character types, our cast might look like this—contented slave: Andy, Fred Sanford, J. J. ("Good Times"); wretched freeman: George Jefferson; comic Negro: Flip Wilson; brute Negro: Mr. T ("The A-Team"), Hawk ("Spenser: for Hire"); tragic mulatto: "Julia," Elvin ("Cosby"), Whitley ("A Different World"); local color Negro: Meschach Taylor ("Designing Women"); exotic primitive: Link ("Mod Squad" 1968–73), most black characters on MTV. If we add the category of Noble Negro (Cliff Huxtable, Benson), our list might be complete.

We can start with George Jefferson, who we might think of as a Kingfish ("Amos 'n' Andy") or as a Fred Sanford ("Sanford and Son") who has finally made it. Jefferson epitomized Richard Nixon's version of black capitalism, bootstrap variety, and all of its terrifying consequences. Jefferson was anything but a man of culture: Unlike the "Cosby" living room, his

East Side apartment had no painting by Jacob Lawrence or Charles White, Romare Bearden or Varnette Honeywood. Despite his new-found wealth, Jefferson was pure street, draped in a Brooks Brothers suit. You did not want to live next to a George Jefferson, and you most certainly did not want your daughter to marry one.

"The Jeffersons" was part of a larger trend in television in the depiction of black men. We might think of this as their domestication, in direct reaction to the questing, macho images of black males shown in the 60's news clips of the civil rights movement, the Black Panthers and the black power movement. While Jefferson (short, feisty, racist, rich, vulgar) represents one kind of domestication, a more curious kind was the cultural dwarfism represented by "Diff'rent Strokes" (1978–86) and "Webster" (1983–87), in which small black "boys" (arrested adolescents who were much older than the characters they played) were adopted by tall, successful white males. These establishment figures represented the myth of the benevolent paternalism of the white upper class, an American myth as old as the abolitionist movement.

Indeed, one central motif of 19th-century American art is a sculpted tall white male (often Lincoln) towering above a crouched or kneeling adult or adolescent slave, in the act of setting them free. "Webster" and "Diff'rent Strokes" depict black orphans who are rescued from blackness and poverty, adopted and raised just like any other upper-middle-class white kid, prep schools and all. These shows can be thought of as TV's fantasy of Lyndon Johnson's "Great Society" and the war on poverty rolled into one.

The formula was not as successful with a female character: An attempt to use the same format with a black woman, Shirley Hemphill ("One in a Million," 1980) lasted only six months. "The White Shadow" (1978–81) was a variation of this paternal motif, in which wild and unruly ghetto kids were tamed with a basketball.

These small black men signaled to the larger American audience that the very idea of the black male could be, and had been, successfully domesticated. Mr. T—whose 1983–87 "A-Team" run paralleled that of "Webster"—might appear to be an exception. We are forced to wonder, however, why such an important feature of his costume—and favorite fetish—was those dazzling gold chains, surely a subliminal suggestion of bondage.

This process of paternal domestication, in effect, made Cliff Huxtable's character a logical next step. In fact, I think of the evolution of the Huxtable character, generationally, in this way: imagine if George Jefferson owned the tenement building in which Florida and her family from "Good Times" lived. After John Amos dies, Jefferson evicts them for nonpayment of rent. Florida, destitute and distraught, tries to kill George. The state puts her children up for adoption.

They are adopted by Mr. Drummond ("Diff'rent Strokes") and graduate from Dalton, Exeter and Howard. Gary Coleman's grandson becomes an obstetrician, marries a lovely lawyer named Clare, and they move to Brooklyn Heights. And there you have it: the transformation of the character type of the black male on television.

And while Clare Huxtable is a refreshingly positive depiction of an intelligent, successful black woman, she is clearly a descendant of "Julia" (1968–71), though a Julia with sensuality and sass. The extent of typecasting of black women as mammy figures, descended from the great Hollywood "Mammy" of "Gone With the Wind," is astonishing: Beulah, Mama in "Amos 'n' Andy," Geraldine ("Flip Wilson," 1970–75), Florida, Nel in "Gimme a Break" (1981–88), Louise ("The Jeffersons"), Eloise ("That's My Mama," 1974–75).

And what is the measure of the Huxtables' nobility? One of the reasons "Cosby" and its spin-off, "A Different World," are so popular is that the black characters in them have finally become, in most respects, just like white people.

While I applaud "Cosby's" success at depicting (at long last) the everyday concerns of black people (love, sex, ambition, generational conflicts, work and leisure) far beyond reflex responses to white racism, the question remains: Has TV managed to depict a truly "different world"? As Mark Crispin Miller puts it, "By insisting that blacks and whites are entirely alike, television denies the cultural barriers that slavery necessarily created; barriers that have hardened over years and years, and that still exist"—barriers that produced different cultures, distinct worlds.

And while "Cosby" is remarkably successful at introducing most Americans to traditional black cultural values, customs and norms, it has not succeeded at introducing America to a truly different world. The show that came closest—that presented the fullest range of black character types—was the 1987–88 series "Frank's Place," starring Tim Reid and his wife Daphne Maxwell Reid and set in a Creole restaurant in New Orleans.

Unfortunately, Mr. Reid apparently has learned his lesson: His new series, "Snoops," in which his wife also stars, is a black detective series suggestive of "The Thin Man." The couple is thoroughly middle class: He is a professor of criminology at Georgetown; she is head of protocol at the State Department. "Drugs and murder and psychotic people," Mr. Reid said in a recent interview. "I think we've seen enough of that in real life."

But it is also important to remember that the early 70's ghetto sitcoms ("Good Times" and "Sanford") were no more realistic than "Cosby" is. In fact, their success made the idea of ghetto life palatable for most Americans, robbing it of its reality as a place of exile, a place of rage, and frustration, and death. And perhaps with "Cosby's" success and the realization that the very structure of the sitcom (in which every character is a type) militates against its use as an agent of social change, blacks will stop looking to TV for our social liberation. As a popular song in the early 70's put it, "The revolution will not be televised."

RACIST STEREOTYPING IN THE ENGLISH LANGUAGE

36

Robert B. Moore

LANGUAGE AND CULTURE

An integral part of any culture is its language. Language not only develops in conjunction with a society's historical, economic and political evolution; it also reflects that society's attitudes and thinking. Language not only *expresses* ideas and concepts but actually *shapes* thought.[1] If one accepts that our dominant white culture is racist, then one would expect our language—an indispensable transmitter of culture—to be racist as well. Whites, as the dominant group, are not subjected to the same abusive characterization by our language that people of color receive. Aspects of racism in the English language that will be discussed in this essay include terminology, symbolism, politics, ethnocentrism, and context.

Before beginning our analysis of racism in language we would like to quote part of a TV film review which shows the connection between language and culture.[2]

> Depending on one's culture, one interacts with time in a very distinct fashion. One example which gives some cross-cultural insights into the concept of time is language. In Spanish, a watch is said to "walk." In English, the watch "runs." In German, the watch "functions." And in French, the watch "marches." In the Indian culture of the Southwest, people do not refer to time in this way.

From: Paula S. Rothenberg (ed.), *Racism and Sexism: An Integrated Study* (New York: St. Martin's Press, 1988), pp. 269–279. Reprinted by permission of the Council on Interracial Books for Children.

The value of the watch is displaced with the value of "what time it's getting to be." Viewing these five cultural perspectives of time, one can see some definite emphasis and values that each culture places on time. For example, a cultural perspective may provide a clue to why the negative stereotype of the slow and lazy Mexican who lives in the "Land of Manana" exists in the Anglo value system, where time "flies," the watch "runs" and "time is money."

A SHORT PLAY ON "BLACK" AND "WHITE" WORDS

Some may blackly (angrily) accuse me of trying to blacken (defame) the English language, to give it a black eye (a mark of shame) by writing such black words (hostile). They may denigrate (to cast aspersions; to darken) me by accusing me of being blackhearted (malevolent), of having a black outlook (pessimistic, dismal) on life, of being a blackguard (scoundrel)—which would certainly be a black mark (detrimental fact) against me. Some may black-brow (scowl at) me and hope that a black cat crosses in front of me because of this black deed. I may become a black sheep (one who causes shame or embarrassment because of deviation from the accepted standards), who will be blackballed (ostracized) by being placed on a blacklist (list of undesirables) in an attempt to blackmail (to force or coerce into a particular action) me to retract my words. But attempts to blackjack (to compel by threat) me will have a Chinaman's chance of success, for I am not a yellow-bellied Indian-giver of words, who will whitewash (cover up or gloss over vices or crimes) a black lie (harmful, inexcusable). I challenge the purity and innocence (white) of the English language. I don't see things in black and white (entirely bad or entirely good) terms, for I am a white man (marked by upright firmness) if there ever was one. However, it would be a black day when I would not "call a spade a spade," even though some will suggest a white man calling the English language racist is like the pot calling the kettle black. While many may be niggardly (grudging, scanty) in their support, others will be honest and decent—and to them I say, that's very white of you (honest, decent).

The preceding is of course a white lie (not intended to cause harm), meant only to illustrate some examples of racist terminology in the English language.

OBVIOUS BIGOTRY

Perhaps the most obvious aspect of racism in language would be terms like "nigger," "spook," "chink," "spic," etc. While these may be facing increasing social disdain, they certainly are not dead. Large numbers of white Americans continue to utilize these terms. "Chink," "gook," and "slant-eyes" were in common usage among U.S. troops in Vietnam. An NBC nightly news broadcast, in February 1972, reported that the basketball team in Pekin, Illinois, was called the "Pekin Chinks" and noted that even though this had been protested by Chinese Americans, the term continued to be used because it was easy, and meant no harm. Spiro Agnew's widely reported "fat Jap" remark and the "little Jap" comment of lawyer John Wilson, during the Watergate hearings, are surface indicators of a deep-rooted Archie Bunkerism.

Many white people continue to refer to Black people as "colored," as for instance in a July 30, 1975 *Boston Globe* article on a racist attack by whites on a group of Black people using a public beach in Boston. One white person was quoted as follows:

> We've always welcomed good colored people in South Boston but we will not tolerate radical blacks or Communists. . . . Good colored people are welcome in South Boston, black militants are not.

Many white people may still be unaware of the disdain many African Americans have for the term "colored," but it often appears that whether used intentionally or unintentionally, "colored" people are "good" and "know their place," while "Black" people are perceived as "uppity" and "threatening" to many whites. Similarly, the term "boy" to refer to African American men is now acknowledged to be a demeaning term, though still in common use. Other terms such as "the pot calling the kettle black" and "calling a spade a spade" have negative racial connotations but are still frequently used, as for example when President Ford was quoted in February 1976 saying that even though Daniel Moynihan had left the U.N., the U.S. would continue "calling a spade a spade."

COLOR SYMBOLISM

The symbolism of white as positive and black as negative is pervasive in our culture, with the black/white words used in the beginning of this essay only one of many aspects. "Good guys" wear white hats and ride white horses, "bad guys" wear black hats and ride black horses. Angels are white, and devils are black. The definition of *black* includes "without any moral light or goodness, evil, wicked, indicating disgrace, sinful," while that of *white* includes "morally pure, spotless, innocent, free from evil intent."

A children's TV cartoon program, *Captain Scarlet*, is about an organization called Spectrum, whose purpose is to save the world from an evil extraterrestrial force called the Mysterons. Everyone in Spectrum has a color name—

Captain Scarlet, Captain Blue, etc. The one Spectrum agent who has been mysteriously taken over by the Mysterons and works to advance their evil aims is Captain Black. The person who heads Spectrum, the good organization out to defend the world, is Colonel White.

Three of the dictionary definitions of white are "fairness of complexion, purity, innocence." These definitions affect the standards of beauty in our culture, in which whiteness represents the norm. "Blondes have more fun" and "Wouldn't you really rather be a blonde" are sexist in their attitudes toward women generally, but are racist white standards when applied to third world women. A 1971 *Mademoiselle* advertisement pictured a curly-headed, ivory-skinned woman over the caption, "When you go blonde go all the way," and asked: "Isn't this how, in the back of your mind, you always wanted to look? All wide-eyed and silky blonde down to there, and innocent?" Whatever the advertising people meant by this particular woman's innocence, one must remember that "innocent" is one of the definitions of the word white. This standard of beauty when preached to all women is racist. The statement "Isn't this how, in the back of your mind, you always wanted to look?" either ignores third world women or assumes they long to be white.

Time magazine in its coverage of the Wimbledon tennis competition between the black Australian Evonne Goolagong and the white American Chris Evert described Ms. Goolagong as "the dusky daughter of an Australian sheepshearer," while Ms. Evert was "a fair young girl from the middle-class groves of Florida." *Dusky* is a synonym of "black" and is defined as "having dark skin; of a dark color; gloomy; dark; swarthy." Its antonyms are "fair" and "blonde." *Fair* is defined in part as "free from blemish, imperfection, or anything that impairs the appearance, quality, or character: pleasing in appearance, attractive; clean; pretty; comely." By defining Evonne Goolagong as "dusky," *Time* technically defined her as the opposite of "pleasing in appearance; attractive; clean; pretty; comely."

The studies of Kenneth B. Clark, Mary Ellen Goodman, Judith Porter and others indicate that this persuasive "rightness of whiteness" in U.S. culture affects children before the age of four, providing white youngsters with a false sense of superiority and encouraging self-hatred among third world youngsters.

ETHNOCENTRISM OR FROM A WHITE PERSPECTIVE

Some words and phrases that are commonly used represent particular perspectives and frames of reference, and these often distort the understanding of the reader or listener. David R. Burgest[3] has written about the effect of using the terms "slave" or "master." He argues that the psychological impact of the statement referring to "the master raped his slave" is different from the impact of the same statement substituting the words: "the white captor raped an African woman held in captivity."

> Implicit in the English usage of the "master-slave" concept is ownership of the "slave" by the "master," therefore, the "master" is merely abusing his property (slave). In reality, the captives (slave) were African individuals with human worth, right and dignity and the term "slave" denounces that human quality thereby making the mass rape of African women by white captors more acceptable in the minds of people and setting a mental frame of reference for legitimizing the atrocities perpetuated against African people.

The term slave connotes a less than human quality and turns the captive person into a thing. For example, two McGraw-Hill Far Eastern Publishers textbooks (1970) stated, "At first it was the slaves who worked the cane and they got only food for it. Now men work cane and get money." Next time you write about slavery or read about it, try transposing all "slaves" into "African people held in captivity," "Black people forced to work for no pay" or "African people stolen from their families and societies." While it is more cumbersome, such phrasing conveys a different meaning.

PASSIVE TENSE

Another means by which language shapes our perspective has been noted by Thomas Greenfield,[4] who writes that the achievements of Black people—and Black people themselves—have been hidden in

> the linguistic ghetto of the passive voice, the subordinate clause, and the "understood" subject. The seemingly innocuous distinction (between active/passive voice) holds enormous implications for writers and speakers. When it is effectively applied, the rhetorical impact of the passive voice—the art of making the creator or instigator of action totally disappear from a reader's perception—can be devastating.

For instance, some history texts will discuss how European immigrants came to the United States seeking a better life and expanded opportunities, but will note that "slaves *were brought* to America." Not only does this omit the destruction of African societies and families, but it ignores the role of northern merchants and southern slaveholders in the profitable trade in human beings. Other books will state that "the continental railroad *was built*," conveniently omitting information about the Chinese laborers who built much of it or the oppression they suffered.

Another example. While touring Monticello, Greenfield noted that the tour guide

> made all the black people of Monticello disappear through her use of the passive voice. While speaking of the architectural achievements of Jefferson in the active voice, she unfailingly shifted to passive when speaking of the work performed by Negro slaves and skilled servants.

Noting a type of door that after 166 years continued to operate without need for repair, Greenfield remarks that the design aspect of the door was much simpler than the actual skill and work involved in building and installing it. Yet his guide stated: "Mr. Jefferson designed these doors . . ." while "the doors were installed in 1809." The workers who installed those doors were African people whom Jefferson held in bondage. The guide's use of the passive tense enabled her to dismiss the reality of Jefferson's slaveholding. It also meant that she did not have to make any mention of the skills of those people held in bondage.

POLITICS AND TERMINOLOGY

"Culturally deprived," "economically disadvantaged" and "underdeveloped" are other terms which mislead and distort our awareness of reality. The application of the term "culturally deprived" to third world children in this society reflects a value judgment. It assumes that the dominant whites are cultured and all others without culture. In fact, third world children generally are bicultural, and many are bilingual, having grown up in their own culture as well as absorbing the dominant culture. In many ways, they are equipped with skills and experiences which white youth have been deprived of, since most white youth develop in a monocultural, monolingual environment. Burgest[5] suggests that the term "culturally deprived" be replaced by "culturally dispossessed," and that the term "economically disadvantaged" be replaced by "economically exploited." Both these terms present a perspective and implication that provide an entirely different frame of reference as to the reality of the third world experience in U.S. society.

Similarly, many nations of the third world are described as "underdeveloped." These less wealthy nations are generally those that suffered under colonialism and neo-colonialism. The "developed" nations are those that exploited their resources and wealth. Therefore, rather than referring to these countries as "underdeveloped," a more appropriate and meaningful designation might be "over exploited." Again, transpose this term next time you read about "underdeveloped nations" and note the different meaning that results.

Terms such as "culturally deprived," "economically disadvantaged" and "underdeveloped" place the responsibility for their own conditions on those being so described. This is known as "Blaming the Victim."[6] It places responsibility for poverty on the victims of poverty. It removes the blame from those in power who benefit from, and continue to permit, poverty.

Still another example involves the use of "non-white," "minority" or "third world." While people of color are a minority in the U.S., they are part of the vast majority of the world's population, in which white people are a distinct minority. Thus, by utilizing the term minority to describe people of color in the U.S., we can lose sight of the global majority/minority reality—a fact of some importance in the increasing and interconnected struggles of people of color inside and outside the U.S.

To describe people of color as "non-white" is to use whiteness as the standard and norm against which to measure all others. Use of the term "third world" to describe all people of color overcomes the inherent bias of "minority" and "non-white." Moreover, it connects the struggles of third world people in the U.S. with the freedom struggles around the globe.

The term third world gained increasing usage after the 1955 Bandung Conference of "non-aligned" nations, which represented a third force outside of the two world superpowers. The "first world" represents the United States, Western Europe and their sphere of influence. The "second world" represents the Soviet Union and its sphere. The "third world" represents, for the most part, nations that were, or are, controlled by the "first world" or West. For the most part, these are nations of Africa, Asia and Latin America.

"LOADED" WORDS AND NATIVE AMERICANS

Many words lead to a demeaning characterization of groups of people. For instance, Columbus, it is said, "discovered" America. The word *discover* is defined as "to gain sight or knowledge of something previously unseen or unknown; to discover may be to find some existent thing that was previously unknown." Thus, a continent inhabited by millions of human beings cannot be "discovered." For history books to continue this usage represents a Eurocentric (white European) perspective on world history and ignores the existence of, and the perspective of, Native Americans. "Discovery," as used in the Euro-American context, implies the right to take what one finds, ignoring the rights of those who already inhabit or own the "discovered" thing.

Eurocentrism is also apparent in the usage of "victory" and "massacre" to describe the battles between Native Americans and whites. *Victory* is defined in the dictionary as "a success or triumph over an enemy in battle or war; the decisive defeat of an opponent." *Conquest* denotes the "taking over of control by the victor, and the obedience of the conquered." *Massacre* is defined as "the unnecessary, indiscriminate killing of a number of human beings, as in barbarous warfare or persecution, or for revenge or plunder." *Defend* is described as "to ward off attack from; guard against assault or injury; to strive to keep safe by resisting attack."

Eurocentrism turns these definitions around to serve the purpose of distorting history and justifying Euro-American conquest of the Native American homelands. Euro-Americans are not described in history books as invading Native American lands, but rather as defending *their* homes against "Indian" attacks. Since European communities were constantly encroaching on land already occupied, then a more honest interpretation would state that it was the Native Americans who were "warding off," "guarding" and "defending" their homelands.

Native American victories are invariably defined as "massacres," while the indiscriminate killing, extermination and plunder of Native American nations by Euro-Americans is defined as "victory." Distortion of history by the choice of "loaded" words used to describe historical events is a common racist practice. Rather than portraying Native Americans as human beings in highly defined and complex societies, cultures and civilizations, history books use such adjectives as "savages," "beasts," "primitive," and "backward." Native people are referred to as "squaw," "brave," or "papoose" instead of "woman," "man," or "baby."

Another term that has questionable connotations is *tribe*. The Oxford English Dictionary defines this noun as "a race of people; now applied especially to a primary aggregate of people in a primitive or barbarous condition, under a headman or chief." Morton Fried,[7] discussing "The Myth of Tribe," states that the word "did not become a general term of reference to American Indian society until the nineteenth century. Previously, the words commonly used for Indian populations were 'nation' and 'people.' " Since "tribe" has assumed a connotation of primitiveness or backwardness, it is suggested that the use of "nation" or "people" replace the term whenever possible in referring to Native American peoples.

The term *tribe* invokes even more negative implications when used in reference to American peoples. As Evelyn Jones Rich[8] has noted, the term is "almost always used to refer to third world people and it implies a stage of development which is, in short, a put-down."

"LOADED" WORDS AND AFRICANS

Conflicts among diverse peoples within African nations are often referred to as "tribal warfare," while conflicts among the diverse peoples within European countries are never described in such terms. If the rivalries between the Ibo and the Hausa and Yoruba in Nigeria are described as "tribal," why not the rivalries between Serbs and Slavs in Yugoslavia, or Scots and English in Great Britain, Protestants and Catholics in Ireland, or the Basques and the Southern Spaniards in Spain? Conflicts among African peoples in a particular nation have religious, cultural, economic and/or political roots. If we can analyze the roots of conflicts among European peoples in terms other than "tribal warfare," certainly we can do the same with African peoples, including correct reference to the ethnic groups or nations involved. For example, the terms "Kaffirs," "Hottentot" or "Bushmen" are names imposed by white Europeans. The correct names are always those by which a people refer to themselves. (In these instances Xhosa, Khoi-Khoin and San are correct.[9])

The generalized application of "tribal" in reference to Africans—as well as the failure to acknowledge the religious, cultural and social diversity of African peoples—is a decidedly racist dynamic. It is part of the process whereby Euro-Americans justify, or avoid confronting, their oppression of third world peoples. Africa has been particularly insulted by this dynamic, as witness the pervasive "darkest Africa" image. This image, widespread in Western culture, evokes an Africa covered by jungles and inhabited by "uncivilized," "cannibalistic," "pagan," "savage" peoples. This "darkest Africa" image avoids the geographical reality. Less than 20 per cent of the African continent is wooded savanna, for example. The image also ignores the history of African cultures and civilizations. Ample evidence suggests this distortion of reality was developed as a convenient rationale for the European and American slave trade. The Western powers, rather than exploiting, were civilizing and Christianizing "uncivilized" and "pagan savages" (so the rationalization went). This dynamic also served to justify Western colonialism. From Tarzan movies to racist children's books like *Doctor Dolittle* and *Charlie and the Chocolate Factory*, the image of "savage" Africa and the myth of "the white man's burden" has been perpetuated in Western culture.

A 1972 *Time* magazine editorial lamenting the demise of *Life* magazine, stated that the "lavishness" of *Life's* enterprises included "organizing safaris into darkest Africa." The same year, the *New York Times*' C. L. Sulzberger wrote that Africa has "a history as dark as the skins of many of its people." Terms such as "darkest Africa," "primitive," "tribe" ("tribal") or "jungle," in reference to Africa, perpetuate myths and are especially inexcusable in such large circulation publications.

Ethnocentrism is similarly reflected in the term "pagan" to describe traditional religions. A February 1973 *Time* magazine article on Uganda stated, "Moslems account for only 500,000 of Uganda's 10 million people. Of the remainder, 5,000,000 are Christians and the rest pagan." *Pagan* is defined as "Heathen, a follower of a polytheistic religion; one that has little or no religion and that is marked by a frank delight in and uninhibited seeking after sensual pleasures and material goods." *Heathen* is defined as "Unenlightened; an unconverted member of a people or nation that does not acknowledge the God of the Bible. A person whose culture or enlightenment is of an inferior grade, especially an irreligious person." Now, the people of Uganda, like almost all Africans, have serious religious beliefs and practices. As used by Westerners, "pagan" connotes something wild, primitive and inferior—another term to watch out for.

The variety of traditional structures that African people live in are their "houses," not "huts." A *hut* is "an often small and temporary dwelling of simple construction." And to describe Africans as "natives" (noun) is derogatory terminology—as in, "the natives are restless." The dictionary definition of *native* includes: "one of a people inhabiting a territorial area at the time of its discovery or becoming familiar to a foreigner; one belonging to a people having a less complex civilization." Therefore, use of "native," like use of "pagan" often implies a value judgment of white superiority.

QUALIFYING ADJECTIVES

Words that would normally have positive connotations can have entirely different meanings when used in a racial context. For example, C. L. Sulzberger, the columnist of the *New York Times*, wrote in January 1975, about conversations he had with two people in Namibia. One was the white South African administrator of the country and the other a member of SWAPO, the Namibian liberation movement. The first is described as "Dirk Mudge, who as senior elected member of the administration is a kind of acting Prime Minister. . . ." But the second person is introduced as "Daniel Tijongarero, an intelligent Herero tribesman who is a member of SWAPO. . . ." What need was there for Sulzberger to state that Daniel Tijongarero is "intelligent"? Why not also state that Dirk Mudge was "intelligent"—or do we assume he wasn't?

A similar example from a 1968 *New York Times* article reporting on an address by Lyndon Johnson stated, "The President spoke to the well-dressed Negro officials and their wives." In what similar circumstances can one imagine a reporter finding it necessary to note that an audience of white government officials was "well-dressed"?

Still another word often used in a racist context is "qualified." In the 1960's white Americans often questioned whether Black people were "qualified" to hold public office, a question that was never raised (until too late) about white officials like Wallace, Maddox, Nixon, Agnew, Mitchell, et al. The question of qualifications has been raised even more frequently in recent years as white people question whether Black people are "qualified" to be hired for positions in industry and educational institutions. "We're looking for a qualified Black" has been heard again and again as institutions are confronted with affirmative action goals. Why stipulate that Blacks must be "qualified," when for others it is taken for granted that applicants must be "qualified."

SPEAKING ENGLISH

Finally, the depiction in movies and children's books of third world people speaking English is often itself racist. Children's books about Puerto Ricans or Chicanos often connect poverty with a failure to speak English or to speak it well, thus blaming the victim and ignoring the racism which affects third world people regardless of their proficiency in English. Asian characters speak a stilted English ("Honorable so and so" or "Confucius say") or have a speech impediment ("roots or ruck," "very solly," "flied lice"). Native American characters speak another variation of stilted English ("Boy not hide. Indian take boy."), repeat certain Hollywood-Indian phrases ("Heap big" and "Many moons") or simply grunt out "Ugh" or "How." The repeated use of these language characterizations functions to make third world people seem less intelligent and less capable than the English-speaking white characters.

WRAP-UP

A *Saturday Review* editorial[10] on "The Environment of Language" stated that language

> . . . has as much to do with the philosophical and political conditioning of a society as geography or climate. . . . people in Western cultures do not realize the extent to which their racial attitudes have been conditioned since early childhood by the power of words to ennoble or condemn, augment or detract,

glorify or demean. Negative language infects the subconscious of most Western people from the time they first learn to speak. Prejudice is not merely imparted or superimposed. It is metabolized in the bloodstream of society. What is needed is not so much a change in language as an awareness of the power of words to condition attitudes. If we can at least recognize the underpinnings of prejudice, we may be in a position to deal with the effects.

To recognize the racism in language is an important first step. Consciousness of the influence of language on our perceptions can help to negate much of that influence. But it is not enough to simply become aware of the effects of racism in conditioning attitudes. While we may not be able to change the language, we can definitely change our usage of the language. We can avoid using words that degrade people. We can make a conscious effort to use terminology that reflects a progressive perspective, as opposed to a distorting perspective. It is important for educators to provide students with opportunities to explore racism in language and to increase their awareness of it, as well as learning terminology that is positive and does not perpetuate negative human values.

NOTES

1. Simon Podair, "How Bigotry Builds Through Language," *Negro Digest*, March '67

2. Jose Armas, "Antonia and the Mayor: A Cultural Review of the Film," *The Journal of Ethnic Studies*, Fall, '75

3. David R. Burgest, "The Racist Use of the English Language," *Black Scholar*, Sept. '73

4. Thomas Greenfield, "Race and Passive Voice at Monticello," *Crisis*, April '75

5. David R. Burgest, "Racism in Everyday Speech and Social Work Jargon," *Social Work*, July '73

6. William Ryan, *Blaming the Victim*, Pantheon Books, '71

7. Morton Fried, "The Myth of Tribe," *National History*, April '75

8. Evelyn Jones Rich, "Mind Your Language," *Africa Report*, Sept./Oct. '74

9. Steve Wolf, "Catalogers in Revolt Against LC's Racist, Sexist Headings," *Bulletin of Interracial Books for Children*, Vol. 6, Nos. 3&4, '75

10. "The Environment of Language," *Saturday Review*, April 8, '67

Also see:

Roger Bastide, "Color, Racism and Christianity," *Daedalus*, Spring '67

Kenneth J. Gergen, "The Significance of Skin Color in Human Relations," *Daedalus*, Spring '67

Lloyd Yabura, "Towards a Language of Humanism," *Rhythm*, Summer '71

UNESCO, "Recommendations Concerning Terminology in Education on Race Questions," June '68

RACE, SEX, AIDS: *The Construction of "Other"*   37

Evelynn Hammonds

In March of this year when Richard Goldstein's article, "AIDS and Race—the Hidden Epidemic" appeared in the *Village Voice*, the following statement in the lead paragraph jumped out at me: "a black woman is thirteen times more likely than a white woman to contract AIDS, says the Centers for Disease Control; a Hispanic woman is at eleven times the risk. Ninety-one percent of infants with AIDS are non-white." My first reaction was shock. I was stunned to discover the extent and rate of spread of AIDS in the black community, especially given the lack of public mobilization either inside or outside the community. My second reaction was anger. AIDS is a disease that for the time being signals a death notice. I am angry because too many people have died and are going to die of this disease. The gay male community over these last several years has been transformed and mobilized to halt transmission and gay men (at least white gay men) with AIDS have been able to live and die with some dignity and self-esteem. People of color need the opportunity to establish programs and interventions to provide education so that the spread of this disease in our communities can be halted, and to provide care so that people of color with AIDS will not live and die as pariahs.

My final reaction was despair. Of course I *knew* why information about AIDS and the black community had been buried—by both the black and white media. The white media, like the dominant power structure, have moved into

From: *Radical America* Vol. 20 No. 6 (1987), "Facing AIDS: A Special Issue": 28–36. Reprinted by permission.

their phase of "color-blindness" as a mark of progress. This ideology buries racism along with race. In the case of AIDS and race, the problem with "color-blindness" becomes clear. Race remains a reality in this society, including a reality about how perception is structured. On the one hand, race blindness means a failure to develop educational programs and materials that speak in the language of our communities and recognize the position of people of color in relation to the dominant institutions of society: medical, legal, etc. Additionally, we must ask why the vast disproportion of people of color in the AIDS statistics hasn't been seen as a remarkable fact, or as worthy of comment. By their silence, the white media fail to challenge the age-old American myth of blacks as carriers of disease, especially sexually transmitted disease. This association has quietly become incorporated into the image of AIDS.

The black community's relative silence about AIDS is in part also a response to this historical association of blacks, disease, and deviance in American society. Revealing that AIDS is prevalent in the black community raises the spectre of blacks being associated with two kinds of deviance: sexually transmitted disease and homosexuality.

As I began to make connections between AIDS and race I slowly began to pull together pieces of information and images of AIDS that I had seen in the media. Immediately I began to think about the forty year-long Tuskegee syphilis experiment on black men. I thought about the innuendoes in media reports about AIDS in Africa and Haiti that hinted at bizarre sexual practices among black people in those countries; I remembered how a black gay man had been portrayed as sexually irresponsible in a PBS documentary on AIDS; I thought about how little I had seen in the black press about AIDS and black gay men; I began to notice the thinly veiled hostility toward the increasing number of i.v. drug users with AIDS. Goldstein's article revealed dramatically, the deafening silence about who was now actually contracting and dying from AIDS—gay/bisexual black and Hispanic men (now about 50% of black and Hispanic men with AIDS); many black and Hispanic i.v. drug users; black and Hispanic women and black and Hispanic babies born to these women.

In this culture, how we think about disease determines who lives and who dies. The history of black people in this country is riddled with episodes displaying how concepts of sickness, disease, health, behavior and sexuality, and race have been entwined in the definition of normalcy and deviance. The power to define disease and normality makes AIDS a political issue.

The average black person on the street may not know the specifics of concepts of disease and race but our legacy as victims of this construction means that we know what it means to have a disease cast as the result of the immoral behavior of a group of people. Black people and other people of color notice, pay attention to what diseases are cast upon us and why. As the saying goes—"when white people get a cold, black people get pneumonia."

In this article I want to address the issues raised by the white media's silence on the connections between AIDS and race; the black media's silence on the connections between AIDS and sexuality/sexual politics, the failure of white gay men's AIDS organizations to reach the communities of people of color, and finally the implications for gay activists, progressives and feminists.

It is very important to outline the historical context in which the AIDS epidemic occurs in regards to race. The dominant media portrayals of AIDS and scientists' assertions about its origins and modes of transmission have everything to do with the history of racial groups and sexually transmitted diseases.

THE SOCIAL CONSTRUCTION OF DISEASE

> A standard feature of the vast majority of medical articles on the health of blacks was a sociomedical profile of a race whose members were rapidly becoming diseased, debilitated, and debauched and had only themselves to blame.[1]

One of the first things that white southern doctors noted about blacks imported from Africa as slaves, was that they seemed to respond differently than whites to certain diseases. Primarily they observed that some of the diseases that were epidemic in the south seemed to affect blacks less severely than whites—specifically, fevers (e.g. yellow fever). Since in the eighteenth and nineteenth centuries there was little agreement about the nature of various illnesses and the causes of many common diseases were unknown, physicians tended to attribute the differences they noted simply to race.

In the 19th century when challenges were made to the institution of slavery, white southern physicians were all too willing to provide medical evidence to justify slavery.

> They justified slavery and, after its abolition, second-class citizenship, by insisting that blacks were incapable of assuming any higher station in life. . . . Thus, medical discourses on the peculiarities of blacks offered, among other things, a pseudoscientific rationale for keeping blacks in their places.[2]

If as these physicians maintained, blacks were less susceptible to fevers than whites, then it seemed fitting that they and not whites should provide most of the labor in the hot, swampy lowlands where southern agriculture was centered. Southern physicians marshalled other "scientific" evidence, such as measurement of brain sizes and other body organs to prove that blacks constituted an inferior race. For many whites these arguments were persuasive because "objective" science offered validity to their personal "observations," prejudices and fears.

The history of sexually transmitted diseases, in particular syphilis, indicates the pervasiveness of racial/sexual stereotyping. The history of syphilis in America is complex, as Allan Brandt discloses in his book *No Magic Bullet*. According to Brandt, "venereal disease has historically been assumed to be the disease of the 'other'." Obviously the complicated interaction of sexuality and disease has deep implications for the current portrayal of AIDS.

Like AIDS, the prevailing nineteenth century view of syphilis was characterized early-on in moral terms—and when it became apparent that a high rate of syphilis occurred among blacks in the South, the morality issue heightened considerably. Diseases that are acquired through immoral behavior were considered in many parts of the culture as punishment from God, the wages of sin. Anyone with such a disease was stigmatized. A white person could avoid this sin by a change in behavior. But for blacks it was different. It was noted that one of the primary differences that separated the races was that blacks were more flagrant and loose in their sexual behavior—behaviors they could not control.

> Moreover, personal restraints on self-indulgence did not exist, physicians insisted, because the smaller brain of the Negro had failed to develop a center for inhibiting sexual behavior.[3]

Therefore blacks deserved to have syphilis, since they couldn't control their behavior and as the Tuskegee experiment carried that logic to extreme—blacks also deserved to die from syphilis.

> [B]lacks suffered from venereal diseases because they would not, or could not, refrain from sexual promiscuity. Social hygiene for whites rested on the assumption that attitudinal changes could produce behavioral changes. A single standard of high moral behavior could be produced by molding sexual attitudes through moral education. For blacks, however, a change in their very *nature* seemed to be required.[4]

If in the above quotation, you change blacks to homosexuals and whites to heterosexuals then the parallel to the media portrayal of people with AIDS is obvious.

The black community's response to the historical construction of sexually transmitted diseases as the result of bad, inherently uncontrollable behavior of blacks—is sexual conservatism. To avoid the stigma of being cast with diseases of the "other," the black media, as well as other institutions in the community, avoid public discussion of sexual behavior and other "deviant" behavior like drug use. The white media on the other hand is often quick to cast blacks and people of color as "other" either overtly or covertly.

BLACK COMMUNITY RESPONSE TO AIDS

Of 38,435 diagnosed cases of AIDS as of July 20, 1987, black and Hispanic people make up 39% of all cases even though they account for only 17 percent of the adult population.[5] Eighty per cent of the pediatric cases are black and Hispanic. The average life expectancy after diagnosis of a white person with AIDS in the US is two years; of a person of color, nineteen weeks.[6]

The leading magazines in the black community, *Ebony* and *Essence* carried no articles on AIDS until the spring of this year. The journal of the National Medical Association, the professional organization of black physicians, carried a short guest editorial article in late 1986 and to date has not published any extensive article on AIDS. The official magazines of the NAACP and the National Urban League make no mention of AIDS throughout 1986 nor to date this year. Only the Atlanta-based SCLC (Southern Christian Leadership Conference) has established an ongoing educational program to address AIDS in the black community.

When I examined the few articles that have been written about AIDS in the national black press, several themes emerged. Almost all the articles I saw tried to indicate that the black people are at risk while simultaneously trying to avoid any implication that AIDS is a "black" disease. The black media has underemphasized, though recognized, that there are significant socioeconomic cofactors in terms of the impact of AIDS in the black community. The high rate of drug use and abuse in the black community is in part a result of many other social factors—high unemployment, poor schools, inadequate housing and limited access to health care, all factors in the spread of AIDS. These affect specifically the fact that people of color with AIDS are diagnosed at more advanced stages of the disease and are dying faster. The national black media have so far also failed to deal with any larger public policy issue that the AIDS crisis will precipitate for the community; and most importantly homosexuality and bisexuality were dealt with in a very conservative and problematic fashion.

TESTING

In terms of testing *Ebony* encourages more opportunity for people to be tested anonymously; *Essence* recommends testing for women thinking of getting pregnant. Both articles mention that exposure of test results could result in discrimination in housing and employment but neither publication discusses the issue at any length. There is no mention of testing that is going on in the military and how those results are being used nor is there mention of testing in prison. It is clear from the sketchy discussion of testing that the political issues around testing are not being faced.

SEXUALITY

The most disappointing aspect of these articles is that by focusing on individual behavior as the cause of AIDS and by setting up bisexuals, homosexuals, and drug users as "other" in the black community, and as "bad," the national black media falls into the trap of reproducing exactly how white society has defined the issue. But unlike the situation for whites, what happens to these groups within the black community will affect the community as a whole. Repressive practices around AIDS in prisons will affect all black men in prison with or without AIDS and their families outside and any other black person facing the criminal justice system; the identification of significant numbers of people of color in the military with AIDS will affect all people of color in the military. Quarantine, suspension of civil liberties for drug users in the black community with AIDS will affect everyone in the community. Healthcare and housing access will be restricted for all of us. If people with AIDS are set-off as "bad" or "other"—no change in individual behavior in relation to them will save any of us. There can be no "us" or "them" in our communities.

The *Ebony* article entitled: "The Truth about AIDS: Dread Disease is Spreading Rapidly through Heterosexual Population," while highlighting the increase of AIDS among heterosexuals in the black community, makes several comments about black homosexuals. The author notes that there is generally a negative attitude towards homosexuals in the community and quotes several physicians who emphasize that the reticence on this issue is a hindrance to AIDS education efforts in the community. It does not emphasize that, because of this "reticence," only now as AIDS is being recognized as striking heterosexuals, is it beginning to be talked about in the black community.

> One of the greatest problems in the black community, other than igno-
> rance about the disease, is the large number of black men who engage in sex
> acts with other men but who don't consider themselves homosexuals.[7]

The point is then that since AIDS was initially characterized as a "gay disease" and many black men don't consider themselves gay in spite of their sexual practices, the black community did not acknowledge the presence of AIDS.

The association of AIDS with "bad" behavior is prominent in this article. Homosexuals and drug users are described as a "physiologically and economically depressed subgroup of the black community."[8]

The message is that to deal with this disease the individual behavior of a deviant subgroup must be changed. Additionally, the recommendation to heterosexuals is to "not have sex" with bisexuals and drug users. There are no recommendations about how the community can find a way to deal with the silence around the issues of homosexuality/bisexuality, sexual practices in general and drug use. The article fails to say what the implications of the sexual practices of black men are for the community.

The *Essence* article, entitled *Nobody's Safe*, avoids the issue as well.[9] The authors describe a scenario of a 38 year-old middle-class professional woman who is suddenly found to have AIDS. Her husband had died two years earlier due to a rare form of pneumonia. After testing positive for AIDS she is told by one of her husband's relatives that he had been bisexual. The text following this scenario goes on to describe how most women contract AIDS; it gives a general sketch of the origins of the disease and discusses the latency period and defines asymptomatic carriers of the virus. There is no mention of bisexuality or homosexuality. The implication is again—just don't have sex with those people if you want to avoid AIDS. It avoids discussion of the prevalence of bisexuality among black men, and consequently the way that AIDS will ultimately change sexual relationships in the black community.

EDUCATION EFFORTS AND SEXUAL
BEHAVIOR IN THE AGE OF AIDS

The implications of this silence on sexuality are obvious when education efforts for black people are being discussed. But there is more at stake here than simply an acknowledgment. Both articles note the desperate need for education and material that speaks directly to the black community, so that black people can recognize that they too are at risk. But the other part of the message one gets from these articles is that black children must be taught the "facts about sex, AIDS and drug use and abuse" not about sexuality. *Essence* reports that a new group has formed in Atlanta which sponsors "Play Safe Parties" to teach women how to practice safer sex. In effect AIDS is described in terms of individual behavior. There are no specific guidelines about what safer sex is—that it is about a community response as much as it is about individual behavior; instead, there is a push for people to return to monogamous, traditional relationships without analysis as to what that means for heterosexuals in a community where women far outnumber men in the population; where traditional patriarchal relationships are not easily accepted anymore. What about discussions about "safer sex" for men? What about sexual pleasure for women and who negotiates it? These articles do not recognize that you can't simply separate sex from AIDS, nor can you respond to it by a call to a return to traditional values while not exploring the implications of that move.

What white gay men have been able to do in the face of the AIDS crisis is to use the connection between sex and community. They succeeded in validating and mobilizing the gay community to the deadly implications of AIDS while preserving their right to define sexual expression and therefore challenge the conception of homosexuality as bad. For the black community, however, "the fear of a racial backlash against minorities as they become more identified with AIDS is one of the reasons the black community has been slow to address this issue, to put it on our agenda."[10] What's at issue here is how to break the dominant culture's association of blacks with disease and immorality. The response so far has been to appeal to blacks to demonstrate our "traditions of respectability," e.g., to embrace monogamy in the face of the dominant culture's association of black people with promiscuity, and to deny the existence of homosexuality in the black community. But such a response means that the racist ideology that gives white culture the power to define morality and immorality remains intact. Black gays are rendered invisible and efforts at educating the community and providing care for people with AIDS are hampered by the need to preserve the notion that gaining respectability involves gaining authority.

Sexuality and sexual politics never came to the forefront of the civil rights agenda because of the reaction of the black community to the way in which race and sex had historically been used against the black community. What the AIDS epidemic raises is that the black political agenda has not been able to dethrone the power of that ideology.

THE MAINSTREAM (WHITE) PRESS

In general the mainstream media has been silent on the rise of AIDS in the black and Hispanic communities. Until very recently, with the exception of a few special reports, such as a quite excellent one on the PBS' MacNeil-Lehrer Report, most media reports on AIDS continue to speak of the disease without mention of its effects on people of color. In recent months specific attention has been paid to the "new" phenomenon of heterosexuals with AIDS or "heterosexual AIDS." This terminology is used without the slightest mention that among Haitians and extensively in Africa, AIDS was never a disease confined to homosexuals.

The assumption in reports about the spread of AIDS to heterosexuals is that these heterosexuals are white—read that as white, middle-class, non-drug-using, sexually-active people. The facts are that there are very few cases of AIDS among this group. As many as 90 percent of the cases of AIDS among heterosexuals are black and Hispanic. In many media reports blacks and Hispanics with AIDS are lumped in the i.v. drug users group. What the media has picked up on is that heterosexual transmission in the US now endangers middle class whites.

A good example of the mainstream media approach is an article by Kate Leishman in the February, 1987 issue of *Atlantic Monthly*. She writes that most Americans, even liberals, have the attitude that AIDS is the result of immoral behavior. Leishman lists the statistics on heterosexual transmission of AIDS at the beginning of her article. Fifteen pages later the following information appears:

> In the case of sexually active gay men [AIDS] is a tragedy—as it is for poor black and Hispanic youths, among whom there is a nationwide epidemic of venereal disease, which is a certain cofactor in facilitating transmission of HIV. This combination with the pervasive use of drugs among blacks and Hispanics ensures that the epidemic will hit them hardest next.[11]

Her first explicit mention of people of color describes them as a group that uses drugs extensively, and as also riddled with venereal disease (a fact she does not support with any data). The image is one of the "unregenerate young street tough" that causes all the trouble in our cities, in short the conventional racist stereotype of black and Hispanic youth displayed in the press almost every day. Her use of the word tragedy because of the risk to blacks, Hispanics and gays is gratuitous at best. The main focus of the article is the risk of AIDS to white heterosexuals and the need for them to face their fears of AIDS so they can effectively change their behavior.

In a passage reminiscent of 19th century physicians' moral advice she notes the problems associated with changing people's behavior and promoting safe sex, and wonders if one can draw any lessons for heterosexual behavior from the gay male experience.

> Many people believe that the intensity or quality of homosexual drives is unique, while others argue that the ability to control sexual impulses varies extraordinarily within groups of any sexual preference.[12]

What I find striking in this passage is that there is still debate over whether certain "groups" of people have the same ability to exercise control over their sexual behavior and drives as "normal" white heterosexuals do. The passage also suggests that white heterosexuals are still the only group who have the strength, the moral fortitude, the inherent ability if educated, to control their sexual and other behavior. After all, is this a disease about behavior and not viruses, right? Leishman doesn't interview any blacks or Hispanics about their fears of AIDS, or how they want to deal with it with respect to sexual practice or other behavior.

Two months later in May several letters to the editors of *Atlantic Monthly* appeared in response to Leishman's article. In particular one reader observed her omission of statistics about the risk of AIDS to blacks and Hispanics. She responded in a fairly defensive manner:

> My article and many others have commented on the high risk of exposure to AIDS among blacks and Hispanics. Mr. Patrick's observations that blacks and Hispanics already account for ninety per cent of the case load seems oddly to suggest that AIDS is on its way to becoming a disease of minorities. But the Centers for Disease Control has stressed that the overrepresentation of blacks and Hispanics in AIDS statistics is related not to race per se but to underlying risk factors.[13]

The risk factor she mentions is intravenous drug use. Leishman fails to deal with the "overrepresentation" of blacks and Hispanics in AIDS statistics. To mention our higher risk only implies that AIDS is a disease of minorities if you believe minorities are inherently different or behave differently in the face of the disease or if you believe that the disease will be confined to the minority community.

So pervasive is the association of race and i.v. drug use, that the fact that a majority of black and Hispanic men who have AIDS are gay or bisexual, and *non* i.v. drug users, has remained buried in statistics.[14] In the face of the statistics, *The New York Times* continues to identify i.v. drug use as the distinguishing mode of transmission among black and Hispanic men, by focusing not on the percentage of black and Hispanic AIDS cases that are drug related, but on the percentage of drug related AIDS cases that are black or Hispanic, which is 94%. This framework, besides blocking information that the black and Hispanic communities need, also functions to keep the white community's image "clean."

CONCLUSION

As this article goes to press, media coverage of the extent of AIDS in the black and Hispanic communities is increasing daily. These latest articles are covering the efforts in the black and Hispanic communities both to raise consciousness in these communities with respect to AIDS and to increase government funding to support culturally specific educational programs. Within the black community, the traditional source of leadership, black ministers, are now publicly expressing the reasons for their previous reluctance to speak out about AIDS. The reasons expressed tend to fall into the areas I have tried to discuss in this article, as indicated by the following comments that recently appeared in the *Boston Globe:*

> Although some black ministers described gays as the children of God and AIDS as just another virus, many more talked about homosexuality as sinful, including some who referred to AIDS as a God-sent plague to punish the sexually deviant.[15]
>
> There's a lot of fear of stigmatization when you stand up. . . . How does this label your church or the people who go to your church? said Rev. Bruce Wall, assistant pastor of Twelfth Baptist Church in Roxbury. Rev. Wall said ministers may also fear that an activist role on AIDS could prompt another question: 'Maybe that pastor is gay.'[16]

The arguments I have made as to the background of these kinds of comments continue to come out in the public discourse on AIDS and race in the national media. As the public discussion and press coverage has increased, one shift is apparent. The media is now focussing on why the black and Hispanic communities have not responded to AIDS before as a "problem" specific to these communities, while there is no acknowledgment that part of the problem is the way the media, the CDC, and the Public Health Service prevented race-specific information about AIDS from being widely disseminated. Or, to say it differently, there is no recognition of how the medical and media construction of AIDS as a "gay disease," or a disease of Haitians has affected the black and Hispanic communities.

Finally, as the black and Hispanic communities mobilize against AIDS, coalitions with established gay groups will be critical. To date, some in the black community have noted the lack of culturally specific educational material produced by these groups. Some gay groups are responding to that criticism. For progressives, feminists and gay activists, the AIDS crisis represents a crucial time when the work we have done on sexuality and sexual politics will be most needed to frame the fight against AIDS in political terms that move the politics of sexuality out of the background and challenge the repressive policies and morality that threaten not only the people with this disease but all of us.

FOOTNOTES

1. James H. Jones, *Bad Blood: The Tuskegee Syphilis Experiment* (New York: Free Press, 1981), p. 21.

2. *Ibid.*, p. 17.

3. *Ibid.*, p. 23.

4. *Ibid.*, p. 48.

5. "High AIDS Rate Spurring Efforts for Minorities," *New York Times*, Sunday, August 2, 1987.

6. *Mother Jones*, Vol. 12, May 1987.

7. *Ebony*, April, 1987, p. 128, quoting a Los Angeles AIDS expert.

8. *Ibid.*, p. 130.

9. *Essence*, June 1987.

10. John Jacob, President, National Urban League, *New York Times*, Sunday, August 2, 1987.

11. *Atlantic Monthly*, February 1987, p. 54.

12. *Ibid.*, p. 40.

13. *Atlantic Monthly*, May 1987, p. 13.

14. *New York Times*, Sunday, August 2, 1987.

15. *Boston Globe*, Sunday, August 9, 1987, p. 1.

16. *Ibid.*, p. 12.

INDIAN HUMOR   **38**

Vine Deloria

One of the best ways to understand a people is to know what makes them laugh. Laughter encompasses the limits of the soul. In humor life is redefined and accepted. Irony and satire provide much keener insights into a group's collective psyche and values than do years of research.

It has always been a great disappointment to Indian people that the humorous side of Indian life has not been mentioned by professed experts on Indian Affairs. Rather the image of the granite-faced grunting redskin has been perpetuated by American mythology.

People have little sympathy with stolid groups. Dick Gregory did much more than is believed when he introduced humor into the Civil Rights struggle. He enabled non-blacks to enter into the thought world of the black community and experience the hurt it suffered. When all people shared the humorous but ironic situation of the black, the urgency and morality of Civil Rights was communicated.

The Indian people are exactly opposite of the popular stereotype. I sometimes wonder how anything is accomplished by Indians because of the apparent overemphasis on humor within the Indian world. Indians have found a humorous side of nearly every problem and the experiences of life have generally been so well defined through jokes and stories that they have become a thing in themselves.

For centuries before the white invasion, teasing was a method of control of social situations by Indian people. Rather than embarrass members of the tribe publicly, people used to tease individuals they considered out of step with the consensus of tribal opinion. In this way egos were preserved and disputes within the tribe of a personal nature were held to a minimum.

Gradually people learned to anticipate teasing and began to tease themselves as a means of showing humility and at the same time advocating a course of action they deeply believed in. Men would depreciate their feats to show they were not trying to run roughshod over tribal desires. This method of behavior served to highlight their true virtues and gain them a place of influence in tribal policy-making circles.

Humor has come to occupy such a prominent place in national Indian affairs that any kind of movement is impossible without it. Tribes are being brought together by sharing humor of the past. Columbus jokes gain great sympathy among all tribes, yet there are no tribes extant who had anything to do with Columbus. But the fact of white invasion from which all tribes have suffered has created a common bond in relation to Columbus jokes that gives a solid feeling of unity and purpose to the tribes.

The more desperate the problem, the more humor is directed to describe it. Satirical remarks often circumscribe problems so that possible solutions are drawn from the circumstances that would not make sense if presented in other than a humorous form.

Often people are awakened and brought to a militant edge through funny remarks. I often counseled people to run for the Bureau of Indian Affairs in case of an earthquake because nothing could shake the BIA. And I would watch as younger Indians set their jaws, determined that they, if nobody else, would shake it. We also had a saying that in case of fire call the BIA and they would handle it because they put a wet blanket on everything. This also got a warm reception from people.

Columbus and Custer jokes are the best for penetration into the heart of the matter, however. Rumor has it that Columbus began his journey with four ships. But one went over the edge so he arrived in the new world with only three. Another version states that Columbus didn't know where he was going, didn't know where he had been, and did it all on someone else's money. And the white man has been following Columbus ever since.

It is said that when Columbus landed, one Indian turned to another and said, "Well, there goes the neighborhood." Another version has two Indians watching Columbus land and one saying to the other, "Maybe if we leave them alone they will go away." A favorite cartoon in Indian country a few years back showed a flying saucer landing while an Indian watched. The caption was "Oh, no, not again."

The most popular and enduring subject of Indian humor is, of course, General Custer. There are probably more jokes about Custer and the Indians than there were participants in the battle. All tribes, even those thousands of miles from Montana, feel a sense of accomplishment when thinking of Custer. Custer binds together implacable foes because he represented the Ugly American of the last century and he got what was coming to him.

Some years ago we put out a bumper sticker which read "Custer Died for Your Sins." It was originally meant as a dig at the National Council of

Churches. But as it spread around the nation it took on additional meaning until everyone claimed to understand it and each interpretation was different.

Originally, the Custer bumper sticker referred to the Sioux Treaty of 1868 signed at Fort Laramie in which the United States pledged to give free and undisturbed use of the lands claimed by Red Cloud in return for peace. Under the covenants of the Old Testament, breaking a covenant called for a blood sacrifice for atonement. Custer was the blood sacrifice for the United States breaking the Sioux treaty. That, at least originally, was the meaning of the slogan.

Custer jokes, however, can barely be categorized, let alone sloganized. Indians say that Custer was well-dressed for the occasion. When the Sioux found his body after the battle, he had on an Arrow shirt.

Many stories are derived from the details of the battle itself. Custer is said to have boasted that he could ride through the entire Sioux nation with his Seventh Calvary and he was half right. He got half-way through. . . .

The years have not changed the basic conviction of the Indian people that they are still dealing with the United States as equals. At a hearing on Civil Rights in South Dakota a few years ago a white man asked a Sioux if they still considered themselves an independent nation. "Oh, yes," was the reply, "we could still declare war on you. We might lose but you'd know you'd been in a terrible fight. Remember the last time in Montana?"

During the 1964 elections Indians were talking in Arizona about the relative positions of the two candidates, Johnson and Goldwater. A white man told them to forget about domestic policies and concentrate on the foreign policies of the two men. One Indian looked at him coldly and said that from the Indian point of view it was all foreign policy.

The year 1964 also saw the emergence of the Indian vote on a national scale. Rumors reached us that on the Navajo reservation there was more enthusiasm than understanding of the political processes. Large signs announced, "All the Way with LJB."

The current joke is that a survey was taken and only 15 percent of the Indians thought that the United States should get out of Vietnam. Eighty-five percent thought they should get out of America!

One of the most popular topics of Indian humor is the Bureau of Indian Affairs. When asked what was the biggest joke in Indian country, a man once said, "The BIA." During the years of termination, no matter how many tribes were being terminated the BIA kept adding employees. Since the thrust of termination was to cut government expenditures, the continual hiring of additional people led Indians to believe that such was not the real purpose. The rumor began that the BIA was phasing out Indians and would henceforth provide services only for its own employees. . . .

Perhaps the most disastrous policy, outside of termination, ever undertaken by the Bureau of Indian Affairs was a program called Relocation. It began as a policy of the Eisenhower administration as a means of getting Indians off the reservation and into the city slums where they could fade away.

Considerable pressure was put on reservation Indians to move into the cities. Reservation people were continually harassed by bureau officials until they agreed to enter the program. Sometimes the BIA relocation officer was so eager to get the Indians moved off the reservation that he would take the entire family into the city himself.

But the Indians came back to the reservation as soon as they learned what the city had to offer. Many is the story by BIA people of how Indians got back to the reservations before the BIA officials who had taken them to the city returned.

When the space program began, there was a great deal of talk about sending men to the moon. Discussion often centered about the difficulty of returning the men from the moon to earth, as re-entry procedures were considered to be very tricky. One Indian suggested that they send an Indian to the moon on relocation. "He'll figure out some way to get back." . . .

Not only the bureau, but other agencies, became the subject of Indian humor. When the War on Poverty was announced, Indians were justly skeptical about the extravagant promises of the bureaucrats. The private organizations in the Indian field, organized as the Council on Indian Affairs, sponsored a Capital Conference on Poverty in Washington in May of 1966 to ensure that Indian poverty would be highlighted just prior to the passage of the poverty program in Congress.

Tribes from all over the nation attended the conference to present papers on the poverty existing on their reservations. Two Indians from the plains area were asked about their feelings on the proposed program.

"Well," one said, "if they bring that War on Poverty to our reservation, they'll know they've been in a fight."

At the same conference, Alex Chasing Hawk, a nationally famous Indian leader from Cheyenne River and a classic storyteller, related the following tale about poverty.

It seemed that a white man was introduced to an old chief in New York City. Taking a liking to the old man, the white man invited him to dinner. The old chief hadn't eaten a good steak in a long time and eagerly accepted. He finished one steak in no time and still looked hungry. So the white man offered to buy him another steak.

As they were waiting for the steak, the white man said, "Chief, I sure wish I had your appetite."

"I don't doubt it, white man," the chief said. "You took my land, you took my mountains and streams, you took my salmon and my buffalo. You took everything I had except my appetite and now you want that. Aren't you ever going to be satisfied?" . . .

People are always puzzled when they learn that Indians are not involved in the Civil Rights struggle. Many expect Indians to be marching up and down like other people, feeling that all problems of poor groups are basically the same.

But Indian people, having treaty rights of long standing, rightly feel that protection of existing rights is much more important to them. Yet intra-group jokes have been increasing since the beginning of the Civil Rights movement and few Indians do not wryly comment on movements among the other groups.

An Indian and a black man were in a bar one day talking about the problems of their respective groups. The black man reviewed all of the progress his people had made over the past decade and tried to get the Indian inspired to start a similar movement of activism among the tribes.

Finally the black man concluded, "Well, I guess you can't do much, there are so few of you."

"Yes," said the Indian, "and there won't be very many of you if they decide to play cowboys and blacks."

Another time, an Indian and a black man were talking about the respective races and how they had been treated by the white man. Each was trying to console the other about the problem and each felt the other group had been treated worse.

The Indian reminded the black man how his people had been slaves, how they had not had a chance to have a good family life, and how they were so persecuted in the South.

The black man admitted all of the sufferings of his people, but he was far more eloquent in reciting the wrongs against the Indians. He reviewed the broken treaties, the great land thefts, the smallpox infected blankets given to the tribes by the English, and the current movement to relocate all the Indians in the cities, far from their homelands.

Listening to the vivid description, the Indian got completely carried away in remorse. As each wrong was recited he nodded sorrowfully and was soon convinced that there was practically no hope at all for his people. Finally he could stand no more.

"And do you know," he told the black man, "there was a time in the history of this country when they used to shoot us *just to get the feathers!*" . . .

Providing information to inquisitive whites has also proved humorous on occasion. . . . Louie Sitting Crow, an old timer from Crow Creek, South

Dakota, used to go into town and watch the tourists who traveled along Highway 16 in South Dakota to get to the Black Hills. One day at a filling station a car from New York pulled up and began filling its tank for the long drive.

A girl came over to talk with Louie. She asked him a great many questions about the Sioux and Louie answered as best he could. Yes, the Sioux were fierce warriors. Yes, the Sioux had once owned all of the state. Yes, they still wished for the old days.

Finally the girl asked if the Indians still scalped people. Louie, weary of the questions, replied, "Lady, remember, when you cross that river and head west, you will be in the land of the fiercest Indians on earth and you will be very lucky to get to the Black Hills alive. And you ask me if they still scalp. Let me tell you, it's worse than that. Now they take the whole head."

As Louie recalled, the car turned around and headed east after the tank was full of gas. . . .

One-line retorts are common in Indian country. Popovi Da, the great Pueblo artist, was quizzed one day on why the Indians were the first ones on this continent. "We had reservations," was his reply. Another time, when questioned by an anthropologist on what the Indians called America before the white man came, an Indian said simply, *"Ours."* A young Indian was asked one day at a conference what a peace treaty was. He replied, "That's when the white man wants a piece of your land."

The best example of Indian humor and militancy I have ever heard was given by Clyde Warrior one day. He was talking with a group of people about the National Indian Youth Council, of which he was then president, and its program for a revitalization of Indian life. Several in the crowd were skeptical about the idea of rebuilding Indian communities along traditional Indian lines.

"Do you realize," he said, "that when the United States was founded, it was only 5 percent urban and 95 percent rural and now it is 70 percent urban and 30 percent rural?"

His listeners nodded solemnly but didn't seem to understand what he was driving at.

"Don't you realize what this means?" he rapidly continued. "It means we are pushing them into the cities. Soon we will have the country back again."

Whether Indian jokes will eventually come to have more significance than that, I cannot speculate. Humor, all Indians will agree, is the cement by which the coming Indian movement is held together. When a people can laugh at themselves and laugh at others and hold all aspects of life together without letting anybody drive them to extremes, then it seems to me that people can survive.

SALSA MUSIC AS A CULTURAL EXPRESSION OF LATINO CONSCIOUSNESS AND UNITY

39

Felix M. Padilla

> *In spite of the conditions of the period,*
> *we're living in good times*
> *because the borders are falling . . .*
> *Our races sing together*
> *with [Latin] American affection.*
> *Our land is fighting*
> *and everyone gives a hand . . .*
> *from Mexico to the Congo, brother*
> *because I'm a Latin American [Latino Americano] and I'm proud.*
>
> (Colon & Miranda, 1980)

The rising awareness described by these two Puerto Rican musicians is part of a political awakening that has been experienced in recent years by Spanish-speaking people in the United States. More and more, members of these groups are coming to the realization that although their distinct nationalities and cultural traditions often set them apart in some matters, there are others that tend to unify them. In those cases giving rise to manifestations of the latter type, thoughts, ideas, and actions are defined from the perspective of a "Latino-conscious bond of identification and unity." For Spanish-speaking people in the United States, Latino consciousness has come to represent a growing awareness of identification with a bond or frame that embraces their shared realities. Thus, in addition to their traditional national and cultural ties and affiliations as individual Mexican Americans, Puerto Ricans, Cubans, or others, the Latino bond is an embodiment of particular social and historical realities Spanish-speaking people share with one another (Padilla, 1985). It is precisely this emerging wide-scale bond of Latino identification and unity that represents the focus of this study. In general terms, the article aims to emphasize the Latino-specific cultural elements found in the work of a

From: *Hispanic Journal of Behavioral Science* 11 (February 1989): 28–45. Reprinted by permission of Sage Publications, Inc.

particular group of cultural artists as a way to highlight different ideas of Latino consciousness and unity being proposed and advanced today. Specifically, the article examines those ideas used by performers of contemporary, popular "Salsa music," originally a New York-Puerto Rican style, in the lyrics of their music for describing certain realities of Spanish-speaking people in Latino terms.

The lyrical content analysis is employed here to represent a distinct avenue through which the following two interconnected questions can be pursued: (1) What are some of the cultural elements of Latino-shared realities delineated by Salsa musicians? (2) Which are the particular social and historical experiences that serve to inform Salsa musicians of a Latino universe that they view to be wider in scope than the groups' individual national and cultural experiences? . . .

The data for this study are drawn from the January 1975 through June 1982 monthly charts of *Billboard*'s top Latin LPs. A total of 501 LPs were reported in these charts for the seven-year period under investigation, of which 20% contained at least one song classified as Latino related. Information and impressions gathered for this study come from two other sources: (1) several interviews I conducted with a Latin music record collector from New York; and (2) a thorough review of available secondary sources, including, in particular, the *New York Latin Magazine*—Salsa music's leading and most popular magazine.

. . . Salsa is created out of the interplay between the economic interests and visions of owners of the Latin music recording industry and the cultural creativity of musicians. Of course, the conflict and resistance implied in this dialectic take place within asymmetrical relations of power that always favor the dominant class, but the essential point is that the lyrical content of Salsa represents a social process through which musicians constantly interact with, shape, and respond to objective forces that represent aspects of the broader social structure of the Latin music recording business and these structures are seen as possessing both enabling and constraining elements that determine and shape the music.

SALSA: A DISTINCTIVE MUSIC FORM

Loosely translated, the word *Salsa* stands for "spice"; literally, it means "sauce." In cultural terms, Salsa is often thought of as Latin essence, much as the word "soul" has been used by black Americans (Baron, 1977, p. 217). As a music expression, Salsa was first used in the mid-1960s by Joe Cuba's Sextet, a New York-based Puerto Rican group in their song, "Salsa y Bembe." Since then, Salsa has come to represent "the force of life that modifies a musician's thoughts and feelings into tones and lyrics" (Ortiz, 1976, p. 25).

Though two traditional Cuban musical elements came to form the basic structural composition and rhythmic arrangement of Salsa, as a music style, its initial creation is distinctively New York-Puerto Rican (Roberts, 1979; Rondon, 1980; Singer, 1982). Salsa was established as a music form in the late 1960s-early 1970s by a group of Puerto Rican musicians whose aim was to create a cultural sound distinctively representative of their New York *barrio* (neighborhood) experience. As such, the musical and cultural foundation of Salsa also incorporated a great deal of early Puerto Rican music styles from the Island as well as others that derived from the social cultural realities of Puerto Rican people in New York.

Indeed, Salsa emerged as the music of *barrio* people—an entertaining, dancing style that also carried a heavily politicized lyrical component, filled with themes and messages concerning the everyday happenings and plight of Puerto Rican people. In fact, the most distinguishing characteristic of Salsa is that the words of the songs are just as essential to the music as its rhythmic dancing sounds. Earlier Latin music, such as the rumba, mambo, and chacha-cha, which were geared primarily to dancing audiences, tended to assign little significance to their lyrical contents. This is also true of Salsa, however, the communication of verbal messages is a major component of the music. . . .

Many unsuccessful attempts were made to "crossover" or Americanize Salsa music (Gurza, 1977; Williams, 1975b), some of which are still being tried in vain today (Fernandez, 1984). It became clearly apparent that the Spanish-language element of the music, as well as its "Hispanic cultural base," pointed toward Central and South America, the Caribbean, and the Spanish-speaking communities in the United States as the most appropriate markets for the dissemination of Salsa music. Thus shortly after its creation as a Puerto Rican ethnic-specific style, a process was undertaken to diversify the Salsa music style, incorporating it into the popular cultures of other Spanish-speaking people. This process, defined here as the "Latinizing" of Salsa, was led by Fania Records that, by this time, held undisputed control over the Latin music recording business (Lopez, 1977, p. 37).

. . . To Fania, the Latinizing of Salsa came to mean homogenizing the product, presenting an all-embracing "Pan-American" or Latino sound with which people from all of Latin American and Spanish-speaking communities in the United States could identify and purchase. . . .

Salsa musicians appeared to have been in agreement with Fania's visions in terms of Latinizing Salsa. They certainly aspired to make a name for themselves the world over. They, too, saw the potential financial rewards behind an international Latino sound. For example, in an interview Willie

Colon, a leading Salsa performer, was asked, "Now that you are arriving at a new stage with your music, do you still consider it somewhat Salsa-like?" to which he responded: "Yes, I do . . . I want to reach Chile, Argentina, reach out to the whole world. As a Puerto Rican, I want to travel through the world and show that this type of music is from people who feel and also think" (Cordova-Ferrer, 1985, p. 37).

For Salsa musicians the Latinizing of Salsa carried another major significance. It came to represent more than just a Pan-American or Latino entertaining, dancing sound—it became a medium through which the different Latino life circumstances could be spoken to. Like the lyrical content of Puerto Rican Salsa, some musicians continued using the songs of their Latino Salsa sound to speak directly to the social, cultural, economic, and political experiences of Latinos as a group. What follows is an examination of the lyrical content of Salsa, emphasizing how musicians speak to the question of Latino consciousness.

CULTURAL MARKERS OF LATINO CONSCIOUSNESS

Identification with the Homeland

The variety of Salsa songs is wide. There are love songs (happy and unhappy romance songs), friendship songs, songs about music, songs of humor, nonsense songs, and others. In discussing the correspondence between Salsa music and Latino consciousness, we've examined exclusively those songs we've labeled "Latino political songs." Latino political songs refer to those songs in which its lyrics carry a very clear political message, involving Spanish-speaking people in a powerful shared experience and thereby making them more aware of themselves and their responsibilities toward each other as Latinos.

To some Salsa singers, the Latino bond is largely a loose configuration of ideas and sentiments as well as aspirations commonly shared by Spanish-speaking groups, though they live in different urban environments and experiences. The basis of Latino consciousness and unity appears universally to be predicated upon the perception of "real or symbolic" cultural features bestowed by people who speak the same language and share or come from the same "homeland." This "we-feeling" as Latinos refers to a "primordialized" attachment to Latin America. In other words, Salsa singers stress that there are some "ready-made" or "inherited" set of endowments and identifications said to be "naturally" shared by the various Spanish-speaking populations and responsible for connecting them to Latin America—their homeland. In addition, these singers share the view that the homeland or past events are essential in present day Latino identity. That is, the determination to restore continuity with the past is of great significance insofar as making the contemporary Latino reality coherent and meaningful.

In "*Antillana Soy*" (I'm Antillian), recorded with *La Sonora Poncena* of Puerto Rico in 1979, Celia Cruz, a Cuban female who for the last twenty years has been one of the leading and more popular performers in the Latin music industry, advances this view very clearly. Although suggestive of a "narrow" Latino identity among the people of the Antilles, the point Celia Cruz tries to make is, nevertheless, applicable to the larger Spanish-speaking universe:

> *Because I feel so Antillian, they've been asking*
> *me for a definition.*
> *And it's impossible to say that I feel, that I*
> *belong to one of them*
> *because Borinquen [Puerto Rico], Cuba, and Quisqueya [Santo*
>   *Domingo]*
> *are one in my heart.*
>
> *There shouldn't be separation.*
> *There cannot be definition.*

This sense of a natural affinity with Latin America is captured once again by Celia Cruz in "*Latinos en Estados Unidos*" (Latinos in the United States). In this song, in which she teamed with Willie Colon, to record in 1981, Celia Cruz creates a Latino bond out of their shared Latin America's historical forebears:

> *Simon Bolivar, Sarmientos, Benito Juarez, Marti,*
> *They left a great beginning for the road to follow.*
> *We should set an example with solidarity.*
> *I'm Latin American, don't be afraid to say it,*
> *For we're all brothers in a different country.*

Celia Cruz closes out the song by driving home this idea even more deeply:

> *We are brothers, it's good to say.*
> *Don't discriminate against your brothers;*
> *whenever you can*
> *offer him your hand.*
> *Latin America, you live in me,*
> *I want this message to reach you,*
> *We must unite so that you can see that we're united;*
> *We'll win the fight.*

Like Celia Cruz, Ruben Blades, a Panamanian lawyer-singer-composer who is perhaps the industry's most recognized performer to the larger American public, has recorded extensively on the idea of a natural attachment to Latin America. . . .

These and other singers seem to be in agreement that the untiring desire for social equality in the United States among Spanish-speaking ethnics (one of the leading topics consistently found in the lyrics of Salsa songs and to be discussed below) should not preclude the validity of and identification with their homeland. To them the Latin American heritage (perhaps the most symbolic dimension of Latino unity and consciousness) becomes a fructifying source of the creative endeavor on the part of Spanish-speaking groups. Just as important is the revelation that this international, global definition of a "Latino people" is intimately related to the view that Latino identification has much to do with defending the originality of their way of life and the dignity of their shared Latin American culture. In its deepest psychological sense, the Latino frame is a sense of self-worth and respect.

The need to affirm the essential human dignity of Spanish-speaking people is well conveyed in several of Ruben Blade's songs. So as not to confuse the meaning of Latin American dignity and pride, in *"Plastico"* (Plastic) recorded in 1978 with Willie Colon, Blades, first, shows how different the American way of life is to that which he advances:

> It was a plastic city, like those I don't want to see
> with cancerous buildings and a tinsel heart
> Where, instead of a sun, a Dollar rises, where no one laughs, where
>   no one cries
> with people with Polyester faces, who listen without hearing and
>   watch without seeing
> people who sold their reason for being and their freedom, for comfort.

The message Blades has to offer Latinos, then, is not to sell their dignity as a people for, what he perceives as, a superficial life-style. He tells them to seek truth and what is right, to work hard, and to be proud of their "race" and to reject foreign inventions:

> Listen, Latino, brother, friend—never sell your future for gold or
>   comfort
> Learn, study, we have a long way to go—always ahead,
> so we can end together the ignorance that keeps us trapped,
> the imported models that aren't the solution
> Don't let yourself get confused—seek the depth and its meaning
> Remember [in America]—you see the faces, but never the heart. . . .

Music and the Latino Identity

Music, itself, represents another leading cultural feature attributed to Latino consciousness and identity by some Salsa musicians. In other words, some Salsa musicians believe that the distinctiveness of a Latino bond is reflected in a commonly shared musical traditional. Like in the case with the "Latin American heritage" discussed above, music has been accorded symbolic significance. It has become mythologized and marked as a defining cultural characteristic of Latino consciousness and unity.

The Latino unifying force of music is quite evident in several of Celia Cruz's songs. Her *"Antillana Soy"* makes clear that the Antille nations share "one rhythm, very much ours: one song excites us" *(bailamos con un compas muy nuestro; nos emociona un mismo son)*. In "Come Down to Miami" (1981), she stresses how *el son* of Cuba, which lives on in Miami, belongs to all:

> *I always think of the Hispanics that live in New York*
> *riding subways, suffering cold and heat*
> *I don't know why they don't come to this, the land of the sun*
> *that looks like my Cuba, with its palm trees and music.*

"Americano Latino" (Latin American), a song by Ismael Miranda, one of Puerto Rico's leading Salsa singers, recorded with Willie Colon in 1980, describes Jamaicans dancing to the Cuban rumba and Venezuelan bomba sung by Puerto Rican voices—suggestive of a "show of Latino unity." In his, *"Me Voy Pa' Colombia"* (I'm Going to Colombia, 1973), Miranda speaks of a Latino unity that derives completely from their common music tradition. "Throughout Latino America," says the song, "the same rhythms, instruments, melodies, and even lyrics unite the people's cultures.". . .

Survival and Injustices

The experiences of survival and injustices shared by some Spanish-speaking groups in American society have been forged together by Salsa singers as another basis for Latino consciousness and unity. In *Juancito* (Little Johnny, 1979), Willie Colon details the everlasting exploitation of Latino workers in New York City—a city filled with so much prosperity and, at the same time, so much hypocrisy and inequality when it comes to Latinos. In a similar way, Celia Cruz speaks of the *"La Tierra Prometida"* (Promised Land, 1982) as nothing more than a dream:

In that precious land, borders aren't known
there is no discrimination of religion or race
it's just one nation
that embraces humanity.
That's why I tell everyone let's go there,
that in that land eternal happiness is enjoyed.
What pain it causes me to tell you
that this land never existed.
I only invented it to hide my pain
I invented that land.
The land I promised never existed
I invented it from a dream I had.

For the Conjunto Clasico, survival and injustice are also essential for describing the Latino way of life. In *"Somos Iguales"* (We are Equals, 1984), the message of this Puerto Rican group is to the point:

If, no one is better than others, according to the land,
why is it that we cannot live?

In *"Pablo Pueblo"* (Peter People, 1979), from another of his many recordings with Willie Colon, Ruben Blades conveys the story of a poor man, attempting to survive in New York City. Although this man "votes in the elections" and even buys lottery tickets, his family suffers from hunger and he cannot support them. His heart and soul are heavy each day as he walks home from the factory, wondering when it will all end:

He reaches the patio, pensive and with his head hung
and his poor man's silence, with the shouts from below
The clothing there on the balcony, the wind is drying it
he hears thunder in the sky, and the sky is getting misty
He enters the room and stands looking at his wife and at his children
     and
he asks himself, "how long?"
Like the way he patches his threadbare dreams with hope,
he makes from hunger a pillow and he lies down with a tired soul.

Unity

Another important symbolic cultural element used in their ideological expression of Latino consciousness and identity by some Salsa singers is that of unity. The appealing symbolism of a unified "Latino population" gives Salsa singers reasons to believe that this dimension can carry the weight necessary to bring these different groups together under one Latino frame. The chorus of *"Latinos en Estados Unidos"* is *"vamos a unirnos"* (let's unite). *"Fuerza Gigante"* says, *"de ver a mi gente unida, eso sera monumento"* (seeing all my people united will be monumental). It was indicated earlier that in "Come Down to Miami," Celia Cruz invites all "Latinos" to join her in the "land of the sun, that is so like my Cuba with its palm trees and music *(la tierra del sol que se parece a mi Cuba son su palmeras y son)*.

It's not surprising to discover that the underlying motive for unification lies with the assumption of a better life for "Latinos." As a "united front, Latinos will be able to get ahead in urban America." A consolidation of their political power will bring about a better future. More specifically, Latino unity may not be easily accomplished, though the political and economic rewards may be substantial—common interests may express the need to unify for mutual benefit. *"Fuerza Gigante"* speaks directly to this point, emphasizing that with a "great force" Latinos will get ahead (*poder echar pa'lante*). *"Plastico"* also speaks of getting ahead, not just as individuals, but as a group—*"siembre hacia adelante para juntos terminar"* (always forward to finish together).

Another goal of Latino unity seems to be a desire to engender respect for Latinos. *"Latinos en Estados Unidos"* points this out when it says, *"al pueblo respetan y le dan valor"* (a unified people will be respected and given value). *"Tiburon"* (Shark, 1980), by Ruben Blades, is all about respect for national boundaries and flags. *"Tiburon"* also speaks of unity as a way to save individual countries from U.S. imperialism, *"Pa' que no se coma nuestro hermano El Salvador"* (so that our brother El Salvador doesn't get eaten up).

But how is unity (the taking-on of a Latino-conscious frame and behavior) to be achieved among Spanish-speaking groups? In direct contrast to those who view Latino identity as given or as ready-made, there are other singers whose songs reflect a recognition that much hard work and time will be necessary. These singers regard Latino unity as an evolving bond, resulting from a formative process in which common matters and goals are identified and defined, but also resolved by the various "interacting groups." In other words, Latino group life necessarily presupposes interaction between group members from different Spanish-speaking populations. The Latino phenomenon occurs predominantly in the relation between the various groups. In *"Fuerza Gigante,"* Ray Barreto recognizes that actual multigroup interaction is of vital importance for the success of the "Latino struggle." He speaks of "years of involvement, struggle, and triumph," with many more to come. The very title of the song suggests the "giant force" needed to "be able to get ahead." In *"Plastico,"* Ruben Blades warns that "we have a lot left to do" *(nos falta andar bastante)*. In a more recent recording, Blades calls upon Spanish-speaking people to become directly active in the pursuit of common interests and goals by suggesting that they *Move On* (Muevete, 1984). He closes out this song with a strong call for Latino participation or interaction that would benefit all:

Everyone looks for comfort, and it's been this way all our lives
he who goes ahead never looks behind to help those who tell him
but the day comes when it's necessary to follow a different path
Come, give us your hand to end evil
you owe the future to the people.

In a similar way, El Gran Combo de Puerto Rico, one of the most widely known Salsa bands the world-over, advances this idea in their *"Prosigue"* (Carry-On) recorded in 1985:

He walks and walks without finding direction
He doesn't have anyone in the world who will give him a hand
The one who said he was his brother came and turned his back on him
Loneliness accompanies him—it is his destiny.

Carry on,
to stop would be to give up
and that can't happen.
He who doesn't walk doesn't arrive
if what you're living is a prison sentence
one day you'll finish your term
You have to carry on
He who doesn't walk doesn't arrive.

In general, Salsa singers tend to define Latino consciousness and unity as a gestalt of factors that predisposes those sharing it to act in a certain matter under specified conditions. The singers tend to count on a wide variation of cultural markers that are real, symbolic, or mythical, most important, they provide Spanish-speaking people with examples and reasons for unifying their effort under one Latino frame. In the main, we have seen how the lyrical content of some Salsa songs have played (and most likely will continue to play) a significant role in aiding with the rise and spread of Latino consciousness and unity. . . .

REFERENCES

Baron, R. (1977). Syncretism and ideology: Latin New York Salsa musicians. *Western Folklore, 36,* 209–225.

Barreto, R. (1980). Fuerza gigante. *Fuerza gigante.* New York: Fania Records.

Blades, R. (1978). Maria Lionza. *Willie Colon and Ruben Blades' siembra.* New York: Fania Records.

Blades, R. (1978). Plastico. *Siembra*. New York: Fania Records.

Blades, R. (1979). Pablo Pueblo. *The last fight*. New York: Fania Records.

Blades, R. (1980). Tiburon. *Tiburon*. New York: Fania Records.

Blades, R. (1984). Todos veulven. *Buscando America*. New York: Elektra/Asylum Records.

Blades, R. (1985). Muevete. *Escenas*. New York: Elektra/Asylum Records.

Carey, J. T. (1969, May). Changing courtship patterns in the popular song. *American Journal of Sociology*, 74, 720–731.

Colon, W. (1979). Juancito. *Willie Colon Solo*. New York: Fania Records.

Colon, W., & Miranda, I. (1980). *Doble energia*. New York: Lo Mejor Records.

Conjunto Clasico. (1979). Somos Iguales. *Los Rodriguez*. New York: Lo Mejor.

Cordova-Ferrer, J. (1985, April). A conversation with Willie Colon. *Neustro Magazine*, 9, 36–38.

Cruz, C., & Poncena, S. (1979). Antillana soy. *Celia Cruz y La Sonora Poncena: La ceiba*. New York: VAYA Records.

Cruz, C., & Poncena, S. (1981). Come down to Miami. *Celia y Willie*. New York: VAYA Records.

Cruz, C., & Poncena, S. (1981). Latinos en Estados Unidos. *Celia y Willie*. New York: VAYA Records.

Cruz, C., & Poncena, S. (1982). Tierra prometida. *Celia Cruz Con La Sonora Matancera: Feliz Encuentro*. New York: Musica Latina International.

DiMaggio, P. (1977). Market structure, the creative process, and popular culture. *Journal of Popular Culture*, 11, 436–452.

El Gran Combo. (1985). Prosigue. *El Gran Combo: Innovations*. Santurce, Puerto Rico: Rico Records.

Fernandez, E. (1984, January 21). Crossover facing tough battle. *Billboard*, p. 52.

Gans, H. J. (1964). The rise of the problem film. *Social Problems*, 11, 327–336.

Gans, H. J. (1967). Popular culture in America: Social problems in a mass society or social asset in a pluralist society? In H. S. Becker (Ed.), *Social problems: A modern approach* (549–620). New York: John Wiley.

Gillett, C. (1973). *The sound of the city*. New York: Outerbridge & Dienstfrey.

Gurza, A. (1977, November 12). Salsa dance music. *Billboard*, 79, 82–83.

Hirsch, P. M. (1970). Sociological approaches to the pop music phenomenon. *American Behavioral Scientist, 14,* 371–388.

Leavitt, R. (1986). Somos el son. *Somos el son.* Santurce, Puerto Rico: Bronco Records.

Lopez, A. (1977, November 7). It don't mean a thing if it ain't got that clave. *Village Voice, 37,* 49–50.

Maisel, R. (1973). The decline of the mass media. *Public Opinion Quarterly, 37,* 59–70.

Miranda, I. (1973). Me voy pa' Colombia. *Ismael Miranda y su org. revelacion, asi se compone un son.* New York: Fania Records.

Miranda, I. (1980). Americano Latino. *Colon/Miranda: Doble energia.* New York: Fania Records.

Ortiz, R. (1976, March). The big business and cultural sides of Salsa music. *Billboard,* pp. 24–28.

Padilla, F. M. (1985). *Latino ethnic consciousness: The case of Mexican Americans and Puerto Ricans in Chicago.* Notre Dame, IN: University of Notre Dame Press.

Padilla, F. M. (1990). Salsa: Puerto Rican and Latino music. *Journal of Popular Culture, 24,* 87–104.

Peterson, R. A., & Berger, D. (1971). Entrepreneurship in organization: Evidence from the popular music industry. *Administrative Science Quarterly, 16,* 97–106.

Peterson, R. A., & Berger, D. (1975). Cycles in symbol production: The case of popular music. *American Sociological Review, 40,* 158–173.

Roberts, J. S. (1979). *The Latin tinge.* New York: Oxford University Press.

Rondon, C. M. (1980). *El libro de la Salsa; cronica de la musica del Caribe urbano.* Caracas, Venezuela: Editorial Arte.

Singer, R. L. (1982). My music is who I am and what I do: Latin popular music and identity in New York City. Unpublished Ph.D. dissertation, Indiana University.

Williams, J. (1975a, May 17). Latin taps soul for Salsa source. *Billboard,* pp. 1, 20.

Williams, J. (1975b, November 27). Latin dilemma, Sal Soul takes an unusual stance in selling product. *Billboard,* p. 55.

Education

EDUCATION AND THE STRUGGLE AGAINST RACE, CLASS, AND GENDER INEQUALITY

40

Roslyn Arlin Mickelson and Stephen Samuel Smith

INTRODUCTION

For the past thirty-five years, policymakers have claimed that federal education policies seek, among other things, to further equality among the races, between the sexes, and, to a much lesser extent, among social classes.[1] In this respect, educational policymakers have shared one of the assumptions that has long been part of the putative dominant ideology: a "good education" is *the* meal ticket. It will unlock the door to economic opportunity and thus enable disadvantaged groups or individuals to improve their lot dramatically. According to the dominant ideology, the United States is basically a meritocracy in which hard work and individual effort are rewarded, especially in financial terms. Related to this central belief are a series of culturally enshrined misconceptions about poverty and wealth. The central one is that poverty and wealth are the result of individual inadequacies or strengths rather than the results of the distributive mechanisms of the capitalist economy. A second misconception is the belief that everyone is the master of her

From: Berch Berberoglu (ed.), *Critical Perspectives In Sociology: A Reader* (Dubuque, Iowa: Kendall/Hunt Publishing, 1991). Copyright 1991 by Kendall/Hunt Publishing Company. Reprinted by permission of the author and the publisher.

or his own fate.[2] The dominant ideology assumes that American society is open and competitive, a place where an individual's status depends on talent and motivation, not inherited position. To compete, everyone must have access to education free of the fetters of family background or ascriptive factors like gender and race.[3] Since the middle of this century the reform policies of the federal government have been designed, at least officially, to enhance individuals' opportunities to acquire education.

We begin this essay by discussing the major educational doctrines and policies of the past thirty-five years that claim to have been aimed at promoting equality through greater equality of educational opportunity. This discussion includes the success and failures of programs such as school desegregation, compensatory education, Title IX, and job training. We then focus on the barriers such programs face in actually promoting equality. Here our point is that inequality is so deeply rooted in the structure and operation of the U.S. political economy that, at best, educational reforms can play only a limited role in ameliorating such inequality. Considerable evidence indicates that the educational system helps legitimate, if not actually reproduce, significant aspects of social inequality.

First, let us distinguish among equality, equality of opportunity, and equality of educational opportunity. The term *equality* has been the subject of extensive scholarly and political debate, much of which is beyond the scope of this essay. Most Americans reject equality of life conditions as a goal, because it would require a fundamental transformation of our basic economic and political institutions, a scenario most are unwilling to accept.[4] In the words of one observer, "So long as we live in a democratic capitalist society—that is, so long as we maintain the formal promise of political and social equality while encouraging the practice of economic inequality—we need the idea of equal opportunity to bridge that otherwise unacceptable contradiction."[5] The distinction between equality of opportunity and equality of outcome is important. Through this country's history, equality has most typically been understood in the former way. Rather than a call for the equal distribution of money, property, or many other social goods, the concern over equality has been with equal opportunity in pursuit of these goods. As Ralph Waldo Emerson put it: "The genius of our country has worked out our true policy—opportunity. Opportunity of civil rights, of education, of personal power, and not less of wealth; doors wide open."[6] To use a current metaphor: If life is a game, the playing field must be level; if life is a race, the starting line must be in the same place for everyone. For the playing field to be level, many believe education is crucial, giving individuals the wherewithal to compete in the allegedly meritocratic system. Thus equality of opportunity hinges on equality of educational opportunity.[7]

THE SPOTTY RECORD OF FEDERAL EDUCATIONAL REFORMS

In the past thirty-five years a series of educational reforms initiated at the national level has been introduced into local school systems. All of the reforms aimed to move education closer to the ideal of equality of educational opportunity. Here we discuss several of these reforms and how the evolution of the concept of equality of educational opportunity, spurred on by the Coleman Report, shaped many of these reforms during the past two decades. Given the importance of race and racism in American social history, many of the federal education policies during this period attempted to redress the most egregious forms of inequality based on race.

School Desegregation

Although American society has long claimed to be based on freedom, justice, and equality of opportunity, the history of race relations has long suggested the opposite. Perhaps the most influential early discussion of this disparity was Gunnar Myrdal's *An American Dilemma*, published in 1944, which vividly exposed the contradictions between the ethos of freedom, justice, equality of opportunity and the actual experiences of African Americans in the United States.[8] Segregated schools presented observers like Myrdal with direct evidence of the shallowness of American claims to equality for all.

The school desegregation movement, whose first phase culminated in the 1954 *Brown* decision outlawing de jure segregation in schools, was the first orchestrated attempt in U.S. history to directly address inequality of educational opportunity.[9] The links among desegregation, equality of educational opportunity, and the larger issue of equality of opportunity are very clear from the history of the desegregation movement. The NAACP strategically chose school segregation to be the camel's nose under the tent of Jim Crow society.[10] That one of the nation's foremost civil rights organizations saw the attack on segregated schools as the opening salvo in the battle against society-wide inequality indicates the pivotal role of education in the American belief system in promoting equality of opportunity.

Has desegregation succeeded? This is really two questions: First, have desegregation efforts integrated public schools? Second, have desegregation efforts enhanced students' educational opportunities? Since 1954 progress toward integrated education has been limited at best. As Hochschild notes, racial isolation has only diminished; it has not gone away. In 1968, 77 percent of African-American students were in schools with student bodies composed of predominantly nonwhite youths. By 1984, 64 percent of African

Americans were in such schools. Moreover, 70.5 percent of Hispanic students attend predominantly minority schools.[11] Furthermore, integrated schools are often resegregated at the classroom level by tracking or ability grouping. Since 1954 racial isolation has declined everywhere but the Northeast. Ironically, today the greatest degree of racial segregation occurs in the Northeast and the least is in the South.[12] The answer to the first question, then, is that desegregation policies have had only a limited effect on overall school integration.

Has desegregation helped to equalize educational outcomes nationwide? As Hochschild points out, a better question might be which desegregation programs under which circumstances accomplish which goals.[13] Where desegregation has succeeded, its effects have been for the most part positive.[14] Evidence from desegregation research suggests that, overall, minority and majority children benefit academically and socially from well-run programs. The city in which we live, Charlotte, North Carolina, is an example of one such success story.[15] Despite these limited but positive outcomes, in the last decade of the twentieth century, most American children attend schools segregated by race, ethnicity, and class. Consequently, thirty-five years of official federal interventions aimed at achieving equality of educational opportunity through school desegregation have not achieved that goal; children from different race and class backgrounds continue to receive significantly segregated and largely unequal educations.[16]

The Coleman Report

Based largely on the massive data introduced in the 1954 *Brown* desegregation case, which showed that resources in black and white schools were grossly unequal, Congress mandated in 1964 a national study of the "lack of availability of equality of educational opportunity for individuals due to race, color, religious, or national origin in public schools." The authors of the study, James Coleman and his associates, expected to find glaring disparities in educational resources available to African-American and white students and that these differences would explain the substantial achievement differences between white and minority students.[17]

Instead, the Coleman Report, released in 1966, produced some very unexpected findings. The researchers found that twelve years after *Brown*, most Americans still attended segregated schools but that the characteristics of black and white schools (such as facilities, books, labs, teacher experience, and expenditures) were surprisingly similar. Apparently, segregated Southern districts upgraded black educational facilities in the wake of the *Brown* decisions. More importantly, Coleman and his colleagues found that school resources had relatively little to do with variations in students' school performance. Instead, they found that family background influenced school achievement more than any other factor, including school characteristics.[18]

The effects of the last finding were dramatic. It deflected attention from how schools operate and instead focused public policy upon poor and minority children and their families as the ultimate sources of unequal school outcomes. Numerous observers concluded that schools were not primarily to blame for black-white educational differences, overlooking another Coleman Report finding that could implicate schools in inequality of educational outcomes. The overlooked finding showed that African-American and white achievement differences increased with every year of schooling. That is, the achievement gap between black and white first graders was much smaller than the gap between twelfth graders. This finding suggests that at best schools reinforce the disadvantages of race and class and at worst are themselves a major source of educational inequality.

Although published a quarter of a century ago, the Coleman Report remains one of the most important and controversial pieces of social research ever completed. One of its many lasting results was a redefinition of the concept of equality of educational opportunity because it made clear that greater inputs into schools were not associated with greater student achievement. No longer were financial inputs a satisfactory measure of equality of opportunity. Only to the extent that academic outcomes of achievement (how well a student performs in school) and attainment (how many years of education a student acquires) are equal can claims be advanced about the putative extent of equality of educational opportunity.[19]

Compensatory Education

A second lasting outcome of the Coleman Report was widespread support for compensatory education. Policymakers interpreted the finding that family background explains more of the variance in students' achievement than any other factor as evidence of "cultural deprivation" among poor and minority families. This notion was consistent with Oscar Lewis's then-popular thesis on the culture of poverty.[20] Such an interpretation of the Coleman Report gave impetus to an education movement to compensate for the alleged cultural deficiencies of non–middle class, nonwhite families so that when so-called disadvantaged children came to school they could compete without the handicap of their background.

Compensatory education refers to the many programs that began with the passage of the Elementary and Secondary Education Act in 1965. These programs target children who are both poor and underachieving and provide them with developmental preschool or a variety of individualized programs in math, reading, and language arts once they are in elementary school. The following are included under the compensatory education rubric:

- Early childhood education such as Head Start
- Follow Through, where Head Start children, now in elementary school, continue to receive special programs
- Bilingual education
- Chapter I (formerly called Title I), which provides language arts and math programs plus food, medicine, and clothing to needy children in primary schools
- Guidance and counseling in secondary schools
- Higher education programs designed to identify potential college students in high schools and special admissions, transition, and retention programs for qualified students going to college[21]

Compensatory education has a controversial history. Initially, critics from the left charged that the underlying premise of compensatory education, that poor and minority families were deficient relative to middle-class white families, was racist and elitist. Compensatory education's most famous critic on the right was Arthur Jensen. His 1969 article on IQ and scholastic achievement argued that compensatory education was a waste of time and money because the lower African-American achievement scores indicated that blacks were less intelligent than whites.[22] This criticism of compensatory education miscast the debate over poverty and education into one about race and education because it ignored the fact that many compensatory education students were white and most African-American children at the time did not participate in the programs.

Despite attacks like Jensen's and an initial absence of evidence that the programs accomplished any of their goals, the compensatory education movement survived the past twenty years. Recent research has begun to demonstrate both the cognitive and social benefits from compensatory education,[23] although the achievement gaps between minority and white and between working- and middle-class children remain. No doubt this is true in part because today only 18 percent of income-eligible students participate in the most famous and successful program, Head Start.[24] While the recent evidence regarding the effects of these programs continues to be positive, we must conclude that compensatory education, like integrated education, has not brought about equality of school outcomes.

Human Capital Theory and Job Training Programs

The notion that "good" education is *the* meal ticket has received theoretical exposition in human capital theory, which views education as a capital investment in human beings. Theodore Schultz, a University of Chicago economist, originally put forth this theory. He argued that "earnings, especially those of minority groups, reflect . . . inadequate investment in their health and education."[25] The social policies developed to remedy shortages in human capital among minority and working-class youth included job training programs like the Comprehensive Education and Training Act (CETA) and its successor, the Job Training and Partnership Act (JTPA). A central problem with both programs is that graduates have few if any jobs once the training is over.[26] The failure of both programs to eradicate inequality stems from the faulty premise that individual, not structural, factors are at the heart of poverty. The poor often have a great deal of skills and education. What they lack is available, well-paying jobs in which to invest their skills.[27] We elaborate on this crucial point later in this article.

These criticisms apply as well to more conventional high school vocational education programs. Vocational students tend to be disproportionately working class and minority, and the courses are highly segregated by gender. Vocational education classes in high school and community colleges are frequently tailored to local businesses' labor force requirements. Too often they train students in obsolete, narrow skills that are virtually useless once the student graduates from the educational program. Much of the recent corporate interest in school reform stems from the results of these processes.[28] The track record of job training programs (CETA and JTPA) and secondary school vocational education programs indicate human capital–based educational reforms do not, and cannot, narrow race, class, and gender differences in equality of educational opportunity in this society.

Title IX

Title IX is the primary federal law prohibiting sex discrimination in education. It states, "No person in the United States shall, on the basis of sex, be excluded from participation in, be denied benefit of, or be subjected to discrimination under any program or activity receiving Federal financial assistance." Until its passage in 1972, gender inequality in educational opportunity received minimal legislative attention. Title IX covers admissions quotas by sex, different courses, and athletic programs. It requires existing school programs be examined for gender-based discrimination and mandates equal treatment of all students in courses, financial aid, counseling services, and employment.[29]

Although Title IX was passed in 1972, it lacked implementing regulations until 1975. Nor was it ever accompanied by substantial federal or state financial assistance. Title IX was potentially damaged in February 1984, when the Supreme Court ruled in *Grove City College* v. *Bell* that coverage of Title IX was limited to programs and activities, rather than entire institutions, receiving federal money.[30] The effects of this ruling remain unclear.[31]

Sexism in education persists despite laws prohibiting it. Even though female achievement and attainment levels are comparable to those of males, many sexist practices remain an integral part of schooling at all levels. For example, curricular materials from kindergarten to college reveal a preponderance of male characters. In addition, male and female characters usually reflect traditional gender roles and behaviors. Although the gap is narrowing, women who graduate from high school are frequently less well prepared in college-level math and science than men are and consequently cannot enroll in math, science, engineering, or computer science courses in the same frequencies as men.[32] Vocational education at the high school and college level remains highly sex segregated. Administrators are overwhelmingly male although most teachers are female. Women in academia face barriers to promotion and continue to earn less than their male colleagues.[33]

Recent civil rights legislation fails to address any of these problems. Like the laws and policies aimed at eliminating race differences in school processes and outcomes, those aiming to eliminate gender differences in educational opportunities have, at best, only narrowed differences. Educational opportunity in the United States remains highly unequal for people of different gender, race, ethnic, and class backgrounds.

EQUALITY OF EDUCATIONAL OPPORTUNITY AND EQUALITY OF INCOME

The educational reforms intended to lessen inequality were not designed primarily to give all students access to better playgrounds, computers, books, teachers, and athletic facilities. Greater equality in the distribution of these resources was seen as a means to better equip minorities, women, and to a lesser extent, working-class whites to improve their chances in life once they become adults. Equality of educational opportunity, as noted earlier, was viewed as means of promoting equality of opportunity.

Whatever increase in the equality of educational opportunity has resulted from the reforms discussed earlier, it has not led to a significantly greater equality of life-chances, at least as measured by income, one of the most telling and broadest gauges of equality in the United States. Much of a person's social

standing depends on income because in a capitalist society income is related to all other forms of inequality. Although this measure does not address the social class basis of inequality, income is one useful and clear measure of inequality in this society.[34] In addition, the disjunction between the greater equality of educational opportunity and lack of a corresponding increase in the equality of incomes can be explained by the nature of the U.S. political economy. The main cause of income inequality is the structure and operation of U.S. capitalism, which have scarcely been affected by the educational reforms discussed earlier.

Several years after the publication of the landmark Coleman Report, Jencks and his associates reanalyzed the data on which it was based to explore the conventional wisdom that a "good education" was how disadvantaged individuals and groups could improve their economic situation. Their findings were published in a now famous book, *Inequality* (1972). Among its conclusions was the following:

> The evidence suggests that equalizing educational opportunity [achievement and attainment] would do very little to make adults more equal. . . . The experience of the past 25 years suggests that even fairly substantial reductions in the range of educational attainments do not appreciably reduce economic inequality among adults.[35]

Almost twenty years of educational reforms have elapsed since those remarks were made. Sadly, the evidence in support of that conclusion is stronger now than it was in 1972. Current statistics on educational and income attainment show that race and gender differences in educational achievement continue to narrow and differences in attainment have all but disappeared.[36] Nevertheless, race and gender differences in income remain stable over time (see Figures 1 and 2).

While race differences in educational attainment have virtually disappeared, and women attain slightly more education than men, both minorities and women remain "less equal" than men—that is, on average they earn significantly less income than white males with comparable educational credentials (see Figure 2). Equality of educational opportunity, indicated by years of attainment, simply has not produced anything resembling equality of income.

The greater equality of educational opportunity has not led to a corresponding increase in the equality of incomes because educational reforms do not create more good-paying jobs, affect sex-segregated and racially segmented occupational structures, or limit the mobility of capital either between regions of the country or between the United States and other countries. For example, no matter how good an education white working-class or minority

Figure 1.   Median Educational Attainment by Sex and Race, 1940–1987

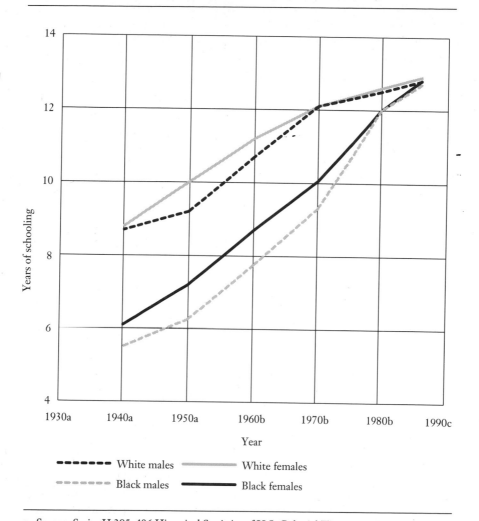

a. Source: Series H 395–406 Historical Statistics of U.S. Colonial Times to 1957. U.S. Dept. of Commerce. Bureau of the Census. Washington, D.C.: U.S. Government Printing Office.

b. Source: U.S. Census of Population 1960, 1970, 1980; Current Population Reports Series P-20 N. 403. U.S. Dept. of Commerce. Bureau of the Census. Washington, D.C.: U.S. Government Printing Office.

c. Source: Current Population Reports Series P-20 N. 428. U.S. Dept. of Commerce. Bureau of the Census. Washington, D.C.: U.S. Government Printing Office.

youth may receive, it does nothing to alter the fact that thousands of relatively good paying manufacturing jobs have left Northern inner cities for Northern suburbs, the Sunbelt, or foreign countries.[37] Perhaps service jobs are left in the wake of such capital flight or have been created in its place, but they pay less than manufacturing jobs. An economy in which McDonald's employs more people than USX Corporation (the former industrial giant U.S. Steel Corporation) is one in which the economic opportunities for minority and working-class youth are limited. Without changes in the structure and operation of the capitalist economy, educational reforms may enable some members of disadvantaged groups to improve their situation, but they cannot markedly improve the social and economic position of these groups in their entirety. This is the primary reason that educational reforms do little to affect the gross social inequalities that inspired them in the first place.

BEYOND ATTAINMENT: THE PERSISTENCE OF EDUCATIONAL INEQUALITY

Educational reforms have not led to greater equality for several additional reasons. Many aspects of school processes and curricular content are deeply connected to race, class, and gender inequality. But gross measures of educational outputs, such as median years of schooling completed, mask these indicators of inequality. The data in Figure 1 indicate that today African Americans as a group have attained essentially as much education as have whites as a group; the same is true for women compared to men. But aggregate data like these obscure gross differences in attainment within race and gender groups. These within-group differences are primarily linked to class and region. For example, in the 1980s children of black farmers averaged 8.65 years of educational attainment; children of black professionals averaged 13.97 years of schooling.[38] Similar differences by class exist for whites. Within-group differences demonstrate the extent to which educational opportunity remains inequitable. Despite significant within-group differences, the comparable median levels of educational attainment by race and gender can illustrate our theoretical point regarding the structural inability of increases in education to reduce income inequality. Were we to compare income by race and by gender for different levels of educational attainment, our argument would be even stronger. For any level of educational attainment, blacks earn less than whites with comparable levels of education and women earn less than men with similar credentials. Furthermore, the disparities in returns to education increase as levels of educational attainment increase.[39]

Figure 2.   Median Individual Earnings by Sex and Race, 1957–1987, in 1987 Constant Dollars

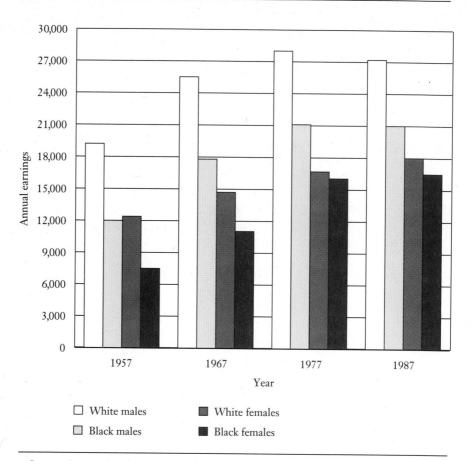

a. Source: Current Population Reports Series P-60 N. 162. U.S. Dept. of Commerce. Bureau of the Census. Washington, D.C.: U.S. Government Printing Office.

Another example of persistent inequality of educational opportunity is credential inflation. Even though women, minorities, and members of the working class now obtain higher levels of education than they did before, the most privileged in society gain even higher levels of education. At the same time, the educational requirements for the best jobs (those with the highest salaries, benefits, agreeable working conditions, autonomy, responsibility) are growing so that only those with the most education from the best schools are eligible for the best jobs. Because the more privileged are almost always in a better position to gain these desirable educational credentials, members of the working class, women, and minorities are still at a competitive disadvantage. Due to credential inflation, previous educational requirements for good jobs, now within the reach of many dispossessed groups, are inadequate and insufficient in today's labor market.[40]

Although gaps in educational attainment between males and females and between minorities and whites have narrowed (see Figure 1), not all educational experiences are alike. Four years of public high school in Beverly Hills are quite different from four years in an inner-city school.[41] Dreeben and Gamoran examined race differences in learning to read among first-grade children in the Chicago area. They concluded that the explanation for why nonblacks learned more than blacks rests, in part, in features of teacher instructional practices, which differ by school. Black children in their sample who attended minority schools were provided with less time in basal instruction—the core activity of primary school reading—and covered fewer new vocabulary words than did black and white children in either integrated or all white schools. The authors concluded, "Blacks learned less than nonblacks . . . mainly because of the instructional inadequacies prevailing in all-black schools."[42]

One additional aspect of these differences is what sociologists of education call the hidden curriculum, which refers to two separate but related processes. The first is that the content and process of education differ for children according to their race, gender, and class. The second is that these differences help reproduce the inequalities based on race, gender, and class that characterize U.S. society.

One aspect of the hidden curriculum is the formal curriculum's ideological content. Anyon's work on U.S. history texts demonstrates that children from more privileged backgrounds are more likely to be exposed to rich, sophisticated, and complex materials than are their working-class counterparts.[43] Another aspect of the hidden curriculum concerns the social organization of the school and the classroom. Some hidden curriculum theorists suggest that tracking, ability grouping, and conventional teacher-centered classroom interactions contribute to the reproduction of the social relations of production at the workplace. This perspective derives from the work of Bowles and Gintis; their seminal work, *Schooling in Capitalist America*, proposes that there is a correspondence among the social relations of the workplace, the home, and the school.[44] Lower-track classrooms are disproportionately filled with working-class and minority students. Students in lower tracks are more likely than those in higher tracks to be assigned repetitive exercises at a very low level of cognitive challenge. Lower-track students are likely to work individually and to lack classroom experience with problem solving or other independent, creative activities.[45] Such activities are more conducive to preparing students for working-class jobs than for professional and managerial positions. Many proponents of the correspondence principle argue that educational experiences from preschool to high school differentially prepare students for their ultimate positions in the work force, and a student's placement in various school programs is based primarily on her or his race and class origin.[46] The correspondence principle has sometimes been applied in too deterministic and mechanical a fashion.[47] Nonetheless, in certain cases, it is a compelling contribution to explanations of how and why school processes and outcomes are so markedly affected by the race, gender, and class of students. . . .

CONCLUSION

In this chapter we have argued that educational reforms cannot eliminate inequality. But education remains important to any struggle to reduce inequality. Moreover, it is more than a meal ticket; it is intrinsically worthwhile. Desegregation, compensatory education, Title IX, and bilingual education all facilitate cognitive growth and promote important nonsexist, nonracist attitudes and practices; they make schools a more humane place for adults and children. Furthermore, education, even reformist liberal education, contains the seeds of individual and social transformation. Those of us committed to the struggle against inequality cannot be paralyzed by the structural barriers that make it impossible for education to eliminate inequality. We must look upon the schools as arenas of struggle. To do otherwise would be to concede what must be contested in every way.

ENDNOTES

1. This essay draws on an article by Roslyn Arlin Mickelson that appeared as "Education and the Struggle Against Race, Class, and Gender Inequality," *Humanity and Society* 11, no. 4 (1987), pp. 440–464. The authors thank Kevin Hawk for his technical assistance in the preparation of the graphs.

2. R. H. deLone, *Small Futures* (New York: Harcourt Brace Jovanovich, 1979). Ascertaining whether a set of beliefs constitutes the dominant ideology in a particular society or social formation involves a host of difficult theoretical and empirical questions. For this reason we use the term *putative dominant ideology*. For discussions of these questions, see Nicholas Abercrombie et al., *The Dominant Ideology Thesis*

(London: George Allen & Unwin, 1980); James C. Scott, *Weapons of the Weak* (New Haven: Yale University Press, 1985); Stephen Samuel Smith, "Political Acquiescence and Beliefs about State Coercion" (unpublished Ph.D. dissertation, Stanford University, 1990).

3. Whether racism and sexism are epiphenomena is too large an issue to address in this article. We take the position that the logic of capitalism breeds sexism and racism, but that both have a quasi-independent cultural history and are therefore important social phenomena in their own right (see C. A. Mackinnon, "Feminism, Marxism, Method, and the State: An Agenda for Theory," in N. O. Keohane et al. (eds.), *Feminist Theory* (Chicago: University of Chicago Press, 1981).

4. Kevin Dougherty, "After the Fall: Research on School Effects Since the Coleman Report," *Harvard Educational Review* 51, no. 2 (1981), pp. 301–308.

5. Jennifer L. Hochschild, "The Double-Edged Sword of Equal Educational Opportunity." Paper presented at the meeting of the American Education Research Association, Washington, D.C., April 22, 1987.

6. Douglas Rae, *Equalities* (Cambridge, Mass.: Harvard University Press, 1981), p. 64.

7. C. J. Hurn, *The Limits and Possibilities of Schooling* (Boston: Allyn and Bacon, 1978).

8. G. Myrdal, *An American Dilemma: The Negro Problem and Modern Democracy* (New York: Harper & Row, 1944).

9. R. Kluger, *Simple Justice* (New York: Knopf, 1975).

10. Ibid.

11. E. B. Fiske, "Integration Lags in Public Schools," *New York Times*, July 26, 1987, pp. 1, 24–25.

12. J. L. Hochschild, *The New American Dilemma* (New Haven: Yale University Press, 1984).

13. Ibid.

14. Jomills H. Braddock II, Robert L. Crain, and James M. McPartland, "A Long-Term View of School Desegregation: Some Recent Studies of Graduates as Adults," in Jeanne H. Ballantine (ed.), *Schools and Society* (Mountain View, Calif.: Mayfield, 1989), pp. 303–313; Robert L. Crain et al., *Making Desegregation Work* (Cambridge, Mass.: Ballinger, 1982); Hochschild, *New American Dilemma;* Charles V. Willie, *Desegregation Plans That Work* (Westport, Conn.: Greenwood Press, 1984).

15. Frye Gaillard, *The Dream Long Deferred* (Chapel Hill: University of North Carolina Press, 1989).

16. Fiske, "Integration Lags."

17. J. Karabel and A. H. Halsey, *Power and Ideology in Education* (New York: Oxford University Press, 1977), p. 20.

18. J. S. Coleman et al., *Equality of Educational Opportunity* (Washington, D.C.: Government Printing Office, 1966); Karabel and Halsey, *Power and Ideology*.

19. B. Heyns, "Educational Effects: Issues in Conceptualization and Measurement," in J. C. Richardson (ed.), *Handbook of Theory and Research for the Sociology of Education* (New York: Greenwood Press, 1986).

20. O. Lewis, "The Culture of Poverty," *Scientific American* (October 1966), pp. 19–25.

21. J. H. Ballantine, *The Sociology of Education* (Englewood Cliffs, N.J.: Prentice-Hall, 1983).

22. A. F. Jensen, "How Much Can We Boost IQ and Scholastic Achievement?" *Harvard Educational Review* 39 (Winter 1969), pp. 1–123. The genetic model of human intelligence Jensen used to substantiate his claims of African Americans' alleged lower levels of intelligence was the work of the late Sir Cyril Burt. In the mid-1970s, however, scientists exposed Burt's work as a major scientific fraud because he had fabricated his data on the IQs of separated identical twins as well as the existence of the two women who supposedly assisted him during his research. Stephen J. Gould's *The Mismeasure of Man* (New York: Norton, 1981) is a masterful exposé of Burt's fakery as well as the scientific and moral bankruptcy of the sexist, classist, and racist underpinnings of much of the intelligence testing movement.

23. J. F. Berrueta-Clement et al., *Changed Lives: The Effects of the Perry Preschool Project on Youths Through Age 19* (Ypsilanti, Mich.: The High/Scope Press, 1985); L. F. Carter, "The Sustaining Effects of Compensatory and Elementary Education," *Educational Researcher* 13, no. 7 (1984), pp. 3–11.

24. Ronald Henkoff, "Now Everyone Loves Head Start," *Fortune*, Special Issue on Saving Our Schools (Spring 1990), pp. 35–43.

25. T. Schultz, "Investment in Human Capital," *American Economic Review* (March 1961), pp. 1–17; Karabel and Halsey, *Power and Ideology*, pp. 313–324.

26. Wilford Wilms, personal communication (1984); Paul Weckstein, personal interview (Washington, D.C., March 8, 1990).

27. B. Bluestone, "Economic Policy and the Fate of the Poor," *Social Policy*, no. 2 (1972): 30–31.

28. Carol A. Ray and Roslyn A. Mickelson, "Corporate Leaders, Resistant Youth, and School Reform in Sunbelt City: The Political Economy of Education," *Social Problems* 37, no. 2 (1990), pp. 178–190.

29. Ballantine, *Sociology of Education;* S. S. Klein, *Handbook for Achieving Sex Equity in Education* (Baltimore: Johns Hopkins University Press, 1985).

30. Klein, *Handbook*, pp. 94–95.

31. Title IX is not the only federal law attempting to achieve gender equity in education through legislative reforms. Other federal programs that target sexism in education include Title IV of the 1964 Civil Rights Act, the Women's Educational Equity Act of 1974 and 1978, an amendment to the 1976 Vocational Education Act, the law authorizing the National Institute of Education, and the laws creating the National Science Foundation and the U.S. Commission on Civil Rights. Klein, *Handbook;* R. Salomone, *Equality of Education Under the Law* (New York: St. Martin's Press, 1986).

32. Elizabeth Fennema and Gilah C. Leder, *Mathematics and Gender* (New York: Teachers College Press, 1990); Klein, *Handbook;* Cornelius Riordan, *Girls and Boys in School: Together or Separate* (New York: Teachers College Press, 1990).

33. L. McMillen, "Women Professors Pressing to Close Salary Gap: Some Colleges Adjust Pay, Others Face Lawsuits," *Chronicle of Higher Education* 33, (1987), p. 1.

34. To be sure, income does not measure class-based inequality, but there is a positive correlation between income and class. Income has the additional advantage of being easily quantifiable. Were we to use another measure of inequality—wealth—the disjuncture between it and increases in educational attainment would appear even larger. The distribution of wealth in U.S. society has remained fairly stable since the Depression, with the richest 10 percent of the population owning about 65 percent of the total wealth. Since the Reagan administration's regressive fiscal and monetary policies have been in effect, the wealth of this country has been further redistributed upward at the expense of the working and middle classes.

35. C. Jencks et al., *Inequality* (New York: Harper & Row, 1972), p. 11.

36. Ira Shor, *Culture Wars* (Boston: Routledge & Kegan Paul, 1986).

37. Lois Weis, *Working Class Without Work: High School Students in a Deindustrialized Economy* (New York: Routledge, 1990); William J. Wilson, *The Truly Disadvantaged* (Chicago: University of Chicago Press, 1988).

38. Hochschild, *New American Dilemma*, pp. 14–16.

39. Reynolds Farley, *Blacks and Whites: Narrowing the Gap?* (Cambridge, Mass.: Harvard University Press, 1984).

40. R. Collins, *Credential Society* (New York: Academic Press, 1979); R. B. Freeman, *The Over-educated American* (New York: Academic Press, 1976).

41. Jean Anyon, "Social Class and the Hidden Curriculum of Work," *Journal of Education* 162, no. 1 (1980), pp. 67–92; Jean Anyon, "Social Class and School Knowledge," *Curriculum Inquiry*, no. 10 (1981), pp. 3–42; Roslyn Mickelson, "The Secondary School's Role in Social Stratification: A Comparison of Beverly Hills High School and Morningside High School," *Journal of Education* 162, no. 4 (1980), pp. 83–112.

42. Robert Dreeben and Adam Gamoran, "Race, Instruction, and Learning," *American Sociological Review* 51, no. 5 (1986), pp. 660–669.

43. Anyon, op. cit.

44. S. Bowles and H. Gintis, *Schooling in Capitalist America: Educational Reform and the Contradictions of Economic Life* (New York: Basic Books, 1976).

45. Jeannie Oakes, *Keeping Track* (New Haven, Conn.: Yale University Press, 1985).

46. Ibid.; S. Lubeck, *Sandbox Society* (Philadelphia: Falmer Press, 1985); Mickelson, "Secondary School's Role"; R. A. Mickelson, "The Case of the Missing Brackets: Teachers and Social Reproduction," *Journal of Education* 169, no. 2 (1987), pp. 78–88.

47. M. Apple and L. Weis (eds.), *Ideology and Practice in Schooling* (Philadelphia: Temple University Press, 1983); H. Giroux, *Theory and Resistance in Education* (Boston: Bergin and Garvey, 1983).

CANTO, LOCURA Y POESIA

41

Olivia Castellano

I am a walking contradiction. I have no Ph.D. yet I'm a full professor of English at a state university. By all definitions and designs I should not even have made it to college. I am the second of five children of a Southern Pacific Railroad worker with a fifth-grade education and a woman who dropped out of the second grade to help raise ten siblings—while her mother worked ten hours a day cleaning houses and doing laundry for rich Texan ranchers.

In Comstock, the Tex-Mex border town about fifteen miles from the Rio Grande where I spent the first twelve years of my life, I saw the despair that

From: *Women's Review of Books* 7, no. 5 (Feb. 1990). Reprinted by permission of the author.

poverty and hopelessness had etched in the faces of young Chicano men who, like my father, walked back and forth on the dusty path between Comstock and the Southern Pacific Railroad station. They would set out every day on rail carts to repair the railroad. The women of Comstock fared no better. Most married early. I had seen them in their kitchens toiling at a stove, with one baby propped on one hip and two toddlers tugging at their skirts. Or they followed their working mothers' route, cleaning houses and doing laundry for rich Texan ranchers who paid them a pittance. I decided very early that this was not the future I wanted.

In 1958 my father, tired of seeing his days fade into each other without promise, moved us to California where we became farmworkers in the San Jose area (then a major agricultural center). I saw the same futile look in the faces of young Chicanos and Chicanas working beside my family. Those faces already lined so young with sadness made me deadly serious about my books and my education.

At a young age—between eleven and fourteen—I began my intellectual and spiritual rebellion against my parents and society. I fell in love with books and created space of my own where I could dare to dream. Yet in school I remained shy and introverted, terrified of my white, male professors. In my adolescence I rebelled against my mother's insistence that Mexican girls should marry young, as she did at eighteen. I told her that I didn't care if my cousins Alicia and Anita were getting married and having babies early. "I was put on this earth to make books, not babies!" I announced and ran into my room.

Books were my obsession. I wanted to read everything that I was not supposed to. By fourteen I was already getting to know the Marquis de Sade, Rimbaud, Lautréamont, Whitman, Dostoyevsky, Marx. I came by these writers serendipitously. To get from home to Sacramento High School I had to walk through one of the toughest neighborhoods in the city, Oak Park. There were men hanging out with liquor in brown paper bags, playing dice, shooting craps and calling from cars: "Hey, baby, get in here with me!" I'd run into a little library called Oak Park Library, which turned out to have a little bit of everything. I would walk around and stare at the shelves, killing time till the shifty-eyed men would go away.

The librarians knew and tolerated me with skepticism: "Are you sure you're going to read the Marquis de Sade? Do your parents know you're checking out this material? What are you doing with the *Communist Manifesto?*" One librarian even forbade me to check the books out, so I'd sit reading in the library for hours on end. Later, at sixteen or seventeen, I was allowed to check anything and everything out.

So it was that I came to grapple with tough language and ideas. These books were hot! Yet I also was obsessed with wanting to be pretty, mysterious, silent and sexy. I wanted to have long curly hair, red lips and long red nails; to wear black tight dresses and high heels. I wanted desperately to look like the sensuous femmes fatales of the Mexican cinema—María Féliz, one of the most beautiful and famous of Mexico's screen goddesses, and Libertad Lamarque, the smoky-voiced, green-eyed Argentinian singer. These were the women I admired when my mother and I went to the movies together. So these were my "outward" models. My "inward" models, the voices of the intellect that spoke to me when I shut the door to my room, were, as you have gathered, a writer of erotica, two mad surrealists, a crazy Romantic, an epileptic literary genius and a radical socialist.

I needed to sabotage society in a major, intellectually radical way. I needed to be a warrior who would catch everyone off guard. But to be a warrior, you must never let your opponent figure you out. When the bullets of racism and sexism are flying at you, you must be very clever in deciding how you want to live. I knew that everything around me—school, teachers, television, friends, men, even my own parents, who in their internalized racism and self-hatred didn't really believe I'd amount to much though they hoped like hell that life would prove them wrong—everything was against me, and I understood this fully.

To protect myself I fell in love with language—all of it, poems, stories, novels, plays, songs, biographies, "cuentos" or little vignettes, movies—all manifestations of spoken and written language. I fell in love with ideas, with essays by writers like Bacon or Montaigne. I began my serious reading crusade around age eleven, when I was already convinced that books were central to my life. Only through them and through songs, I felt, would I be free to structure some kind of future for myself.

I wanted to prove to anyone who cared to ask (though by now I was convinced no one gave a damn) that I, the daughter of a laborer-farmworker, could dare to be somebody. Try to imagine what it is like to be always full of rage—rage at everything: at white teachers who could never even pronounce my name (I was often called anything from "Odilia" to "Otilia" to "Estela"); rage at those teachers who asked me point-blank, "But how did you get to be so smart? You are Mexican, aren't you?"; rage at my eleventh-grade English teacher who said to me in front of the class, "You stick to essay writing; never try to write a poem again because a poet you are not!" (This, after I had worked for two diligent weeks on an imitation of "La Belle Dame Sans Merci"! Now I can laugh. Then it was pitiful.)

From age thirteen I was also angry at boys who hounded me for dates. When I'd reject them they'd yell, "So what do you plan to do for the rest of your life, fuck a book?" I was angry at my Chicana classmates in high school who, perhaps jealous of my high grades, would say, "What are you trying to do, be like the whites?" I regret to say that I was also angry at my parents, exasperated by their docility, their limited expectations of me. Oh, I knew they were proud; but sometimes, in their own misdirected rage (maybe afraid of my little successes), they would make painful comments. "Te vas a volver loca con esos jodidos libros" ("You'll go nuts with those fucking books") was my mother's frequent statement. Or the even more sickening, "Esta nunca se va a casar." ("Give up on this one; she'll never get married.") This was the tenor of my adolescent years. When nothing on either side of the two cultures, Mexican or Anglo-American, affirms your existence, that is how rage is shaped.

While I managed to escape at least from the obvious entrapments—a teen pregnancy, a destructive early marriage—I did not escape years of being told I wasn't quite right, that because of my ethnicity and gender I was somehow defective, incomplete. Those years left wounds on my self-esteem, wounds so deep that even armed with my books and stolen knowledge I could not entirely escape deep feelings of unworthiness.

By the time I graduated from high school and managed to get a little scholarship to California State University in Sacramento, where I now teach (in 1962 it was called Sacramento State College), I had become very unassertive, immensely shy. I was afraid to look unfeminine if I raised my hand in class, afraid to seem ridiculous if I asked a "bad" question and all eyes turned on me. A deeper part of me was afraid that my rage might rear its ugly head and I would be considered "an angry Mexican accusing everybody of racism." I was painfully concerned with my physical appearance: wasn't I supposed to look beautiful like Féliz and Lamarque? Yet while I wanted to look pretty for the boys, the thought of having sex terrified me. What if I got pregnant, had to quit college and couldn't read my books any more? The more I feared boys, the more I made myself attractive for them and the more they would make advances, the more I rejected them.

The constant tension sapped my energy and distracted me from my creative journeys into language. Oh, I would write little things (poems, sketches for stories, journal entries), but I was afraid to show them to anyone. Besides, no one knew I was writing them. I was so frightened by my white, male professors, especially in the English department—they looked so arrogant and were so ungiving of their knowledge—that I didn't have the nerve to major in English, though it was the major I really wanted.

Instead, I chose to major in French. The "Parisiens" and "Québecois" in the French department faculty admired my French accent: "Mademoiselle, êtes-vous certaine que vous n'êtes pas parisienne?" they would ask. In short, they cared. They engaged me in dialogue, asked why I preferred to study

French instead of Spanish. ("I already know Spanish," I'd say.) French became my adopted language. I could play with it, sing songs in it and sound exotic. It complemented my Spanish; besides, I didn't have to worry about speaking English with my heavy Spanish accent and risk being ridiculed. At one point, my spoken French was better than my oral Spanish; my written French has remained better than my written Spanish.

At 23, armed with a secondary school teaching credential and B.A. in French with an English minor, I became a high school teacher of French and English. Soon after that I began to work for a school district where the majority of the students were Chicanos and Blacks from families on welfare and/or from households run by women.

After two years of high school teaching, I returned to Cal State at Sacramento for the Master's degree. Professionally and artistically, it was the best decision I have ever made. The Master's program to which I applied was a pilot program in its second year at CSUS. Called the Mexican American Experienced Teachers' Fellowship, it was run by a team of anthropology professors, central among whom was Professor Steven Arvizu. The program was designed to turn us into "agents of cultural change." It was 1969 and the program was one of the first federally funded (Title V) ones to address Mexican American students' needs by re-educating their teachers.

My interests were literary, but all twenty of us " fellows" had to get an M.A. in social anthropology, since this experiment took the "anthropologizing education" approach. We studied social dynamics, psycholinguistics, history of Mexico, history of the American Southwest, community activism and confrontational strategies and the nature of the Chicano movement. The courses were eye-openers. I had never heard the terms Chicano, biculturalism, marginality, assimilation, Chicanismo, protest art. I had never heard of Cesar Chavez and the farmworkers nor of Luis Valdez and the Teatro Campesino. I had never studied the nature of racism and identity. The theme of the program was that culture is a powerful tool for learning, self-expression, solidarity and positive change. Exploring it can help Chicano students under-stand their bicultural circumstances.

The program brought me face to face with nineteen other Chicano men and women, all experienced public school teachers like myself, with back-grounds like mine. The program challenged every aspect of my life. Through group counseling, group encounter, classroom interaction, course content and community involvement I was allowed to express my rage and to examine it in the company of peers who had a similar anger. Most of our instructors, moreover, were Chicano or white professors sensitive to Chicanos. For the first time, at 25, I had found my role models. I vowed to do for other students what these people had done for me.

Eighteen years of teaching primarily white women students, Chicanos and Blacks at California State University, Sacramento, have led me to see myself less as a teacher and more as a cultural worker, struggling against society to undo the damage of years of abuse. I continue to see myself as a warrior empowered by my rage. Racism and sexism leave two clear-cut scars on my students; internalized self-hatred and fear of their own creative passion, in my view the two most serious obstacles in the classroom. Confronting this two-headed monster has made me razor-sharp. Given their tragic personal stories, the hope in my students' eyes reconfirms daily the incredible beauty, the tenacity of the human spirit.

Teaching white women students (ages 30–45) is no different from working with Chicano and Black students (both men and women): you have to bring about changes in the way they view themselves, their abilities, their right to get educated and their relation to a world that has systematically oppressed them simply for being who they are. You have to help them channel and understand the seething rage they carry deep inside, a rage which, left unexpressed, can make them turn against each other and, more sadly, against themselves.

I teach four courses per semester: English 109G, Writing for Proficiency for Bilingual/Bidialectal Students (a course taken mainly by Chicano and Black students, ages 19–24); English 115A, Pedagogy/Language Arts for Prospective Elementary School Teachers (a course taken mainly by women aged 25–45, 50 percent white, 50 percent Chicano); English 180G, Chicano Literature, an advanced studies General Education course for non-English majors (taken by excellent students, aged 24–45, about 40 percent white, 40 percent Chicano, 20 percent Black/Vietnamese/Filipino/South American). The fourth course is English 1, Basic Language Skills, a pre-freshman composition course taken primarily by Black and Chicano freshmen, male and female, aged 18–22, who score too low on the English Placement Test to be placed in "regular" Freshman Composition.

Mine is a teaching load that, in my younger days at CSUS, used to drive me close to insanity from physical, mental and spiritual exhaustion—spiritual from having internalized my students' pain. Perhaps not fully empowered myself, not fully emplumed in the feathers of my own creativity (to borrow the wonderful "emplumada" metaphor coined by Lorna Dee Cervantes, the brilliant Chicana poet), I allowed their rage to become part of mine. This kind of rage can kill you. And so through years of working with these kinds of students I have learned to make my spirit strong with "canto, locura y poesia" (song, madness, and poetry). Judging from my students' progress, the songs have worked.

Truly, it takes a conjurer, a magus with all her teaching cards up her sleeve, to deal with the fragmented souls that show up in my classes. Among the Chicanos and Blacks I get ex-offenders (mostly men but occasionally a woman who has done time), orphans, single women heads of household, high school dropouts who took years to complete their Graduation Equivalency Diploma.

I get women who have been raped and/or who have been sexually abused either by a father figure or by male relatives—Sylvia Tracey, for example, a 30-year-old Chicana feminist, mother of two, whose parents pressured her to marry her (white) rapist and who is going through divorce after ten years of marriage. I get women who have been battered. And, of course, I get the young Chicano and Black little yuppies who don't believe the world existed before 1970, who know nothing about the sixties' history of struggle and student protest, who—in the case of the Chicanos—feel ashamed that their parents speak English with an accent or were once farmworkers. I get Chicanos, Blacks and white women, especially, who are ashamed of their writing skills, who have never once been told that they could succeed in school.

Annetta Jones is typical. A 45-year-old Black woman, who single-handedly raised three children, all college-educated and successful, she is still married to a man who served ten years in prison for being a "hit man." She visited him faithfully in prison and underwent all kinds of humiliation at the hands of correctional officers—even granting them sexual favors just to be allowed to have conjugal visits. When her husband completed his time he fell in love with a young woman from Chicago, where he now lives.

Among my white women students (ranging in age from 25 to 40, though occasionally I get a 45-year-old woman who wants to be an elementary or high school teacher and "help out young kids so they won't have to go through what I went through"—their exact words) I get women who are either divorced or divorcing; rarely do I get a "happily" married woman. This is especially true of the white women who take my Chicano literature and my credential-pedagogy classes. Take Lynne Trebeck, for instance, a white woman about 40 years old who runs a farm. When she entered the university her husband objected, so she divorced him! They continue to live in the same house (he refused to leave), "but now he has no control over me," she told me triumphantly midway through the semester. She has two sons, fifteen and eighteen years old; as a young woman she did jail time as the accomplice of a convicted drug dealer.

Every semester I get two or three white lesbian feminists. This semester there was Vivianne Rose, about 40, in my Chicano literature class. Apparently sensing too much conservatism in the students, and knowing that she wanted to be an elementary school teacher, she chose to conceal her sexual orientation.

On the first day of class she wore Levi pants, a baggy sweat shirt, white tennis shoes and a beige baseball cap. By the end of the first week she had switched to ultrafeminine dresses and skirts, brightly colored blouses, nylons and medium-heeled black shoes, not to mention lipstick and eye makeup. When she spoke in class she occasionally made references to "my husband who is Native American." She and Sylvia Tracey became very close friends. Halfway through the course they informed me that "Shit, it's about time we tell her." (This, from Sylvia.) "Oh hell, why not," Vivianne said; "my 'husband' is a woman." The woman *is* Native American; Vivianne Rose lived on a reservation for years and taught young Native American children to read and write. She speaks "Res" talk (reservation speech) and has adopted her "husband's" last name.

Among my white women students there are also divorced women who are raising two to four children, usually between the ages of eight and seventeen. Sometimes I get older widowed white women who are taking classes for their own enjoyment, not for a degree. These women also tell stories of torment: rapes, beatings, verbal and emotional harassment from their men. On occasion I get women who have done jail time, usually for taking the rap for drug-connected boyfriends. I rarely get a married woman, but when I do there is pain: "My husband doesn't really want me in school." "My husband doesn't really care what I do in college as long as I take care of his needs and the kids' needs." "My husband doesn't really know what I'm studying—he has never asked and I've never told him."

Most of the white women as well as the minority students come to the university under special programs. There is the "Educational Opportunity Program" for students who do not meet all university entrance requirements or whose grade point average is simply too low for regular admission. There is the "Student Affirmative Action Program" for students who need special counseling and tutoring to bring their academic skills up to par or deal with emotional trauma. There is the "College Assistance Migrant Program" for students whose parents are migrant farmworkers in the agricultural areas surrounding Sacramento. There is a wonderful program called PASAR for older women students entering the university for the first time or returning after a multiple-year absence. The Women's Resource Center also provides small grants and scholarships for re-entry women. A large number of my students (both white and minority women) come severely handicapped in their basic language, math and science skills; many have never used a computer. It is not uncommon (especially among Chicanos and Blacks) to get an incoming student who scores at the fifth- and sixth-grade reading levels.

The task is herculean, the rewards spiritually fulfilling. I would not have it any other way. Every day is a lesson in humility and audacity. That my students have endured nothing but obstacles and putdowns, yet still have the courage and strength to seek a college education, humbles me. They are, like me, walking paradoxes. They have won against all the odds (their very presence on campus attests to that). Yet really they haven't won: they carry a deeply ingrained sense of inferiority, a firm conviction that they are not worthy of success.

This is my challenge: I embrace it wholeheartedly. There is no place I'd rather be, no profession more noble. Sure, I sometimes have doubts: every day something new, sad, even tragic comes up. Just as I was typing this article, for instance, Vicky, one of the white students in my Chicano literature class, called in tears, barely able to talk. "Professor, I can't possibly turn in my paper to your mailbox by four o'clock," she cried. "Everything in my house is falling apart! My husband just fought with my oldest daughter [from a previous marriage], has thrown her out of the house. He's running up and down the street, yelling and threatening to leave us. And I'm sitting here trying to write your paper! I'm going crazy. I feel like walking away from it all!" I took an hour from writing this article to help her contain herself. By the end of our conversation, I had her laughing. I also put her in touch with a counselor friend of mine and gave her a two-day extension for her final paper. And naturally I was one more hour late with my own writing!

I teach in a totally non-traditional way. I use every trick in the book: lots of positive reinforcement, both oral and written; lots of one-on-one conferences. I network women with each other, refer them to professor friends who can help them; connect them to graduate students and/or former students who are already pursuing careers. In the classroom I force my students to come up in front of their classmates, explain concepts or read their essays aloud. I create panels representing opposing viewpoints and hold debates—lots of oral participation, role-playing, reading their own texts. Their own writing and opinions become part of the course. On exams I ask them questions about their classmates' presentations. I meet with individual students in local coffeehouses or taverns: it's much easier to talk about personal pain over coffee or a beer or a glass of wine than in my office. My students, for the most part, do not have a network of support away from the university. There are no supportive husbands, lovers (except on rare occasions, as with my lesbian students), no relatives saying, "Yes, you can do it."

Is it any wonder that when these students come to me they have a deep sense of personal shame about everything—poor skills, being older students? They are also very angry, not only at themselves but at the schools for having victimized them; at poor, uninspired teaching; at their parents for not having had high enough expectations of them or (in the case of the women) for having allowed them to marry so young. Sylvia, my Chicana feminist student, put it best when I was pointing out incomplete sentences in her essay: "Where the hell was I when all this was being taught in high school? And why didn't anybody give a damn that I wasn't learning it?"

I never teach content for the first two weeks of any of my courses. I talk about anger, sexism, racism and the sixties—a time when people believed in something larger than themselves. We dialogue—about prisons and why so many Chicano and Black young men are behind bars in California; why people fear differences; why they are so homophobic. I give my students a chance to talk about their anger ("coraje" in Spanish). I often read them the poem by my friend and colleague Jose Montoya, called "Eslipping and Esliding," where he talks about "locura" (craziness) and says that with a little locura, a little eslipping and esliding, we can survive the madness that surrounds us. We laugh at ourselves, sharing our tragic, tattered pasts; we undo everything and let the anger out. "I know why so many of you are afraid of doing well," I say. "You've been told you can't do it, and you're so pissed off about it, you can't concentrate." Courage takes pure concentration. By the end of these initial two or three weeks we have become friends and defined our mutual respect. Only then do we enter the course content.

I am not good at endings; I prefer to celebrate beginnings. The struggle continues and the success stories abound. Students come back, year after year, to say "Thank you." Usually I pull these visitors into the classroom: "Tell my class that they can do it. Tell them how you did it!" They start talking and can't stop. "Look, Olivia, when I first came into your class," said Sylvia, "I couldn't even put a fucking sentence together. And now look at me, three years later I'm even writing poetry!"

REMINISCENCE OF A POST-INTEGRATION KID: *Or, Where Have We Come Since Then?*

42

Gaye Williams

I want to dedicate this to the young woman who sat in the University of Tennessee dining hall while a table of seven white kids—who would share her microbiology class an hour later—stood to leave as she sat down. They stood to prove that they were too good to sit next to a Black woman. However, one of them (her lab partner) could later laugh and joke with her by the safety of the microscope where no one could see them, as if nothing had happened. Sharing space were the young man and the woman, who was smarter but darker, and who knew what it was to be hurt.

Post-segregation. I asked my mother why, when I got around to attending schools, everything had calmed down. "After the whites realized they had lost," she said, "they mostly gave up fighting desegregation." So, no mobs lined up to keep me out of North Roebuck School's third grade class, or my Black teacher from her job teaching all those white kids. I even won Top Scholar of my class.

Someone asked me when I first began to identify as a feminist. I realized then that I was outraged about the unequal treatment of women in relation to men long before I understood what racism meant. Before being asked the question, I had not thought about the fact that I lacked a racial consciousness growing up in Birmingham, Alabama, in the sixties. I thought some more.

The absence of a racial consciousness was a result of my being a post-integration kid. I came up through a conspiracy to silence the Black movement, which was not a topic in the white schools I attended. Even though one of my babysitters was among the girls killed in the 16th Street Baptist Church bombing, everything was fine, or so the silence suggested. There were no bombs, no riots, no state troopers taking me to school. There was also no one to reinforce the radio's message that Black was beautiful, just James Brown shouting as I got ready for school "Say It Loud, I'm Black and I'm Proud!"

From: *Sage: A Scholarly Journal on Black Women* 1 (Spring, 1984): 20–21. Reprinted by permission.

But JB's message did not sink in. In elementary school, I thought the white kids would not know I was Black if I did not tell them, although I am not at all light enough to pass. I made myself invisible and pretended I was someone else, for protection from the self-hatred that I had learned from somewhere. The fact that my imaginary self was always male, and more often white than Black, says something about the effects of curriculum, climate, and the availability of suitable role models to my sense of self-validation. Very little in my pre-college schooling gave me an alternative to hating my Blackness and femaleness, although at the time I am sure I would not have spoken of it that way. I retreated into identities I felt were safer, more attractive than my own.

Was that all the fault of curriculum, climate, lack of suitable role models? Maybe not, but I spent the great bulk of my pre-college time either in school or studying, with very little free time left over. When I was not studying, I was acting, and the classes and plays were little different in content from my school lessons.

Very early in my education, the lines were drawn between the kids singled out as smart and the others. I think about the church schools I attended—no rods spared nor children spoiled there. Being "good" and "smart" were my best defenses. From there I went to public elementary school for second grade, where I wandered outside of class to the school library and the reading specialist's lab. I was a favored child, along with my friend Eric. We were taught at home by our school teacher/administrator families. We both advanced beyond the other kids and were treated something like a prince and princess—"golden" children.

I thought I was rich, with my light skin and proper talk, because I was set apart by the teacher, attractive to boys, and picked on by at least one girl. I knew, even while she made me cry, that Debra was as much attracted to me as she was envious or curious. That was the year when the teacher performed a wedding ceremony for Eric and me in front of all the others.

The chance to develop my talent also set me apart from other Black kids. I was not a singer, coming along in the bosom of a Black church choir, but acting in plays that had Black characters only because their actors happened to be Black. After a successful audition, I went to the Alabama School of the Fine Arts in drama. The number of Black kids in the school slowly grew, but most of them were musicians. Even among the Black actors, I was still set apart by my lack of a Black or southern accent.

The other side of being a golden child marked for success was the feeling of being separated from my peers. I was held up for praise and vulnerable to disdain. One problem of post-integration kids is that the divisions between us of class, sex, and color have become more virulent. These differences have always been present in the Black community, and their resulting hierarchy a divisive problem. But this distancing effect of the combination of light skin, brains and opportunity became much greater post-integration because the possibility of admission to white society became much more probable. With post-integration came more options.

I came from a family that sent its children, daughters included, to the best schools the Black community had to offer, at whatever sacrifice. They considered education the necessary ticket to advancement. By the time I was ready for college, even the Ivy League was within reach. My admission was bought by sit-ins, marches, riots, freedom rides, and legislation, but I had only the vaguest understanding of the importance of these occurrences.

My mother once said that she wondered whether she had done the best thing sending me to mostly white private schools. Which is more important—that kids have the best opportunity to develop their minds in language, art and science, or that their souls and spirits benefit from the best the Black tradition has to offer, so that they face the world's hostility feeling part of a strong community and heritage? She could not ask nor answer then the question of why we should have to choose between the two.

It was in college that I began to gain a full sense of what it meant to me to be born Black and female. Knowing that the Ivy League probably had little idea of what a young Black girl/woman from the South needed or wanted so far away from home, I had the sense to build a community of friends around me very soon. Convinced that I was not prepared to be in this prestigious university and that I was going to have a difficult time academically (even though I never before had trouble in school), I surrounded myself with people and activities to help see me through. First, I found upperclass women students who were intrigued, I think, by my boldness and always ready with advice and comfort. They were my survival, along with special teachers, the Boston women's community, and the Black children and their families I met in the Intergenerational Outreach Saturday Educational Program.

I met older Black kids who had a strong racial and feminist consciousness. But they had also felt separated from most Blacks for the same reasons I had. These folks were discovering together how to bridge gaps, knowing that these were the most important lessons to learn. I grew from a base of self-love to alliances and friendships with students who were Chicano, Puerto Rican, African, Asian and American Indian, and the gay folks of all ethnicities.

The most important thing about going to college when I did and where I did was that I began to broaden my idea of education. Thinking about what education has meant to me seems almost the same as thinking about what being young means. There is the education that happens inside classrooms or other clearly designated learning places. But it is difficult, and perhaps undesirable, to separate the learning I did there from the constant process of figuring out what I was doing in this world. The point to consider is how the learning in everyday life and that of school fit together. Then I can begin to answer questions of how my racial/feminist consciousness was shaped.

I went to a lot of conferences and events in the Boston area while in school. The most significant one was the 1981 Women and Law Conference. Meeting feminist women of color there had a catalytic effect on my education, helping to bring everything together. Afterwards, I began demanding that my course work in school complement the questions I was framing and hearing outside the classroom. I insisted that this expensive schooling give me something that would help me understand the meaning of my life as a Black woman. From the example of the women I met there and at subsequent events, I gained the inspiration and courage necessary to run successfully for president of the Harvard-Radcliffe Black Students Association, and learned to bring the force that women's work embodied onto the campus and into the lives of the other students.

I have not liked feeling cut off from people, especially from Black folks. It has been my good fortune to make friendships that showed me how silly and immaterial were the barriers which I thought kept me apart. With the help of my friends of all races I have come to insist that the post-integration decades be just that: a time that allows me to "integrate" and to use all the parts of myself. I insist on it being a time that does not demand that I be either Black **or** female, but recognizes that I am both, **all** of the time. From there I can go on to the business of helping make this world fit for all of us to live in.

Of course, my education does not end with the close of classes. The beat, I know, will keep going on.

TAKING WOMEN STUDENTS SERIOUSLY

43

Adrienne Rich

I see my function here today as one of trying to create a context, delineate a background, against which we might talk about women as students and students as women. I would like to speak for awhile about this background, and then I hope that we can have, not so much a question period, as a raising of concerns, a sharing of questions for which we as yet may have no answers, an opening of conversations which will go on and on.

When I went to teach at Douglass, a women's college, it was with a particular background which I would like briefly to describe to you. I had graduated from an all-girls' school in the 1940s, where the head and the majority of the faculty were independent, unmarried women. One or two held doctorates, but had been forced by the Depression (and by the fact that they were women) to take secondary school teaching jobs. These women cared a great deal about the life of the mind, and they gave a great deal of time and energy—beyond any limit of teaching hours—to those of us who showed special intellectual interest or ability. We were taken to libraries, art museums, lectures at neighboring colleges, set to work on extra research projects, given extra French or Latin reading. Although we sometimes felt "pushed" by them, we held those women in a kind of respect which even then we dimly perceived was not generally accorded to women in the world at large. They were vital individuals, defined not by their relationships but by their personalities; and although under the pressure of the culture we were all certain we wanted to get married, their lives did not appear empty or dreary to us. In a kind of cognitive dissonance, we knew they were "old maids" and therefore supposed to be bitter and lonely; yet we saw them vigorously involved with life. But despite their existence as alternate models of women, the *content* of the

The talk that follows was addressed to teachers of women. . . . It was given for the New Jersey College and University Coalition on Women's Education, May 9, 1978.

education they gave us in no way prepared us to survive as women in a world organized by and for men.

From that school, I went on to Radcliffe, congratulating myself that now I would have great men as my teachers. From 1947 to 1951, when I graduated, I never saw a single woman on a lecture platform, or in front of a class, except when a woman graduate student gave a paper on a special topic. The "great men" talked of other "great men," of the nature of Man, the history of Mankind, the future of Man; and never again was I to experience, from a teacher, the kind of prodding, the insistence that my best could be even better, that I had known in high school. Women students were simply not taken very seriously. Harvard's message to women was an elite mystification: we were, of course, part of Mankind; we were special, achieving women, or we would not have been there; but of course our real goal was to marry—if possible, a Harvard graduate.

In the late sixties, I began teaching at the City College of New York—a crowded, public, urban, multiracial institution as far removed from Harvard as possible. I went there to teach writing in the SEEK Program, which predated Open Admissions and which was then a kind of model for programs designed to open up higher education to poor, black, and Third World students. Although during the next few years we were to see the original concept of SEEK diluted, then violently attacked and betrayed, it was for a short time an extraordinary and intense teaching and learning environment. The characteristics of this environment were a deep commitment on the part of teachers to the minds of their students; a constant, active effort to create or discover the conditions for learning, and to educate ourselves to meet the needs of the new college population; a philosophical attitude based on open discussion of racism, oppression, and the politics of literature and language; and a belief that learning in the classroom could not be isolated from the student's experience as a member of an urban minority group in white America. Here are some of the kinds of questions we, as teachers of writing, found ourselves asking:

1. What has been the student's experience of education in the inadequate, often abusively racist public school system, which rewards passivity and treats a questioning attitude or independent mind as a behavior problem? What has been her or his experience in a society that consistently undermines the selfhood of the poor and the nonwhite? How can such a student gain that sense of self which is necessary for active participation in education? What does all this mean for us as teachers?

2. How do we go about teaching a canon of literature which has consistently excluded or depreciated nonwhite experience?

3. How can we connect the process of learning to write well with the student's own reality, and not simply teach her/him how to write acceptable lies in standard English?

When I went to teach at Douglass College in 1976, and in teaching women's writing workshops elsewhere, I came to perceive stunning parallels to the questions I had first encountered in teaching the so-called disadvantaged students at City. But in this instance, and against the specific background of the women's movement, the questions framed themselves like this:

1. What has been the student's experience of education in schools which reward female passivity, indoctrinate girls and boys in stereotypic sex roles, and do not take the female mind seriously? How does a woman gain a sense of her *self* in a system—in this case, patriarchal capitalism—which devalues work done by women, denies the importance and uniqueness of female experience, and is physically violent toward women? What does this mean for a woman teacher?
2. How do we, as women, teach women students a canon of literature which has consistently excluded or depreciated female experience, and which often expresses hostility to women and validates violence against us?
3. How can we teach women to move beyond the desire for male approval and getting "good grades" and seek and write their own truths that the culture has distorted or made taboo? (For women, of course, language itself is exclusive: I want to say more about this further on.)

In teaching women, we have two choices: to lend our weight to the forces that indoctrinate women to passivity, self-depreciation, and a sense of powerlessness, in which case the issue of "taking women students seriously" is a moot one; or to consider what we have to work against, as well as with, in ourselves, in our students, in the content of the curriculum, in the structure of the institution, in the society at large. And this means, first of all, taking ourselves seriously: Recognizing that central responsibility of a woman to herself, without which we remain always the Other, the defined, the object, the victim; believing that there is a unique quality of validation, affirmation, challenge, support, that one woman can offer another. Believing in the value and significance of women's experience, traditions, perceptions. Thinking of ourselves seriously, not as one of the boys, not as neuters, or androgynes, but *as women.*

Suppose we were to ask ourselves, simply: What does a woman need to know? Does she not, as a self-conscious, self-defining human being, need a knowledge of her own history, her much-politicized biology, an awareness of the creative work of women of the past, the skills and crafts and techniques and powers exercised by women in different times and cultures, a knowledge of women's rebellions and organized movements against our oppression and how they have been routed or diminished? Without such knowledge women live and have lived without context, vulnerable to the projections of male fantasy, male prescriptions for us, estranged from our own experience because our education has not reflected or echoed it. I would suggest that not biology, but ignorance of our selves, has been the key to our powerlessness.

But the university curriculum, the high-school curriculum, do not provide this kind of knowledge for women, the knowledge of Womankind, whose experience has been so profoundly different from that of Mankind. Only in the precariously budgeted, much-condescended-to area of women's studies is such knowledge available to women students. Only there can they learn about the lives and work of women other than the few select women who are included in the "mainstream" texts, usually misrepresented even when they do appear. Some students, at some institutions, manage to take a majority of courses in women's studies, but the message from on high is that this is self-indulgence, soft-core education: the "real" learning is the study of Mankind.

If there is any misleading concept, it is that of "coeducation": that because women and men are sitting in the same classrooms, hearing the same lectures, reading the same books, performing the same laboratory experiments, they are receiving an equal education. They are not, first because the content of education itself validates men even as it invalidates women. Its very message is that men have been the shapers and thinkers of the world, and that this is only natural. The bias of higher education, including the so-called sciences, is white and male, racist and sexist; and this bias is expressed in both subtle and blatant ways. I have mentioned already the exclusiveness of grammar itself: "The student should test himself on the above questions"; "The poet is representative. He stands among partial men for the complete man." Despite a few half-hearted departures from custom, what the linguist Wendy Martyna has named "He-Man" grammar prevails throughout the culture. The efforts of feminists to reveal the profound ontological implications of sexist grammar are routinely ridiculed by academicians and journalists, including the professedly liberal *Times* columnist, Tom Wicker, and the professed humanist, Jacques Barzun. Sexist grammar burns into the brains of little girls and young women a message that the male is the norm, the standard, the central figure beside which we are the deviants, the marginal, the dependent variables. It lays the foundation for androcentric thinking, and leaves men safe in their solipsistic tunnel-vision.

Women and men do not receive an equal education because outside the classroom women are perceived not as sovereign beings but as prey. The

growing incidence of rape on and off the campus may or may not be fed by
the proliferations of pornographic magazines and X-rated films available to
young males in fraternities and student unions; but it is certainly occurring in
a context of widespread images of sexual violence against women, on billboards
and in so-called high art. More subtle, more daily than rape is the verbal abuse
experienced by the woman student on many campuses—Rutgers for example—where, traversing a street lined with fraternity houses, she must run a
gauntlet of male commentary and verbal assault. The undermining of self, of
a woman's sense of her right to occupy space and walk freely in the world, is
deeply relevant to education. The capacity to think independently, to take
intellectual risks, to assert ourselves mentally, is inseparable from our physical
way of being in the world, our feelings of personal integrity. If it is dangerous
for me to walk home late of an evening from the library, *because I am a woman
and can be raped*, how self-possessed, how exuberant can I feel as I sit working
in that library? how much of my working energy is drained by the subliminal
knowledge that, as a woman, I test my physical right to exist each time I go
out alone? Of this knowledge, Susan Griffin has written:

> . . . more than rape itself, the fear of rape permeates our lives. And what
> does one do from day to day, with *this* experience, which says, without words
> and directly to the heart, *your existence, your experience, may end at any mo-
> ment*. Your experience may end, and the best defense against this is not to
> be, to deny being in the body, as a self, to . . . avert your gaze, make yourself,
> as a presence in the world, less felt.[1]

Finally, rape of the mind. Women students are more and more often now
reporting sexual overtures by male professors—one part of our overall growing consciousness of sexual harassment in the workplace. At Yale a legal suit
has been brought against the university by a group of women demanding an
explicit policy against sexual advances toward female students by male professors. Most young women experience a profound mixture of humiliation and
intellectual self-doubt over seductive gestures by men who have the power to
award grades, open doors to grants and graduate school, or extend special
knowledge and training. Even if turned aside, such gestures constitute mental
rape, destructive to a woman's ego. They are acts of domination, as despicable
as the molestation of the daughter by the father.

But long before entering college the woman student has experienced her
alien identity in a world which misnames her, turns her to its own uses, denying

---

1. Quoted from the manuscript of her forthcoming book, *Rape: The Power of Consciousness*; to be
published in 1979 by Harper & Row.

her the resources she needs to become self-affirming, self-defined. The nuclear family teaches her that relationships are more important than selfhood or work; that "whether the phone rings for you, and how often," having the right clothes, doing the dishes, take precedence over study or solitude; that too much intelligence or intensity may make her unmarriageable; that marriage and children—service to others—are, finally, the points on which her life will be judged a success or a failure. In high school, the polarization between feminine attractiveness and independent intelligence comes to an absolute. Meanwhile, the culture resounds with messages. During Solar Energy Week in New York I saw young women wearing "ecology" T-shirts with the legend: CLEAN, CHEAP AND AVAILABLE; a reminder of the 1960s antiwar button which read: CHICKS SAY YES TO MEN WHO SAY NO. Department store windows feature female mannequins in chains, pinned to the wall with legs spread, smiling in positions of torture. Feminists are depicted in the media as "shrill," "strident," "puritanical," or "humorless," and the lesbian choice—the choice of the woman-identified woman—as pathological or sinister. The young woman sitting in the philosophy classroom, the political science lecture, is already gripped by tensions between her nascent sense of self-worth, and the battering force of messages like these.

Look at a classroom: look at the many kinds of women's faces, postures, expressions. Listen to the women's voices. Listen to the silences, the unasked questions, the blanks. Listen to the small, soft voices, often courageously trying to speak up, voices of women taught early that tones of confidence, challenge, anger, or assertiveness, are strident and unfeminine. Listen to the voices of the women and the voices of the men; observe the space men allow themselves, physically and verbally, the male assumption that people will listen, even when the majority of the group is female. Look at the faces of the silent, and of those who speak. Listen to a woman groping for language in which to express what is on her mind, sensing that the terms of academic discourse are not her language, trying to cut down her thought to the dimensions of a discourse not intended for her *(for it is not fitting that a woman speak in public)*; or reading her paper aloud at breakneck speed, throwing her words away, deprecating her own work by a reflex prejudgment: *I do not deserve to take up time and space.*

As women teachers, we can either deny the importance of this context in which women students think, write, read, study, project their own futures; or try to work with it. We can either teach passively, accepting these conditions, or actively, helping our students identify and resist them.

One important thing we can do is *discuss* the context. And this need not happen only in a women's studies course; it can happen anywhere. We can refuse to accept passive, obedient learning and insist upon critical thinking. We can become harder on our women students, giving them the kinds of "cultural prodding" that men receive, but on different terms and in a different style. Most young women need to have their intellectual lives, their work, legitimized against the claims of family, relationships, the old message that a woman is always available for service to others. We need to keep our standards very high, not to accept a woman's preconceived sense of her limitations; we need to be hard to please, while supportive of risk-taking, because self-respect often comes only when exacting standards have been met. At a time when adult literacy is generally low, we need to demand more, not less, of women, both for the sake of their futures as thinking beings, and because historically women have always had to be better than men to do half as well. A romantic sloppiness, an inspired lack of rigor, a self-indulgent incoherence, are symptoms of female self-depreciation. We should help our women students to look very critically at such symptoms, and to understand where they are rooted.

Nor does this mean we should be training women students to "think like men." Men in general think badly: in disjuncture from their personal lives, claiming objectivity where the most irrational passions seethe, losing, as Virginia Woolf observed, their senses in the pursuit of professionalism. It is not easy to think like a woman in a man's world, in the world of the professions; yet the capacity to do that is a strength which we can try to help our students develop. To think like a woman in a man's world means thinking critically, refusing to accept the givens, making connections between facts and ideas which men have left unconnected. It means remembering that every mind resides in a body; remaining accountable to the female bodies in which we live; constantly retesting given hypotheses against lived experience. It means a constant critique of language, for as Wittgenstein (no feminist) observed, "The limits of my language are the limits of my world." And it means that most difficult thing of all: listening and watching in art and literature, in the social sciences, in all the descriptions we are given of the world, for the silences, the absences, the nameless, the unspoken, the encoded—for there we will find the true knowledge of women. And in breaking those silences, naming our selves, uncovering the hidden, making ourselves present, we begin to define a reality which resonates to *us*, which affirms *our* being, which allows the woman teacher and the woman student alike to take ourselves, and each other, seriously: meaning, to begin taking charge of our lives.

Violence and Social Control

"THE MIND THAT BURNS IN EACH BODY": *Women, Rape, and Racial Violence*

44

Jacquelyn Dowd Hall

HOSTILITY FOCUSED ON HUMAN FLESH

> FLORIDA TO BURN NEGRO AT STAKE: SEX CRIMINAL SEIZED FROM JAIL, WILL BE MUTILATED, SET AFIRE IN EXTRA-LEGAL VENGEANCE FOR DEED
>
> —Dothan (Alabama) *Eagle,* October 26, 1934

> After taking the nigger to the woods . . . they cut off his penis. He was made to eat it. Then they cut off his testicles and made him eat them and say he liked it.
>
> —Member of a lynch mob, 1934[1]

Lynching, like rape, has not yet been given its history. Perhaps it has been too easily relegated to the shadows where "poor white" stereotypes dwell. Perhaps the image of absolute victimization it evokes has been too difficult to

From: Ann Snitow, Christine Stansell, and Sharon Thompson (eds.), *Powers of Desire: The Politics of Sexuality* (New York: Monthly Review, 1983), pp. 328–349. Copyright © 1983 by Ann Snitow, Christine Stansell, and Sharon Thompson. Reprinted by permission.

reconcile with what we know about black resilience and resistance. Yet the impact of lynching, both as practice and as symbol, can hardly be underestimated. Between 1882 and 1946 almost 5,000 people died by lynching. The lynching of Emmett Till in 1955 for whistling at a white woman, the killing of three civil rights workers in Mississippi in the 1960s, and the hanging of a black youth in Alabama in 1981 all illustrate the persistence of this tradition of ritual violence in the service of racial control, a tradition intimately bound up with the politics of sexuality.

Vigilantism originated on the eighteenth-century frontier where it filled a vacuum in law enforcement. Rather than passing with the frontier, however, lynching was incorporated into the distinctive legal system of southern slave society.[2] In the nineteenth century, the industrializing North moved toward a modern criminal justice system in which police, courts, and prisons administered an impersonal, bureaucratic rule of law designed to uphold property rights and discipline unruly workers. The South, in contrast, maintained order through a system of deference and customary authority in which all whites had informal police power over all blacks, slave owners meted out plantation justice undisturbed by any generalized rule of law, and the state encouraged vigilantism as part of its overall reluctance to maintain a strong system of formal authority that would have undermined the planter's prerogatives. The purpose of one system was class control, of the other, control over a slave population. And each tradition continued into the period after the Civil War. In the North, factory-like penitentiaries warehoused displaced members of the industrial proletariat. The South maintained higher rates of personal violence than any other region in the country and lynching crossed over the line from informal law enforcement into outright political terrorism.

White supremacy, of course, did not rest on force alone. Routine institutional arrangements denied to the freedmen and women the opportunity to own land, the right to vote, access to education, and participation in the administration of the law. Lynching reached its height during the battles of Reconstruction and the Populist revolt; once a new system of disfranchisement, debt peonage, and segregation was firmly in place, mob violence gradually declined. Yet until World War I, the average number of lynchings never fell below two or three a week. Through the twenties and thirties, mob violence reinforced white dominance by providing planters with a quasi-official way of enforcing labor contracts and crop lien laws and local officials with a means of extracting deference, regardless of the letter of the law. Individuals may have lynched for their own twisted reasons, but the practice continued only with tacit official consent.[3]

Most importantly, lynching served as a tool of psychological intimidation aimed at blacks as a group. Unlike official authority, the lynch mob was unlimited in its capriciousness. With care and vigilance, an individual might avoid situations that landed him in the hands of the law. But a lynch mob could strike anywhere, any time. Once the brush fire of rumor began, a manhunt was organized, and the local paper began putting out special editions announcing a lynching in progress, there could be few effective reprieves. If the intended victim could not be found, an innocent bystander might serve as well.

It was not simply the threat of death that gave lynching its repressive power. Even as outbreaks of mob violence declined in frequency, they were increasingly accompanied by torture and sexual mutilation. Descriptions of the first phase of Hitler's death sweep are chillingly applicable to lynching: "Killing was ad hoc, inventive, and in its dependence on imagination, peculiarly expressive . . . this was murder uncanny in its anonymous intimacy, a hostility so personally focused on human flesh that the abstract fact of death was not enough."[4]

At the same time, the expansion of communications and the development of photography in the late nineteenth and early twentieth centuries gave reporting a vividness it had never had before. The lurid evocation of human suffering implicated white readers in each act of aggression and drove home to blacks the consequences of powerlessness. Like whipping under slavery, lynching was an instrument of coercion intended to impress not only the immediate victim but all who saw or heard about the event. And the mass media spread the imagery of rope and faggot far beyond the community in which each lynching took place. Writing about his youth in the rural South in the 1920s, Richard Wright describes the terrible climate of fear:

> The things that influenced my conduct as a Negro did not have to happen to me directly; I needed but to hear of them to feel their full effects in the deepest layers of my consciousness. Indeed, the white brutality that I had not seen was a more effective control of my behavior than that which I knew. The actual experience would have let me see the realistic outlines of what was really happening, but as long as it remained something terrible and yet remote, something whose horror and blood might descend upon me at any moment, I was compelled to give my entire imagination over to it.[5]

A penis cut off and stuffed in a victim's mouth. A crowd of thousands watching a black man scream in pain. Such incidents did not have to occur very often, or be witnessed directly, to be burned indelibly into the mind.

NEVER AGAINST HER WILL

> White men have said over and over—and we have believed it because it was repeated so often—that not only was there no such thing as a chaste Negro woman—but that a Negro woman could not be assaulted, that it was never against her will.
>
> —Jessie Daniel Ames (1936)

Schooled in the struggle against sexual rather than racial violence, contemporary feminists may nevertheless find familiar this account of lynching's political function, for analogies between rape and lynching have often surfaced in the literature of the anti-rape movement. To carry such analogies too far would be to fall into the error of radical feminist writing that misconstrues the realities of racism in the effort to illuminate sexual subordination.[6] It is the suggestion of this essay, however, that there is a significant resonance between these two forms of violence. We are only beginning to understand the web of connections among racism, attitudes toward women, and sexual ideologies. The purpose of looking more closely at the dynamics of repressive violence is not to reduce sexual assault and mob murder to static equivalents but to illuminate some of the strands of that tangled web.

The association between lynching and rape emerges most clearly in their parallel use in racial subordination. As Diane K. Lewis has pointed out, in a patriarchal society, black men, as men, constituted a potential challenge to the established order.[7] Laws were formulated primarily to exclude black men from adult male prerogatives in the public sphere, and lynching meshed with these legal mechanisms of exclusion. Black women represented a more ambiguous threat. They too were denied access to the politico-jural domain, but since they shared this exclusion with women in general, its maintenance engendered less anxiety and required less force. Lynching served primarily to dramatize hierarchies among men. In contrast, the violence directed at black women illustrates the double jeopardy of race and sex. The records of the Freedmen's Bureau and the oral histories collected by the Federal Writers' Project testify to the sexual atrocities endured by black women as whites sought to reassert their command over the newly freed slaves. Black women were sometimes executed by lynch mobs, but more routinely they served as targets of sexual assault.

Like vigilantism, the sexual exploitation of black women had been institutionalized under slavery. Whether seized through outright force or voluntarily granted within the master-slave relation, the sexual access of white men to black women was a cornerstone of patriarchal power in the South. It was used as a punishment or demanded in exchange for leniency. Like other forms of

deference and conspicuous consumption, it buttressed planter hegemony. And it served the practical economic purpose of replenishing the slave labor supply.

After the Civil War, the informal sexual arrangements of slavery shaded into the use of rape as a political weapon, and the special vulnerability of black women helped shape the ex-slaves' struggle for the prerequisites of freedom. Strong family bonds had survived the adversities of slavery; after freedom, the black family served as a bulwark against a racist society. Indeed, the sharecropping system that replaced slavery as the South's chief mode of production grew in part from the desire of blacks to withdraw from gang labor and gain control over their own work, family lives, and bodily integrity. The sharecropping family enabled women to escape white male supervision, devote their productive and reproductive powers to their own families, and protect themselves from sexual assault.[8]

Most studies of racial violence have paid little attention to the particular suffering of women.[9] Even rape has been seen less as an aspect of sexual oppression than as a transaction between white and black men. Certainly Claude Lévi-Strauss's insight that men use women as verbs with which to communicate with one another (rape being a means of communicating defeat to the men of a conquered tribe) helps explain the extreme viciousness of sexual violence in the post-emancipation era.[10] Rape *was* in part a reaction to the effort of the freedmen to assume the role of patriarch, able to provide for and protect his family. Nevertheless, as writers like Susan Griffin and Susan Brownmiller and others have made clear, rape is first and foremost a crime against women.[11] Rape sent a message to black men, but more centrally, it expressed male sexual attitudes in a culture both racist and patriarchal. . . .

In the United States, the fear and fascination of female sexuality was projected onto black women; the passionless lady arose in symbiosis with the primitively sexual slave. House slaves often served as substitute mothers; at a black woman's breast white men experienced absolute dependence on a being who was both a source of wish-fulfilling joy and of grief-producing disappointment. In adulthood, such men could find in this black woman a ready object for the mixture of rage and desire that so often underlies male heterosexuality. The black woman, already in chains, was sexually available, unable to make claims for support or concern; by dominating her, men could replay the infant's dream of unlimited access to the mother.[13] The economic and political challenge posed by the black patriarch might be met with death by lynching, but when the black woman seized the opportunity to turn her maternal and sexual resources to the benefit of her own family, sexual violence met her assertion of will. Thus rape reasserted white dominance and control in the private arena as lynching reasserted hierarchical arrangements in the public transactions of men.

LYNCHING'S DOUBLE MESSAGE

The crowds from here that went over to see [Lola Cannidy, the alleged rape victim in the Claude Neal lynching of 1934] said he was so large he could not assault her until he took his knife and cut her, and also had either cut or bit one of her breast [sic] off.

—Letter to Mrs. W. P. Cornell, October 29, 1934, Association of Southern Women for the Prevention of Lynching Papers

. . . more than rape itself, the fear of rape permeates our lives. . . . and the best defense against this is not to be, to deny being in the body, as a self, to . . . avert your gaze, make yourself, as a presence in the world, less felt.

—Susan Griffin, *Rape: The Power of Consciousness* (1979)

In the 1920s and 1930s, the industrial revolution spread through the South, bringing a demand for more orderly forms of law enforcement. Men in authority, anxious to create a favorable business climate, began to withdraw their tacit approval of extralegal violence. Yet lynching continued, particularly in rural areas, and even as white moderates criticized lynching in the abstract, they continued to justify outbreaks of mob violence for the one special crime of sexual assault. For most white Americans, the association between lynching and rape called to mind not twin forms of white violence against black men and women, but a very different image: the black rapist, "a monstrous beast, crazed with lust";[13] the white victim—young, blond, virginal; her manly Anglo-Saxon avengers. Despite the pull of modernity, the emotional logic of lynching remained: only swift, sure violence, unhampered by legalities, could protect white women from sexual assault.

The "protection of white womanhood" was a pervasive fixture of racist ideology. In 1839, for example, a well-known historian offered this commonly accepted rationale for lynching: black men find "something strangely alluring and seductive . . . in the appearance of the white woman; they are aroused and stimulated by its foreignness to their experience of sexual pleasures, and it moves them to gratify their lust at any cost and in spite of every obstacle." In 1937, echoing an attitude that characterized most local newspapers, the Jackson, Mississippi, *Daily News* published what it felt was the *coup de grace* to anti-lynching critics: "What would you do if your wife, daughter, or one of your loved ones was ravished? You'd probably be right there with the mob." Two years later, 65 percent of the white respondents in an anthropological survey believed that lynching was justified in cases of sexual assault.[14] Despite its tenacity, however, the myth of the black rapist was never founded on objective reality. Less than a quarter of lynch victims were even accused of rape or attempted rape. Down to the present, almost every study has underlined the fact that rape is overwhelmingly an intraracial crime, and the victims are more often black than white.[15]

A major strategy of anti-lynching reformers, beginning with Ida B. Wells in the 1880s and continuing with Walter White of the NAACP and Jessie Daniel Ames of the Association of Southern Women for the Prevention of Lynching, was to use such facts to undermine the rationalizations for mob violence. But the emotional circuit between interracial rape and lynching lay beyond the reach of factual refutation. A black man did not literally have to attempt sexual assault for whites to perceive some transgression of caste mores as a sexual threat. White women were the forbidden fruit, the untouchable property, the ultimate symbol of white male power. To break the racial rules was to conjure up an image of black over white, of a world turned upside down.

Again, women were a means of communication and, on one level, the rhetoric of protection, like the rape of black women, reflected a power struggle among men. But impulses toward women as well as toward blacks were played out in the drama of racial violence. The fear of rape was more than a hypocritical excuse for lynching; rather, the two phenomena were intimately intertwined. The "southern rape complex" functioned as a means of both sexual and racial suppression.[16]

For whites, the archetypal lynching for rape can be seen as a dramatization of cultural themes, a story they told themselves about the social arrangements and psychological strivings that lay beneath the surface of everyday life. The story such rituals told about the place of white women in southern society was subtle, contradictory, and demeaning. The frail victim, leaning on the arms of her male relatives, might be brought to the scene of the crime, there to identify her assailant and witness his execution. This was a moment of humiliation. A woman who had just been raped, or who had been apprehended in a clandestine interracial affair, or whose male relatives were pretending that she had been raped, stood on display before the whole community. Here was the quintessential Woman as Victim: polluted, "ruined for life," the object of fantasy and secret contempt. Humiliation, however, mingled with heightened worth as she played for a moment the role of the Fair Maiden violated and avenged. For this privilege—if the alleged assault had in fact taken place—she might pay with suffering in the extreme. In any case, she would pay with a lifetime of subjugation to the men gathered in her behalf.

Only a small percentage of lynchings, then, revolved around charges of sexual assault; but those that did received by far the most attention and publicity—indeed, they gripped the white imagination far out of proportion to their statistical significance. Rape and rumors of rape became the folk pornography of the Bible Belt. As stories spread the rapist became not just a black man but a ravenous brute, the victim a beautiful young virgin. The experience of the woman was described in minute and progressively embellished detail, a public fantasy that implied a group participation in the rape as cathartic as the subsequent lynching. White men might see in "lynch law" their ideal selves: patriarchs, avengers, righteous protectors. But, being men themselves, and sometimes even rapists, they must also have seen themselves in the lynch mob's prey.

The lynch mob in pursuit of the black rapist represented the trade-off implicit in the code of chivalry: for the right of the southern lady to protection presupposed her obligation to obey. The connotations of wealth and family background attached to the position of the lady in the antebellum South faded in the twentieth century, but the power of "ladyhood" as a value construct remained. The term denoted chastity, frailty, graciousness. "A lady," noted one social-psychologist, "is always in a state of becoming: one acts like a lady, one attempts to be a lady, but one never *is* a lady." Internalized by the individual, this ideal regulated behavior and restricted interaction with the world.[17] If a woman passed the tests of ladyhood, she could tap into the reservoir of protectiveness and shelter known as southern chivalry. Women who abandoned secure, if circumscribed, social roles forfeited the claim to personal security. Together the practice of ladyhood and the etiquette of chivalry controlled white women's behavior even as they guarded caste lines. . . .

THE DECLINE OF CHIVALRY

> As male supremacy becomes ideologically untenable, incapable of justifying itself as protection, men assert their domination more directly, in fantasies and occasionally in acts of raw violence.
>
> —Christopher Lasch, *Marxist Perspectives* (1978)

In the 1970s, for the second time in the nation's history, rape again attracted widespread public attention. The obsession with interracial rape, which peaked at the turn of the nineteenth century but lingered from the close of the Civil War into the 1930s, became a magnet for racial and sexual oppression. Today the issue of rape has crystallized important feminist concerns.

Rape emerged as a feminist issue as women developed an independent politics that made sexuality and personal life a central arena of struggle. First in consciousness-raising groups, where autobiography became a politicizing technique, then in public "speakouts," women broke what in retrospect seems a remarkable silence about a pervasive aspect of female experience. From that beginning flowed both an analysis that held rape to be a political act by which men affirm their power over women and strategies for change that ranged from the feminist self-help methods of rape crisis centers to institutional reform of the criminal justice and medical care systems. After 1976, the movement broadened to include wife-battering, sexual harassment, and, following the lead of Robin Morgan's claim that "pornography is the theory, rape the practice," media images of women.[18]

By the time Susan Brownmiller's *Against Our Will: Men, Women and Rape* gained national attention in 1975, she could speak to and for a feminist constituency already sensitized to the issue by years of practical, action-oriented work. Her book can be faulted for supporting a notion of universal patriarchy and timeless sexual victimization; it leaves no room for understanding the reasons for women's collaboration, their own sources of power (both self-generated and derived), the class and racial differences in their experience of discrimination and sexual danger. But it was an important milestone, pointing the way for research into a subject that has consistently been trivialized and ignored. Many grass-roots activists would demur from Brownmiller's assertion that all men are potential rapists, but they share her understanding of the continuum between sexism and sexual assault.[19]

The demand for control over one's own body—control over whether, when, and with whom one has children, control over how one's sexuality is expressed—is central to the feminist project because, as Rosalind Petchesky persuasively argues, it is essential to "a sense of being a person, with personal and bodily integrity," able to engage in conscious activity and to participate in social life.[20] It is the right to bodily integrity and self-determination that rape, and the fear of rape, so thoroughly undermines. Rape's devastating effect on individuals derives not so much from the sexual nature of the crime (and anti-rape activists have been concerned to revise the idea that rape is a "fate worse than death" whose victims, if no longer "ruined for life," are at least so traumatized that they must rely for recovery on therapeutic help rather than on their own resources) as from the experience of helplessness and loss of control, the sense of one's self as an object of rape. And women who may never be raped share, by chronic attrition, in the same helplessness, "otherness," lack of control. The struggle against rape, like the anti-lynching movement, addresses not only external dangers but also internal consequences: the bodily muting, the self-censorship that limits one's capacity to "walk freely in the world."[21]

The focus on rape, then, emerged from the internal dynamics of feminist thought and practice. But it was also a response to an objective increase in the crime. From 1969 to 1974, the number of rapes rose 49 percent, a greater increase than for any other violent crime. Undoubtedly rape statistics reflect general demographic and criminal trends, as well as a greater willingness of victims to report sexual attacks (although observers agree that rape is still the most underreported of crimes).[22] But there can be no doubt that rape is a serious threat and that it plays a prominent role in women's subordination. Using recent high-quality survey data, Allan Griswold Johnson has estimated that, at a minimum, 20 to 30 percent of girls now twelve years old will suffer a violent attack sometime in their lives. A woman is as likely to be raped as she is to experience a divorce or to be diagnosed as having cancer.[23]

In a recent anthology on women and pornography, Tracey A. Gardner has drawn a parallel between the wave of lynching that followed Reconstruction and the increase in rapes in an era of anti-feminist backlash.[24] Certainly, as women enter the workforce, postpone marriage, live alone or as single heads of households, they become easier targets for sexual assault. But observations like Gardner's go further, linking the intensification of sexual violence directly to the feminist challenge. Such arguments come dangerously close to blaming the victim for the crime. But they may also contain a core of truth. Sociological research on rape has only recently begun, and we do not have studies explaining the function and frequency of the crime under various historical conditions; until that work is done we cannot with certainty assess the current situation. Yet it seems clear that just as lynching ebbed and flowed with new modes of racial control, rape—both as act and idea—cannot be divorced from changes in the sexual terrain.

In 1940, Jessie Ames released to the press a statement that, for the first time in her career, the South could claim a "lynchless year," and in 1942, convinced that lynching was no longer widely condoned in the name of white womanhood, she allowed the Association of Southern Women for the Prevention of Lynching to pass quietly from the scene. The women's efforts, the larger, black-led anti-lynching campaign, black migration from the rural South, the spread of industry—these and other developments contributed to the decline of vigilante justice. Blacks continued to be victimized by covert violence and routinized court procedures that amounted to "legal lynchings." But after World War II, public lynchings, announced in the papers, openly accomplished, and tacitly condoned, no longer haunted the land, and the black rapist ceased to be a fixture of political campaigns and newspaper prose.

This change in the rhetoric and form of racial violence reflected new attitudes toward women as well as toward blacks. By the 1940s few southern leaders were willing, as Jessie Ames put it, to "lay themselves open to ridicule" by defending lynching on the grounds of gallantry, in part because gallantry itself had lost conviction.[25] The same process of economic development and national integration that encouraged the South to adopt northern norms of authority and control undermined the chivalric ideal. Industrial capitalism on the one hand and women's assertion of independence on the other weakened paternalism and with it the conventions of protective deference.[26] This is not to say that the link between racism and sexism was broken; relations between white women and black men continued to be severely sanctioned, and black men, to the present, have drawn disproportionate punishment for sexual assault. The figures speak for themselves: of the 455 men executed for rape since 1930, 405 were black, and almost all the complainants were white.[27] Nevertheless, "the protection of white womanhood" rang more hollow in the postwar New South and the fear of interracial rape became a subdued theme in the nation at large rather than an openly articulated regional obsession.

The social feminist mainstream, of which Jessie Ames and the anti-lynching association were a part, thus chipped away at a politics of gallantry that locked white ladies in the home under the guise of protecting them from the world. But because such reformers held to the genteel trappings of their role even as they asserted their autonomous citizenship, they offered reassurance that women's influence could be expanded without mortal danger to male prerogatives and power. Contemporary feminists have eschewed some of the comforting assumptions of their nineteenth-century predecessors: women's passionlessness, their limitation to social housekeeping, their exclusive responsibility for childrearing and housekeeping. They have couched their revolt in explicit ideology and unladylike behavior. Meanwhile, as Barbara Ehrenreich has argued, Madison Avenue has perverted the feminist message into the threatening image of the sexually and economically liberated woman. The result is a shift toward the rapaciousness that has always mixed unstably with sentimental exaltation and concern. Rape has emerged more clearly into the sexual domain, a crime against women most often committed by men of their own race rather than a right of the powerful over women of a subordinate group or a blow by black men against white women's possessors.[28]

It should be emphasized, however, that the connection between feminism and the upsurge of rape lies not so much in women's gains but in their assertion of rights within a context of economic vulnerability and relative powerlessness. In a perceptive article published in 1901, Jane Addams traced lynching in part to "the feeling of the former slave owner to his former slave, whom he is now bidden to regard as his fellow citizen."[29] Blacks in the post-Reconstruction era were able to express will and individuality, to wrest from their former masters certain concessions and build for themselves supporting institutions. Yet they lacked the resources to protect themselves from economic exploitation and mob violence. Similarly, contemporary feminist efforts have not yet succeeded in overcoming women's isolation, their economic and emotional dependence on men, their cultural training toward submission. There are few restraints against sexual aggression, since up to 90 percent of rapes go unreported, 50 percent of assailants who are reported are never caught, and seven out of ten prosecutions end in acquittal.[30] Provoked by the commercialization of sex, cut loose from traditional community restraints, and "bidden to regard as his fellow citizen" a female being whose subordination has deep roots in the psyches of both sexes, men turn with impunity to the use of sexuality as a means of asserting dominance and control. Such fear and rage are condoned when channeled into right-wing attacks on women's claim to a share in public power and control over their bodies. Inevitably they also find expression in less acceptable behavior. Rape, like lynching, flourishes in an atmosphere in which official policies toward members of a subordinate group give individuals tacit permission to hurt and maim.

In 1972 Anne Braden, a southern white woman and long-time activist in civil rights struggles, expressed her fear that the new anti-rape movement might find itself "objectively on the side of the most reactionary social forces" unless it heeded a lesson from history. In a pamphlet entitled *Open Letter to Southern White Women*—much circulated in regional women's liberation circles at the time—she urged anti-rape activists to remember the long pattern of racist manipulation of rape fears. She called on white women, "for their own liberation, to refuse any longer to be used, to act in the tradition of Jessie Daniel Ames and the white women who fought in an earlier period to end lynching," and she went on to discuss her own politicization through left-led protests against the prosecution of black men on false rape charges. Four years later, she joined the chorus of black feminist criticism of *Against Our Will*, seeing Brownmiller's book as a realization of her worst fears.[31]

Since this confrontation between the Old Left and the New, between a white woman who placed herself in a southern tradition of feminist anti-racism and a radical feminist from the North, a black women's movement has emerged, bringing its own perspectives to bear. White activists at the earliest "speakouts" had acknowledged "the racist image of black men as rapists," pointed out the large number of black women among assault victims, and debated the contradictions involved in looking for solutions to a race and class-biased court system. But not until black women had developed their own autonomous organizations and strategies were true alliances possible across racial lines.

A striking example of this development is the Washington, D.C., Rape Crisis Center. One of the first and largest such groups in the country, the center has evolved from a primarily white self-help project to an aggressive interracial organization with a multifaceted program of support services, advocacy, and community education. In a city with an 80 percent black population and more than four times as many women as men, the center has recruited black leadership by channeling its resources into staff salaries and steering clear of the pitfalls of middle-class voluntarism on the one hand and professionalism on the other. It has challenged the perception of the anti-rape movement as a "white woman's thing" by stressing not only rape's devastating effect on women but also its impact on social relations in the black community. Just as racism undermined working-class unity and lynching sometimes pitted poor whites against blacks, sexual aggression now divides the black community against itself. In a society that defines manhood in terms of power and possessions, black men are denied the resources to fulfill their expected roles. Inevitably, they turn to domination of women, the one means of manhood within their control. From consciousness-raising groups for convicted rapists to an intensive educational campaign funded by the city's public school system and aimed at both boys and girls from elementary through high school, the center has tried to alter the cultural plan for both sexes that makes men potential rapists and women potential victims.[32]

As the anti-rape movement broadens to include Third World women, analogies between lynching and rape and the models of women like Ida B. Wells and Jessie Daniel Ames may become increasingly useful. Neither lynching nor rape is the "aberrant behavior of a lunatic fringe."[33] Rather, both grow out of everyday modes of interaction. The view of women as objects to be possessed, conquered, or defiled fueled racial hostility; conversely, racism has continued to distort and confuse the struggle against sexual violence. Black men receive harsher punishment for raping white women, black rape victims are especially demeaned and ignored, and, until recently, the different historical experience of black and white women has hindered them from making common cause. Taking a cue from the women's anti-lynching campaign of the 1930s as well as from the innovative tactics of black feminists, the anti-rape movement must not limit itself to training women to avoid rape or depending on imprisonment as a deterrent, but must aim its attention at changing the behavior and attitudes of men. Mindful of the historical connection between rape and lynching, it must make clear its stand against *all* uses of violence in oppression.

NOTES

My title comes from Adrienne Rich, "Disloyal to Civilization: Feminism, Racism, Gynephobia," in Rich, *On Lies, Secrets and Silences: Selected Prose, 1966–1978* (New York: W. W. Norton, 1979), p. 299. Parts of this essay are taken from Jacquelyn Down Hall, *Revolt Against Chivalry: Jessie Daniel Ames and the Women's Campaign Against Chivalry* (New York: Columbia University Press, 1979), and full documentation can be found in that work. See also Hall, " 'A Truly Subversive Affair': Women Against Lynching in the Twentieth-Century South," in *Women of America:*

A History, eds. Carol Berkin and Mary Beth Norton (Boston: Houghton Mifflin, 1979). Thanks to Rosemarie Hester, Walter Dellinger, Loretta Ross, Nkenge Toure, Janet Colm, Kathleen Dowdy, and Nell Painter for their help and encouragement.

1. Quoted in Howard Kester, *The Lynching of Claude Neal* (New York: National Association for the Advancement of Colored People, 1934).

2. Michael Stephen Hindus, *Prison and Plantation: Crime, Justice, and Authority in Massachusetts and South Carolina, 1767–1878* (Chapel Hill: University of North Carolina Press, 1980), pp. xix, 31, 124, 253.

3. For recent overviews of lynching, see Robert L. Zangrando, *The NAACP Crusade Against Lynching, 1909–1950* (Philadelphia: Temple University Press, 1980); McGovern, *Anatomy of a Lynching*; and Hall, *Revolt Against Chivalry*.

4. Terrence Des Pres, "The Struggle of Memory," *The Nation*, 10 April 1982, p. 433.

5. Quoted in William H. Chafe, *Women and Equality: Changing Patterns in American Culture* (New York: Oxford University Press, 1977), p. 60.

6. Margaret A. Simons, "Racism and Feminism: A Schism in the Sisterhood," *Feminist Studies* 5 (Summer 1979): 384–401.

7. Diane K. Lewis, "A Response to Inequality: Black Women, Racism, and Sexism," *Signs* 3 (Winter 1977): 341–42.

8. Jacqueline Jones, *Freed Women?: Black Women, Work, and the Family During the Civil War and Reconstruction*, Working Paper No. 61, Wellesley College, 1980; Roger L. Ransom and Richard Sutch, *One Kind of Freedom: The Economic Consequences of Emancipation* (New York: Cambridge University Press, 1977), pp. 87–103.

9. Gerda Lerner, *Black Women in White America: A Documentary History* (New York: Random House, 1972), is an early and important exception.

10. Robin Morgan, "Theory and Practice: Pornography and Rape," *Take Back the Night: Women on Pornography*, ed. Laura Lederer (New York: William Morrow, 1980), p. 140.

11. Susan Griffin, "Rape: The All-American Crime," *Ramparts* (September 1971): 26–35; Susan Brownmiller, *Against Our Will: Men, Women, and Rape* (New York: Simon and Schuster, 1975). See also Kate Millet, *Sexual Politics* (Garden City, N.Y.: Doubleday & Co., 1970).

12. Dorothy Dinnerstein, *The Mermaid and the Minotaur: Sexual Arrangements and Human Malaise* (New York: Harper and Row, 1977). See also Phyllis Marynick Palmer, "White Women/Black Women: The Dualism of Female Identity and Experience," unpublished paper presented at the American Studies Association, September 1979, pp. 15–17. Similarly, British Victorian eroticism was structured by class relations in which upper-class men were nursed by lower-class country women. . . .

13. A statement made in 1901 by George T. Winston, president of the University of North Carolina, typifies these persistent images: "The southern woman with her helpless little children in a solitary farm house no longer sleeps secure. . . . The black brute is lurking in the dark, a monstrous beast, crazed with lust. His ferocity is almost demoniacal. A mad bull or a tiger could scarcely be more brutal" (quoted in Charles Herbert Stember, *Sexual Racism: The Emotional Barrier to an Integrated Society* [New York: Elsevier, 1976], p. 23).

14. Philip Alexander Bruce, *The Plantation Negro as a Freeman* (New York: Putnam's, 1889), pp. 83–84; Jackson *Daily News*, 27 May 1937; Hortense Powdermaker, *After Freedom: A Cultural Study in the Deep South* (1939; New York: Atheneum, 1969), pp. 54–55, 389.

15. For a contradictory view, see, for example, S. Nelson and M. Amir, "The Hitchhike Victim of Rape: A Research Report," in *Victimology: A New Focus. Vol. 5: Exploiters and Exploited*, eds. M. Agopian, D. Chappell, and G. Geis, and I. Drapkin and E. Viano (1975), p. 47; and "Black Offender and White Victim: A Study of Forcible Rape in Oakland, California," in *Forcible Rape: The Crime, the Victim, and the Offender* (New York: Columbia University Press, 1977).

16. Winthrop Jordan, *White over Black: American Attitudes Toward the Negro, 1550–1812* (Baltimore: Penguin Books, 1969); W. J. Cash, *The Mind of the South* (New York: Knopf, 1941), p. 117.

17. This reading of lynching as a "cultural text" is modeled on Clifford Geertz, "Deep Play: Notes on the Balinese Cockfight," in *The Interpretation of Cultures: Selected Essays by Clifford Geertz* (New York: Basic Books, 1973), pp. 412–53. For "ladyhood," see Greer Litton Fox, " 'Nice Girl': Social Control of Women Through a Value Construct," *Signs* 2 (Summer 1977): 805–17.

18. Noreen Connell and Cassandra Wilsen, eds., *Rape: The First Sourcebook for Women* (New York: New American Library, 1974); Morgan, "Theory and Practice."

19. Interview with Janet Colm, director of the Chapel Hill-Carrboro (North Carolina) Rape Crisis Center, April 1981. Two of the best recent analyses of rape are Ann Wolbert Burgess and Lynda Lytle Holmstrom, *Rape: Crisis and Recovery* (Bowie, Md.: Robert J. Brady Co., 1979) and Lorenne M. G. Clark and Debra J. Lewis, *Rape: The Price of Coercive Sexuality* (Toronto: Canadian Women's Educational Press, 1977).

20. Rosalind Pollack Petchesky, "Reproductive Freedom: Beyond 'A Woman's Right to Choose,' " *Signs* 5 (Summer 1980): 661–85.

21. Adrienne Rich, "Taking Women Students Seriously," in *Lies, Secrets and Silences*, p. 242.

22. Vivian Berger, "Man's Trial, Woman's Tribulation: Rape Cases in the Courtroom," *Columbia Law Review* 1 (1977): 3–12. Thanks to Walter Dellinger for this reference.

23. Allan Griswold Johnson, "On the Prevalence of Rape in the United States," *Signs* 6 (Fall 1980): 136–46.

24. Tracey A. Gardner, "Racism in Pornography and the Women's Movement," in *Take Back the Night*, p. 111.

25. Jessie Daniel Ames, "Editorial Treatment of Lynching," *Public Opinion Quarterly* 2 (January 1938): 77–84.

26. For a statement of this theme, see Christopher Lasch, "The Flight from Feeling: Sociopsychology of Sexual Conflict," *Marxist Perspectives* 1 (Spring 1978): 74–95.

27. Berger, "Man's Trial, Woman's Tribulation," p. 4. For a recent study indicating that the harsher treatment accorded black men convicted of raping white women is not limited to the South and has persisted to the present, see Gary D. LaFree, "The Effect of Sexual Stratification by Race on Official Reactions to Rape," *American Sociological Review* 45 (October 1980): 842–54. Thanks to Darnell Hawkins for this reference.

28. Barbara Ehrenreich, "The Women's Movement: Feminist and Antifeminist," *Radical America* 15 (Spring 1981): 93–101; Lasch, "Flight from Feeling." Because violence against women is so inadequately documented, it is impossible to make accurate racial comparisons in the incidence of the crime. Studies conducted by Menachen Amir in the late 1950s indicated that rape was primarily intraracial, with 77 percent of rapes involving black victims and black defendants and 18 percent involving whites. More recent investigations claim a somewhat higher percentage of interracial assaults. Statistics on reported rapes show that black women are more vulnerable to assault than white women. However, since black women are more likely than white women to report assaults, and since acquaintance rape, most likely to involve higher status white men, is the most underreported of crimes, the vulnerability of white women is undoubtedly much greater than statistics indicate (Berger, "Man's Trial, Woman's Tribulation," p. 3, n. 16; LaFree, "Effect of Sexual Stratification," p. 845, n. 3; Johnson, "On the Prevalence of Rape," p. 145).

29. Quoted in Aptheker, *Lynching and Rape*, pp. 10–11.

30. Berger, "Woman's Trial, Man's Tribulation," p. 6; Johnson, "On the Prevalence of Rape," p. 138.

31. Anne Braden, "A Second Open Letter to Southern White Women," *Generations: Women in the South*, a special issue of *Southern Exposure* 4 (Winter 1977), edited by Susan Angell, Jacquelyn Dowd Hall, and Candace Waid.

32. Interview with Loretta Ross and Nkenge Toure, Washington, D.C., May 12, 1981. See also Rape Crisis Center of Washington, D.C., *How to Start a Rape Crisis Center* (1972, 1977).

33. Johnson, "On the Prevalence of Rape," p. 137.

FRATERNITIES AND RAPE ON CAMPUS   45

Patricia Yancey Martin and Robert A. Hummer

Rapes are perpetrated on dates, at parties, in chance encounters, and in specially planned circumstances. That group structure and processes, rather than individual values or characteristics, are the impetus for many rape episodes was documented by Blanchard (1959) 30 years ago (also see Geis 1971), yet sociologists have failed to pursue this theme (for an exception, see Chancer 1987). A recent review of research (Muehlenhard and Linton 1987) on sexual violence, or rape, devotes only a few pages to the situational context of rape events, and these are conceptualized as potential risk factors for individuals rather than qualities of rape-prone social contexts.

Many rapes, far more than come to the public's attention, occur in fraternity houses on college and university campuses, yet little research has analyzed fraternities at American colleges and universities as rape-prone contexts (cf. Ehrhart and Sandler 1985). Most of the research on fraternities reports on samples of individual fraternity men. One group of studies compares the values, attitudes, perceptions, family socioeconomic status, psychological traits (aggressiveness, dependence), and so on, of fraternity and nonfraternity men (Bohrnstedt 1969; Fox, Hodge, and Ward 1987; Kanin 1967; Lemire 1979; Miller 1973). A second group attempts to identify the effects of fraternity membership over time on the values, attitudes, beliefs, or moral precepts of members (Hughes and Winston 1987; Marlowe and Auvenshine 1982; Miller 1973; Wilder, Hoyt, Doren, Hauck, and Zettle 1978; Wilder, Hoyt, Surbeck, Wilder, and Carney 1986). With minor exceptions, little research addresses the group and organizational context of fraternities or the social construction of fraternity life (for exceptions, see Letchworth 1969; Longino and Kart 1973; Smith 1964).

From: *Gender & Society* 3 (December 1989): 457–473. Reprinted by permission of Sage Publications, Inc.

Authors' note: We gratefully thank Meena Harris and Diane Mennella for assisting with data collection. The senior author thanks the graduate students in her fall 1988 graduate research methods seminar for help with developing the initial conceptual framework. Judith Lorber and two anonymous *Gender & Society* referees made numerous suggestions for improving our article and we thank them also.

Gary Tash, writing as an alumnus and trial attorney in his fraternity's magazine, claims that over 90 percent of all gang rapes on college campuses involve fraternity men (1988, p. 2). Tash provides no evidence to substantiate this claim, but students of violence against women have been concerned with fraternity men's frequently reported involvement in rape episodes (Adams and Abarbanel 1988). Ehrhart and Sandler (1985) identify over 50 cases of gang rapes on campus perpetrated by fraternity men, and their analysis points to many of the conditions that we discuss here. Their analysis is unique in focusing on conditions in fraternities that make gang rapes of women by fraternity men both feasible and probable. They identify excessive alcohol use, isolation from external monitoring, treatment of women as prey, use of pornography, approval of violence, and excessive concern with competition as precipitating conditions to gang rape (also see Merton 1985; Roark 1987).

The study reported here confirmed and complemented these findings by focusing on both conditions and processes. We examined dynamics associated with the social construction of fraternity life, with a focus on processes that foster the use of coercion, including rape, in fraternity men's relations with women. Our examination of men's social fraternities on college and university campuses as groups and organizations led us to conclude that fraternities are a physical and sociocultural context that encourages the sexual coercion of women. We make no claims that all fraternities are "bad" or that all fraternity men are rapists. Our observations indicated, however, that rape is especially probable in fraternities because of the kinds of organizations they are, the kinds of members they have, the practices their members engage in, and a virtual absence of university or community oversight. Analyses that lay blame for rapes by fraternity men on "peer pressure" are, we feel, overly simplistic (cf. Burkhart 1989; Walsh 1989). We suggest, rather, that fraternities create a sociocultural context in which the use of coercion in sexual relations with women is normative and in which the mechanisms to keep this pattern of behavior in check are minimal at best and absent at worst. We conclude that unless fraternities change in fundamental ways, little improvement can be expected.

METHODOLOGY

Our goal was to analyze the group and organizational practices and conditions that create in fraternities an abusive social context for women. We developed a conceptual framework from an initial case study of an alleged gang rape at Florida State University that involved four fraternity men and an 18-year-old coed. The group rape took place on the third floor of a fraternity house and ended with the "dumping" of the woman in the hallway of a neighboring fraternity house. According to newspaper accounts, the victim's blood-alcohol concentration, when she was discovered, was .349 percent, more than three times the legal limit for automobile driving and an almost lethal amount. One law enforcement officer reported that sexual intercourse occurred during the time the victim was unconscious: "She was in a life-threatening situation" (*Tallahassee Democrat*, 1988b). When the victim was found, she was comatose and had suffered multiple scratches and abrasions. Crude words and a fraternity symbol had been written on her thighs (*Tampa Tribune*, 1988). When law enforcement officials tried to investigate the case, fraternity members refused to cooperate. This led, eventually, to a five-year ban of the fraternity from campus by the university and by the fraternity's national organization.

In trying to understand how such an event could have occurred, and how a group of over 150 members (exact figures are unknown because the fraternity refused to provide a membership roster) could hold rank, deny knowledge of the event, and allegedly lie to a grand jury, we analyzed newspaper articles about the case and conducted open-ended interviews with a variety of respondents about the case and about fraternities, rapes, alcohol use, gender relations, and sexual activities on campus. Our data included over 100 newspaper articles on the initial gang rape case; open-ended interviews with Greek (social fraternity and sorority) and non-Greek (independent) students (N = 20); university administrators (N = 8, five men, three women); and alumni advisers to Greek organizations (N = 6). Open-ended interviews were held also with judges, public and private defense attorneys, victim advocates, and state prosecutors regarding the processing of sexual assault cases. Data were analyzed using the grounded theory method (Glaser 1978; Martin and Turner 1986). In the following analysis, concepts generated from the data analysis are integrated with the literature on men's social fraternities, sexual coercion, and related issues.

FRATERNITIES AND THE SOCIAL CONSTRUCTION OF MEN AND MASCULINITY

Our research indicated that fraternities are vitally concerned—more than with anything else—with masculinity (cf. Kanin 1967). They work hard to create a macho image and context and try to avoid any suggestion of "wimpishness," effeminacy, and homosexuality. Valued members display, or are willing to go along with, a narrow conception of masculinity that stresses competition, athleticism, dominance, winning, conflict, wealth, material possessions, willingness to drink alcohol, and sexual prowess vis-à-vis women.

Valued Qualities of Members

When fraternity members talked about the kind of pledges they prefer, a litany of stereotypical and narrowly masculine attributes and behaviors was recited and feminine or woman-associated qualities and behaviors were expressly denounced (cf. Merton 1985). Fraternities seek men who are "athletic," "big guys," good in intramural competition, "who can talk college sports." Males "who are willing to drink alcohol," "who drink socially," or "who can hold their liquor" are sought. Alcohol and activities associated with the recreational use of alcohol are cornerstones of fraternity social life. Nondrinkers are viewed with skepticism and rarely selected for membership.[1]

Fraternities try to avoid "geeks," nerds, and men said to give the fraternity a "wimpy" or "gay" reputation. Art, music, and humanities majors, majors in traditional women's fields (nursing, home economics, social work, education), men with long hair, and those whose appearance or dress violate current norms are rejected. Clean-cut, handsome men who dress well (are clean, neat, conforming, fashionable) are preferred. One sorority woman commented that "the top ranking fraternities have the best looking guys."

One fraternity man, a senior, said his fraternity recruited "some big guys, very athletic" over a two-year period to help overcome its image of wimpiness. His fraternity had won the interfraternity competition for highest grade-point average several years running but was looked down on as "wimpy, dancy, even gay." With their bigger, more athletic recruits, "our reputation improved; we're a much more recognized fraternity now." Thus a fraternity's reputation and status depends on members' possession of stereotypically masculine qualities. Good grades, campus leadership, and community service are "nice" but masculinity dominance—for example, in athletic events, physical size of members, athleticism of members—counts most.

Certain social skills are valued. Men are sought who "have good personalities," are friendly, and "have the ability to relate to girls" (cf. Longino and Kart 1973). One fraternity man, a junior, said: "We watch a guy [a potential pledge] talk to women . . . we want guys who can relate to girls." Assessing a pledge's ability to talk to women is, in part, a preoccupation with homosexuality and a conscious avoidance of men who seem to have effeminate manners or qualities. If a member is suspected of being gay, he is ostracized and informally drummed out of the fraternity. A fraternity with a reputation as wimpy or tolerant of gays is ridiculed and shunned by other fraternities. Militant heterosexuality is frequently used by men as a strategy to keep each other in line (Kimmel 1987).

Financial affluence or wealth, a male-associated value in American culture, is highly valued by fraternities. In accounting for why the fraternity involved in the gang rape that precipitated our research project had been recognized recently as "the best fraternity chapter in the United States," a university official said: "They were good-looking, a big fraternity, had lots of BMWs [expensive, German-made automobiles]." After the rape, newspaper stories described the fraternity members' affluence, noting the high number of members who owned expensive cars (*St. Petersburg Times*, 1988).

The Status and Norms of Pledgeship

A pledge (sometimes called an associate member) is a new recruit who occupies a trial membership status for a specific period of time. The pledge period (typically ranging from 10 to 15 weeks) gives fraternity brothers an opportunity to assess and socialize new recruits. Pledges evaluate the fraternity also and decide if they want to become brothers. The socialization experience is structured partly through assignment of a Big Brother to each pledge. Big Brothers are expected to teach pledges how to become a brother and to support them as they progress through the trial membership period. Some pledges are repelled by the pledging experience, which can entail physical abuse; harsh discipline; and demands to be subordinate, follow orders, and engage in demeaning routines and activities, similar to those used by the military to "make men out of boys" during boot camp.

Characteristics of the pledge experience are rationalized by fraternity members as necessary to help pledges unite into a group, rely on each other, and join together against outsiders. The process is highly masculinist in execution as well as conception. A willingness to submit to authority, follow orders, and do as one is told is viewed as a sign of loyalty, togetherness, and unity. Fraternity pledges who find the pledge process offensive often drop out. Some do this by openly quitting, which can subject them to ridicule by brothers and other pledges, or they may deliberately fail to make the grades necessary for initiation or transfer schools and decline to reaffiliate with the fraternity on the new campus. One fraternity pledge who quit the fraternity he had pledged described an experience during pledgeship as follows:

> This one guy was always picking on me. No matter what I did, I was wrong. One night after dinner, he and two other guys called me and two other pledges into the chapter room. He said, "Here, X, hold this 25 pound bag of ice at arms' length 'til I tell you to stop." I did it even though my arms and hands were killing me. When I asked if I could stop, he grabbed me around the throat and lifted me off the floor. I thought he would choke me to death. He cussed me and called me all kinds of names. He took one of my fingers and twisted it until it nearly broke. . . . I stayed in the fraternity for a few more days, but then I decided to quit. I hated it. Those guys are sick. They like seeing you suffer.

Fraternities' emphasis on toughness, withstanding pain and humiliation, obedience to superiors, and using physical force to obtain compliance contributes to an interpersonal style that de-emphasizes caring and sensitivity but fosters intragroup trust and loyalty. If the least macho or most critical pledges drop out, those who remain may be more receptive to, and influenced by, masculinist values and practices that encourage the use of force in sexual relations with women and the covering up of such behavior (cf. Kanin 1967).

Norms and Dynamics of Brotherhood

Brother is the status occupied by fraternity men to indicate their relations to each other and their membership in a particular fraternity organization or group. Brother is a male-specific status; only males can become brothers, although women can become "Little Sisters," a form of pseudomembership. "Becoming a brother" is a rite of passage that follows the consistent and often lengthy display by pledges of appropriately masculine qualities and behaviors. Brothers have a quasi-familial relationship with each other, are normatively said to share bonds of closeness and support, and are sharply set off from nonmembers. Brotherhood is a loosely defined term used to represent the bonds that develop among fraternity members and the obligations and expectations incumbent upon them (cf. Marlowe and Auvenshine [1982] on fraternities' failure to encourage "moral development" in freshman pledges).

Some of our respondents talked about brotherhood in almost reverential terms, viewing it as the most valuable benefit of fraternity membership. One senior, a business-school major who had been affiliated with a fairly high-status fraternity throughout four years on campus, said:

> Brotherhood spurs friendship for life, which I consider its best aspect, although I didn't see it that way when I joined. Brotherhood bonds and unites. It instills values of caring about one another, caring about community, caring about ourselves. The values and bonds [of brotherhood] continually develop over the four years [in college] while normal friendships come and go.

Despite this idealization, most aspects of fraternity practice and conception are more mundane. Brotherhood often plays itself out as an overriding concern with masculinity and, by extension, femininity. As a consequence, fraternities comprise collectivities of highly masculinized men with attitudinal qualities and behavioral norms that predispose them to sexual coercion of women (cf. Kanin 1967; Merton 1985; Rapaport and Burkhart 1984). The norms of masculinity are complemented by conceptions of women and femininity that are equally distorted and stereotyped and that may enhance the probability of women's exploitation (cf. Ehrhart and Sandler 1985; Sanday 1981, 1986).

Practices of Brotherhood

Practices associated with fraternity brotherhood that contribute to the sexual coercion of women include a preoccupation with loyalty, group protection and secrecy, use of alcohol as a weapon, involvement in violence and physical force, and an emphasis on competition and superiority.

Loyalty, group protection, and secrecy. Loyalty is a fraternity preoccupation. Members are reminded constantly to be loyal to the fraternity and to their brothers. Among other ways, loyalty is played out in the practices of group protection and secrecy. The fraternity must be shielded from criticism. Members are admonished to avoid getting the fraternity in trouble and to bring all problems "to the chapter" (local branch of a national social fraternity) rather than to outsiders. Fraternities try to protect themselves from close scrutiny and criticism by the Interfraternity Council (a quasi-governing body composed of representatives from all social fraternities on campus), their fraternity's national office, university officials, law enforcement, the media, and the public. Protection of the fraternity often takes precedence over what is procedurally, ethically, or legally correct. Numerous examples were related to us of fraternity brothers' lying to outsiders to "protect the fraternity."

Group protection was observed in the alleged gang rape case with which we began our study. Except for one brother, a rapist who turned state's evidence, the entire remaining fraternity membership was accused by university and criminal justice officials of lying to protect the fraternity. Members consistently failed to cooperate even though the alleged crimes were felonies, involved only four men (two of whom were not even members of the local chapter), and the victim of the crime nearly died. According to a grand jury's findings, fraternity officers repeatedly broke appointments with law enforcement officials, refused to provide police with a list of members, and refused to cooperate with police and prosecutors investigating the case (*Florida Flambeau*, 1988).

Secrecy is a priority value and practice in fraternities, partly because full-fledged membership is premised on it (for confirmation, see Ehrhart and Sandler 1985; Longino and Kart 1973; Roark 1987). Secrecy is also a boundary-maintaining mechanism, demarcating in-group from out-group, us from them. Secret rituals, handshakes, and mottoes are revealed to pledge brothers as they are initiated into full brotherhood. Since only brothers are supposed to know a fraternity's secrets, such knowledge affirms membership in the fraternity and separates a brother from others. Extending secrecy tactics from protection of private knowledge to protection of the fraternity from criticism is a predictable development. Our interviews indicated that individual members knew the difference between right and wrong, but fraternity norms that emphasize loyalty, group protection, and secrecy often overrode standards of ethical correctness.

Alcohol as weapon. Alcohol use by fraternity men is normative. They use it on weekdays to relax after class and on weekends to "get drunk," "get crazy," and "get laid." The use of alcohol to obtain sex from women is pervasive—in other words, it is used as a weapon against sexual reluctance. According to several fraternity men whom we interviewed, alcohol is the major tool used to gain sexual mastery over women (cf. Adams and Abarbanel 1988; Ehrhart and Sandler 1985). One fraternity man, a 21-year-old senior, described alcohol use to gain sex as follows: "There are girls that you know will fuck, then some you have to put some effort into it. . . . You have to buy them drinks or find out if she's drunk enough. . . ."

A similar strategy is used collectively. A fraternity man said that at parties with Little Sisters: "We provide them with 'hunch punch' and things get wild. We get them drunk and most of the guys end up with one." " 'Hunch punch,' " he said, "is a girls' drink made up of overproof alcohol and powdered Kool-Aid, no water or anything, just ice. It's very strong. Two cups will do a number on a female." He had plans in the next academic term to surreptitiously give hunch punch to women in a "prim and proper" sorority because "having sex with prim and proper sorority girls is definitely a goal." These women are a challenge because they "won't openly consume alcohol and won't get openly drunk as hell." Their sororities have "standards committees" that forbid heavy drinking and easy sex.

In the gang rape case, our sources said that many fraternity men on campus believed the victim had a drinking problem and was thus an "easy make." According to newspaper accounts, she had been drinking alcohol on the evening she was raped; the lead assailant is alleged to have given her a bottle of wine after she arrived at his fraternity house. Portions of the rape occurred in a shower, and the victim was reportedly so drunk that her assailants had difficulty holding her in a standing position (*Tallahassee Democrat*, 1988a). While raping her, her assailants repeatedly told her they were members of another fraternity under the apparent belief that she was too drunk to know the difference. Of course, if she was too drunk to know who they were, she was too drunk to consent to sex (cf. Allgeier 1986; Tash 1988).

One respondent told us that gang rapes are wrong and can get one expelled, but he seemed to see nothing wrong in sexual coercion one-on-one. He seemed unaware that the use of alcohol to obtain sex from a woman is grounds for a claim that a rape occurred (cf. Tash 1988). Few women on campus (who also may not know these grounds) report date rapes, however; so the odds of detection and punishment are slim for fraternity men who use alcohol for "seduction" purposes (cf. Byington and Keeter 1988; Merton 1985).

Violence and physical force. Fraternity men have a history of violence (Ehrhart and Sandler 1985; Roark 1987). Their record of hazing, fighting, property destruction, and rape has caused them problems with insurance companies (Bradford 1986; Pressley 1987). Two university officials told us that fraternities "are the third riskiest property to insure behind toxic waste dumps and amusement parks." Fraternities are increasingly defendants in legal actions brought by pledges subjected to hazing (Meyer 1986; Pressley 1987) and by women who were raped by one or more members. In a recent alleged gang rape incident at another Florida university, prosecutors failed to file charges but the victim filed a civil suit against the fraternity nevertheless (*Tallahassee Democrat*, 1989).

Competition and superiority. Interfraternity rivalry fosters in-group identification and out-group hostility. Fraternities stress pride of membership and superiority over other fraternities as major goals. Interfraternity rivalries take many forms, including competition for desirable pledges, size of pledge class, size of membership, size and appearance of fraternity house, superiority in intramural sports, highest grade-point averages, giving the best parties, gaining the best or most campus leadership roles, and, of great importance, attracting and displaying "good looking women." Rivalry is particularly intense over members, intramural sports, and women (cf. Messner 1989).

FRATERNITIES' COMMODIFICATION OF WOMEN

In claiming that women are treated by fraternities as commodities, we mean that fraternities knowingly, and intentionally, *use* women for their benefit. Fraternities use women as bait for new members, as servers of brother's needs, and as sexual prey.

Women as bait. Fashionably attractive women help a fraternity attract new members. As one fraternity man, a junior, said, "They are good bait." Beautiful, sociable women are believed to impress the right kind of pledges and give the impression that the fraternity can deliver this type of woman to its members. Photographs of shapely, attractive coeds are printed in fraternity brochures and videotapes that are distributed and shown to potential pledges. The women pictured are often dressed in bikinis, at the beach, and are pictured hugging the brothers of the fraternity. One university official says such recruitment materials give the message: "Hey, they're here for you, you can have whatever you want," and, "we have the best looking women. Join us and you can have them too." Another commented: "Something's wrong when males join an all-male organization as the best place to meet women. It's so illogical."

Fraternities compete in promising access to beautiful women. One fraternity man, a senior, commented that "the attraction of girls [i.e., a fraternity's success in attracting women] is a big status symbol for fraternities." One university official commented that the use of women as a recruiting tool is so well entrenched that fraternities that might be willing to forgo it say they cannot afford to unless other fraternities do so as well. One fraternity man said, "Look, if we don't have Little Sisters, the fraternities that do will get all the good pledges." Another said, "We won't have as good a rush [the period during which new members are assessed and selected] if we don't have these women around."

In displaying good-looking, attractive, skimpily dressed, nubile women to potential members, fraternities implicitly, and sometimes explicitly, promise sexual access to women. One fraternity man commented that "part of what being in a fraternity is all about is the sex" and explained how his fraternity uses Little Sisters to recruit new members:

> We'll tell the sweetheart [the fraternity's term for Little Sister], "You're gorgeous; you can get him." We'll tell her to fake a scam and she'll go hang all over him during a rush party, kiss him, and he thinks he's done wonderful and wants to join. The girls think it's great too. It's flattering for them.

Women as servers. The use of women as servers is exemplified in the Little Sister program. Little Sisters are undergraduate women who are rushed and selected in a manner parallel to the recruitment of fraternity men. They are affiliated with the fraternity in a formal but unofficial way and are able, indeed required, to wear the fraternity's Greek letters. Little Sisters are not full-fledged fraternity members, however; and fraternity national offices and most universities do not register or regulate them. Each fraternity has an officer called Little Sister Chairman who oversees their organization and activities. The Little Sisters elect officers among themselves, pay monthly dues to the fraternity, and have well-defined roles. Their dues are used to pay for the fraternity's social events, and Little Sisters are expected to attend and hostess fraternity parties and hang around the house to make it a "nice place to be." One fraternity man, a senior, described Little Sisters this way: "They are very social girls, willing to join in, be affiliated with the group, devoted to the fraternity." Another member, a sophomore, said: "Their sole purpose is social—attend parties, attract new members, and 'take care' of the guys."

Our observations and interviews suggested that women selected by fraternities as Little Sisters are physically attractive, possess good social skills, and are willing to devote time and energy to the fraternity and its members.

One undergraduate woman gave the following job description for Little Sisters to a campus newspaper:

> It's not just making appearances at all the parties but entails many more responsibilities. You're going to be expected to go to all the intramural games to cheer the brothers on, support and encourage the pledges, and just be around to bring some extra life to the house. [As a Little Sister] you have to agree to take on a new responsibility other than studying to maintain your grades and managing to keep your checkbook from bouncing. You have to make time to be a part of the fraternity and support the brothers in all they do. (*The Tomahawk,* 1988)

The title of Little Sister reflects women's subordinate status; fraternity men in a parallel role are called Big Brothers. Big Brothers assist a sorority primarily with the physical work of sorority rushes, which, compared to fraternity rushes, are more formal, structured, and intensive. Sorority rushes take place in the daytime and fraternity rushes at night so fraternity men are free to help. According to one fraternity member, Little Sister status is a benefit to women because it gives them a social outlet and "the protection of the brothers." The gender-stereotypic conceptions and obligations of these Little Sister and Big Brother statuses indicate that fraternities and sororities promote a gender hierarchy on campus that fosters subordination and dependence in women, thus encouraging sexual exploitation and the belief that it is acceptable.

Women as sexual prey. Little Sisters are a sexual utility. Many Little Sisters do not belong to sororities and lack peer support for refraining from unwanted sexual relations. One fraternity man (whose fraternity has 65 members and 85 Little Sisters) told us they had recruited "wholesale" in the prior year to "get lots of new women." The structural access to women that the Little Sister program provides and the absence of normative supports for refusing fraternity members' sexual advances may make women in this program particularly susceptible to coerced sexual encounters with fraternity men.

Access to women for sexual gratification is a presumed benefit of fraternity membership, promised in recruitment materials and strategies and through brothers' conversations with new recruits. One fraternity man said: "We always tell the guys that you get sex all the time, there's always new girls. . . . After I became a Greek, I found out I could be with females at will." A university official told us that, based on his observations, "no one [i.e., fraternity men] on this campus wants to have 'relationships.' They just want to have fun [i.e., sex]." Fraternity men plan and execute strategies aimed at obtaining sexual gratification, and this occurs at both individual and collective levels.

Individual strategies include getting a woman drunk and spending a great deal of money on her. As for collective strategies, most of our undergraduate interviewees agreed that fraternity parties often culminate in sex and that this outcome is planned. One fraternity man said fraternity parties often involve sex and nudity and can "turn into orgies." Orgies may be planned in advance, such as the Bowery Ball party held by one fraternity. A former fraternity member said of this party:

> The entire idea behind this is sex. Both men and women come to the party wearing little or nothing. There are pornographic pinups on the walls and usually porno movies playing on the TV. The music carries sexual overtones. . . . They just get schnockered [drunk] and, in most cases, they also get laid.

When asked about the women who come to such a party, he said: "Some Little Sisters just won't go. . . . The girls who do are looking for a good time, girls who don't know what it is, things like that."

Other respondents denied that fraternity parties are orgies but said that sex is always talked about among the brothers and they all know "who each other is doing it with." One member said that most of the time, guys have sex with their girlfriends "but with socials, girlfriends aren't allowed to come and it's their [members'] big chance [to have sex with other women]." The use of alcohol to help them get women into bed is a routine strategy at fraternity parties.

CONCLUSIONS

In general, our research indicated that the organization and membership of fraternities contribute heavily to coercive and often violent sex. Fraternity houses are occupied by same-sex (all men) and same-age (late teens, early twenties) peers whose maturity and judgment is often less than ideal. Yet fraternity houses are private dwellings that are mostly off-limits to, and away from scrutiny of, university and community representatives, with the result that fraternity house events seldom come to the attention of outsiders. Practices associated with the social construction of fraternity brotherhood emphasize a macho conception of men and masculinity, a narrow, stereotyped conception of women and femininity, and the treatment of women as commodities. Other practices contributing to coercive sexual relations and the cover-up of rapes include excessive alcohol use, competitiveness, and normative support for deviance and secrecy (cf. Bogal-Allbritten and Allbritten 1985; Kanin 1967).

Some fraternity practices exacerbate others. Brotherhood norms require "sticking together" regardless of right or wrong; thus rape episodes are unlikely to be stopped or reported to outsiders, even when witnesses disapprove. The ability to use alcohol without scrutiny by authorities and alcohol's frequent association with violence, including sexual coercion, facilitates rape in fraternity houses. Fraternity norms that emphasize the value of maleness and masculinity over femaleness and femininity and that elevate the status of men and lower the status of women in members' eyes undermine perceptions and treatment of women as persons who deserve consideration and care (cf. Ehrhart and Sandler 1985; Merton 1985).

Androgynous men and men with a broad range of interests and attributes are lost to fraternities through their recruitment practices. Masculinity of a narrow and stereotypical type helps create attitudes, norms, and practices that predispose fraternity men to coerce women sexually, both individually and collectively (Allgeier 1986; Hood 1989; Sanday 1981, 1986). Male athletes on campus may be similarly disposed for the same reasons (Kirshenbaum 1989; Telander and Sullivan 1989).

Research into the social contexts in which rape crimes occur and the social constructions associated with these contexts illuminate rape dynamics on campus. Blanchard (1959) found that group rapes almost always have a leader who pushes others into the crime. He also found that the leader's latent homosexuality, desire to show off to his peers, or fear of failing to prove himself a man are frequently an impetus. Fraternity norms and practices contribute to the approval and use of sexual coercion as an accepted tactic in relations with women. Alcohol-induced compliance is normative, whereas, presumably, use of a knife, gun, or threat of bodily harm would not be because the woman who "drinks too much" is viewed as "causing her own rape" (cf. Ehrhart and Sandler 1985).

Our research led us to conclude that fraternity norms and practices influence members to view the sexual coercion of women, which is a felony crime, as sport, a contest, or a game (cf. Sato 1988). This sport is played not between men and women but between men and men. Women are the pawns or prey in the interfraternity rivalry game; they prove that a fraternity is successful or prestigious. The use of women in this way encourages fraternity men to see women as objects and sexual coercion as sport. Today's societal norms support young women's right to engage in sex at their discretion, and coercion is unnecessary in a mutually desired encounter. However, nubile young women say they prefer to be "in a relationship" to have sex while young men say they prefer to "get laid" without a commitment (Muehlenhard and Linton 1987). These differences may reflect, in part, American puritanism and men's fears of sexual intimacy or perhaps intimacy of any kind. In a fraternity context, getting sex without giving emotionally demonstrates "cool" masculinity. More important, it poses no threat to the bonding and loyalty of the fraternity brotherhood (cf. Farr 1988). Drinking large quantities of alcohol before having sex suggests that "scoring" rather than intrinsic sexual pleasure is a primary concern of fraternity men.

Unless fraternities' composition, goals, structures, and practices change in fundamental ways, women on campus will continue to be sexual prey for fraternity men. As all-male enclaves dedicated to opposing faculty and administration and to cementing in-group ties, fraternity members eschew any hint of homosexuality. Their version of masculinity transforms women, and men with womanly characteristics, into the out-group. "Womanly men" are ostracized; feminine women are used to demonstrate members' masculinity. Encouraging renewed emphasis on their founding values (Longino and Kart 1973), service orientation and activities (Lemire 1979), or members' moral development (Marlowe and Auvenshine 1982) will have little effect on fraternities' treatment of women. A case for or against fraternities cannot be made by studying individual members. The fraternity qua group and organization is at issue. Located on campus along with many vulnerable women, embedded in a sexist society, and caught up in masculinist goals, practices, and values, fraternities' violation of women—including forcible rape—should come as no surprise.

NOTE

1. Recent bans by some universities on open-keg parties at fraternity houses have resulted in heavy drinking before coming to a party and an increase in drunkenness among those who attend. This may aggravate, rather than improve, the treatment of women by fraternity men at parties.

REFERENCES

Allgeier, Elizabeth. 1986. "Coercive Versus Consensual Sexual Interactions." G. Stanley Hall Lecture to American Psychological Association Annual Meeting, Washington, DC, August.

Adams, Aileen and Gail Abarbanel. 1988. *Sexual Assault on Campus: What Colleges Can Do.* Santa Monica, CA: Rape Treatment Center.

Blanchard, W. H. 1959. "The Group Process in Gang Rape." *Journal of Social Psychology* 49:259–66.

Bogal-Allbritten, Rosemarie B. and William L. Allbritten. 1985. "The Hidden Victims: Courtship Violence Among College Students." *Journal of College Student Personnel* 43:201–4.

Bohrnstedt, George W. 1969. "Conservatism, Authoritarianism and Religiosity of Fraternity Pledges." *Journal of College Student Personnel* 27:36–43.

Bradford, Michael. 1986. "Tight Market Dries Up Nightlife at University." *Business Insurance* (March 2): 2, 6.

Burkhart, Barry. 1989. Comments in Seminar on Acquaintance/Date Rape Prevention: A National Video Teleconference, February 2.

Burkhart, Barry R. and Annette L. Stanton. 1985. "Sexual Aggression in Acquaintance Relationships." Pp. 43–65 in *Violence in Intimate Relationships*, edited by G. Russell. Englewood Cliffs, NJ: Spectrum.

Byington, Diane B. and Karen W. Keeter. 1988. "Assessing Needs of Sexual Assault Victims on a University Campus." Pp. 23–31 in *Student Services: Responding to Issues and Challenges*. Chapel Hill: University of North Carolina Press.

Chancer, Lynn S. 1987. "New Bedford, Massachusetts, March 6, 1983-March 22, 1984: The 'Before and After' of a Group Rape." *Gender & Society* 1:239–60.

Ehrhart, Julie K. and Bernice R. Sandler. 1985. *Campus Gang Rape: Party Games?* Washington, DC: Association of American Colleges.

Farr, K. A. 1988. "Dominance Bonding Through the Good Old Boys Sociability Network." *Sex Roles* 18:259–77.

Florida Flambeau. 1988. "Pike Members Indicted in Rape." (May 19):1, 5.

Fox, Elaine, Charles Hodge, and Walter Ward. 1987. "A Comparison of Attitudes Held by Black and White Fraternity Members." *Journal of Negro Education* 56:521–34.

Geis, Gilbert. 1971. "Group Sexual Assaults." *Medical Aspects of Human Sexuality* 5:101–13.

Glaser, Barney G. 1978. *Theoretical Sensitivity: Advances in the Methodology of Grounded Theory*. Mill Valley, CA: Sociology Press.

Hood, Jane. 1989. "Why Our Society Is Rape-Prone." *New York Times*, May 16.

Hughes, Michael J. and Roger B. Winston, Jr. 1987. "Effects of Fraternity Membership on Interpersonal Values." *Journal of College Student Personnel* 45:405–11.

Kanin, Eugene J. 1967. "Reference Groups and Sex Conduct Norm Violations." *The Sociological Quarterly* 8:495–504.

Kimmel, Michael, ed. 1987. *Changing Men: New Directions in Research on Men and Masculinity*. Newbury Park, CA: Sage.

Kirshenbaum, Jerry. 1989. "Special Report, An American Disgrace: A Violent and Unprecedented Lawlessness Has Arisen Among College Athletes in all Parts of the Country." *Sports Illustrated* (February 27): 16–19.

Lemire, David. 1979. "One Investigation of the Stereotypes Associated with Fraternities and Sororities." *Journal of College Student Personnel* 37:54–57.

Letchworth, G. E. 1969. "Fraternities Now and in the Future." *Journal of College Student Personnel* 10:118–22.

Longino, Charles F., Jr., and Cary S. Kart. 1973. "The College Fraternity: An Assessment of Theory and Research." *Journal of College Student Personnel* 31:118–25.

Marlowe, Anne F. and Dwight C. Auvenshine. 1982. "Greek Membership: Its Impact on the Moral Development of College Freshmen." *Journal of College Student Personnel* 40:53–57.

Martin, Patricia Yancey and Barry A. Turner. 1986. "Grounded Theory and Organizational Research." *Journal of Applied Behavioral Science* 22:141–57.

Merton, Andrew. 1985. "On Competition and Class: Return to Brotherhood." *Ms.* (September): 60–65, 121–22.

Messner, Michael. 1989. "Masculinities and Athletic Careers." *Gender & Society* 3:71–88.

Meyer, T. J. 1986. "Fight Against Hazing Rituals Rages on Campuses." *Chronicle of Higher Education* (March 12):34–36.

Miller, Leonard D. 1973. "Distinctive Characteristics of Fraternity Members." *Journal of College Student Personnel* 31:126–28.

Muehlenhard, Charlene L. and Melaney A. Linton. 1987. "Date Rape and Sexual Aggression in Dating Situations: Incidence and Risk Factors." *Journal of Counseling Psychology* 34:186–96.

Pressley, Sue Anne. 1987. "Fraternity Hell Night Still Endures." *Washington Post* (August 11):B1.

Rapaport, Karen and Barry R. Burkhart. 1984. "Personality and Attitudinal Characteristics of Sexually Coercive College Males." *Journal of Abnormal Psychology* 93:216–21.

Roark, Mary L. 1987. "Preventing Violence on College Campuses." *Journal of Counseling and Development* 65:367–70.

Sanday, Peggy Reeves. 1981. "The Socio-Cultural Context of Rape: A Cross-Cultural Study." *Journal of Social Issues* 37:5–27.

———. 1986. "Rape and the Silencing of the Feminine." Pp. 84–101 in *Rape*, edited by S. Tomaselli and R. Porter. Oxford: Basil Blackwell.

St. Petersburg Times. 1988. "A Greek Tragedy." (May 29):1F, 6F.

Sato, Ikuya. 1988. "Play Theory of Delinquency: Toward a General Theory of 'Action.'" *Symbolic Interaction* 11:191–212.

Smith, T. 1964. "Emergence and Maintenance of Fraternal Solidarity." *Pacific Sociological Review* 7:29–37.

Tallahassee Democrat. 1988a. "FSU Fraternity Brothers Charged" (April 27):1A, 12A.

————. 1988b. "FSU Interviewing Students About Alleged Rape" (April 24):1D.

————. 1989. "Woman Sues Stetson in Alleged Rape" (March 19):3B.

Tampa Tribune. 1988. "Fraternity Brothers Charged in Sexual Assault of FSU Coed." (April 27):6B.

Tash, Gary B. 1988. "Date Rape." *The Emerald of Sigma Pi Fraternity* 75(4):1–2.

Telander, Rick and Robert Sullivan. 1989. "Special Report, You Reap What You Sow." *Sports Illustrated* (February 27):20–34.

The Tomahawk. 1988. "A Look Back at Rush, A Mixture of Hard Work and Fun" (April/May):3D.

Walsh, Claire. 1989. Comments in Seminar on Acquaintance/Date Rape Prevention: A National Video Teleconference, February 2.

Wilder, David H., Arlyne E. Hoyt, Dennis M. Doren, William E. Hauck, and Robert D. Zettle. 1978. "The Impact of Fraternity and Sorority Membership on Values and Attitudes." *Journal of College Student Personnel* 36:445–49.

Wilder, David H., Arlyne E. Hoyt, Beth Shuster Surbeck, Janet C. Wilder, and Patricia Imperatrice Carney. 1986. "Greek Affiliation and Attitude Change in College Students." *Journal of College Student Personnel* 44:510–19.

AMERICAN ARCHIPELAGO: *Blacks and Criminal Justice*

46

Mary Frances Berry and John Blassingame

The American criminal justice system has put blacks and other minorities behind bars out of all proportion to their numbers in the general population. The celebrated acquittals of Angela Davis, Bobby Seale, Huey P. Newton, Joanne Little, and others in the 1970s changed neither the fact of discrimination against blacks nor the system itself. The system remained rotted through with two centuries of substantive and procedural injustice, incarceration of the innocent, and unconscionable mistreatment of the guilty. Even the meaning of "guilt" in a system run by and for white people was distorted for blacks. On April 6, 1970, *Time* magazine stated the essential facts:

> Whites often assume that civil rights acts and court decisions made law the black man's redeemer. In practice, many blacks see the law as something different: a white weapon that white policemen, white judges and white juries use against black people. Indeed, blacks are clearly under-represented in law enforcement and over-represented in crime and punishment. . . . Blacks are arrested between three and four times more than whites, partly because police stop and search blacks far more frequently than they do whites. . . . Most of the victims of black crimes are black. Example: black women are 18 times more likely to be raped than white women, and usually by black assailants.
>
> Once caught, black suspects are more likely than whites to be convicted than acquitted, and more likely to receive stiff sentences. . . . According to many experts, one factor in this disproportion is poverty: few black defendants can afford skilled lawyers.

RACIAL DISPARITIES IN PUNISHMENT FOR CRIMES AGAINST PROPERTY

From the beginning of their history in the United States, blacks raised critical issues concerning the criminal justice system: procedural fairness in trials of blacks, the inequities in administration of justice (from arrest to sentencing after trial to postconviction remedies), the punishment of whites for mistreatment of blacks, and the sentences blacks and whites received for the same offense. They questioned whether economic conditions were more important than race in determining treatment and whether black-on-black crime was punished. In addition, blacks raised serious questions about whether the entire legal system had any legitimate role to play when so-called crimes were perpetrated against private property in a capitalist society where the poor did not have equal opportunity to acquire material possessions. In such a setting, crimes aimed directly or indirectly at acquiring equal access to property take place primarily because private property exists. Poor black criminals, according to this analysis, were slaves of a capitalist system without other means of accumulating capital.

The criminal justice system punished and harassed black political prisoners whose crimes might have been ostensibly against property but whose basic offense to the system was their race. Racism imprisoned small-time thieves, among whom blacks were disproportionally represented but released white-collar swindlers or political operatives with a reprimand. And the system has come under fire despite the fact that a black and a white might be given the same sentences for similar crimes in some cases, for the deeper realities are: (1) that blacks suffered measurable oppression as defendants, as prison inmates, as victims of official mistreatment, and even as crime victims for whom there was often no legal redress; and (2) that the oppression of blacks was facilitated by the legal definition of what is a criminal offense and what is not. How many blacks have been in a position to swindle huge fortunes from their corporations in the past century? The severe penalties for crimes against property were reserved for just those offenses which black people were in the best position to commit most often.

When a corporate executive received a $1,000 fine for evading $60,000 in income taxes and a poor black man was sentenced to jail for four years for stealing a Social Security check from the mails, serious questions were raised about the equity of treatment within the criminal justice system. For example, in 1969 in a federal court in New York City, a stockbroker pleaded guilty to an indictment charging him with $20 million in illegal trading with Swiss banks. He hired a prestigious lawyer who described the offense in court as comparable to breaking a traffic law. Judge Irving Cooper gave the stockbroker a tongue lashing, a $30,000 fine, and a suspended sentence. A few days later, the same judge sentenced an unemployed black shipping clerk who pleaded guilty to stealing a television set worth $100 to one year in jail.

An analysis of sentencing in the southern district of New York from May 1, 1972, to October 31, 1972, indicates that white-collar defendants, predominantly white, received more lenient treatment as a general rule than defendants charged with common crimes, largely unemployed and undereducated blacks, who were more likely to receive prison sentences. There was little differentiation in sentencing between blacks and whites charged with the same offense. However, most whites were charged with white-collar crime, and the only certain punishment even after conviction was a suspended sentence or a very short prison term. The same criminal justice system mandates certain incarceration for the so-called common crimes, with which most blacks were charged.

In fact, some judges seemed not to believe that white-collar offenders were criminals. A prime example is the famous electrical equipment price-rigging case of 1961. The defendants, including several vice presidents of General Electric and Westinghouse, had committed flagrant criminal offenses in conspiring to fix prices. They even employed secret codes. General Electric alone set aside $225 million to settle damage claims that resulted from the conspiracy. In court after they pleaded no contest, the defendants were fined and sentenced to thirty days in jail. Even this short period of incarceration offended one defense attorney, who said he could not understand why his client should be put "behind bars with common criminals who have been convicted of embezzlement and other serious crimes."

As a holdover from the period when a certain amount of brigandage, as typified in the expression "robber baron," was accepted as the price of economic growth, a lack of integrity and fair dealing in business, even when it cheated the government, consumers, or shareholders, seemed to be expected. The perpetrator of white-collar crimes such as tax evasion or fraud was likely to be winked at or confined to plush quarters in a minimum security Allenwood prison for a short period. The black numbers operator, dope dealer, or other successful criminal was cited as an example that blacks were just naturally criminal or preferred to pursue a criminal way of life, instead of as an example of an entrepreneur in the best tradition of American economic development.

The ruling classes defined crime in such a way that they themselves usually escaped scrutiny and punishment. For example, in compiling the Uniform Crime Statistics, the Federal Bureau of Investigation (FBI) had no categories for white-collar crimes (embezzlement, bribery, price fixing, and consumer fraud). The Uniform Crime Statistics misled the public by highlighting the least costly crimes. The crimes with which blacks were usually associated accounted, according to a 1974 *U.S. News and World Report* study, for less than 10 percent of the cost of crime. Organized crime (gambling, narcotics, hijacking, and loan sharking) accounted for $37.2 billion, white-collar crimes (embezzlement, fraud, forgery, kickbacks, and business thefts) accounted for $17 billion, and drunken driving accounted for $6.5 billion, but the crimes commonly associated with blacks (robbery, burglary, theft, shoplifting, homicide, and assault) accounted for only $6.0 billion, or less than 10 percent of the estimated total of $66.7 billion for crime. When one adds the $20.6 billion for law enforcement to the total, the black percentage falls even lower. Consistent with the economic history of blacks, one would expect the crime rate for blacks to be higher than the measured rate for whites. So long as economic oppression and racial prejudice thwarted black potential and ambitions, it would be extraordinary indeed if the black crime rate did not exceed that for whites who, whatever their economic condition, did not have to overcome the burden of racial oppression.

THE LEGACY OF SLAVERY

Twentieth-century blacks caught in the criminal justice system were scarred as a group by instruments of oppression derived from punitive laws that buttressed slavery in the South and continued to oppress blacks, North and South, after emancipation. After the Civil War the criminal justice system was corrupted in that it assumed the controlling role formerly played by the institution of slavery. Many blacks walked away from the chains of slavery only to become ensnared in the faceless and, in many respects, more horrible oppression of courts, executions, prisons, poverty, and despair.

In the period before the Civil War, each of the slave states had elaborate and severe laws dealing with black criminals. Blacks, free and slave, were not permitted to testify against whites and were punished for failure to accord them respect. The statutory punishment for most crimes was much more severe for slaves than for whites. Whites were executed for rape and murder alone, but slaves could be executed for stealing; a slave who struck a white person was flogged and, during the eighteenth century, often maimed or castrated. Slaves conspiring to rebel or engaging in revolts were sometimes tortured to extract a confession and could be convicted on the flimsiest evidence. There were a small number of reported trials of slaves, but often trials were held only to determine the compensation to be provided to a master when his slave was convicted of killing the slave of another slaveowner or of killing a white person.

Laws restrained the movement and conduct of free blacks as they attempted to maintain a semblance of freedom. They were forced to give bond or register in local communities upon penalty of deportation, forbidden to assemble in groups for fear of slave insurrections, and punished more severely than whites for teaching slaves to read and write, "the use of figures excepted."

Laws also forbade or regulated the use of firearms and "any ardent spirits" by free blacks. Because the lack of facilities for criminals made imprisonment unpopular, fines and whippings were the punishments of choice as alternatives to all or part of a sentence. A free black found guilty of threatening a white man with a deadly weapon in North Carolina was "sentenced to three months imprisonment, to stand two hours in the stocks on two different days and to give bond, with good security, in the sum of 18 pounds."

The impoverished state of most free blacks made fines an unrealistic proposed punishment. Some of the laws which imposed fines on free blacks stated that an alternative of whipping or imprisonment could be meted out at the discretion of the court. In response to this problem the North Carolina assembly in 1831 enacted a measure providing that "when any free Negro or free person of color should be hereafter connected in any offense against the criminal laws of the state and sentenced to pay a fine, and it shall appear to the satisfaction of the court that the free Negro . . . so convicted is unable to pay the fine imposed, the court shall direct the sheriff . . . to hire out the free Negro . . . so convicted to any person who will pay the fine for his services for the shortest space of time."

CONTROLLING FREED BLACKS THROUGH THE CRIMINAL JUSTICE SYSTEM, 1865–1920

After emancipation, the statistics reported by the U.S. Census Bureau indicated an increase in black criminality. This was predictable. No longer valuable property, the former slaves became despised free blacks. The criminal law was used to control and harass them. . . .

In the criminal court system in the South after emancipation, case loads increased substantially, with the major part of the courts' time taken up with trying cases involving blacks. Increasingly, the law was used to restrain or punish blacks as a substitute for the constraints of slavery. Many blacks became familiar with the courts not as protective institutions but rather as places where labor contracts which reduced them to peonage were enforced. Many observers and participants in the process believed that blacks usually received procedural fairness but that whites would often be acquitted for offenses which when committed by blacks brought certain conviction. After ten years as a trial judge in Montgomery, Alabama, Judge W. H. Thomas told the Southern Sociological Congress at Nashville, in 1912, "It is not that the Negro fails to get justice before the courts, . . . but too often it is that the native white man escapes it." The judge went on to point out that minority groups would not accept this uneven status before the law as fair, and that a distrust of the law would be the result.

With the failure of Reconstruction, penal systems picked up the oppression of blacks where slavery left off, except that the prisons made no provision for handling black female offenders. The prisons were transformed surreptitiously into a far-flung routing system—imitating that of the slave trade— through which poor blacks passed on their way to serving as the property of whites in need of cheap labor. There were large numbers of able-bodied blacks in prisons, there was a great demand for labor throughout the South, and maintaining a prison system was a great financial burden for the state. By leasing prisoners to contractors, the state was relieved of the responsibility of supporting the prisoners and acquired a source of profit for the state treasury. Some planters paid the fines of black prisoners directly to state officials and were permitted to work them until their sentences expired. Each state soon had an interest in increasing the number of convicts in order to lease them. Furthermore, many of the convicts were mistreated by the lessors, who were interested only in profits and not in the health and welfare of their charges. Indeed, the lessors had even less concern for the convicts than the master had had for slaves who were, after all, his valuable property.

The pardoning power of executives in the southern states was also utilized inequitably. A 1901 study reported that "the last reports of Virginia and Louisiana show: In the former, one out of every 3½ white men receives a pardon, while only one out of every 14 Negroes obtained such clemency. In the latter, for the whites it is one to every 4½ white men, and one to every 49 Negroes." Furthermore, the study showed that the complete absence of white women in prisons was the result of judges who deemed prison conditions unfit for them. There were, however, sixty black women in the prisons of the two states at that time.

The criminal justice system reinforced the oppression of blacks in other ways. Large numbers of black workers signed contracts to work for white planters who underpaid, overcharged, and cheated them and then prosecuted them for contract violations when they attempted to leave the plantation. Many black peons appealed to the Justice Department to protect them. Despite the federal antipeonage law of 1867, the Justice Department failed to abolish debt slavery, which continued to flourish until the 1940s. . . .

DISPARITIES IN ARREST AND SENTENCING, 1920–50

Despite the protests of Afro-American leaders, the reported black crime rate continued to be higher than that of whites. For instance, in the first half of 1924 in Philadelphia, blacks, who made up 7.4 percent of the population, accounted for 24.4 percent of the arrests. During the first six months of 1926 in Detroit, the black crime rate was 3.9 per 10,000 as opposed to 1 per 10,000 for whites. In the superior courts of North Carolina in 1922–25, there were 4.65 indictments per 1,000 for whites and 8.71 per 1,000 for blacks. Nationwide, the U.S. Census Bureau reported in 1923 that blacks formed 31.3 percent of the total prison population and 23.3 percent of the commitments, contrasted to only 9.3 percent of the total adult population. Racism—pure and simple—generated these statistics.

The Jackson, Mississippi, *Daily News* reported in 1916, "We allow petty officers of the law to harass and oppress our Negro labor, deprive them of their wages, assessing stiff fines on trivial charges and often they are convicted on charges which if preferred against a white man would result in prompt acquittal." The Chicago Commission on Race Relations reported in 1922,

"The testimony is practically unanimous that Negroes are much more liable to arrest than whites, since police officers share in the general public opinion that Negroes are more criminal than whites." Studies of criminal trials of blacks confirm the observation that when blacks were arrested, their conviction rate was higher than that of whites. In Alabama, the percentage of acquittals based on cases brought to trial in 1920–22 was much lower for blacks than for whites for all serious crimes except robbery. A 1926 Detroit study found that the rate of conviction of blacks for burglary, armed robbery, simple larceny, assault and battery, disturbing the peace, accosting and soliciting, prostitution, sex crimes, offenses against the state and prohibition laws, embezzling, and forgery was much higher than the rate for whites.

Sentencing patterns gave even stronger evidence of racial discrimination. In the Detroit study 48.6 percent of the black defendants compared with 43.8 percent of the whites were convicted of felonies. Of the blacks, only 7.1 percent were given the alternative of a fine or prison sentence, compared with 13.5 percent of the whites. Only 7.2 percent of blacks were given probation, while 12.2 percent of the whites received it. Altogether, 30.9 percent of the blacks and 15.5 percent of the whites were sentenced to imprisonment. Of course, it could be argued that fewer blacks had opportunities for proper probation work, also a result of discrimination, or that blacks committed offenses calling for heavier penalties.

Blacks were not only convicted more often than whites but also received longer sentences. For example, a 1927 study of 1,521 chain gang prisoners in North Carolina found that 7 percent of the white prisoners and 11 percent of the blacks were serving sentences shorter than three months. On the other hand, 6 percent of the white prisoners and 11 percent of the blacks were serving sentences of three years. It may be argued that blacks had committed more serious offenses, but that is not evident from the statistics.

By the 1940s it was well established that the black crime rate was consistently higher than that for whites, and more emphasis was placed on studying the causes of crime and the relationship of blacks to criminal justice agencies. Scholars theorized that one cause of black crime was that "slavery in a sense dehumanized the Negro." Furthermore, "slavery nurtured a set of habits and attitudes which still affect many thousands of Negroes." Among these were lack of self-respect, lack of self-confidence, a distaste for hard work, a habit of dependence upon white friends, lack of regard for the property of others, a feeling that "the white folks owe us a living," disdain for the white man's law, and a tendency to "let tomorrow take care of itself." Scholars agreed that after slavery blacks were subjected to continuous social and economic deprivation which made them large contributors to crime. Since ecological studies had demonstrated the relationship among socially disordered neighborhoods, vice, and crime, it was easy to extrapolate from the fact that 90 percent of all blacks in the North and West in 1940 were urban dwellers, and that about 90 percent of these lived in or adjacent to disorganized areas, the assumption that consistent criminality would result.

In the South, violation of segregation customs could result in arrest: "recklessly eyeballing" a white woman, disputing a white man's word, or refusing to leave a public place when asked. Furthermore, blacks were useful targets for scapegoating and frame-ups. A white person could commit a crime with his face blackened or arrange a situation so that a particular black would appear to be guilty. If the hapless black escaped lynching, he would go to prison. Whites murdered blacks and successfully pinned a serious crime—actually committed by the murderer—on the dead victim.

Even more significant than scapegoating and frame-ups was the differential punishment of blacks whose victims were white. M. D. Richardson described the process in the Atlanta *World* in 1933: "When a Negro is arrested for a crime and brought to trial, the first question is against whom it was committed, white or colored. If against a white, the sentence is severe, usually far severer than it deserves. . . . If against a Negro, however, the whole complexion of the case is different. A meager sentence is very likely to be imposed, and in some cases no sentence at all." A 1941 study of Richmond, Virginia, five counties in North Carolina, and one county in Georgia pointed out the disparity of conviction and sentencing in homicide cases when blacks allegedly killed other blacks and when blacks allegedly killed whites. There were few interracial murders, but the conviction rate was higher and the sentences more severe in cases where blacks allegedly killed whites. . . .

The data indicated that blacks who killed other blacks literally got away with murder. This effect helped to make blacks even more contemptuous of the law. They knew how little whites cared for black life and property. The Chief of the Atlanta Police Department put it best in 1933: "One reason for the high percentage of killings among Negroes is that few of them are electrocuted for slaying members of their own race. We bring them before the courts charged with murder, and the verdict is usually manslaughter. This does not serve as a sufficient deterrent." . . .

Blacks were still decidedly ill-treated in prisons in the 1940s. In the South, black women, juvenile offenders, hardened criminals, and the criminally insane were often imprisoned together. The chain gang system was still in use for highway work, and it led to terrible accidents, such as the burning of twenty men in a truck cage because they were trying to warm themselves by setting fire to some gasoline. In another incident, convicts had their feet amputated after they were frostbitten during solitary confinement in a cage on a cold night.

Most black prisoners served out their time and did not receive the benefit of pardon or parole. Blacks generally lacked the influence to obtain pardons, and the disposition of many parole cases followed the example in which the butler for a white man murdered a black woman who spurned his attentions. He was defended by his employer, received a light sentence, and then was paroled to his employer. The major factor in the release of blacks was the interest of some white person in using them. Letters such as these were received by parole officials in Alabama: "I can use a Negro full time . . . will see that he has something to eat, and keep him at work all the time clearing land, cutting wood, and helping cultivate the land. . . . I am in need of a Negro farm hand and I am depending on one from you and if you have one for me, you may write what prison I can get him and when. . . . I understand that the state is letting out prisoners on parole, if so I would like to get a Negro named G——— W———."

EXPLORING THE CLASS BASIS
OF BLACK CRIME IN THE 1950s

By the mid-1950s social scientists had reached a consensus that crime statistics had more to do with class than with race. The existing significant difference was still attributed to such variables as police discrimination toward blacks, discrimination in the sentencing process, differences in treatment inside prison, differences in education and job opportunities, and the effect of migratory patterns on criminal behavior. Any of the social and economic indicators used by experts showed that the black condition was not expected to improve to any substantial degree so long as racism and an unwillingness to provide opportunities to relieve the effects of past discrimination existed among the white majority. Unlike white immigrants of an earlier day or even more recent immigrants, blacks could scarcely hope that the majority of their numbers would be provided opportunities for advancement based solely on merit. White liberals were patronizing more often than helpful. A 1958 *Time* editorial is typical: "This pervasive discrimination holds down capable Negroes at the top of the social ladder, dims their voices among their own people, builds up tensions and resentments inside the Negro Society, and keeps great masses of Negroes segregated in ghettos where the standards of personal morality, discipline and responsibility are lower than those in the white world outside." San Francisco's black deputy city attorney, R. J. Reynolds, put it best when he said, "Slam enough doors in a man's face, and he may break one of them down." Despite the increased awareness, little was done to ameliorate social and economic conditions among blacks so as to reduce criminal actions against white persons and rising crime rates against the property of blacks. Blacks remained largely a people without capital, property, or jobs in a capitalist system and were often driven to prey on those just as disadvantaged who lived in close proximity to them.

INCREASED PUBLIC ATTENTION
TO BLACK CRIME IN THE 1960s AND 1970s

Several events occurred in the criminal justice system to focus increased public concern on black crime rates in the 1960s. First, the Supreme Court rendered a series of decisions which served to apply most of the due process requirements of federal criminal procedures to state criminal justice systems. Since the Tenth Amendment to the Constitution left the punishment of crimes to the states, enjoining federal constitutional procedures in the state criminal justice system was a matter of great controversy. The Court had held earlier that the Fourteenth Amendment did not make all of the provisions of the U.S. Bill of Rights applicable to the states' legal systems. But the Court had recognized that some of the rights safeguarded in the Bill of Rights might be protected against state infringement because to deny them might be a denial of due process of law.

By 1969 the specific earlier rulings had been overruled, but the Court still rejected the total incorporation theory. However, in a series of separate decisions, most of the Bill of Rights had been selectively incorporated to apply to the states. The Fourth Amendment right to be free from unreasonable searches and seizures and to have excluded from criminal trials any evidence illegally seized was applied to the state investigation procedures. The Fifth Amendment right to be free from self-incrimination was applied, as well as the Sixth Amendment right to counsel, the right to a speedy and public trial, the right to confront opposing witnesses, the right to compulsory process for obtaining witnesses, and the right to trial by jury. The Court went on to extend the right to counsel during the interrogation stage and to rule out the use of a confession obtained in the absence of the opportunity to counsel and on effective waivers of the right.

The climate in which abuse of law enforcement in the streets of Selma, Montgomery, Bogalusa, and other cities was blatantly obvious and in which there was continuous controversy over police brutality, dragnet arrests, and discriminatory official conduct in the North possibly accelerated the Court's willingness to enlarge due process protections. Liberal lawyers and the Court succeeded in restraining the power of the police to treat suspects arbitrarily and in enlarging the scope of due process protection. Policemen viewed liberal efforts to restrain their discretion as an unconscionable effort to make their jobs more difficult and to increase the physical danger to which they were exposed in enforcing the law.

The 1960s rebellions, riots, and insurrections in the cities, carried out by blacks in reaction to the failure of both the legal civil rights changes and the Johnson administration's War on Poverty to improve their social and economic condition, erupted usually in response to perceived police brutality. As defenders of the social order, police were in the most exposed position among blacks in the cities and were thus more likely to have their activities become the precipitating cause of any rebellion. In Detroit, police efforts to close a "blind pig," an illegal after-hours drinking establishment, resulted in a large-scale riot; in Watts, it was the arrest of a black man in the midst of a crowd and in other cities the shooting of black suspected criminals. During the rebellions, blacks destroyed and appropriated the property of businessmen and store owners in what many whites regarded as needless, irrational rage. The spectacle reinforced the notion that blacks were likely to be criminals, violators of law and order.

Blacks viewed the police in the 1960s and 1970s as a white alien army occupying their neighborhoods. Statistics supported their characterization. For example, in 1970 blacks made up between 27 and 63 percent of the total population of Detroit, Atlanta, Chicago, and Washington, D.C., but represented only between 5 and 21 percent of the police forces in those cities. An overwhelming majority of the policemen lived in the suburbs. The novelist James Baldwin correctly described black attitudes toward the police in *Nobody Knows My Name* (1962):

> The only way to police a ghetto is to be oppressive. None of the Police Commissioner's men, even with the best will in the world, have any way of understanding the lives led by the people they swagger about in twos and threes controlling. Their very presence is an insult, and it would be, even if they spent their entire day feeding gumdrops to children. They represent the force of the white world, and that world's criminal profit and ease, to keep the Black man corralled up here, in his place. The badge, the gun in the holster, and the swinging club make vivid what will happen should his rebellion become overt. . . . He moves through Harlem, therefore, like an occupying soldier in a bitterly hostile country, which is precisely what, and where he is, and is the reason he walks in twos and threes.

Speaking in 1973, Benjamin Ward, deputy commissioner of the New York City Police Department, echoed Baldwin's sentiments: "Blacks in America are jailed first and bailed last. The police discretionary power is used least in the ghettos. Police there are viewed as an army of invaders, and, in turn, the police often view black people as inferiors."

White police not only viewed blacks as inferiors, they also frequently beat and killed them. During the 1920s, according to historian Arthur Raper, 50 percent of the blacks killed by whites were murdered by policemen. A Department of Justice study of reported cases of police brutality against private citizens from January 1, 1958, through June, 1960, found that out of 1,328 incidents, 461 or 34 percent were against blacks. Afro-Americans found little redress for their grievances from either the police or the few police review boards. Without regard to class, blacks were mistreated by the police with impunity.

During this period, scholars and the public became more aware of the problem of urban poverty and the need for law enforcement to reckon with the consequences of continued social and economic injustice. But many white Americans opposed or betrayed the War on Poverty and began asserting that the new measures were not working even before they were really tried. Significantly, the liberal economic solutions of the War on Poverty were not designed to redistribute the wealth and overturn the existing structure, but merely to provide blacks with better education to enable them to compete within the existing system. Even this change was more than many white Americans would support, especially when it became apparent that the provision of better education and social welfare was costly and that when blacks became competitors for a wide variety of opportunities they would be competing with whites who already had such opportunities. The whites were just not willing to provide justice for blacks if it led to greater competition for jobs.

Increasingly, some whites began to assert that it was the inadequacy of punitive measures that caused the high black crime rate, not continued oppression by the white majority. Predictably, law and order became a pungent issue in the 1968 presidential campaign. American party candidate George Wallace in his campaign preached incessantly about a high black crime rate. Democrat Hubert Humphrey talked about black crime but was careful to stress that most of the victims were blacks. Republican Richard Nixon tried "law and order with justice" in his speeches as a compromise, but the phrase "with justice" got lost in the final weeks of his campaign.

Even before the campaign, federal officials began to emphasize crime control. President Johnson had created a Commission of Law Enforcement and the Administration of Justice in July, 1965, which published many volumes of reports in the spring of 1967. In March and June, 1967, respectively, the First International Congress on Crime Control and the National Conference on Juvenile Delinquency were convened to determine what the next steps should be. These conferences concluded that support should be provided to individual states to implement the recommendations of the President's Commission. Congress enacted the omnibus Crime Control and Safe Streets Act of 1968, authorizing unprecedented federal funding, and established the Law Enforcement Assistance Administration (LEAA) as a key instrument for the national response to the crime problem. The LEAA distributed $870 million to state and local police for fiscal year 1975.

In mid-September, 1968, when the election campaign was at its height, Attorney General Ramsey Clark, testifying before the National Commission on the Causes and Prevention of Violence, pointed out that blacks, 12 percent of the population, were involved in 59 percent of the arrests for murder. Fifty-four percent of the victims were black; nearly 50 percent of the persons arrested for aggravated assault were black, and blacks were the primary victims; 47 percent of those arrested for rape were blacks, and again blacks were the primary victims; 61 percent of those arrested for robbery were black, but less than 33 percent of the persons arrested for other property crimes such as embezzlement were black. The picture was that of a crime-ridden black community with blacks striking out at those closest to them—other blacks. The arrest rate among blacks for murder, robbery, carrying concealed weapons, prostitution, and gambling was about five times that for whites. Most of the data on black crime had been analyzed by scholars for years, but it began to penetrate the white community only when whites noticed blacks coming out of their communities to attack whites or attacking white persons and their property in the black community. Clark, unlike the winner in the presidential campaign, emphasized that the reasons for black crime could be found in the economic and social deprivation perpetuated in communities where they lived.

Racism accounted, in part, for what occurred thereafter. Instead of focusing on efforts to improve the conditions and prospects of blacks in order to stop breeding crime, politicians focused on efforts to stamp out the criminal behavior involved and to punish the criminals. "Law and order" should be enforced by courts, more police officers, and stronger punitive measures adopted in prisons. As the LEAA poured more and more money into the training and education of police and prison officials, the crime rate continued to increase. . . .

MORE POWER THAN WE WANT:

Masculine Sexuality and Violence

47

Bruce Kokopeli and George Lakey

Masculine sexuality involves the oppression of women, competition among men, and homophobia (fear of homosexuality). Patriarchy, the systematic domination of women by men through unequal opportunities, rewards, punishments, and the internalization of unequal expectations through sex role differentiation, is the institution which organizes these behaviors. Patriarchy is men having more power, both personally and politically, than women of the same rank. This imbalance of power is the core of patriarchy, but definitely not the extent of it.

Sex inequality cannot be routinely enforced through open violence or even blatant discriminatory agreements—patriarchy also needs its values accepted in the minds of people. If as many young *women* wanted to be physicians as men, and as many young men *wanted* to be nurses as women, the medical schools and the hospitals would be hard put to maintain the masculine domination of health care; open struggle and the naked exercise of power would be necessary. Little girls, therefore, are encouraged to think "nurse" and boys to think "doctor."

Patriarchy assigns a list of human characteristics according to gender: women should be nurturant, gentle, in touch with their feelings, etc.; men should be productive, competitive, super-rational, etc. Occupations are valued according to these gender-linked characteristics, so social work, teaching, housework, and nursing are of lower status than business executive, judge, or professional football player.

When men do enter "feminine" professions they disproportionately rise to the top and become chefs, principals of schools, directors of ballet, and teachers of social work. A man is somewhat excused from his sex role deviation if he at least dominates within the deviation. Domination, after all, is what patriarchy is all about.

From: *Off Their Backs . . . and on Our Own Two Feet* (Philadelphia: New Society Publishers, 1983), pp. 17–24. Reprinted by permission.

Access to powerful positions by women (i.e., those positions formerly limited to men) is contingent on the women adopting some masculine characteristics, such as competitiveness. They feel pressure to give up qualities assigned to females (such as gentleness) because those qualities are considered inherently weak by patriarchal culture. The existence, therefore, of a woman like Indira Gandhi in the position of a dictator in no way undermines the basic sexist structure which allocates power to those with masculine characteristics.

Patriarchy also shapes men's sexuality so it expresses the theme of domination. Notice the masculine preoccupation with size. The size of a man's body has a lot to say about his clout or his vulnerability, as any junior high boy can tell you. Many of these schoolyard fights are settled by who is bigger than whom, and we experience in our adult lives the echoes of intimidation and deference produced by our habitual "sizing up" of the situation.

Penis size is part of this masculine preoccupation, this time directed toward women. Men want to have large penises because size equals power, the ability to make a woman "really feel it." The imagery of violence is close to the surface here, since women find penis size irrelevant to sexual genital pleasure. "Fucking" is a highly ambiguous word, meaning both intercourse and exploitation/assault.

It is this confusion that we need to untangle and understand. Patriarchy tells men that their need for love and respect can only be met by being masculine, powerful, and ultimately violent. As men come to accept this, their sexuality begins to reflect it. Violence and sexuality combine to support masculinity as a character ideal. To love a woman is to have power over her and to treat her violently if need be. The Beatles' song "Happiness Is A Warm Gun" is but one example of how sexuality gets confused with violence and power. We know one man who was discussing another man who seemed to be highly fertile—he had made several women pregnant. "That guy," he said, "doesn't shoot any blanks."

Rape is the end logic of masculine sexuality. Rape is not so much a sexual act as an act of violence expressed in a sexual way. The rapist's mind-set—that violence and sexuality *can* go together—is actually a product of patriarchal conditioning, for most of us men understand the same, however abhorrent rape may be to us personally.

In war, rape is astonishingly prevalent even among men who "back home" would not do it. In the following description by a marine sergeant who witnessed a gang rape in Vietnam, notice that nearly all the nine-man squad participated:

They were supposed to go after what they called a Viet Cong whore. They went into her village and instead of capturing her, they raped her—every man raped her. As a matter of fact, one man said to me later that it was the first time he had ever made love to a woman with his boots on. The man who led the platoon, or the squad, was actually a private. The squad leader was a sergeant but he was a useless person and he let the private take over his squad. Later he said he took no part in the raid. It was against his morals. So instead of telling his squad not to do it, because they wouldn't listen to him anyway, the sergeant went into another side of the village and just sat and stared bleakly at the ground, feeling sorry for himself. But at any rate, they raped the girl, and then, the last man to make love to her, shot her in the head. [Vietnam Veterans Against the War, statement by Michael McClusker in *The Winter Soldier Investigation: An Inquiry Into American War Crimes.*]

Psychologist James Prescott adds to this account:

What is it in the American psyche that permits the use of the word "love" to describe rape? And where the act of love is completed with a bullet in the head! [*Bulletin of the Atomic Scientists,* November 1975, p. 17.]

MASCULINITY AGAINST MEN: THE MILITARIZATION OF EVERYDAY LIFE

Patriarchy benefits men by giving us a class of people (women) to dominate and exploit. Patriarchy also oppresses men, by setting us at odds with each other and shrinking our life space.

The pressure to win starts early and never stops. Working class gangs fight over turf; rich people's sons are pushed to compete on the sports field. British military officers, it is said, learned to win on the playing fields of Eton.

Competition is conflict held within a framework of rules. When the stakes are really high, the rules may not be obeyed; fighting breaks out. We men mostly relate through competition, but we know what is waiting in the wings. John Wayne is not a cultural hero by accident.

Men compete with each other for status as masculine males. Because masculinity equals power, this means we are competing for power. The ultimate proof of power/masculinity is violence. A man may fail to "measure up" to the macho stereotype in important ways, but if he can fight successfully with the person who challenges him on his deviance, he is still all right. The television policeman Baretta is strange in some ways: he is gentle with women and he cried when a man he loved was killed. However, he has what are probably the largest biceps in television and he proves weekly that he can beat up the toughs who come his way.

The close relationship between violence and masculinity does not need much demonstration. War used to be justified partly because it promoted "manly virtue" in a nation. Those millions of people in the woods hunting deer, in the National Rifle Association, and cheering on the bloodiest hockey teams are overwhelmingly men.

The world situation is so much defined by patriarchy that what we see in the wars of today is competition between various patriarchal ruling classes and governments breaking into open conflict. Violence is the accepted masculine form of conflict resolution. Women at this time are not powerful enough in the world situation for us to see mass overt violence being waged on them. But the violence is in fact there; it is hidden through its legitimization by the state and by culture.

In everyday middle-class life, open violence between men is of course rare. The defining characteristics of masculinity, however, are only a few steps removed from violence. Wealth, productivity, or rank in the firm or institution translate into power—the capacity (whether or not exercised) to dominate. The holders of power in even polite institutions seem to know that violence is at their fingertips, judging from the reactions of college presidents to student protest in the 1960s. We know of one urban "pacifist" man, the head of a theological seminary, who was barely talked out of calling the police to deal with a nonviolent student sit-in at "his" seminary!

Patriarchy teaches us at very deep levels that we can never be safe with other men (or perhaps with anyone!), for the guard must be kept up lest our vulnerability be exposed and we be taken advantage of. At a recent Quaker conference in Philadelphia, a discussion group considered the value of personal sharing and openness in the Quaker Meeting. In almost every case the women advocated more sharing and the men opposed it. Dividing by gender on that issue was predictable; men are conditioned by our life experience of masculinity to distrust settings where personal exposure will happen, especially if men are present. Most men find emotional intimacy possible only with women; many with only one woman; some men cannot be emotionally intimate with anyone.

Patriarchy creates a character ideal—we call it masculinity—and measures everyone against it. Many men as well as women fail the test and even men who are passing the test today are carrying a heavy load of anxiety about tomorrow. Because masculinity is a form of domination, no one can really rest secure. The striving goes on forever unless you are actually willing to give up and find a more secure basis for identity.

MASCULINITY AGAINST GAY MEN: PATRIARCHY FIGHTS A REAR GUARD ACTION

Homophobia is the measure of masculinity. The degree to which a man is thought to have gay feelings is the degree of his unmanliness. Because patriarchy presents sexuality as men over women (part of the general dominance theme), men are conditioned to have only that in mind as a model of sexual expression. Sex with another man must mean being dominated, which is very scary. A non-patriarchal model of sexual expression as the mutuality of equals doesn't seem possible; the transfer of the heterosexual model to same-sex relations can at best be "queer," at worst, "perverted."

In the recent book *Blue Collar Aristocrats*, by E. E. LeMasters, a working class tavern is described in which the topic of homosexuality sometimes comes up. Gayness is never defended. In fact, the worst thing you can call a man is homosexual. A man so attacked must either fight or leave the bar.

Notice the importance of violence in defending yourself against the charge of being a "pansy." Referring to your income or academic degrees or size of your car is no defense against such a charge. Only fighting will re-establish your respect as a masculine male. Because "gay" appears to mean "powerless," one needs to go to the masculine source of power—violence—for adequate defense.

Last year, the Argentinian government decided to persecute gays on a systematic basis. The Ministry of Social Welfare offered the rationale for this policy in an article in its journal, which also attacked lesbians, concluding that they should be put in jail or killed:

> As children they played with dolls. As they grew up, violent sports horrified them. As was to be expected, with the passage of time and the custom of listening to foreign mulattos on the radio, they became conscientious objectors. [*El Caudillo*, February 1975, excerpted in *Peace News*, July 11, 1975, p. 5]

The Danish government, by contrast with Argentina, has liberal policies on gay people. There is no government persecution and all government jobs are open to gays—except in the military and the diplomatic service! Two places where the nation-state is most keen to assert power are places where gays are excluded as a matter of policy.

We need not go abroad to see the connections between violence and homophobia. In the documentary film *Men's Lives*, a high school boy is interviewed on what it is like to be a dancer. While the interview is conducted, we see him working out, with a very demanding set of acrobatic exercises. The boy mentions that other boys think he must be gay. "Why is that?" the interviewer asks. "Dancers are free and loose," he replies; they are not big like football players; and "you're not trying to kill anybody."

Different kinds of homosexual behavior bring out different amounts of hostility, curiously enough. That fact gives us further clues to violence and female oppression. In prisons, for example, men can be respected if they fuck other men, but not if they are themselves fucked. (We use the word "fucked" intentionally for its ambiguity.) Often prison rapes are done by men who identify as heterosexual; one hole substitutes for another in this scene, for sex is in either case an expression of domination for the masculine mystique.

But for a man to be entered sexually, or to use effeminate gestures and actions, is to invite attack in prison and hostility outside. Effeminate gay men are at the bottom of the totem pole because they are *most like women*, which is nothing less than treachery to the Masculine Cause. Even many gay men shudder at drag queens and vigilantly guard against certain mannerisms because they, too, have internalized the masculinist dread of effeminacy.

John Braxton's report of prison life as a draft resister is revealing on this score. The other inmates knew immediately that John was a conscientious objector because he did not act tough. They also assumed he was gay, for the same reason. (If you are not masculine, you must be a pacifist and gay, for masculinity is a package which includes both violence and heterosexuality.)

A ticket of admission to masculinity, then, is sex with women, and bisexuals can at least get that ticket even if they deviate through having gay feelings as well. This may be why bisexuality is not feared as much as exclusive gayness among men. Exclusively gay men let down the Masculine Cause in a very important way—those gays do not participate in the control of women through sexuality. Control through sexuality matters because it is flexible; it usually is mixed with love and dependency so that it becomes quite subtle. (Women often testify to years of confusion and only the faintest uneasiness at their submissive role in traditional heterosexual relationships and the role sex plays in that.)

Now we better understand why women are in general so much more supportive of gay men than non-gay men are. Part of it of course is that heterosexual men are often paralyzed by fear. Never very trusting, such men find gayness one more reason to keep up the defenses. But heterosexual women are drawn to active support for the struggles of gay men because there is a common enemy—patriarchy and its definition of sexuality as domination. Both heterosexual women and gay men have experienced first hand the violence of sexism; we all have experienced its less open forms such as put-downs and discrimination, and we all fear its open forms such as rape and assault.

Patriarchy, which links characteristics (gentleness, aggressiveness, etc.) to gender, shapes sexuality as well, in such a way as to maintain male power. The Masculine Cause draws strength from homophobia and resorts habitually to violence in its battles on the field of sexual politics. It provides psychological support for the military state and is in turn stimulated by it.

PATRIARCHY AND THE MILITARY STATE

The parallels between these two powerful institutions are striking. Both prefer more subtle means of domination but insist on violence as a last resort. Both institutions provide role models for socialization: the masculine man, the feminine woman, the patriotic citizen. Both are aided by other institutions in maintaining their legitimacy—religion, education, business, sport. . . .

The interplay at the top levels of the state between violence and masculinity is becoming clearer. Political scientist Richard Barnet refers to the "hairy chest syndrome" among National Security Managers in government agencies:

> The man who is ready to recommend using violence against foreigners, even where he is overruled, does not damage his reputation for prudence, soundness, or imagination, but the man who recommends putting an issue to the UN, seeking negotiations or—horror of horrors—"doing nothing" quickly becomes known as "soft." To be "soft"—that is, unbelligerent, compassionate, willing to settle for less—or simply to be repelled by homicide, is to be "irresponsible." It means walking out of the club. [*Men and Masculinity*, by Joseph Pleck and Jack Sawyer, p. 136]

. . . The struggle for a world without war must also be a struggle against patriarchy with its masculine character ideal and its oppression of women and gays. Pacifist men, by rejecting violence, have taken a healthy first step in dropping out of masculinity. Some have sought to compensate for that by being more rigorously "tough" in other ways and by participating in the oppression of women and gays. This must stop. The feminist and gay struggles are other dimensions of the same cause: an end to violence. . . .

IV

Social Change and the Politics of Empowerment

Power is typically equated with domination and control over people or things. Social institutions depend on this version of power to reproduce hierarchies of race, class, and gender. Exploration of the experiences of African-Americans, Latinos, women, Native Americans, Asian Americans, and the poor reveals much about how dominant groups exercise power. But centering on the experiences of historically marginalized groups also reveals much about resistance because members of these groups engage in individual acts of resistance and organized political activism to challenge race, class, and gender oppression.

Dominant ideologies and the social institutions they defend try to obscure the individual and collective political activism of everyday citizens. By making the political activism of historically marginalized groups invisible, social institutions aim to suppress the strength of these groups and render them more easily exploited. The articles in "Political Activism: Making a Difference" address this forced invisibility. Each article explores a different dimension of empowerment in the context of everyday life, demonstrating that individuals can and do work for social change. Although academic credentials, positions of authority, and economic resources can do much to help individuals challenge hierarchies of race, class, and gender, these articles suggest that individual and collective actions of ordinary persons form the bedrock for any lasting social change.

For Chang Jok Lee, the elderly immigrant Chinese-American mother of eight and grandmother of eleven interviewed in "From Homemaker to Housing Advocate," political activism is not a theoretical issue but part of her everyday life. Her story demonstrates how individuals with ostensibly few resources for resistance can exercise political power. In "Sharing the Shop Floor," Stan Gray provides a firsthand account of the daily issues he confronted as a union organizer. He discusses the importance of holistic analyses of race, class, and gender in political activism and the necessity of collective action. Kathleen Kautzer's account of how older women organized on a national level to improve their lives parallels Stan Gray's rendition of the difficulties of organizing for change. Once again we see how individuals deemed least likely to organize on their own behalf not only were effective but also addressed the interlocking nature of race, class, and gender in their activism. Roberta Praeger, a mother dependent on welfare, gives a compelling account of her own successful struggle to become an activist working for "A World Worth Living In." Praeger's narrative demonstrates the importance of community and the value of collective struggle in empowering oneself and in working to empower others. Praeger found that she had to resist oppressive beliefs and actions from those closest to her daily life. Oppression accompanied by love is often difficult to see, let alone resist. Praeger engaged in a silent, internal struggle to reject dominant ideologies telling her that she was lesser. She offers us an inside view of resisting internalized oppression, where racist, sexist, homophobic, or other dominant ideologies aim to recruit the victims of oppression to collude in their own domination.

Because existing institutions are structured around race, class, and gender oppression, gaining power within them as they currently exist is unlikely to improve significantly the lives of African-Americans, Native Americans, women, Asian Americans, the poor, gays and lesbians, Latinos, and other historically marginalized groups. Replacing one type of dominant group with another of a different color or gender may improve the lives of some without addressing the fundamental inequalities that pervade existing social institutions.

Investigating forms of power used by historically marginalized groups offers one way of rethinking social change and reconceptualizing the politics of empowerment. As Black feminist theorist Bell Hooks suggests, "Sexism has never rendered women powerless. It has either suppressed their strength or exploited it. Recognition of that strength, that power, is a step women together can take toward liberation."[1] Thus, African-Americans, Native Americans, women, Latinos, gays and lesbians, and the poor and working class have never been powerless; the question is one of how to identify and use those forms of power that often go unrecognized.

Reenvisioning and exercising power to bring about social change requires a sense of purpose and a vision that encourages us to look beyond what already exists. We must learn to question what is possible. For example, what type of housing would result if Chang Jok Lee were central in her community's decision-making process? If men and women truly learned to "share the shop floor," how might economic security be better provided for all? What would distinguish a "world worth living in" from the one we now have?

The three essays in "Envisioning Change" provide new visions about what is possible. Each offers inclusive thinking, reconstructed knowledge, and a distinctive perspective on the kinds of questions we should be considering in working toward Praeger's "world worth living in." One theme that pervades the concluding essays is rethinking the nature of difference. "We have *all* been programmed to respond to the human differences between us with fear and loathing," contends Audre Lorde, "and to handle that difference in one of three ways: ignore it, and if that is not possible, copy it if we think it is dominant, or destroy it if we think it is subordinate." Race, class, and gender have created distinctive histories among us and have encouraged us to think about differences in ways that provide few models for relating across differences as equals.

These essays envision how we might address this question of difference. Rayna Green's "Culture and Gender in Indian America" suggests that Native American culture offers alternative ways of conceptualizing difference that might enrich Western social institutions. "In Indian cultures I go back to my families and there is no division," observes Green. "There are distinctions, certainly, about the way people are treated, and the authority they have, but I want to reclaim the power to move through categories, so that I do not have to stay fixed in any one place." Her account of the utility of reclaiming all parts of her past provides a model for allowing diverse groups to speak for themselves. It allows us to imagine alternative ways of being that are not based on hierarchical distinctions among race, class, and gender groups. For example, one such distinction—the vast differences in wealth that characterize the class system—is viewed quite differently in Native American culture. According to Green, in Native American traditions, real wealth lies in "our own hearts, and not in something that is a commodity beyond it." Thus the richest person is the one who "gives the most away, not the person who keeps the most for themselves."

Through the image of the barred room in "Coalition Politics: Turning the Century," Bernice Johnson Reagon explores the creation of nurturing spaces and communities where we can recover from the damaging effects of race, class, and gender oppression. "Nationalism is crucial to a people if you are going to ever impact as a group in your interest," suggests Reagon. African-American communities, for example, offer a space where Blacks can retreat from the difficulties of oppression, learn ways of supporting one another, and identify the positive qualities of difference based on group identity. But Reagon also points to the limited value of these spaces. Nationalism and the celebration of difference that can accompany it become limiting if a group does not look beyond its own room and learn to appreciate differences of other groups.

A second theme that pervades these essays is the necessity of building coalitions across differences and the difficulty of doing so. As Reagon points out, coalition building requires hard work that creates tensions and discomforts. Green illustrates this problem in her discussion of the tensions created at a women's studies conference when white feminists misunderstood the actions of Native American people because of their lack of knowledge of Native American culture. This tension can be further aggravated when groups of different power within hierarchies of race, class, and gender try to build coalitions. Although the white feminists in Green's example had good intentions, they also wanted to retain their power to define the conference. They wanted to include Native American women but only on terms acceptable to them. As a result, effective communication was limited by differences in power that allowed one group to define the terms of the discourse.

Audre Lorde offers another view of how coalitions can be built across differences generated by different histories and varying amounts of power. Lorde cautions us to reject the so-called mythical norm, one key indicator of group power. Usually defined as white, thin, male, young, heterosexual, Christian, and financially secure, within this norm reside the trappings of power. Coalition building in such a context requires not just trying to relate across differences, but identifying the differences in power that accrue to groups based on their proximity to the mythical norm. Thus, truly effective coalition building involves rejecting the entire norm, not just that part of it that oppresses one's own group. African-Americans of both genders must resist sexism, antiracist policies must inform feminist political activism, and poverty cannot be eliminated without challenging its race, class, and age-specific dimensions.

"Change means growth, and growth can be painful," observes Audre Lorde. "But we sharpen self-definition by exposing the self in work and struggle together with those whom we define as different from ourselves, although sharing the same goals." Building coalitions across differences and empowering historically marginalized groups requires seeing the connections among groups currently differentiated by inequalities of race, class, and gender. Doing so fosters much-needed social change and eventually empowers us all.

1. Bell Hooks, *From Margin to Center* (Boston: South End Press, 1984), p. 93.

Political Activism: Making a Difference

GROWING NUMBERS, GROWING FORCE: *Older Women Organize*

48

Kathleen Kautzer

We have played the game according to rules you set down. Now the rules have changed and we're called out, but we have one half to one third of our lives still to go, and we will not be shelved.

—Tish Sommers, "Epilogue"[1]

With these words, Tish Sommers, a self-described "free-lance agitator," aptly summarized the spirit and message of the Older Women's movement that she labored to initiate and build over the past fifteen years. (Sommers died in the fall of 1985.)

Sommers described her generation of American women as "playing by the rules" because her cohorts, by and large, accepted traditional female roles in both the family and the labor market. This generation had very

From: Rochelle Lefkowitz and Ann Withorn (eds.), *For Crying Out Loud: Women and Poverty in the United States* (New York: Pilgrim Press, 1986), pp. 89–98. Reprinted by permission.

[1]This essay is based on ongoing work for my dissertation on the Older Women's League (OWL). It could not have been written without the collaboration and support of Tish Sommers and Alice Quinlan.

limited exposure to feminism because their youth and adolescence occurred between 1930 and 1950, when the first wave of the feminist movement had subsided, and the second wave had not yet coalesced. During World War II many had enjoyed brief stints of employment as "Rosie, the Riveter" recruited to replace male workers who entered military service. However, at the end of the war, many women were persuaded, with varying degrees of reluctance and resistance, to relinquish their lucrative and challenging jobs to returning soldiers, or as was often the situation, to continue to work at less well-paid "women's jobs." In order to achieve this transition, American producers and public officials subjected this generation to an intense propaganda campaign extolling the homemaker role as the most suitable and rewarding occupation available to women.

Now that Sommers' generation has reached late adulthood many of her cohorts are discovering that "the rules have changed and we've been called out." In other words, contrary to their expectations, older women are encountering penalties rather than rewards for their lifelong service in female roles because of changing demographic and social trends and discriminatory social policies. Rising divorce rates and increasing gaps in the longevity rates of males and females have left today's generation of older women more likely than earlier generations to survive over an extended period without spousal companionship or support. After being socialized to view their husband as their provider, many older women find themselves lacking the resources needed to insure their own economic survival. As a result of the combined effects of age and sex discrimination in the labor market, older women are frequently unable to find employment or earn adequate wages. Equally important, older women find their retirement security jeopardized by both Social Security and pension programs, which penalize women for their lower lifetime earnings and/or their status as dependent spouses. Lastly, the passive, self-effacing, and subservient behavior women acquire during their lengthy playing of female roles inhibits their ability to assert their rights and protest the omnipresent discrimination they encounter.

Fortunately, Sommers' assertion that her generation of American women "will not be shelved" is being echoed by many of her cohorts, more than 13,000 of whom have become members of the Older Women's League (OWL), the first and only advocacy organization in the United States for mid-life and older women. Founded in 1981 by Tish Sommers and Laurie Shields, OWL is dedicated to the goal of "bridging the gap between the women's movement and aging activism." . . .

EMERGENCE AND GROWTH OF
THE OLDER WOMEN'S MOVEMENT

With the rallying slogan of "Don't Agonize, Organize," Tish Sommers attained wide recognition among both feminist and aging activists for her keen political instincts, her witty and captivating speaking style, her energetic and persistent leadership, and her path-breaking insights regarding the problems and potentialities of older women.

The origins of Sommers' interest in social justice and political activism can be traced to her experience when, as a young, foreign, exchange dance student residing with a Jewish family during the 1930s, she witnessed Hitler's rise to power. Following this early encounter with the horrors of racism and militarism in Nazi Germany, Sommers pursued a lifelong career as a volunteer community organizer supporting poverty programs and the Civil Rights Movement. Sommers' organizing talents reached their most complete expression when her own encounters with discriminatory treatment sparked her interest in launching a collective protest movement of older women.

When Sommers became divorced at age fifty-seven she experienced many of the problems of other displaced homemakers: she had difficulty getting credit in her own name and was unable to purchase medical insurance because of medical history. She also found that her background as a former homemaker and community organizer commanded little respect from employers and society as a whole. As an experienced political activist, Sommers quickly recognized herself to be the victim of structural inequities that negatively affected many women of her generation. Shortly thereafter she concluded that her peers were clearly "ripe" for political mobilization based on their overwhelmingly positive response to her public appeals for collective protest by and for older women.

Sommers' formal career as an advocate for older women began in 1973 when she convinced the National Organization for Women (NOW) to form a Task Force on Older Women. As coordinator of this task force, Sommers attracted a dedicated group of older women activists. Although Sommers and her colleagues maintained an ongoing dialogue with organizations representing women and the elderly, they eventually recognized the need to build their own advocacy organization focused exclusively on the unique problems of older women that remained largely ignored or misunderstood, even by feminist and aging activists.

Sommers' first attempt at organization building focused on displaced homemakers. In 1974 she formed a partnership with Laurie Shields, a former advertising executive and recently widowed displaced homemaker, and together they founded the Alliance for Displaced Homemakers (ADH). At present the ADH has been supplanted by the Displaced Homemaker Network (DHN), with headquarters in Washington, which serves as an information clearinghouse and national advocacy organization for displaced homemakers.

The women who became participants in the displaced-homemaker movement represented a wide range of backgrounds including (1) middle- and upper-income women who entered the ranks of the "new poor" upon loss of spousal support; (2) welfare mothers who lost Aid to Families with Dependent Children benefits when their eldest child turned eighteen; (3) homemakers with graduate degrees whose credentials were considered "outdated" by employers; and (4) women of color who remained "underemployed" as a result of their dual burdens as a family wage earner and care giver.

In spite of its limited resources and small membership base, ADH compiled an impressive list of legislative victories: by 1980, thirty states had passed displaced-homemaker legislation, and the U.S. Congress had officially recognized displaced homemakers as a "disadvantaged group" eligible for priority services under the 1978 Comprehensive Employment and Training Act (CETA) Reauthorization Act. . . .

Shields and Sommers always viewed the displaced-homemaker movement as a first step toward their long-term goal of building a mass membership organization for older women. In 1978 they laid the groundwork for realizing this goal by establishing the Older Women's League Education Fund (OWLEF), to engage in public education and consciousness raising regarding the problems shared by today's generation of older women.

Documenting the problems of older women proved to be a challenging task for OWLEF because of the lack of prior research. Feminist researchers had focused primarily on issues of concern to younger women (child care, reproductive rights, hiring policies) and had barely tapped issues of concern to women during the latter stages of the life cycle (retirement policies, health insurance, tending disabled family members, nursing home care, age-sex discrimination). Gerontological research was even more disappointing. For example, in the field of retirement research, inclusion of female subjects was "almost unheard of" before 1975. Many gerontologists justified their preoccupation with male retirees by arguing that retirement was primarily a "male" problem because of the role discontinuity men experience when forced to abandon their lifelong role as family wage earner. Even when women were included as research subjects, gerontologists usually failed to explain or highlight the high rates of unemployment, poverty, and institutionalization encountered by older women.[2] Lastly, government statistics are organized into categorical schemes that disguise the disadvantaged status of older women. For example, the Department of Labor does not cross-classify their employment statistics by age and sex, thereby making it impossible to pinpoint how older women fare relative to other employee groups. Similarly, homemakers are not recognized as an occupational category, thereby making it impossible to identify the number of older women who are full-time homemakers or displaced homemakers.

Shields and Sommers recognized that as long as the problems of older women remain undocumented and unpublicized, they would remain invisible. After all, the very existence of displaced homemakers had escaped public attention and concern until the displaced-homemaker's movement emerged and provided them with an official label and evidence of their disadvantaged status. Consequently, OWLEF prepared a series of policy papers outlining inequities in divorce settlements, Social Security, pension plans, the labor market, and health insurance. These papers—the OWLEF Gray Papers—received favorable reviews from policymakers in the field of the aging. In turn, this heightened awareness and receptivity to OWL issues on the part of professionals concerned with aging greatly enhanced efforts to solicit funds and find prestigious sponsors for OWLEF activities from organizations that serve the elderly.

In 1980 Sommers served as convenor of the Mini-Conference on Older Women (funded by the U.S. Administration on Aging) and invited delegates to remain an extra day at the close of the conference to participate in the launching of the Older Women's League. Three hundred of the four hundred conference delegates responded to this appeal, and the Older Women's League (OWL) was born.

To date OWL has attracted more than 13,000 members and has established ninety-five local chapters. The composition of OWL's membership is not, however, truly representative of the older female population. According to a recent membership survey, only 4 percent of OWL members are ethnic minorities and only 8 percent are full-time homemakers. A majority of OWL members have college degrees, are currently employed, and are between the ages of fifty and sixty-five. In the interest of building a more representative organization, OWL leaders are currently experimenting with a variety of strategies for increasing the number of members who have low incomes and/or belong to minority groups.

Shields and Sommers take pride in OWL's expanding capacity to engage in organizing and advocacy activities. For example, OWL's staff currently includes a government-relations specialist and several field organizers. Grants from private and public foundations enable OWL to provide grants and leadership training to local chapters and to publish an extensive range of consciousness-raising and educational material. OWL also receives pro-bono services from a prestigious media consulting firm, which designs public-service ads that cleverly dramatize OWL's mission. (One popular ad features a picture of a weeping Statue of Liberty with a caption that reads: "When it comes to older women, this country takes a lot of liberties.")

In discussing OWL's political objectives, OWL leaders consistently emphasize that genuine and enduring equity for older women can be accomplished only by eliminating structural inequities that are responsible for the multiple forms of discrimination they presently encounter. Reforms viewed necessary to achieve this long-range goal include the following:

- Social Security coverage for homemakers to eliminate the penalties imposed on them as a result of their "dependent" status
- full employment and expanded employment training programs to ensure employment to displaced homemakers and other older women who are subject to widespread discrimination in the current labor market
- comparable pay legislation to establish more equitable pay scales in traditionally female occupations

It should be noted that none of these reforms can be characterized as exclusively older women's issues; instead they would eliminate inequities encountered by women of all age groups. A variety of feminist organizations consequently include such proposals on their reform agendas. Needless to say, however, OWL leaders recognize that reforms of this magnitude can be achieved only as a result of an intensive and protracted struggle, led by a broad-based coalition of organizations representing women, the elderly, and their allies. . . .

Sommers' own words best describe the guiding principles of the older women's movement:

> One way we have worked in OWL is to take our experience, some of it bitter, and turn it into good energy to make this a better society for ourselves and those who will follow us. "We build a new road to aging and the road to aging builds us." Facing death and planning for it, squeezing the sweet juice out of adversity, is part of what OWL is all about.[3]

NOTES

1. Tish Sommers, "Epilogue" in *Displaced Homemakers: Organizing for a New Life*, Laurie Shields (New York: McGraw-Hill, 1981). This book is a firsthand account of the genesis and evolution of the displaced-homemakers' movement.

2. Maximilian Szinovacz, ed., *Women's Retirement* (Beverly Hills, Calif.; Sage Publications, 1982). This anthology documents and criticizes the sexist biases of many

gerontologists and presents summaries of a variety of recent research studies focused exclusively on female retirees. Another excellent feminist critique of gerontological research is Diane Beeson, "Women in Studies of Aging: A Critique and Suggestion," *Social Problems* 23 (1975): 52–59. Since the Older Women's League Education Fund (OWLEF) was founded in 1978, gerontologists have expressed an increasing interest and concern with older women's issues. Owing to a recent influx of female scholars in the field, there has also been a dramatic expansion of research focused exclusively on older women. This research is summarized in *The Mature Women in America, A Selected Annotated Bibliography 1979–1982* (available from the National Council on the Aging, Inc., Washington, DC 20004).

3. Letter to Older Women's League membership "On Death and Dying" by Tish Sommers, May 1985. (Copies may be obtained from OWL, 1325 G. Street, N.W., Washington, D.C. 20005.)

SHARING THE SHOP FLOOR   49

Stan Gray

On an October evening in 1983, a group of women factory workers from Westinghouse came to the United Steelworkers hall in Hamilton, Ontario, to tell their story to a labor federation forum on affirmative action. The women told of decades of maltreatment by Westinghouse—they had been confined to job ghettoes with inferior conditions and pay, and later, when their "Switchgear" plant was shut down, they had fought to be transferred to the other Westinghouse plants in the city. They had to battle management and the resistance of some, though not all, of their brothers in the shops. They won the first round, but when the recession hit, many were laid off regardless of seniority and left with little or no income in their senior years.

By the night of the forum I had worked at Westinghouse for ten years and had gone through the various battles for equality in the workplace. As I listened to the women, I thought of how much their coming into our plant had changed me, my fellow workers, and my brother unionists.

From: *Canadian Dimension* 18 (June 1984). Reprinted by permission.

The women were there to tell their own story because the male staff officials of their union, United Electrical Workers, had prevented the women's committee of the local labor council from presenting their brief. The union claimed it was inaccurate, the problems weren't that bad, and it didn't give union officials the credit for leading the fight for women's rights. The Westinghouse women gave their story and then the union delivered a brief of its own, presenting a historical discussion of male-female relations in the context of the global class struggle, without mentioning Westinghouse or Hamilton or any women that it represented.[1]

This kind of thing happens in other cities and in other unions. The unanimous convention resolutions in support of affirmative action tend to mask a male resistance within the unions and on the shop floor. Too many men pay lip service to women's rights but leave the real fighting to the women. They don't openly confront the chauvinism of their brothers on the shop floor and in the labor movement. Yet an open fight by men against sexism is an important part of the fight for sexual equality. It is also important because sexism is harmful for working men, in spite of whatever benefits they gain in the short term; it runs counter to their interests and undermines the quality of their trade unionism.

I was one of those unionists who for years sat on the fence in this area until sharp events at work pushed me off. I then had to try to deal with these issues in practice. The following account of the debates and struggles on the shop floor at Westinghouse concentrates on the men rather than on the women's battle; it focuses on the men's issues and tries to bring out concretely the interests of workingmen in the fight against sexism.

MY EDUCATION BEGINS

My education in the problems of the Westinghouse women began in November 1978, when I was recalled to work following a bitter and un-successful five-month strike. The union represented eighteen hundred workers in three plants that produced turbines, motors, transformers, and switchgear equipment. When I was recalled to work it wasn't to my old Beach Road plant—where I had been a union steward and safety rep—but to an all-female department in the Switchgear plant and to a drastic drop in my labor grade. The plant was mostly segregated; in other words, jobs (and many departments) were either male or female. There were separate seniority lists and job descriptions. The dual-wage, dual-seniority system was enshrined in the collective agreement signed and enforced by both company and union.

At Switchgear I heard the complaints of the women, who worked the worst jobs in terms of monotony, speed, and work discipline but received lower pay, were denied chances for promotion, and were frequently laid off. They complained too of the union, accusing the male leadership of sanctioning and policing their inferior treatment. In cahoots with management, it swept the women's complaints under the carpet. From the first day it was obvious to me that the company enforced harsher standards for the women. They worked harder and faster, got less break time, and were allowed less leeway than the men. When I was later transferred to the all-male machine shop, the change was from night to day.

Meanwhile the men's club that ran the union made its views known to me early and clearly. The staff rep told me that he himself would never work with women. He boasted that he and his friends in the leadership drank in the one remaining all-male bar in the city. The local president was upset when he heard that I was seriously listening to the complaints of the women workers. He told me that he always just listened to their unfounded bitching, said "yes, yes, yes," and then completely ignored what he had been told. I ought to do the same, was his advice. Although I had just been elected to the executive in a rank-and-file rebellion against the old guard, he assumed that a common male bond would override our differences. When I persisted in taking the women's complaints seriously, the leadership started to ridicule me, calling me "the Ambassador" and saying they were now happy that I was saving them the distasteful task of listening to the women's bitching.

Then in 1979 the boom fell at Switchgear: the company announced it would close the plant. For the women, this was a serious threat. In the new contract the seniority and wage lists had been integrated, thanks to a new Ontario Human Rights Code. But would the women be able to exercise their seniority and bump or transfer to jobs in the other Hamilton plants, or would they find themselves out in the street after years at Switchgear?

DIVIDE AND CONQUER

By this time I had been recalled to my old department at the Beach Road plant, thanks to shop-floor pressure by the guys. There was a lot of worry in the plants about the prospect of large-scale transfers of women from Switchgear. A few women who had already been transferred had met with harassment and open hostility from the men. Some of us tried to raise the matter in the stewards' council, but the leadership was in no mood to discuss and confront sexism openly. The union bully boys went after us, threatening, shouting, breast beating, and blaming the women for the problems.

Since the union structures weren't going to touch the problem, we were left to our own resources in the shop. I worked in the Transformer Division, which the management was determined to keep all male. As a steward I insisted that the Switchgear women had every right to jobs in our department, at least to training and a trial period as stipulated by seniority. Since this was a legal and contractual right, management developed a strategy of Divide and Rule: present the women as a threat to men's jobs; create splits and get the hourly men to do the bosses' dirty work for them. Management had a secondary objective here, which was to break our shop-floor union organization. Since the trauma of the strike and post-strike repression, a number of stewards and safety reps had patiently rebuilt the union in the plant, block by block—fighting every grievance, hazard, and injustice with a variety of tactics and constructing some shop-floor unity. We did so in the teeth of opposition from both company and union, whose officials were overly anxious to get along peacefully with each other. A war of the sexes would be a weapon in management's counteroffensive against us.

For months before the anticipated transfers, foremen and their assorted rumor mongers stirred up the pot with the specter of the Invasion of the Women. Two hundred Switchgear women would come and throw all Beach Road breadwinners out in the street; no one's job would be safe. Day after day, week after week, we were fed the tales: for example, that fourteen women with thirty years' seniority were coming to the department in eight days and no male would be protected. Better start thinking now about unemployment insurance.

In the department next to mine a few transfers of women were met with a vicious response from the men. Each side, including the militant steward, ended up ratting on the other to the boss. The men were furious and went all over the plant to warn others against allowing any "cunts" or "bitches" into their departments.

Meanwhile I had been fighting for the women to be called into new jobs opening up in the iron-stacking area of my department. The union's business agent had insisted that women couldn't physically handle those and other jobs. But I won the point with the company. The major influx of women would start here.

For weeks before their arrival, the department was hyper-alive, everyone keyed to the Invasion of the Women. I was approached by one of the guys, who said that a number of them had discussed the problem and wanted me, as their steward, to tell management the men didn't want the women in here and would fight to keep them out.

The moment was a personal watershed for me. As I listened to him, I knew that half measures would no longer do. I would now have to take the bull by the horns.

Over the years I had been dealing with male chauvinism in a limited fashion. As a health and safety rep, I had to battle constantly with men who would knowingly do dangerous work because it was "manly" to do so and because it affirmed their masculine superiority. The bosses certainly knew how to use guys like that to get jobs done quickly. With a mixture of sarcasm, force, and reason, I would argue, "It's stupidity not manliness to hurt yourself. Use your brains, don't be a hero and cripple yourself; you're harming all of us and helping the company by breaking the safety rules we fought so hard to establish, rules that protect all of us."

From this I was familiar with how irrational, self-destructive, and anti-collective the male ego could be. I also felt I had learned a great deal from the women's movement, including a never-ending struggle with my own sexism. Off and on I would have debates with my male co-workers about women's liberation. But all this only went so far. Now with the approaching invasion and the Great Fear gripping the department, I had to deal with an angry male sexism in high gear. I got off the fence.

I told this guy, "No. These women from Switchgear are our sisters, and we have fought for them to come into our department. They are our fellow workers with seniority rights, and we want them to work here rather than get laid off. If we deny them their seniority rights, it hurts us, for once that goes down the drain, none of us has any protection. It is our enemies, the bosses, who are trying to do them out of jobs here. There's enough work for everyone; even if there weren't, seniority has to rule. For us as well as for them. The guys should train the women when they come and make them feel welcome."

And with that reply, the battle was on. For the next few weeks the debate raged hot and heavy, touching on many basic questions, drawing in workers from all over the plant. Many men made the accusation that the women would be the bosses' fifth column and break our unity. They would side with the foremen, squeal on us, outproduce us, and thereby force speed-ups. The women were our enemy, or at least agents of the enemy, and would be used by *them* against *us*. Many of them pointed to the experience of the next department over, where, since the influx of a few women, the situation had been steadily worsening.

The reply was that if we treated the women as sisters and friends they'd side with us not the boss. Some of us had worked in Switchgear and knew it was the *men* there who got favored treatment. What's more, our own shop-floor unity left a lot to be desired and many of our male co-workers engaged in squealing and kowtowing to the boss. Some of us argued sarcastically that women could never equal some of our men in this area.

We argued that we had common class interests with our sisters against the company, particularly in protecting the seniority principle.

It was easy to tease guys with the contradictions that male double standards led them to. Although they were afraid the women would overproduce, at the same time they insisted that women wouldn't be physically strong enough to do our "man's work." Either they could or they couldn't was the answer to that one, and if they could, they deserved the jobs. It would be up to us to initiate them into the department norms. Many of the guys said that the women would never be able to do certain of the heavy and rotten jobs. As steward and safety rep I always jumped on that one: we shouldn't do those jobs either. Hadn't we been fighting to make them safer and easier for ourselves? Well, they answered, the women would still not be able to do all the jobs. Right, I would say, but how many guys here have we protected from doing certain jobs because of back or heart problems, or age, or simply personal distaste? If the women can't do certain jobs, we treat them the same way as men who can't. We don't victimize people who can't do everything the company wants them to. We protect them: as our brothers, and as our sisters.

By pointing out the irrationalities of the sexist double standards, we were pushing the guys to apply their class principles—universal standards of equal treatment. Treat the women just as we treat men regarding work tasks, seniority, illness, and so on.

COUNTERING SEXISM

Male sexist culture strives to degrade women to nothing but pieces of flesh, physical bodies, mindless animals . . . something less than fully human, which the men can then be superior to. Name-calling becomes a means of putting women in a different category from *us*, to justify different and inferior treatment.

Part of the fight to identify the women as co-workers was therefore the battle against calling them "cunts" or "bitches." It was important to set the public standard whereby the women were labeled as part of us, not *them*. I wouldn't be silent with anyone using these sexist labels and pushed the point very aggressively. Eventually everyone referred to "the women."

After a while most of the men in the department came to agree that having the women in and giving them a chance was the right thing to do by any standard of fairness, unionism, or solidarity, and was required by the basic human decency that separates *us* from *them*. But then the focus shifted to other areas. Many men came back with traditional arguments against women in the work force. They belong at home with the kids, they're robbing male bread-winners of family income and so forth. But others disagreed: most of the guys' wives worked outside the home or had done so in the past; after all a family needed at least two wages these days. Some men answered that in bad times a family should have only one breadwinner so all would have an income. Fine, we told them, let's be really fair and square: you go home and clean the house and leave your wife at work. Alright, they countered, they could tolerate women working who supported a family, but not single women. And so I picked out four single men in our department and proposed they be immediately sacked.

Fairness and equality seemed to triumph here too. The guys understood that everyone who had a job at Westinghouse deserved equal protection. But then, some men found another objection. As one, Peter, put it, "I have no respect for any women who could come in to work here in these rotten conditions." The comeback was sharp: "What the hell are *you* putting up with this shit for? Why didn't *you* refuse to do that dirty job last month? Don't *you* deserve to be treated with respect?"[2]

As the Invasion Date approached I got worried. Reason and appeals to class solidarity had had a certain impact. Most of the guys were agreeing, grudgingly, to give the women a chance. But the campaign had been too short; fear and hostility were surfacing more and more. I was worried that there would be some ugly incident the first day or two that would set a pattern.

Much of the male hostility had been kept in check because I, as the union steward, had fought so aggressively on the issue. I decided to take this one step further and use some intimidation to enforce the basics of public behavior. In a tactic I later realized was a double-edged sword, I puffed myself up, assumed a cocky posture, and went for the jugular. I loudly challenged the masculinity of any worker who was opposed to the women. What kind of man is afraid of women? I asked. Only sissies and wimps are threatened by equality. A *real man* has nothing to be afraid of; he wants strong women. Any man worth his salt doesn't need the crutch of superiority over his sisters; he fears no female. A real man lives like an equal, doesn't step on women, doesn't degrade his sisters, doesn't have to rule the roost at home in order to affirm his manhood. Real men fight the boss, stand up with self-respect and dignity, rather than scapegoat our sisters.

I was sarcastic and cutting with my buddies: "This anti-woman crap of yours is a symbol of weakness. Stand up like a real man and behave and work as equals. The liberation of the women is the best thing that ever came along. . . . It's in *our* interests." To someone who boasted of how he made his wife cook his meals and clean his floors, I'd ask if she wiped his ass too? To the porno addicts I'd say, "You like that pervert shit? What's wrong with the real thing? Can you only get it up with those fantasies and cartoon women? Afraid of a real woman?" I'd outdo some of the worst guys in verbal intimidation and physical feats. Then I'd lecture them on women's equality and on welcoming our sisters the next week. I zeroed in on one or two of the sick types and physically threatened them if they pulled off anything with the women.

All of this worked, as I had hoped. It established an atmosphere of intimidation; no one was going to get smart with the women. Everyone would stand back for a while, some would cooperate, some would be neutral, and those I saw as "psycho-sexists" would keep out.

The tactic was effective because it spoke directly to a basic issue. But it was also effective because it took a leaf from the book of the psycho-sexists themselves.

At Westinghouse as elsewhere, some of the men were less chauvinistic and more sensible than others, but they often kept quiet in a group. They allowed the group pattern to be set by the most sexist bullies, whose style of woman baiting everyone at least gave in to. The psycho-sexists achieved this result because they challenged, directly or by implication, the masculinity of any male who didn't act the same way. All the men, whatever their real inclinations, are intimidated into acting or talking in a manner degrading to women. I had done the same thing, but in reverse. I had challenged the masculinity of any worker who would oppose the women. I had scared them off.

THE DAY THE WOMEN ARRIVED

The department crackled with tension the morning The Women arrived. There were only two of them to start with. The company was evidently scared by the volatile situation it had worked so hard to create. They backed off a direct confrontation by assigning my helper George and me to work with the women.

The two women were on their guard: Betty and Laura, in their late thirties, were expecting trouble. They were pleasantly shocked when I said matter-of-factly that we would train them on the job. They were overjoyed when I explained that the men had wanted them in our department and had fought the bosses to bring them here.

It was an unforgettable day. Men from all corners of the plant crept near the iron-stacking area to spy on us. I explained the work and we set about our tasks. We outproduced the standard rate by just a hair so that the company couldn't say the women weren't able to meet the normal requirements of the job.

My strategy was to get over the hump of the first few days. I knew that once the guys got used to the women being there, they'd begin to treat them as people, not as "women" and their hysteria would go away. It was essential to avoid incidents. Thus I forced the guys to interact with them. Calling over one of the male opponents, I introduced him as Bruce the Slinger who knew all the jobs and was an expert in lifts and would be happy to help them if asked and could always be called on to give a hand. This put him on the spot. Finally he flashed a big smile, and said, "Sure, just ask and I'd be pleased to show you anything, and to begin with, here's what to watch out for. . . ."

The morning went by. There were no incidents. From then on it was easy. More guys began to talk to the two women. They started to see them as Betty with four kids who lived on the mountain and knew wiring and was always cheerful; or Laura, who was a friend of John's uncle and was cranky early in the morning, who could easily operate the crane but had trouble with the impact gun, and who liked to heat up meat pies for lunch. After all, these men lived and worked with women all of their lives outside the plant—mothers, sisters, wives, in-laws, friends, daughters, and girlfriends. Having women at work was no big deal once they got over the trauma of the invasion of this male preserve. Just like helping your sister-in-law hang some wallpaper.

As the news spread, more and more women applied to transfer to our department. They were integrated with minimum fuss. The same thing happened in several adjoining departments. Quickly, men and women began to see each other as people and co-workers, not as enemies. Rather than man vs. woman it was John, Mary, Sue, Peter, Alice, George, and Laura. That Christmas we had a big party at someone's home—men and women of the department, drinking and dancing. The photos and various raucous tales of that night provided the basis for department storytelling for the next three months.

Was this, then, peace between the sexes? The integration of men and women as co-workers in the plant? Class solidarity triumphing over sex antagonism? Not quite. Although they were now together, it was not peace. The result was more complicated, for now the war between the sexes was being extended from the community into the workplace.

WORKPLACE CULTURE

As our struggle showed, sexism coexists and often is at war with class consciousness and with the trade union solidarity that develops among factory men. Our campaign was successful to the extent that it was able to sharply polarize and push the contradictions between these two tendencies in each individual. With most of the men, their sense of class solidarity triumphed over male chauvinism.

Many of the men had resisted the female invasion of the workplace because for them it was the last sanctum of male culture. It was somewhere they could get away from the world of women, away from responsibility and children and the civilized society's cultural restraints. In the plant they could revel in the rough and tumble of a masculine world of physical harshness, of constant swearing and rough behavior, of half-serious fighting and competition with each other and more serious fighting with the boss. It was eight hours full of filth and dirt and grease and grime and sweat—manual labor and a manly atmosphere. They could be vulgar and obscene, talk about football and car repairs, and let their hair down. Boys could be boys.

The male workplace culture functions as a form of rebellion against the discipline of their society. Outside the workplace, women are the guardians of the community. They raise the kids and enforce some degree of family and collective responsibility. They frequently have to force this upon men, who would rather go drinking or play baseball while the women mind the kids, wash the family's clothes, attend to problems with the neighbors and in-laws, and so on. Like rebellious teenage sons escaping mother's control, male wage earners enter the factory gates, where in their male culture they feel free of the restraints of these repressive standards.

Even if all factory men don't share these attitudes, a large proportion do, to a greater or lesser degree.

The manly factory culture becomes an outlet for accumulated anger and frustration. But this is a vicious circle because the tedious work and the subordination to the bosses is in large part the very cause of the male worker's dissatisfaction. He is bitter against a world that has kept him down, exploited his labor power, bent him to meet the needs of production and profit, cheated him of a better life, and made the daily grind so harsh. Working men are treated like dirt everywhere: at work they are at the bottom of the heap and under the thumb of the boss; outside they are scorned by polite society. But, the men can say, we are better than them all in certain ways; we're doing men's work; it's physically tough; women can't do it; neither can the bankers and politicians. Tough work gives a sense of masculine superiority that compensates for being stepped on and ridiculed. All that was threatened by the Women's Invasion.

However, this male workplace culture is not one-sided, for it contains a fundamentally positive sense of class value. The workingmen contrast themselves to other classes and take pride in having a concrete grasp of the physical world around them. The big shots can talk fancy and manipulate words, flout their elegance and manners. But we control the nuts and bolts of production, have our hands on the machines and gears and valves, the wires and lathes and pumps, the furnaces and spindles and batteries. We're the masters of the real and the concrete; we manipulate the steel and the lead, the wood, oil, and aluminum. What we know is genuine, the real and specific world of daily life.

Workers are the wheels that make a society go round, the creators of social value and wealth. There would be no fancy society, no civilized conditions if it were not for our labor.

The male workers are contemptuous of the mild-mannered parasites and soft-spoken vultures who live off our daily sweat: the managers and directors, the judges and entertainers, the lawyers, the coupon clippers, the administrators, the insurance brokers, the legislators . . . all those who profit from the shop floor, who build careers for themselves with the wealth we create. All that social overhead depends upon our mechanical skills, our concrete knowledge, our calloused hands, our technical ingenuity, our strained muscles and backs.

The Dignity of Labor, but society treats us like a pack of dumb animals, mere bodies with no minds or culture. We're physical labor power; the intelligence belongs to the management class. Workers are sneeringly regarded as society's bodies, the middle class as society's mind. One is inferior; the other is superior and fully human. The workers are less than human, close to animals, society's beasts of burden.

The male workplace culture tends to worship this self-identity of vulgar physicalness. It is as if the men enjoy wallowing in a masculine filth. They They brag of being the wild men of the factory. Say it loud: I'm a brute and I'm proud.

Sexism thus undermines and subverts the proud tradition of the dignity of labor. It turns a class consciousness upside down by accepting and then glorifying the middle-class view of manual labor and physical activity as inferior, animalistic, and crude. When workers identify with the savages that the bosses see them as, they develop contempt for themselves. It is self-contempt to accept the scornful labels, the negative definitions, the insulting dehumanized treatment, the cartoon stereotypes of class chauvinism: the super-masculine menials, the industrial sweathogs.

Remember Peter, who couldn't respect a woman who would come to work in this hellhole. It was obviously a place where he felt he had lost his own self-respect. My reply to him was that he shouldn't put up with that rotten treatment, *that the men also deserved better.* We should be treated with dignity. Respect yourself—fight back like a man, not a macho fool who glorifies that which degrades him.

Everything gets turned inside out. It is seen as manly to be treated as less than a man, as just a physical, instinctual creature. But this is precisely how sexist society treats women: as mindless bodies, pieces of flesh . . . "biology is destiny." You would think that male factory workers and the women's movement would be natural allies, that they'd speak the same language. They share a common experience of being used as objects, dehumanized by those on top.

Men in the factory are treated not as persons, but as bodies, replaceable numbers, commodities, faceless factors of production. The struggles of workingmen and of women revolve around similar things. The right to choice on abortion, for example, revolves around the right for women to control their own bodies. Is this not what the fight for health and safety on the shop floor is all about? To have some control over our bodies, not to let the bastards do what they want with our lives and limbs, to wreck us in their search for higher profits.

But male chauvinism turns many workingmen away from their natural allies, away from a rational and collective solution to their problems, diverting them from class unity with their sisters into oppressors and degraders of their sisters. Robbed of their real manhood—their humanity as men—they get a false sense of manhood by lording over women.

PLAYING THE FOREMAN AT HOME

Many men compensate for their wage-labor status in the workplace by becoming the boss at home. Treated terribly in the factory, he plays foreman after work and rules with authority over his wife and kids. He thus gains at home that independence he loses on the shop floor. He becomes a part-time boss himself with women as his servants. This becomes key to his identity and sense of self-esteem. Working-class patriarchs, rulers of the roost.

This sense of authority has an economic underpinning. The male worker's role as primary breadwinner gives him power over the family and status in society. It also makes him the beneficiary of the woman's unpaid labor in the household.

A wage laborer not only lacks independence, he also lacks property, having nothing but his labor power to sell. Sexism gives him the sense of property, as owner of the family. His wife or girlfriend is his sexual property. As Elvis sang, "You are my only possession, you are my everything." This domination and ownership of a woman are basic to how he sees himself.

These things are powerful pressures toward individualism, a trait of the business class: foreman of the family, man of property, possessiveness. They elevate the wage earner above the category of the downtrodden common laborer, and in doing so divert him from the collective struggle with his brothers and sisters to change their conditions. Capitalism is based on competitiveness and encourages everyone to be better than the next guy, to rise up on the backs of your neighbors. Similarly the male chauvinist seeks superiority over others, of both sexes. Men tend to be competitive, always putting one another down, constantly playing one-upmanship. Men even express appreciation and affection for each other through good-natured mutual insults.

Sexist culture thus undermines the working-class traditions of equality and solidarity and provides a recruiting ground for labor's adversaries. Over the years at Westinghouse I had noticed that a high proportion of workers who became foremen were extreme chauvinists—sexual braggarts, degraders of women, aggressive, individualistic, ambitious, ever willing to push other workers around. Male competition is counterproductive in the shop or union, where we ought to cooperate as equals and seek common solutions. The masculine ego makes for bad comradeship, bad brotherhood. It also makes it difficult for chauvinistic men to look at and deal objectively with many situations because their fragile egos are always on the line. They have to keep up a facade of superiority and are unable to handle criticism, no matter how constructive. Their chauvinistic crutches make them subjective, irrational, unreliable, and often self-destructive, as with men who want to work or drive dangerously.

Workingmen pay a high price for the limited material benefits they get from sexist structures. It is the bosses who make the big bucks and enjoy the real power from the inferior treatment of women.

THE NEXT ROUND AND A PEEK
INTO THE WOMEN'S WORLD

Battles continued about the women getting a crack at the more skilled and high-paying assembly jobs up the floor. Next we won the fight against the company, which was trying to promote junior men. This time women were there to fight for themselves, and there were male stewards from other departments who backed them up. The shop floor was less hostile, many of the men being sympathetic or neutral.

But despite the general cooperation, most men still maintained that the women were inferior workers. The foremen did their best to foster sex divisions by spreading stories of all the mistakes the women supposedly made. They would reserve the worst jobs for the men, telling them the women couldn't do them. The men would thus feel superior while resenting the women's so-called privileges and the women would feel grateful for not having to do these jobs. The supervisors forged a common cause with some of the guys against the women. They fed their male egos and persuaded them to break safety rules, outproduce, and rat on other workers. The male bond often proved stronger than the union bond, and our collective strength suffered as a result.

As for myself, I was learning and changing a lot as a result of my experiences. I would often meet with the women at the lunch table to plan strategy. These sessions affected me in many ways. They were good talks, peaceful and constructive, with no fighting and argument, no competition, all of us talking sensibly about a common problem and figuring out how to handle it as a group. It was a relaxed and peaceful half hour, even when we had serious differences.

This was in marked contrast to the men's lunch tables, which were usually boisterous and raucous during those months. There was a lot of yelling and shouting, mutual insults, fists pounding, and throwing things at one another. When you ate at the women's table, you sat down to rest and relax. When you ate at the men's table, you sat down to fight.

I had read and heard a lot from my feminist friends about this so-called woman's world of warmth, cooperation, and friendship, as contrasted to men's norm of aggression, violence, and competition. Although I had always advocated women's liberation and respected the women's movement, I paid only lip service, if that, to this distinction, and was in fact more often scornful of this "women's world." Over the years I had become a more aggressive male, which I saw as distinct from being a chauvinist or sexist male. In the world of constant struggle, I thought, you had to be aggressive or go under. We'd have peace and love in the socialist future, some distant day.

As a unionist it became very clear to me that the women almost automatically acted like a collective. And in those months of going back and forth between the men's and women's tables, I took a long and serious look at this women's world. It was an unnerving but pleasant experience to sit down among friends, without competition and put-downs, not to have to watch out for flying objects, not to be on the alert for nerve-shattering noises, to be in a non-threatening atmosphere. There was obviously something genuine there and it seemed to offer a better way. It also became obvious to me that the gap between the sexes was enormous and that men and women were far from speaking a common language.

NEW STRUGGLES AND THE RECESSION

In the months ahead there were new struggles. There was the fight to form a women's committee in the union in order to bring women's demands to the fore, to combat sexism among the male workers, and to give women a forum for developing their own outlook, strategy, and leadership. We launched that fight in the fall of 1981, with Mary, a militant woman in our rank-and-file group, in the lead. The old guard, led by the union's national president, fought us tooth and nail. The battle extended over a number of months and tumultuous membership meetings, and we eventually lost as the leadership railroaded through its chauvinistic policy. No women's committee was formed. In time, however, the leadership came to support women's rights formally, even though they did little to advance the cause in practice.

In the spring of 1982 the recession finally caught up with us at Westinghouse and there were continuous layoffs in every division. Our bargaining power shrank, everyone was afraid for his or her own job, and the contract became little more than a piece of paper as the company moved aggressively to roll back the clock on our hard-won traditions on seniority rules, health and safety regulations, and so on. Bitterness and frustration were everywhere.

The company went after the women. Their seniority rights were blatantly ignored as they were transferred to "chip and grind" duties—the least skilled, the heaviest, dirtiest, and most unpleasant jobs. The progress the men had made also seemed to vanish. From the first day of the layoff announcements, many rallied to the call of "Get the women out first." Those most hostile to women came back out in the open and campaigned full blast. They found many sympathetic responses on the shop floor: protect the breadwinners and, what's more, no women should be allowed to bump a male since they're not physically capable of doing the jobs anyway. It was the war of the sexes all over again, but far worse now because the situation allowed little leeway. There was some baiting of the women, and the plant became a tension-ridden, hateful place for all workers.

The bosses managed to seize back many of the powers the shop floor had wrenched away from them over the years, and even to create newer and deeper divisions within the workforce. But the recession was not all-powerful. We still managed to win all our battles on health and safety, and the shop floor continued to elect our militant shop stewards.

Some of the women gave in to the inevitable and were laid off despite their seniority. But others fought back and fought well. Some of them were even able to gain the sympathy of the male workers who had at first stood aside or resisted them. In some cases, the men joined in and helped the women retain their jobs.

Obviously, things had changed a great deal amongst the men since the first women began to come into the division. *When the chips were down, many men took their stand with their sisters against the company—despite the recession. . . .*

Workingmen share basic common interests with our sisters. When more of us recognize this, define and speak about these interests in our own way, and act in common with women, then we will be able to start moving the mountains that stand in our way.

NOTES

1. United Electrical Workers (UEW) is a union whose militant rhetoric is rarely matched by its actual behavior. For example, it has passed resolutions at its national conventions favoring the formation of women's committees at the national and local levels, but what is on paper often does not match daily reality. Some leaders have a habit of advocating a position that suits the political needs of the moment rather than consistent principles. These limitations are not peculiar to UEW, which is much like the rest of the labor movement, despite its sometimes radical rhetoric. Like most of the labor movement, it has its good and its bad locals, its good and its bad leaders. Like a lot of other unions it has moved toward a better position on "women's" issues, although with a lot of sharp contradictions and see-saws in behavior along the way, given its authoritarian style.

2. The names of the plant workers in this article are not their real ones.

FROM HOMEMAKER TO HOUSING ADVOCATE: *An Interview with* *Mrs. Chang Jok Lee*

50

Nancy Diao

I first met Mrs. Lee in 1976 at a rally in front of the International Hotel and then again in 1985 in the midst of a financial crisis in the San Francisco Housing Authority. The agency was more than $9 million in debt, and its executive director Carl Williams had been asked to resign by Mayor Diane Feinstein. During this time, the Ping Yuen Residents Improvement Association (PYRIA) remained the best organized and most effective tenant association in the city.[1] Much of its strength was due to the consistent participation of Mrs. Lee. She had been the backbone of a monumental effort to protect the rights of low-income tenants in San Francisco's Chinatown. This is an unusual role for an immigrant woman whose Chinese tradition frowns upon women activists.

What struck me was Mrs. Lee's dedication to working for social change, an unusual choice for a woman her age. Instead of playing mah-jongg with her contemporaries, she prefers to attend community meetings, testify at city hearings, and help fellow tenants settle disputes. Mrs. Lee is in her late fifties, but looks much younger. With glasses and short black hair, permed and fashionably kept, she is always well groomed and impeccably dressed. For a Chinese woman, she is rather big-framed, but looks sturdy and confident. She speaks her mind freely, from telling stories about her favorite granddaughter to tales about growth pains with the tenant association or gossip in the Chinese community. Though she speaks a combination of Chinese dialects, with a mixture of some English words, she looks you straight in the eye when she talks. You can't help but notice her sincerity and passion.

GROWING UP IN JAPAN

In a 1985 interview, Mrs. Lee told of how poverty and discrimination have plagued her since her childhood in Japan. Born in 1927, in Kobe, she was the third of eight children, and the second girl. Her family suffered the hard life of Chinese immigrants in Japan, and she remembers growing up poor, segregated from the Japanese.

> My family was very poor when I was born. We didn't even have money to buy soy sauce. When I was two years old, my father got a job as a chef in the Egyptian Embassy, so our entire family lived in the servants' quarters of the embassy. My mother helped out with the housecleaning and ironing.
> We didn't have much contact with the Japanese except when we went shopping. In Kobe, the Chinese operated pastry, coffee, tailoring, and other shops and had two Chinese schools. I went to the Mandarin school until the sixth grade, but we didn't have enough money for me to continue; my sister went only to night school.

The heavy responsibilities she assumed as a girl helped to groom her for her later leadership role in the Chinatown tenants' group. When her family returned to the Zhongshan district in southeastern China during the Sino-Japanese War, and while her father and older brother remained in Japan, Mrs. Lee had to bear the bulk of caring for the family though she was only eleven years old. This responsibility continued even after the family reunited in Japan one year later. More aggressive and verbal than her older, frail sister, Mrs. Lee represented the family at air raid exercises and in food ration lines. After the sixth grade, she worked in a Taiwanese-owned shoe factory and then in a candy factory to help with the family income.

Along with other Chinese in Japan, she and her family were subjected to many forms of discrimination because Japan and China were on opposite sides of a war.

> Some pharmacies would use slogans like "Can even kill the Nanking Bloodsuckers" as advertisements for the effectiveness of pesticides.[2] In many Japanese shops we would have to wait until the Japanese customers were served first. We were also discriminated against in employment and were only able to get lower class jobs regardless of our education, skills, and abilities. This situation forced many of us to start our own small businesses such as cafe/restaurants, tailor shops, and painting stores.

When the United States began bombing Kobe in 1944, life became even harsher for Mrs. Lee's family.

> Whole families died in air raid shelters, smothered by smoke. When the planes came, everyone in my family went into caves or shelters; only my older brother and I stayed behind to watch our house. One time our house was fire-bombed, and I tried to put out the fire by stomping, but in vain. My brother went looking for me all over the place, but the fire and smoke had spread so fast that he couldn't see anything. Fortunately I had escaped, and he did thereafter. We lost our house, and our family split up. I was sent to live with a family friend who came from the Fukien province.

ROMANCE LEADS TO AMERICA

While living with the Fukienese family and working for them to earn her keep, Mrs. Lee met her future husband, George, through her first boyfriend. George was a Chinese American GI who was stationed in Yokohama after the surrender of the Japanese government at the end of World War II. When asked how she met George, Mrs. Lee giggled. Her face lit up and she blushed. Then her eyes softened with a watery glow. Compared to her first boyfriend, who treated her like a "good little workhorse," George was considerate and romantic, though they didn't talk much in those days.

> George always treated me with kindness and respect, very different from my first boyfriend. He always saved me a seat on the bus and gave me little gifts, whereas my boyfriend never showed any appreciation. [For instance], when my boyfriend's family's house was bombed, and he lost all of his belongings, I stayed up all night to knit him a sweater. He never even said "thank you."

Mrs. Lee and George married in 1946, and their first son was born one year later. When the son was just six months old, George returned to the United States while Mrs. Lee remained in Japan with her parents till her husband came back to get her. They arrived in San Francisco in 1950, and in two years moved into one of the Ping Yuen public housing apartments in Chinatown. She remembers her life being full, but also one of poverty.

> We were so poor that most of the time we didn't even have a penny in the house, but I wasn't scared or worried. We raised eight children, four boys and four girls, and from them I learned some English.

When the children were small, Mrs. Lee spent all of her time raising them; but as they grew older, she found more time to think about her own needs and interests. She began to become more active in the community, beginning first with just singing and socializing, and then onto more serious work.

> When the children were all grown up, I started learning Mandarin and singing songs at the Asian Community Center.[3] Since I went to a Mandarin school in Japan, I wanted to keep it up. While I was learning Mandarin, I had the opportunity to read a lot of newspapers and books, and went to May Day celebrations with George. Ever since George got disabled from a car accident in 1972, he has had a lot of free time to get involved in community issues.

CONFRONTATION WITH HOUSING ISSUES

The Asian Community Center was a commercial tenant of the International Hotel block, which soon became the focal point of the early conflict of interests between low-income tenants and land developers.[4] Mrs. Lee's association with the center eventually led to her involvement with community housing issues.

> In 1977, when my youngest daughters, Sylvia, Patricia, and Teresa, were twenty-one, nineteen, and ten, I became involved in the International Hotel struggle. I would take my youngest daughter, Teresa, to meetings and classes with me. Because I knew some of the tenants who lived in the International Hotel, I got upset when I saw leaflets about the possibility of them being evicted; I did not want to see them homeless. The young people at the Asian Community Center encouraged me to go to meetings on the third floor of the I-Hotel. It took me a while to get used to meetings and rallies, but eventually I even spoke with bullhorns at demonstrations.

> On August 3, 1977, the night of the eviction, George, Teresa, Patricia, and I were there. It was a warm night; there were four hundred policemen on horses, in addition to the tactical squad. The I-Hotel was surrounded by thousands of people—Asian, white, black, young and old, including many from Reverend Jim Jones's church who came in busloads. It seemed that we all stood on the sidewalk for hours. Suddenly the horses charged. I screamed, and everywhere there was yelling, screaming, and crying. We wanted the horses to stop charging, but the tactical squad used their billy clubs to hold us back on the sidewalk. As the horses rushed and trampled, the human chain around the hotel broke. People fell down. Tears poured out of my eyes as I heard Hongisto (then chief of police) breaking down the door to the I-Hotel. We stayed in front of the I-Hotel until three in the morning—watching every tenant being either dragged out or carried out of the hotel; then we went to Portsmouth Square.

Even as Mrs. Lee's support of the I-Hotel continued, she transferred more energy toward improving living conditions in Ping Yuen. In 1977 all the pipes in Ping Yuen were rotting, but in spite of repeated calls to the San Francisco Housing Authority, nothing was being done to fix the problem. Eventually George and some members of the tenant association initiated a massive petition drive to get the plumbing repaired. At the end of 1977, the housing authority finally repaired all of the pipes and painted the exterior walls of half of the buildings. And George was elected president of the association.

A year later, when the housing authority proved unresponsive to meeting the tenants' demands for better security, Mrs. Lee participated in the Ping Yuen tenants' first rent strike. The action was instigated by the brutal rape and murder of tenant Judy Wong.[5] It was an intense period for Mrs. Lee.

> I remember passing out leaflets door to door, talking to the tenants, attending lots of meetings, and collecting rent for fifteen days of each month at the association office on Pacific Avenue. The strike lasted for four months, with numerous press conferences and tedious negotiations with the housing authority, at the end of which we got our security guards.

The second strike followed at the end of 1979, when housing authority groundskeepers and office workers struck for higher pay. The city-wide Public Housing Tenants Association (PHTA) wanted to strike in support, but only the Ping Yuen tenants actually did. When the city employees went back to work, the Public Housing Tenants Association withdrew their support. But the Ping Yuen group continued to strike for maintenance issues, such as fixing apartment interiors and elevators, repairing floors, and painting. It was a long and drawn-out fight, but the tenants' persistence brought them victory.

> We started with eighty households, but some tenants discontinued their
> strike support for fear of eviction. We held many meetings and visited people
> door to door. We also had membership drives and sponsored activities to
> keep the striking tenants together. Since I was the treasurer, I collected the
> rent, put it in escrow, and kept the books. After two years, we finally got our
> demands met.

At the end of the strike, most of the tenants chose to donate 50 percent
of the escrow interest, about ten thousand dollars, to PYRIA for a color
television in the community room and a banquet at Asia Garden. At the
banquet the tenants surprised Mrs. Lee and George with two round-trip
tickets to Japan to show their appreciation for the couple's efforts in the
strike.

During her husband's term as president of the improvement association,
from 1979 to 1981, Mrs. Lee worked on two major projects that brought
additional benefits to the Ping Yuen tenants. In 1979, at the request of the
tenant population, Mrs. Lee went door to door at least two hours a day to sign
up enough tenants to pressure Cablevision to install cable television services.
Second, Mrs. Lee took over the coordination of the vegetable garden and
established new rules: each member had an opportunity to have a garden and
the size of all the lots was made equal. She thereby abolished all favoritism in
the distribution of garden plots.

REACTIONS TO ACTIVISM

Though Mrs. Lee can now act fearlessly, this was not so when she first became
active in the community.

> At first I was scared, or rather, kind of embarrassed. I didn't speak Eng-
> lish and was not used to speaking in front of people. But after a while, I got
> used to it. As long as I am fighting for a just cause, then I am not scared.

Since Mrs. Lee's own family has remained in Japan, and George is also
alone in the United States, neither has had to face pressure and criticism from
relatives, who traditionally might have frowned on women's activism. She and
her husband have, however, had some run-ins with the more conservative
element of the community.

> I didn't really get much reaction from getting involved in I-Hotel, but when
> I became active in the business of the association, I started getting a lot of
> harassment. The wall near our apartment was often spray painted with the

word "commies!" with a black arrow pointing to our apartment. Everytime we challenged the previous PYRIA administration's way of doing things, we were called "commies." There were also flyers and posters attacking us.

Neither have her relationships with other tenants always been smooth. Some have criticized her for "doing too much." Take, for example, the laundromat project.[6]

One of the officers of the association says that I am stupid to sweep the floors of the laundryroom. But when the laundryroom is dirty, I just can't stand it. It took so much out of us to get this project done; I feel like it's my own. So, when people don't clean up after themselves and youths abuse the furniture and write on walls, it really hurts me. But what hurts me more is when other officers nag at me for "doing too much." If they do some and if everybody does something, then I wouldn't have to do so much. Sometimes I squeeze in the sweeping when the baby is taking a nap.

After a recent officers' meeting, Mrs. Lee went home crying. The stress brought her a few sleepless nights and some additional white hair. At times like these, she wonders about whether her efforts are worth all the headaches and talks about quitting, but she stays. She remains undaunted about making Ping Yuen a better place to live and confident about the tenants' overall good feelings towards her.

Deep down, I know a lot of tenants really like me. They respect me and support George. The maintenance worker, Mr. Wong, complains about the youths not listening to him, but I don't have any problems with them. I just tell them to get out [of the laundryrooms] and they do. Most of the tenants listen to me, and whenever there is something bothering them, they always either ask me questions or ask me to help them.

Sometimes even her children scold her for "wasting her time." Yet other times they have helped out by protecting her at demonstrations or doing errands.

Some of my children get down on me for doing so much volunteer work. They say that I am crazy for spending so much time on the association when I don't get paid. They don't really understand me. I am happier when I am active, though there is nothing material to gain. It keeps me young. I don't have much white hair or wrinkles [*she points to her head*], do I?

Sylvia doesn't get down on me for doing so much. She just doesn't want me and George to be taken advantage of; she helps me out a lot. She is the one who taught me how to do books, how to do a membership drive, and keep a membership list. Her husband took off work a couple of times to take care of their daughter whom I watch [five days a week], so that I could be freed up to go to the public hearings on the Orangeland Project at the City Planning Commission.[7]

Teresa . . . knows that I am happier when I am active. She doesn't complain when I am not home to cook dinner, and sometimes she even translates for me.

CONCLUSION: BALANCING LIFE'S DEMANDS

When asked if it has been hard to balance all the demands in her life—being a wife, mother of eight, grandmother of eleven now (eight when she was interviewed), and a housing activist—she laughed:

From these activities, I learned that there is nothing to fear. I feel alive when I come out to do things. But I do take a lot of abuse from people— gripes, complaints, blames, and a lot of headaches. Even George and I have differences sometimes, and he is very stubborn. But basically we are alike, so things don't get too bad at home. At least he doesn't bug me about housework or cooking; sometimes we just go out to eat. . . .

In the past a lot of the community leaders courted George and me. They always invited us to events and asked us to help. Now no one comes. I guess they realize that they can't just use us anymore. I try to keep up with the issues. Sometimes I get upset about association business, and I can't sleep at night. But most of the time, being active keeps me alive. I don't play mah-jongg or go to Reno, so I take care of my granddaughter, and I go to meetings.

On 10 July 1985, Mrs. Chang Jok Lee was honored for her dedication and hard work with the Ping Yuen Residents Improvement Association at the eighth anniversary celebration of the Chinatown Neighborhood Improvement Resources Center, which has spearheaded much of the effort to retain housing in San Francisco's Chinatown. In front of 550 people, she said in Chinese, "I don't really deserve this, but I know that if we all work together, anything can be done." Then, the fifty-eight-year-old grandmother smiled and curtsied.

NOTES

1. The Ping Yuen Residents Improvement Association (PYRIA), formed in 1966, serves as the official representative of 430 households of mostly monolingual Chinese public housing tenants in San Francisco's Chinatown. The Pings, as the four buildings are commonly called, constitute 15 percent of the low-income housing in Chinatown, have

a waiting list with more than two thousand names, and a waiting period of five to ten years.

2. Nanking (Namking) is a city in the southern part of China. Nanking bloodsuckers are particularly poisonous and vicious worms from the area.

3. The Asian Community Center was a volunteer community service and advocacy organization which provided English, Mandarin, and singing lessons for community people. The center is now closed.

4. The International Hotel, or I-Hotel, was a San Francisco residential hotel in the last foothold of Manilatown and on the edge of Chinatown. In 1965 Four Seas Corporation, owned by real estate investors from Thailand, bought the hotel with plans to demolish the building and convert the space into mixed-use development, including offices. It became the rallying point for a concerted community-wide effort to stem the loss of low-income housing in the area.

5. Judy Wong was raped and murdered in North Ping Yuen in 1978. The elevators had not been functioning for six months, forcing Wong to use the stairs, where she was attacked.

6. In 1983 PYRIA received city funds to renovate the Ping Yuen laundromats.

7. The Orangeland Project was designed to include both low income housing and mixed-use commercial development. But its construction would have involved the dislocation of 195 elderly and family tenants residing on the site and fourteen commercial and neighborhood shops. The Ping Yuen tenants supported the Orangeland tenants' efforts to keep their homes. With communitywide support, the Orangeland tenants were able to stay in their homes, and the original development project was relocated to another site.

A WORLD WORTH LIVING IN

51

Roberta Praeger

As an impoverished woman I live with the exhaustion, the frustration, the deprivation of poverty. As a survivor of incest I struggle to overcome the emotional burden. One thing has led to another in my life as the causes of poverty, of incest, of so many issues have become increasingly clear. My need to personalize has given way to a realization of social injustice and a commitment to struggle for social change.

LIVING ON WELFARE

I live alone with my four-year-old child, Jamie. This state (Massachusetts) allocates $328 a month to a family of two living on Aid to Families with Dependent Children (AFDC). This sum places us, along with other social service recipients, at an income 40 percent below the federal poverty line. In today's economy, out of this sum of money, we are expected to pay for rent, utilities, clothing for two, child-care expenses, food not covered by food stamps, and any other expenses we may incur.

My food stamps have been cut to the point where they barely buy food for half the month. I have difficulty keeping up with the utility bills, and my furniture is falling apart. Furniture breaks, and there is no money to replace it. Things that others take for granted, such as sheets and towels, become irreplaceable luxuries.

Chaos exists around everything, even the most important issues, like keeping a roof over one's head. How are people expected to pay rent for their families on the shameful amount of income provided by the Welfare Department? The answer, in many cases, is reflected in the living conditions of welfare recipients. Some of us live in apartments that should be considered uninhabitable. We live with roaches, mice, sometimes rats, and floors about to cave in. I live in subsidized housing. It's that or the street. My rent without the subsidy is $400 a month, $72 more than my entire monthly income. It took

From: Rochelle Lefkowitz and Ann Withorn (eds.), *For Crying Out Loud: Women and Poverty in the U.S.* (New York: Pilgrim Press, 1986). Reprinted by permission.

over a year of red tape between the time of my first application to the time of final acceptance into the program, all the while watching the amount of my rent climb higher and higher. What becomes of the more than 80 percent of AFDC recipients who are not subsidized because there isn't enough of this housing available?

Emergencies are dealt with in the best way possible. One cold winter day, Jamie broke his ankle in the day-care center. It was the day my food stamps were due to arrive. With no food in the house, I had to take him, on public transportation, to the hospital emergency room and then walk to the super-market with my shopping cart in a foot of snow. This was not an unusual event in my life. All AFDC mothers get caught up in situations like this, because we are alone, because we have few resources and little money.

Ronald Reagan's war on the poor has exacerbated an already intolerable situation. Human service programs have been slashed to the bone. Regulations governing the fuel assistance program have been changed in ways that now make many of the impoverished ineligible. Energy assistance no longer pays my utility bills. For some these changes have meant going without needed fuel, thereby forcing people to endure freezing temperatures.

The food stamp situation has gone from bad to worse. The amount of money allocated for the program has been drastically reduced. My situation reflects that of most welfare recipients. Last year, my food stamps were cut back from $108 to $76 a month, barely enough to buy food for two weeks. Reagan doesn't even allow us to work to supplement our meager income. His reforms resulted in a law, the Omnibus Budget Reconciliation Act, that, in one fell swoop, instituted a number of repressive work-related changes. Its main impact came when it considerably lowered the amount of money a recipient can earn before the termination of benefits. Under this new law even a low-paying, part-time job can make a person no longer eligible for assistance.

The complexity of our lives reaches beyond economic issues. Monday through Friday, I work as an undergraduate student at the University of Massachusetts. On weekends, when in two-parent families, one parent can sometimes shift the responsibility to the other, I provide the entertainment for my child. All the household chores are my responsibility, for I have no one to share them with. When Jamie is sick I spend nights awake with him. When I am sick, I have no one to help me. I can't do things others take for granted, such as spend an evening out at the movies, because I don't have enough money to pay both the admission fee and for child care. Even if I did, I would be too exhausted to get out the front door. Often I wind up caught in a circle of isolation.

What kind of recognition do I and other welfare mothers get for all this hard work? One popular image of welfare recipients pictures us as lazy, irresponsible women, sitting at home, having babies, and living off the government. Much of society treats us like lepers, degrading and humiliating us at every turn, treating us as if we were getting something for nothing. One day I walked into a small grocery store wearing a button that read "Stop Reagan's War on the Poor." The proprietor of the store looked at my button and said to me, "You know, all those people on welfare are rich." Most welfare recipients would say anything rather than admit to being on welfare because of the image it creates. My brother-in-law had the audacity to say to me in conversation one day, "People are poor because they're lazy. They don't want to work."

And the Welfare Department shares this image of the recipient with the general public. From the first moment of contact with the department, the client is treated with rudeness, impatience, mistrust, and scorn. She is intimidated by constant redeterminations, reviews, and threats of being cut off. Her life is controlled by a system wracked with ineptness and callous indifference. Two years ago, unable to pay my electric bill, I applied for emergency assistance. It took the Welfare Department so long to pay the bill that the electric company turned the power off. We lived for two days without electricity before my constant badgering of the Welfare Department and the utility company produced results.

The department gives out information that is misleading and/or incomplete. The recipient is made to feel stupid, guilty, and worthless, a "problem" rather than a person. When I first applied I had to answer all sorts of questions about my personal life time and again. Many of my replies were met with disbelief. I sat there for hours at a time, nine months pregnant, waiting to be interviewed. And that was just the beginning of hours and hours of waiting, of filling in forms for the programs that keep us and our children alive.

THE PERSONAL IS POLITICAL

For most women in this situation, suffering is nothing new. Poverty is seldom an isolated issue. It's part of a whole picture. Other issues complicate our lives. For myself, as for many of us, suffering is complicated by memories, the results of trauma brought forward from childhood. Under frilly pink dresses and little blue sailor suits lay horror stories shared by many. The memories I bring with me from my childhood are not very pretty.

I was born in a Boston neighborhood in 1945. My father was a linoleum installer, my mother a homemaker. I want to say that my childhood was colored by the fact that I was an abused child. It's still difficult for me to talk about some things to this day.

My mother didn't give me a life of my own. When I was an infant she force-fed me. At age nine, she was still spoon-feeding me. Much of the time she didn't let me out of her sight. She must have seen school as a threat to her control, for she kept me home half the time. In me she saw not a separate person but an extension of herself. She felt free to do as she wished with my body. Her attempts to control my elimination process have had a lasting impact on my sexuality. The methods she used have been documented for their use in cases of mother-daughter incest. She had an obsessive-compulsive desire to control what went into me, to control elimination, to control everything about me. I had no control over anything. I couldn't get out from under what was happening to me psychologically. Powerlessness, frustration, and emotional insecurity breed a chain of abuse as men abuse women and children and women abuse children.

In the face of all the adverse, perverted attention received from my mother, I turned to my father for love and affection. We became close. In time, though, it became clear he knew as little about child rearing as my mother. His own deprived childhood had taught him only bitterness.

Throughout the years I knew him, he had gambled literally thousands of dollars away at the horse track. He left me alone outside the track gate at age five or six when the sign read "No children allowed." When I was twelve, he set fire to our house. He had run out of money for gambling purposes, and the house was insured against fire. When the insurance money arrived, my mother somehow managed to intercept it and bought new furniture. When my father found out what she had done, he went on a rampage. I had a knickknack shelf, charred from the fire. He threw it across the room, splinters of glass flying everywhere, and then he hit my mother. This was not an uncommon scene in my childhood.

By the time I reached eleven, my father was beginning to see me in a different light. At this point, the closeness that had developed between him and me still existed. And he proceeded to take advantage of it.

My mother belonged to a poker club, and once a week she would leave the house to go to these sessions. On these occasions my father would come over to me and remove both my clothes and his. He would then use my body to masturbate until he reached orgasm. He attempted to justify these actions by saying, "A man has to have sex and your mother won't." This occurred a number of times when I was between the ages of eleven and thirteen. I cried the last time he did this and he stopped molesting me sexually. In incestuous situations there doesn't have to be any threat; very often there isn't, because parents are in a position of trust, because parents are in a position of power, and because the child needs love. Children are in a developmental stage where they have no choice.

I went to public school and did very well. When I was sixteen, the school authorities told me that no matter how well I did, no matter how high my grades were, they could not keep me in school if I appeared only half the time. So I dropped out. I just spent the whole time sitting in front of the television until my mother died.

I didn't understand the extent of my mother's sickness in her treatment of me. Fear that if my mother knew what my father was doing she would kill him seemed realistic to me at the time. And so, I kept silent. I looked at my parents, as all children do, as authority figures. Longing for a way out of the situation, I felt trapped. In the face of all this I felt overwhelmed, afraid, and isolated. I retreated from reality into a world of fantasy. For only through my imagination could I find any peace of mind or semblance of happiness. The abuse I had taken all these years began to manifest itself in psychosomatic symptoms. Periodically, I started suffering intense abdominal pain. Once I fainted and fell on the bathroom floor. There were three visits to the hospital emergency room. My doctor had misdiagnosed the symptoms as appendicitis.

When I was seventeen, my father, after a major argument with my mother, moved out. Without money to pay the rent, with no job training or other resources, we rented out a room. Ann, the young woman renting the room, was appalled at the situation she discovered. She began to teach me some basic skills such as how to wash my own clothes. For the first time in my life I related positively to someone. My father moved back two months later. For two years this is how the situation remained, my mother, father, Ann, and I all living together.

In 1965 my mother was diagnosed as having lung cancer. Three months later she was dead. I felt nothing, no sorrow, no anger, no emotion. I had long ago learned how to bury my emotions deep down inside of me. I packed my belongings and moved out with Ann, in the midst of my father's ranting and raving.

Living in an apartment with Ann made things seem to improve on the surface. My life was quieter. I held a steady job for the first time. There was a little money to spend. I could come and go as I pleased. It felt good, and I guess, at that point I thought my life had really changed. It took me a long time to realize what an adult who has had this kind of childhood must still go through. I had nightmares constantly. There were times when I went into deep depressions. I didn't know what was going on, what was happening to me, or why.

After holding my first job for three years, I went through a series of jobs in different fields: sales, hairdressing, and, after a period of training, nursing. It seemed I was not functioning well in any area. I fell apart in any situation where demands were made of me. I had no tolerance for hierarchy. I discovered that I performed best when I was acting as charge nurse. Unfortunately, in my role as a Licensed Practical Nurse, I usually wound up low person on the totem pole, generally having to answer to someone else. In time, it became clear to me, that control was a major factor in a variety of situations that I encountered.

My self-confidence and self-esteem were abysmally low. Every time something went wrong my first thought was, "There must be something wrong with me." I didn't know then, what I know now. Children never blame their parents for the wrong that is done. They blame themselves. This feeling carries on into adulthood until it is difficult not to blame oneself for everything that does not go right.

I was depressed, suicidal, frightened out of my wits, and completely overwhelmed by life. After a series of failed relationships and a broken marriage, I wound up alone, with a small child, living on welfare. The emotional burden I carried became complicated by the misery and exhaustion of poverty.

Why have I survived? Why am I not dead? Because I'm a survivor. Because I have Jamie and I love him more than words can say. In him I see the future, not the past.

A MAJOR CHANGE

I survived because in the midst of all this something happened, something that was to turn out to be the major guiding force in my life. In 1972 the owner of my building sent out notices threatening eviction if the tenants did not pay a huge rent increase. Everyone in the building was aghast at the prospect and so formed a tenant union to discuss alternatives. Through my activities with the union, I learned of an organization that did community work throughout the city. Cambridge Tenants Organizing Committee (CTOC) was a multi-faceted organization involved in work around issues such as tenants' rights, welfare advocacy, antiracist work, and education concerning sexism in society. I began working with a group of people unlike any that I had been exposed to in the past. They treated me as a person capable of assuming responsibility and doing any job well. My work with CTOC included organizing tenant unions throughout the city, counseling unemployed workers, and attending countless demonstrations, marches, picketings, and hearings. As a group we organized and/or supported eviction blocking, we helped defend people against physical racist attacks, and we demonstrated at the state house for continuation of rent control. I wasn't paid for my work. What I earned was far more important than money. I learned respect for myself as a woman. I learned the joys and pitfalls of working collectively and began assimilating more information than I had at any other time of my life.

And I flourished. I went to meeting after meeting until they consumed almost all of my nonwork time. Over the years I joined other groups. One of my major commitments was to a group that presented political films. My politics became the center of my life.

Through counseling and therapy groups with therapists who shared my political perspective, the guilt I had shouldered all these years began to lessen. Within a period of three years, through groups and conventions, I listened to and/or spoke with more than three hundred other survivors of incest. I heard stories that would make your hair stand on end. New learning led to making connections. Although the true extent of incest is not known, owing to the fact that sexual abuse within families usually goes unreported, various statistics estimate that 100,000 to 250,000 children are sexually molested each year in the United States. Other studies show that one out of every three to four women in this country is a victim of sexual abuse as a child. Incest Resources, my primary resource for group counseling, believes these statistics heavily underestimate the extent of actual abuse. So do I. Although the guilt for the abuse lies with the abuser, the context of the problem reaches far beyond, beyond me or my parents, into society itself as power and inequality surround us.

Connections with other people have become part and parcel of my life as my life situation has led me into work surrounding the issue of poverty. Although I had known for years of the existence of the Coalition for Basic Human Needs (CBHN)—a progressive group composed almost totally of welfare recipients—my political work, reflecting my life situation, had led me in other directions. Now I found myself alone with a toddler, living on AFDC. When Jamie was two, I returned to school to acquire additional skills. My academic work led me into issues concerning poverty as I became involved in months of activity, along with students and faculty and a variety of progressive women's groups, constructing a conference on the issue of women and poverty. Members of CBHN were involved in work on the conference, and we connected.

Social change through welfare-rights struggles became a major focus in my life as I began working with CBHN. Collectively, we sponsored legislative bills that would improve our lives financially while, at the same time, we taught others how we actually live. Public education became intertwined with legislative work as I spoke at hearings on the reality of living on AFDC. Political support became intertwined with public education as I spoke on the work of CBHN to progressive groups and their constituencies, indicting this country's political system for the impoverishment of its people.

CBHN is composed of chapters representing various cities and towns across Massachusetts. Grass-roots organizing of welfare recipients takes place within local chapters, while the organization as a whole works on statewide issues. We mail out newsletters, hold press conferences, and initiate campaigns. We are currently involved in our most ambitious effort. Whereas in the past our work has been directed toward winning small goals such as a clothing allowance or a small increase in benefits, this time we have set about to bring welfare benefits up to the poverty level, a massive effort involving all of our past strategies and more. We have filed a bill with the state legislature. Public education has become concentrated in the campaign as we plan actions involving the work of welfare-rights groups and individuals throughout the state.

The courage we share as impoverished women has been mirrored throughout this effort. At a press conference to announce the campaign a number of us gave truth to the statement that we and our children go without the basic necessities of life. One woman spoke of sending her child to school without lunch because there was no food in the house. Others had no money for winter jackets or shoes for their children. Sharing the reality of living at 40 percent below the poverty level brings mutual support as well as frustration and anger. In mid-April hundreds of welfare recipients—women carrying infants, the disabled, and the homeless—came from all over Massachusetts to rally in front of the state house along with our supporters and testify to the legislature in behalf of our "Up to the Poverty Level" bill. Courage and determination rang out in statements such as this:

> Take the cost of implementing this program and weigh it, if it must be weighed at all; then weigh it against the anguish suffered by the six-month-old twins who starved to death in a Springfield housing project.
> The day that the state legislature has to scrape the gilt off the dome of the state house and sell if for revenue is the day that this state can answer to us that there is not the means to do this.

The complexity of the situation comes home to me again and again as I sit in the CBHN office answering the telephone and doing welfare advocacy work. I've spoken with women on AFDC who have been battered to within an inch of their lives, some who are, like myself, survivors of child abuse, and others who are reeling from the effects of racism as well as poverty.

In this society so many of us internalize oppression. We internalize the guilt that belongs to the system that creates the conditions people live in. When we realize this and turn our anger outward in an effort to change society, then we begin to create a world worth living in.

The work isn't easy. Many of us become overwhelmed as well as overextended. It takes courage and fortitude to survive. For we live in a society laden with myths and an inequality that leads to human suffering. In order to alleviate the suffering and provide the equality each and every one of us deserves, we must effect social change. If we are to effect social change, then we must recognize social injustice and destroy the myths it creates. Little did I realize, years ago, when I first began this work how far it reached beyond my own survival. For those of us involved in creating a new society are doing the most important work that exists.

Envisioning Change

AGE, RACE, CLASS, AND SEX: *Women Redefining Difference*

52

Audre Lorde

Much of Western European history conditions us to see human differences in simplistic opposition to each other: dominant/subordinate, good/bad, up/down, superior/inferior. In a society where the good is defined in terms of profit rather than in terms of human need, there must always be some group of people who, through systematized oppression, can be made to feel surplus, to occupy the place of the dehumanized inferior. Within this society, that group is made up of Black and Third World people, working-class people, older people, and women.

As a forty-nine-year-old Black lesbian feminist socialist mother of two, including one boy, and a member of an interracial couple, I usually find myself a part of some group defined as other, deviant, inferior, or just plain wrong. Traditionally, in american society, it is the members of oppressed, objectified groups who are expected to stretch out and bridge the gap between the actualities of our lives and the consciousness of our oppressor. For in order to survive, those of us for whom oppression is as american as apple pie have always had to be watchers, to become familiar with the language and manners of the oppressor, even sometimes adopting them for some illusion of protection.

From: Audre Lorde, *Sister Outsider* (Freedom, Calif.: Crossing Press, 1984), pp. 114–123. Reprinted by permission.

Paper delivered at the Copeland Colloquium, Amherst College, April 1980.

Whenever the need for some pretense of communication arises, those who profit from our oppression call upon us to share our knowledge with them. In other words, it is the responsibility of the oppressed to teach the oppressors their mistakes. I am responsible for educating teachers who dismiss my children's culture in school. Black and Third World people are expected to educate white people as to our humanity. Women are expected to educate men. Lesbians and gay men are expected to educate the heterosexual world. The oppressors maintain their position and evade responsibility for their own actions. There is a constant drain of energy which might be better used in redefining ourselves and devising realistic scenarios for altering the present and constructing the future.

Institutionalized rejection of difference is an absolute necessity in a profit economy which needs outsiders as surplus people. As members of such an economy, we have *all* been programmed to respond to the human differences between us with fear and loathing and to handle that difference in one of three ways: ignore it, and if that is not possible, copy it if we think it is dominant, or destroy it if we think it is subordinate. But we have no patterns for relating across our human differences as equals. As a result, those differences have been misnamed and misused in the service of separation and confusion.

Certainly there are very real differences between us of race, age, and sex. But it is not those differences between us that are separating us. It is rather our refusal to recognize those differences, and to examine the distortions which result from our misnaming them and their effects upon human behavior and expectation.

Racism, the belief in the inherent superiority of one race over all others and thereby the right to dominance. Sexism, the belief in the inherent superiority of one sex over the other and thereby the right to dominance. Ageism. Heterosexism. Elitism. Classism.

It is a lifetime pursuit for each one of us to extract these distortions from our living at the same time as we recognize, reclaim, and define those differences upon which they are imposed. For we have all been raised in a society where those distortions were endemic within our living. Too often, we pour the energy needed for recognizing and exploring difference into pretending those differences are insurmountable barriers, or that they do not exist at all. This results in a voluntary isolation, or false and treacherous connections. Either way, we do not develop tools for using human difference as a springboard for creative change within our lives. We speak not of human difference, but of human deviance.

Somewhere, on the edge of consciousness, there is what I call a *mythical norm*, which each one of us within our hearts knows "that is not me." In america, this norm is usually defined as white, thin, male, young, heterosexual, christian, and financially secure. It is with this mythical norm that the trappings of power reside within this society. Those of us who stand outside that power often identify one way in which we are different, and we assume that to be the primary cause of all oppression, forgetting other distortions around difference, some of which we ourselves may be practicing. By and large within the women's movement today, white women focus upon their oppression as women and ignore differences of race, sexual preference, class, and age. There is a pretense to a homogeneity of experience covered by the word *sisterhood* that does not in fact exist.

Unacknowledged class differences rob women of each others' energy and creative insight. Recently a women's magazine collective made the decision for one issue to print only prose, saying poetry was a less "rigorous" or "serious" art form. Yet even the form our creativity takes is often a class issue. Of all the art forms, poetry is the most economical. It is the one which is the most secret, which requires the least physical labor, the least material, and the one which can be done between shifts, in the hospital pantry, on the subway, and on scraps of surplus paper. Over the last few years, writing a novel on tight finances, I came to appreciate the enormous differences in the material demands between poetry and prose. As we reclaim our literature, poetry has been the major voice of poor, working class, and Colored women. A room of one's own may be a necessity for writing prose, but so are reams of paper, a typewriter, and plenty of time. The actual requirements to produce the visual arts also help determine, along class lines, whose art is whose. In this day of inflated prices for material, who are our sculptors, our painters, our photographers? When we speak of a broadly based women's culture, we need to be aware of the effect of class and economic differences on the supplies available for producing art.

As we move toward creating a society within which we can each flourish, ageism is another distortion of relationship which interferes without vision. By ignoring the past, we are encouraged to repeat its mistakes. The "generation gap" is an important social tool for any repressive society. If the younger members of a community view the older members as contemptible or suspect or excess, they will never be able to join hands and examine the living memories of the community, nor ask the all important question, "Why?" This gives rise to a historical amnesia that keeps us working to invent the wheel every time we have to go to the store for bread.

We find ourselves having to repeat and relearn the same old lessons over and over that our mothers did because we do not pass on what we have learned, or because we are unable to listen. For instance, how many times has this all been said before? For another, who would have believed that once again our daughters are allowing their bodies to be hampered and purgatoried by girdles and high heels and hobble skirts?

Ignoring the differences of race between women and the implications of those differences presents the most serious threat to the mobilization of women's joint power.

As white women ignore their built-in privilege of whiteness and define *woman* in terms of their own experience alone, then women of Color become "other," the outsider whose experience and tradition is too "alien" to comprehend. An example of this is the signal absence of the experience of women of Color as a resource for women's studies courses. The literature of women of Color is seldom included in women's literature courses and almost never in other literature courses, nor in women's studies as a whole. All too often, the excuse given is that the literatures of women of Color can only be taught by Colored women, or that they are too difficult to understand, or that classes cannot "get into" them because they come out of experiences that are "too different." I have heard this argument presented by white women of otherwise quite clear intelligence, women who seem to have no trouble at all teaching and reviewing work that comes out of the vastly different experiences of Shakespeare, Molière, Dostoyefsky, and Aristophanes. Surely there must be some other explanation.

This is a very complex question, but I believe one of the reasons white women have such difficulty reading Black women's work is because of their reluctance to see Black women as women and different from themselves. To examine Black women's literature effectively requires that we be seen as whole people in our actual complexities—as individuals, as women, as human— rather than as one of those problematic but familiar stereotypes provided in this society in place of genuine images of Black women. And I believe this holds true for the literatures of other women of Color who are not Black.

The literatures of all women of Color recreate the textures of our lives, and many white women are heavily invested in ignoring the real differences. For as long as any difference between us means one of us must be inferior, then the recognition of any difference must be fraught with guilt. To allow women of Color to step out of stereotypes is too guilt provoking, for it threatens the complacency of those women who view oppression only in terms of sex.

Refusing to recognize difference makes it impossible to see the different problems and pitfalls facing us as women.

Thus, in a patriarchal power system where whiteskin privilege is a major prop, the entrapments used to neutralize Black women and white women are not the same. For example, it is easy for Black women to be used by the power structure against Black men, not because they are men, but because they are

Black. Therefore, for Black women, it is necessary at all times to separate the needs of the oppressor from our own legitimate conflicts within our communities. This same problem does not exist for white women. Black women and men have shared racist oppression and still share it, although in different ways. Out of that shared oppression we have developed joint defenses and joint vulnerabilities to each other that are not duplicated in the white community, with the exception of the relationship between Jewish women and Jewish men.

On the other hand, white women face the pitfall of being seduced into joining the oppressor under the pretense of sharing power. This possibility does not exist in the same way for women of Color. The tokenism that is sometimes extended to us is not an invitation to join power; our racial "otherness" is a visible reality that makes that quite clear. For white women there is a wider range of pretended choices and rewards for identifying with patriarchal power and its tools.

Today, with the defeat of ERA, the tightening economy, and increased conservatism, it is easier once again for white women to believe the dangerous fantasy that if you are good enough, pretty enough, sweet enough, quiet enough, teach the children to behave, hate the right people, and marry the right men, then you will be allowed to co-exist with patriarchy in relative peace, at least until a man needs your job or the neighborhood rapist happens along. And true, unless one lives and loves in the trenches it is difficult to remember that the war against dehumanization is ceaseless.

But Black women and our children know the fabric of our lives is stitched with violence and with hatred, that there is no rest. We do not deal with it only on the picket lines, or in dark midnight alleys, or in the places where we dare to verbalize our resistance. For us, increasingly, violence weaves through the daily tissues of our living—in the supermarket, in the classroom, in the elevator, in the clinic and the schoolyard, from the plumber, the baker, the saleswoman, the bus driver, the bank teller, the waitress who does not serve us.

Some problems we share as women, some we do not. You fear your children will grow up to join the patriarchy and testify against you, we fear our children will be dragged from a car and shot down in the street, and you will turn your backs upon the reasons they are dying.

The threat of difference has been no less blinding to people of Color. Those of us who are Black must see that the reality of our lives and our struggle does not make us immune to the errors of ignoring and misnaming difference. Within Black communities where racism is a living reality, differences among us often seem dangerous and suspect. The need for unity is often misnamed as a need for homogeneity, and a Black feminist vision mistaken for betrayal of our common interests as a people. Because of the continuous battle against racial erasure that Black women and Black men share, some Black women still refuse to recognize that we are also oppressed as women, and that sexual hostility against Black women is practiced not only by the white racist society, but implemented within our Black communities as well. It is a disease striking the heart of Black nationhood, and silence will not make it disappear. Exacerbated by racism and the pressures of powerlessness, violence against Black women and children often becomes a standard within our communities, one by which manliness can be measured. But these woman-hating acts are rarely discussed as crimes against Black women.

As a group, women of Color are the lowest paid wage earners in america. We are the primary targets of abortion and sterilization abuse, here and abroad. In certain parts of Africa, small girls are still being sewed shut between their legs to keep them docile and for men's pleasure. This is known as female circumcision, and it is not a cultural affair as the late Jomo Kenyatta insisted, it is a crime against Black women.

Black women's literature is full of the pain of frequent assault, not only by a racist patriarchy, but also by Black men. Yet the necessity for and history of shared battle have made us, Black women, particularly vulnerable to the false accusation that anti-sexist is anti-Black. Meanwhile, womanhating as a recourse of the powerless is sapping strength from Black communities, and our very lives. Rape is on the increase, reported and unreported, and rape is not aggressive sexuality, it is sexualized aggression. As Kalamu ya Salaam, a Black male writer points out, "As long as male domination exists, rape will exist. Only women revolting and men made conscious of their responsibility to fight sexism can collectively stop rape."*

Differences between ourselves as Black women are also being misnamed and used to separate us from one another. As a Black lesbian feminist comfortable with the many different ingredients of my identity, and a woman committed to racial and sexual freedom from oppression, I find I am constantly being encouraged to pluck out some one aspect of myself and present this as the meaningful whole, eclipsing or denying the other parts of self. But this is a destructive and fragmenting way to live. My fullest concentration of energy is available to me only when I integrate all the parts of who I am, openly, allowing power from particular sources of my living to flow back and forth freely through all my different selves, without the restrictions of externally imposed definition. Only then can I bring myself and my energies as a whole to the service of those struggles which I embrace as part of my living.

---

*From "Rape: A Radical Analysis, An African-American Perspective" by Kalamu ya Salaam in *Black Books Bulletin*, vol. 6, no. 4 (1980).

A fear of lesbians, or of being accused of being a lesbian, has led many Black women into testifying against themselves. It has led some of us into destructive alliances, and others into despair and isolation. In the white women's communities, heterosexism is sometimes a result of identifying with the white patriarchy, a rejection of that interdependence between women-identified women which allows the self to be, rather than to be used in the service of men. Sometimes it reflects a die-hard belief in the protective coloration of heterosexual relationships, sometimes a self-hate which all women have to fight against, taught us from birth.

Although elements of these attitudes exist for all women, there are particular resonances of heterosexism and homophobia among Black women. Despite the fact that woman-bonding has a long and honorable history in the African and African-american communities, and despite the knowledge and accomplishments of many strong and creative women-identified Black women in the political, social and cultural fields, heterosexual Black women often tend to ignore or discount the existence and work of Black lesbians. Part of this attitude has come from an understandable terror of Black male attack within the close confines of Black society, where the punishment for any female self-assertion is still to be accused of being a lesbian and therefore unworthy of the attention or support of the scarce Black male. But part of this need to misname and ignore Black lesbians comes from a very real fear that openly women-identified Black women who are no longer dependent upon men for their self-definition may well reorder our whole concept of social relationships.

Black women who once insisted that lesbianism was a white woman's problem now insist that Black lesbians are a threat to Black nationhood, are consorting with the enemy, are basically un-Black. These accusations, coming from the very women to whom we look for deep and real understanding, have served to keep many Black lesbians in hiding, caught between the racism of white women and the homophobia of their sisters. Often, their work has been ignored, trivialized, or misnamed, as with the work of Angelina Grimke, Alice Dunbar-Nelson, Lorraine Hansberry. Yet women-bonded women have always been some part of the power of Black communities, from our unmarried aunts to the amazons of Dahomey.

And it is certainly not Black lesbians who are assaulting women and raping children and grandmothers on the streets of our communities.

Across this country, as in Boston during the spring of 1979 following the unsolved murders of twelve Black women, Black lesbians are spearheading movements against violence against Black women.

What are the particular details within each of our lives that can be scrutinized and altered to help bring about change? How do we redefine difference for all women? It is not our differences which separate women, but our reluctance to recognize those differences and to deal effectively with the distortions which have resulted from the ignoring and misnaming of those differences.

As a tool of social control, women have been encouraged to recognize only one area of human difference as legitimate, those differences which exist between women and men. And we have learned to deal across those differences with the urgency of all oppressed subordinates. All of us have had to learn to live or work or coexist with men, from our fathers on. We have recognized and negotiated these differences, even when this recognition only continued the old dominant/subordinate mode of human relationship, where the oppressed must recognize the masters' difference in order to survive.

But our future survival is predicated upon our ability to relate within equality. As women, we must root out internalized patterns of oppression within ourselves if we are to move beyond the most superficial aspects of social change. Now we must recognize differences among women who are our equals, neither inferior nor superior, and devise ways to use each others' difference to enrich our visions and our joint struggles.

The future of our earth may depend upon the ability of all women to identify and develop new definitions of power and new patterns of relating across difference. The old definitions have not served us, nor the earth that supports us. The old patterns, no matter how cleverly rearranged to imitate progress, still condemn us to cosmetically altered repetitions of the same old exchanges, the same old guilt, hatred, recrimination, lamentation, and suspicion.

For we have, built into all of us, old blueprints of expectation and response, old structures of oppression, and these must be altered at the same time as we alter the living conditions which are a result of those structures. For the master's tools will never dismantle the master's house.

As Paulo Freire shows so well in *The Pedagogy of the Oppressed*,* the true focus of revolutionary change is never merely the oppressive situations which we seek to escape, but that piece of the oppressor which is planted deep within each of us, and which knows only the oppressors' tactics, the oppressors' relationships.

Change means growth, and growth can be painful. But we sharpen self-definition by exposing the self in work and struggle together with those whom we define as different from ourselves, although sharing the same goals. For Black and white, old and young, lesbian and heterosexual women alike, this can mean new paths to our survival.

---

*Seabury Press, New York, 1970.

We have chosen each other
and the edge of each others battles
the war is the same
if we lose
someday women's blood will congeal
upon a dead planet
if we win
there is no telling
we seek beyond history
for a new and more possible meeting. *

COALITION POLITICS: *Turning the Century* **   53

Bernice Johnson Reagon

I've never been this high before. I'm talking about the altitude. There is a lesson in bringing people together where they can't get enough oxygen, then having them try to figure out what they're going to do when they can't think properly. I'm serious about that. There probably are some people here who can breathe, because you were born in high altitudes and you have big lung cavities. But when you bring people in who have not had the environmental conditioning, you got one group of people who are in a strain—and the group of people who are feeling fine are trying to figure out why you're staggering around, and that's what this workshop is about this morning.

I wish there had been another way to graphically make me feel it because I belong to the group of people who are having a very difficult time being here. I feel as if I'm gonna keel over any minute and die. That is often what it feels

From: Barbara Smith (ed.), *Home Girls: A Black Feminist Anthology* (New York: Kitchen Table Press, 1983), pp. 356–368. Reprinted by permission.

*From "Outlines," unpublished poem.

**Based upon a presentation at the West Coast Women's Music Festival 1981, Yosemite National Forest, California.

like if you're *really* doing coalition work. Most of the time you feel threatened to the core and if you don't, you're not really doing no coalescing.

I'm Bernice Reagon. I was born in Georgia, and I'd like to talk about the fact that in about twenty years we'll turn up another century. I believe that we are positioned to have the opportunity to have something to do with what makes it into the next century. And the principles of coalition are directly related to that. You don't go into coalition because you just *like* it. The only reason you would consider trying to team up with somebody who could possibly kill you, is because that's the only way you can figure you can stay alive.

A hundred years ago in this country we were just beginning to heat up for the century we're in. And the name of the game in terms of the dominant energy was technology. We have lived through a period where there have been things like railroads and telephones, and radios, TV's and airplanes, and cars, and transistors, and computers. And what this has done to the concept of human society and human life is, to a large extent, what we in the latter part of this century have been trying to grapple with. With the coming of all that technology, there was finally the possibility of making sure no human being in the world would be unreached. You couldn't find a place where you could hide if somebody who had access to that technology wanted to get to you. Before the dawning of that age you had all these little cute villages and the wonderful homogeneous societies where everybody looked the same, did things the same, and believed the same things, and if they didn't, you could just kill them and nobody would even ask you about it.

We've pretty much come to the end of a time when you can have a space that is "yours only"—just for the people you want to be there. Even when we have our "women-only" festivals, there is no such thing. The fault is not necessarily with the organizers of the gathering. To a large extent it's because we have just finished with that kind of isolating. There is no hiding place. There is nowhere you can go and only be with people who are like you. It's over. Give it up.

Now every once in awhile there is a need for people to try to clean out corners and bar the doors and check everybody who comes in the door, and check what they carry in and say, "Humph, inside this place the only thing we are going to deal with is X or Y or Z." And so only the X's or Y's or Z's get to come in. That place can then become a nurturing place or a very destructive place. Most of the time when people do that, they do it because of the heat of trying to live in this society where being an X or Y or Z is very difficult, to say the least. The people running the society call the shots as if they're still living in one of those little villages, where they kill the ones they don't like or put them in the forest to die. (There are some societies where babies are born and if they are not wanted for some reason they are put over in a corner. They do that here too, you know, put them in garbage cans.) When somebody else is running a society like that, and you are the one who would be put out to die, it gets too hard to stay out in that society all the time. And that's when you find a place, and you try to bar the door and check all the people who come in. You come together to see what you can do about shouldering up all of your energies so that you and your kind can survive.

There is no chance that you can survive by staying *inside* the barred room. (Applause) That will not be tolerated. The door of the room will just be painted red and then when those who call the shots get ready to clean house, they have easy access to you.

But that space while it lasts should be a nurturing space where you sift out what people are saying about you and decide who you really are. And you take the time to try to construct within yourself and within your community who you would be if you were running society. In fact, in that little barred room where you check everybody at the door, you act out community. You pretend that your room is a world. It's almost like a play, and in some cases you actually grow food, you learn to have clean water, and all of that stuff, you just try to do it all. It's like, "If *I* was really running it, this is the way it would be."

Of course the problem with the experiment is that there ain't nobody in there but folk like you, which by implication means you wouldn't know what to do if you were running it with all of the other people who are out there in the world. Now that's nationalism. I mean it's nurturing, but it is also nationalism. At a certain stage nationalism is crucial to a people if you are going to ever impact as a group in your own interest. Nationalism at another point becomes reactionary because it is totally inadequate for surviving in the world with many peoples. (Applause)

Sometimes you get comfortable in your little barred room, and you decide you in fact are going to live there and carry out all of your stuff in there. And you gonna take care of everything that needs to be taken care of in the barred room. If you're white and in the barred room and if everybody's white, one of the first things you try to take care of is making sure that people don't think that the barred room is a racist barred room. So you begin to talk about racism and the first thing you do is say, "Well, maybe we better open the door and let some Black folks in the barred room." Then you think, "Well, how we gonna figure out whether they're X's or not?" Because there's nothing in the room but X's. (Laughter) You go down the checklist. You been working a while to sort out who you are, right? So you go down the checklist and say, "If we can find Black folk like that we'll let them in the room." You don't really want Black folks, you are just looking for yourself with a little color to it.

And there are those of us Black folk who are like that. So if you're lucky you can open the door and get one or two. Right? And everything's wonderful. But no matter what, there will be one or two of us who have not bothered to be like you and you know it. We come knocking on your door and say, "Well, you let them in, you let me in too." And we will break your door down trying to get in. (Laughter) As far as we can see we are also X's. Cause you didn't say, "THIS BARRED ROOM IS FOR WHITE X'S ONLY." You just said it was for X's. So everybody who thinks they're an X comes running to get into the room. And because you trying to take care of everything in this room, and you know you're not racist, you get pressed to let us all in.

The first thing that happens is that the room don't feel like the room anymore. (Laughter) And it ain't home no more. It is not a womb no more. And you can't feel comfortable no more. And what happens at that point has to do with trying to do too much in it. You don't do no coalition building in a womb. It's just like trying to get a baby used to taking a drink when they're in your womb. It just don't work too well. Inside the womb you generally are very soft and unshelled. You have no covering. And you have no ability to handle what happens if you start to let folks in who are not like you.

Coalition work is not work done in your home. Coalition work has to be done in the streets. And it is some of the most dangerous work you can do. And you shouldn't look for comfort. Some people will come to a coalition and they rate the success of the coalition on whether or not they feel good when they get there. They're not looking for a coalition; they're looking for a home! They're looking for a bottle with some milk in it and a nipple, which does not happen in a coalition. You don't get a lot of food in a coalition. You don't get fed a lot in a coalition. In a coalition you have to give, and it is different from your home. You can't stay there all the time. You go to the coalition for a few hours and then you go back and take your bottle wherever it is, and then you go back and coalesce some more.

It is very important not to confuse them—home and coalition. Now when it comes to women—the organized women's movement—this recent thrust— we all have had the opportunity to have some kind of relationship with it. The women's movement has perpetuated a myth that there is some common experience that comes just cause you're women. And they're throwing all these festivals and this music and these concerts happen. If you're the same kind of women like the folk in that little barred room, it works. But as soon as some other folk check the definition of "women" that's in the dictionary (which you didn't write, right?) they decide that they can come because they are women, but when they do, they don't see or hear nothing that is like them. Then they charge, "This ain't no women's thing!" (Applause) Then if you try to address that and bring them in, they start to play music that ain't even women's music!

(Laughter and hoots) And you try to figure out what happened to your wonderful barred room. It comes from taking a word like "women" and using it as a code. There is an in-house definition so that when you say "women only" most of the time that means you had better be able—if you come to this place—to handle lesbianism and a lot of folks running around with no clothes on. And I'm being too harsh this morning as I talk to you, but I don't want you to miss what I'm trying to say. Now if you come and you can't handle that, there's another term that's called "woman-identified." They say you might be a woman but you're not woman-identified, and we only want women who are "woman-identified." That's a good way to leave a lot of women out of your room.

So here you are and you grew up and you speak English and you know about this word "woman" and you know you one, and you walk into this "woman-only" space and you ain't there. (Laughter) Because "woman" in that space does not mean "woman" from your world. It's a code word and it traps, and the people that use the word are not prepared to deal with the fact that if you put it out, everybody that thinks they're a woman may one day want to seek refuge. And it ain't no refuge place! And it's not safe! It should be a coalition! It may have been that in its first year the Michigan National "Women-Only" festival was a refuge place. By the fourth year it was a place of coalition, and it's not safe anymore. (Applause) It ain't safe for nobody who comes. When you walk in there you in trouble—and everybody who comes is trying to get to their home there. At this festival [Yosemite] they said: whatever you drink, bring it with you—tea, honey, you know, whatever it is—and we will provide hot water. Now I understand that you got here and there was no hot water. Can't get nothing! That is the nature of coalition. (Laughter) You have to give it all. It is not to feed you; you have to feed it. And it's a monster. It never gets enough. It always wants more. So you better be sure you got your home someplace for you to go to so that you will not become a martyr to the coalition. Coalition *can* kill people; however, it is not by nature fatal. You do not have to die because you are committed to coalition. I'm not so old, and I don't know nothing else. But you do have to know how to pull back, and you do have to have an old-age perspective. You have to be beyond the womb stage.

None of this matters at all very much if you die tomorrow—that won't even be cute. It only matters if you make a commitment to be around for another fifty more years. There are some grey haired women I see running around occasionally, and we have to talk to those folks about how come they didn't commit suicide forty years ago. Don't take everything they say because some of the stuff they gave up to stay around ain't worth considering. But be sure you get on your agenda some old people and try to figure out what it will be like if you are a raging radical fifty years from today.

Think about yourself that way. What would you be like if you had white hair and had not given up your principles? It might be wise as you deal with coalition efforts to think about the possibilities of going for fifty years. It calls for some care. I'm not gonna be suicidal, if I can help it. Sometimes you don't even know you just took a step that could take your head off cause you can't know everything when you start to coalesce with these people who sorta look like you in just one aspect but really they belong to another group. That is really the nature of women. It does not matter at all that biologically we have being women in common. We have been organized to have our primary cultural signals come from some other factors than that we are women. We are not from our base acculturated to be women people, capable of crossing our first people boundaries—Black, White, Indian, etc.

Now if we are the same women from the same people in this barred room, we never notice it. That stuff stays wherever it is. It does not show up until somebody walks into the room who happens to be a woman but really is also somebody else. And then out comes who we really are. And at that point you are not a woman. You are Black or you are Chicana or you are Disabled or you are Racist or you are White. The fact that you are a woman is not important at all and it is not the governing factor to your existence at that moment. I am now talking about bigotry and everybody's got it. I am talking about turning the century with some principles intact. Today wherever women gather together it is not necessarily nurturing. It is coalition building. And if you feel the strain, you may be doing some good work. (Applause) So don't come to no women's festival looking for comfort unless you brought it in your little tent. (Laughter) And then if you bring it in your tent don't be inviting everybody in because everybody ain't your company, and then you won't be able to stand the festival. Am I confusing you? Yes, I am. If coalition is so bad, and so terrible, and so uncomfortable, why is it necessary? That's what you're asking. Because the barred rooms will not be allowed to exist. They will all be wiped out. That is the plan that we now have in front of us.

Now these little rooms were created by some of the most powerful movements we have seen in this country. I'm going to start with the Civil Rights movement because of course I think that that was the first one in the era we're in. Black folks started it, Black folks did it, so everything you've done politically rests on the efforts of my people—that's my arrogance! Yes, and it's the truth; it's my truth. You can take it or leave it, but that's the way I see it. So once we did what we did, then you've got women, you've got Chicanos, you've got the Native Americans, and you've got homosexuals, and you got all of these people who also got sick of somebody being on their neck. And maybe if they come together, they can do something about it. And I claim all of you as coming from something that made me who I am. You can't tell me that you ain't in the Civil Rights movement. You are in the Civil Rights movement that we created that just rolled up to your door. But it could not stay the same, because if it was gonna stay the same it wouldn't have done you no good. Some of you would not have caught yourself dead near no Black folks walking around talking about freeing themselves from racism and lynching. So by the time our movement got to you it had to sound like something you knew about. Like if I find out you're gay, you gonna lose your job.

There were people who came South to work in the movement who were not Black. Most of them were white when they came. Before it was over, that category broke up—you know, some of them were Jewish, not simply white, and some others even changed their names. Say if it was Mary when they came South, by the time they were finished it was Maria, right? It's called finding yourself. At some point, you cannot be fighting oppression and be oppressed yourself and not feel it. Within the Black movement there was also all of the evils of the society, so that anything that was happening to you in New York or the West Coast probably also happened to you in another way, within the movement. And as you became aware of that you tried to talk to these movement people about how you felt. And they say, "Well let's take that up next week. Because the most important thing now is that Black people are being oppressed and we must work with that." Watch these mono-issue people. They ain't gonna do you no good. I don't care who they are. And there are people who prioritize the cutting line of the struggle. And they say the cutting line is this issue, and more than anything we must move on this issue and that's automatically saying that whatever's bothering you will be put down if you bring it up. You have to watch these folks. Watch these groups that can only deal with one thing at a time. On the other hand, learn about space within coalition. You can't have everybody sitting up there talking about everything that concerns you at the same time or you won't get no place. . . .

It must become necessary for all of us to feel that this is our world. And that we are here to stay and that anything that is here is ours to take and to use in our image. And watch that "our"—make it as big as you can—it ain't got nothing to do with that barred room. The "our" must include everybody you have to include in order for you to survive. You must be sure you understand that you ain't gonna be able to have an "our" that don't include Bernice Johnson Reagon, cause I don't plan to go nowhere! That's why we have to have coalitions. Cause I ain't gonna let you live unless you let me live. Now there's danger in that, but there's also the possibility that we can both live—if you can stand it. . . .

CULTURE AND GENDER IN INDIAN AMERICA   **54**

Rayna Green

I don't have a theory or line of argument this morning. I want to go through a series of vignettes, all of which cast a different light, cast a different slant, and give a slightly different ear to each other.

My first story is about two friends of mine, both Sioux women who were up at the Capitol one day. Up on top of the Capitol there's a statue. It's a marvelous statue. If you get very close to that statue, you'll see that it's clearly a female figure, and it might look something like Miss Liberty standing out in New York Harbor. Nobody knows much about her. These two young Sioux women I know went up to the guard and they said, "What's the statue? What's it about?" He said, "Well, you know, that statue, a lot of people seem to think it's an Indian. Her name is Freedom. But Freedom isn't an Indian. She's a woman." And my two friends laughed to think that in this country freedom could be either. But the truth is, in this country freedom is both. And that's what I want to talk about today. And I want to talk about justice and liberty, and about America. I want to talk about home, family, and about women. I want to talk about changing our names, and taking hold of our names. And I want to talk about coming home.

Freedom is an Indian and a woman. She's also Black and a woman. She's also Jewish, Vietnamese, and Salvadoran, and a woman. She is all of those things. But her iconography is clear. She comes from the fifteenth century, when the first images of the New World went back to Europe. Freedom, in the early days of America, was pictured as this large, bare-breasted Indian woman. She was a queen. She was our kind of girl. She was pictured with her foot on the head of an alligator, her spear in her hands. Pineapples, corn, all these wonderful bounteous crops spilling out of her arms. Her warriors stood behind her. She was in control; she was the New World, the promise of everything that everyone wanted.

And they took her away from us. As the two centuries moved forward and things happened here that we now must pay for, dearly, she changed. They took away her flesh. They covered her breasts. She couldn't be naked, the symbol of innocence in the fifteenth, sixteenth century; the symbol of virtue.

From: *Sojourner: The Women's Forum* 15 (September 1989): 20–22. Reprinted by permission.

They had to cover her and make her less savage, less pagan. They took away her alligator. I mean, can you imagine taking a girl's alligator away? She must have been angry. They took away all of the fruits of her fields. And she became a Renaissance little wonder woman icon, like Minerva, draped in little tasteful white garments with her breasts covered. And they wouldn't even let her be like Minerva; they robbed her of her power. Thin and powerless, with a tiny little diadem on her head. She never needed a crown to know she was a queen. But now, she's changed. And that's who stands in the New York harbor. Someone who changed. And that's who stands on top of the Capitol. But we need to know her name. Her name is Freedom, and she is who I have described. And we need to go back to her to begin to look to the future.

That future is vague and muddy, though. That future is opaque. We all have difficulties now knowing who we are, and what our names are. We try to put on different names, give ourselves a kind of identity. We struggle through various ways of looking at an identity. Indian people have been forced to confront lots of different faces in the mirror, and those faces are confusing for all of us. At one level, Indians are totally insignificant. They exist in no number to matter—to the economy, to the judicial system, to anything else. There are fewer Indians in America than Vietnamese. And so why do Indians matter? I'll tell you why they matter: simply because of the history I've spoken of.

But Indians cannot simply be functions of the historic past. They can't simply be reminders of an America that once was, bad or good. They can't simply function as vague, ghostly reminders of poverty index levels, of hunger and homelessness in America; that's irrelevant. What is relevant is that there is a metaphor here that stands for all of us in some ways and doesn't encompass the experience of others in another. What is relevant is that as my friend Roberta Hill Whiteman says, "Indians know how to wait." And it is the waiting that will dignify us all. The waiting for freedom and justice to come in the form of an Indian woman, once again, to reclaim us all. In Roberta's words:

> Look west long enough, the moon will grow
> inside you.
> Coyote hears her song, he'll
> teach you now.
> Mirrors follow trails of blood and lightning.
> Mother needs the strength of one like you.
> Let blood
> dry, but seize the lightning. Hold it like your
> mother
> rocks the trees. In your fear, watch the road,
> breathe deeply.
> Indians know how to wait.
>
> (from "Lines for Marking Time")

What are we waiting for? Are we waiting for a moment like that which happened at the National Women's Studies Association Conference in Minneapolis last year? The planning group invited a young Indian girl to dance for the opening event. Typically, and profoundly, she came with her uncle, and a group of young men who drummed for her. In Indian culture, an uncle is like your father. An uncle raises you. An aunt raises you. Your own father and mother are perhaps even less significant in some ways. Her uncle came with her because her father had just died. And her uncle, to honor her, and to honor the women who had come to see her, spoke for her.

In our world, people speak for you when you're honored. It's a gift to speak for someone. And when that man, who was honoring everyone there by his presence, rose to speak for her, he was booed. Because in an environment where we've gotten our signals crossed, we don't know the faces of other people, we don't know how they live, and we cannot speak to them directly. He gave them even a further gift, he explained to them why she was not wearing her jingle dress. (A jingle dress is a wonderful buckskin or cloth dress filled with little tin coins that make a marvelous noise when a young lady dances.) She was in her menstrual period, and a girl does not wear a jingle dress when she's menstruating, because the noise of those coins, you see, is a prayer, and it's a prayer for power. Music goes up, music calls down the spirits to look at you, and asks for power. Because a menstruating woman is already so powerful, to wear the jingle dress is to really risk a problem; to call down uncontrolled power, perhaps. He gave them the gift of telling them this. He was explaining something rather arcane, something that people don't just discuss in public. It was a women's event. He wanted to reach out. And they booed him for that, because they thought he was talking about pollution.

I'm not here, as I said, to accuse. This is not accusatory. That is not what Indian women and Indian men are about. This is about knowing our own names and knowing our faces. A gift was refused because no one knew it was a gift. We have got to come forward and know the gifts that different people give us. And that's why a meeting like this is essential—to look in the face of different gifts and to learn to honor each other, by accepting the terms on which those gifts are given.

Sometimes, because things get so confused in moments like that, we're forced to change our names. Sometimes we have to change our shape. Shape shifters are important for all of us; all of our worlds have shape shifters. Sometimes we have to shift shape because guns are aimed at us, and we must escape. Sometimes the old shape has become too uncomfortable. Sometimes, like the queen in the early days, our original form is taken—we're sent to the diet center, forced on cultural aerobics until we change. And I say it's time to change our shape because we want to, to change our names because we want to.

Sometimes when we're forced to change those shapes it's painful; sometimes it's a joy. In Indian cultures, there is a tradition of name-changing and shape-shifting, and it's an important tradition to look to for all of us because it enables us to be empowered; it enables us to be in control. We are all women, certainly; we are all men; we are all gay; we are all straight; we are all old; we are all young. And in Indian cultures I go back to my families and there is no division. There are distinctions, certainly, about the way people are treated, and the authority they have, but I want to reclaim the power to move through categories, so that I do not have to stay fixed in any one place. Jesse [Jackson] said a couple of years ago, in the presidential elections, "God ain't finished with me yet, she never will be finished." We can all move and grow.

Some of the categories become so restrictive, we have to be able to move out of them. One category that Indian people suffer from is that of "half-breed." It's staggering to think about that kind of marginality; to suggest that someone is a quart low of whatever it is that makes them real is to take their life and breath and squeeze it until it stops. We're all half-breeds, if you come right down to it. As my mom used to say, "Heinz 57." We locate our internal space, perhaps, in one place that gives us a name to call ourselves that we're proud of, but we are all out there on the margins (and there are no people on the margin like women, because we have to shift into so many shapes). But the category of "half-breed" is tragic, damaging in so many ways, we've got to give it up. It is like Freedom. We've got to put a name to it that enables us to stand up again.

I am a German Jew. I feel comfortable with that. I've lived my life as a German Jew. One of my grandmothers was a German Jew who became a profound Texan. I will not deny her. I will not look at my mother, with her blue eyes, her white skin, and deny her. My father is only one part of me. He must be claimed, too. And I gravitate toward that part of him, and his world, and my other grandmother, who gave me a name and space. But I will not deny any one part of that world to force Indian people, native people, any people to live on a margin, where they cannot define their own existence as a whole, whatever parts may be there, just to rob them of a future, and to force them to die somewhere in a past.

My German grandmother was a remarkable person. She is my mother, the primary character in my life. She shaped and formed me; she gave me stories, language, and songs. In many ways, she gave me more than my Indian grandmother, who was afraid because of all the things that had happened to her; afraid to sing, to breathe, to leave town. Her pain transferred over, so I took joy from the maternal grandmother, and I took the name from the other one. We take what we can from each one of our relatives and honor them.

My German grandmother was an extraordinary woman who loved to dance, loved to sing, loved to tell dirty stories. She was the mistress of them all. She wanted to be a dancer on the Palace stage. Dressed to kill, she'd play whorehouse songs on the piano, or sad ones that would make us cry and beg for more. On that summer porch, we believed she could have been anything, living in her ruby pleasures. Oh, she glittered then, dancing across that summer porch, dancing the stories that made me dream over her shattered breath. She is mine, and she is yours, too. Never walk away from all the faces you've known in your life, who gave you birth. That's the Indian way, certainly. But it's all of our way. If we only can have the courage to look back for them.

Some of the shape-shifting sometimes makes it important to walk away from being female. Being female is painful. Being male is painful, never more than lately, as we look into the faces of our young men on the streets of urban cities. We see death in their faces, and it pains us. If only they had the freedom we have, to walk into a female body, into a female metaphor, and say, "That's not my world. Those guns, that dope, those drugs are not my world. That world that lures me only because my name is man, that world that pains me because I have to live trapped in a metaphor, that will not work for me."

We have an option that makes us live, an option women have always had, an extraordinary option. Some women take it in different ways. Some women call themselves mothers, some sisters, some lovers. Some women call themselves men, and walk into Coyote's terrible dream, which enables us to move through the changes. We can take any of those options at any one time. But to take those options means we have to teach our baby boys to grow up and be all those things, too. We don't have to claim the men in us by being tough. We only have to look in our children's and our brothers' faces, and bring them up to live with us.

There's a gift that moves in Indian country, and that gift is an extraordinary gift. It is the gift of giving itself. All of us have it in our worlds. At dances, various ceremonial occasions, you'll see women walk over and put shawls on other people's backs—men's backs, too. In ceremonial occasions these shawls get piled so high, you never know how anybody stands up under them. (I want to eartag a shawl during a powwow season sometime like biologists do animals, see how it migrates across the room.) Those gifts are extraordinary.

I want to take the metaphor of that shawl, and I want to wrap it around your shoulders now, and say you are my sister, you are my mother, you are my friend, you are my brother, you are my husband, you are my uncle, you are my aunt, come into that dance circle. It is the gift that keeps on moving, because it brings us into the circle. The richest person in Indian country is the person who gives the most away, not the person who keeps the most for themselves. And this is a gift that America needs. We would not have homeless people on our streets, if we truly believed we lived in Indian country. If freedom was really the Indian woman we know she is, we would not have people living out on the margin, children selling themselves for one shot, for a pint of Thunderbird. We have got to wrap that shawl around the rest of us, and women can do that.

To talk about culture in this country, to talk about gender, is to talk about giving. And it is in the heart and face of our own cultures, and our own passions that we can look and see the gift that we have to wrap again, and keep moving, and keep giving. But in order to do that, we have to know what real wealth is. Real wealth lies in our own hearts, and not in something that is a commodity beyond it. Indian country knows that. The gift that moves will carry us to that place. I think of the warrior women who reputedly used to carry their husbands' and brothers' and friends' bodies off the field and take up the bow or the gun or the spear themselves. And I say, this is not militance, this is not warrior behavior (although at one level it is: it is what is required to survive). All of us in our communities now are carrying those boys' bodies off the field. What will we do when there are no more of them? Will we become the warriors? Are we willing to take that battle on? Perhaps the gift is not to keep thinking of it as a battle, but to think of it as a role for us all, in the survival of our people, in the raising of our children. What is a real warrior woman—in Indian terms, even? Certainly, it is not to take up a spear. If you have to, you do, to defend your life or that of your children. But I don't want to talk about defensiveness; I want to talk about survival. And there are keys to survival.

In 1642, a group of British got off a boat in Virginia somewhere and migrated to what we call North Carolina; and there they met a delegation of Cherokees, led by a man who had been a warrior. His name was Outacitty, which means man-killer. He was a great warrior, a red chief, sent by the Beloved Woman and the clan-mothers to make war. But this time they had asked him not to make war. The Beloved Woman of the Nation, Ghigau had asked him to become a white chief, a peace chief, and to go and make peace with these people. And so Outacitty rode up to meet them. The first thing he said to them was, "Where are your women?" These men had come to do serious business, and they had no women with them. Peace is a very serious business. No act of war, no act of peace in my country is made without the women there. And Outacitty was shocked: the British dared to come without their women. "Where are your women?" he said. And he went back and reported that there was a problem here. "We cannot do business with these men," he said. They were clearly missing half of the people needed to do business with.

And in 1987, a young woman named Wilma Mankiller was elected principal chief of the Cherokee nation, and I say to you she is him, come back, and she knows it. And the old people knew it. When we'd go out to campaign with her, the old ladies would say, "Good name, good name." And they didn't mean war. They didn't mean hunting; they didn't mean power. They meant she's back. She has returned; the Beloved has returned. You see, she is all of those converged together. Like all of us can be. Warrior, peacemaker, mother, father, Beloved woman, Beloved man, the white and the red merged together, to take our own story back.

And that's an interesting story. It's a story about family. Everybody in Indian country talks about the family as the center of their lives, just as in Black culture, in Irish-American communities. Because to talk about family is to talk about community, about survival, about the future.

The central figure in this next story about family is a woman called Buffalo Birdwoman who could not give up the old way. She was a great farmer. When the time came to make her change, they brought in the tractors, they brought in the freight wagons, and she said, "I don't want to do that. I'll stick to my digging stick. Because I grow corn better than your corn. I know how to grow corn, and I will not give up on corn songs. I will not forget the corn songs. The corn is my family, my mother, my grandmother, the corn gave me birth. And to give up my corn songs is to give up my family." Tradition is not a yoke around our neck, if we know its name. Tradition is not the chains that bind us, if we know how to use it. Tradition is not the deadly past wrapped around us like a coffin. Tradition, for the Indian family, for the Indian woman, is simply remembering who you are, and it is that story we must reclaim once more. Hear Linda Hogan, Chickasaw:

> *calling myself home*
>
> *There were old women*
> *who lived on amber.*
> *Their dark hands*
> *laced the shells of turtles*
> *together, pebbles inside*
> *and they danced*
> *with rattles strong on their legs.*
>
> *There is a dry river*
> *between them and us.*
> *Its banks divide up our land.*
> *Its bed was the road*
> *I walked to return.*

We are plodding creatures like the turtle
born of an old people.
We are nearly stone
turning slow as the earth.
Our mountains are underground
they are so old.

This land is the house
we have always lived in.
The women,
their bones are holding up the earth.

The red tail of a hawk
cuts open the sky
and the sun
brings their faces back
with the new grass.

Dust from yarrow
is in the air,
the yellow sun.
Insects are clicking again.

I came back to say good-bye
to the turtle
to those bones
to the shells locked together
on his back
gold atoms dancing underground.

The turtle in the stories of some Indian people is our mother. On her back the earth grew. We were born in the mud of her back. It doesn't matter which story you claim. Whether you think it was Corn or the Turtle Mother or the Spider Woman that gave you birth. Coyote came from all these. His tricking lies give us the ability to change our shapes. He is necessary to us. But the earth and where we were born is that woman's back and that woman's breast; she cuts it open to feed us and make us whole again.

Sun over the horizon, a sweating yellow force, our continuance. The uncountable distance that sweeps through our hands, the first prayers in the morning. It is this that I believe in. The galloping sun. In my whole life, a rider. It is that round earth—I call it Indian country, you call it the name you need to call it—the moon, the stars, and that sweating sun, that enables me to be the writer I am. If I choose not to climb on that galloping horse, that galloping sun, it is my own choice. But it is a choice I cannot make. I need to come home. I need my family. I need you, my brothers and sisters, my father, my uncle, and I need my aunties. The metaphor of family is simply one that works in Indian country because it brings that circle round. We all join in the dance that brings us to a place called America, where Freedom may be lots of things. And you can put the shape and face to her you wish.

The bottom line is very simple; it is morning once more. And that galloping sun races across the horizon. For me to come home to Indian country means I must climb on that sun and race across the horizon, with other people. I don't want to leave any of you behind. America has a way of leaving some of us out on the edge. I say it's time for the women of America, all of us—we're not separate, we belong with each other—to reclaim our families. To climb on that sun with me in that eternal morning. Once again, your whole life, a rider.

Ed. note: The poems quoted in this article are from *That's What She Said* edited by Rayna Green (Indiana University Press, 1984).